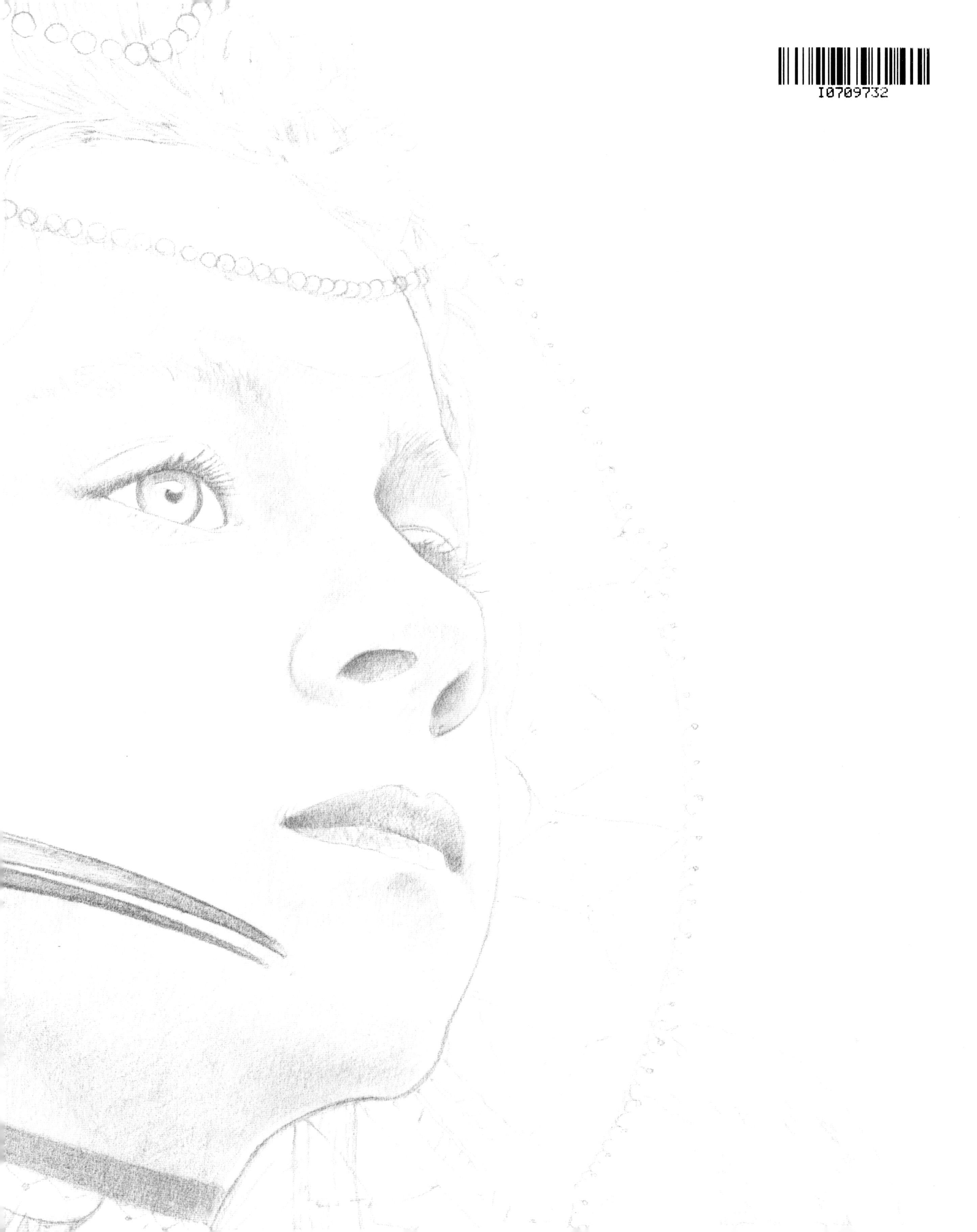

Master SKETCHBOOKS

Legendary artists of the entertainment industry reveal their secrets

3dtotal Publishing

3dtotal Publishing

Correspondence: **publishing@3dtotal.com**
Website: **store.3dtotal.com**

First published in the United Kingdom, 2025,
by 3dtotal Publishing.

Address: 3dtotal.com Ltd,
29 Foregate Street, Worcester,
WR1 1DS, United Kingdom.

Hard cover ISBN: 978-1-915992-13-0

Printed and Bound in Shanghai, China,
by KS Printing.

Visit **store.3dtotal.com** for a complete list
of available book titles.

Editor: Philippa Barker
Designer: Fiona Tarbet
Lead Editor: Samantha Rigby
Lead Designer: Joseph Cartwright
Studio Manager: Simon Morse
Managing Director: Tom Greenway

Dust jacket: All images copyrighted as noted
throughout the book
End papers: Images © Darrell Warner

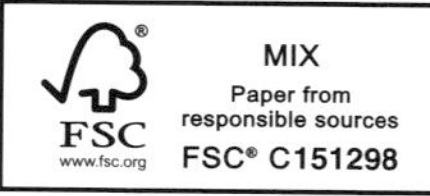

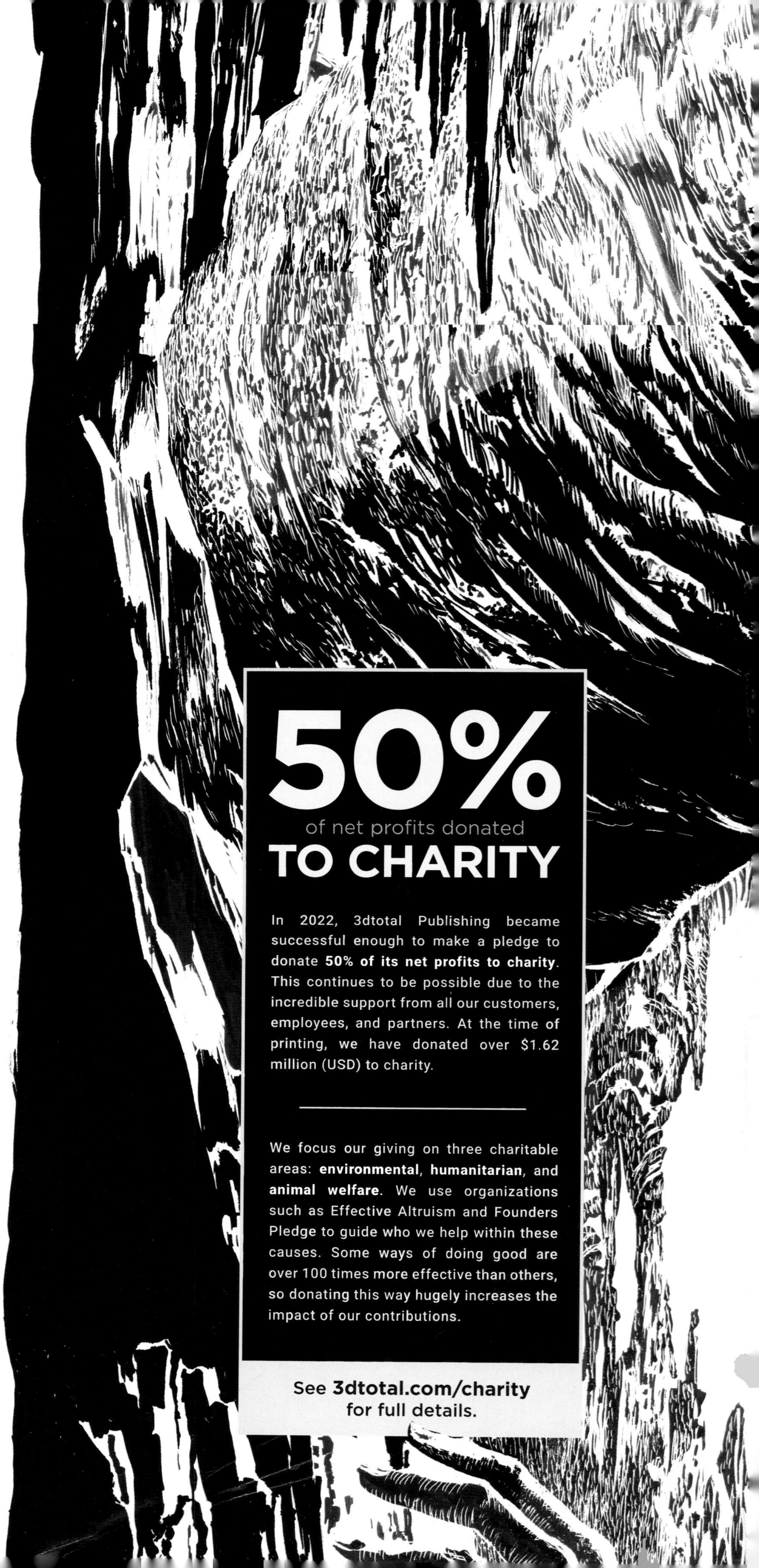

50%
of net profits donated
TO CHARITY

In 2022, 3dtotal Publishing became
successful enough to make a pledge to
donate **50% of its net profits to charity**.
This continues to be possible due to the
incredible support from all our customers,
employees, and partners. At the time of
printing, we have donated over $1.62
million (USD) to charity.

We focus our giving on three charitable
areas: **environmental**, **humanitarian**, and
animal welfare. We use organizations
such as Effective Altruism and Founders
Pledge to guide who we help within these
causes. Some ways of doing good are
over 100 times more effective than others,
so donating this way hugely increases the
impact of our contributions.

See **3dtotal.com/charity**
for full details.

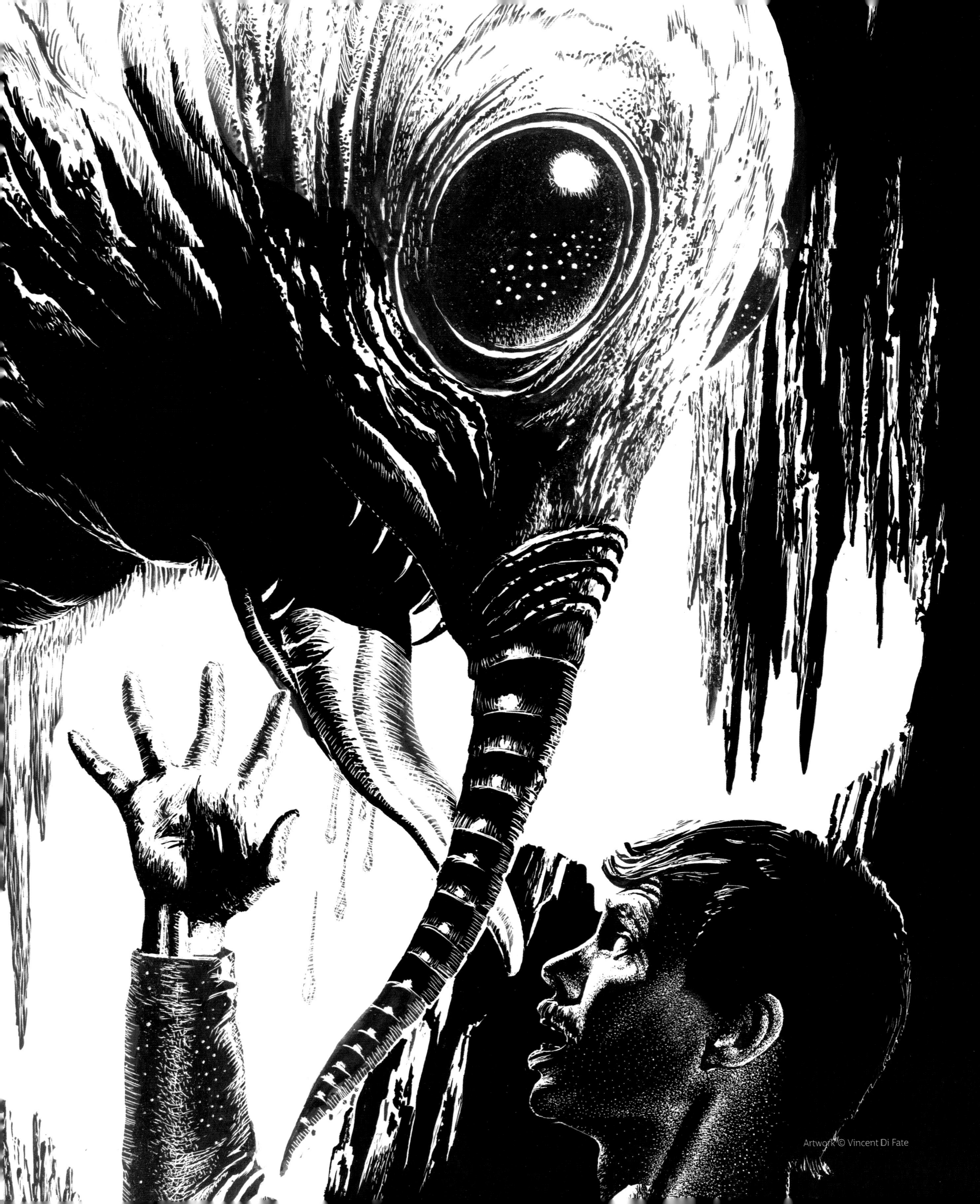

Artwork © Vincent Di Fate

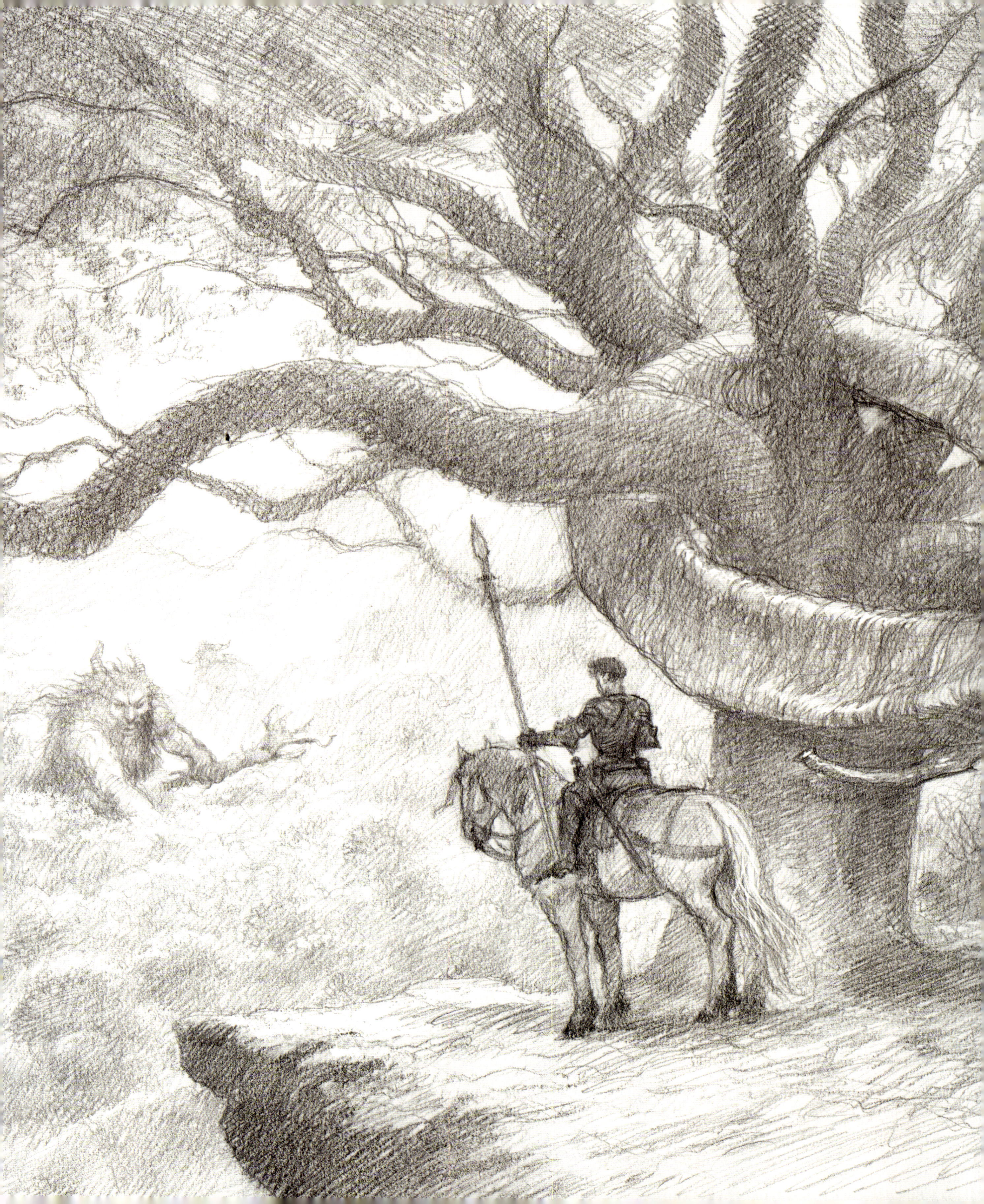

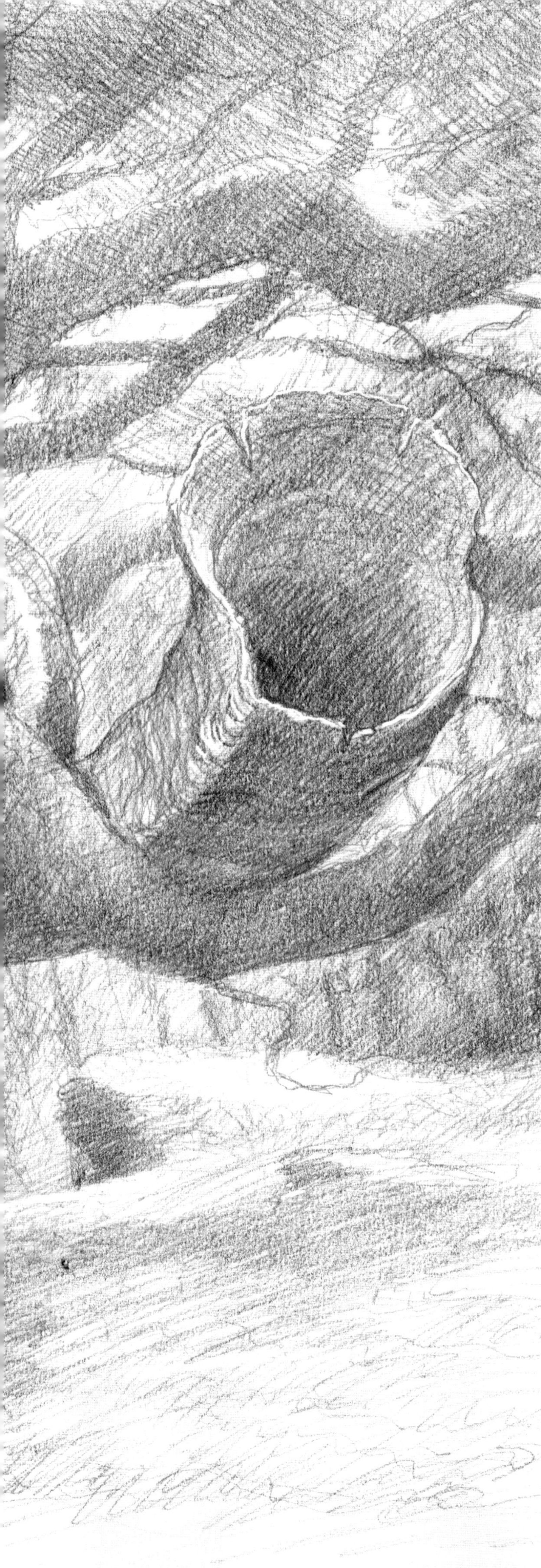

Contents

Artwork © John Howe

Introduction

Few things compel an aspiring artist to pick up a pencil like seeing the work of an artist they admire. We fall in love with characters, creatures, and worlds crafted by artists whose names we may not discover until many years later, whether they are printed in books, comics, and magazines, or lighting up the big or small screen.

In this book, we invite you to explore the sketchbooks and 'behind-the-scenes' work of ten living legends whose influence on the art industry has been felt across decades. Their fantastical designs have made a unique mark on entertainment as we know it and will continue to inspire readers and audiences for years to come.

World-renowned science-fiction and fantasy artist **Wayne Barlowe** has created artwork for books, magazines, and films such as *Pacific Rim*, *Hellboy*, and *Avatar*. He has also written novels and art books, including his retrospective infernal art book, *PSYCHOPOMP*. Over the following pages he pulls back the curtain on his creative workflow and shares a series of 'digital sketchbooks', revealing how he develops his otherworldly pieces from rough forms to final full-colour illustrations.

Brazilian animator and character designer **Sandro Cleuzo** has worked for Don Bluth, Disney, and DreamWorks on films such as *Anastasia*, *The Emperor's New Groove*, and *The Princess and the Frog*. In his chapter, Sandro shares how his animation career began when he was a teen, setting him on the path to working with a host of major animation studios on iconic films and characters. Accompanying his insight and advice are a collection of characters from his sketchbooks – evidence of years of dedicated sketching practice.

Emmy-winning **David Colman** currently works as Head of Story at DreamWorks Pictures. As well as working on projects with Sony, Paramount, Netflix, Legendary, Skydance, and Apple, he is widely known for his animal illustration and has published seven art books. David's chapter charts his career beginnings, early lessons and inspirations, and the importance of keeping a sketchbook for growing as an artist, accompanied by a gallery of beautiful animal artwork. The sketches showcase a range of different materials and techniques, made possible by persistent practice.

Renowned science-fiction illustrator **Vincent Di Fate** is an inductee of the Science Fiction Hall of Fame and the Illustrators Hall of Fame. He has worked for clients including *Reader's Digest*, The National Geographic Society, and NASA, and has received numerous awards for his art. Vincent's chapter showcases a collection of his book covers and interior illustrations, alongside the early development sketches and thumbnails that led to the final artwork. He shares the backstory to each piece, the pros and cons of keeping a sketchbook, and his love of the genre that continually asks, 'What if?'

Number-one New York Times bestselling author and illustrator **Tony M. DiTerlizzi** has been creating children's books for twenty-five years, including *The Spiderwick Chronicles*, which has sold millions of copies worldwide and was adapted into a feature film and television series. His bestselling trilogy, *WondLa*, is now streaming globally on Apple TV+. Alongside a gallery of whimsical character sketches, Tony shares his formative inspirations, the practice of having dedicated sketchbooks for different stories, and the idea of sketchbooks as a kind of memoir.

Creator of the award-winning *Dinotopia* book series, as well as several popular art books, **James Gurney** is known for his realistic renderings of imaginative scenes, from dinosaurs to ancient civilizations. He has created numerous pieces for *National Geographic* magazine, in addition to multiple covers for science-fiction and fantasy novels. His chapter explores his key artistic influences, the benefits of self-taught learning, and the fascinating studies that can be found within the pages of his sketchbooks.

Internationally acclaimed book illustrator and concept designer **John Howe** is primarily known for illustrating many of the works of J. R. R. Tolkien. One of the chief conceptual designers on *The Lord of the Rings* trilogy and *The Hobbit* film series, most recently he has worked as a concept artist for *The Lord of the Rings: The Rings of Power* television series. His chapter is full of well-earned insight and wisdom from a life of sketching, interspersed with a gallery of his striking sketches of fantastical isles, magical characters, and long-admired creatures from Middle-earth.

Dave McKean has illustrated over ninety groundbreaking books and graphic novels, collaborating with the likes of Ray Bradbury and David Almond. He is the creator of *Cages* and *Black Dog: The Dreams of Paul Nash*, and has directed both short and feature films, including *MirrorMask* and *Luna*. His chapter showcases striking cover artwork created for books, albums, and Blu-ray, demonstrating how he developed the designs from rough sketches and ideas to the final products.

With over fifty major film titles to his name, **Darrell Warner** has worked in costume and character development, plus costume illustration, on motion pictures including *Wicked* and *Pirates of the Caribbean*. He won the Award for Excellence at the 2023 Royal Institute of Painters in Water Colours and was a semi-finalist for Sky Arts Portrait Artist of the Year 2013. Alongside a series of beautiful greyscale sketches, he shares his transition from illustration to film, how he uses sketchbooks for problem-solving, and his loyalty to traditional media throughout a varied career.

Terryl Whitlatch is an iconic creature designer who has worked with Lucasfilm on the *Star Wars* film series, as well as with Disney, Paramount, and Sony. She holds a Professorship of Illustration at the Savannah College of Art & Design and is a sought-after instructor in creature design and animal drawing. Her chapter reveals how she fuses knowledge of ancient animal species with the science-fiction genre to develop her truly unique creature designs. Combining traditional and digital media, her pages show the development of rough exploratory sketches into a full-colour illustration, with steps for reference-finding and anatomical studies.

PHILIPPA BARKER
Editor

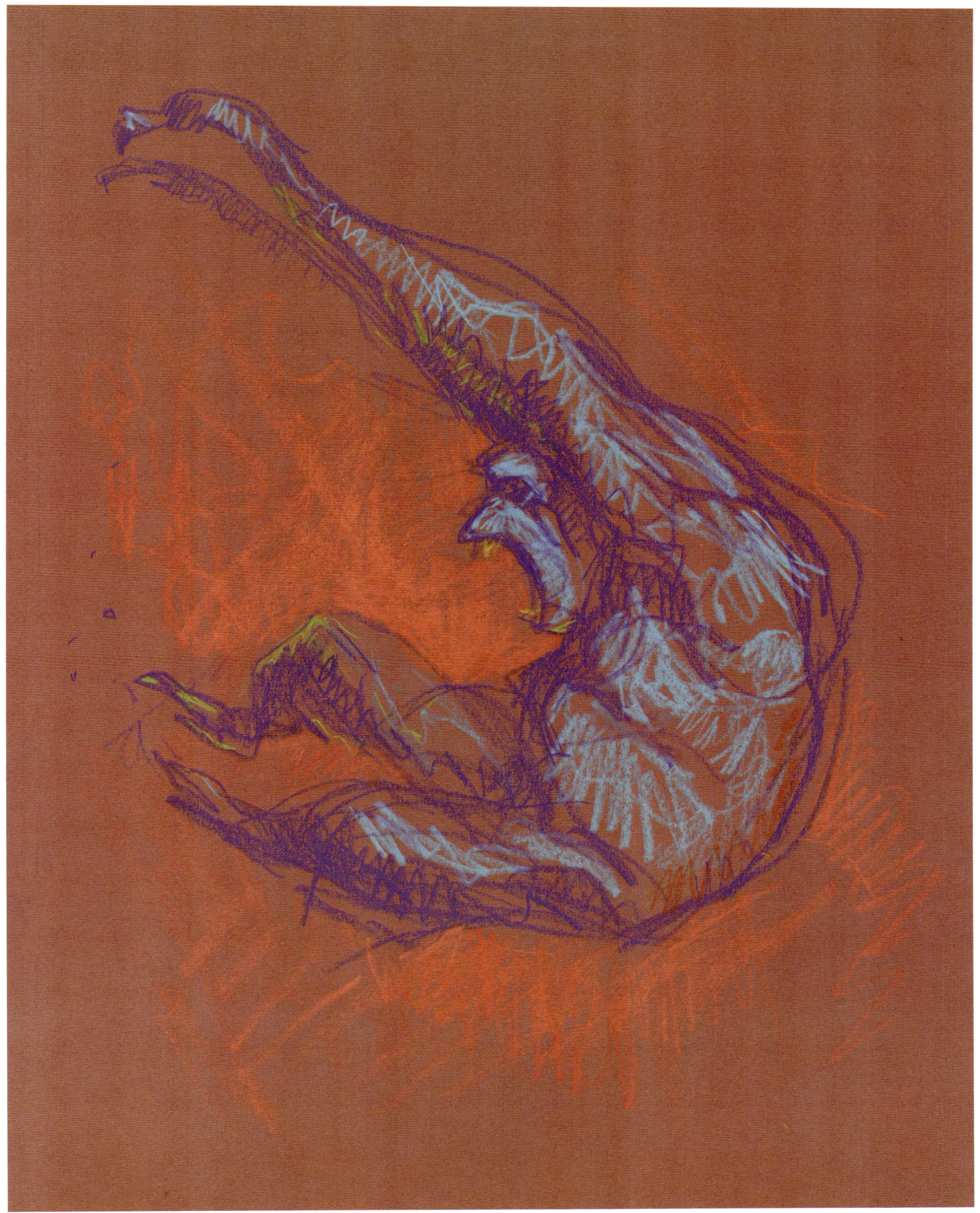

John Howe

CLEAR ON ONE SIDE

When I was small, I endlessly pestered my mother for paper that was 'clear on one side'. Growing up on a farm in western (and very rural) British Columbia meant that real drawing paper was out of the question, but I happily scribbled on the back of anything else. The other side of the paper was usually occupied by untidy columns of farm accounting or school papers my older brother no longer needed.

I drew all the time and, naturally, my very first memory connected to art is of a drawing I couldn't get right. Growing up on a farm, I, of course, drew farm animals and on this occasion had set my sights on Polly, our milk cow. I must have been about five at the time. Milk cows have none of the sturdy, rounded-out profiles of beef cattle, with their broad haunches, sturdy legs, and trim udders. Milk cows seem to defy gravity. With huge bellies and udders, they sag ponderously, as well as being astonishingly bony, with ribs, vertebrae, and leg bones that seem about to poke through the skin. This complex anatomy was so far beyond my skills that I turned to my mom for help. (As a five-year-old, I assumed adults knew everything!) Unfortunately her efforts were no more satisfying than mine and I burst into tears, wailing, 'That's not a cowwwwww!'

I suppose that day I learned two lessons: adults can't do everything and, when it comes to drawing, you are on your own. Bovine frustrations aside, I, of course, continued. I have since graduated to paper that's clear on *both* sides and am still happily sketching and drawing.

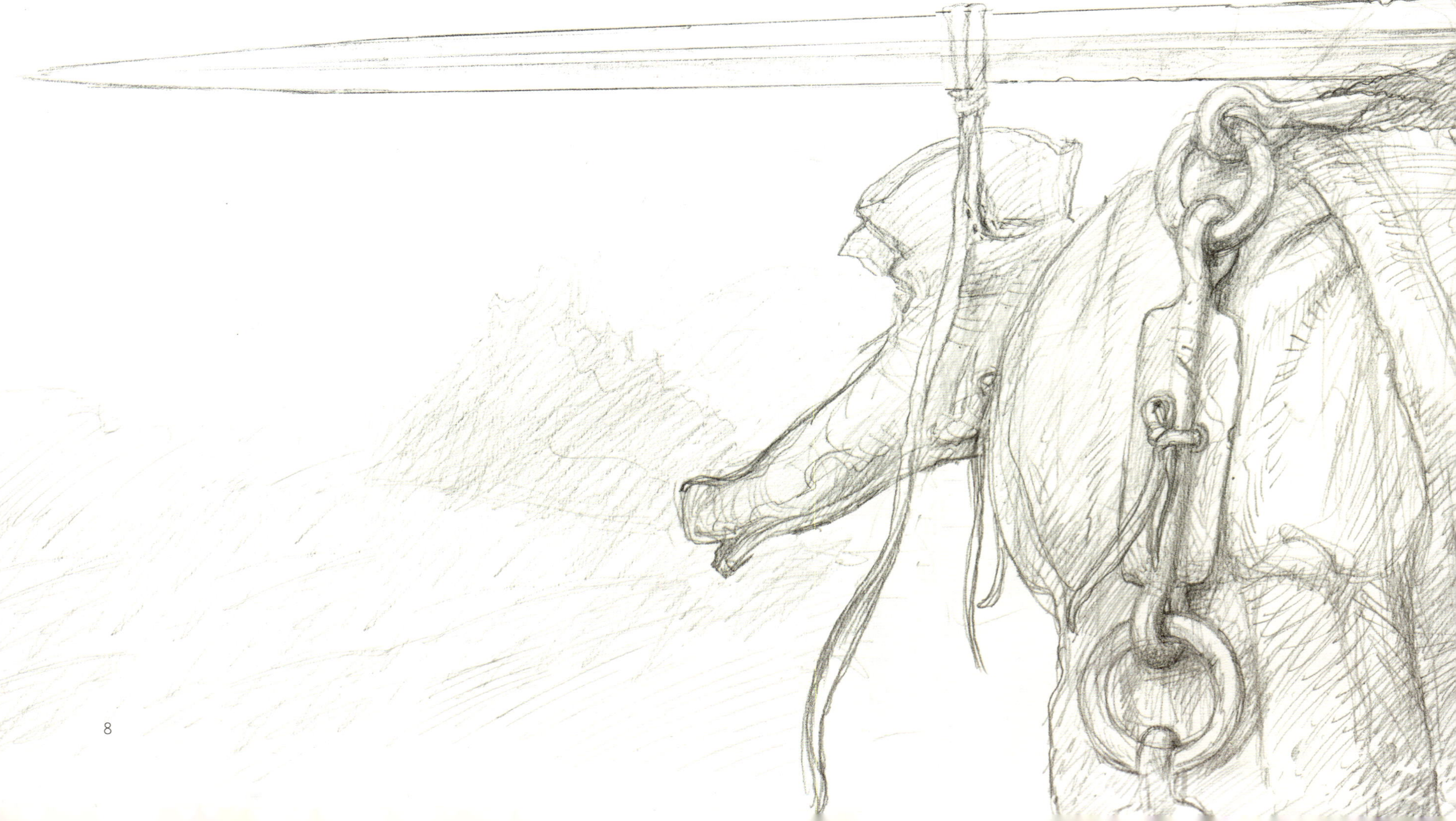

BOOK ILLUSTRATOR & CONCEPT DESIGNER
john-howe.com

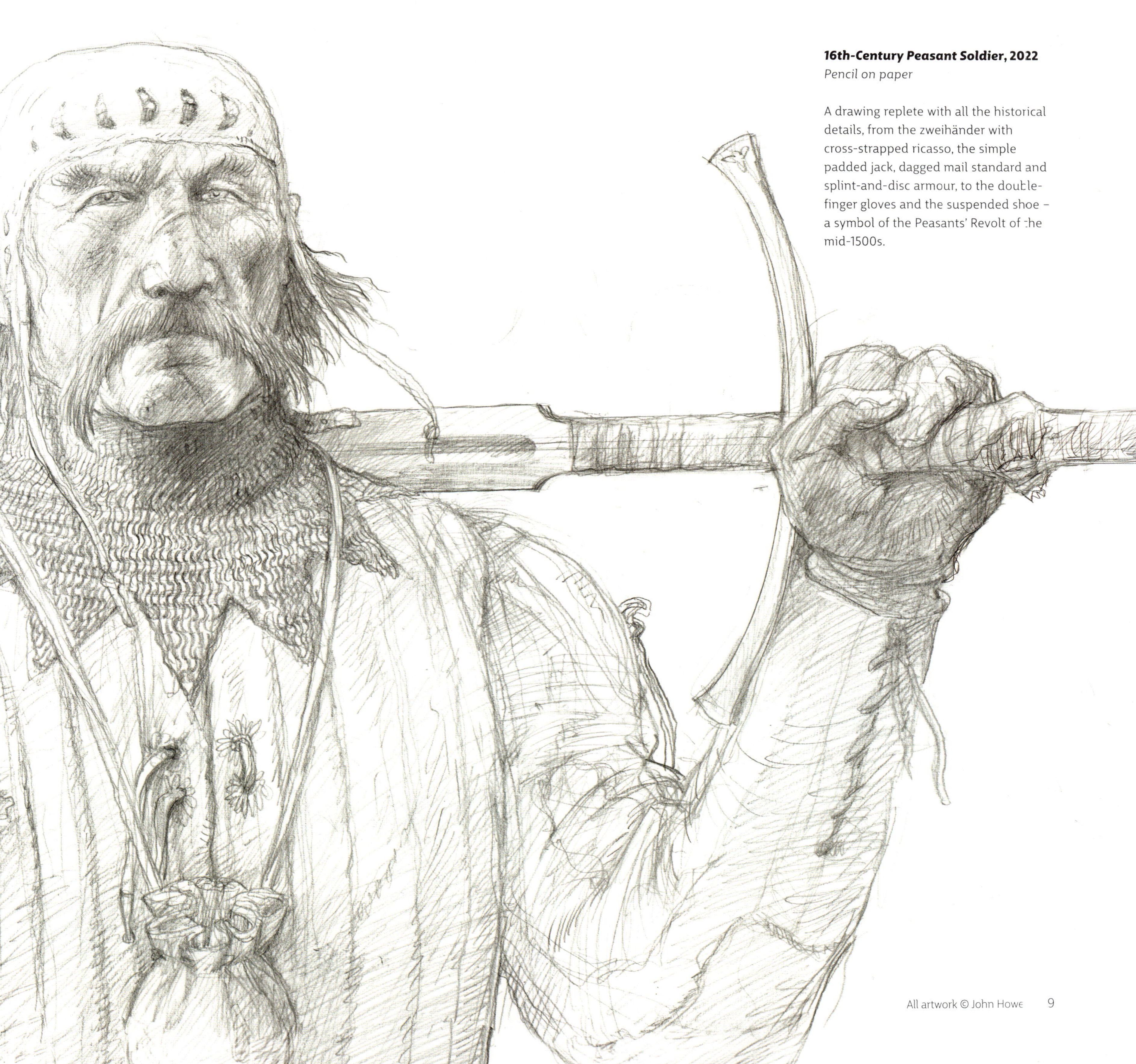

16th-Century Peasant Soldier, 2022
Pencil on paper

A drawing replete with all the historical details, from the zweihänder with cross-strapped ricasso, the simple padded jack, dagged mail standard and splint-and-disc armour, to the double-finger gloves and the suspended shoe – a symbol of the Peasants' Revolt of the mid-1500s.

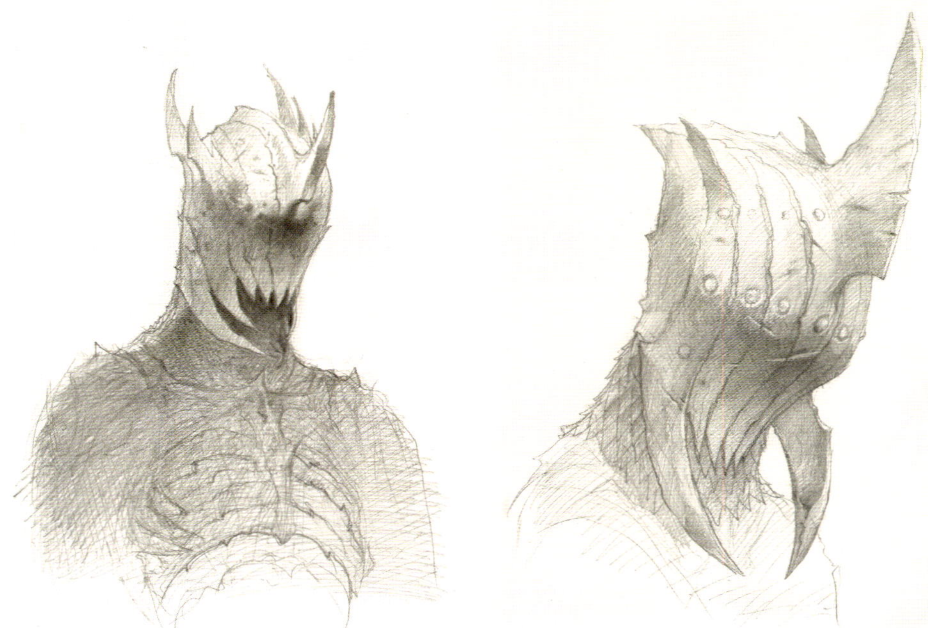

ART CLASS

I had trouble getting into art class in high school. Two family moves meant I arrived in my new school partway through the year and the art classes were already full. I finally secured a place in the twelfth grade, where I was a member of a rowdy trio that must have dismayed our teacher no end. Nonetheless, I owe her what progress I made and her constant encouragement and eagle-eyed criticism helped me prepare for real art school.

Outside of the classroom, I discovered the first Tolkien calendars and realized that you could actually illustrate these books and see your work published. I would redraw each month's calendar image in my own style (at the time I used oil pastels, of all things!). I also copied the work of artists I admired, most notably Frank Frazetta and Roy G. Krenkel. A year after my first high-school art class, I enrolled at an American college in France and the following year in a real art school, graduating three years later.

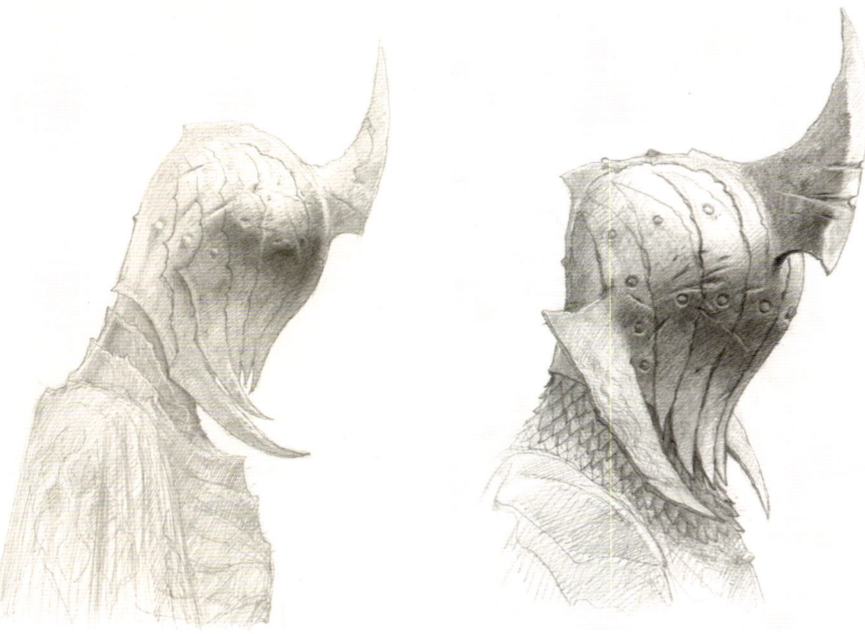

The Mouth of Sauron, Autumn 2024
Sketchbook, 30 × 40 cm

This is what happens when one pursues a theme to see where it might lead. I created all of these after work, so to speak (yes, artists unwind from work by … working!) – a drawing each evening, until another subject came along.

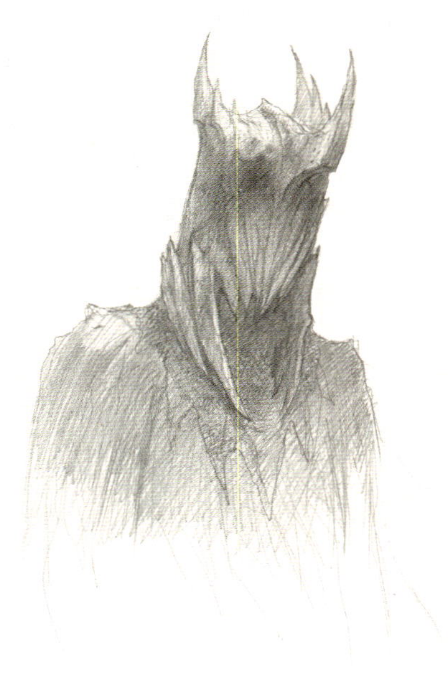

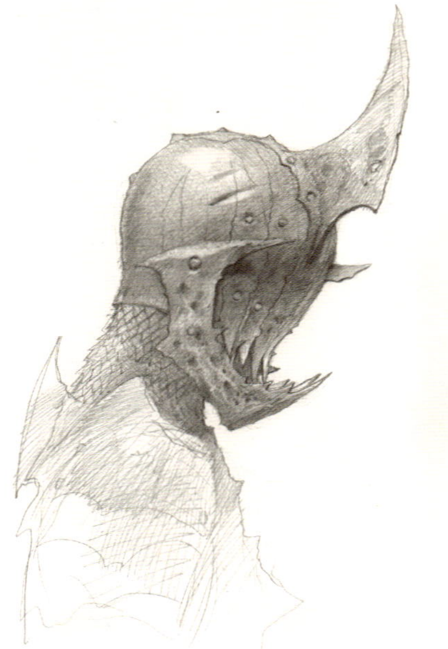

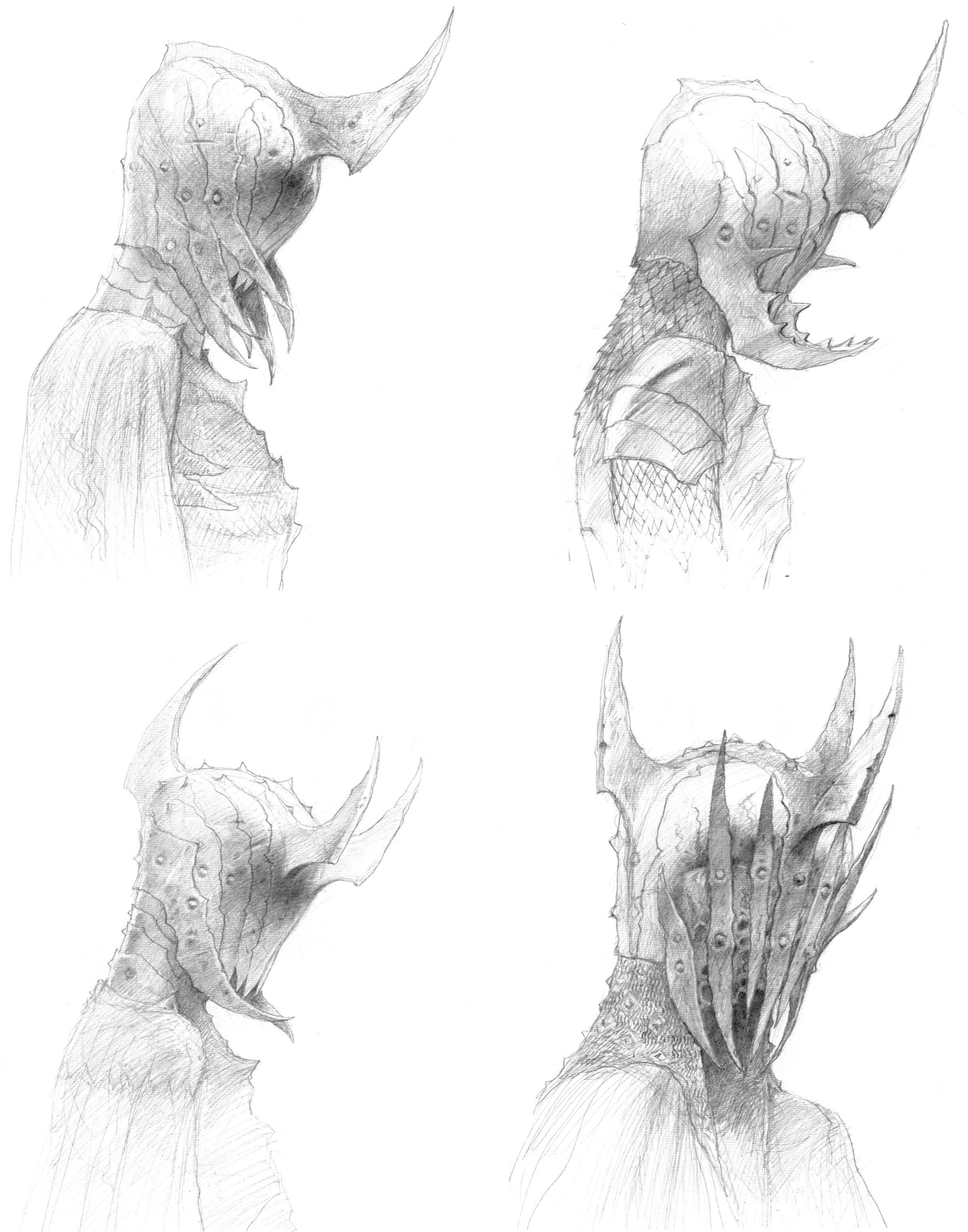

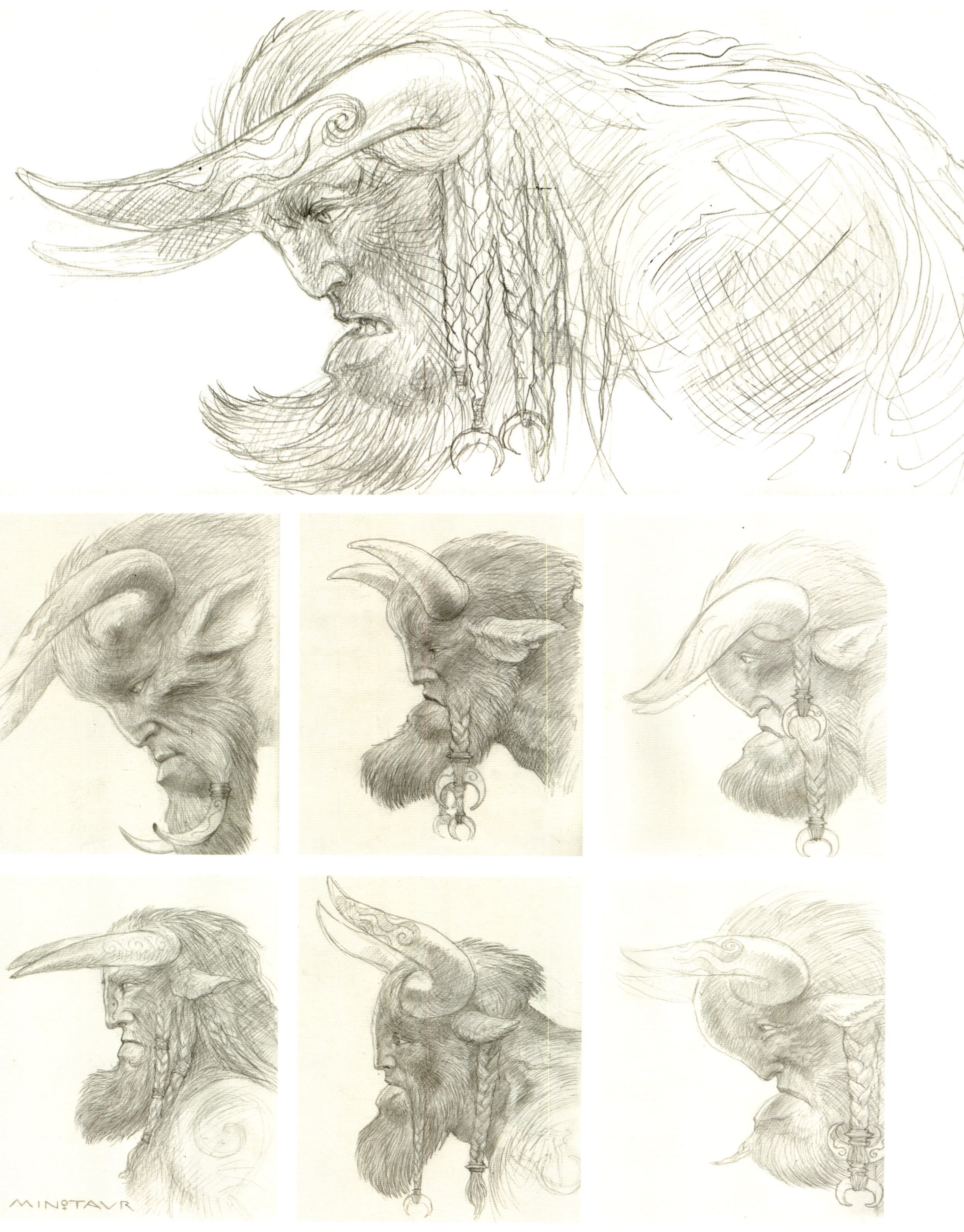

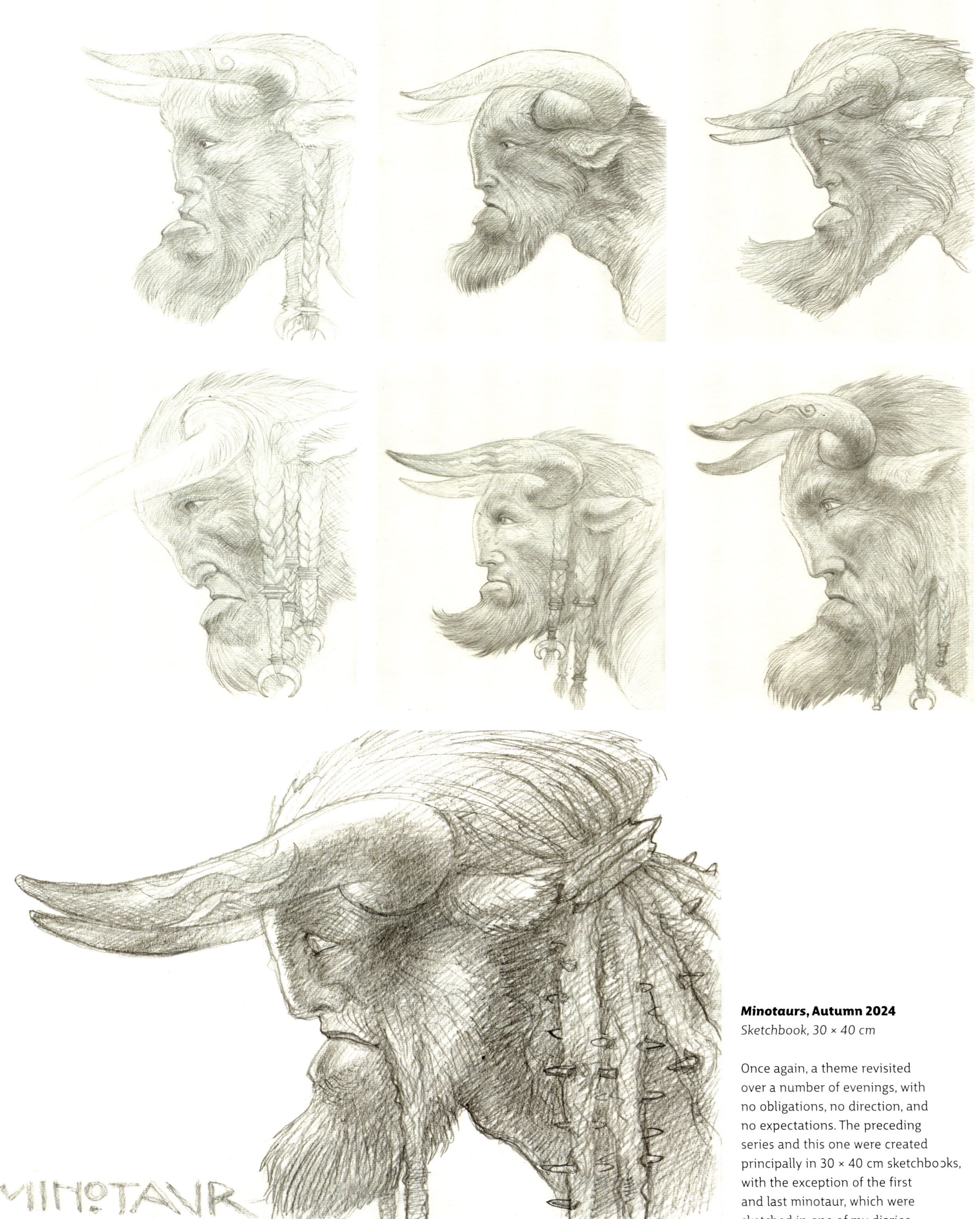

Minotaurs, Autumn 2024
Sketchbook, 30 × 40 cm

Once again, a theme revisited
over a number of evenings, with
no obligations, no direction, and
no expectations. The preceding
series and this one were created
principally in 30 × 40 cm sketchbooks,
with the exception of the first
and last minotaur, which were
sketched in one of my diaries.

TRADITIONAL MATERIALS

There was a long period after high school where I did not use sketchbooks regularly. For decades I worked on tracing paper or separate sheets. I started using them again when my colleague Alan Lee offered me a sketchbook during early pre-production on *The Lord of the Rings*. Since then, I have filled up over 150 of them. If you imagine between thirty and forty drawings per sketchbook, that makes a healthy number.

I generally use A3 hardbound sketchbooks, both portrait and landscape formats, which usually have about forty or fifty pages of top-quality paper. I also keep a smaller diary that is filled with sketches, depending on circumstance. When I travel, these materials – sketchbook, diary, pencils – all live in a small backpack that I purchased expressly because it can hold the A3 sketchbook. As for the paper, rough or smooth, I don't necessarily have a preference; although it does determine the selection of pencils I use. I am happy to draw on anything, as long as it is sturdy. I also enjoy little accordion sketchbooks for more whimsical drawings.

I confess to a prejudice against spiral-bound sketchbooks; they make it too tempting to tear out pages when the sketch goes wrong. Keeping the sketches that didn't work is even more important, in a way, than preserving the ones that did. Since you cannot tear out pages in a hardbound sketchbook, you must conserve the sketches that didn't work out, rather than pretending they don't exist.

I exclusively use pencil in my sketchbooks, though I do have watercolour sketchbooks for colour sketching. For the pencils themselves, I habitually use anything from a 7 or 8H to a 4B, depending on the nature of the paper or the drawing.

There are two key advantages to using pencils and traditional sketchbooks. While digital tools (such as tablets) are wonderful devices, the option to 'undo' means that you are not offered the chance to make decisions that are final. Traditional materials also mean that if you draw something lovely that is just not quite in the right spot, you cannot simply lasso and move it. You must erase and redraw. Irreversibility encourages clarity of thought and line.

Lastly, sketchbooks are resolutely low-tech, never crash, and don't need updates. It's almost as though maintaining this contact with materials that have been used by artists for centuries is something of an antidote to the seductiveness of digital tools.

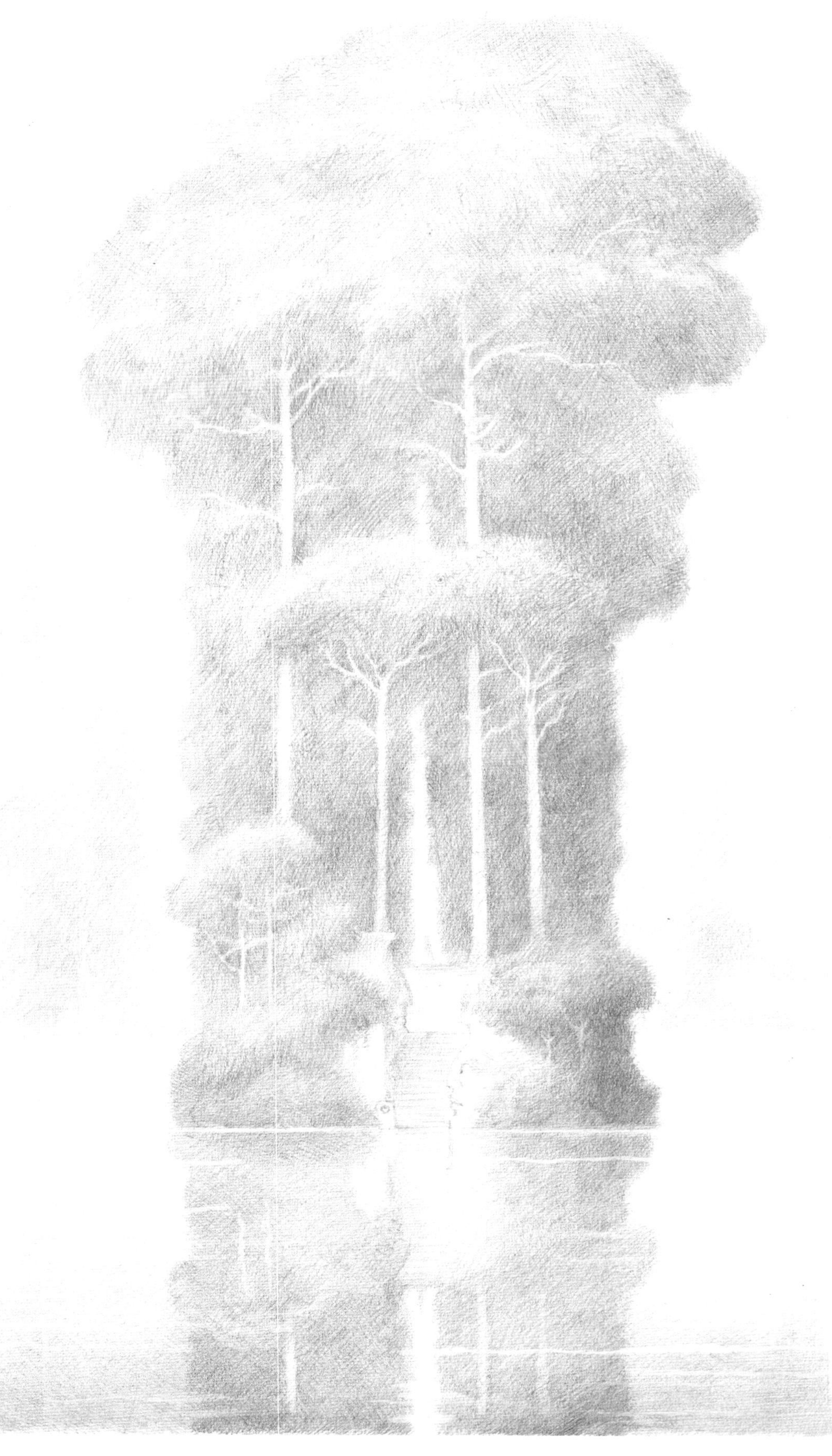

Opposite page | *Thanatos' Isle*, **2017**
Pencil on paper

Another theme I often return to,
inspired by the Swiss Symbolist
painter Arnold Böcklin's *Toteninsel*.
(Böcklin painted four of them,
one is lost.) Themes such as these are
a never-ending source of inspiration.

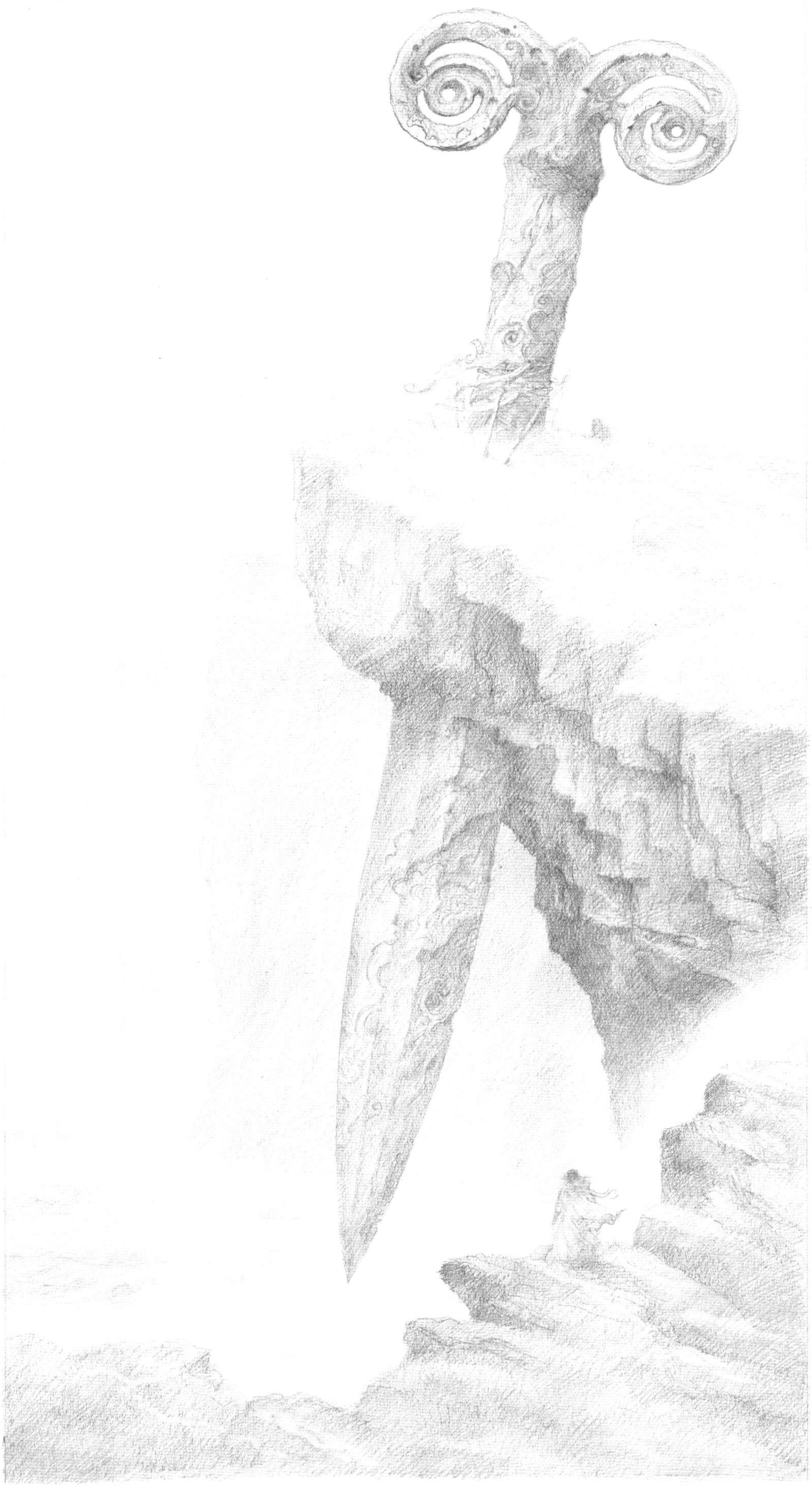

The Dagger, 2017
Pencil on paper

One of a series of drawings created for
an exhibition. I am always late, so the
gallery owners and I decided on the
formats (matte boards and frames
had to be prepared in advance) and
I did thirty pencil drawings, delivered
a couple of days before the opening.

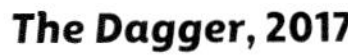

Witches' Beach I, 2017
Pencil on paper

Each of these drawings carries with it a handful of words, all in response to the
narrative already hinted at in the image. Sometimes, several images follow one another,
each in response to this narrative.

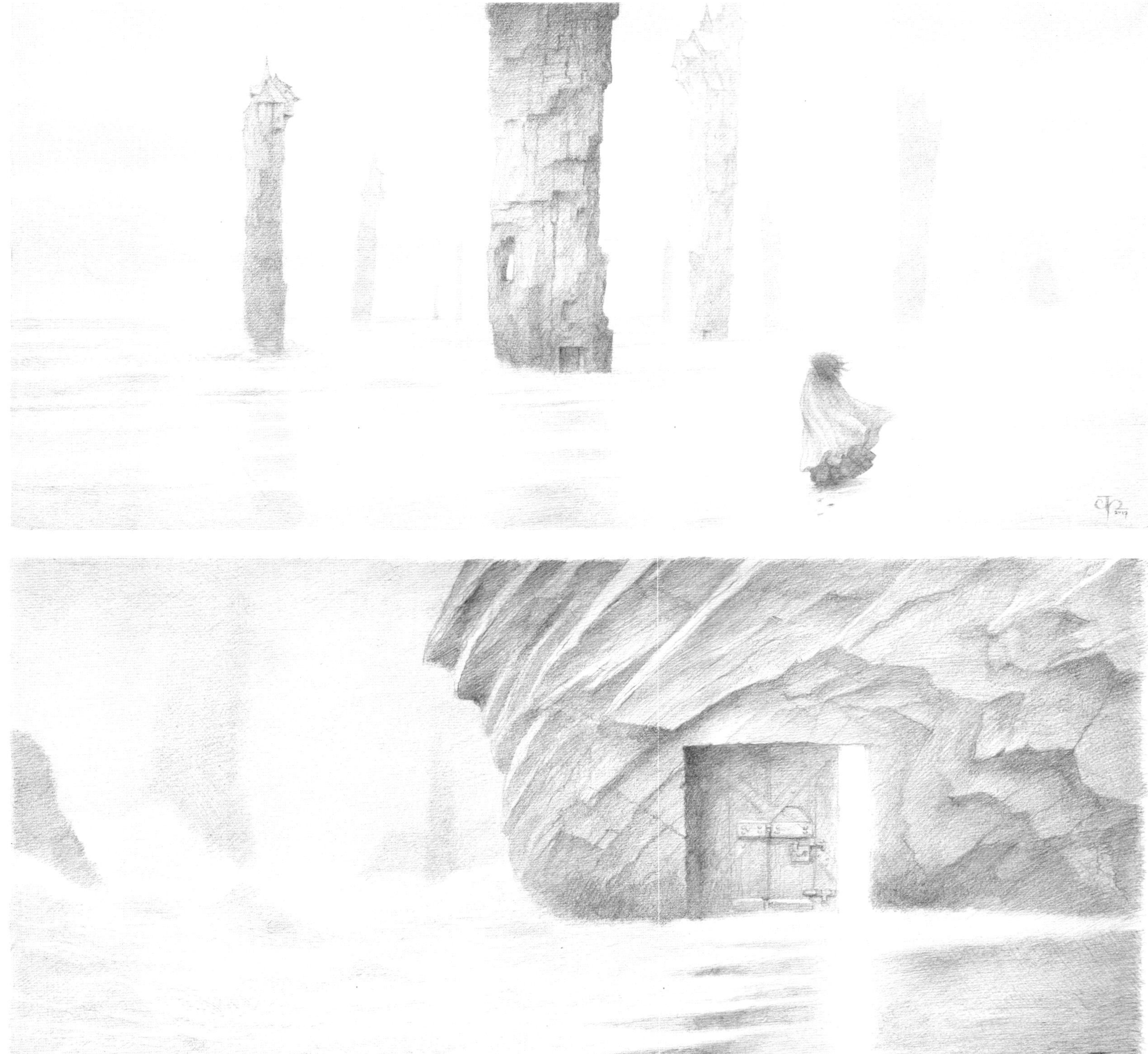

Witches' Beach II, 2017
Pencil on paper

The door is open, but what is at the top of the steps, wherever they lead? It is now part
of the story, but I've not quite got around to drawing my way up that winding stair.

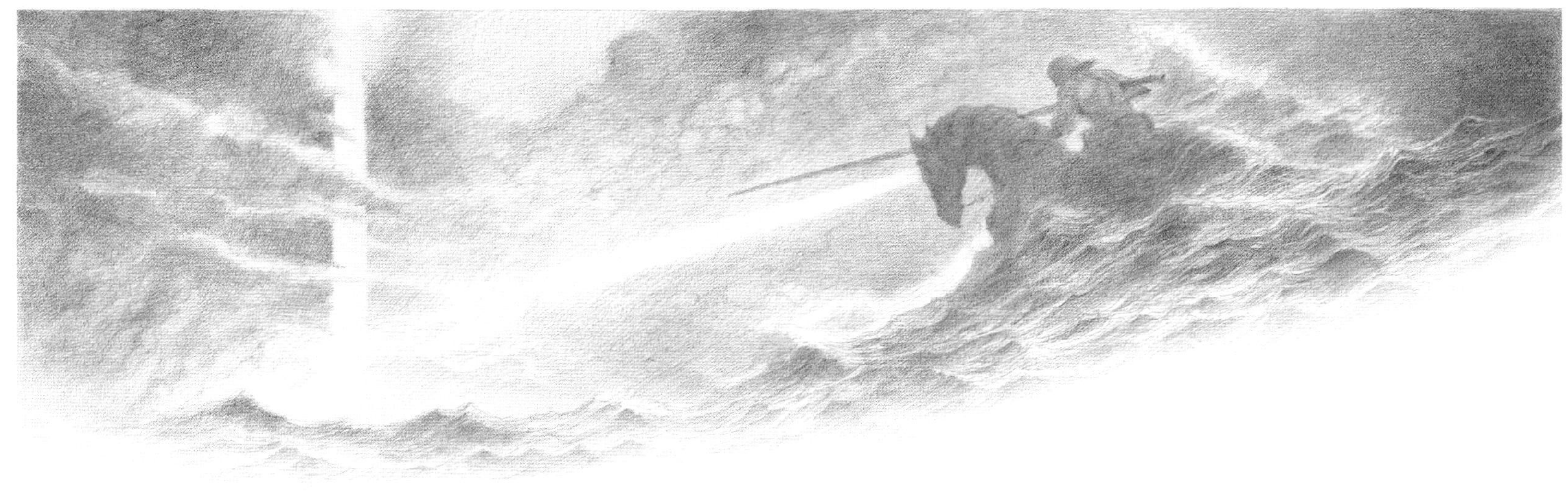

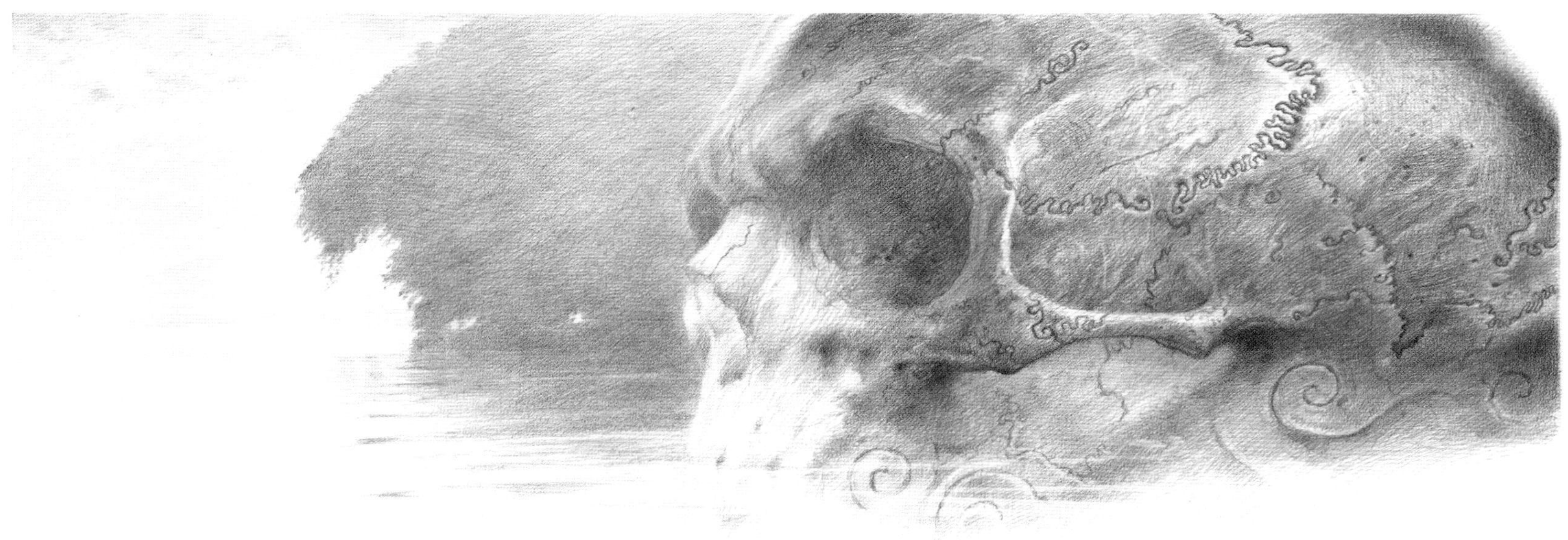

The Stormjaeger, 2015
Sketchbook, 30 × 40 cm

These beings grew from a story that appeared through an image, before taking on an existence of their own. I enjoy this back-and-forth navigation between word and picture, where ideas may take either path, figurative or literary. Although reading words and contemplating pictures are distinctly different activities, the initial spark of inspiration can go either way.

͵Thanatos' Isle, 2017
Pencil on paper

Another narrative within a narrative: I began a series of paintings several years ago, accompanied by a pencil drawing along the bottom edge of each. Each successive drawing provided the theme of the next painting, followed by another drawing – often on a new tangent – weaving in and out of the series.

Irreversibility encourages clarity of thought and line

INVESTING IN A SKETCHBOOK

While of course you can, and are sometimes obliged, to draw anywhere, on anything, with whatever you have to hand, when you purchase a sketchbook it is a clear recognition that your sketch work, without becoming self-conscious about its preservation, deserves the best materials.

As I mentioned earlier, I would insist on a properly bound sketchbook rather than spiral binding, principally because with spiral bound it is far too tempting to tear out a sketch that didn't work. Conserving your worst work is important; it is a precious witness of your progress and evolution. Also, don't buy a small sketchbook, unless it's specifically for travelling light. I see many students working in tiny sketchbooks, A4 or even A5, which don't allow much elbow room or space for improvement.

If you have just bought a beautiful sketchbook and find yourself hesitating for fear your very first drawing in it won't be good enough, simply start ten or twenty pages in. If that drawing doesn't work out, it won't be the first one you see on opening it.

Dragon Shores I, 1996

Sketch originally created for a book on dragons. I imagined the shores of a land covered in dragons, inspired by the marine iguanas of the Galapagos. Dragon Shores … it is a theme I have returned to often. These are scenes that I see as a film sequence – from the point of view of a small sailing craft, a sable and torn shoreline, underscored by a brushstroke of crashing foam, emerges from the mist. As we approach, the rocks begin to stir, vast heads lift; ragged crests silhouetted against the sky. The whole shoreline is lined with dragons...

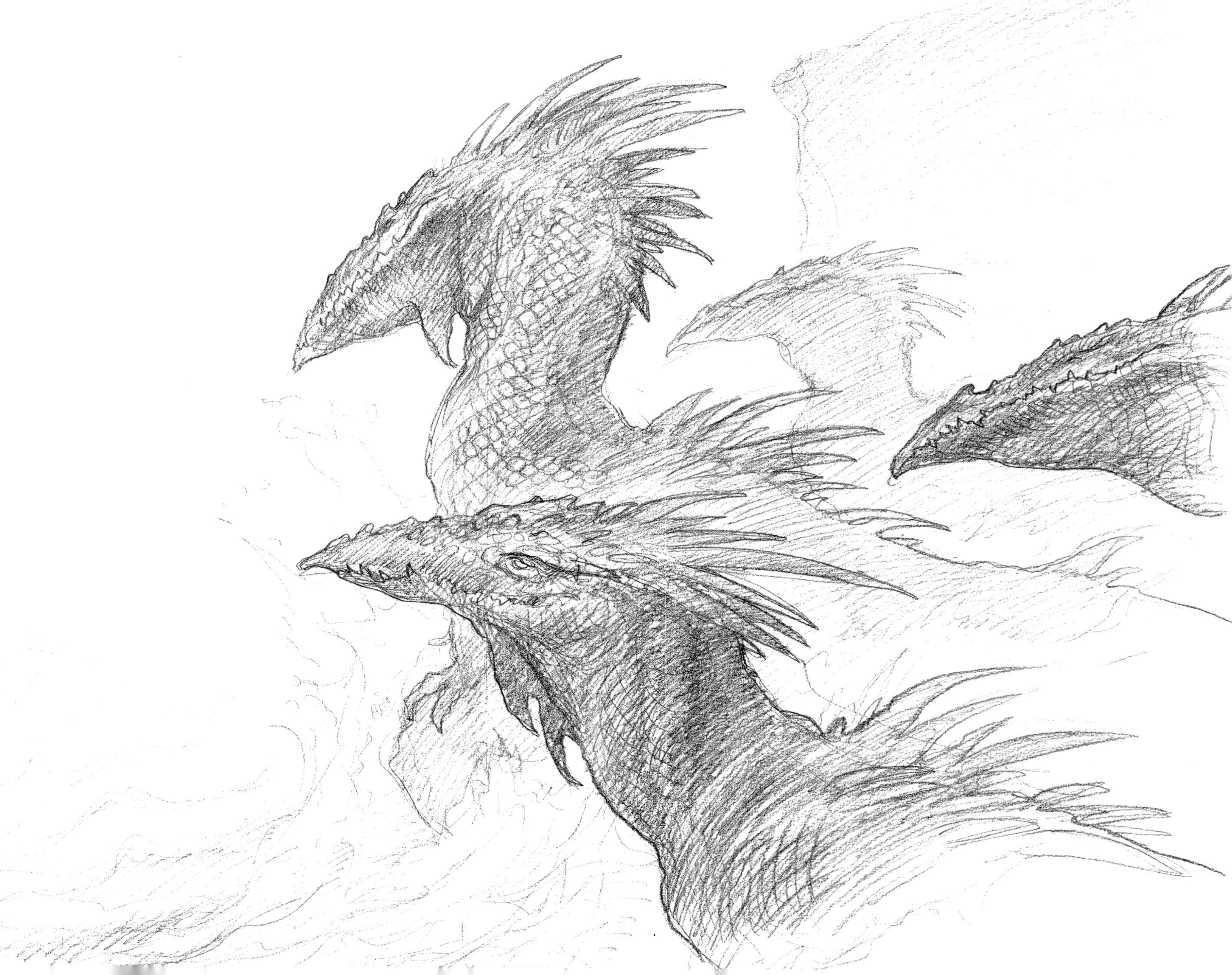

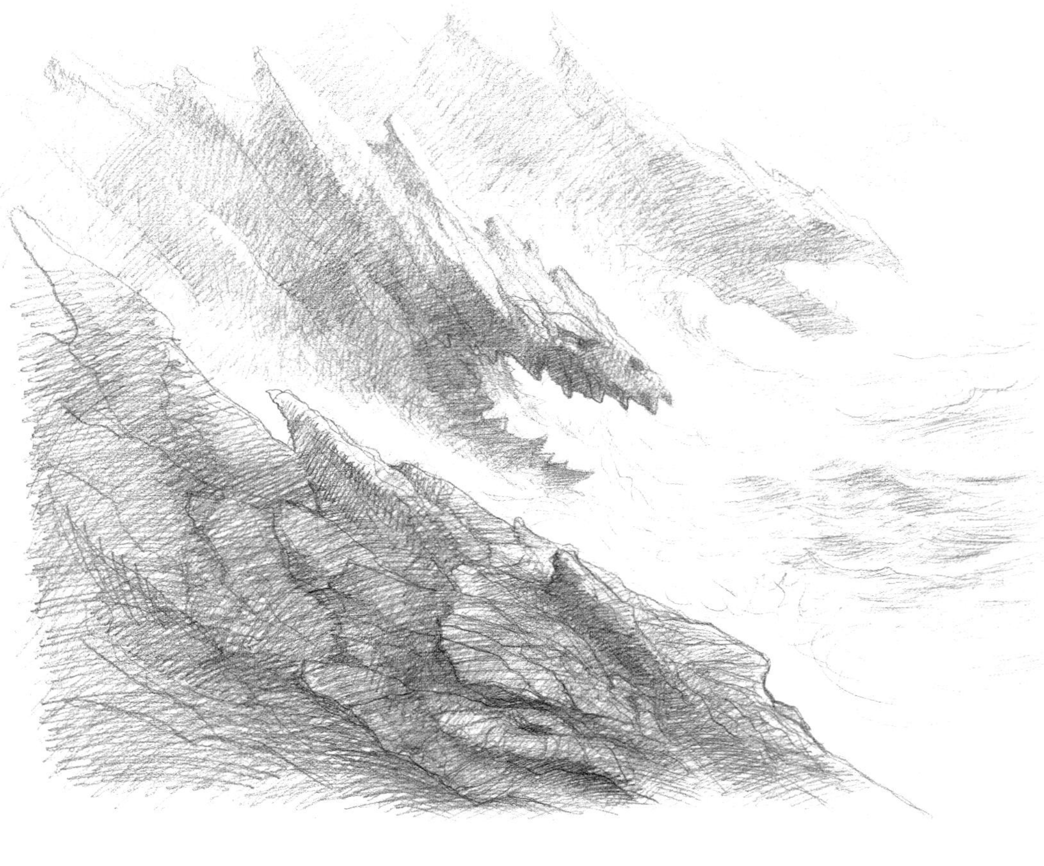

Dragon Shores II, 1996

I've always been enamoured by the striking spectacle of lava flowing into the ocean in Hawaii. This black-and-white sketch was meant to be the beginning of a series of paintings depicting dragons of stone spouting fire into the waves.

Book cover sketch, 1991

A rapid rough sketch for a fantasy novel. These are quickly done, intended tc provide the publisher with enough information so that the final artwork can be created.

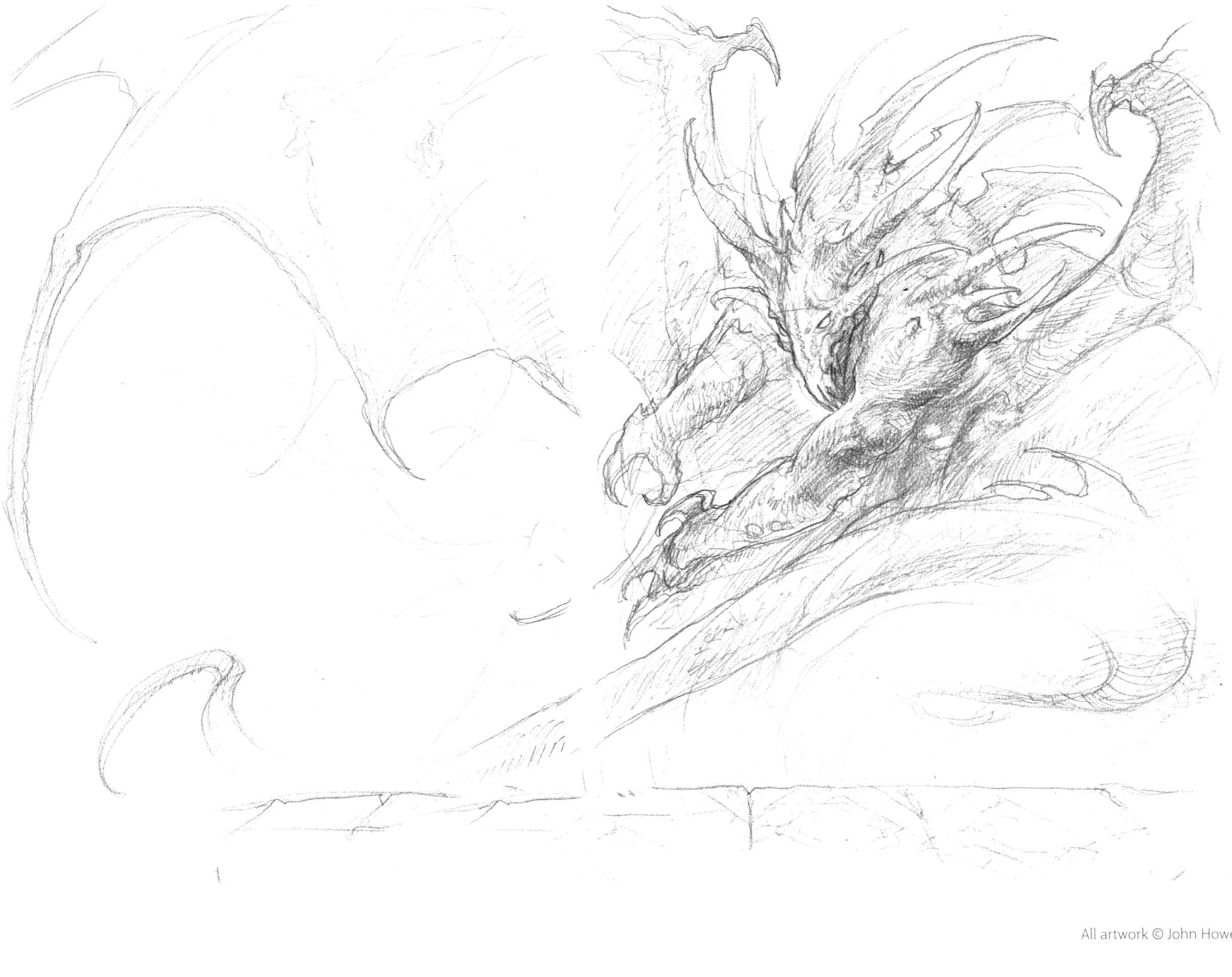

King Lir, 2016

Drawing for *Two Hearts*, the short
sequel to the marvellous book *The
Last Unicorn* by Peter Beagle (a book
I would absolutely love to illustrate one
day). The project was unfortunately
abandoned.

King Lir is TM & © Peter Beagle, printed with the
permission of Project Uni LLC

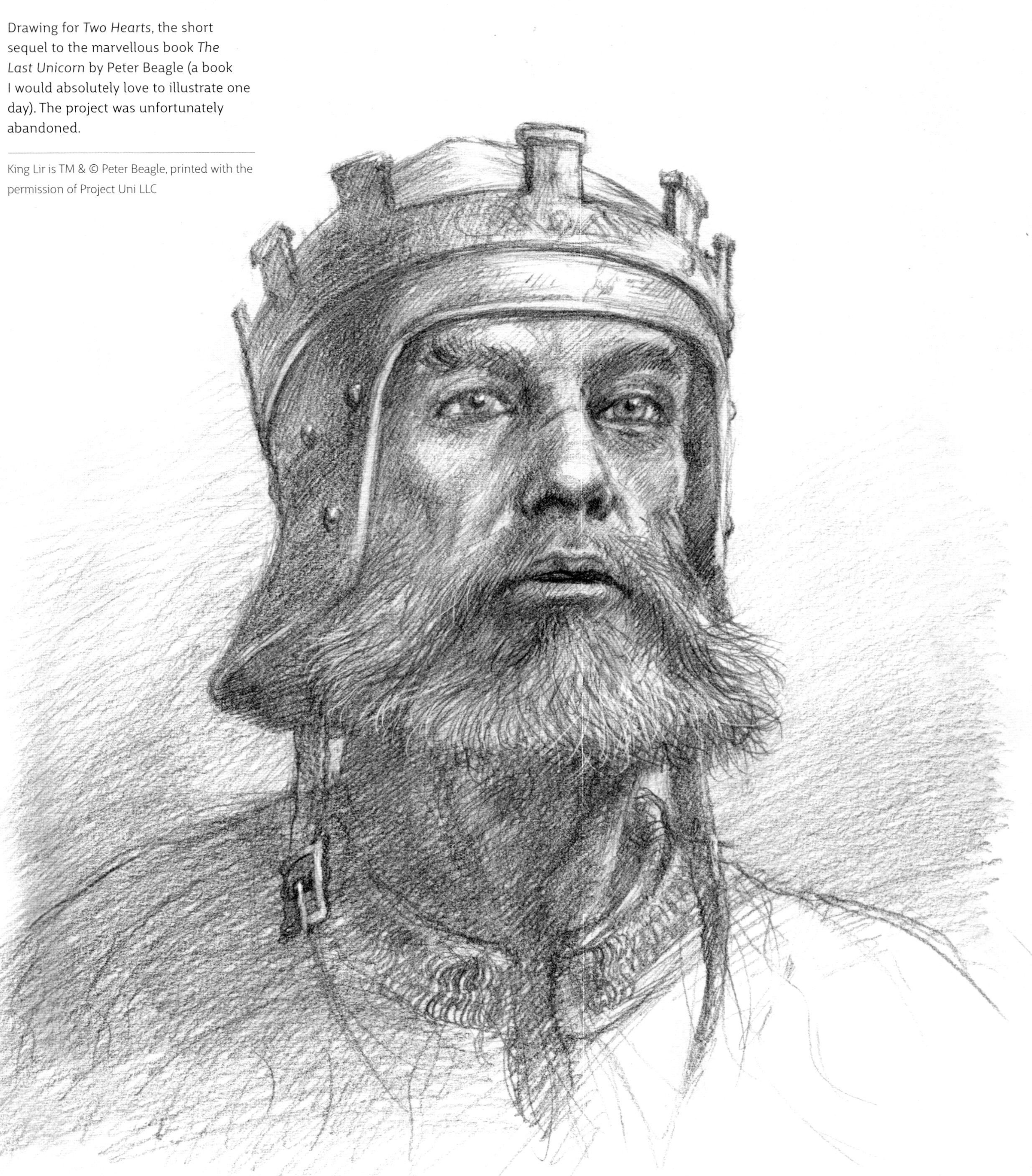

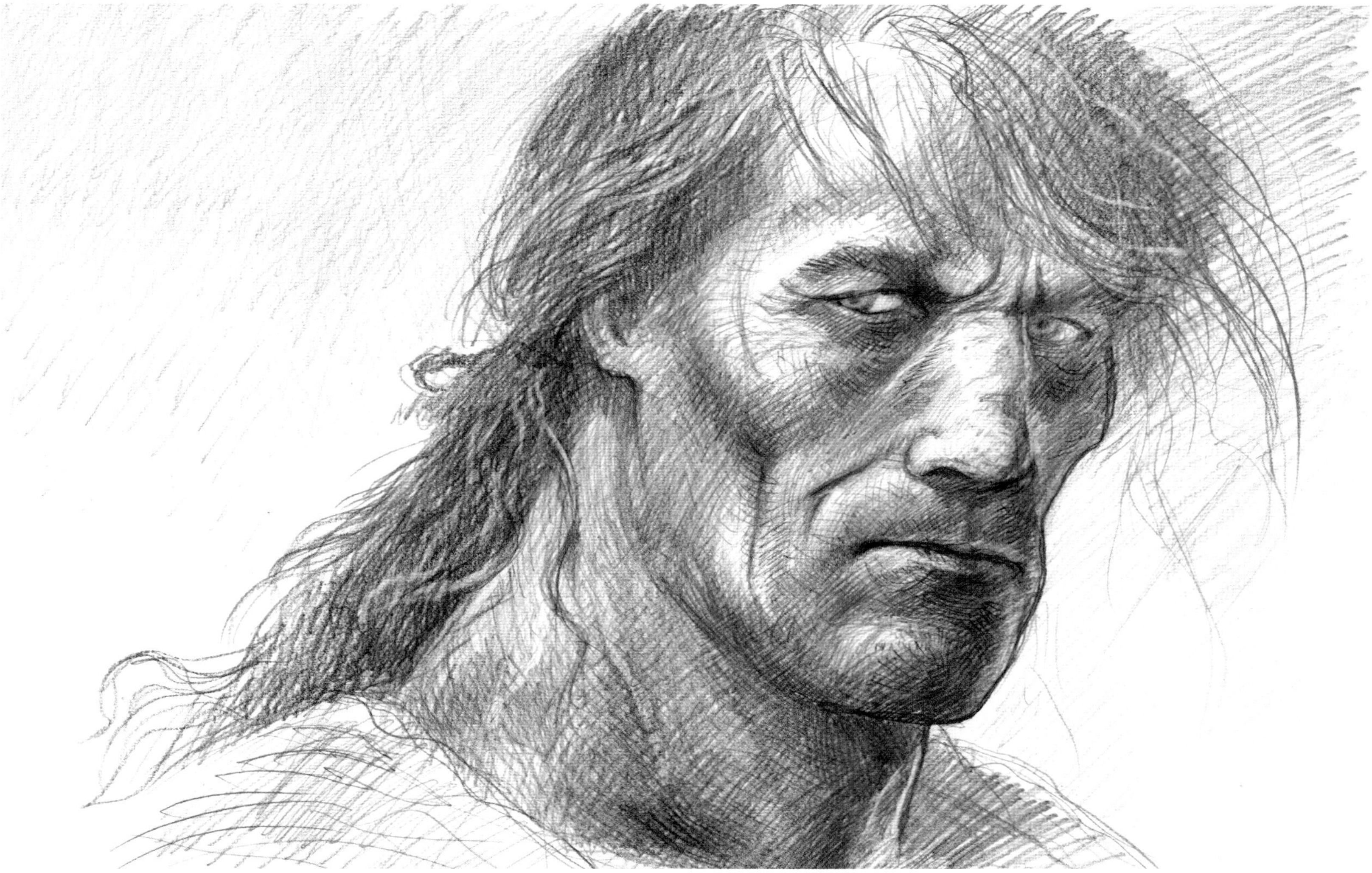

Frankenstein's Monster

The first in a series of sketches
depicting the famous creation of
Doctor Frankenstein.

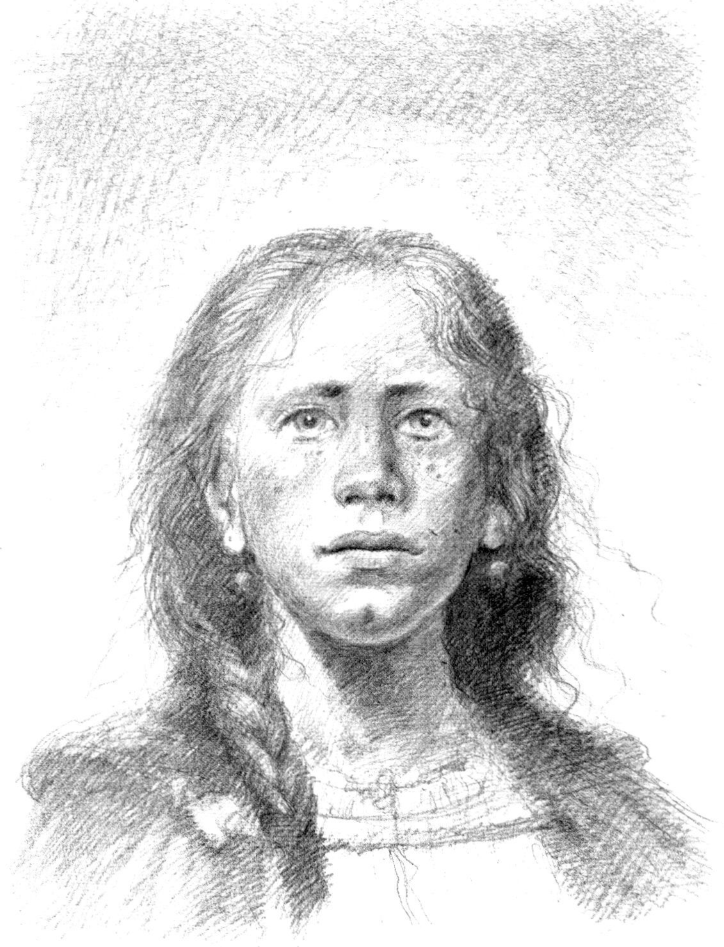

Sooz, 2016

Another character from *The Last
Unicorn* sequel.

Sooz is TM & © Peter Beagle, printed with the
permission of Project Uni LLC

Nightmare Raven, 2004

A sketch I created to accompany a
limited edition of *A Clash of Kings*
by George R. R. Martin.

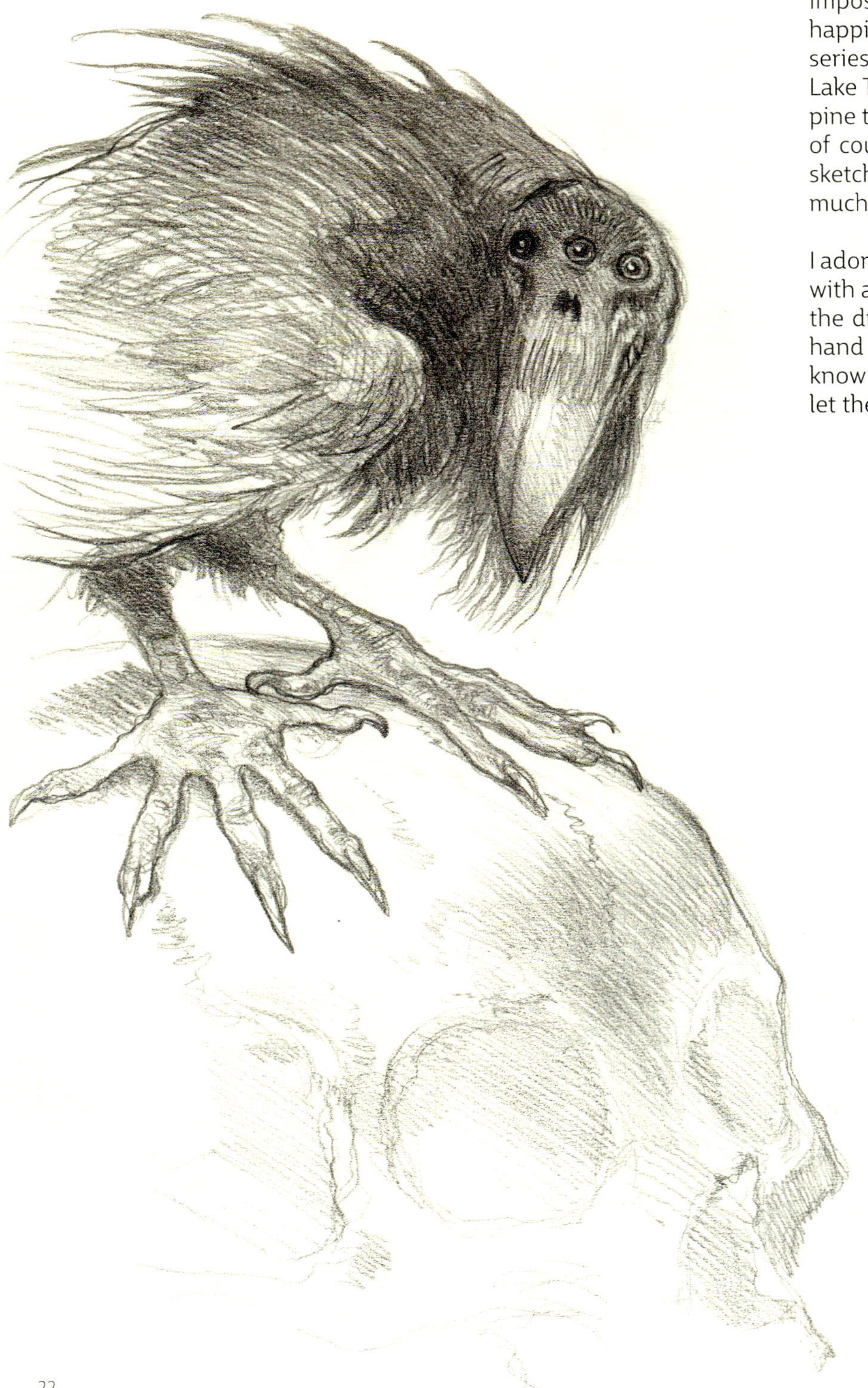

THE PERFECT PERSONAL WORKSPACE

The sketchbook is, of course, the perfect travel companion and personal workspace. It never needs charging or updates. I try to use mine very spontaneously and usually carry one with me wherever I go. It is also a way of escaping the traditional posture of sitting hunched over a table, as you can lounge anywhere with a sketchbook on your knees. I have no systematic approach to anything where sketches are involved; I value the incidental and spontaneous process. A more measured approach may be necessary when preparing a painting, but sketches should remain free of any obligation.

When I was working on *The Hobbit* film in New Zealand, we would occasionally have to track down Peter Jackson on location to show him recent concept art. On-location film shooting being what it is, the most precious commodity is the right weather, and some days it was impossible for him to stop for half an hour to look at art. So, we would happily find a shady spot and draw while waiting. I created a whole series of sketches of Bilbo under the Lonely Mountain on the shores of Lake Tekapo on the South Island, comfortably seated in the shade of a pine tree. Other times, we would wait in a corner of a sound stage, and, of course, you never stop drawing. I had never considered choosing sketchbooks for their sound before those moments. (Smooth paper is much less noisy than rough!)

I adore using sketchbooks for film concept work. I suppose I think better with a pencil and sketchbook than I do with a tablet. Afterwards, I scan the drawings and work them up digitally. I also keep a sketchbook to hand late evenings when the mind can vagabond freely. You never know what will appear when you simply shut down all thoughts and let the pencil wander.

I have no systematic approach to anything where sketches are involved; I value the incidental and spontaneous process

Skavven Shaman, 2017
Pencil on paper

Ravens have always been a source of inspiration. I draw dozens of them, continually,
always searching for what it is that attracts me so much.

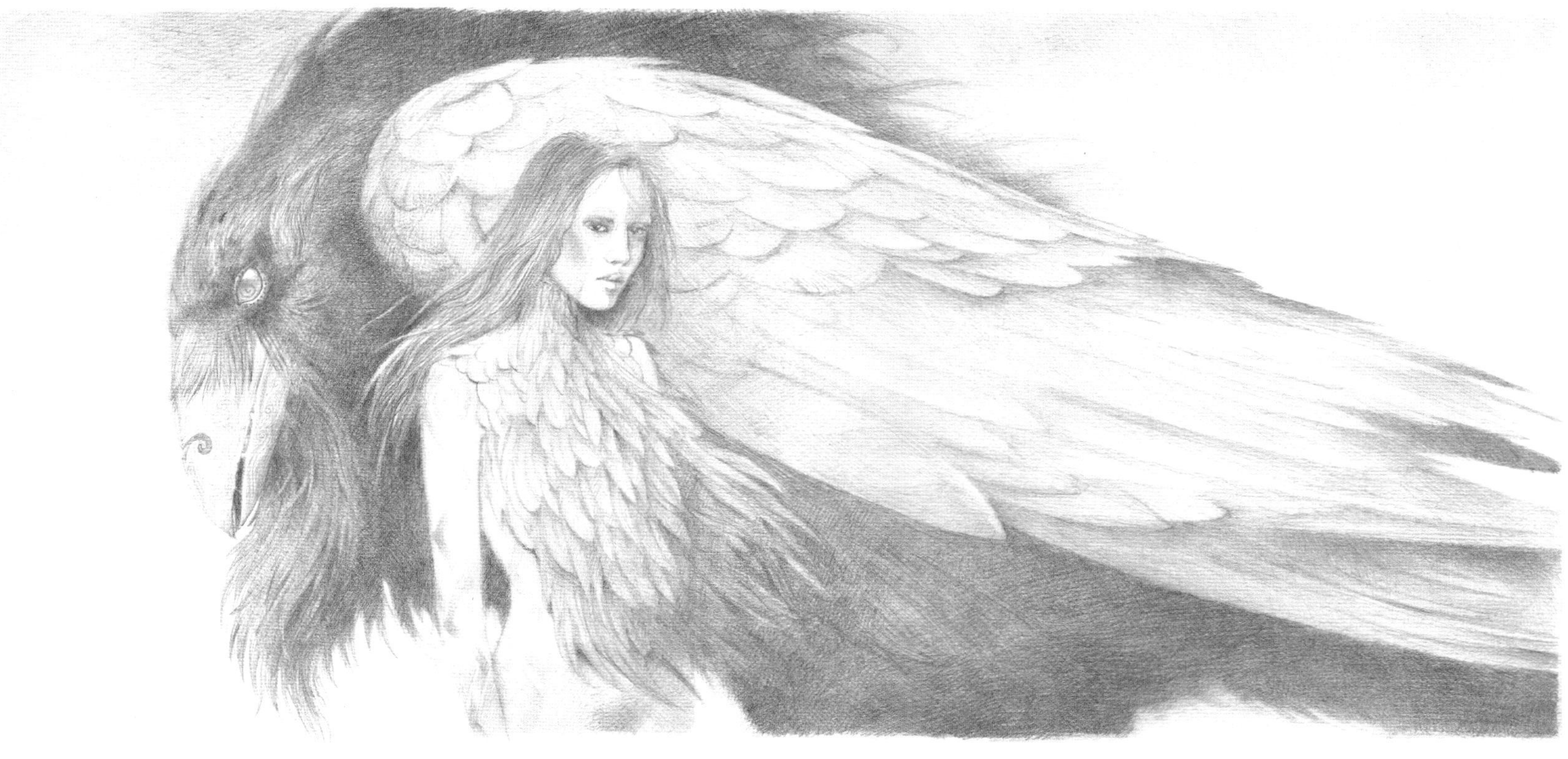

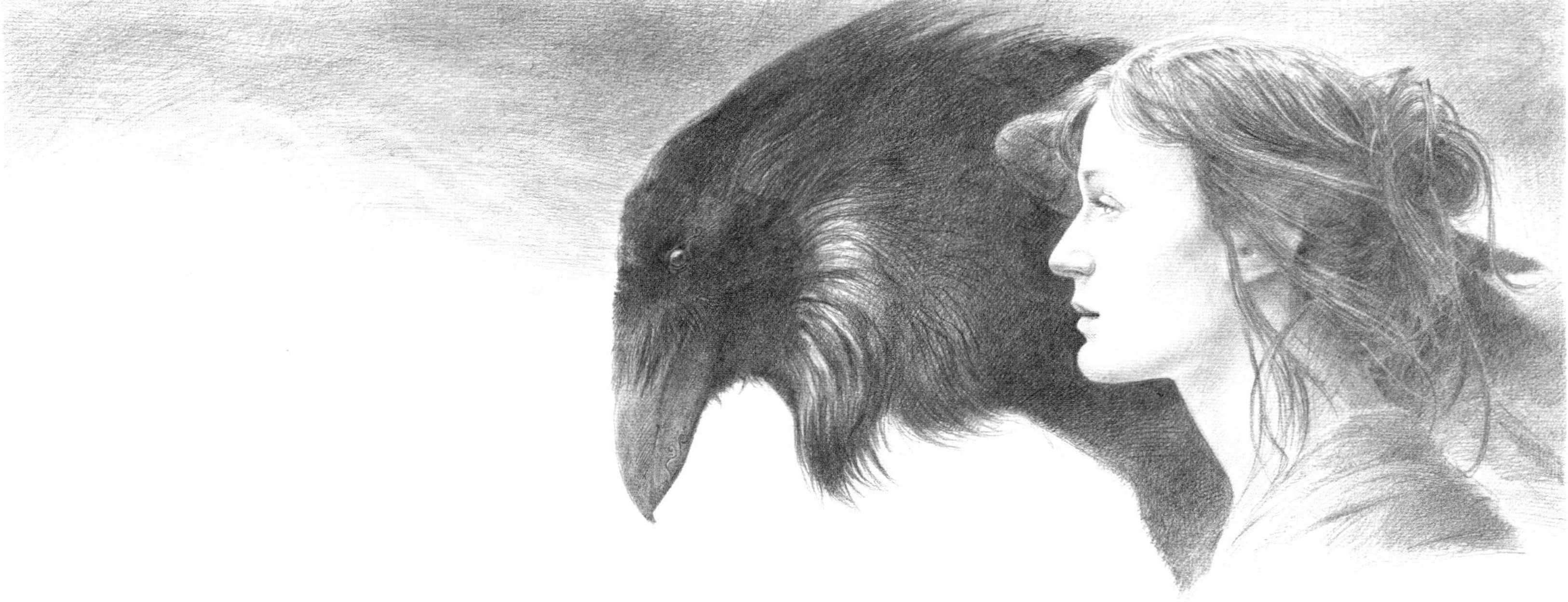

Llora and the Ravven, 2015
Pencil on paper

Perhaps the best way to understand the subjects or themes about
which one feels passionate is to draw them. Capturing the likeness
brings you nearer; beyond that is the elusive realm of the archetype.

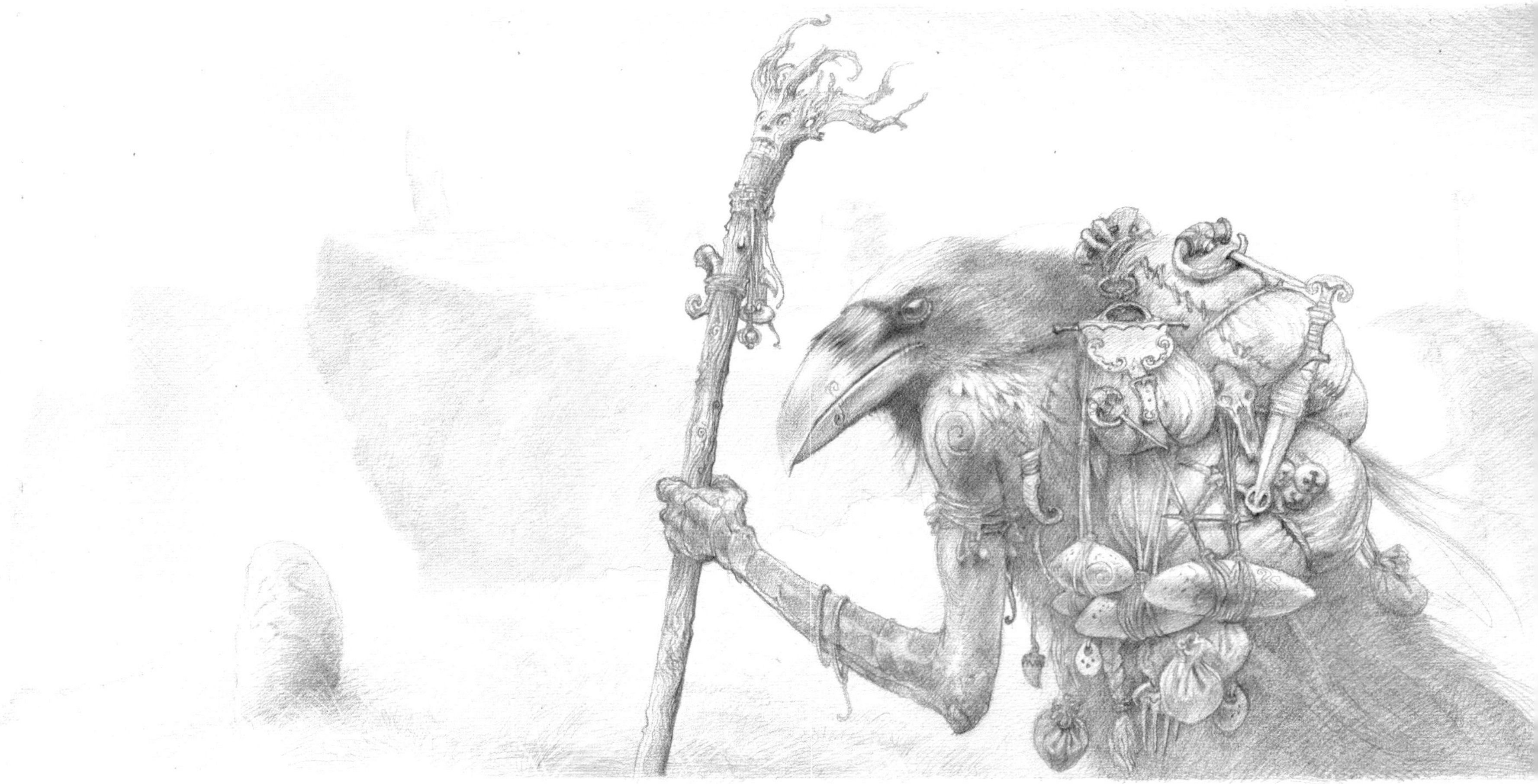

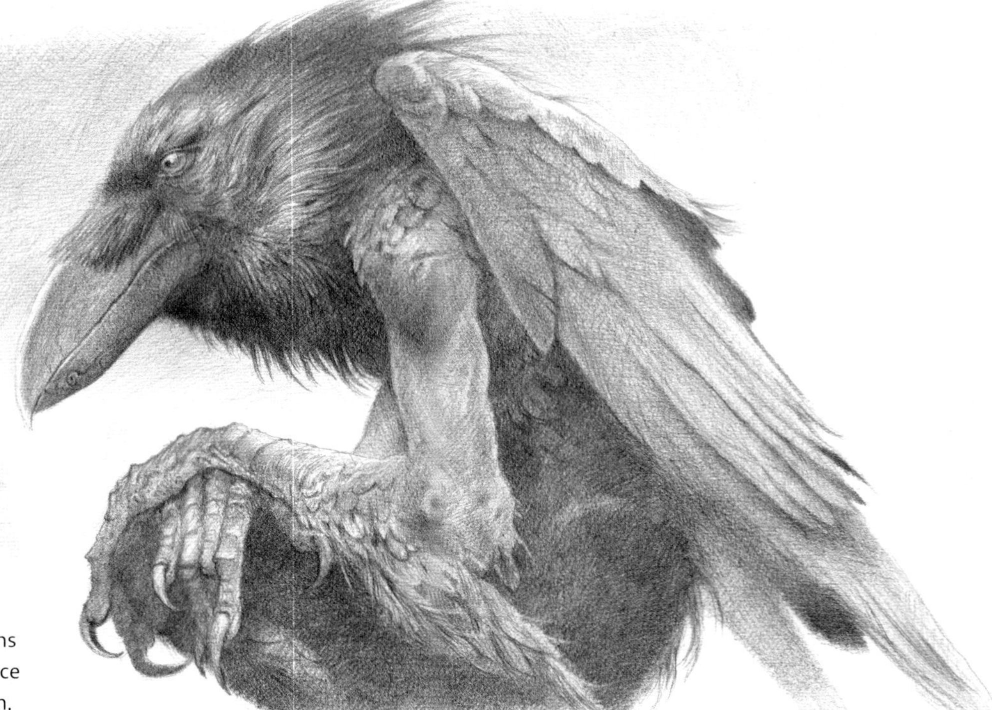

Skavven Voyager, 2017
Pencil on paper

These drawings were created, purposefully, without a clear idea of what I wished to draw. I had a nominal, and imprecise, notion of the theme, but there is no layout. This conscientious lack of planning means that the drawing appears through the dialogue between myself, the theme, and the drawing itself as it takes shape.

Skavven Hunter, 2017
Pencil on paper

These drawings appear on the paper in stages, the relaxing portions being the accumulation of details and complexity in a defined space or form. Other elements appear out of nowhere, like the musk oxen, who are now the preferred mounts of the skavven hunters.

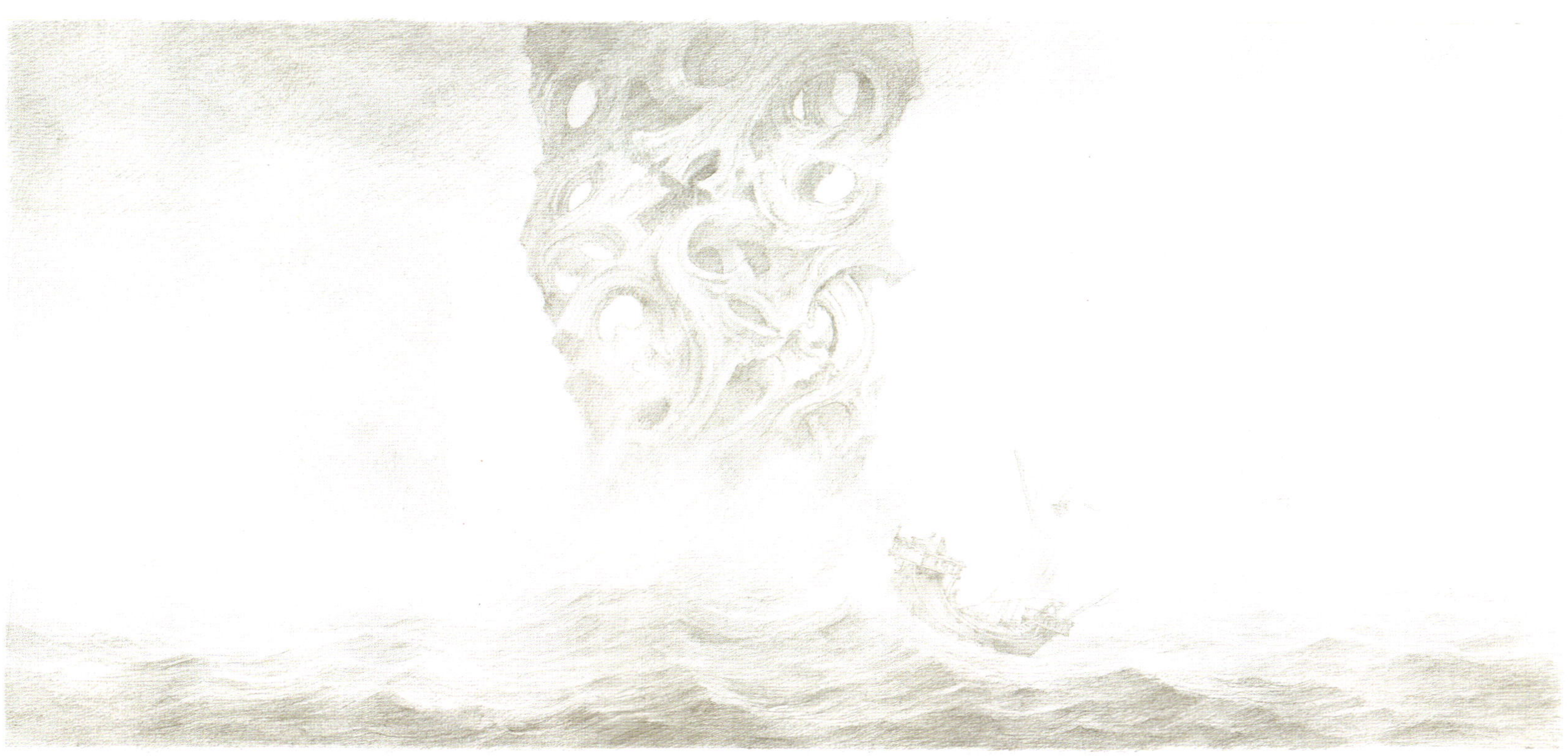

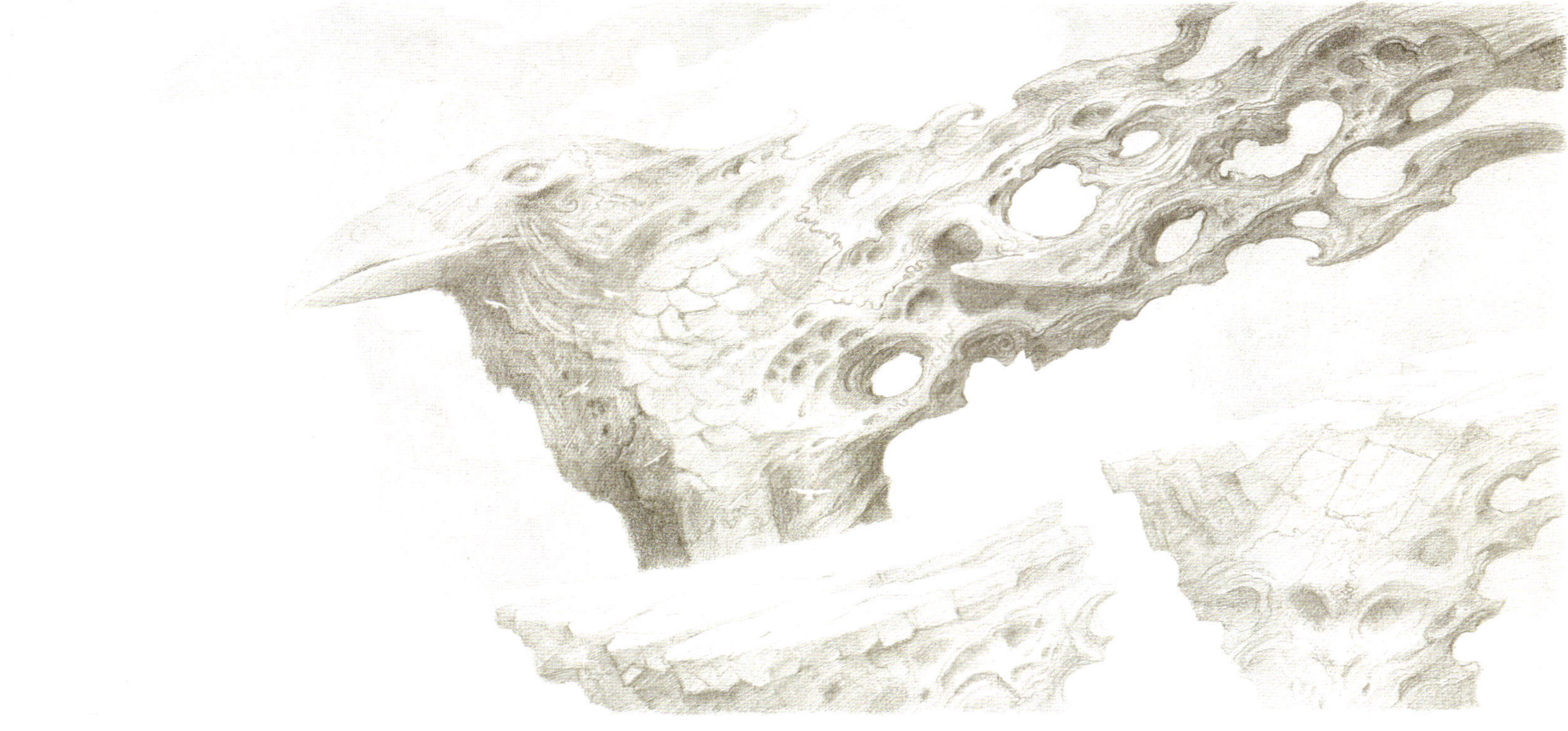

Llora's Quest, 2017
Pencil on paper

On Strasbourg Cathedral, almost at street level, there
is an extraordinary series of statue bases entirely
composed of interlaced gothic leaf shapes. They have
been there half a millennium and are weathered,
aged, and incredibly beautiful. I return to them often
for inspiration. (They are not to go on any bucket list,
though – restoration of that section has begun, so they
will ultimately be replaced by modern copies.)

Ravven Dreaming, 2017
Pencil on paper

Another theme I return to: that of
beings both rooted in the land and
dreaming the land, as if towering cliffs
were formed not by erosion, but by
dreams of stone and verticality, to form
a fantastical landscape that shapes
nature before being shaped by it.

EXPLORATION & SPONTANEITY

My sketchbooks are as spontaneous and disorganized as my life in general, I fear. The idea of having a selection of sketchbooks, each one dedicated to a specific genre or task, is something I cannot even imagine. A sketchbook is meant to be picked up on a whim, or filled diligently on a project. My sketchbooks are an unpredictable mix of everything.

In a sense, a sketchbook only exists as an object after it is filled up. I could never imagine keeping a selection of sketchbooks for predetermined subjects or genres. I think I would find it stifling and counterproductive. Occasionally there will be a series on a theme, following one idea to another, often interrupted by a sketch for a specific commission. My last sketchbook has, in order, nine finished drawings for a calendar, a sketch for a watch design, three sketches for a book cover, five drawings of leaves, another cover sketch, two ravens, a giant, a sketch for a slipcase, thirteen minotaurs (for no reason at all), and a landscape sketch drawn near a river.

I don't care for the idea of curating the contents of a sketchbook. The goal of a sketchbook is exploration and spontaneity, which sits poorly with planning or having an idea of the sketchbook as a whole. Each time I have decided to save a sketchbook for a particular theme or project, it has always ended up being a mix of work. The only way to ensure homogenous content is to fill it up quickly, which usually happens on film projects. In those cases, a sketchbook can last a week or ten days.

I must confess, I don't do a lot of drawing from nature or practise any particular techniques. I do distinguish between sketches and drawings; the former are incidental, spontaneous, and often abandoned in favour of a new sketch, whereas the latter are more thoroughly planned and generally more detailed throughout. I do occasionally do quick sketches as visual notes, but those are generally in my diaries. (I have a few hundred of those diaries, indifferently filled with writing and sketches. They are all in an A5 format, or square.)

Grendel, 2004
Pencil on paper

Grendel, the terrible devourer of men that attacks the Hall of Heorot. Sea otters were the inspiration for the shape of Grendel's skull, and lampreys for his mouth and teeth.

The goal of a sketchbook is exploration and spontaneity

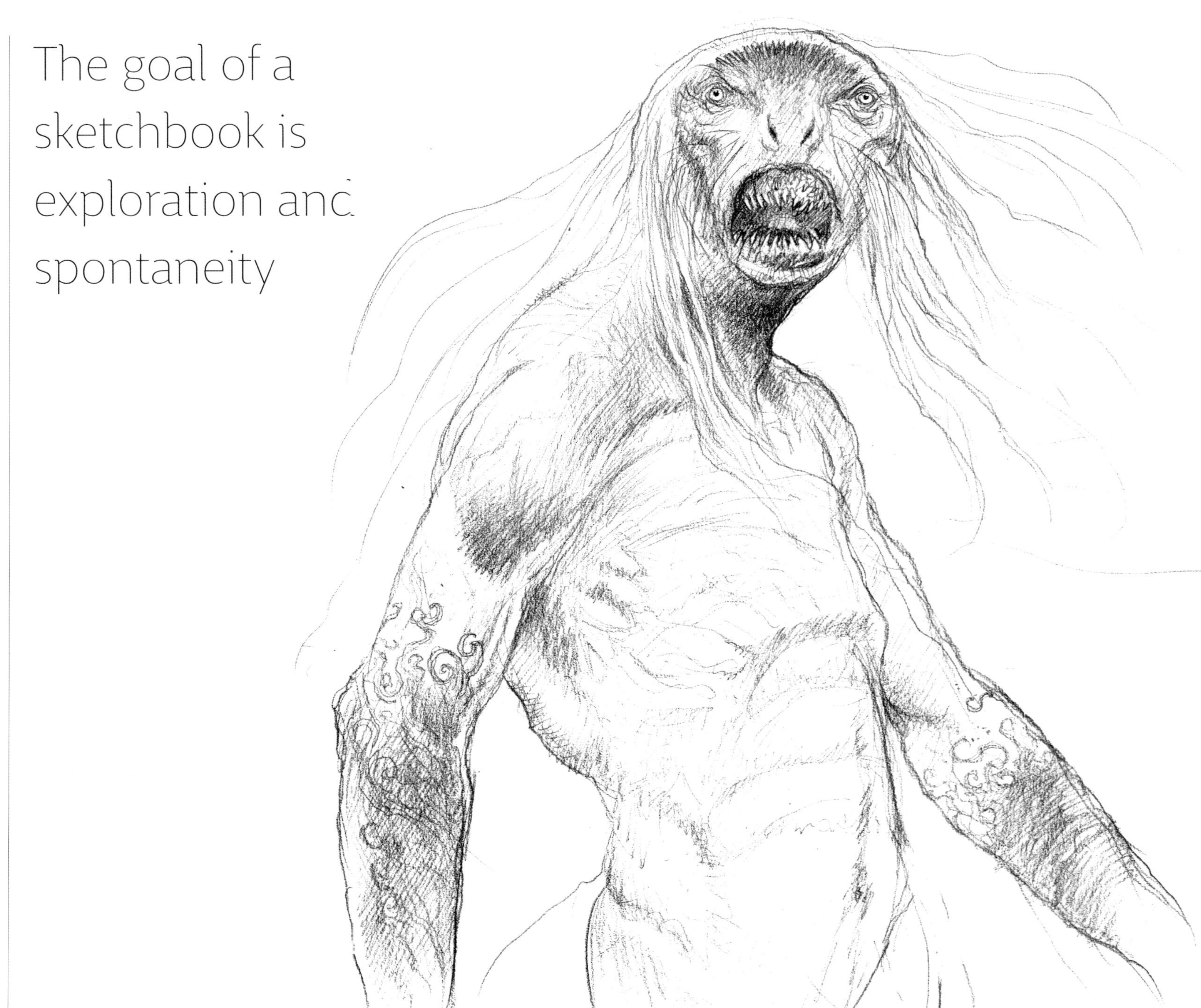

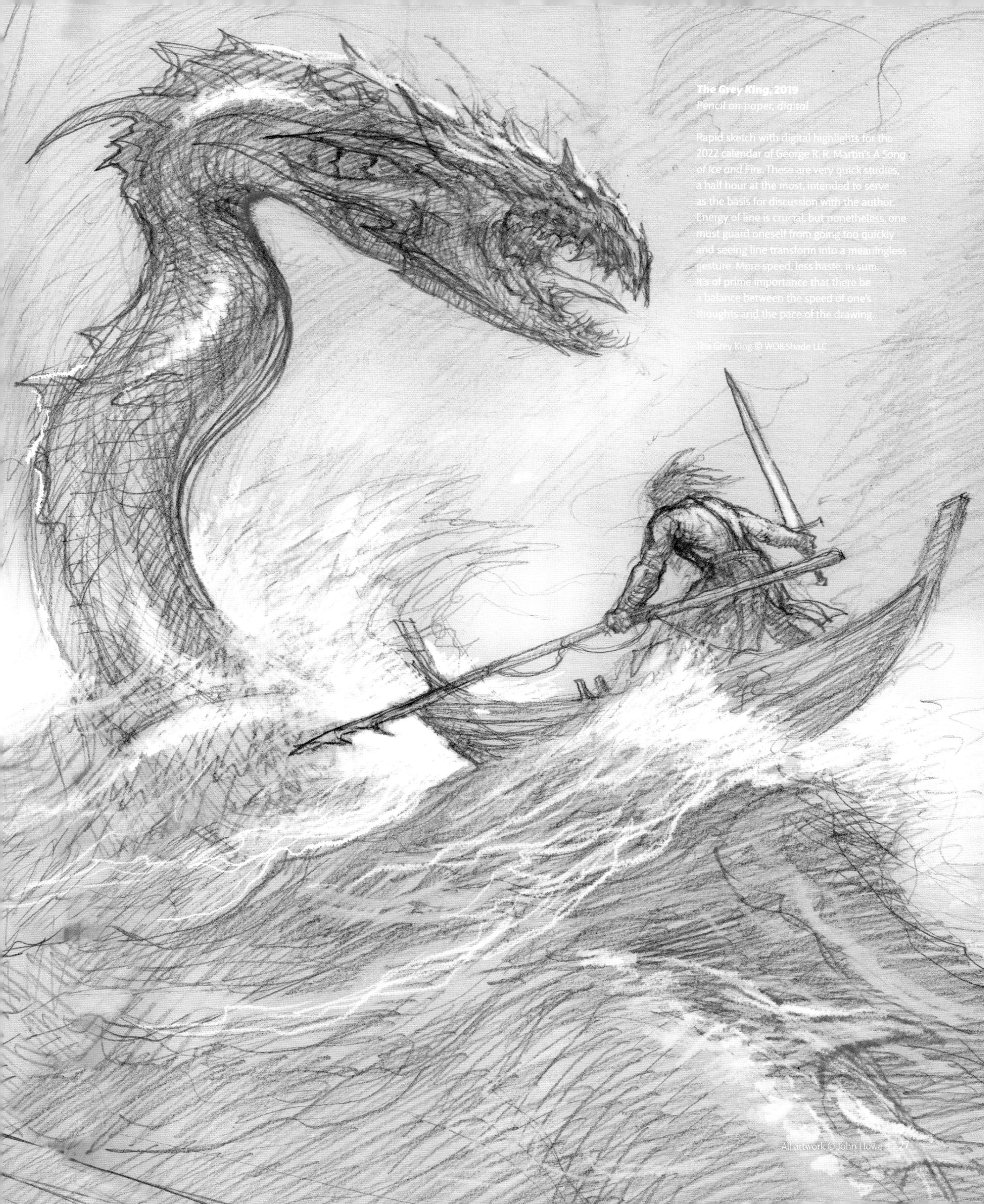

The Grey King, 2019
Pencil on paper, digital

Rapid sketch with digital highlights for the
2022 calendar of George R. R. Martin's A Song
of Ice and Fire. These are very quick studies,
a half hour at the most, intended to serve
as the basis for discussion with the author.
Energy of line is crucial, but nonetheless, one
must guard oneself from going too quickly
and seeing line transform into a meaningless
gesture. More speed, less haste, in sum.
It's of prime importance that there be
a balance between the speed of one's
thoughts and the pace of the drawing.

The Grey King © WO&Shade LLC

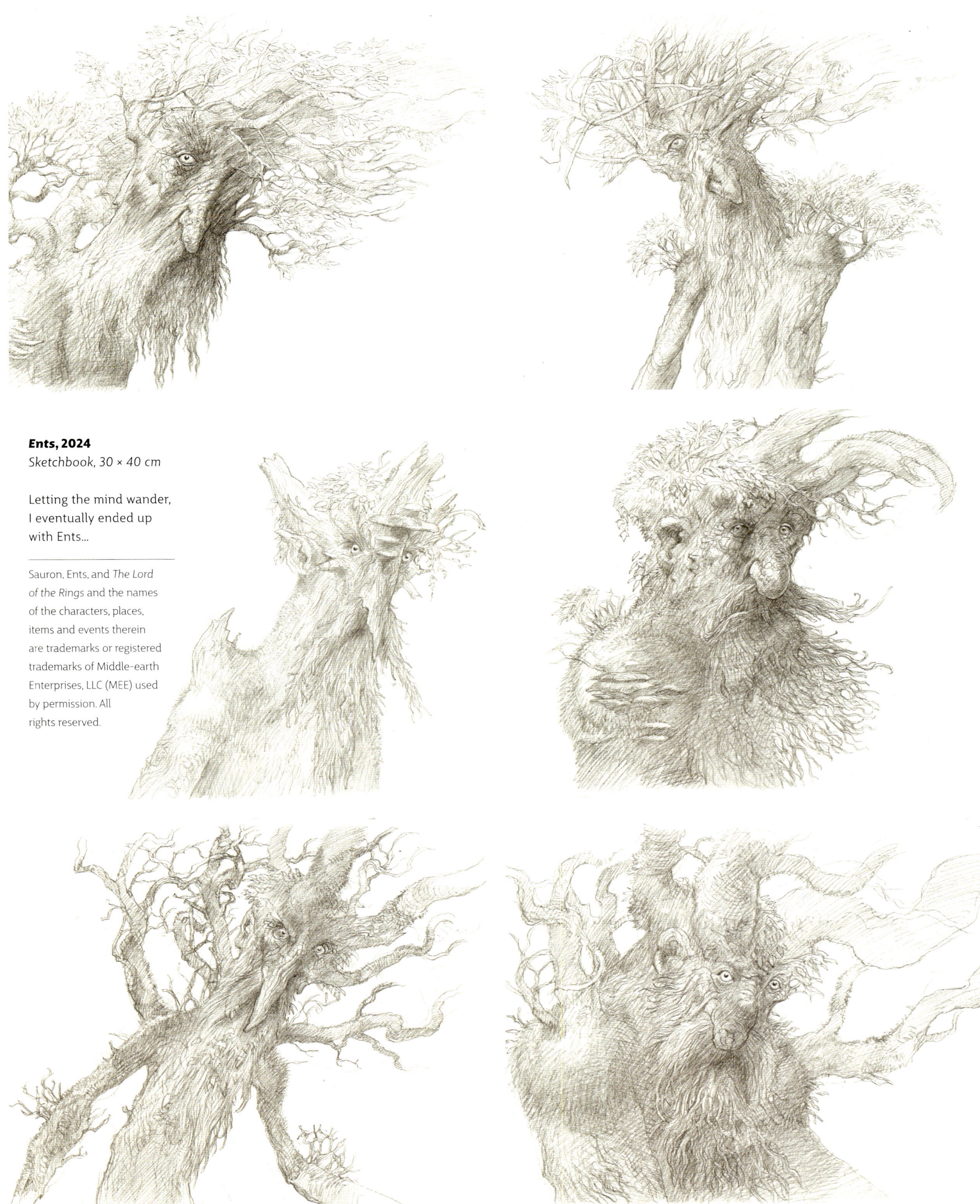

Ents, 2024
Sketchbook, 30 × 40 cm

Letting the mind wander,
I eventually ended up
with Ents...

Sauron, Ents, and *The Lord
of the Rings* and the names
of the characters, places,
items and events therein
are trademarks or registered
trademarks of Middle-earth
Enterprises, LLC (MEE) used
by permission. All
rights reserved.

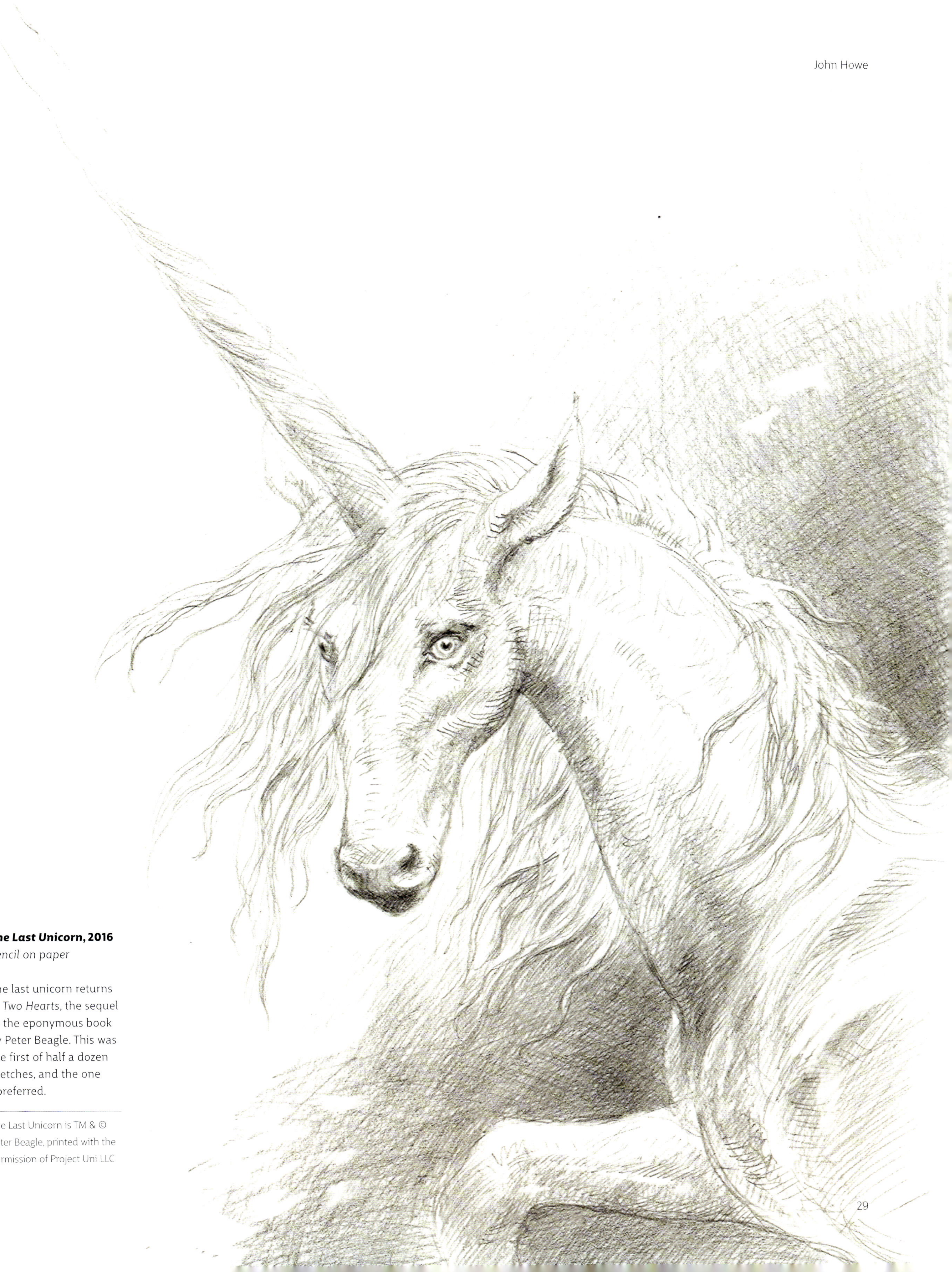

The Last Unicorn, 2016
Pencil on paper

The last unicorn returns
in *Two Hearts*, the sequel
to the eponymous book
by Peter Beagle. This was
the first of half a dozen
sketches, and the one
I preferred.

The Last Unicorn is TM & ©
Peter Beagle, printed with the
permission of Project Uni LLC

SKETCHING AS A CONVERSATION

Sketchbooks are useful for learning to allow your thoughts and your pencil to evolve at the same rhythm. If you are thinking too far ahead of your sketch, your pencil will struggle to keep up and the sketch will be hurried. Conversely, if your pencil outpaces your thoughts, you will end up with a sketch that lacks spontaneity and energy. A sketch is a conversation between three entities: you, the theme you are pursuing, and the drawing itself. As in any conversation, if one of the three does all the talking, a true exchange is no longer possible. Allowing the sketch itself the possibility to inform your thoughts is crucial to its development. Because the sketch, as opposed to a drawing, is incidental, it is finished when it stops either asking or answering questions. Sketches are made to be abandoned.

One of the most magical moments when sketching is when a chance line suddenly opens an avenue of thought, and you completely change direction and pursue a new idea, one that you might never have found if you hadn't allowed the sketch itself a certain amount of freedom.

Opposite page | *The High Castle, 2006*
Pencil on paper

Drawing done on site, from the main tower of the neogothic castle of Haut-Koenigsbourg in the Alsace, looking down on the castle's 'high garden' or upper courtyard. A certain amount of artistic licence was involved, especially when a story occurred to me as I was drawing.

Stormjaeger II, 2016
Sketchbook, 30 × 40 cm

A sketchbook page created, if I recall correctly, while waiting for a flight. Sketchbooks are the perfect travelling accessory. (You do have to sharpen your pencils in advance, though, as craft knives must travel in checked luggage.)

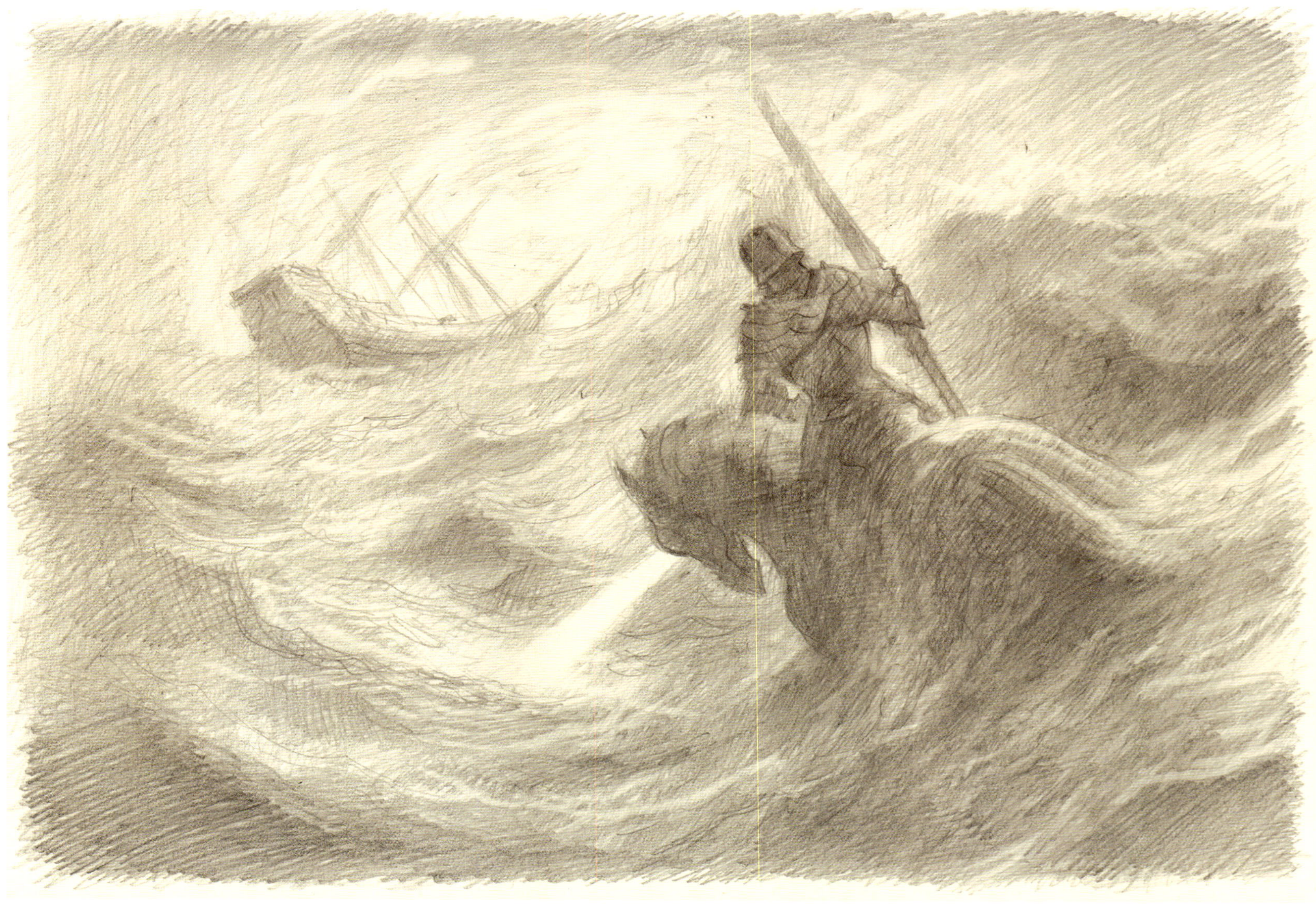

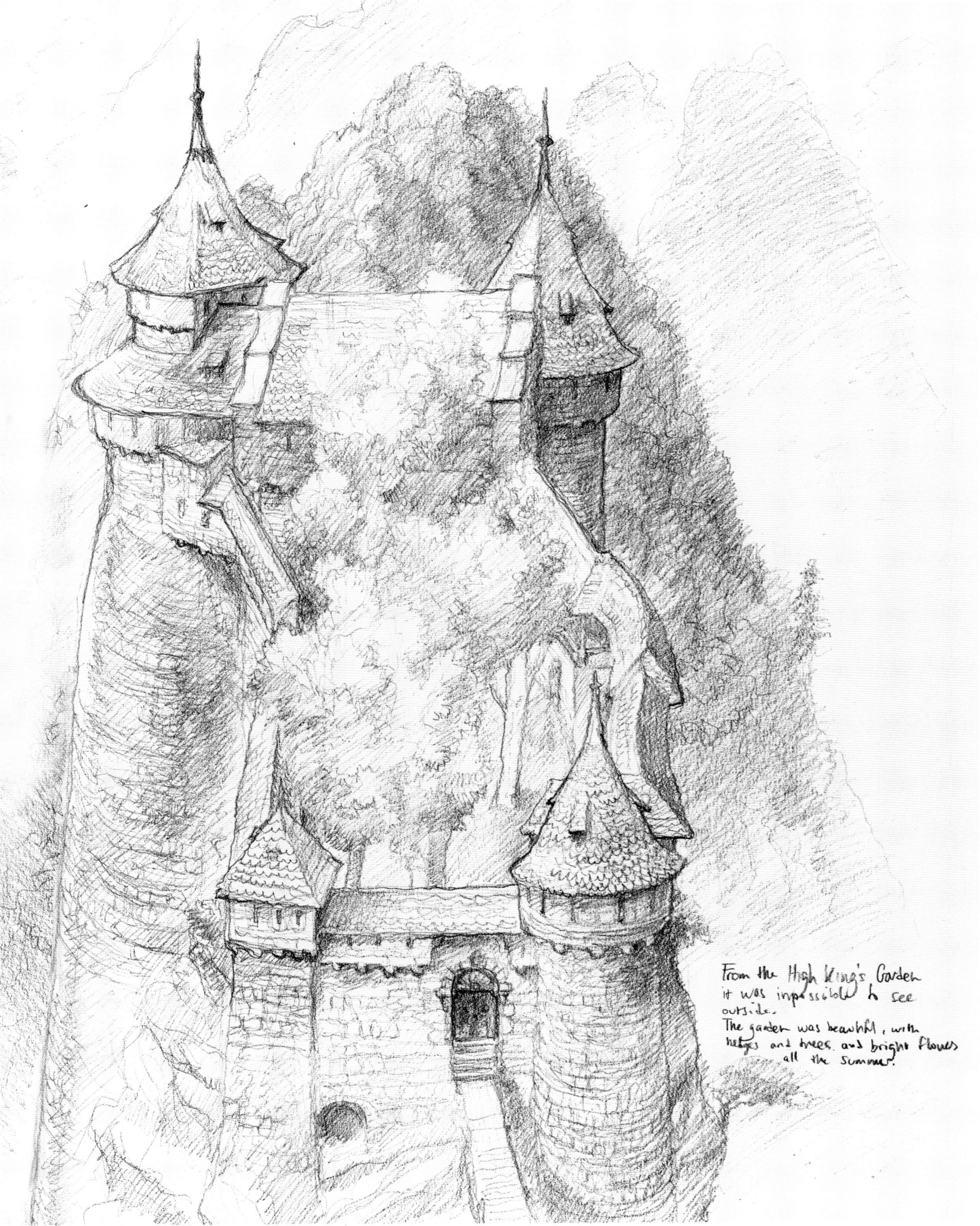

From the High King's Garden
it was impossible to see
outside.
The garden was beautiful, with
hedges and trees and bright flowers
all the summer.

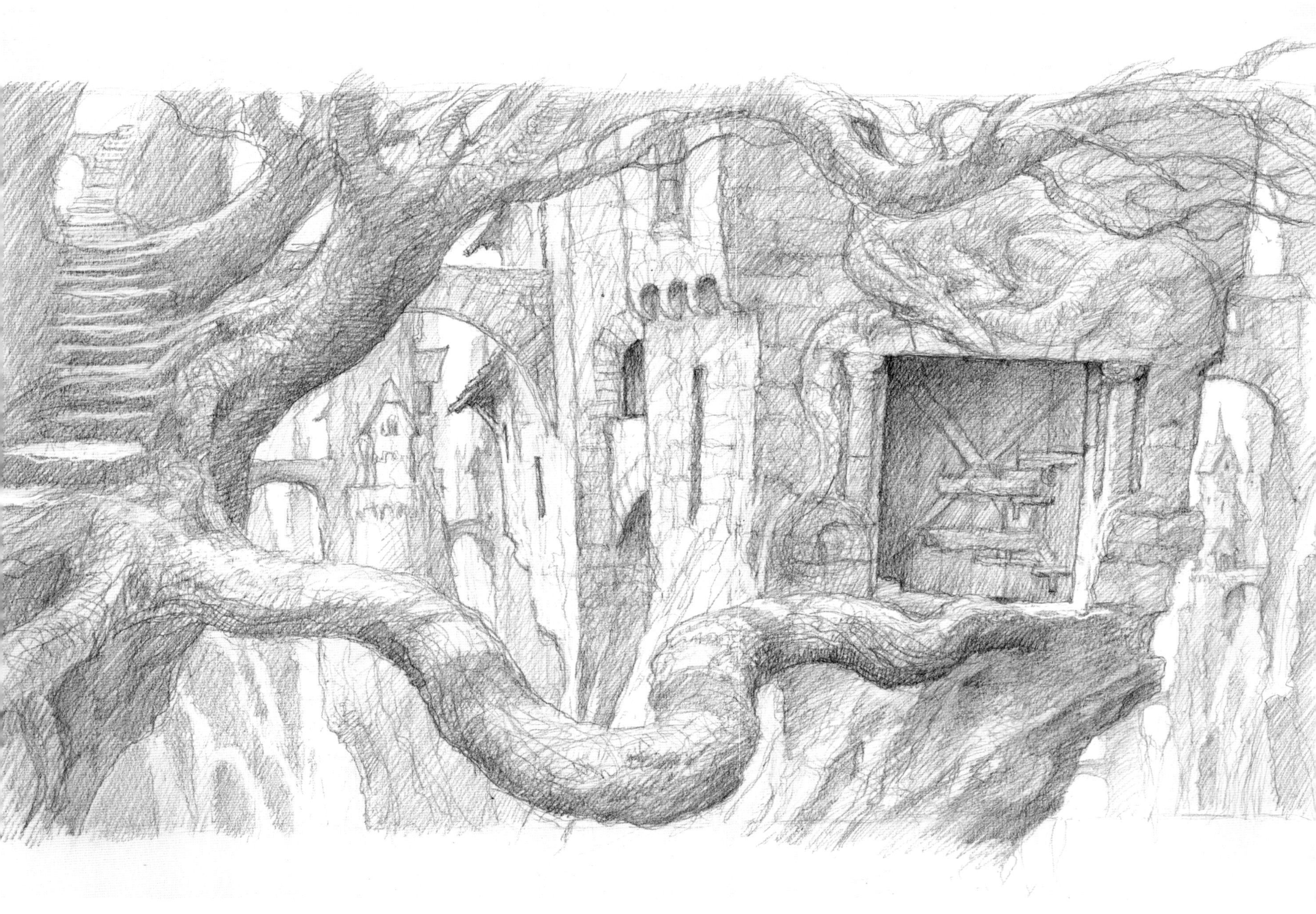

The Magic Door, 2010
Pencil on paper

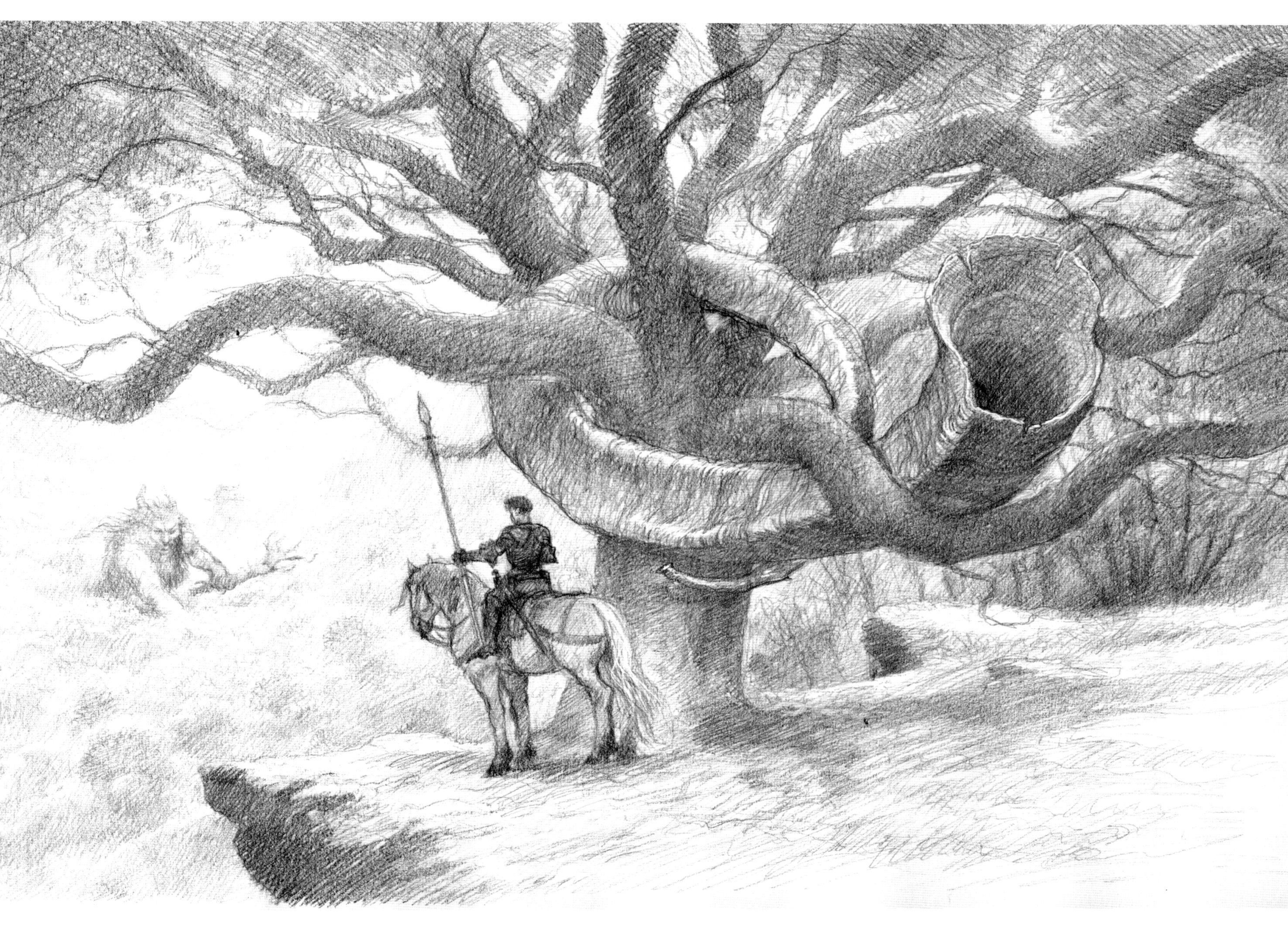

The Edge of the Wild, 2010
Pencil on paper

A drawing created for a film project.

© John Howe / Cerigo Films, Strasbourg, France

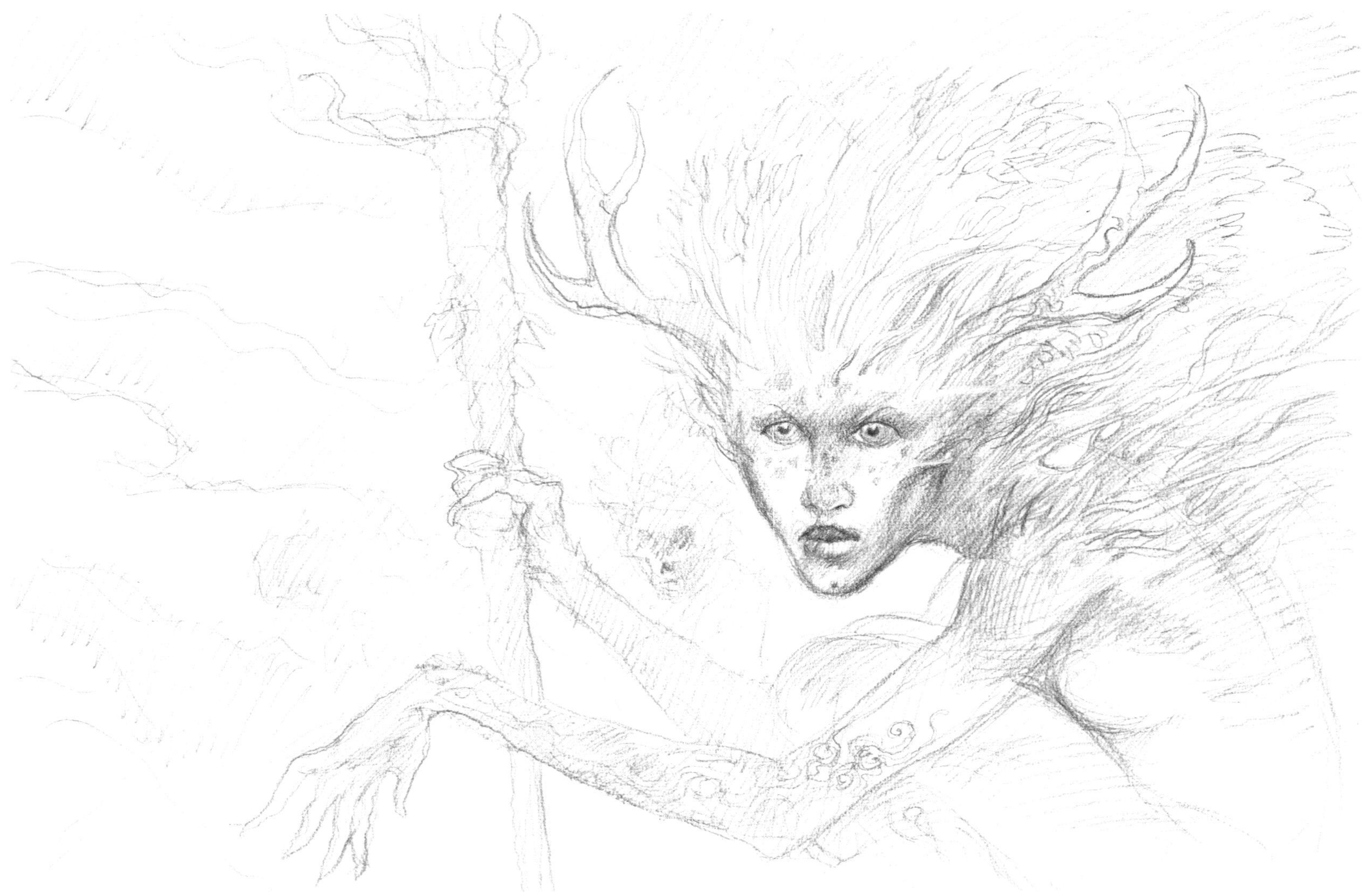

Above | *Forest People, 2019*
Sketchbook, 30 × 40 cm

Sketch for the 2022 calendar of George
R. R. Martin's *A Song of Ice and Fire.*

HABITS TO CULTIVATE

I would love to have a more efficient and logical cataloguing system. While I do number my diaries, my sketchbooks are less chronological and linear. I have taken to putting in the odd date here and there, to help situate them in time. Most of my archiving is sedimentary in nature – I pile up sketchbooks as they are filled and take the next sketchbook from the stack of new ones. From time to time, I do my best to arrange them properly. On the other hand, I am diligent in my scanning, and every sketchbook is scanned as I work my way through it.

My number-one piece of advice to artists just starting out would be to conserve your work, without being too precious about it. Date your work when you can and above all, scan your work as you go. It's a good habit to cultivate. If you let it go too long, it becomes a chore and it is hard to catch up. Do your best to keep your digital files organized on two external drives. Having the misfortune to lose work really drives home how important this is.

Another good habit is to set aside a little time regularly to cultivate your own garden – to do work, not for a client, but to explore worlds of your own. Not only is this an investment in your future, but it will also allow you to progress rapidly on a personal level.

In addition, if you are not in the habit of writing (many visual people are not), then adopt it as a regular exercise. You may find that you can establish a second line of communication with the worlds you have in your head. A drawing can evoke a snippet of text, which can in turn inspire a drawing.

Set aside a little time regularly to cultivate your own garden – to do work, not for a client, but to explore worlds of your own

Below | *Green Man, 2005*
Pencil on paper, digital

In this sketch I only drew half the face, and then mirrored it in Photoshop.

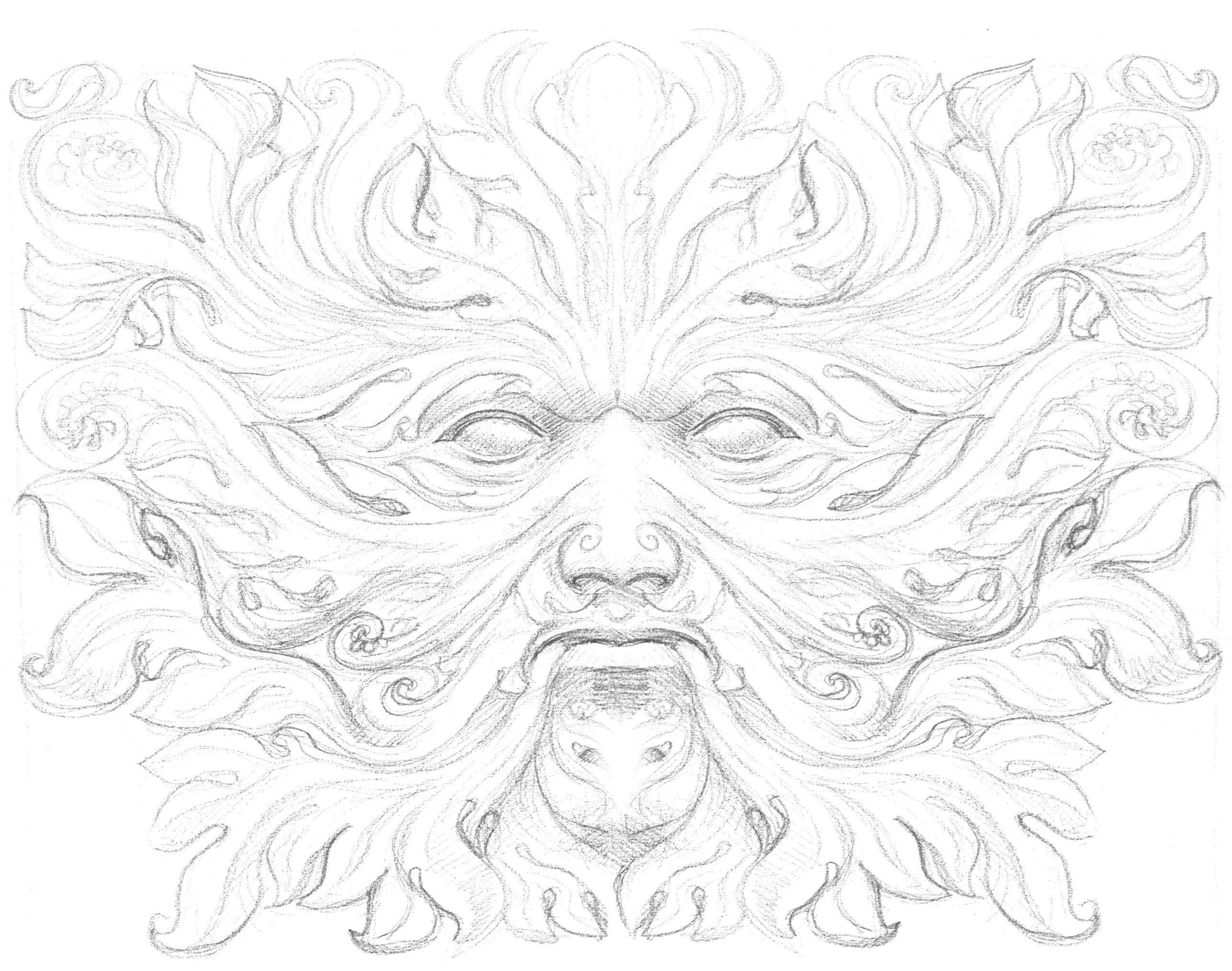

CONSTANT APPRECIATION

It's hard to say which part of my career stands out as my proudest, not because there are outstanding episodes or achievements, but because I find it difficult to establish a scale of values. Often, lovely sketches will be done for low-profile projects, and vice-versa. I think the things I most value, as an exceedingly timid person who is ill at ease with crowds, is that drawing, sketching, and painting have brought me into a more comfortable and close relationship with myself and the world. Drawing and sketching, and the 'magic' that accompanies the ability to put thoughts into images, whether quickly sketched or painstakingly detailed, are witness to the journey both inwards and outwards. Inwards to the materialization of the imagination, and outwards by reaching out into the world, first for inspiration, and secondly to share one's views, passions, and beliefs.

This patient layering of experience, of an ever-renewed regard, of a constant appreciation of light, atmosphere, form, and colour, of the opportunity to kindle one's own interest and that of one's viewers, is a gift. For that I am always grateful.

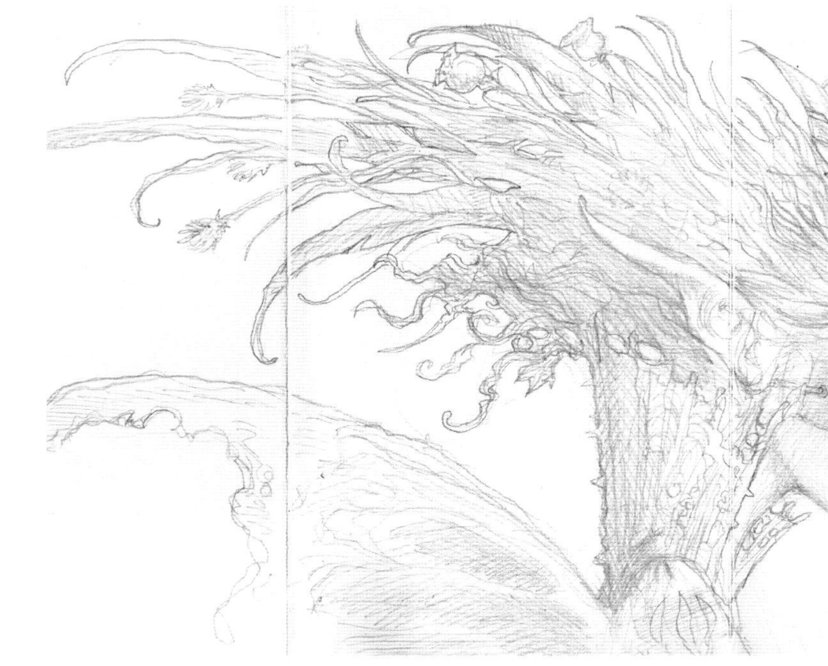

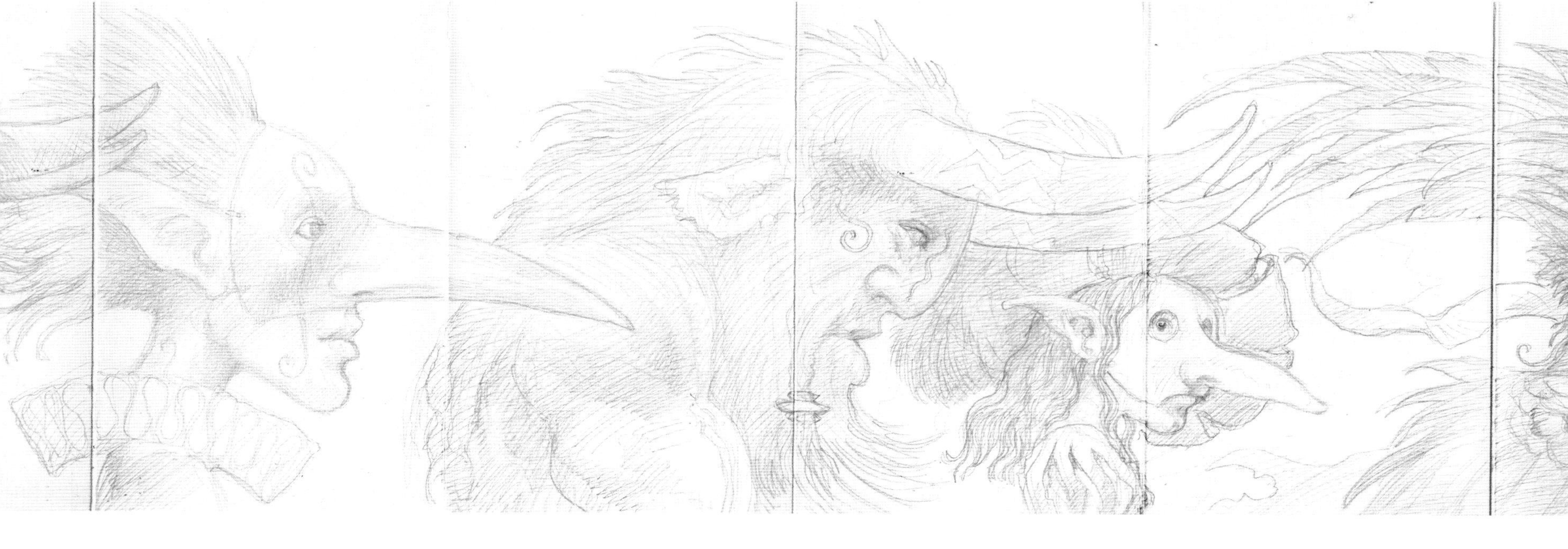

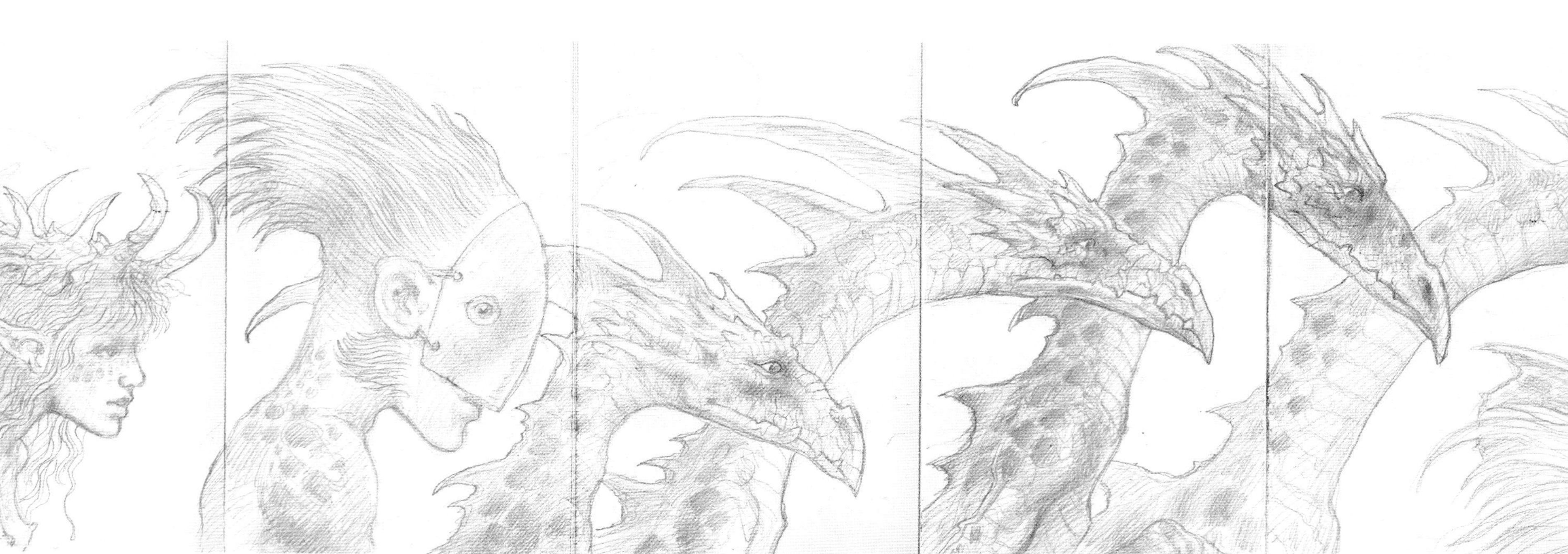

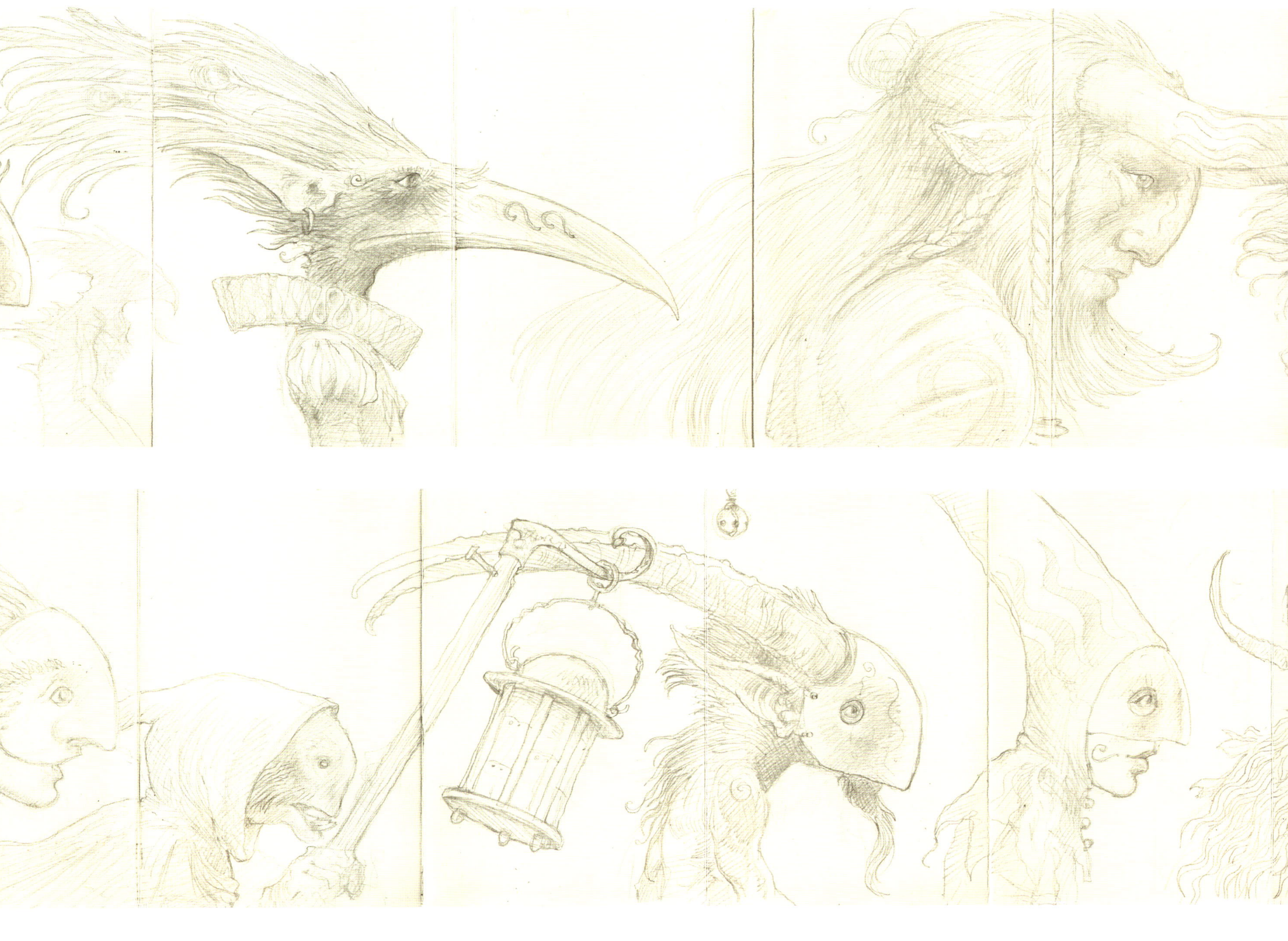

Accordion Sketchbook, 2014
Accordion sketchbook, 9 × 12 cm

I love those little fold-out sketchbooks, which often accompany me to long meetings. I find that drawing while listening liberates the mind from distractions, while concentrating on the intuitive process of making lines sharpens the attention. It's almost more efficient than taking notes.

James Gurney

EVERYTHING BEGINS AS A DRAWING

My dad was a mechanical engineer. His drawings were of machine parts and crazy inventions. He would build windmills from old bicycle wheels and mount them on the roof of our house. He also designed and built recumbent bicycles using a welding set. (I was honoured when he trusted me to use the welder when I was only in fifth grade!) He told me that everything begins as a drawing, and that anything you imagine becomes a little more real if you can make a sketch of it.

Both my mom and dad dabbled in 'artistic' painting – figure drawings, oil landscapes. But none of us cared for making pretty easel pictures. Drawing was more of a step to building or inventing things.

My older brother, Dan, would collaborate with me on big drawings of sailing boats and clipper ships. We were real experts on every bit of the rigging because we did a lot of sailing on our own boats. Whenever we saw someone else's drawing of a boat or ship, we would look it over very carefully and gleefully point out all the mistakes. We would design our own model sailing boats and race them in the duck pond in Palo Alto. We were very competitive about it, and launching a new boat was a big event.

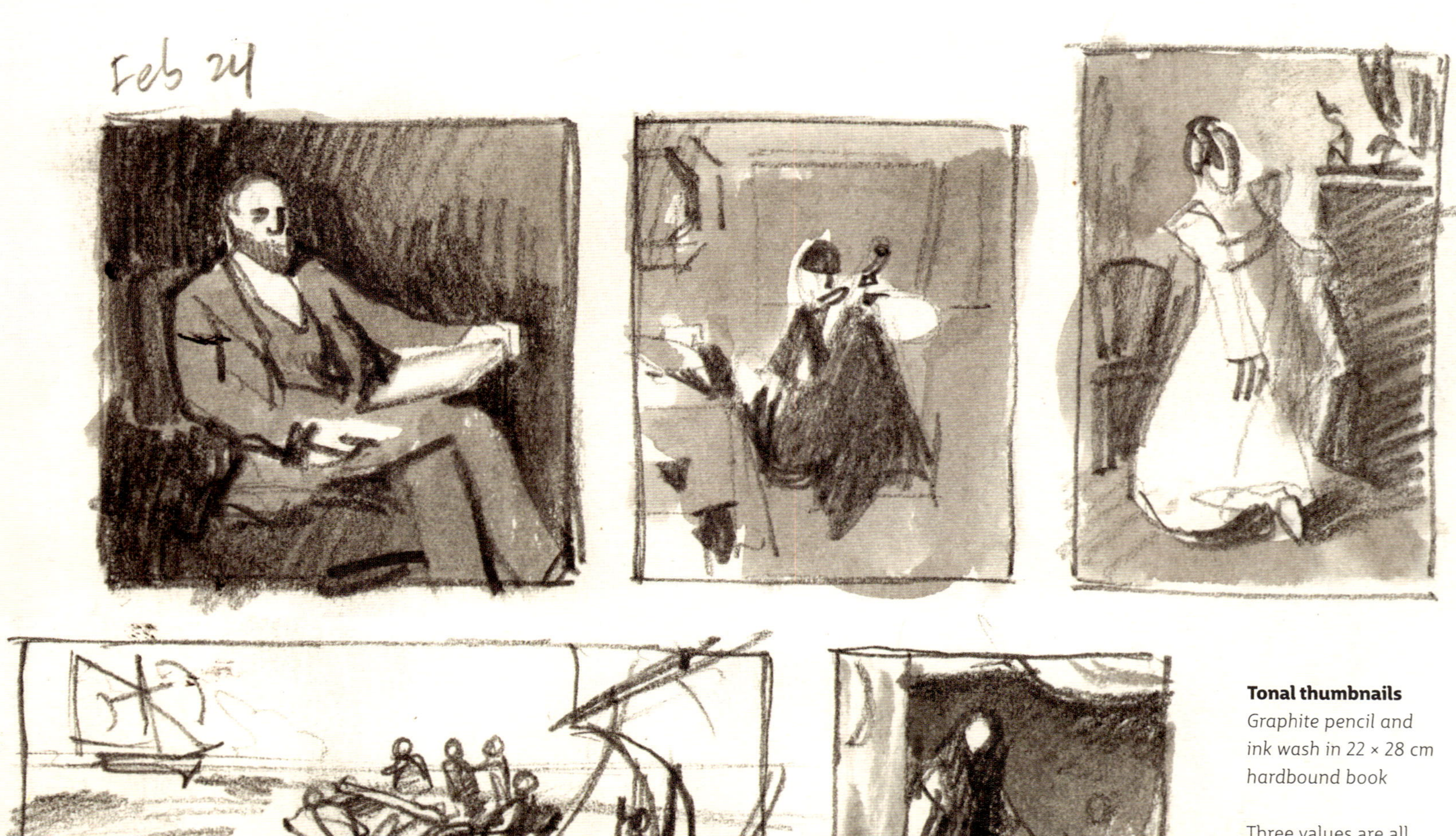

Tonal thumbnails

Graphite pencil and ink wash in 22 × 28 cm hardbound book

Three values are all you need to analyse compositions: the white of the paper, the dark or black tone of the pencil, and the middle tone from a pre-mixed tint of ink.

My parents often took me up to San Francisco to see the dinosaurs in the museum and the paintings in the art gallery. I didn't understand how artists could make paintings look so real – I thought there was some magic involved. I still remember seeing a Rembrandt out of the corner of my eye; it seemed to watch me walking along, and I could swear it winked at me.

My two heroes were Norman Rockwell and M. C. Escher, both of whom obviously put a tremendous amount of thought into their work. When I was in eighth grade or so, I started to realize that they did a lot of sketches before arriving at their famous designs. I began riding my bicycle to the library to check out every book I could about art and illustration to learn the secrets of this magical process.

Our family also had a set of the old adventure classics by Robert Louis Stevenson and Jules Verne – books like *Treasure Island* and *Twenty Thousand Leagues Under the Sea*. Once in a while my dad would read aloud from them, and I would look forward to each of the glorious illustrations by N. C. Wyeth.

Cornwell studies
Soft graphite pencil in 22 × 28 cm hardbound book

I learned a lot from filling a series of 'study books' with notes from readings and copies in pencil from works I admired, either from the original or from a reproduction.

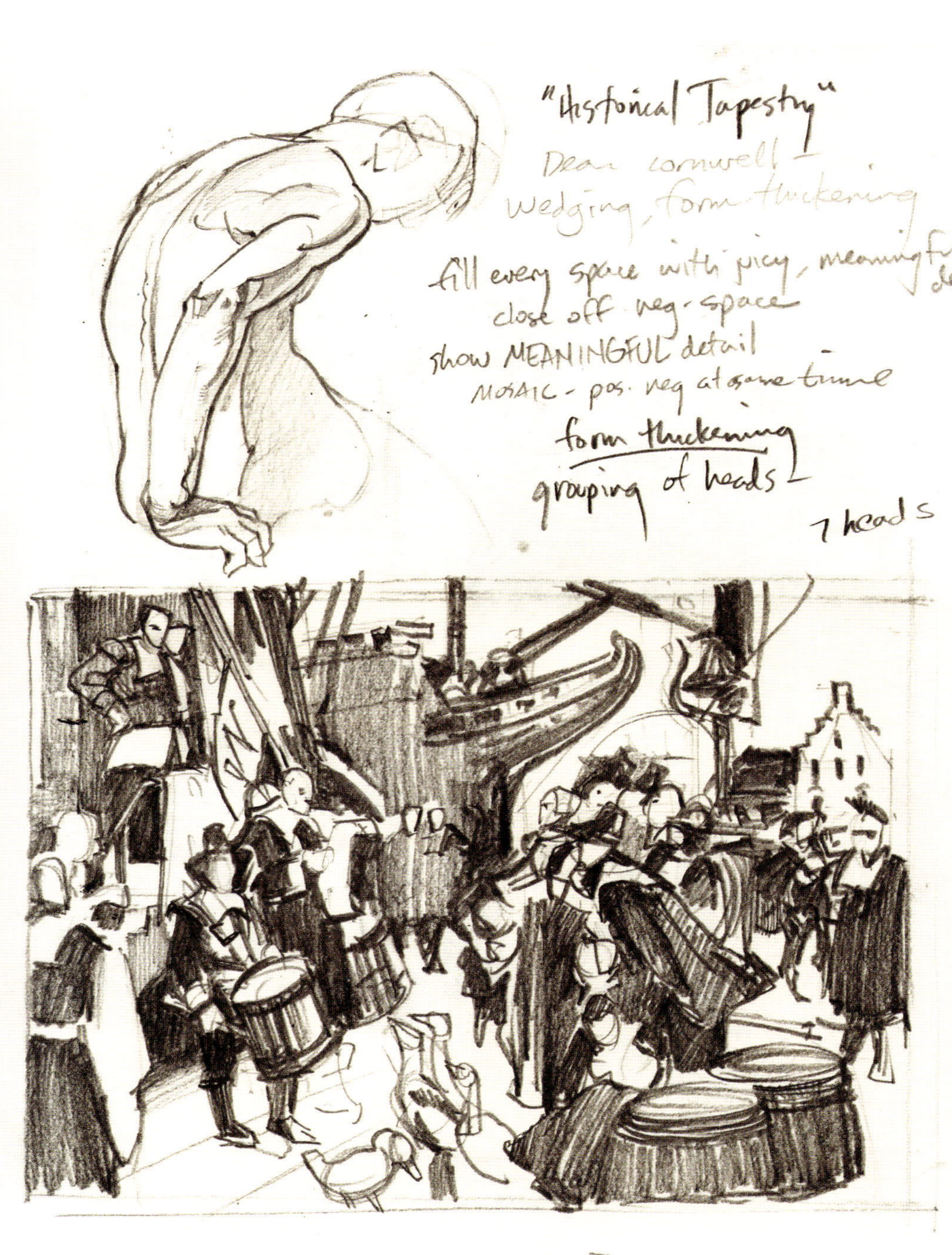

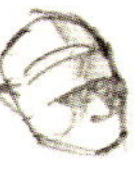

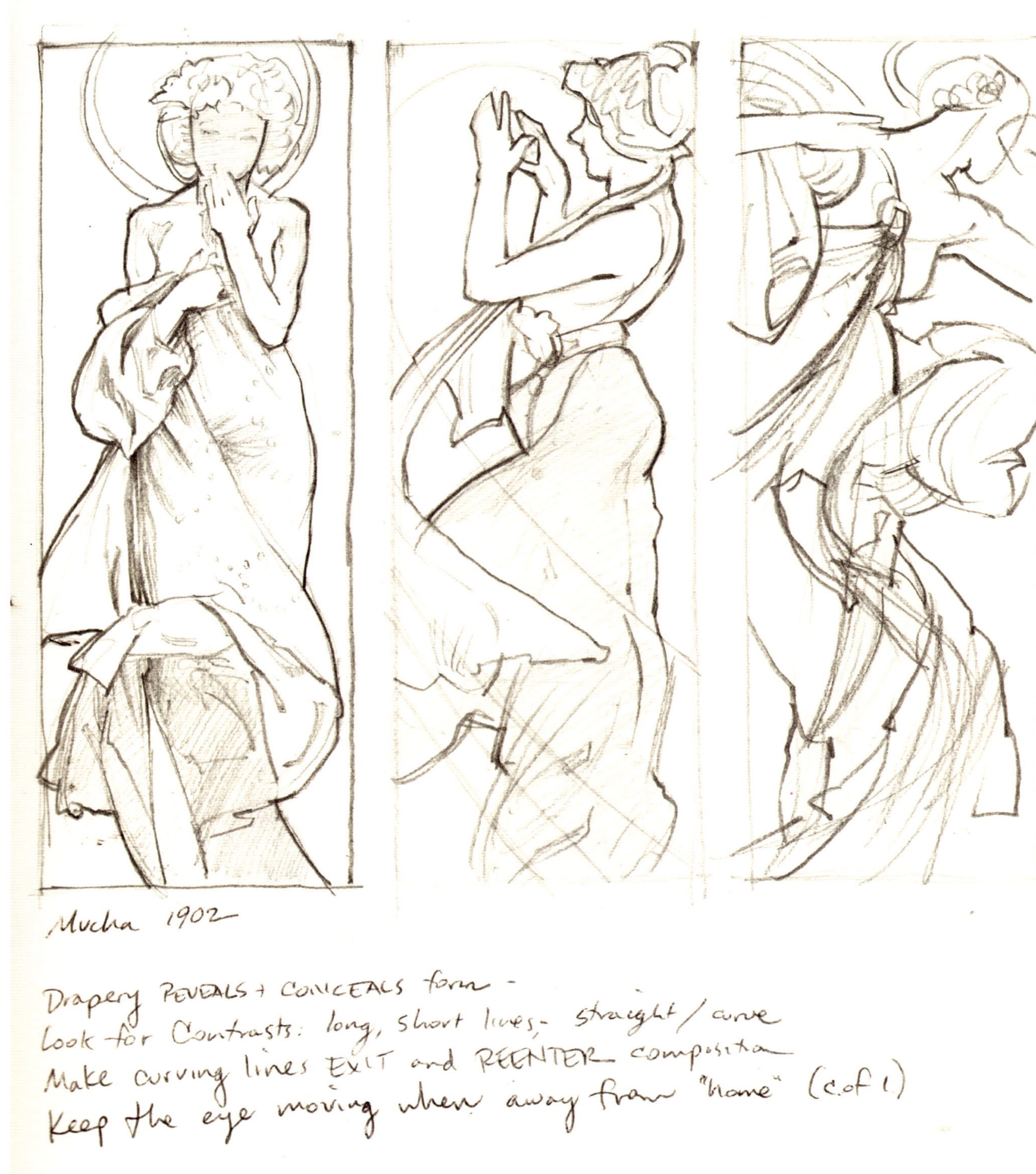

Mucha studies
Graphite pencil in 22 × 28 cm hardbound book

All this academic work was combined with daily outdoor sketching, which became such a passion that I ended up co-authoring a book on the subject for Watson-Guptill called *The Artist's Guide to Sketching* in 1982.

SELF-TAUGHT LEARNING

I took time off from my art ambitions to go to the University of California, Berkeley, where I majored in archaeology, a subject that always fascinated me. I then went to school for a couple of semesters at ArtCenter College of Design in Pasadena, where I learned some very helpful material about perspective. I wanted to learn animal anatomy, animation, and multi-figure composition, but the art school wasn't equipped to teach those things in 1980, so I had to blaze my own trail into the darkness.

Most of what I have learned has been self-taught, as I found that art school only got in the way of my education. After I left art school, I bought a membership to the zoo and the natural history museum and went to both twice a week. I developed my own curriculum of self-teaching based on the 'Famous Artist's Course' from the 1950s, Andrew Loomis's book *Creative Illustration*, and the teaching methods from the 19th-century French Academy, which involved fairly detailed anatomy and cast drawing.

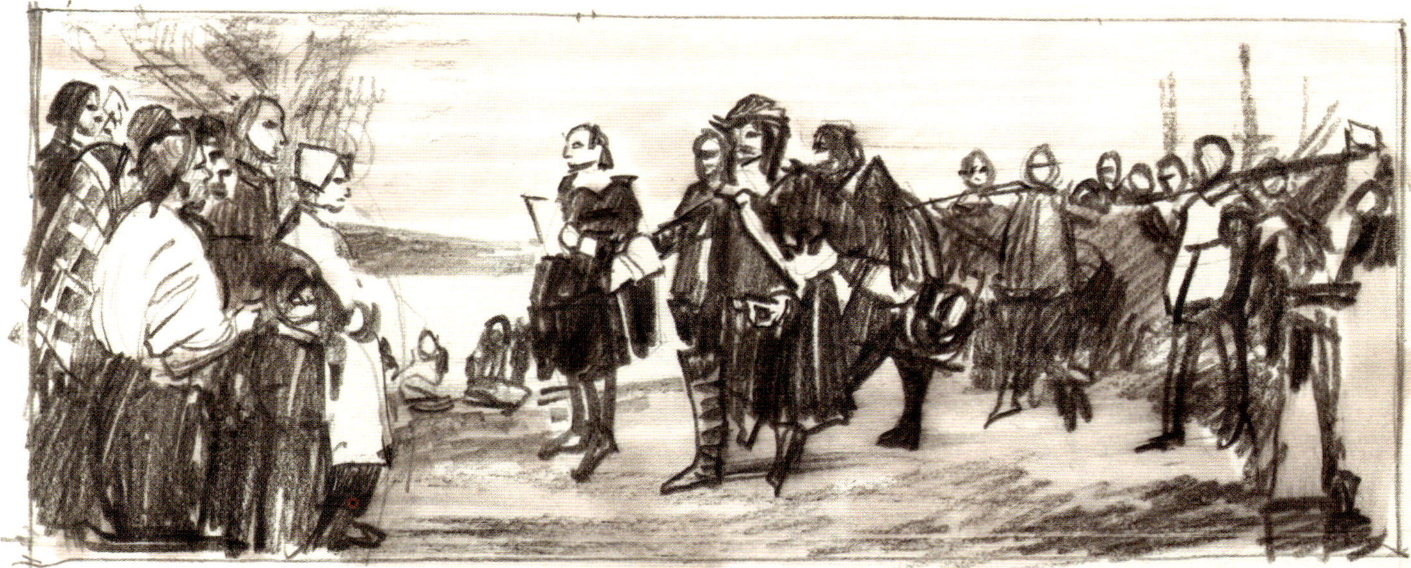

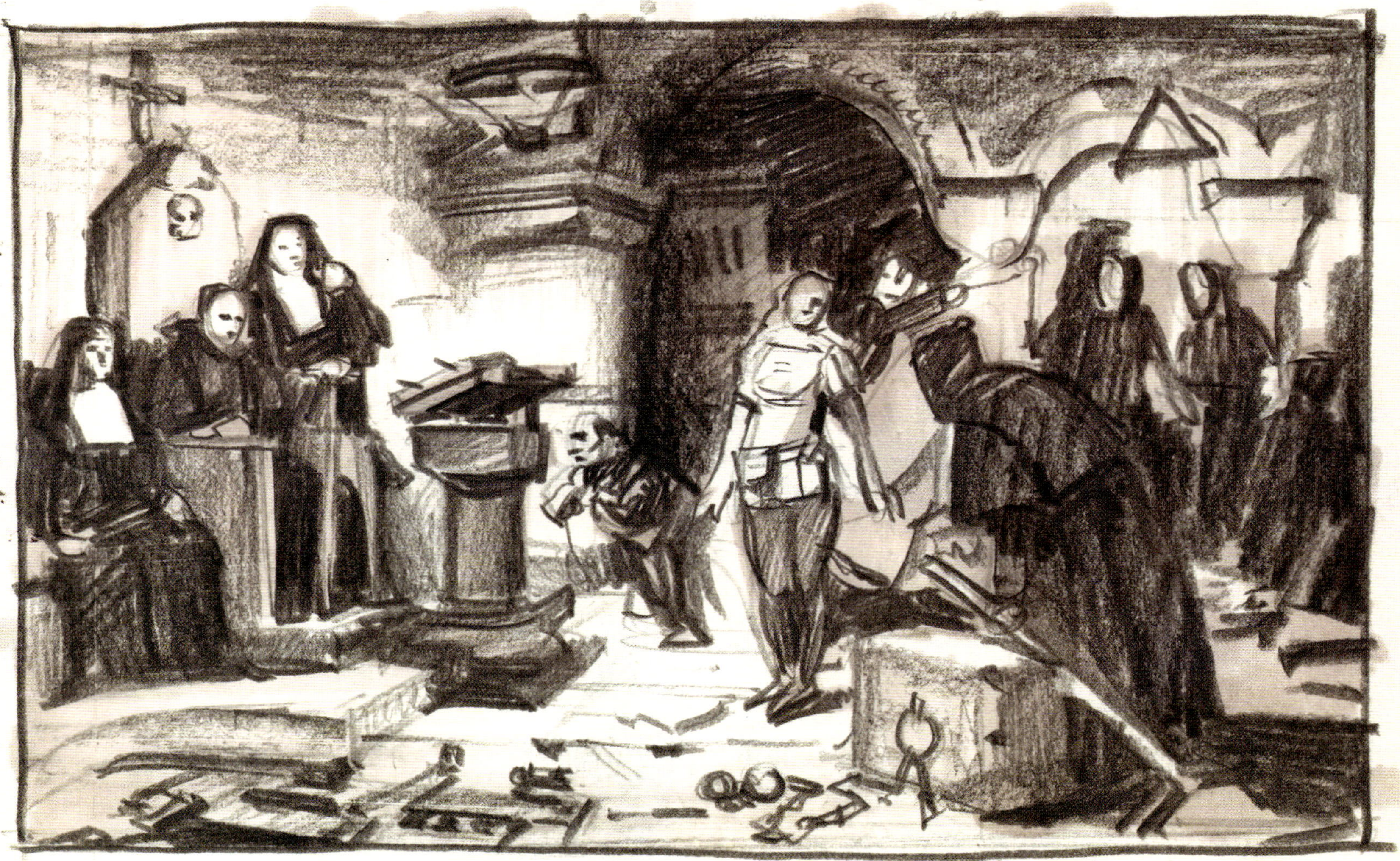

Pyle studies

Soft graphite pencil in 22 × 28 cm hardbound book

Making a compositional copy in graphite is like injecting the artists I revere directly into my creative veins. What I admire most about Howard Pyle is his ability to conjure imaginary worlds in such a convincing way, both in his writing and in his artwork. Pyle has always been the standard in American illustration for well-researched and well-imagined recreations of historical scenes. He was interested in capturing a mood and transporting you through a picture into another world.

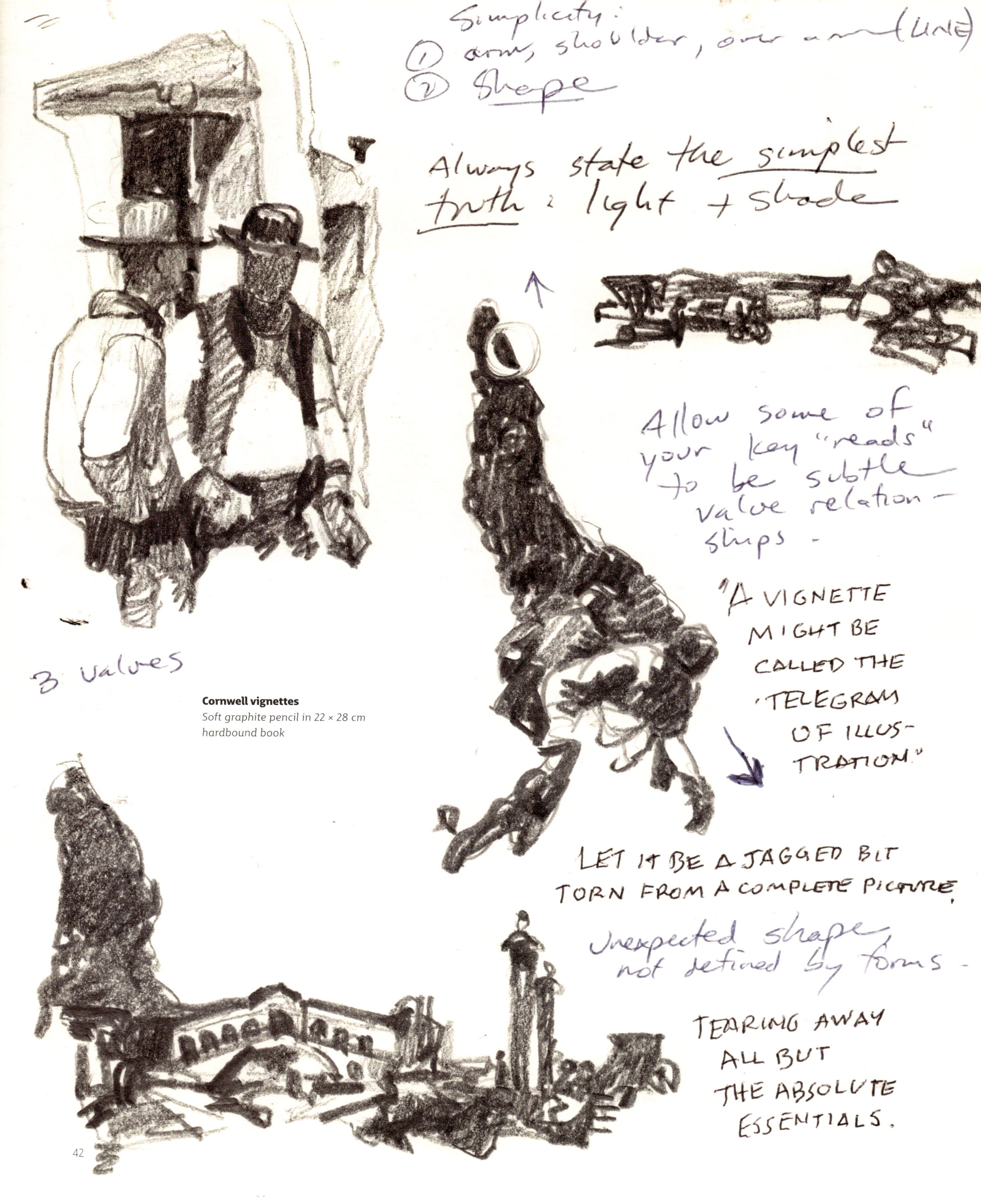

Cornwell vignettes
*Soft graphite pencil in 22 × 28 cm
hardbound book*

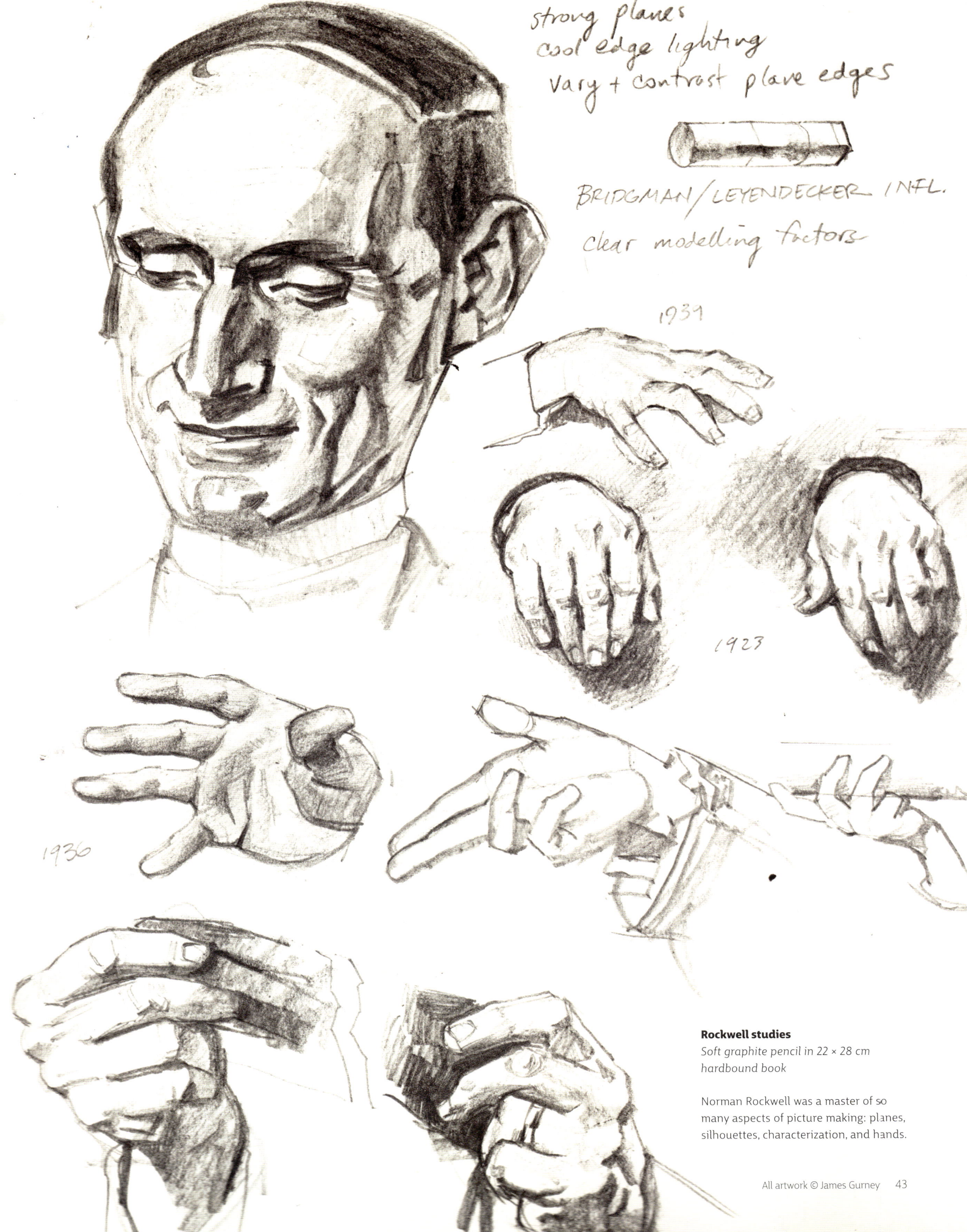

Rockwell studies

Soft graphite pencil in 22 × 28 cm hardbound book

Norman Rockwell was a master of so many aspects of picture making: planes, silhouettes, characterization, and hands.

 43

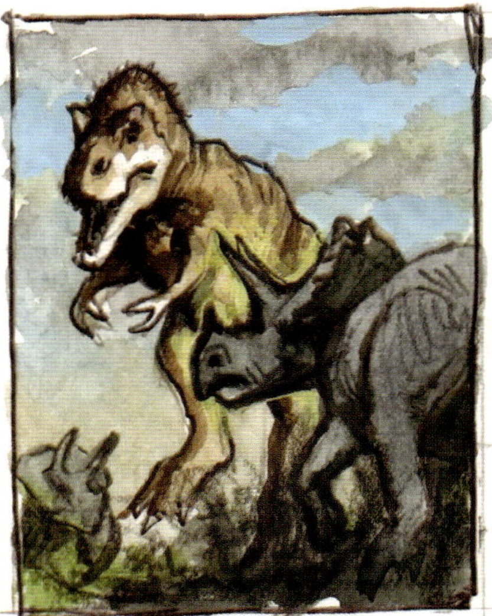

T. REX CONFRONTS
TRICERATOPS

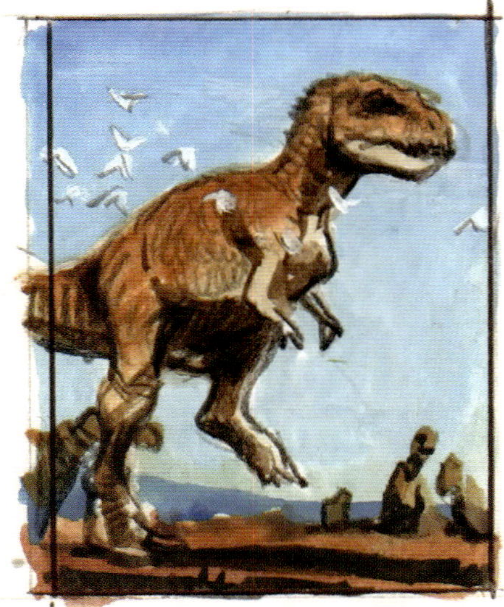

GIANT T. REX WITH
FLOCK OF WHITE BIRDS

T. rex sketches
Coloured pencils and gouache

When I was about eight, my parents took me to a science museum where I saw a life-size skeleton of a big carnivorous dinosaur. I was bowled over to learn such a fantastic and scary-looking creature had really existed. I imagined it coming to life at night, stepping off the platform, and wandering around the empty museum. I was also inspired by a series of dinosaur illustrations by Zdeněk Burian that looked as real as photos to me.

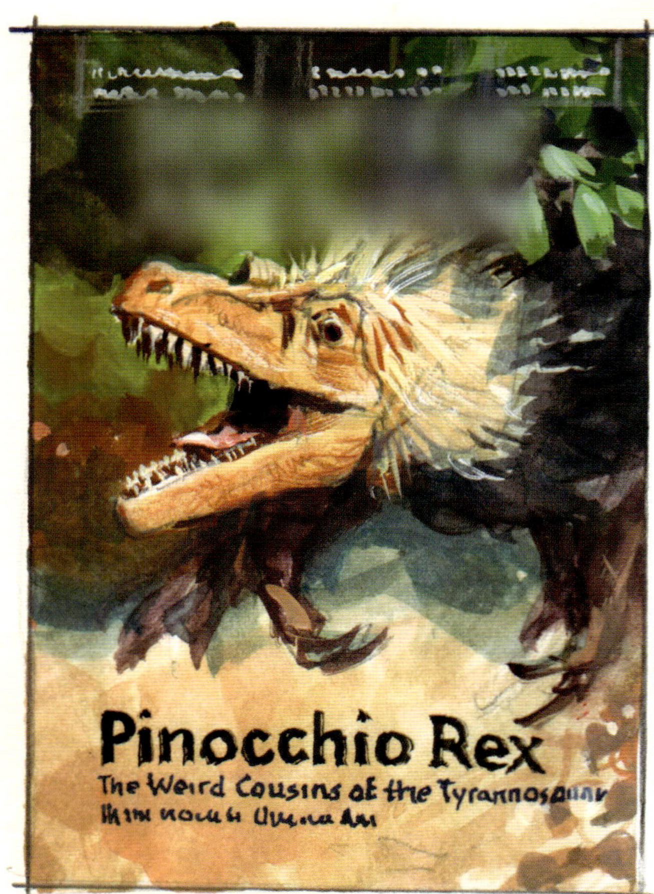

① CROUCHING DRAGON WITH MANE
OF FEATHERS, LEAF CANOPY ABOVE

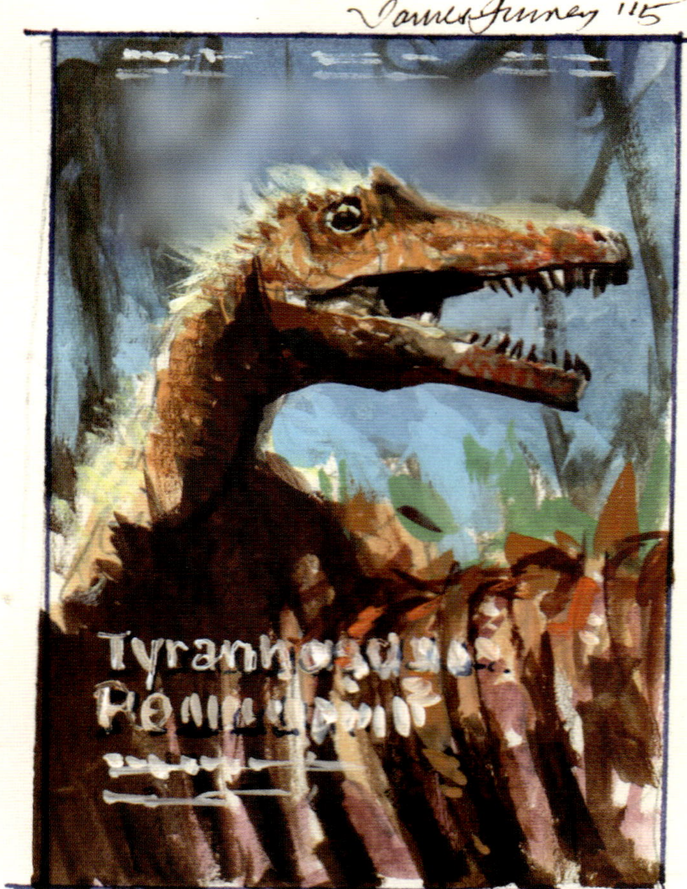

② QIANZHOUSAURUS LOOKS UP
WARILY WHILE DEVOURING KILL.

Cover thumbnails
Gouache, pencil and pens, 7.5 × 10 cm

Scientific American asked me to help visualize some relatives of T. rex, a broader group known as Tyrannosaurids. To sell the basic visual idea to the editors and consultants of the magazine, I wanted to do some initial ideas using colour. We hoped to get the art on the cover, so we featured the recently discovered Qianzhousaurus, aka 'Pinocchio Rex', a strange long-snouted tyrannosaurid that happens to be one of the most celebrated finds. As fun as any of these would be to paint, none of them were really striking or simple enough in their design.

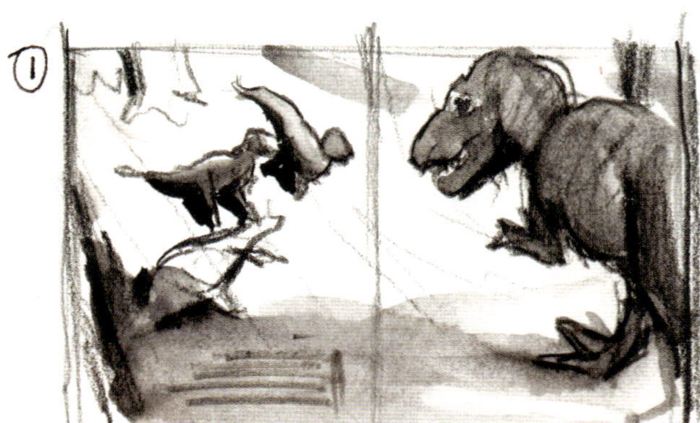

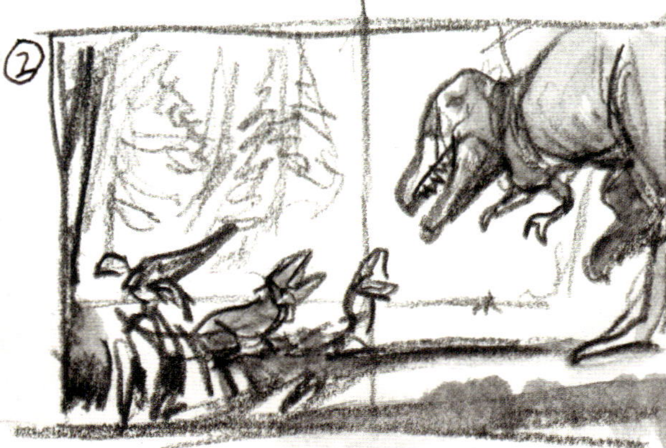

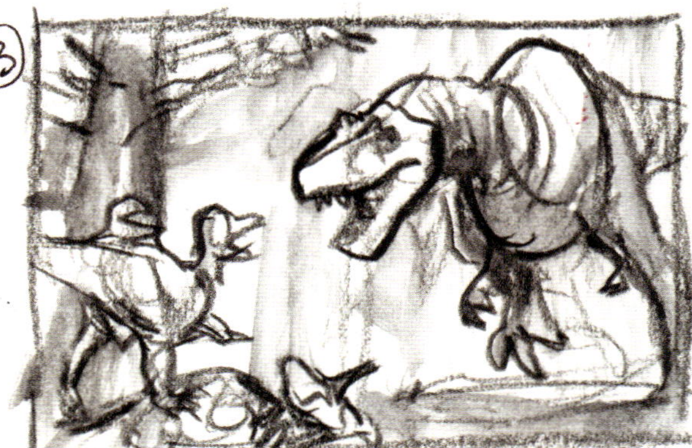

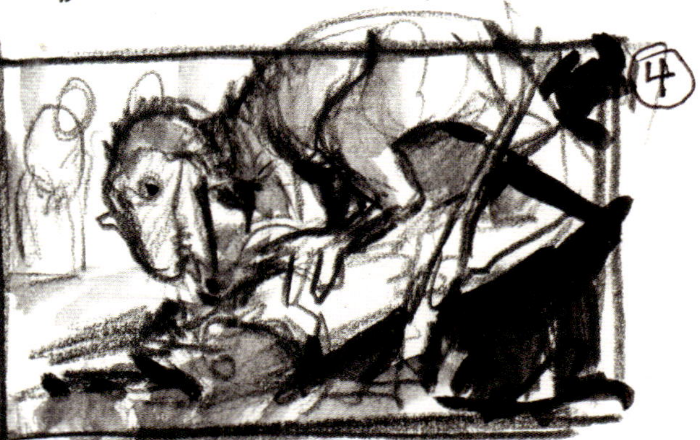

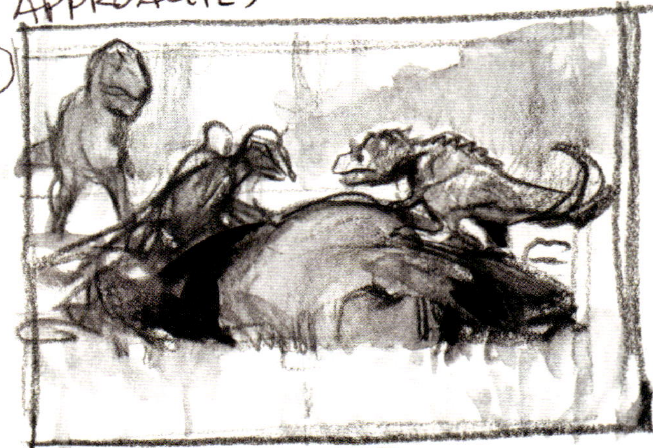

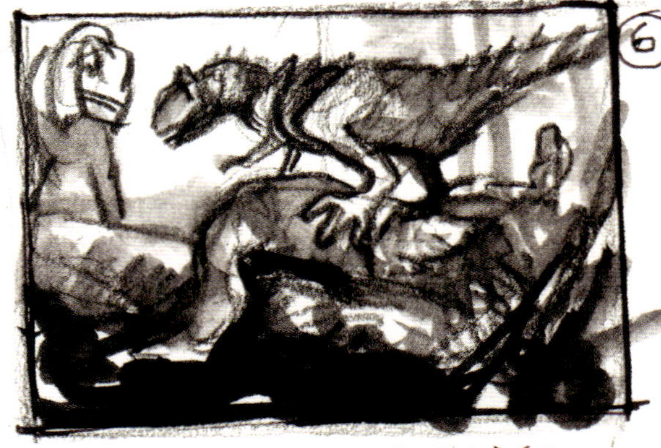

KLEPTOPARASITISM = PREDATORY PIRACY

Tyrannosaurid sketches

Black watercolour pencils and pen, 20 × 28 cm

Freelance Art Director Juan Velasco and *Scientific American's* Design Director Michael Mrak suggested expanding the art to fill the entire spread, with allowance for the headline to reverse out of the art. I did these black watercolour-pencil sketches to explore various points of view, almost as if I was a movie director planning a shot.

Additional sketches

Watercolour, gouache, coloured pencils, and markers, 7.5 × 10 cm

I used gouache for these sketches, which is a good medium for rapid visualizing in colour. I generated ideas for compositions by researching behavioural scenarios of analogous land predators. One of the best sources for this research is watching nature videos about wolves, bears, big cats, and other carnivores.

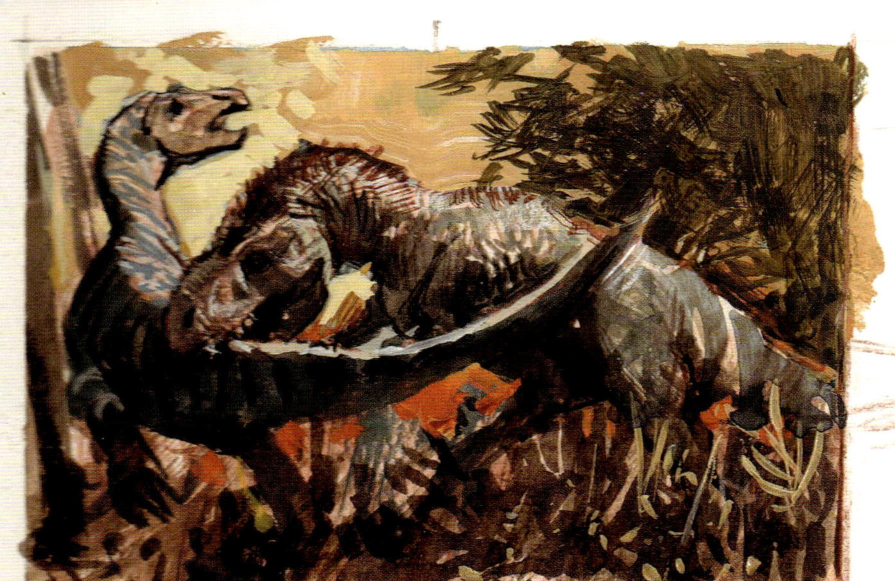

FUZZY T·REX ATTACKS EDMONTOSAURUS

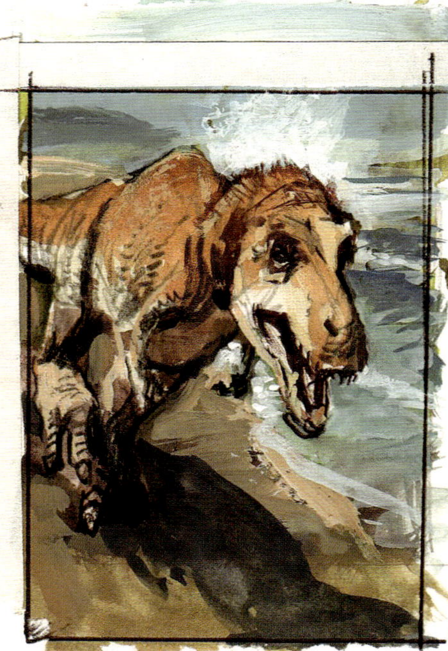

RUNNING ALONG BEACH

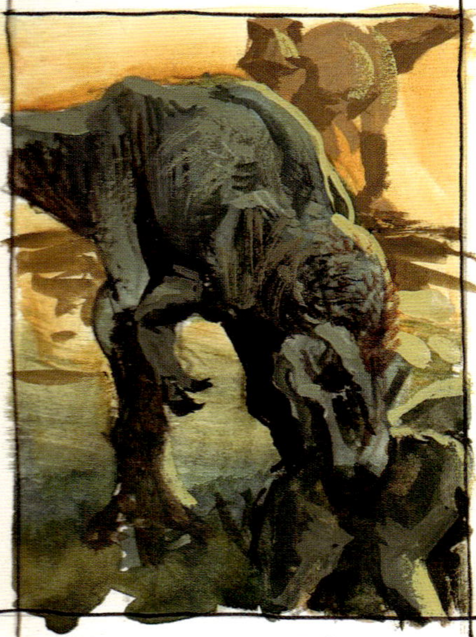

T. REX DEVOURS FALLEN TRICERATOPS —

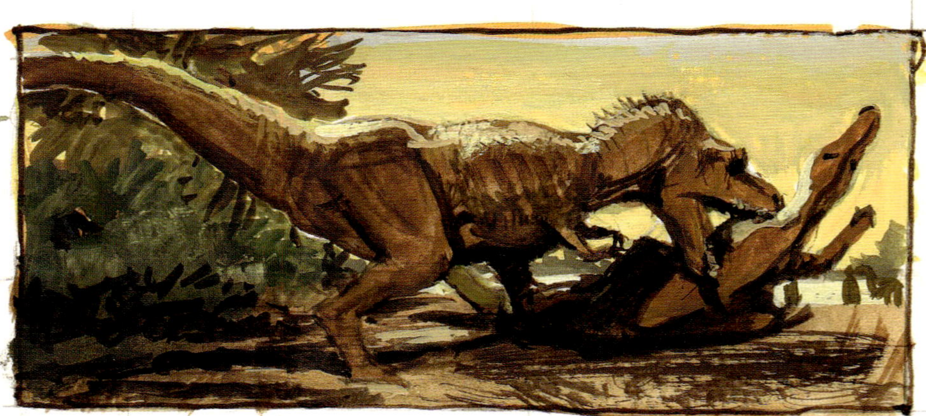

"PUNCTURE-PULL" ATTACK ON EDMONTOSAURUS —

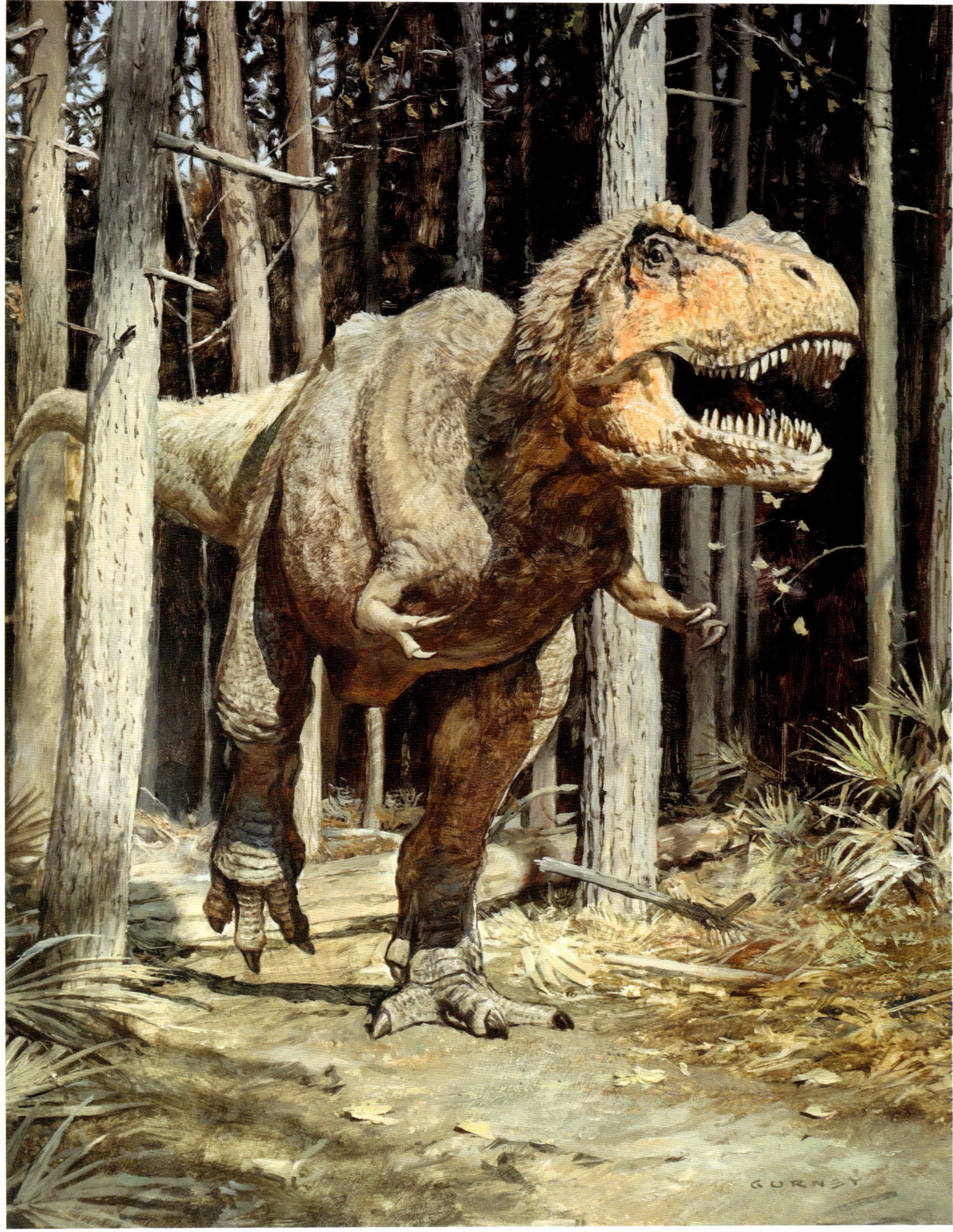

T. rex in Forest
Oil on board, 46 × 36 cm

A T. rex emerges from the shadows of the forest into the light. He's got some
feathers on his neck and his face has a reddish tinge, as many birds and reptiles do.

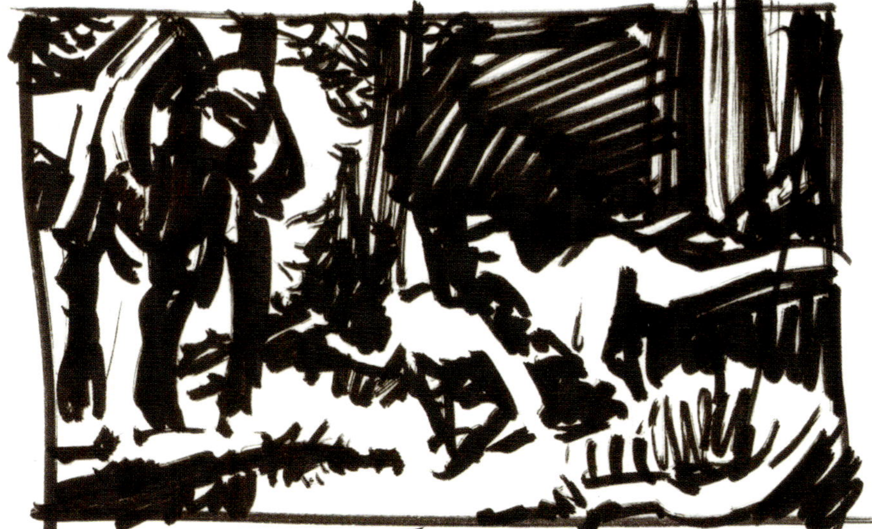

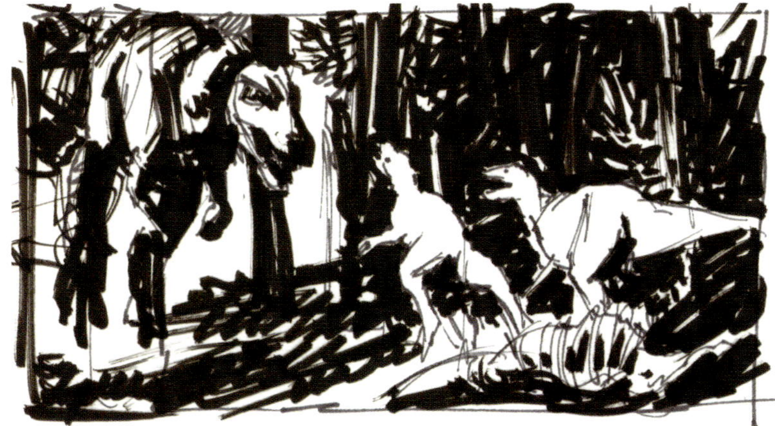

Notan thumbnails
Brush pen on paper, 7.5 × 10 cm each

The idea with these sketches was to reduce the variables to black and white. Mindful of the risk of getting carried away with too much detail and middle tones, I reminded myself to keep it simple. These black-and-white thumbnail sketches were done with a pigmented brush marker, which forced me to reduce the image to its tonal essentials.

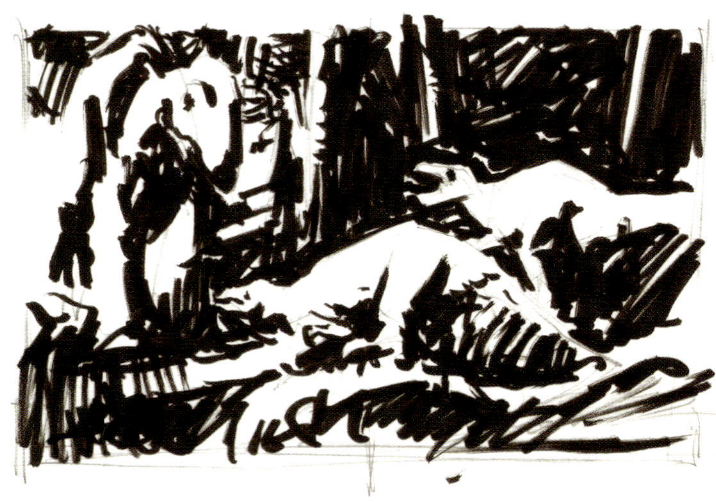

Comp sketches with graphics
Casein, 13 × 18 cm

We settled on the idea of smaller tyrannosaurids trying to defend their kill from a powerful Yutyrannus. The art director created a digital overlay where he indicated headline and text blocks to imagine the final effect of the page.

I painted this small comprehensive sketch in casein to give the art director something more complete that he could use for the layout. We decided to stage the scene inside a forest rather than in the open plains. The art director wanted to make sure the little Dilongs didn't get too close to that gutter, and that the back of the Yutyrannus wasn't tangent to the top of the frame.

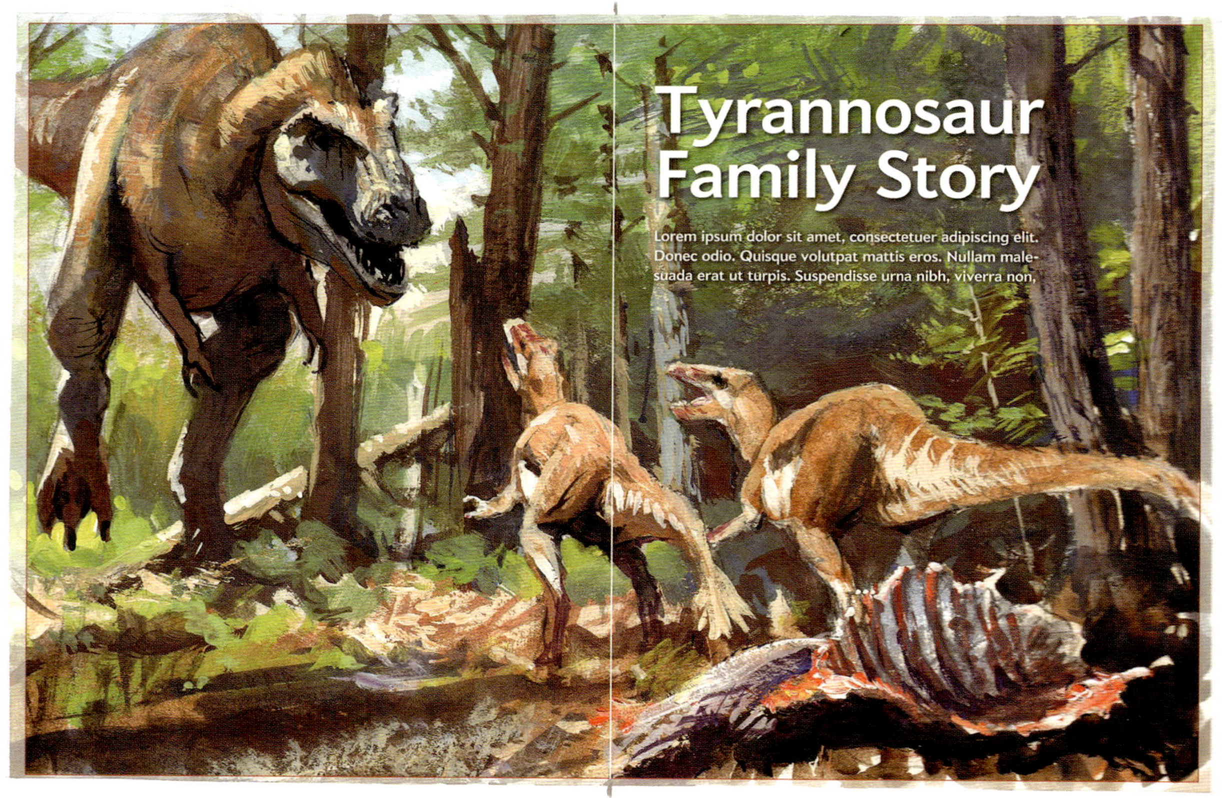

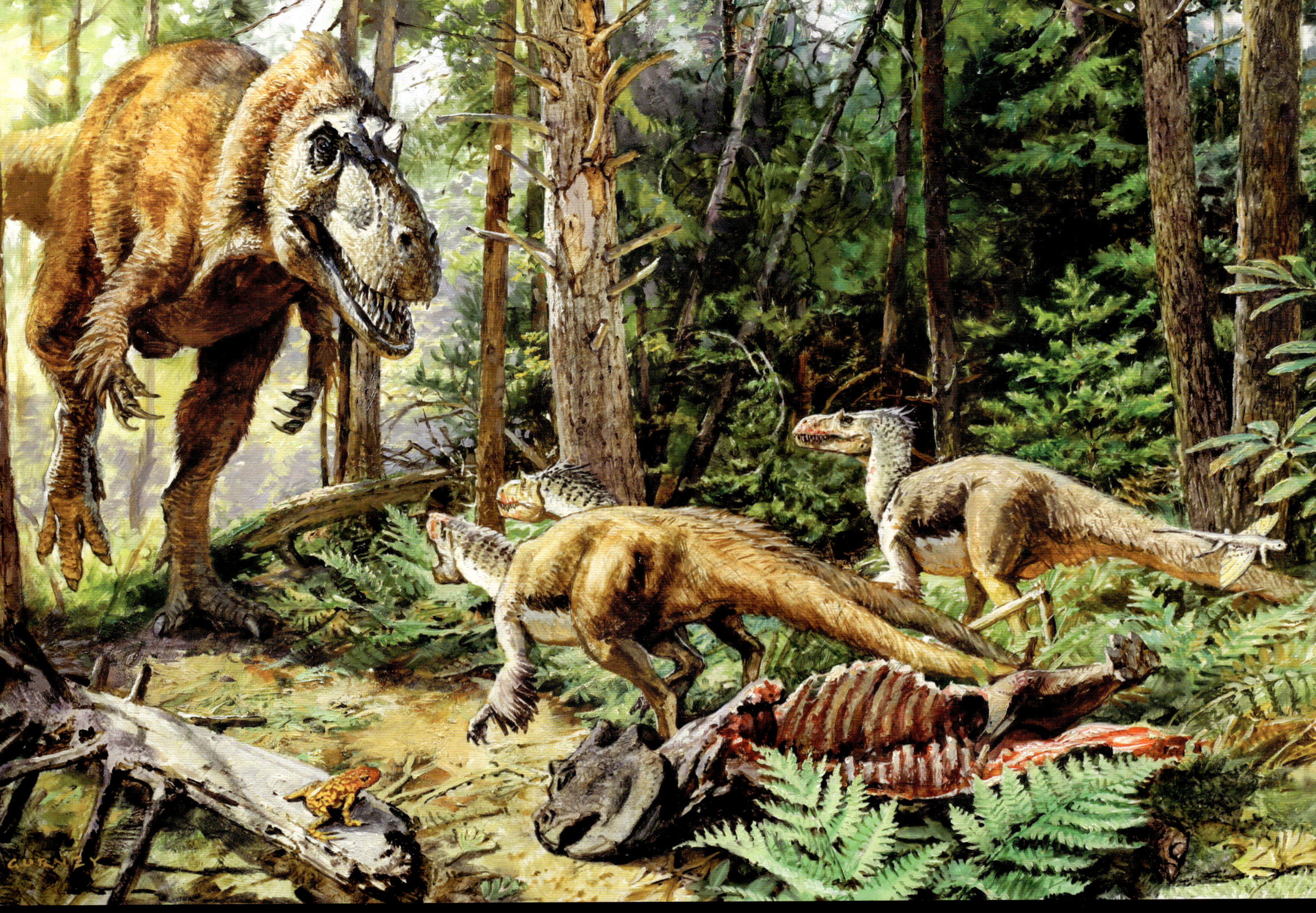

Yutyrannus vs. Dilong
Oil on panel, 36 × 46 cm

A situation that often happens among animals is that a larger meat eater will steal a kill from smaller predators. I followed the layout of the comp fairly closely and based the forest on the wild woods near where I live in upstate New York.

Right | Etruscan reference

I had the opportunity to travel on a research assignment to the newly discovered Blue Devil Tomb in Tarquinia for *National Geographic*, working on an archaeology story about the Etruscans. It wasn't hard to imagine the clock turning back to a time before photography was invented, when artists were necessary members of archaeological expeditions.

The tomb was recently discovered, but unfortunately the tomb robbers had got there first and cleaned out all the artefacts and human remains. We had no choice but to speculatively reconstruct what might have been in there based on other tombs that had been found intact.

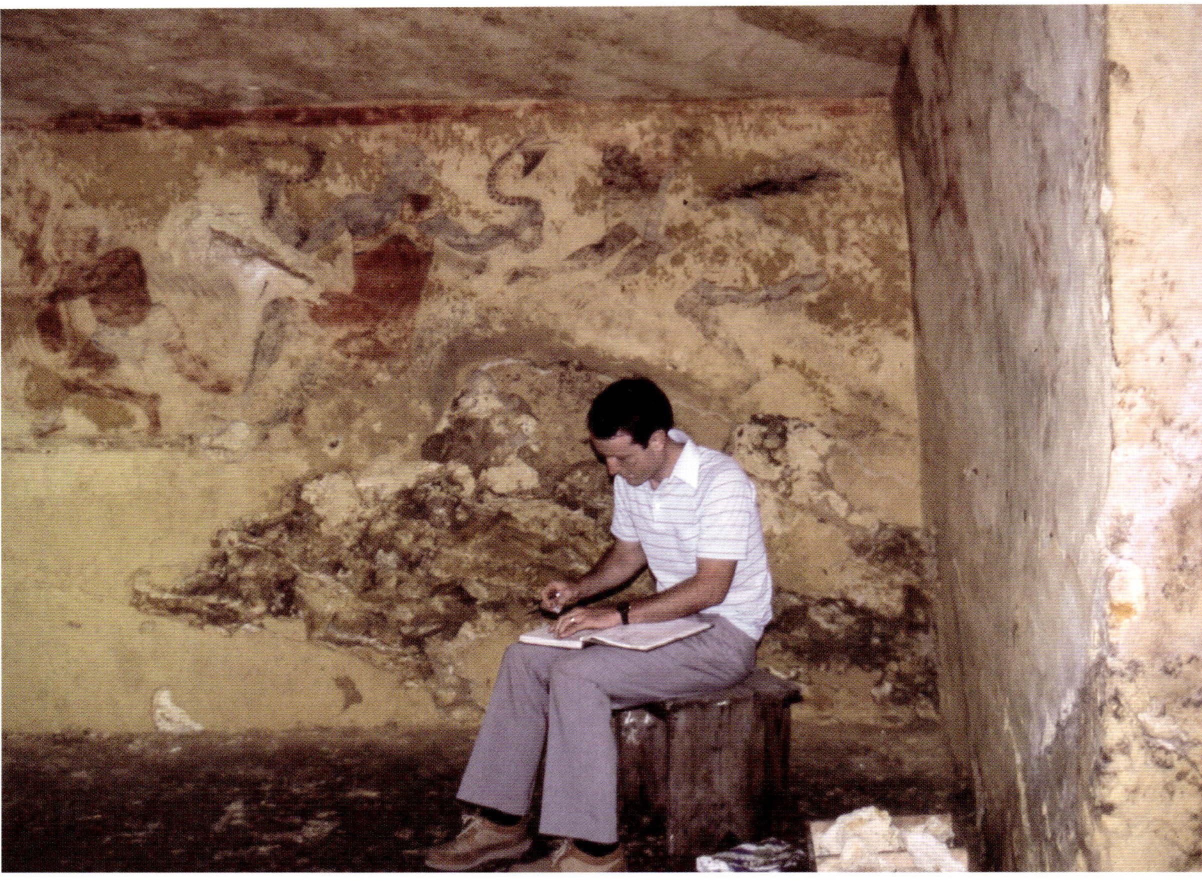

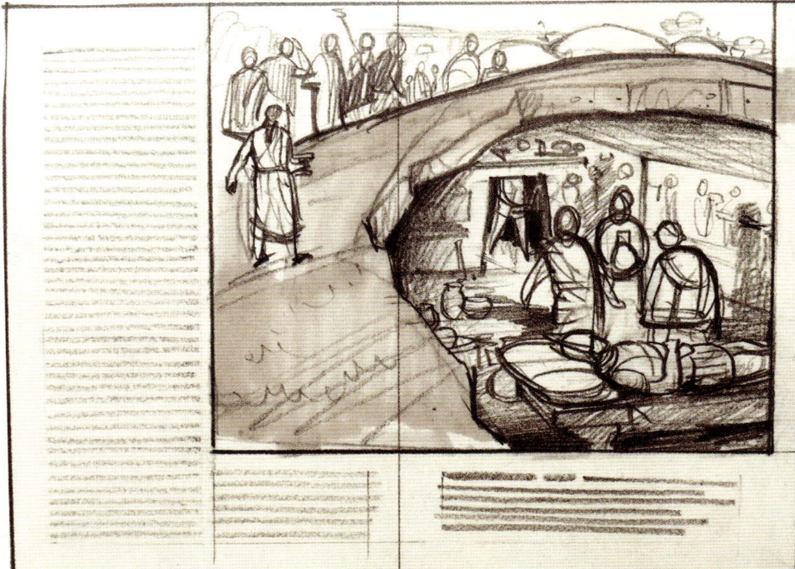

Left | Tomb sketch
Pencil and grey ink on bond paper, 15 × 20 cm

After visiting the site and reading the science papers, I was ready to start visualizing. At *National Geographic*, the artists must compete for page space against the world's best photographers. Page space is so valuable that almost everything ends up on the cutting room floor. We had the best luck getting the editor's approval when we showed comprehensive drawings in layout settings.

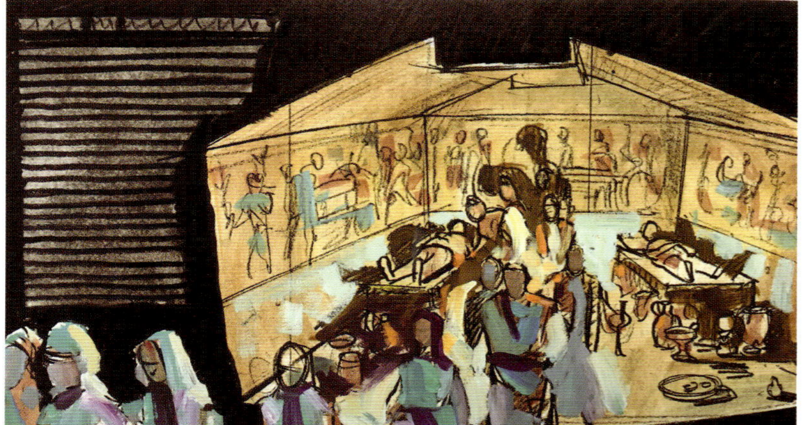

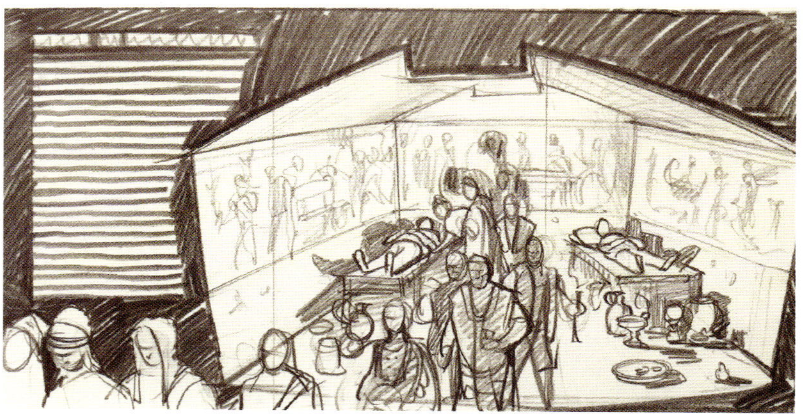

Left | New tomb sketch
Pencil on paper, 15 × 20 cm

The approved layout shows the outline of the tomb with the living relatives of the dead spilling across the bottom of the frame as they exit the tomb, dancing and playing instruments.

Above | Colour sketch
Oil over photocopy, 15 × 20 cm

I glued a copy of the last sketch onto a piece of board, sealed it with acrylic matte medium, and then applied oils over it to see how it might look in finished form.

Right | Tomb layout
Pencil on layout board

The pencil sketch shows the figures as I first imagined them, still without reference to models. The sketch had to be comprehensive enough to sell the editor on setting aside a double-page spread in the article layout.

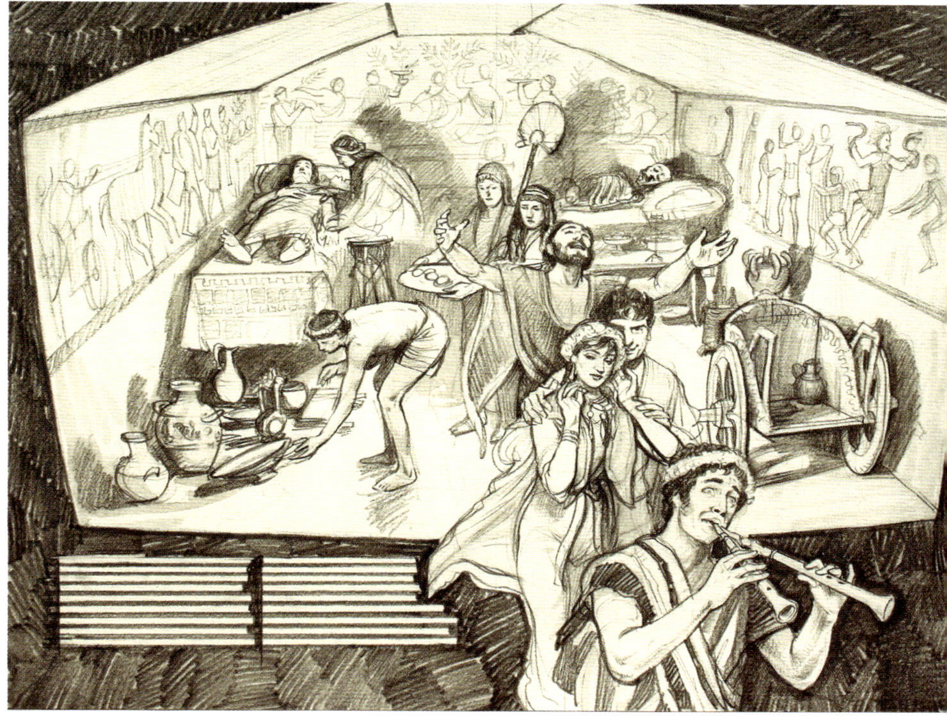

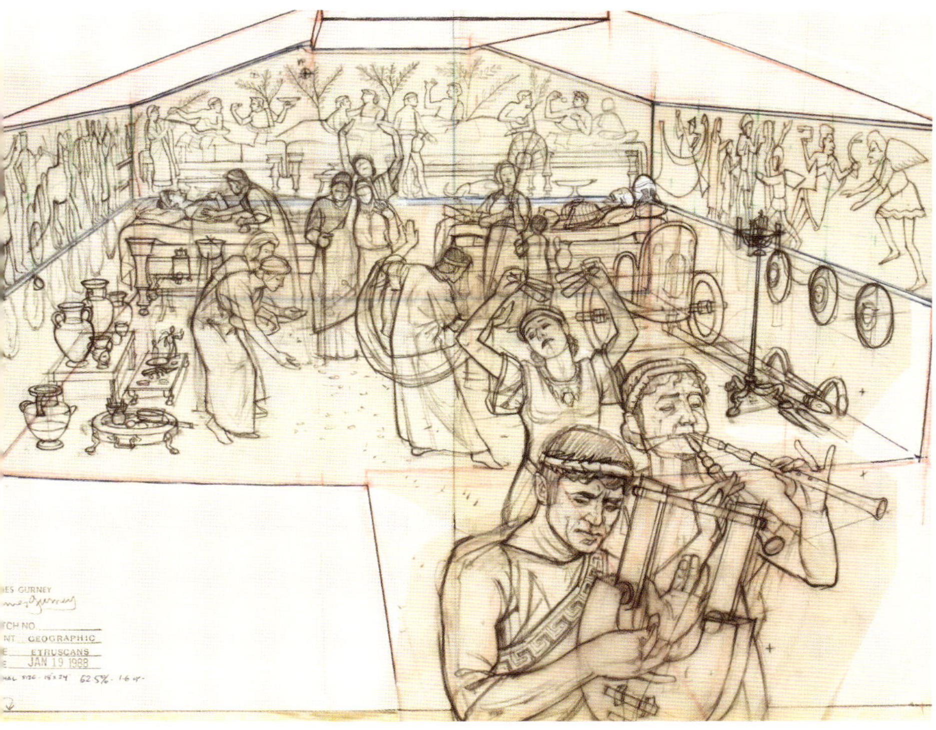

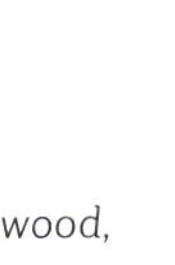

Left | Tarquinia layout
Charcoal on tracing paper, 46 × 61 cm

For the charcoal comprehensive, I drew each figure grouping on a separate layer of tracing paper. This way I could experiment with overlapping without erasing or affecting the layers beneath. Of course, you could do all this in Photoshop, but working in pencil or charcoal is deliciously tactile and just as fast.

Right | Tarquinia Tomb
Oil on canvas mounted on plywood, 46 × 61 cm

The final painting takes us back to around 700 BC to show a family departing the tomb, accompanied by musicians and dancers.

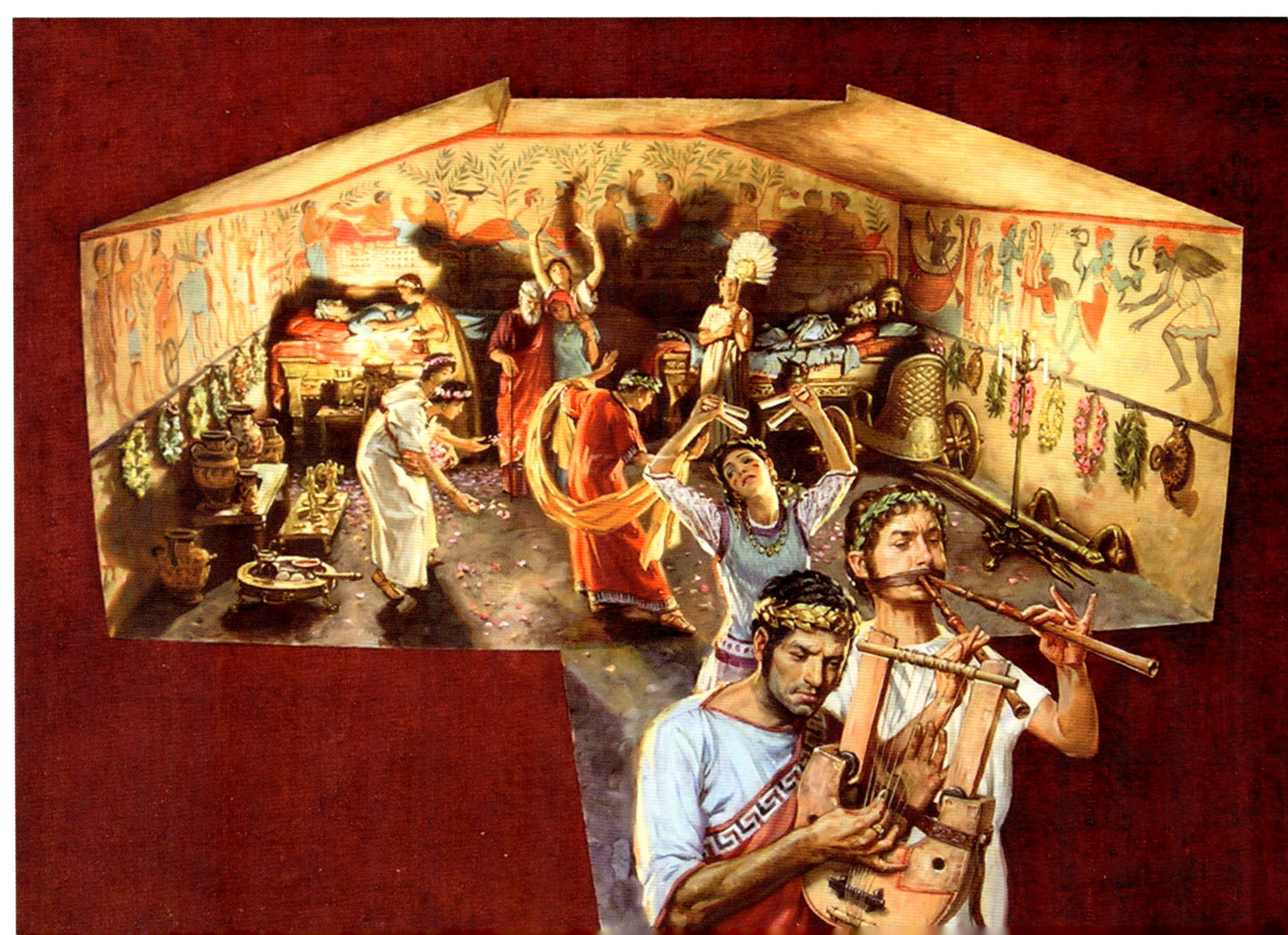

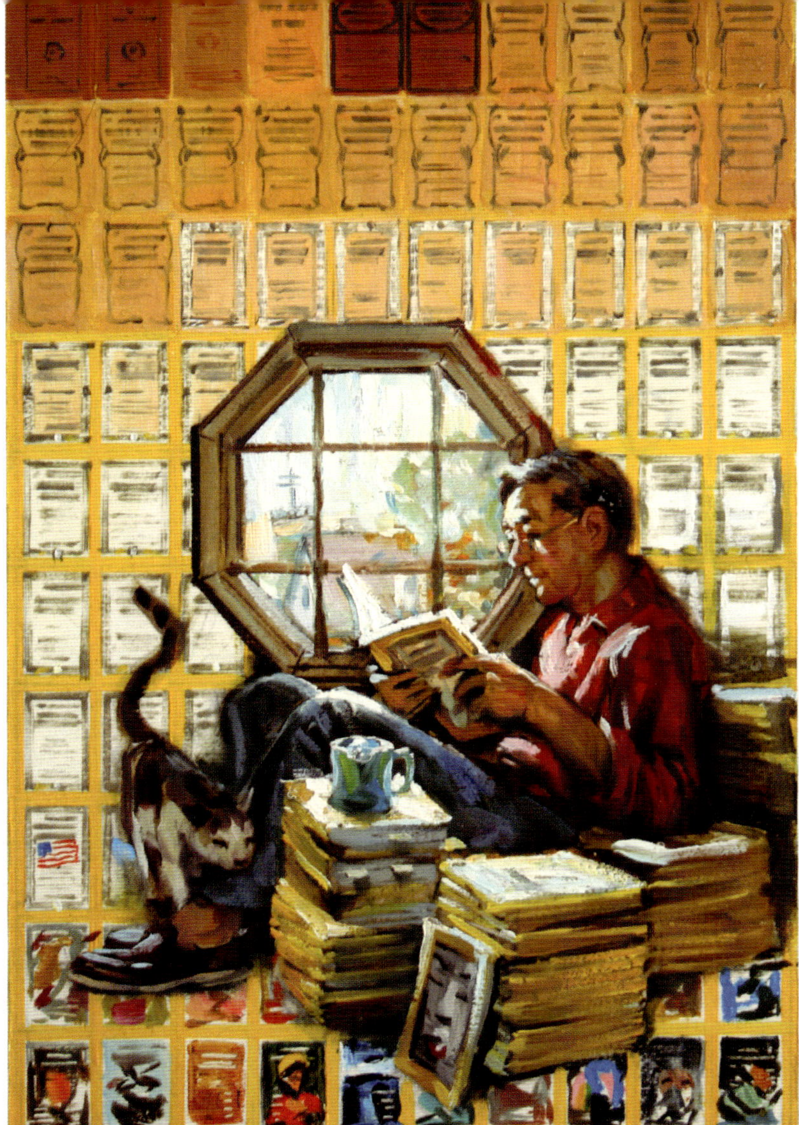

Left | **First concept sketch**
Oil on board, 23 × 15 cm

To honour its centennial in 1988, *National Geographic* asked me to paint a picture expressing the magazine's legacy of adventure and discovery. Instead of portraying some bold explorer, I thought it would be fun to show something more poignant and homespun: a man sitting in an attic looking back on his life and his world through the pages of old magazines. In my first concept for the painting, the man sat all by himself. The first colour sketch shows the man against a background of magazine covers. I had hoped the octagonal window would convey the idea that he was sitting in an attic. But it was confusing. It wasn't clear where he was sitting.

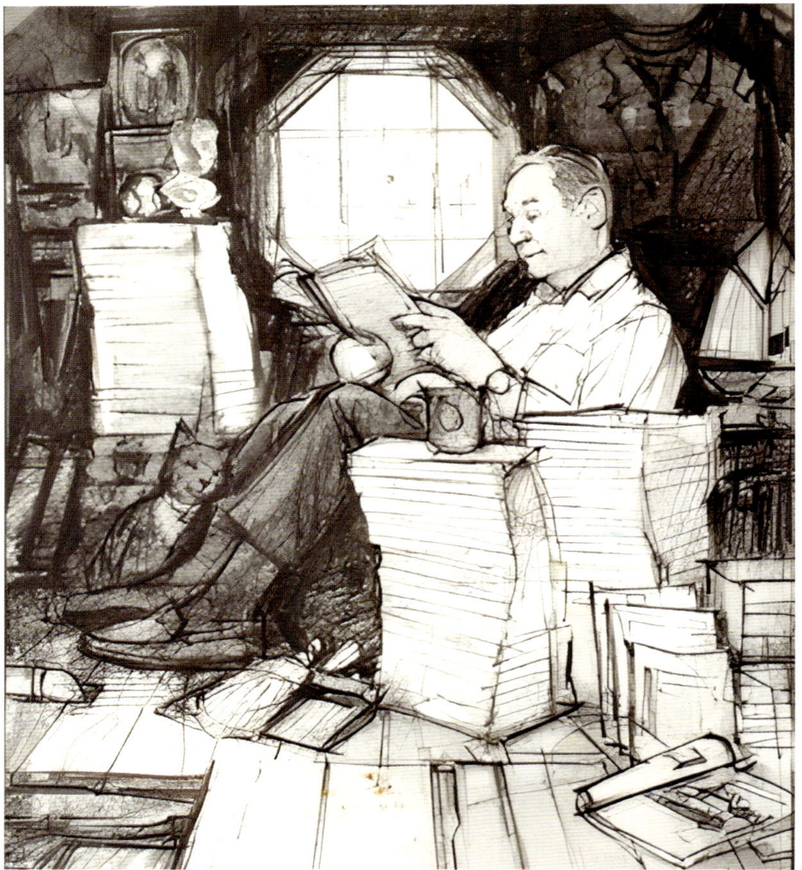

Above | **Charcoal pencil sketch**
Pencil on bond paper, 23 × 15 cm

To cure the loneliness problem, I drew the composition again in charcoal and returned to the idea of a cat rubbing against his leg. But that still wasn't enough. I needed to show that he was passing his memories on to someone.

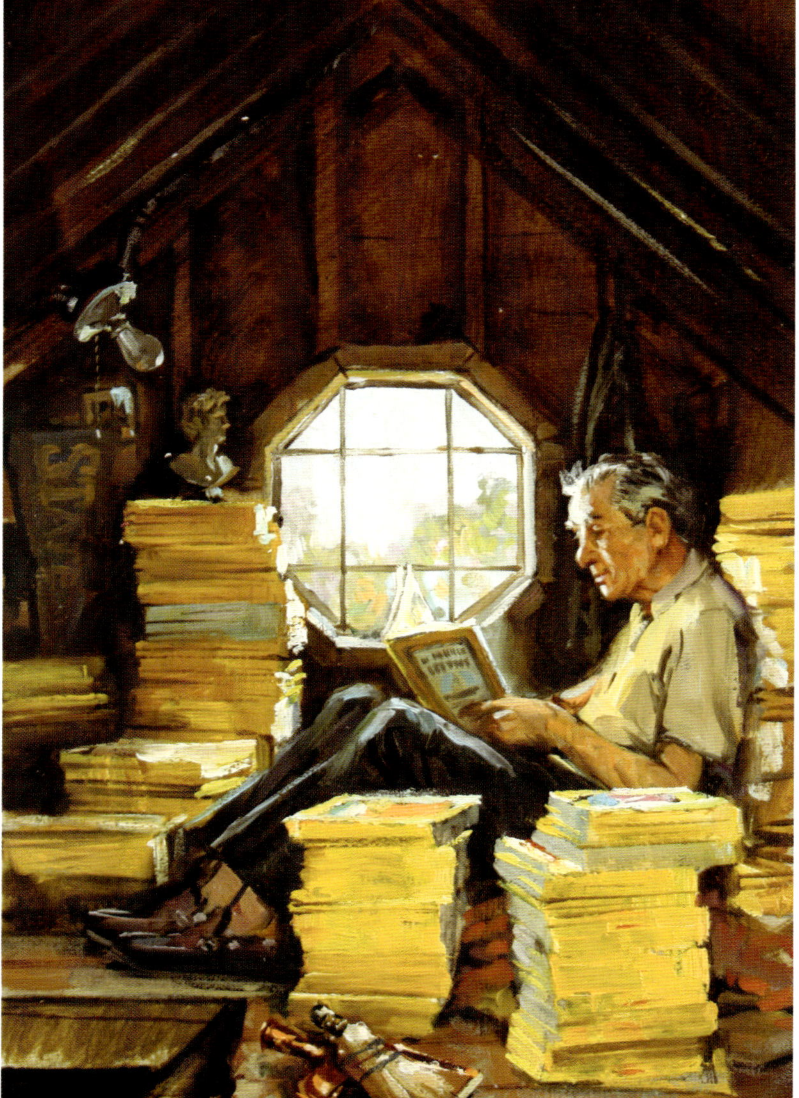

Left | **Second concept sketch**
Oil on board, 23 × 15 cm

In the second sketch, I placed him in an attic and used the broom and dustpan to show that he was distracted in the process of cleaning up. But I wasn't happy with this idea either. It was depressing to think of this old man sitting up there all by himself.

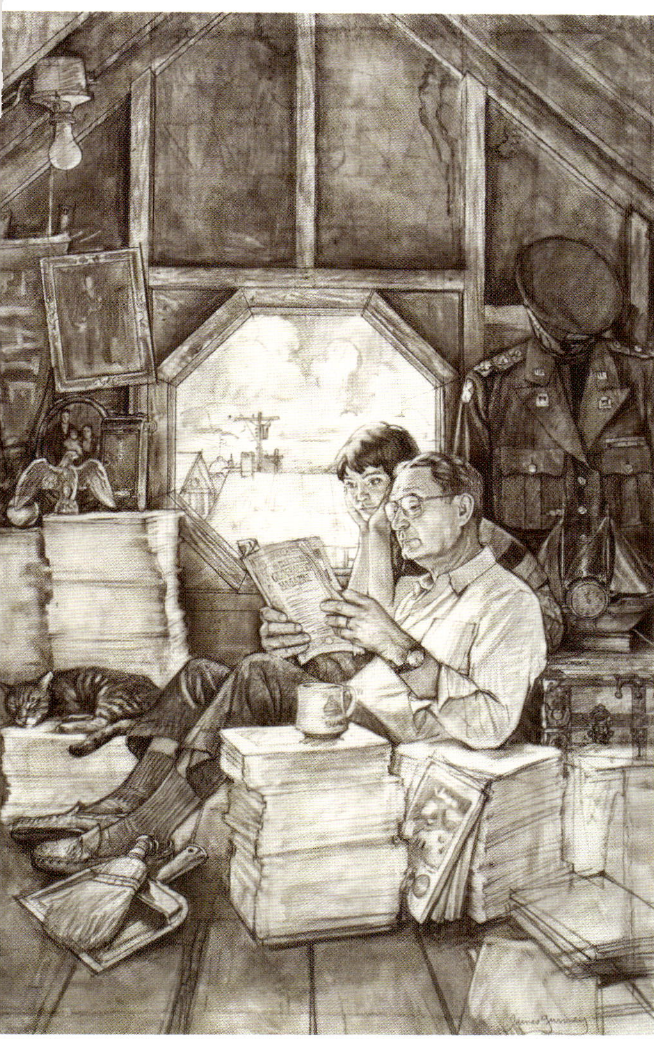

Above | Charcoal comprehensive
Charcoal on vellum, 91 × 61 cm

So, I added a grandson. I had models pose and drew the charcoal comprehensive at the size of the final painting. The idea of preparing a charcoal drawing at the full size of the final painting was inspired by Norman Rockwell, though he wasn't the first to do it.

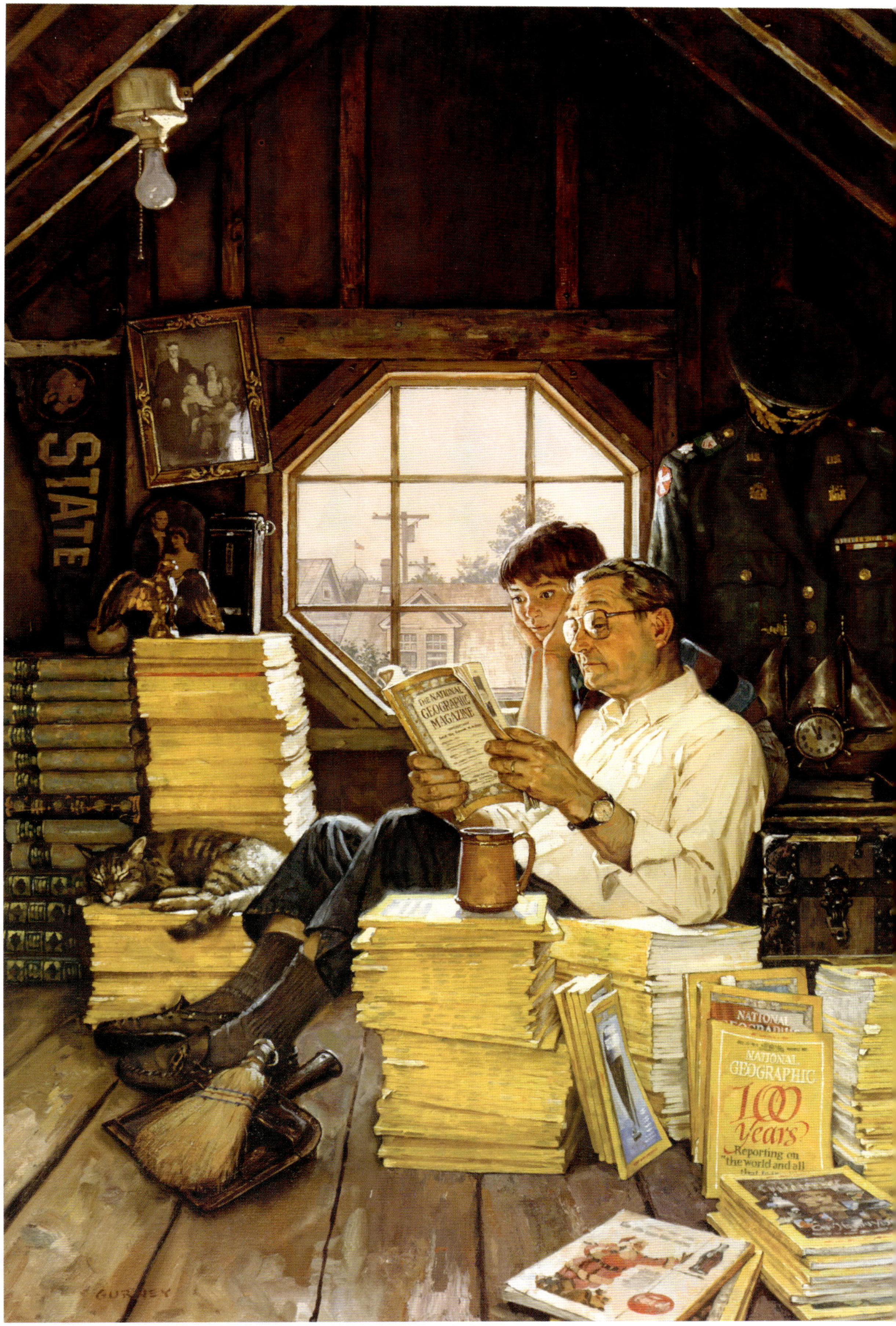

Right | Published in *National Geographic*, February 1989
Oil on canvas, 91 × 61 cm

The final painting shows the two figures surrounded by mementos of the man's life: a military uniform, an old family photo, and a ship clock. When I started the project, I knew I would have to search out all those items from real attics in my home town. In the finished painting, I was interested in the cool light from the window and the warm illumination bouncing back from the attic space. I tried to capture the boy's faraway expression, as if the magazine and his grandfather's memories are transporting him to another world.

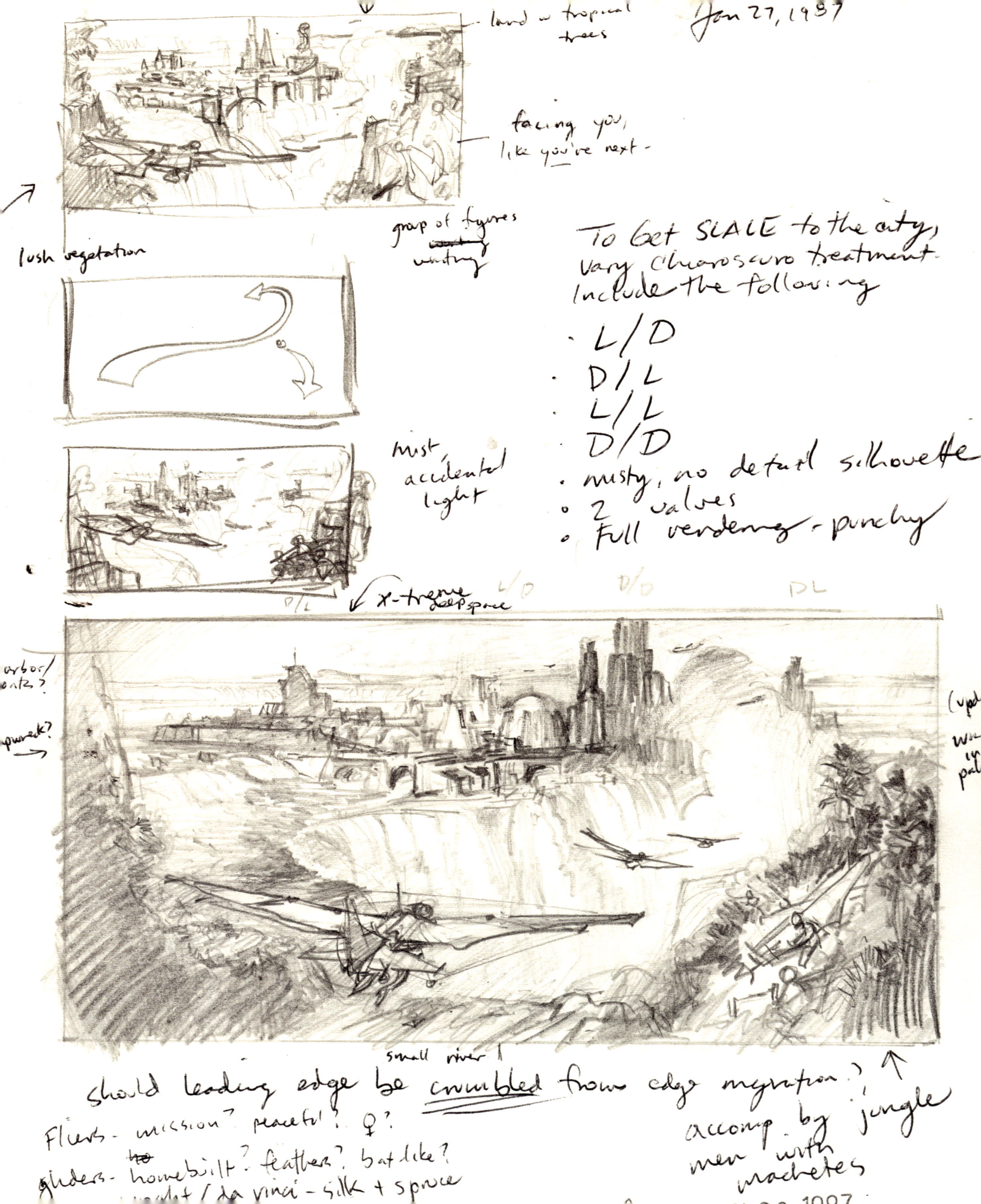

land w/ tropical trees
Jan 27, 1997
facing you, like you're next
lush vegetation
group of figures waiting
To Get SCALE to the city, vary chiaroscuro treatment. Include the following
· L/D
· D/L
· L/L
· D/D
· misty, no detail silhouette
○ 2 values
○ full verdens - punchy
mist accidental light
x-treme deep space
L/D
D/D
DL
arbor/ onts?
pwreck?
small river
Should leading edge be crumbled from edge migration?
Fliers - mission? peaceful? Q?
gliders - homebuilt? feathers? bat like?
da vinci - silk + spruce
accomp. by jungle men with machetes
1997

SKETCHBOOK PRACTICE

My sketchbooks are a mixed bag of field notes, thumbnail sketches, compositional breakdowns, and shopping lists. A lot of what you see in this chapter was created before the birth of social media and its consciousness of sharing the process.

I like graphite for quick sketches and studies, but I'm a mixed-media guy at heart. In my urban-sketching kit, I've got art supplies that are cross-compatible. I might use pen, brush pen, coloured pencil, gouache, watercolour, casein, or acrylic – and even coffee rings or glued-on bits of paper – if they can give me the effect I'm looking for.

I get going with certain sketchbook formats and fill a bunch of books to make a series. Lately it has been 12.5 × 20 cm horizontal-format watercolour books. In the past I've filled a series of 20 × 20 cm drawing books with pencil sketchbooks. On my studio shelves I have a whole series of 'study books' for concepts, ideas, notes, and diagrams. Those are 21.5 × 28 cm hardbound books.

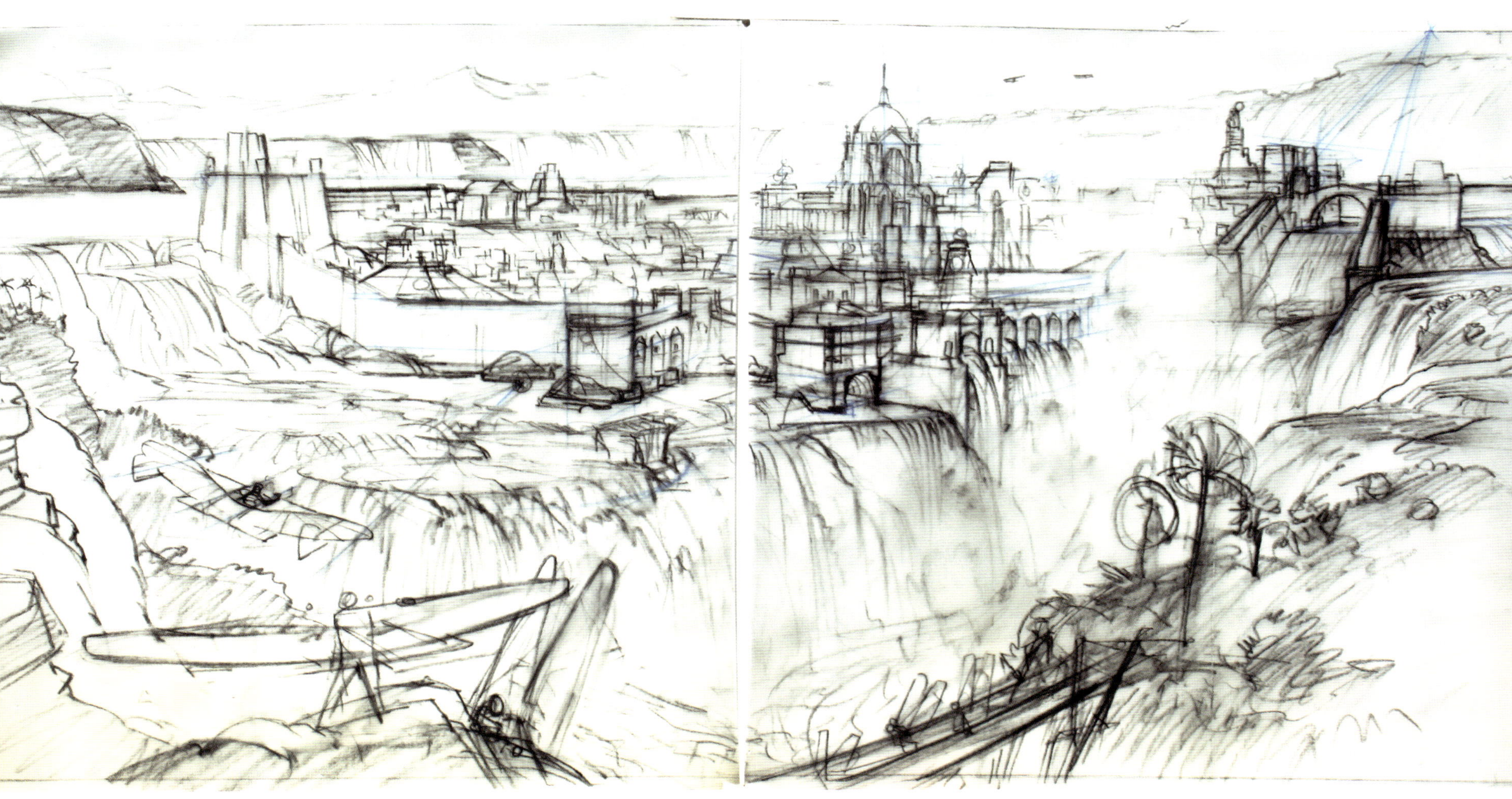

Opposite page | Sketch for *Waterfall City*
Pencil on paper

Above | Line study
Charcoal on vellum, 30 × 61 cm

This charcoal-on-vellum line drawing is about half the size of the final painting of *Waterfall City*. This is the step where I figure out perspective, placement, and storytelling, thinking about how those gliders could get across the gorge, which areas to lose in mist, and which architectural forms are repeated.

Right | **Sketch in oil,
Niagara Falls from Goat Island**
*Oil on canvas mounted
to panel, 15 × 30 cm*

There's only so much I can do from my
imagination alone. To go beyond that,
I have to 'fill the bucket', which is what
I call the process of gathering reference.
One key step was painting at Niagara
Falls. I set up my painting gear on Goat
Island with a bunch of kids watching.
The studies helped me understand how
the water should look, something that's
hard to get from photos.

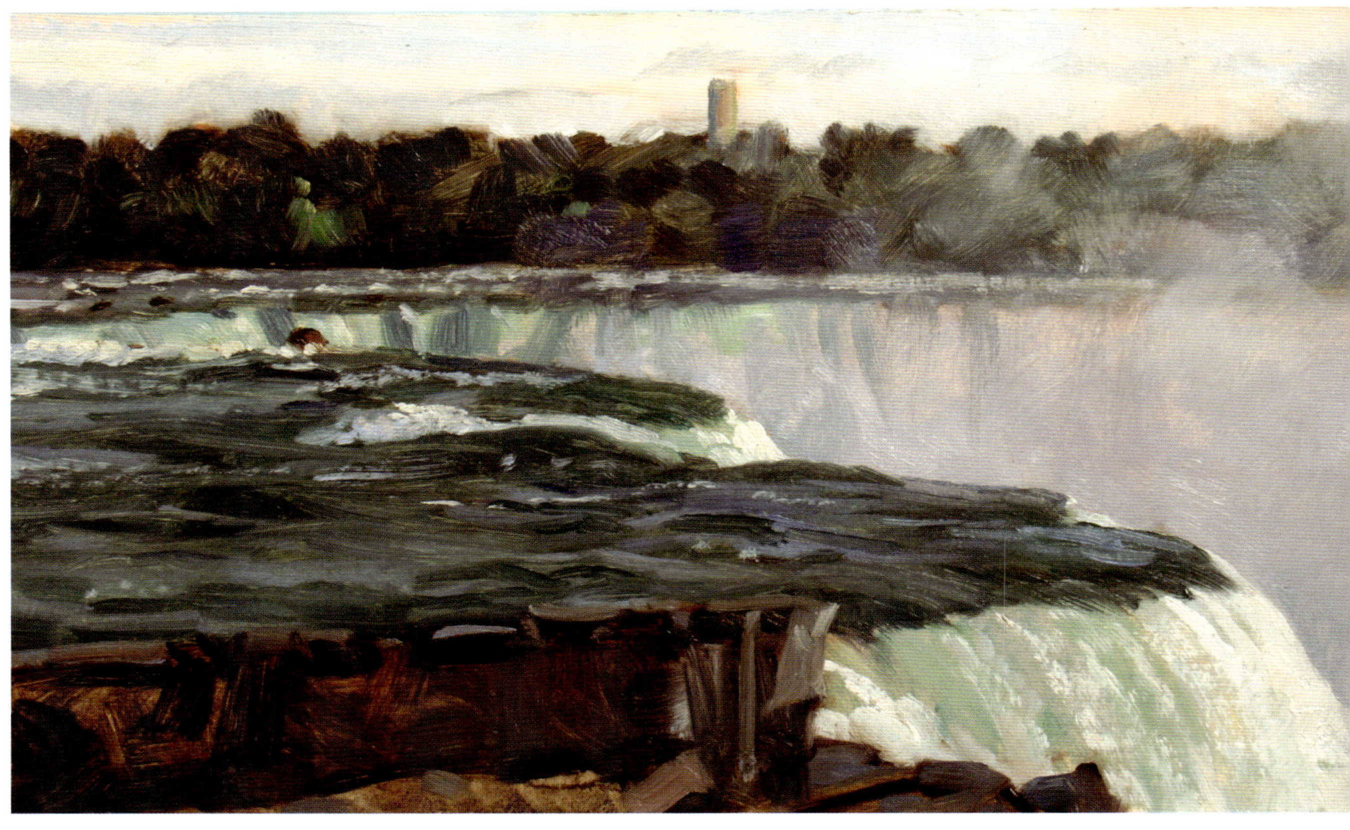

Left | **Schematic maquette**
Grey-painted foam, 51 × 51 cm

This schematic maquette is made out
of Styrofoam, cardboard, and a wood
ball, spray-painted with grey spray-on
primer. It helped me as a designer to
keep Waterfall City visually consistent
when it appears in various angles.
The real benefit of such a schematic
maquette is that you can turn it around
to any angle to see how the light plays
on it. This kind of model is a great
help for entertainment designers or
sequential artists who need to imagine
a complex form consistently from a
variety of angles.

Right | **Painted maquette**
Mixed media, 28 × 36 × 20 cm

I also built a more detailed maquette.
This maquette is made from cardboard,
Styrofoam, and epoxy putty, painted
in acrylic. It helped me imagine
perspective and lighting on this near
corner of Waterfall City, which appeared
from many angles in my books
Dinotopia: The World Beneath and
Dinotopia: Journey to Chandara.

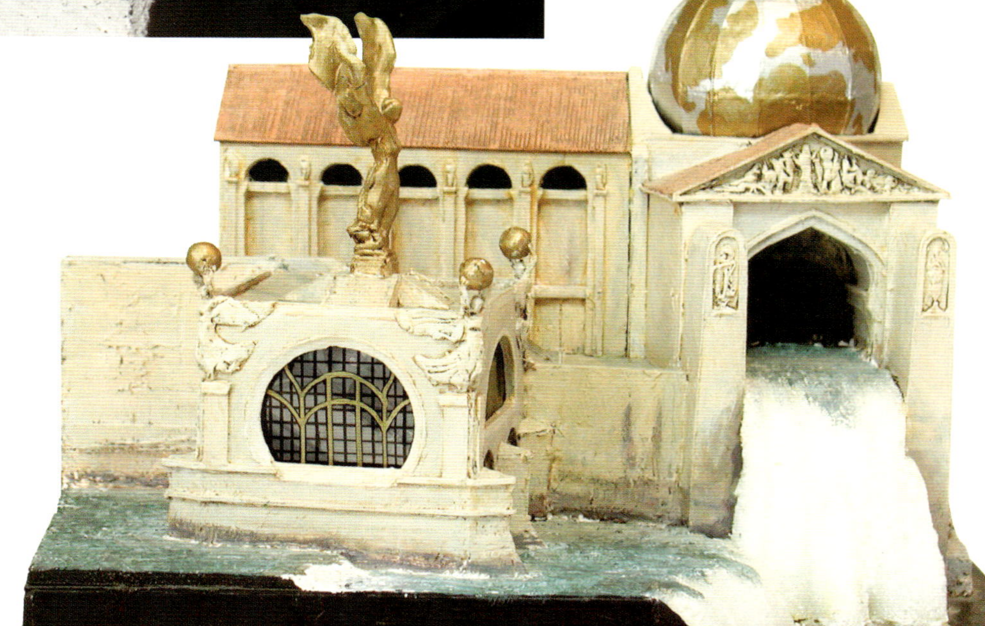

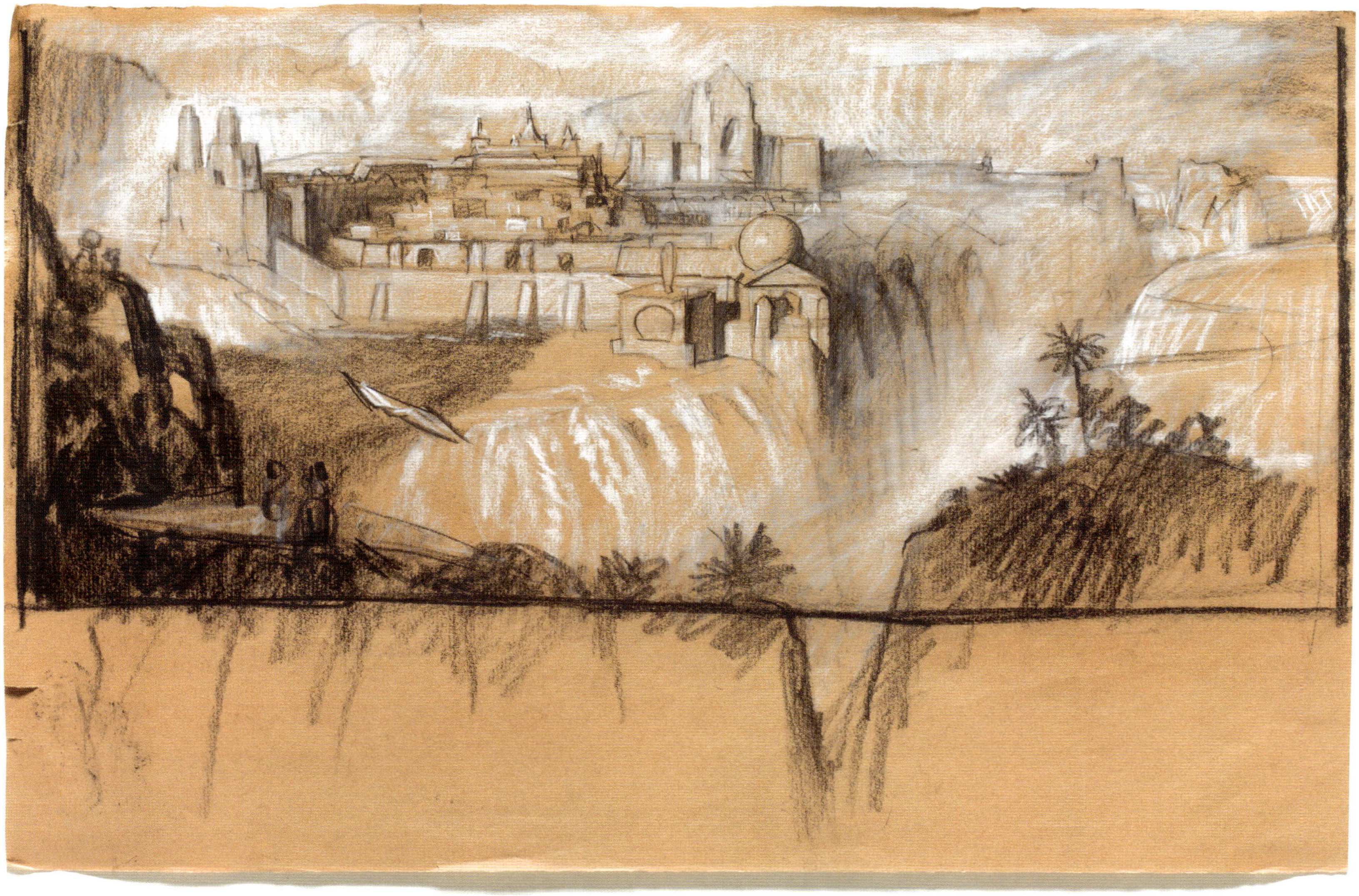

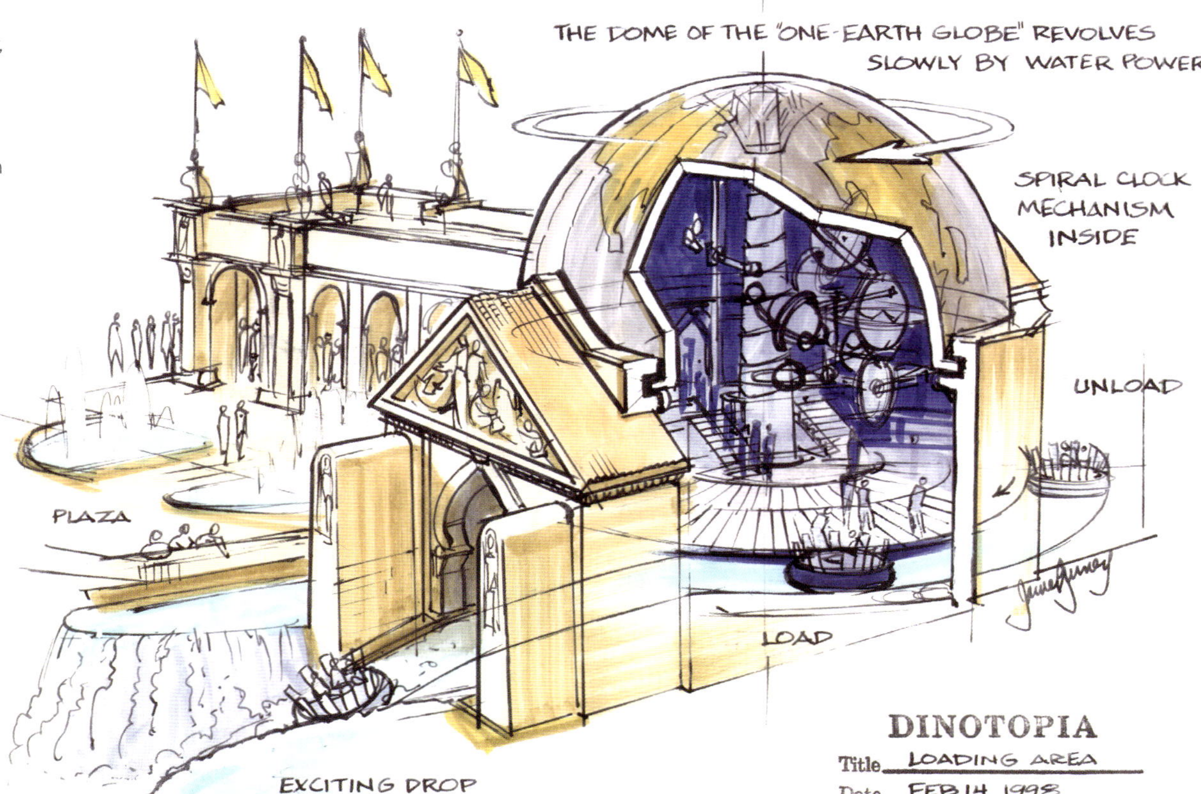

Above | **Tone study**

Charcoal and white chalk on brown paper,
25 × 41 cm

After studying the maquettes, I drew a
study on toned paper to solidify my vision
of how the city would look veiled in mist.

Right | **Rapids ride**

Pen and markers on paper, 22 × 28 cm

A theme-park company wanted to build
a water ride based on Waterfall City,
so I made this sketch of the loading
area under the One-Earth Globe.

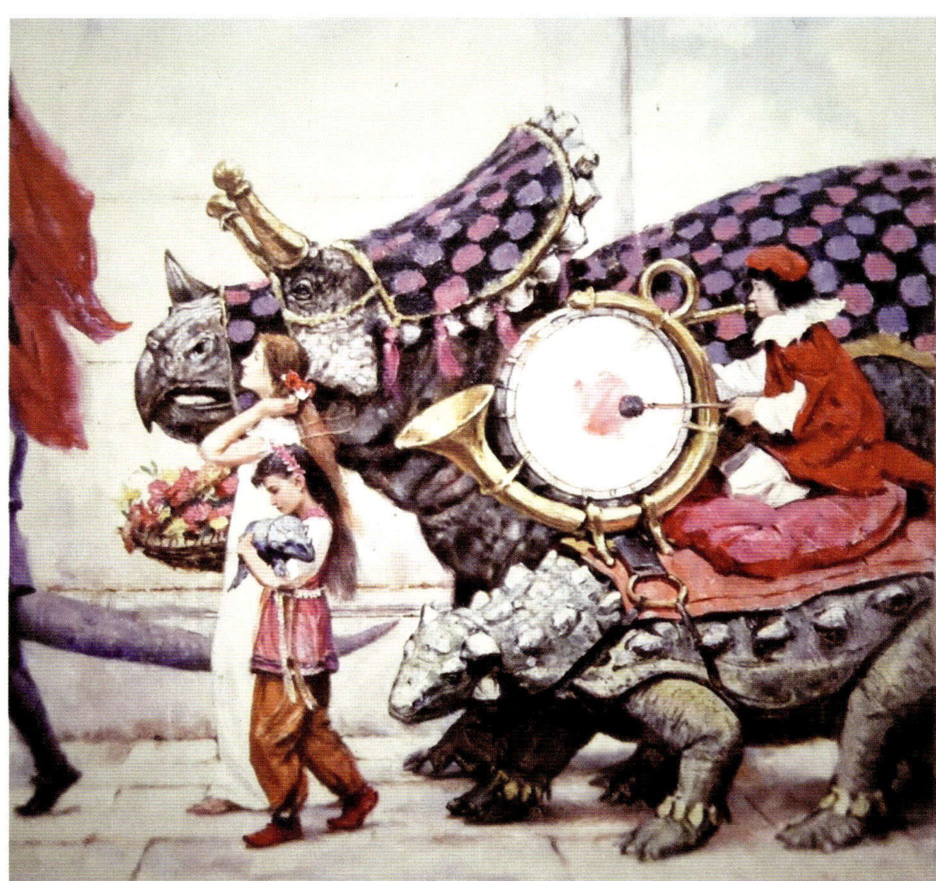

Dinotopia Parade
Oil on panel, 30 × 30 cm

In an early concept for a dinosaur parade scene, I tried a profile view of a small group of humans and dinosaurs bedecked in colourful costumes, with a horn-drum on an Ankylosaurus to set the tempo. I realized I needed to pull back the view to show the whole parade.

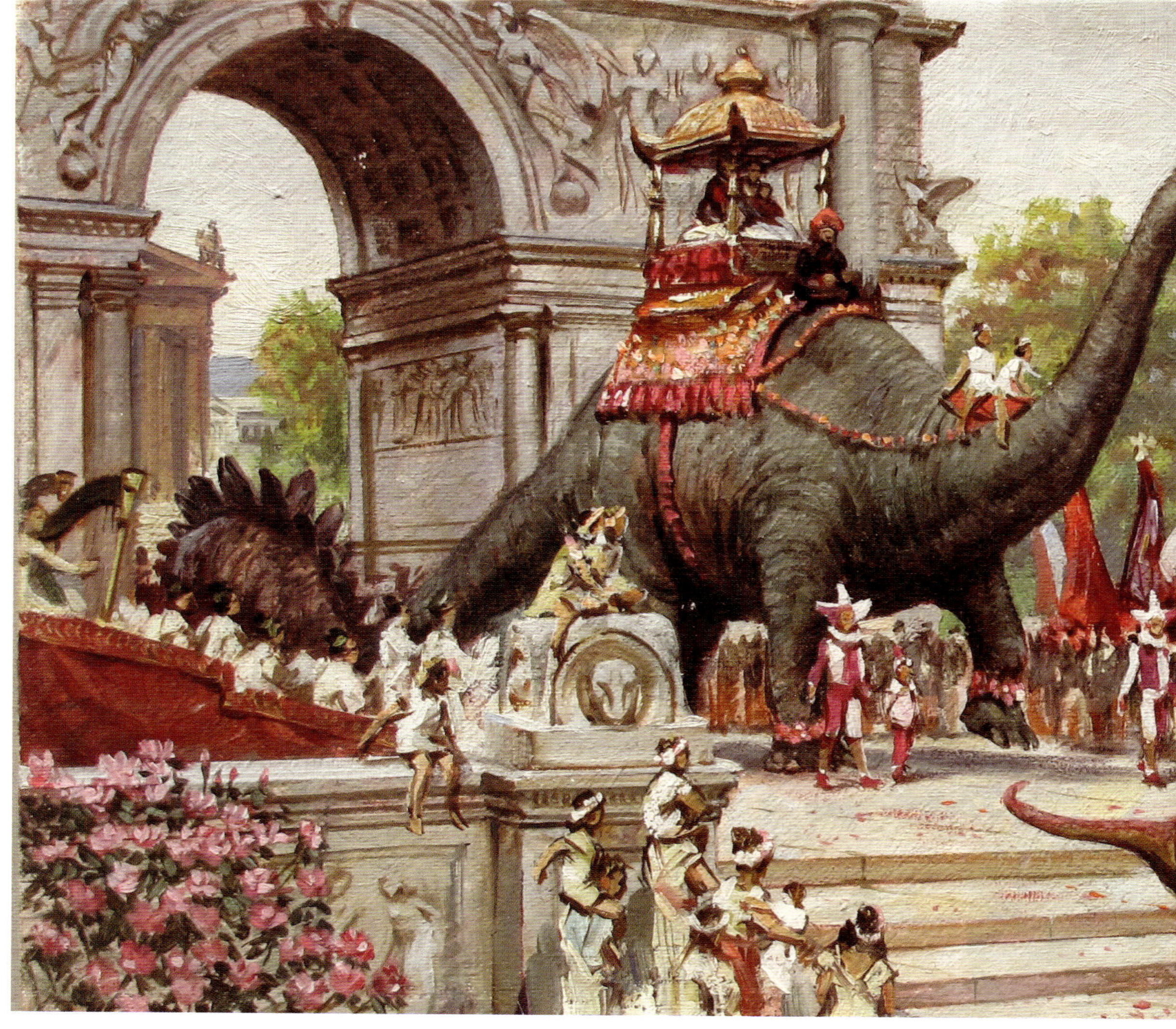

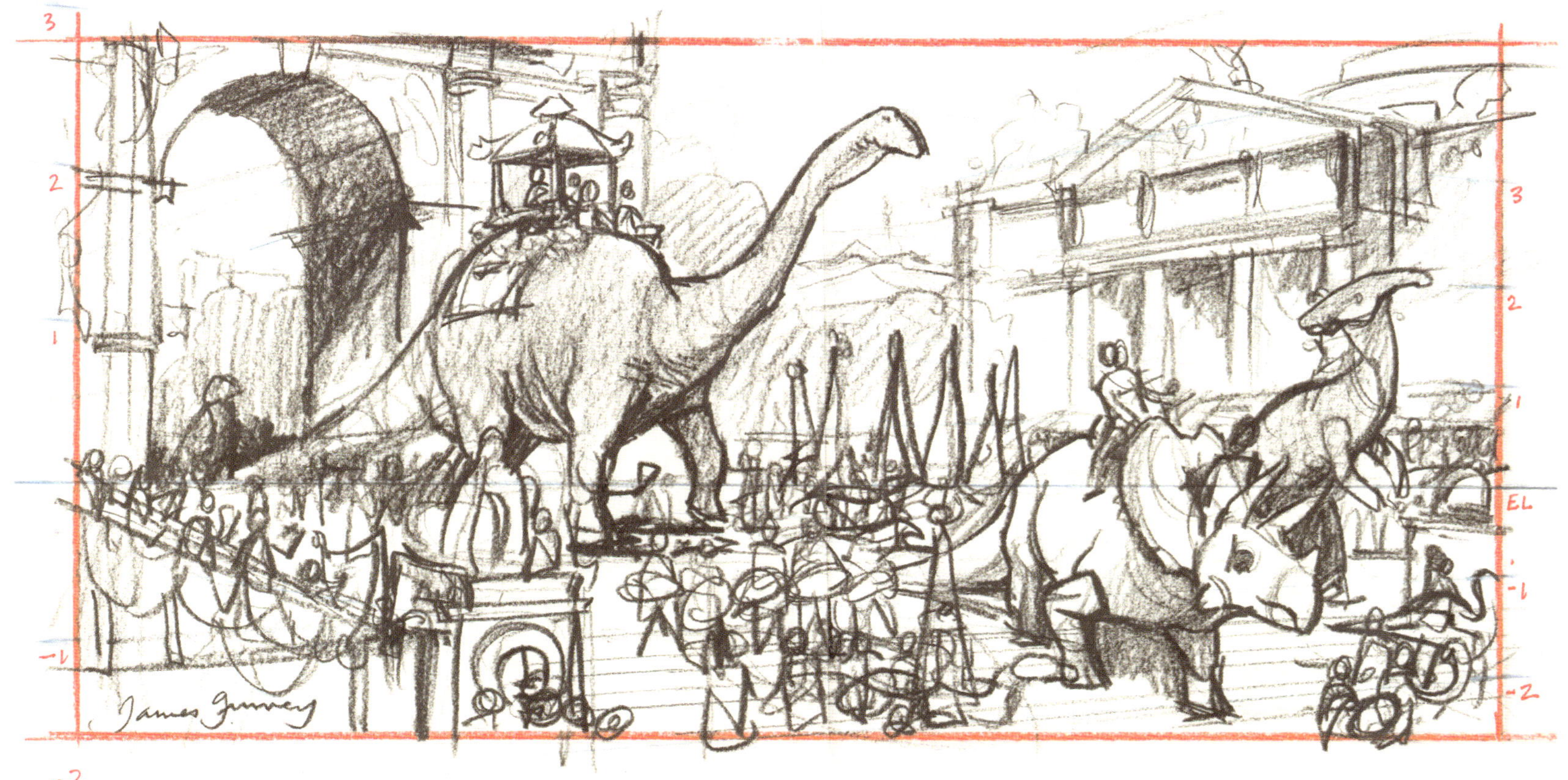

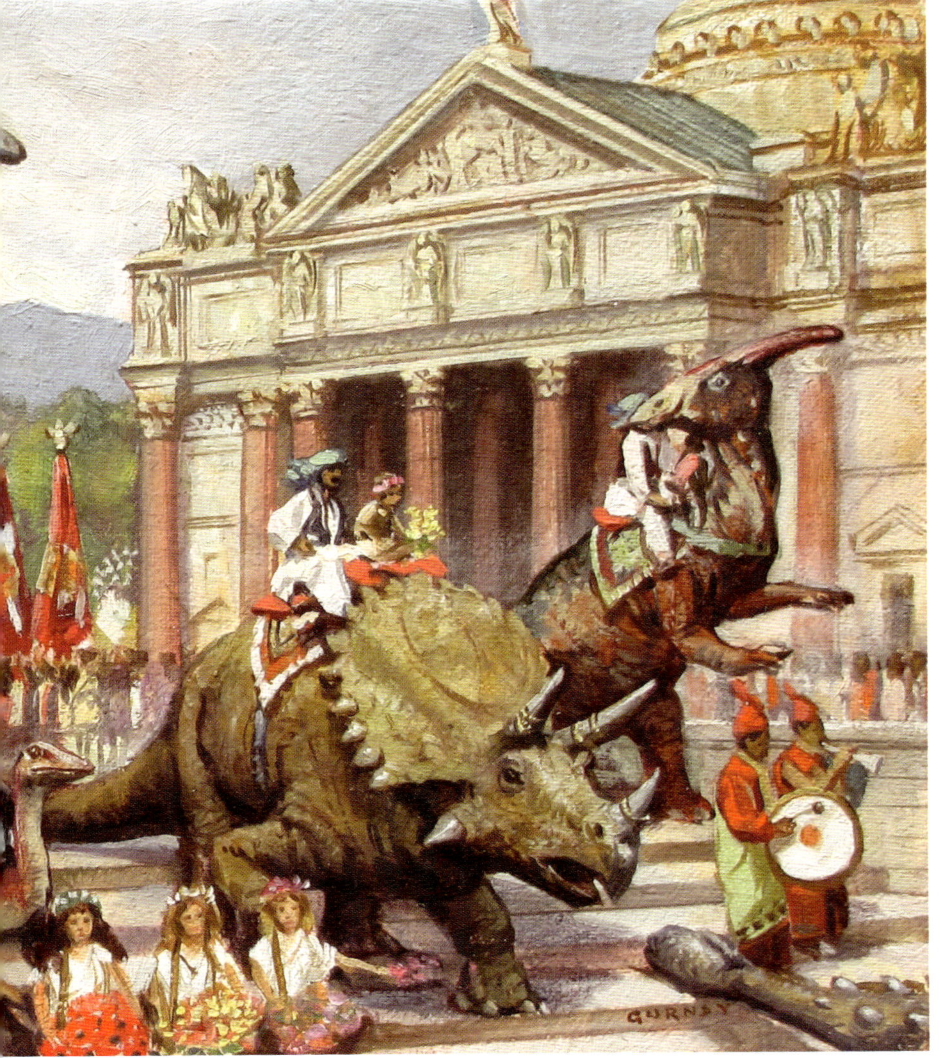

Layout

Pencil on bond paper, 15 × 30 cm

This planning sketch was drawn entirely
from my imagination. I established
the eye level to help work out the
perspective, even though the horizon
wasn't visible from this viewpoint.

Mini comp

Oil on canvas mounted to plywood, 15 × 30 cm

Once I knew where to place the various elements,
I made this tiny comprehensive study to see how the
scene would work as an ensemble. Using oil gave me
a chance to think about how to light the scene with an
overcast sky and how to restrict the colour palette to
cool reds, gold ochres, and viridian greens. At this point
I was still working almost entirely from my imagination.

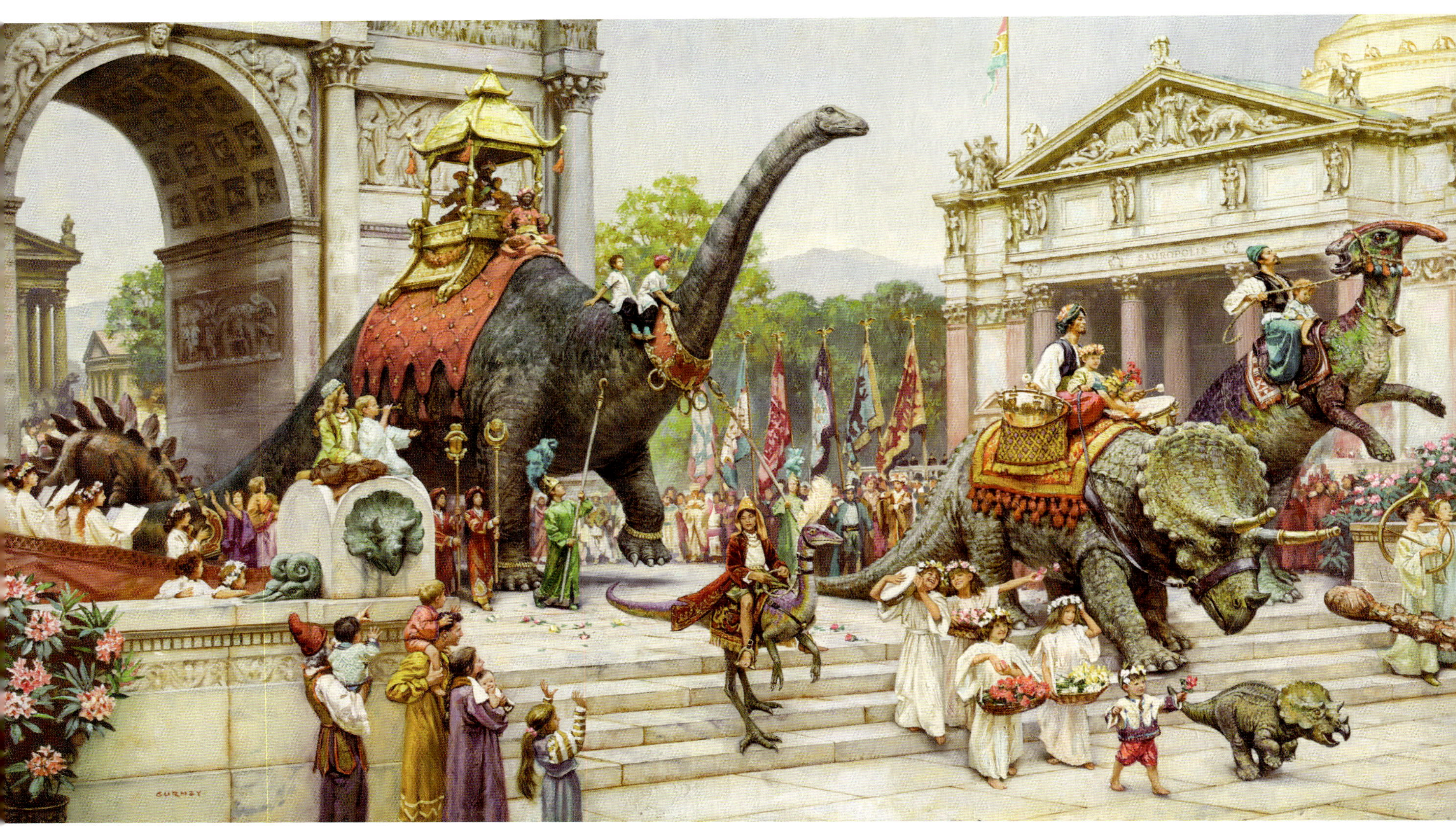

Dinosaur Parade

Oil on canvas mounted to board,
61 × 122 cm

The final painting was aided by
photographic reference that I shot using
the mini comp as a guide. For models,
I enlisted the help of friends and
neighbours wearing costumes that we
bought from a New York rental company.

Paper Play Set

Pen and markers on bond paper,
22 × 28 cm

The original *Dinotopia* book was
published in 1992 in thirty-two
countries and eighteen languages.
The success of the books created
demand for other products, such
as coffee mugs, audio adaptations,
calendars, and pop-up books.
To imagine the possibility of spin-offs,
I did quick renderings to visualize
what the potential might be, but we
didn't go forward with most of them.

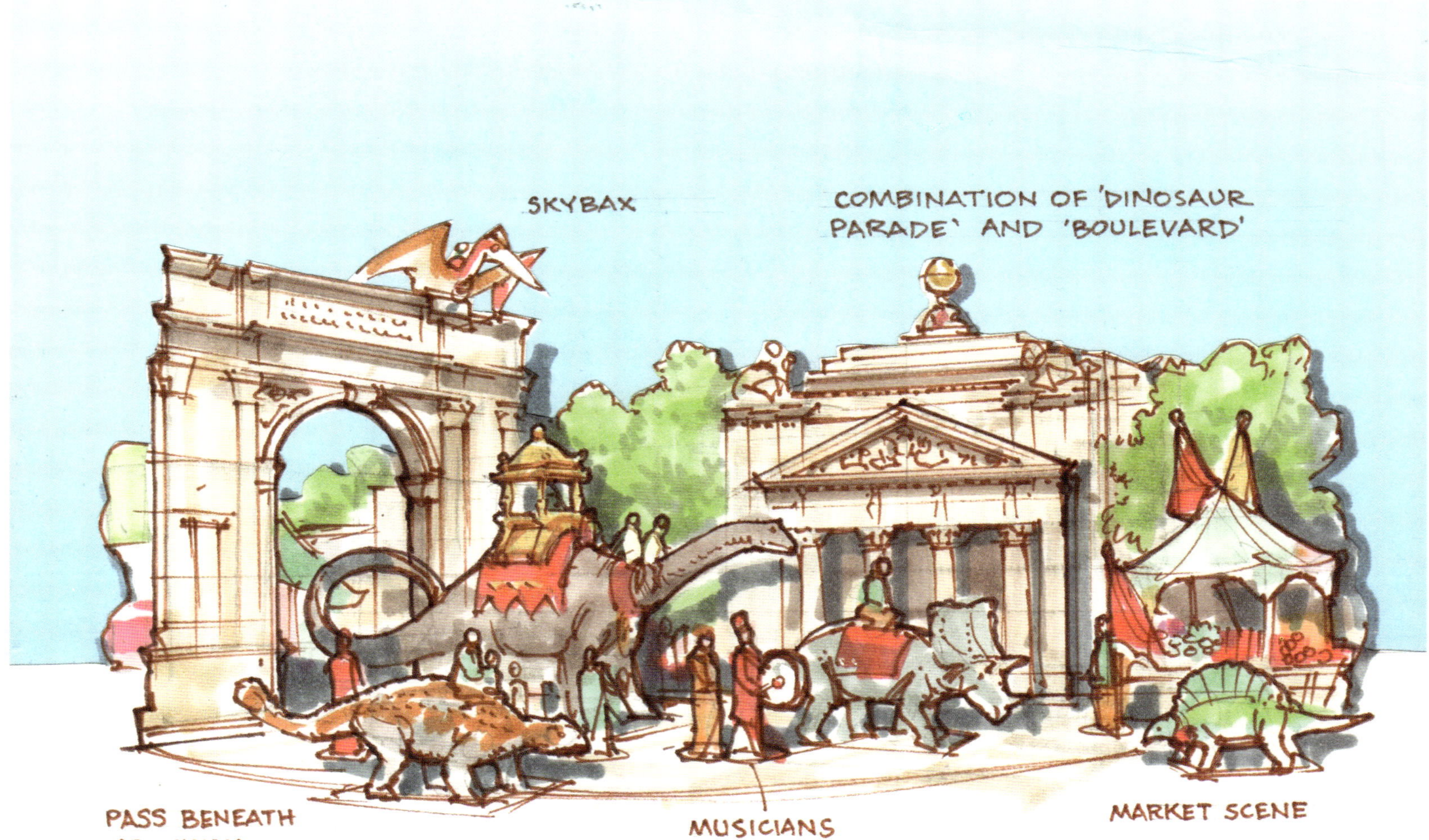

PAPER PLAY SET

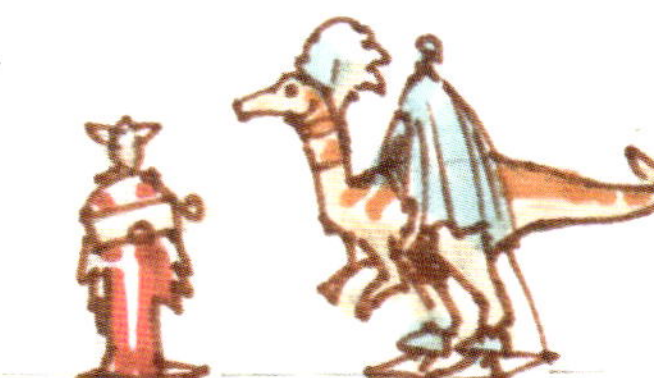

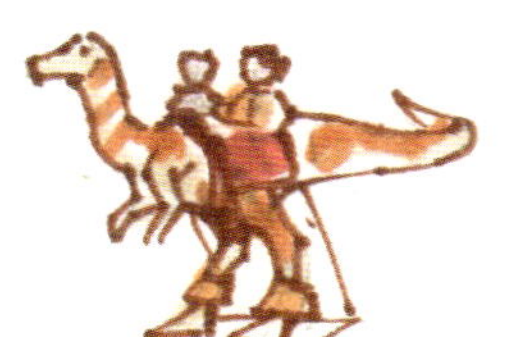

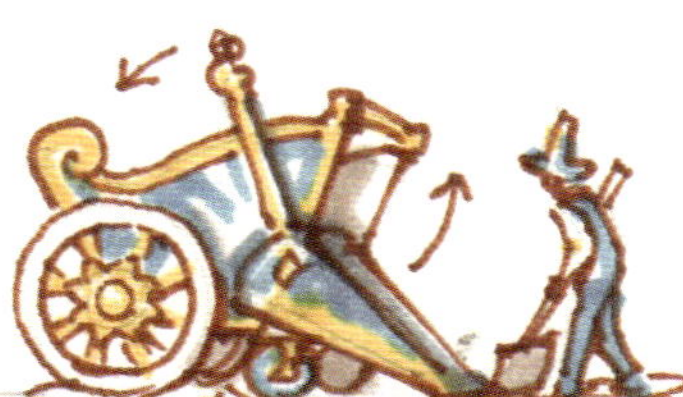

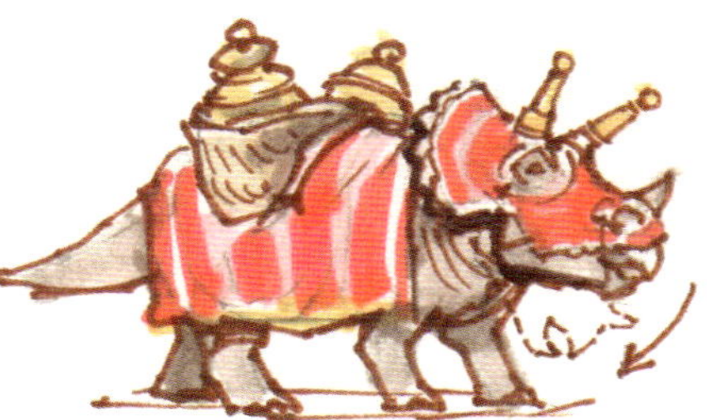

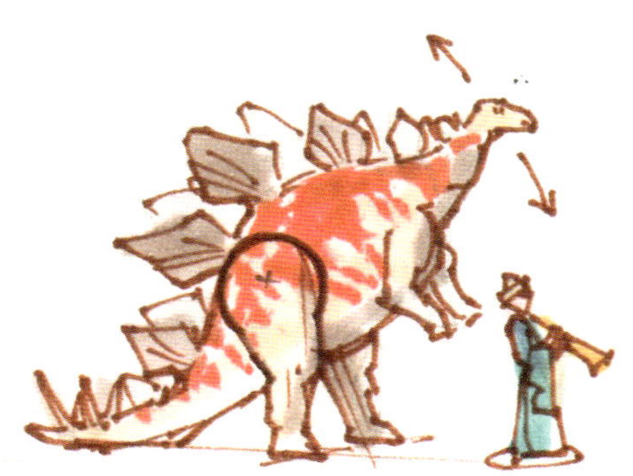

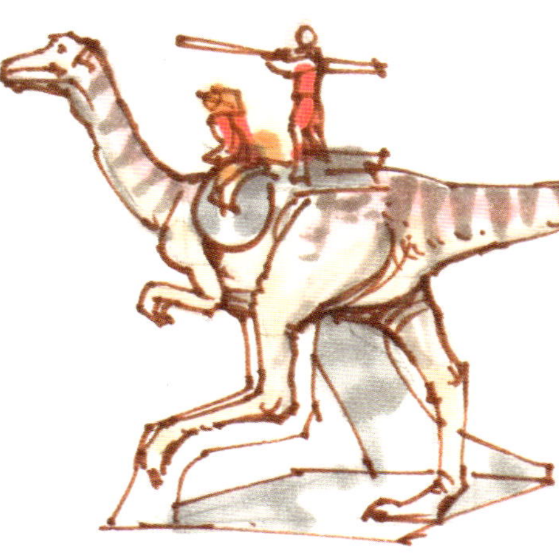

REALISM & IMAGINATION

Some people have called my kind of artwork 'imaginative realism' or 'reality-based fantasy', but I think it's really what artists have always done throughout history in portraying scenes from myth, literature, and the Bible. What I'm trying to do is create a realistic image of a scene that could never be photographed.

My guiding philosophy is the old Latin saying: *Ars est celare artem*, which roughly translates as: true art conceals the artifice of its making. For me, creating depth and illusion is one of the most exciting goals of painting, but it's just a first step. The higher goal is to select, accentuate, and subordinate all the elements of the picture to communicate a particular mood or feeling, and that goes beyond mere illusionism.

I've learned that an imaginative idea starts out as a fragile flame, easily blown out. But if you trust your muse and feed your idea, that flame can grow into a blazing fire. Feeding that candle flame requires both patience and persistence. There are so many temptations to immediately Google something, or look at photographs, before we've even lit the match of our imagination. There's nothing wrong with using these tools a little later, but I think what people want from artists today is what they've always wanted from us: to be able to dream out loud with us and to see the world through our eyes.

You've got to trust your mental image and let it guide you through the sketch stage. Take the idea as far as you can from your own imagination before you expand your reference gathering. Even if the initial sketches don't look very promising, keep going. Try switching media when sketching: pencil, pen, marker, gouache. Use them as a foundation to build upon.

When I'm not sketching I feel like I'm seeing the world around me, but when I'm sketching, I feel like my eyes open up and I begin really seeing what's around me for the first time.

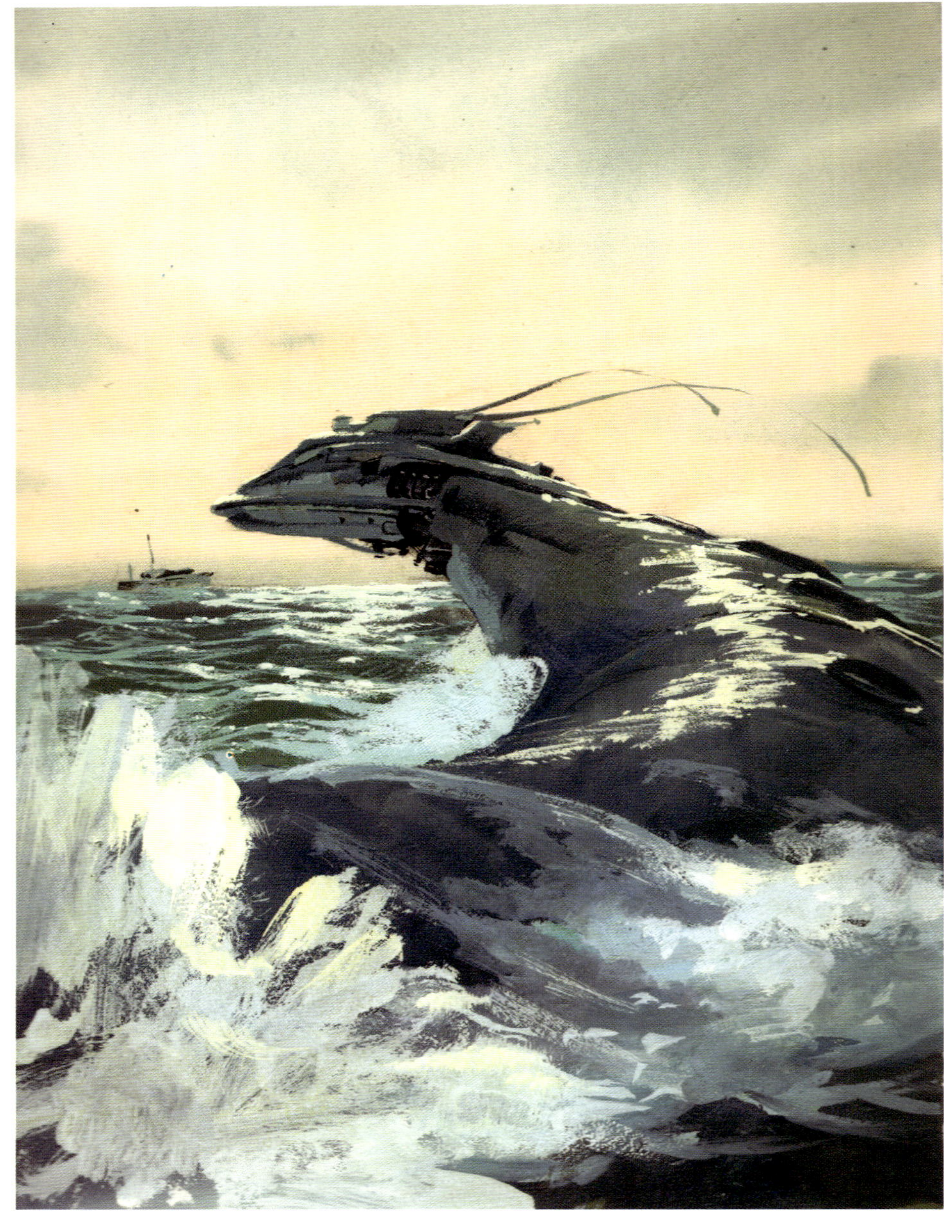

Above | **Colour sketch, 1981**
Gouache, 28 × 20 cm

In this quick sketch I explored the afternoon light shimmering off the water.

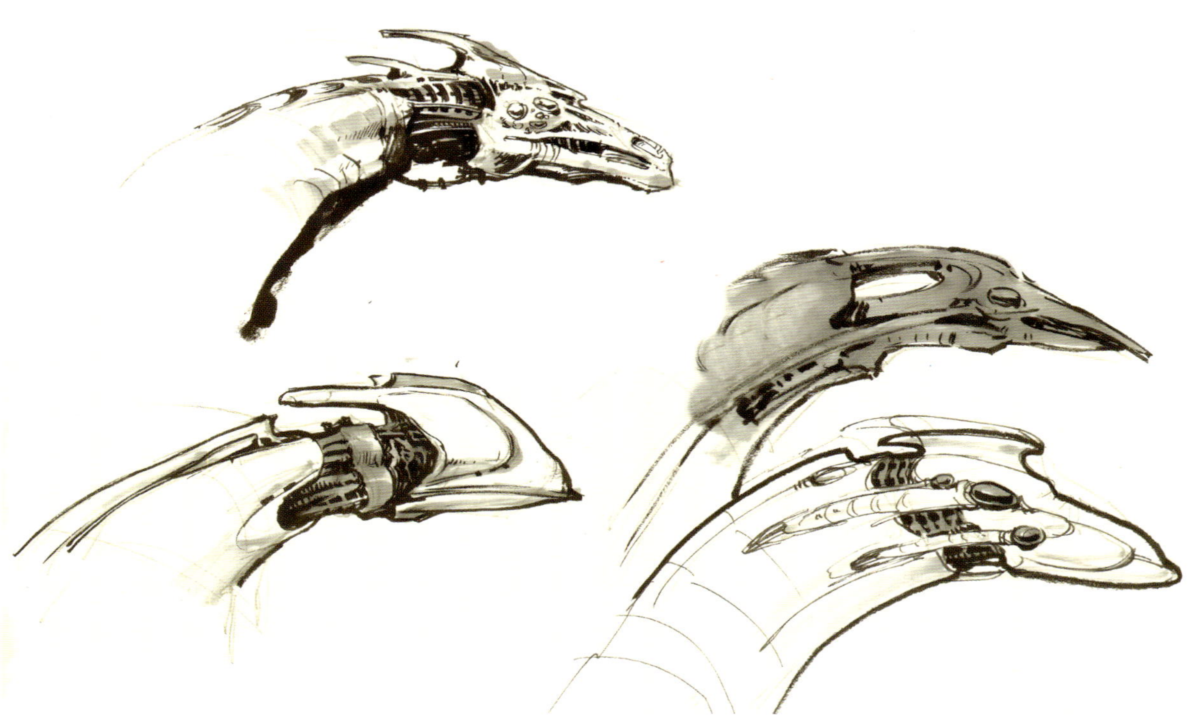

Left | **Head sketches**
Pen and markers, 18 × 30 cm

What would happen if this sea monster were half biological and half mechanical? A kind of mechanical juggernaut invading the human world to take vengeance. I loved the idea that the creature had a smooth outer skin protecting its more delicate inner structure and that it was injured somehow, making it act recklessly and unpredictably.

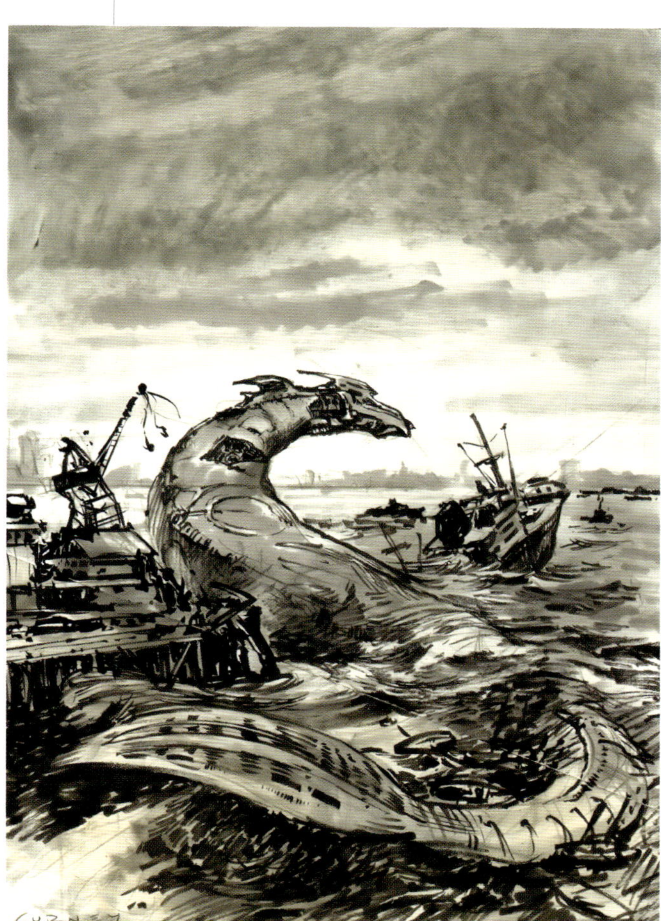

Tonal sketch
Pencil and pen, 29 × 22 cm

I tried staging the mayhem in a harbour,
with smashed piers and sinking ships.
I established the basic idea for the
S-shaped gesture, but I realized that
seeing the full body including the tail
was too obvious and undramatic.

Sea Monster
Gouache and acrylic on board, 102 × 76 cm

I brought the action across the foreground,
disorientating the viewer and making it hard to tell
how big the monster really is. Painting a cyborg
is satisfying because cyborgs serve as a measure
of, or convey a discomfort with, the increased
mechanization and depersonalization of life.

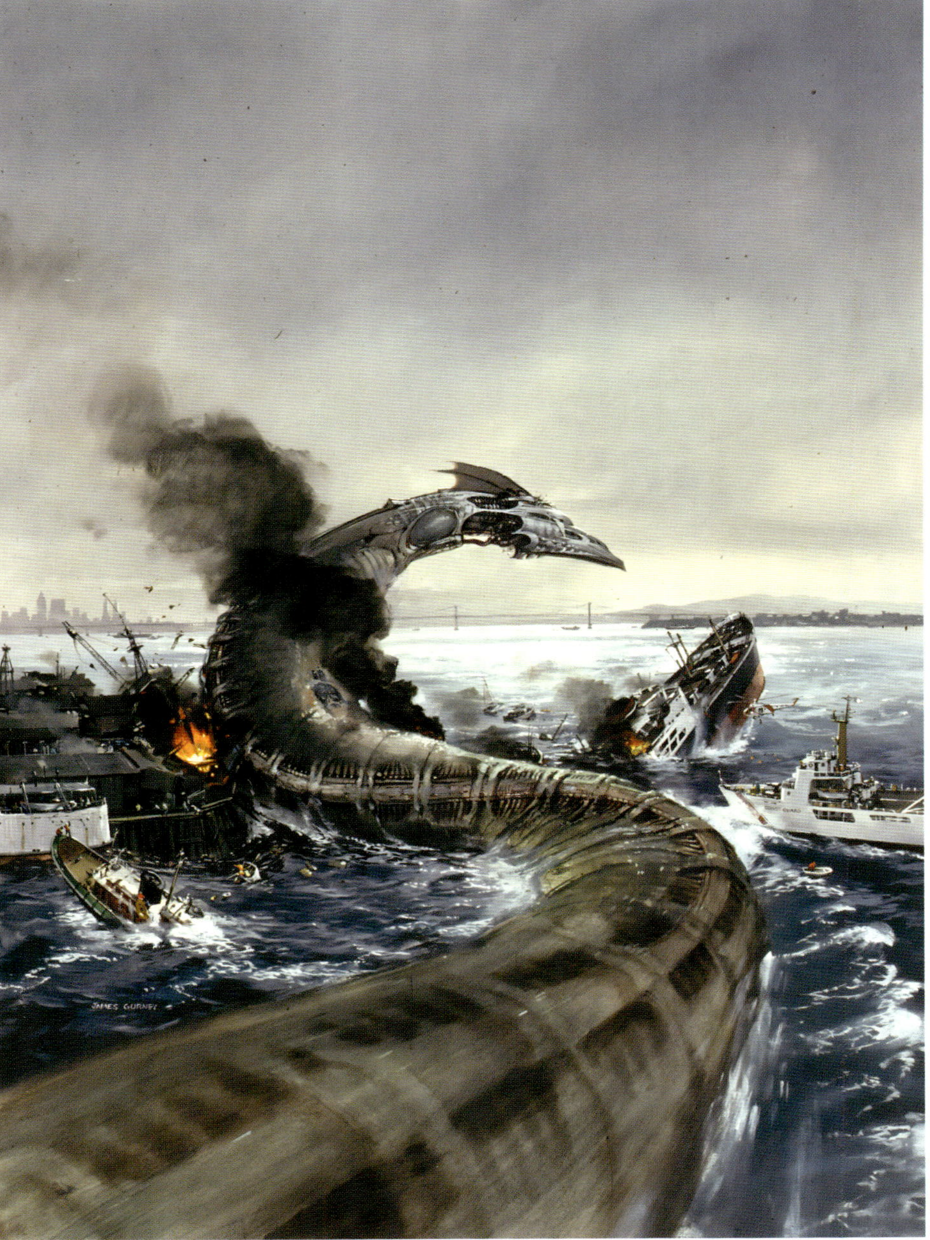

When I'm
sketching, I feel
like my eyes
open up and
I begin really
seeing what's
around me for
the first time

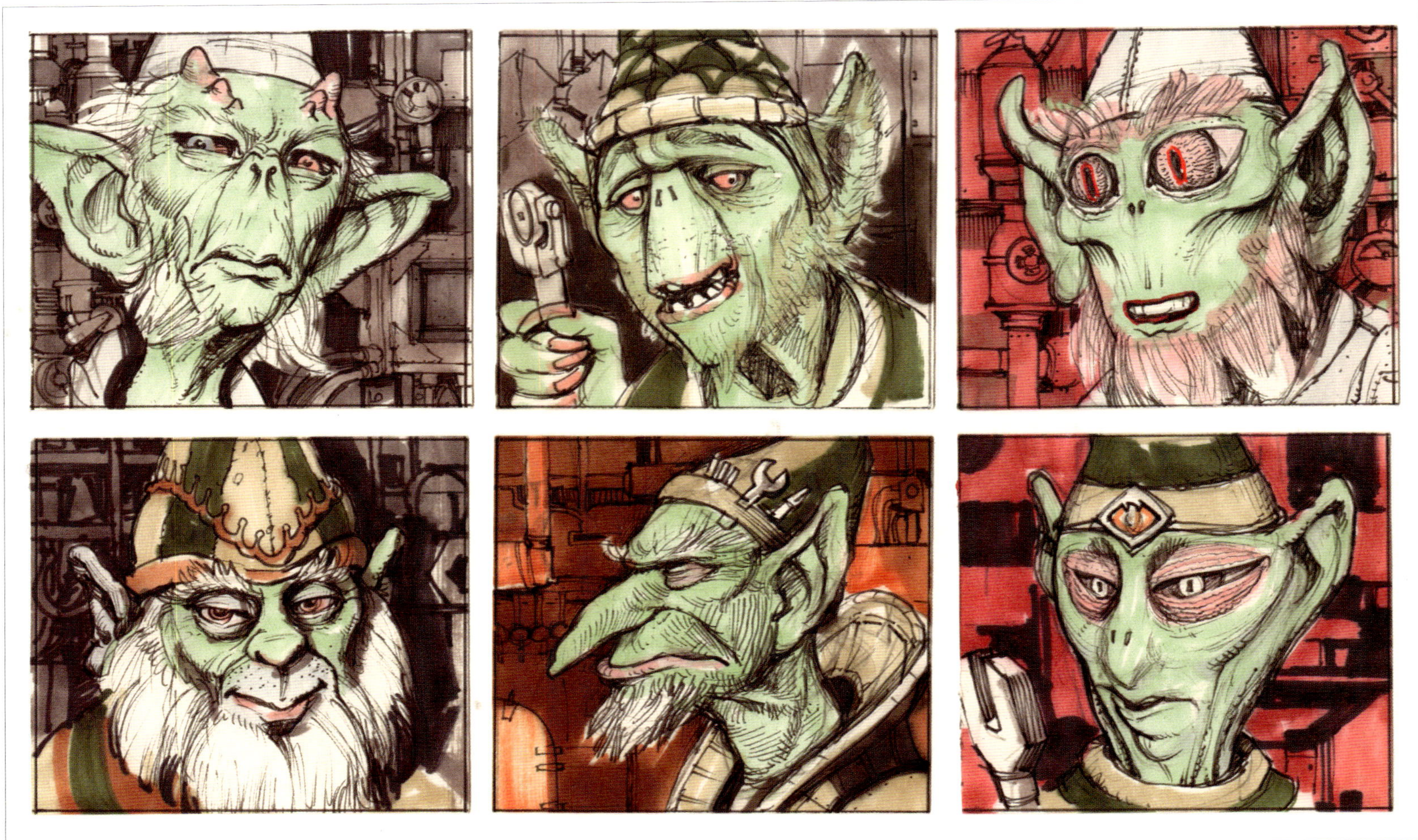

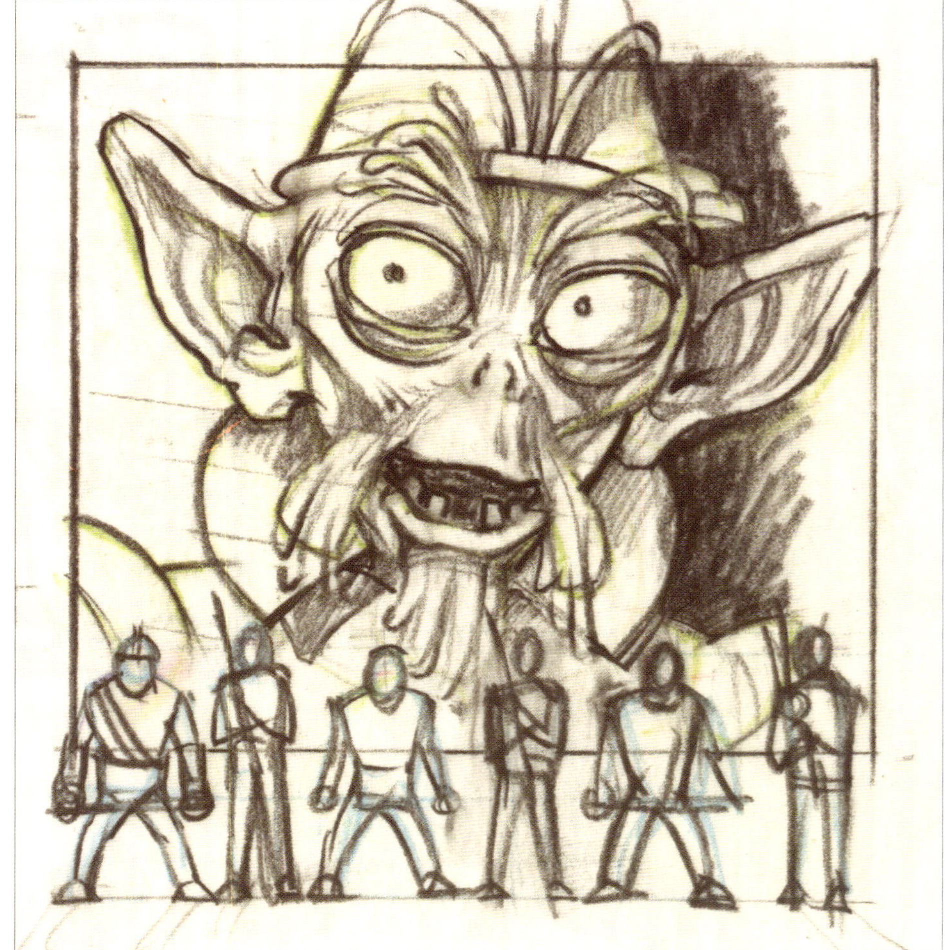

Alien thumbnails
Marker and pen, 6.5 ×6.5 cm each

I was commissioned to create the cover for a science-fiction paperback anthology called *The Fleet: Sworn Allies*. These are the thumbnail sketches I showed the art director after I read the manuscript of the original science-fiction novel about intergalactic war. The little elf-like alien was an important character in the story, but the author wasn't very specific about what he looked like. Eventually I settled on a frog-like look.

Line drawing

Based on the marker sketch the art director and I liked best, I kept the tighter cropping on his face, with a row of warriors painted in front of him.

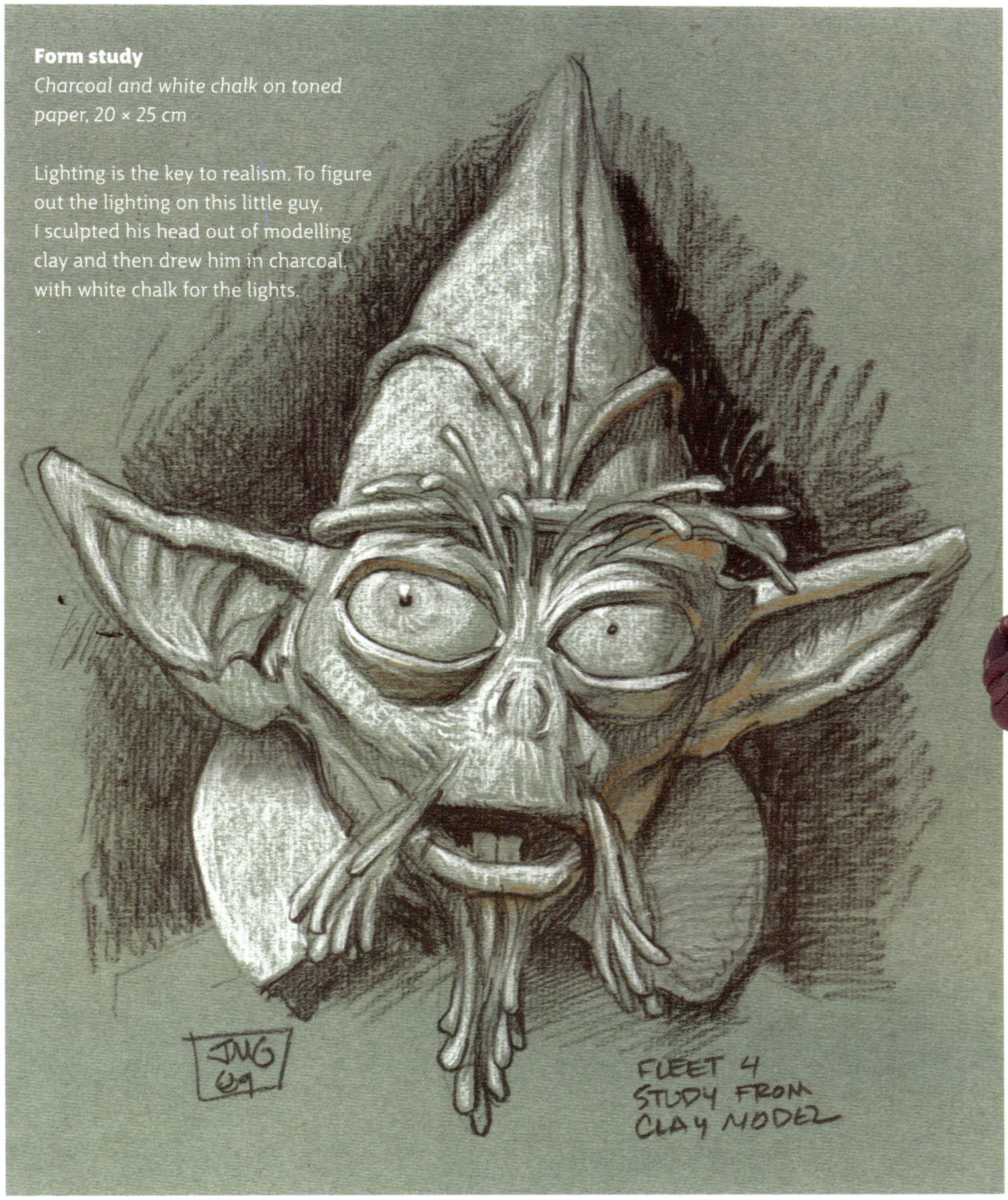

Form study
Charcoal and white chalk on toned paper, 20 × 25 cm

Lighting is the key to realism. To figure out the lighting on this little guy, I sculpted his head out of modelling clay and then drew him in charcoal, with white chalk for the lights.

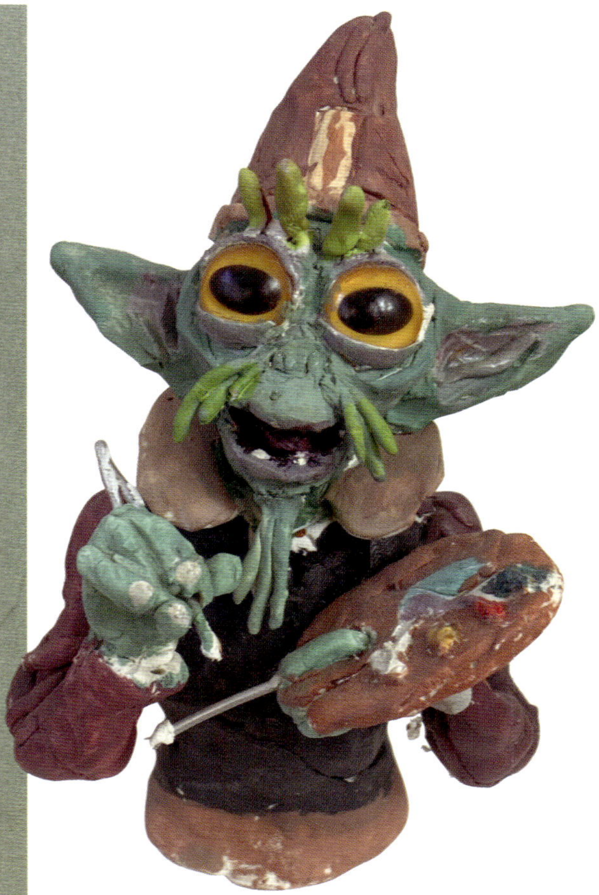

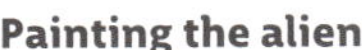

Alien maquette
Polymer clay, 10 cm tall

I decided to repaint the frog-like alien to be on the cover of my book *Imaginative Realism: How to Paint What Doesn't Exist*. I don't usually go back into old paintings, but I wanted to explore the little guy's character more. I made this little maquette out of Sculpey, an oven-hardening clay, and painted him with acrylic. Crude as he is, he gave me lots of information about light and shadow.

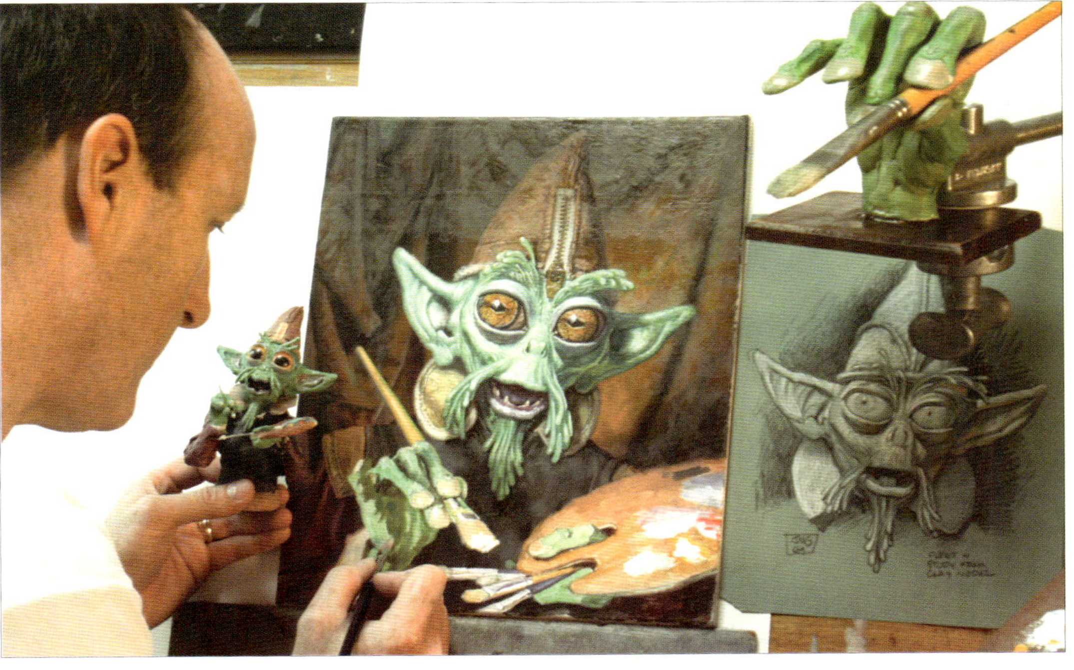

Painting the alien

Creating the final oil painting was much easier once I had done all these sculpts, sketches, and studies. It almost felt like I was looking at the actual character.

SKETCHING FROM LIFE

My speciality is painting realistic scenes that can't be photographed, either for paleoart, historical illustration, or fantasy/science fiction. In my sketching life, I draw *everything*. I also paint everything: portraits, landscapes, and animals. Artists from the past that I admire always tackled the most difficult subjects. They would jump out of the safe zone as much as possible.

Sketching from life definitely builds my visual vocabulary, which helps when I'm trying to conjure a fantasy world from thin air. I often dig into my sketchbooks for poses, rock formations, trees, landscape effects, or other details. That's one of the reasons I like to draw everything. As Adolph Menzel put it: '*Alles Zeichnen ist nützlich, und Alles zeichnen auch*', which roughly translates as: 'All sketching is useful, as is sketching everything.'

I suppose my sketchbooks tell a story, though it's not very obvious to me while I'm filling them. In a broad sense, they tell the story of my visual life: what I've noticed, where I've travelled, my struggle to give shape to a dream. I use my sketchbooks for recording the evolution of ideas, testing out new techniques, and giving me something to do while I'm waiting around, especially when I'm travelling. My sketchbooks are not just a collection of random drawings; they are a visual diary, a record of my artistic process, and a place to capture snapshots from my inner and outer life. Some of my sketchbooks have collaborative drawings that I've done with friends, and looking at them immediately brings back a laugh.

As I fill a sketchbook, I can see how my concepts develop, how my skills improve, and how my interests and inspirations shift over time. If there's a bad sketch or a half-finished effort, I leave it in. Each sketchbook reflects the highs and lows, breakthroughs, and challenges that I encounter along the way.

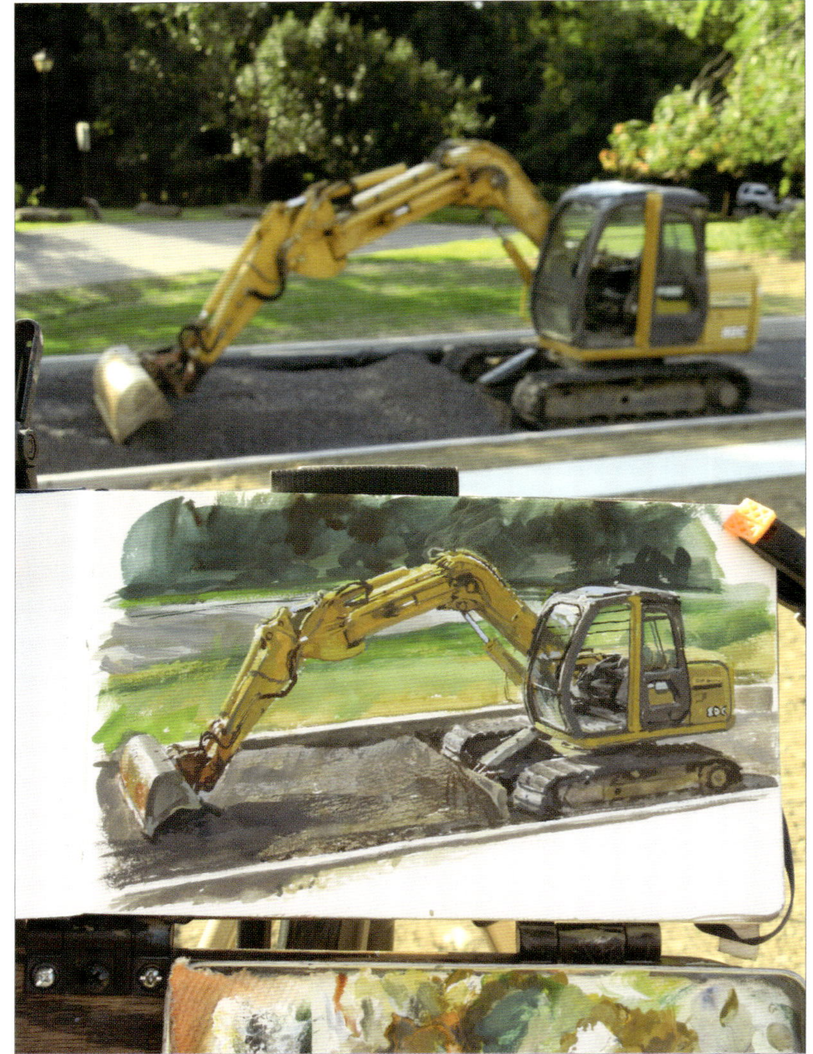

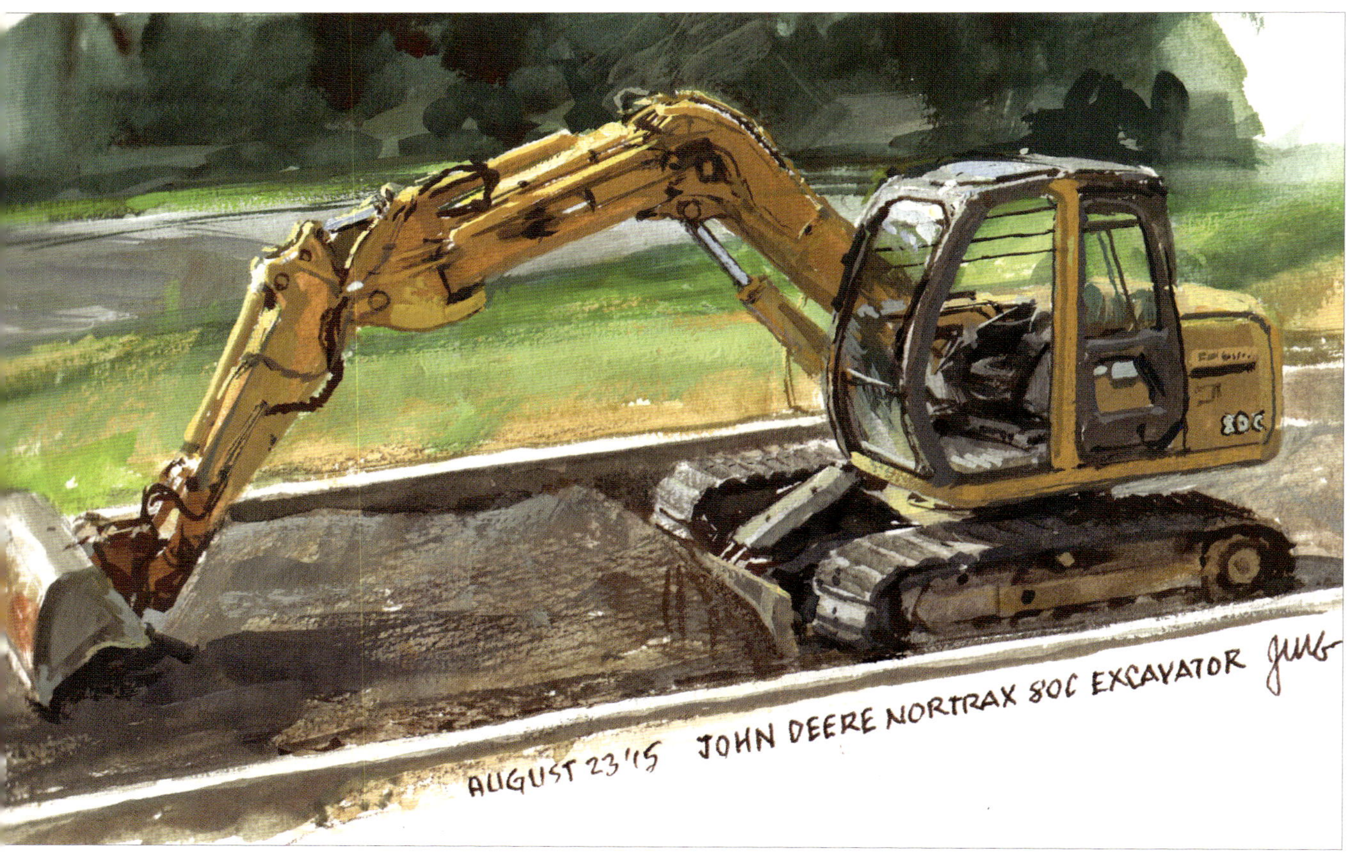

Excavator study
Gouache, 12.5 × 20 cm

At a construction site, I decided to invent a giant robot based on the design of construction equipment. I started by doing a careful study of one of the excavators to absorb the mechanics into my design vocabulary.

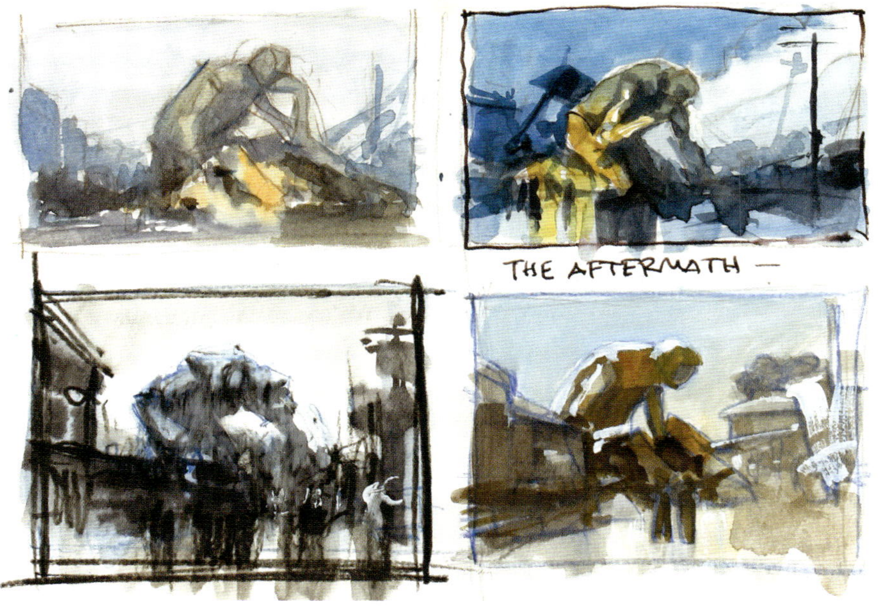

Aftermath of disaster
Watercolour, gouache, and pen,
23 × 15 cm overall

Each little sketch is like a seed that could grow into a larger idea. Story drives the choices. Instead of having the robot fighting or marauding, I wanted to show that he feels sad because maybe he accidentally broke something.

My sketchbooks are not just a collection of random drawings; they are a visual diary, a record of my artistic process, and a place to capture snapshots from my inner life and my outer life

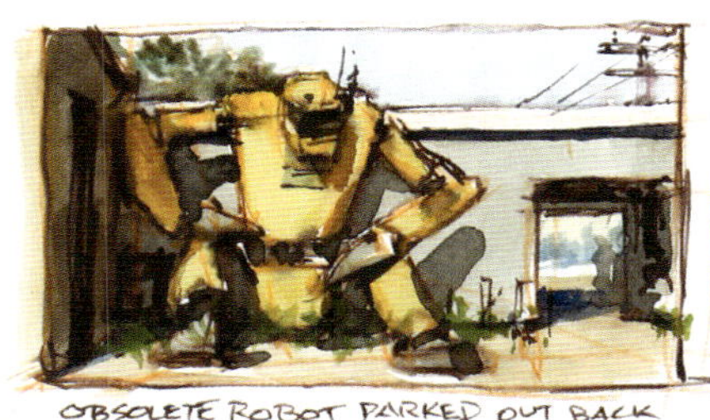

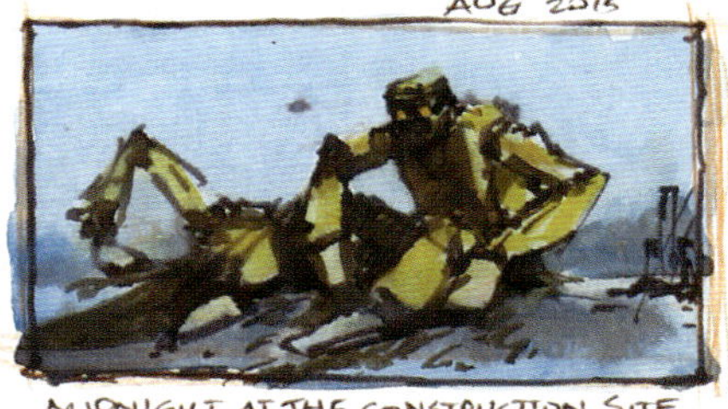

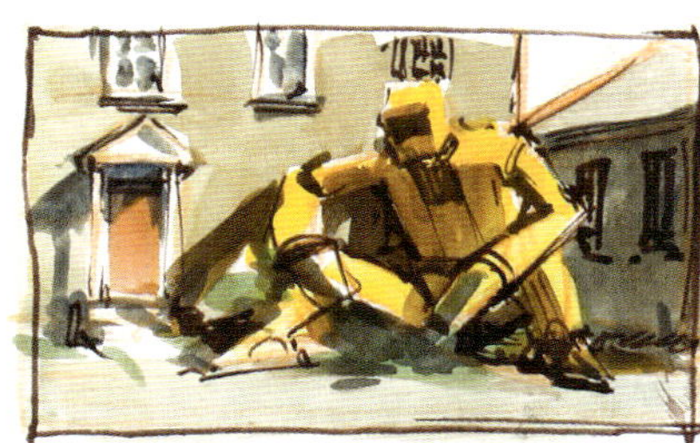

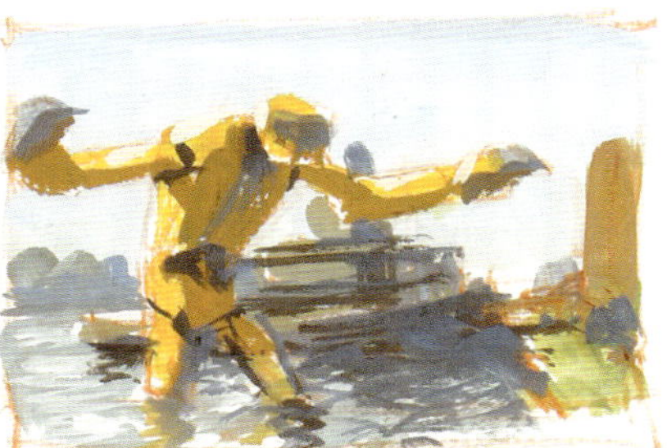

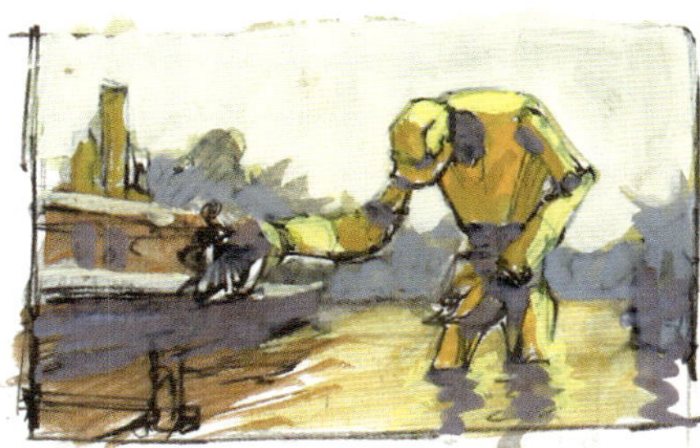

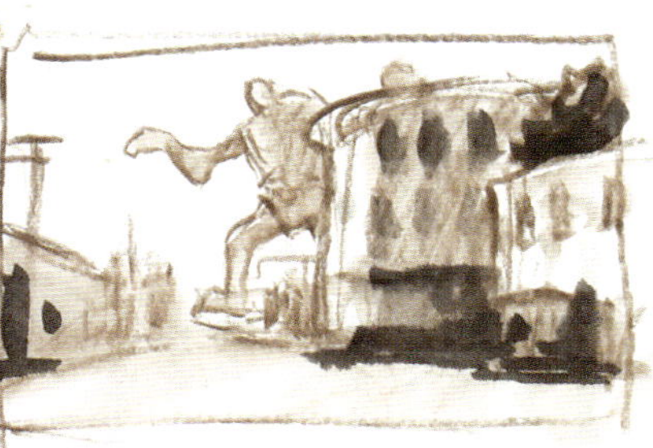

Obsolete robot
Gouache, casein, pen, and coloured pencil, 23 × 30 cm overall

With each little colour concept thumbnail, I tried out a different lighting, pose, composition, and story. By working small I could execute these ideas quickly without being committed to details.

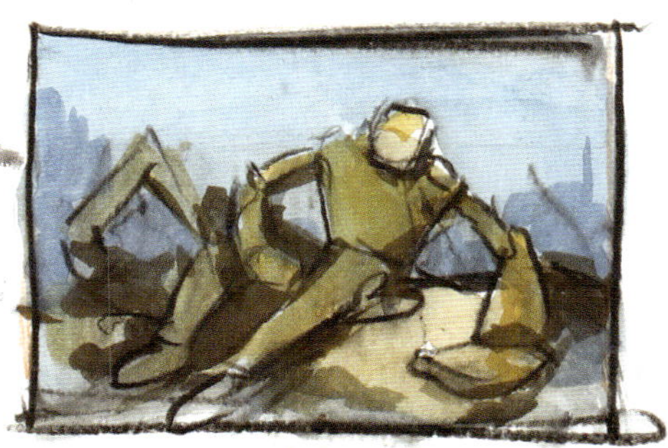

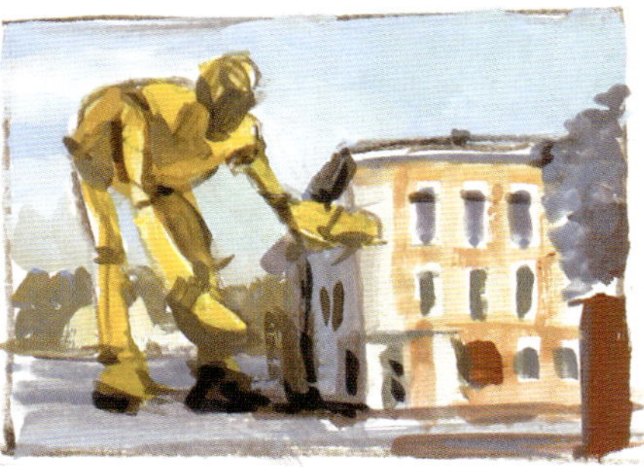

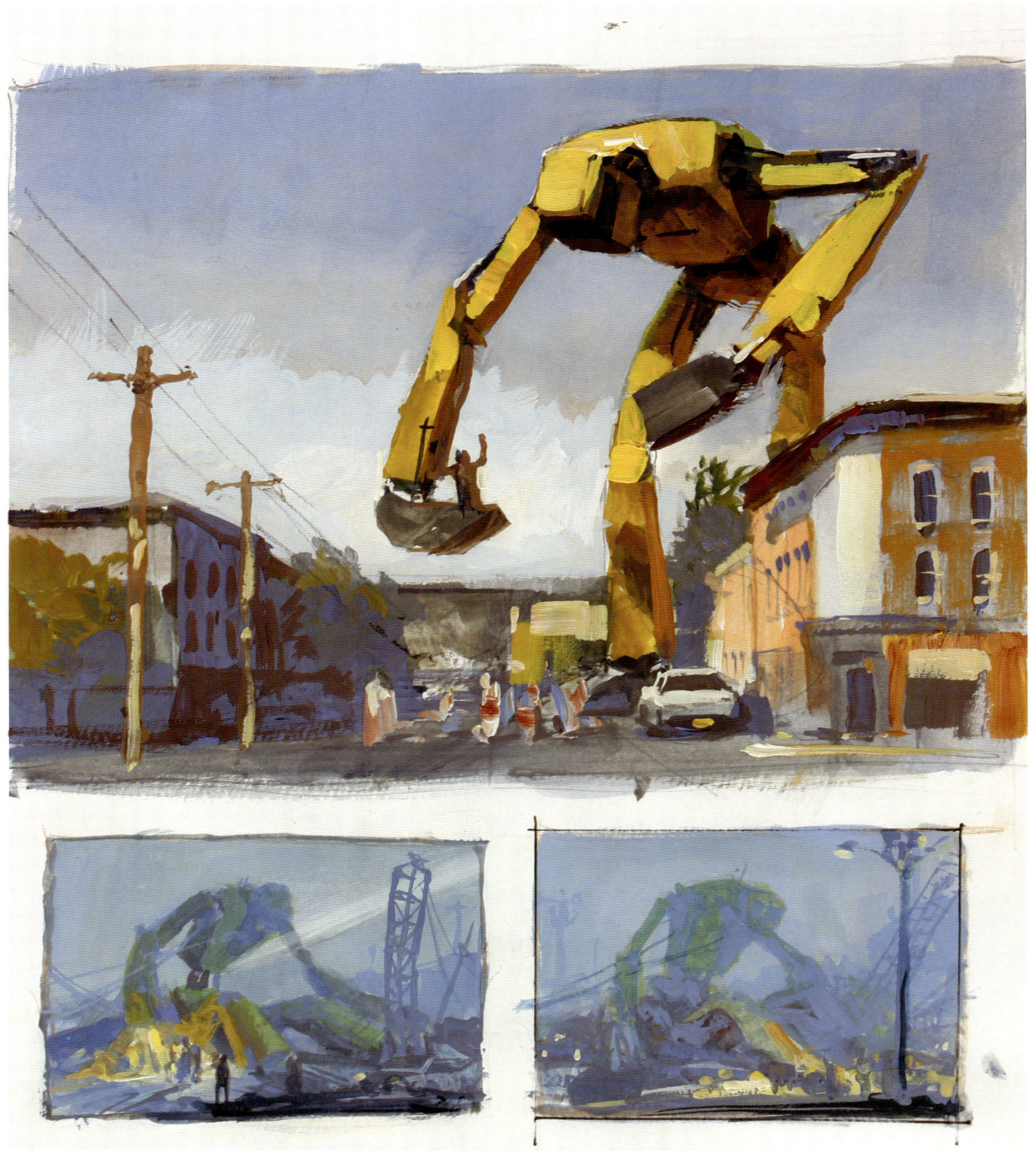

Robot encounter
Casein and gouache, 30 × 23 cm overall

Further explorations in small, loose
colour thumbnail sketches. Should the
scene be staged in broad daylight or
in a foggy twilight?

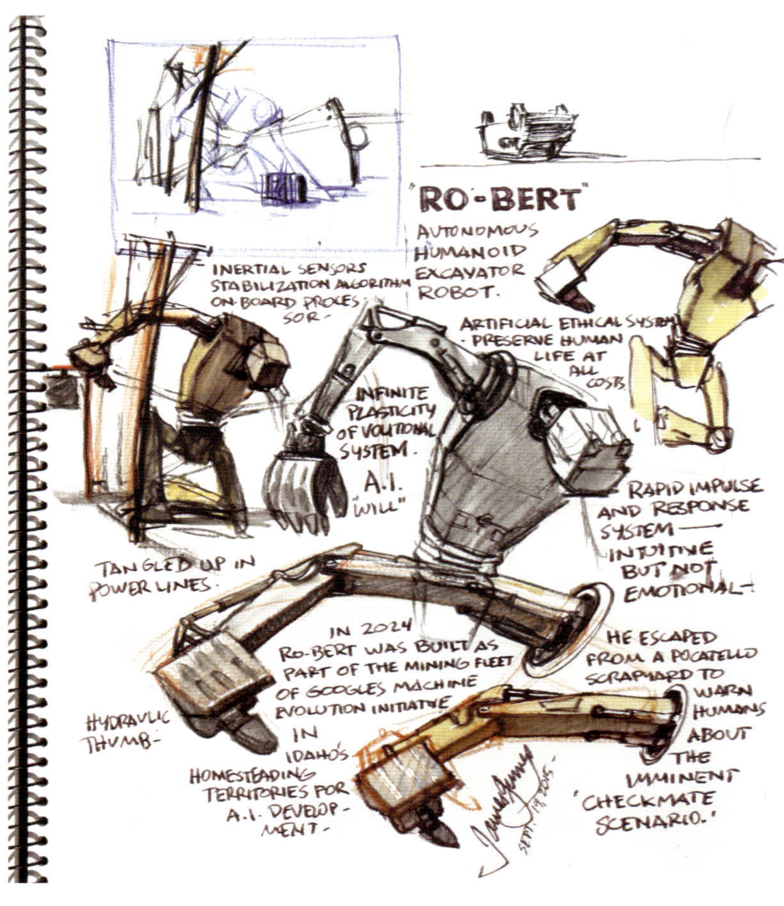

'Digger Drone' sketch and maquette

Markers, wire, and construction foam, 15 × 15 cm

While I've loved drawing since I was a child (from both observation and my imagination), I was always more comfortable with making things in 3D out of wood, paper, and metal. I especially liked making models of ships and aeroplanes.

Here I built a maquette of the giant robot. The skeleton was made from aluminium armature wire so I could put the figure into any pose, and the body was made from craft foam held together with a hot glue gun. This method of construction is very fast. Because of the wire armature, I didn't have to worry about hinged joint mechanics.

Robot backstory

Fountain pen and watercolour, 23 × 30 cm

I invented a scenario involving a giant robot that escapes from a factory and heads into the human world. I worked my way through a lot of sketches, developing the backstory as I went. The autonomous robot is actually a good guy who wants to aid humans. In trying to help, he gets tangled in the wires and wreaks havoc.

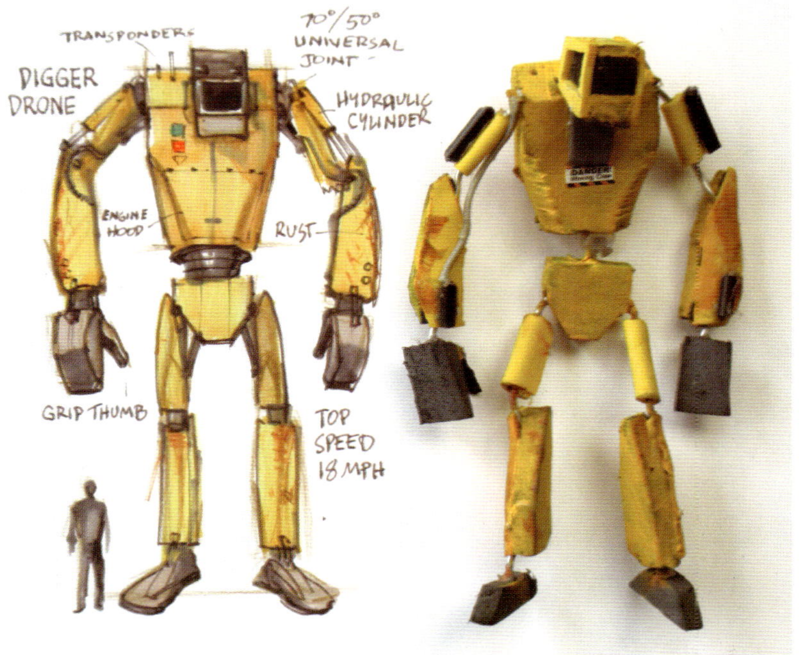

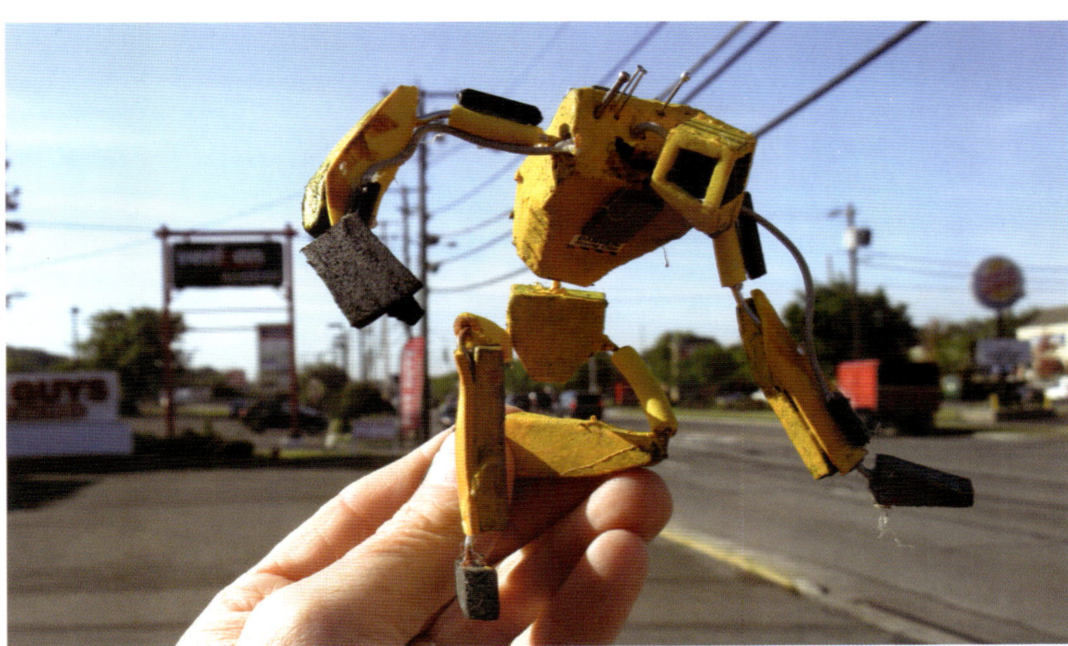

Maquette on location

Bringing a maquette to the location was a big help, because I could see it in the same light that illuminated the actual scene. By holding it up against the background and squinting through one eye, I could imagine the correct perspective. In visual effects this would be called a 'foreground miniature'.

Robot colour comps
Casein and gouache, 30 × 23 cm overall

I was getting closer to a workable story and a clearer concept of the character.
With these elements established, I could figure out the ensemble and the details.
Grid lines would help me to scale up the sketch to the final size.

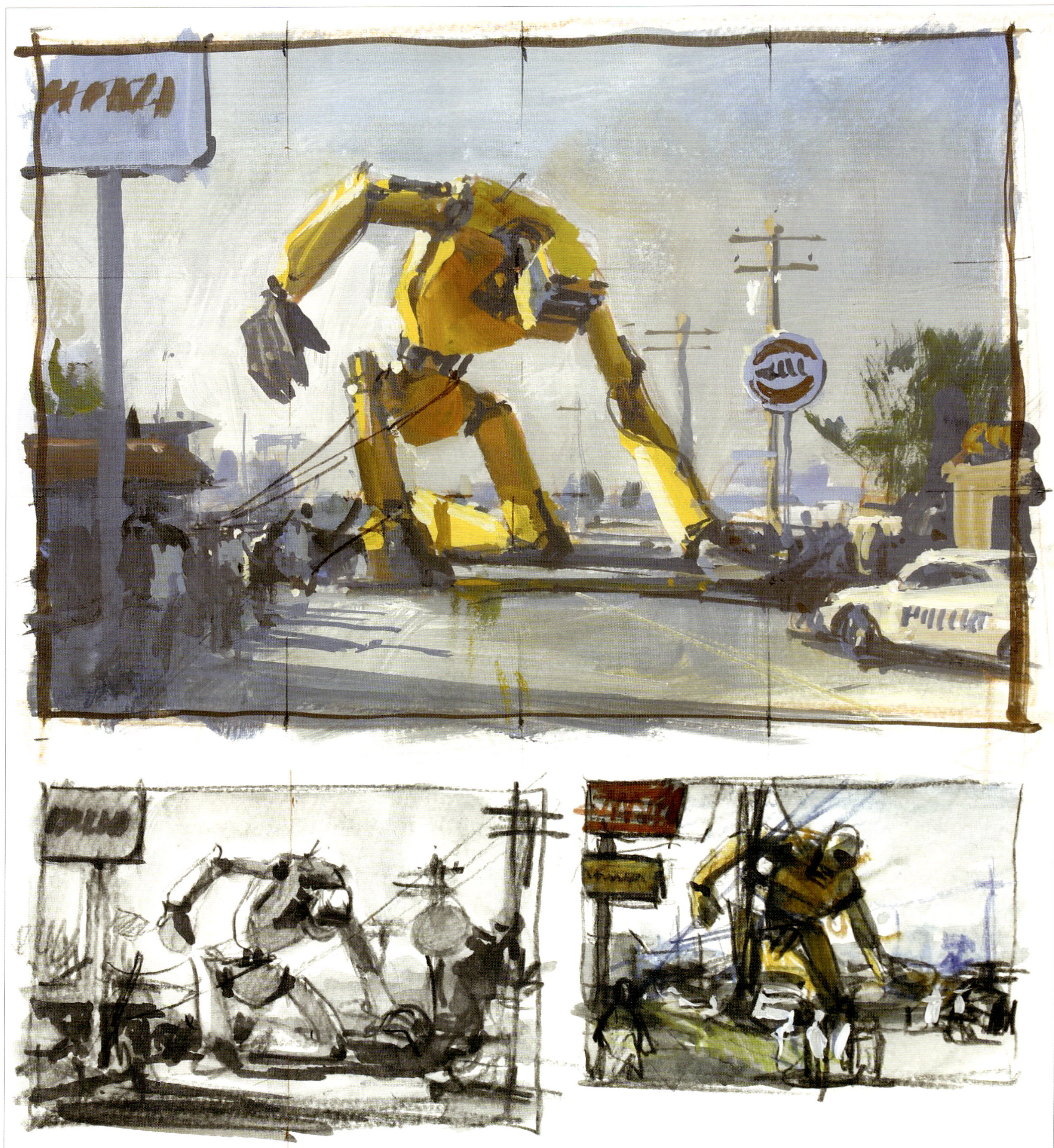

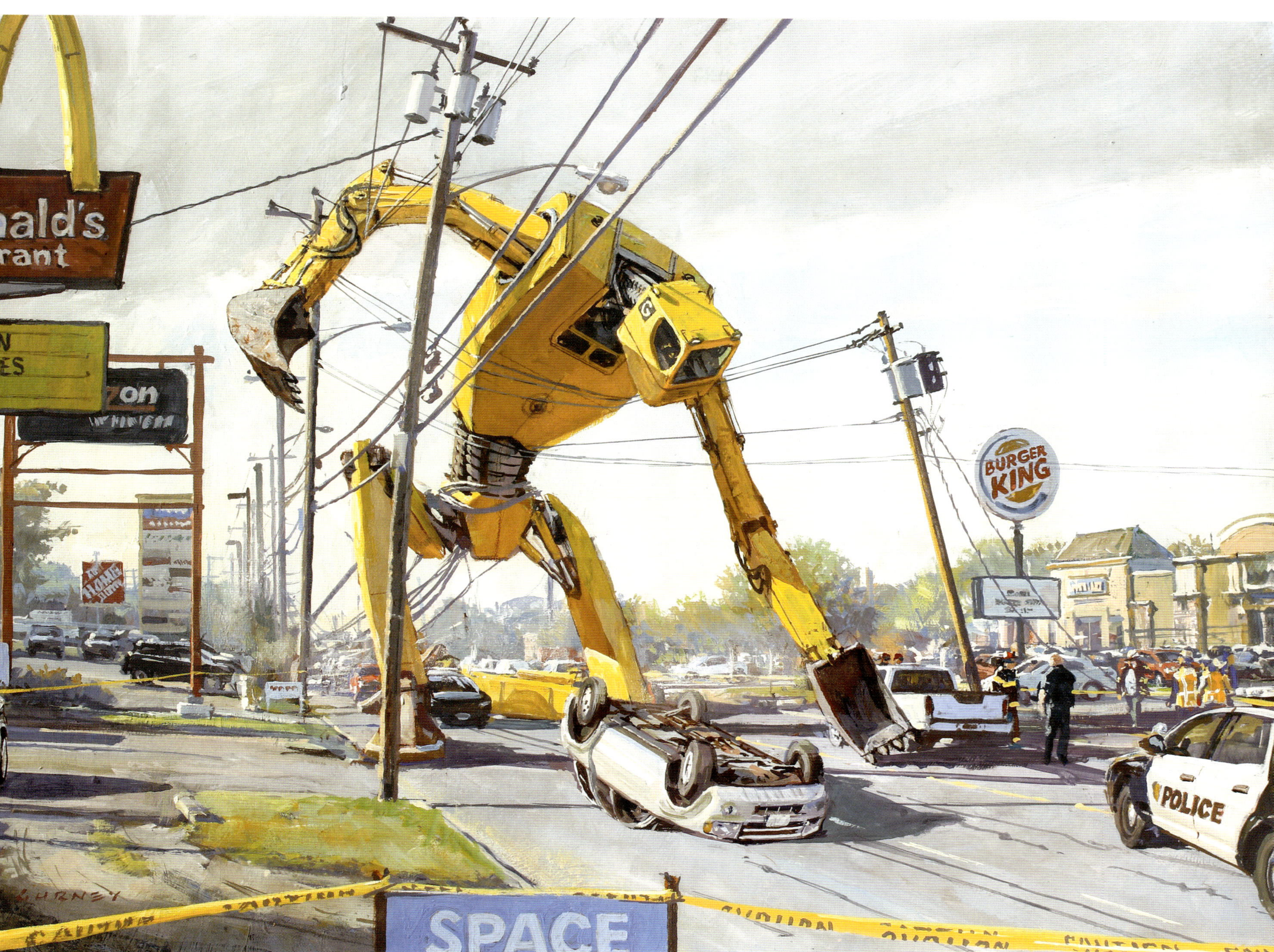

Aftermath

Casein, 30 × 41 cm

I painted the robot at a construction site. In another
session, I painted the fast-food setting along a
commercial strip near where I live. I documented the
design process on a video called *Fantasy in the Wild*,
which followed the idea all the way from the first sketch
to the final painting.

DreamWorks demo easel

When DreamWorks Animation asked me to give a
workshop to a group of their artists about imaginative
realism and worldbuilding, I came up with a crazy
plan: Why not ask them to fire up their imagination
out of doors? I invited eighteen of their top concept
artists to join me in an alley behind a Jack in the Box
restaurant. The artists were from various departments:
visual development, lighting, story, and matte painting.
Each artist brought their favourite toy figurine, along
with their art supplies. The challenge was to enlarge
their toy and place it in a real life scene. The hero
of my painting was my own sculpted stop-motion
character named Otis the Ocelot.

Otis maquette
Wood and epoxy, painted with acrylic, 10 cm tall

My maquette of Otis the Ocelot has glass beads for
eyes, wooden spheres for the head and hips (modified
with epoxy sculpting compound), and neodymium
micro-magnets for his shoulders, hips, and knee joints.
I set him on top of my easel in the same light as the
fast-food restaurant in the background.

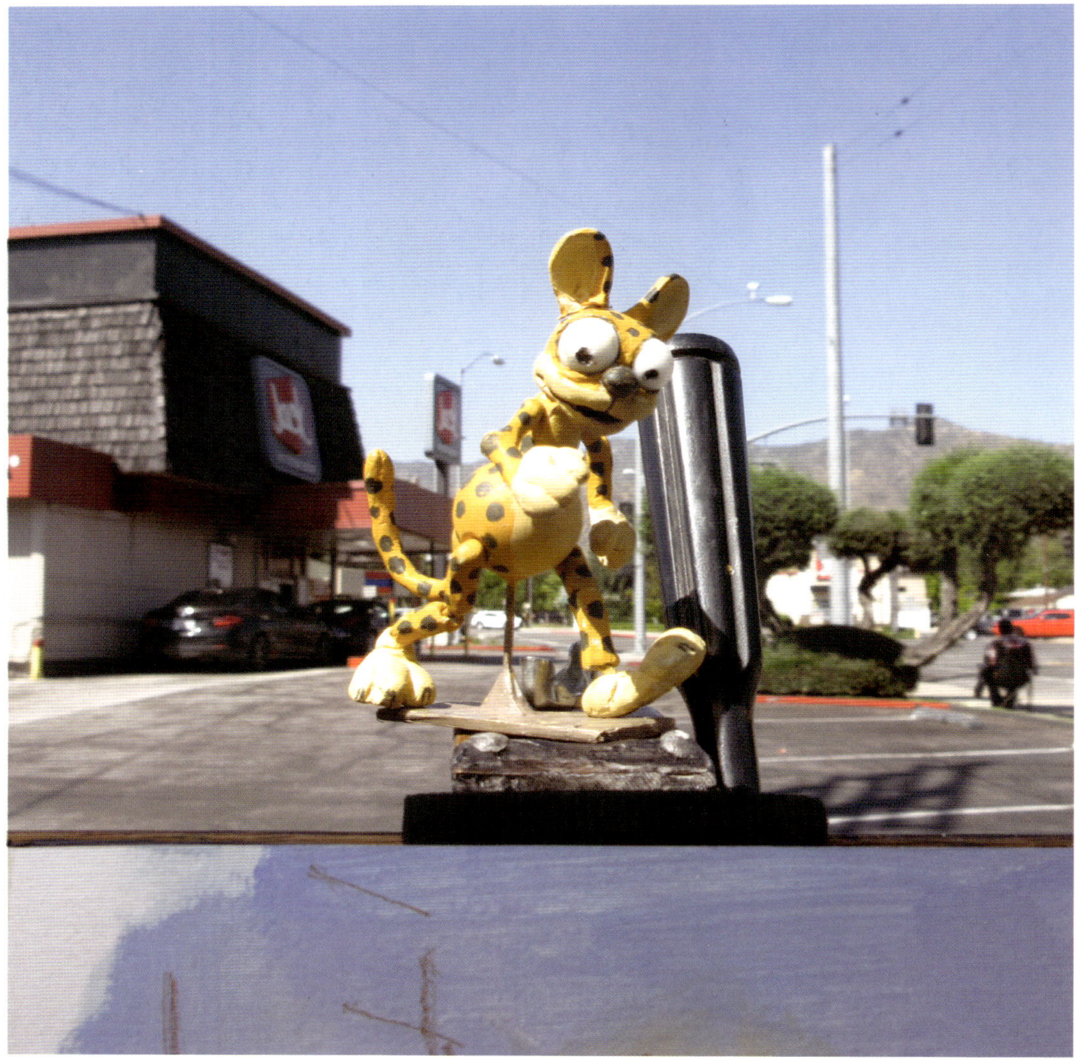

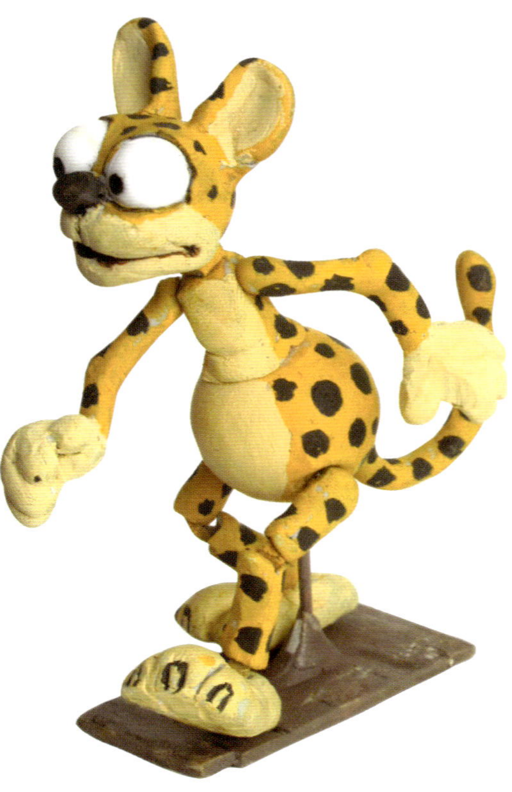

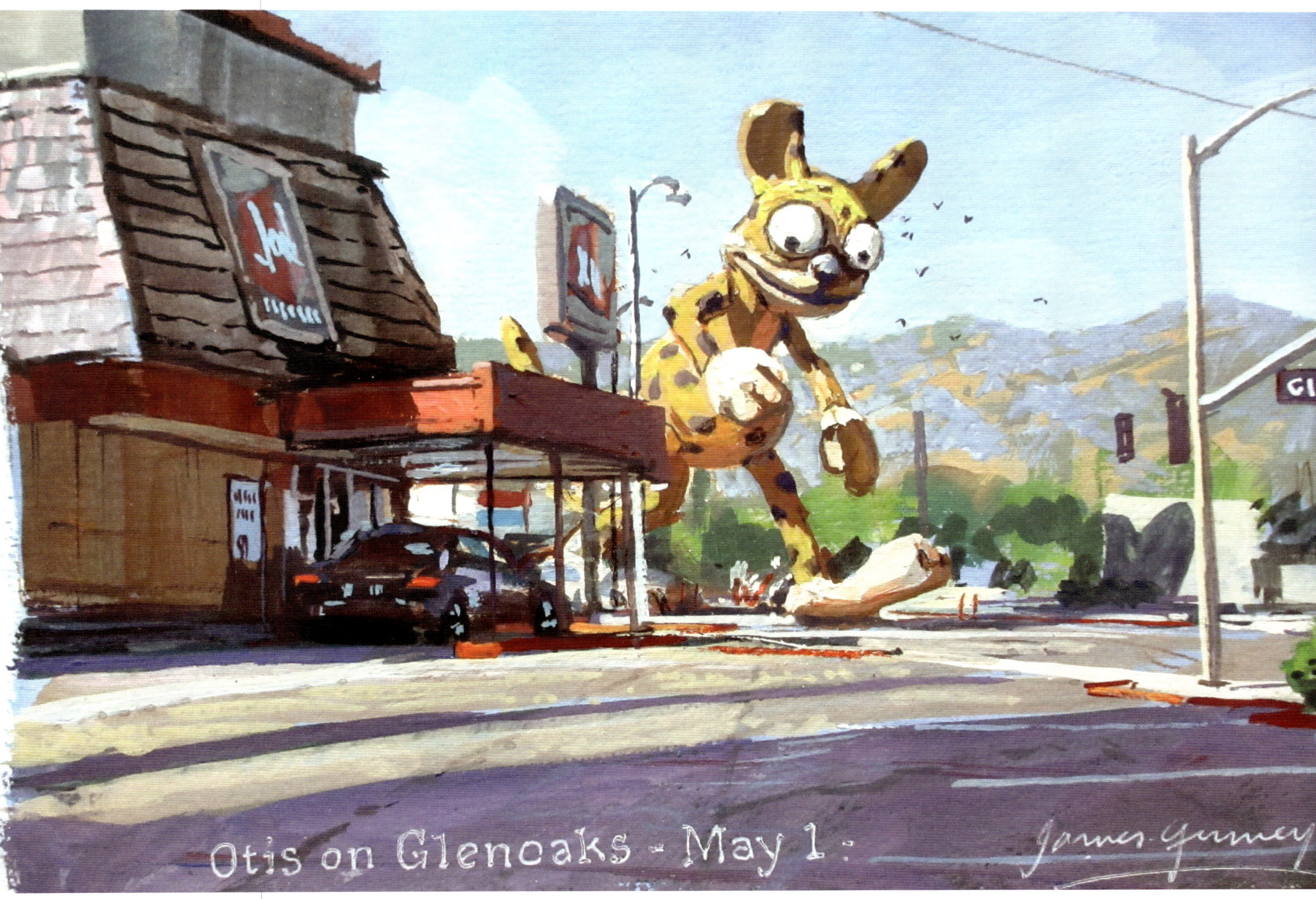

Otis on Glenoaks
Gouache, 12.5 × 20 cm

The maquette helped me to visualize
the pose, perspective, and lighting.
The cast shadows on the left leg were
especially helpful. I probably wouldn't
have imagined them without the actual
physical reference in front of me.

Sketching from life
definitely builds my
visual vocabulary, which
helps when I'm trying to
conjure a fantasy world
from thin air

Tony M. DiTerlizzi

THE STORY SO FAR

I am a *New York Times* bestselling author and illustrator who has created books for young readers for over twenty-five years. From fanciful picture books like *The Spider and the Fly* to chapter books like *The WondLa Trilogy*, I try to imbue every story with imagination. With my friend, author Holly Black, we created the middle-grade series, *The Spiderwick Chronicles*, which has sold millions of copies around the world and has been adapted into a feature film, a video game, and a television series. My work has been showcased in several touring exhibitions, including a retrospective at the Norman Rockwell Museum that featured artwork from the beginning of my career as a contributing artist for *Dungeons & Dragons* and *Magic: The Gathering*.

I've created little bound books of drawings since I was a child. The earliest was a field guide to insects I'd collected and another about dinosaurs. When I was twelve, I spent the summer filling a notebook with detailed accounts of fantastic monsters that lived on an imaginary island. Twenty years later, this notebook, brimming with sketches and drawings, became the seed for *The Spiderwick Chronicles*.

I would say that my proudest moments aren't tied to awards or commercial achievements, but rather to instances where my work sparks imagination in others. This could be through connecting with young fans, such as seeing my books inspire children to create their own stories, or simply witnessing the joy my creations bring to readers. I find fulfilment in fostering a love for fantasy and reminding people of the boundless potential of imagination.

I find fulfilment in fostering a love for fantasy and reminding people of the boundless potential of imagination

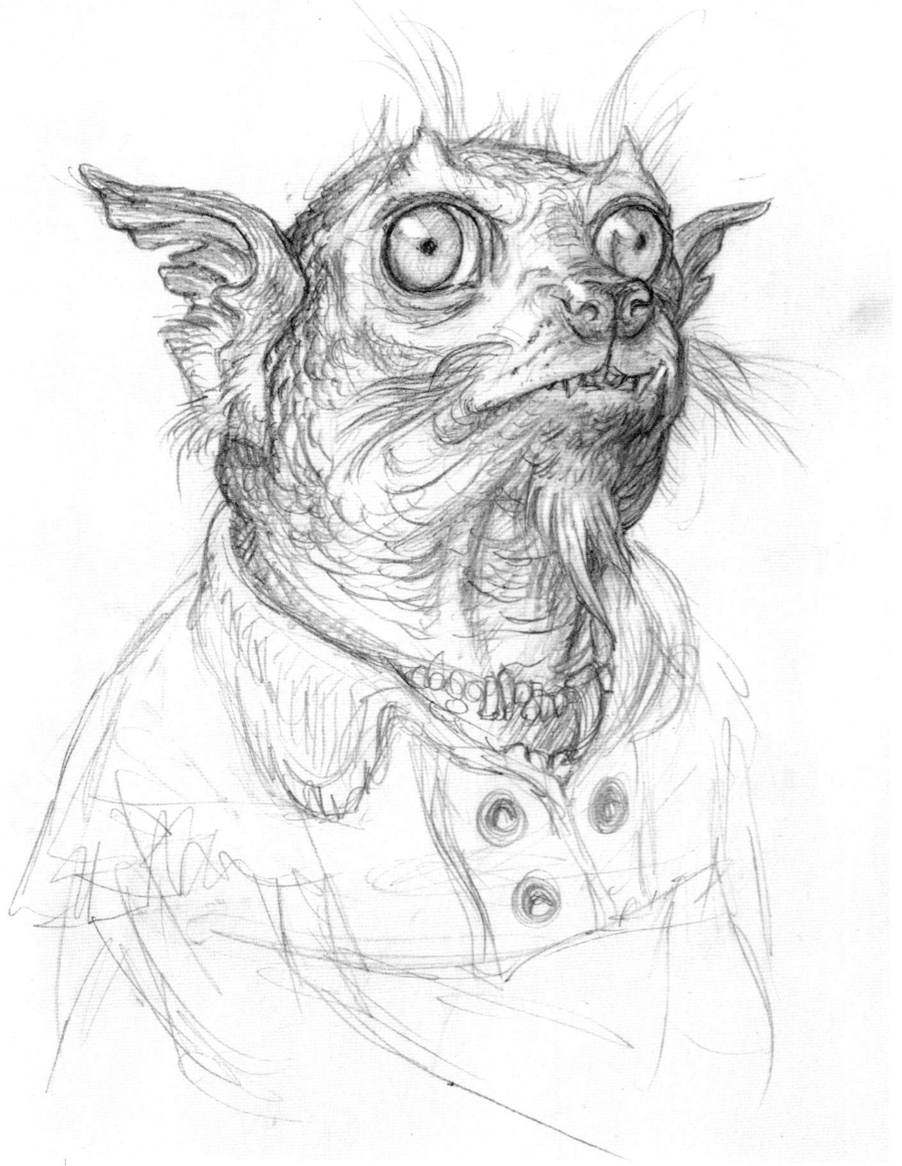

Study for *Borderlands Kobold*, 2014

A lifelike representation of the kobold, with inspiration from a hairless chihuahua.

AUTHOR & ILLUSTRATOR
diterlizzi.com

Final sketch of
Borderlands Kobold, 2014

Preparatory drawing for the final painting of the Borderlands Kobold printed in the book, *REALMS: The Roleplaying Game Art of Tony DiTerlizzi*. Whereas early sketches focused on canine reference, I drew this pose using multiple photographic references, including me swinging a sword and one of my daughter's stuffed animals dressed in a similar costume.

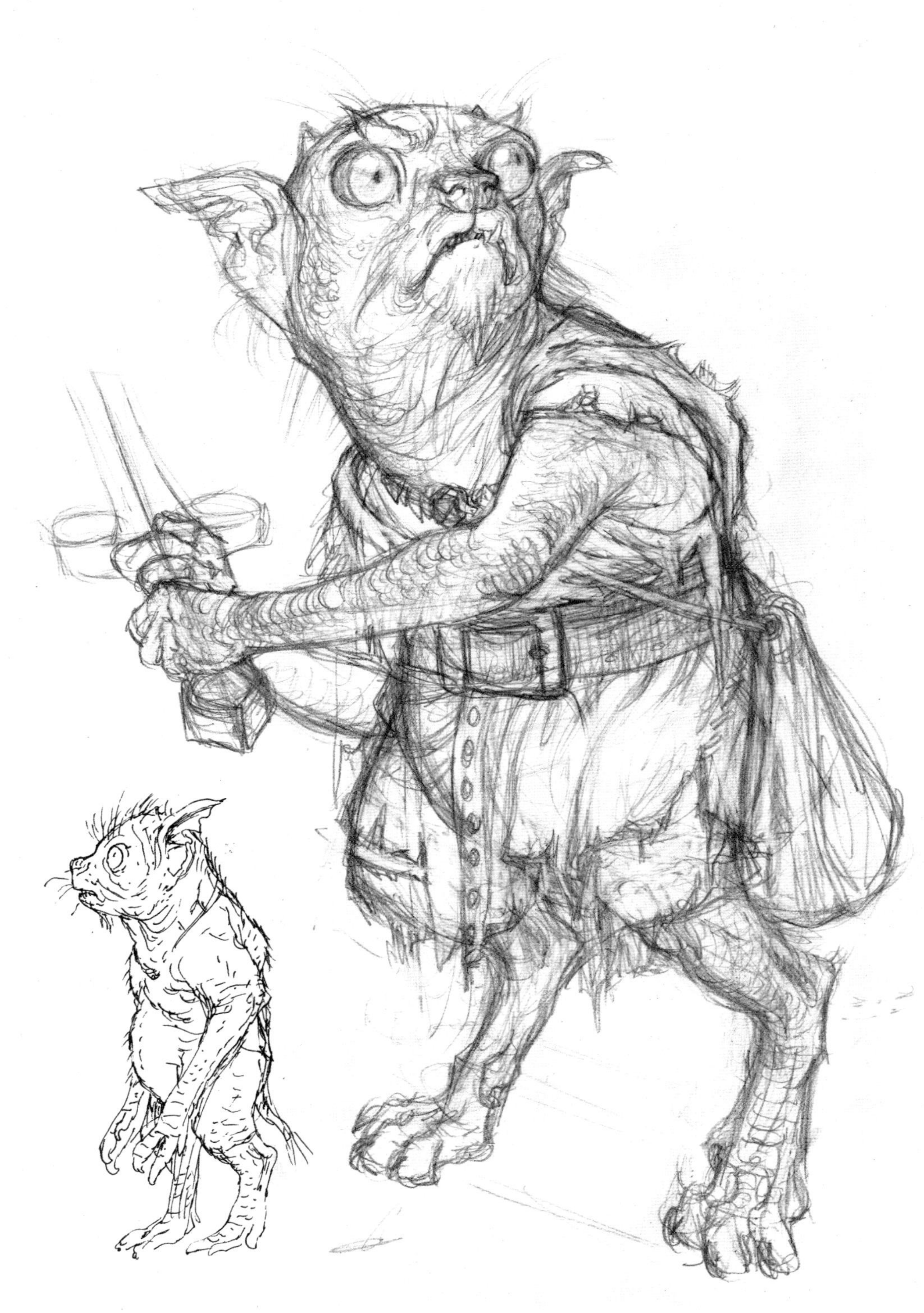

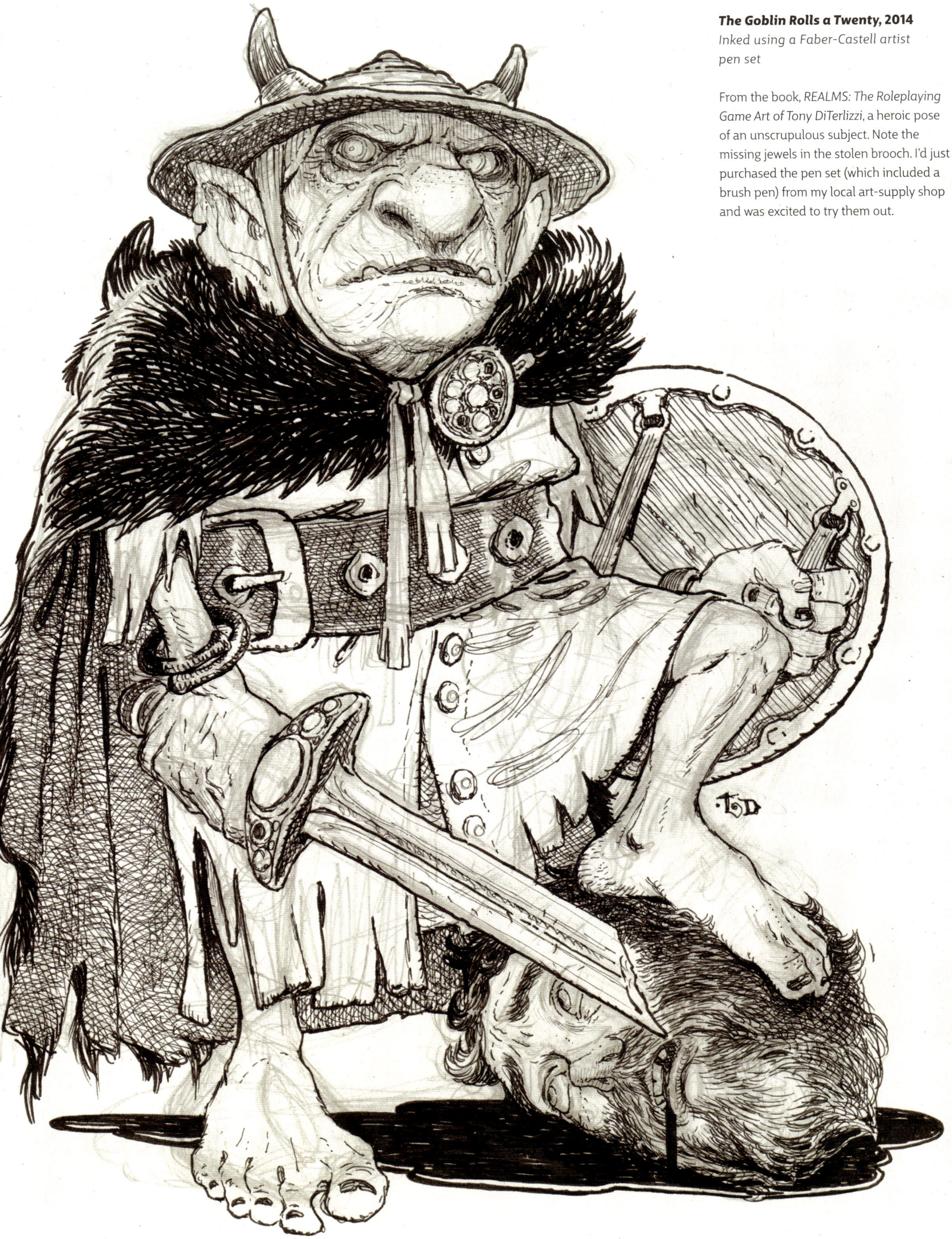

The Goblin Rolls a Twenty, 2014
Inked using a Faber-Castell artist pen set

From the book, *REALMS: The Roleplaying Game Art of Tony DiTerlizzi*, a heroic pose of an unscrupulous subject. Note the missing jewels in the stolen brooch. I'd just purchased the pen set (which included a brush pen) from my local art-supply shop and was excited to try them out.

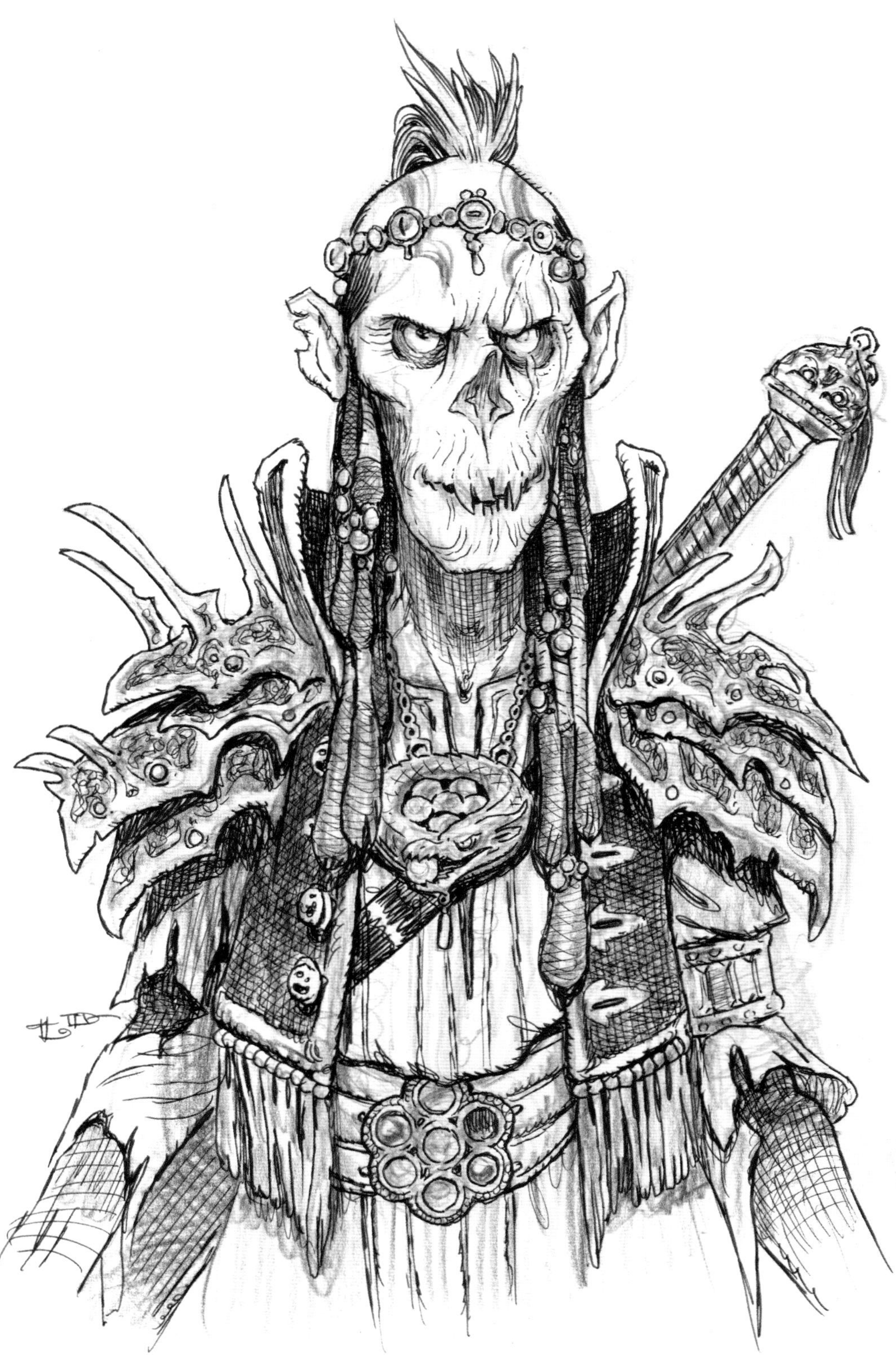

Githyanki, 2023
Inked using Pilot Precise rollerball pens

I've sketched the astral marauders of
Dungeons & Dragons since I first played
the game in the 1980s. His headband
holds the eyes of his fallen foes so
they can watch as he carries on with
his nefarious business. His circular belt
buckle harks back to the first depiction
of the Githyanki on the cover of the
AD&D Fiend Folio, published in 1981.

INSPIRATION

Growing up in an artistic household, my mom would buy art books
that all of us DiTerlizzi kids had to share. We had a few that were
highly coveted, such as *Norman Rockwell: Artist and Illustrator*, but
the one that blew my mind was Brian Froud and Alan Lee's *Faeries*,
published in 1978. I vividly remember copying the fantastic drawings in
that book. Right out of art school I discovered Heinrich Kley's pen and
ink drawings in a pair of books collecting his work. As I'd done before,
I copied his energetic line work in the hope of understanding how he
thought while putting pen to paper.

Nowadays, I have a bookshelf loaded with convention sketchbooks from
contemporaries that I admire, including Jean Giraud, Chris Sanders, Peter
de Sève, Claire Wendling, William Stout, and many more.

Sophia the Sprite (and Dart), 2019
Inked using Pilot Precise rollerball pens

A drawing of my daughter's first *Dungeons & Dragons* character. Elements of her design – from the acorn-cap buckler to the greaves comprised of discarded bits of insect – remind the viewer of her diminutive size. This is certainly one of those drawings that feels as if it's an illustration for a yet-to-be-told story.

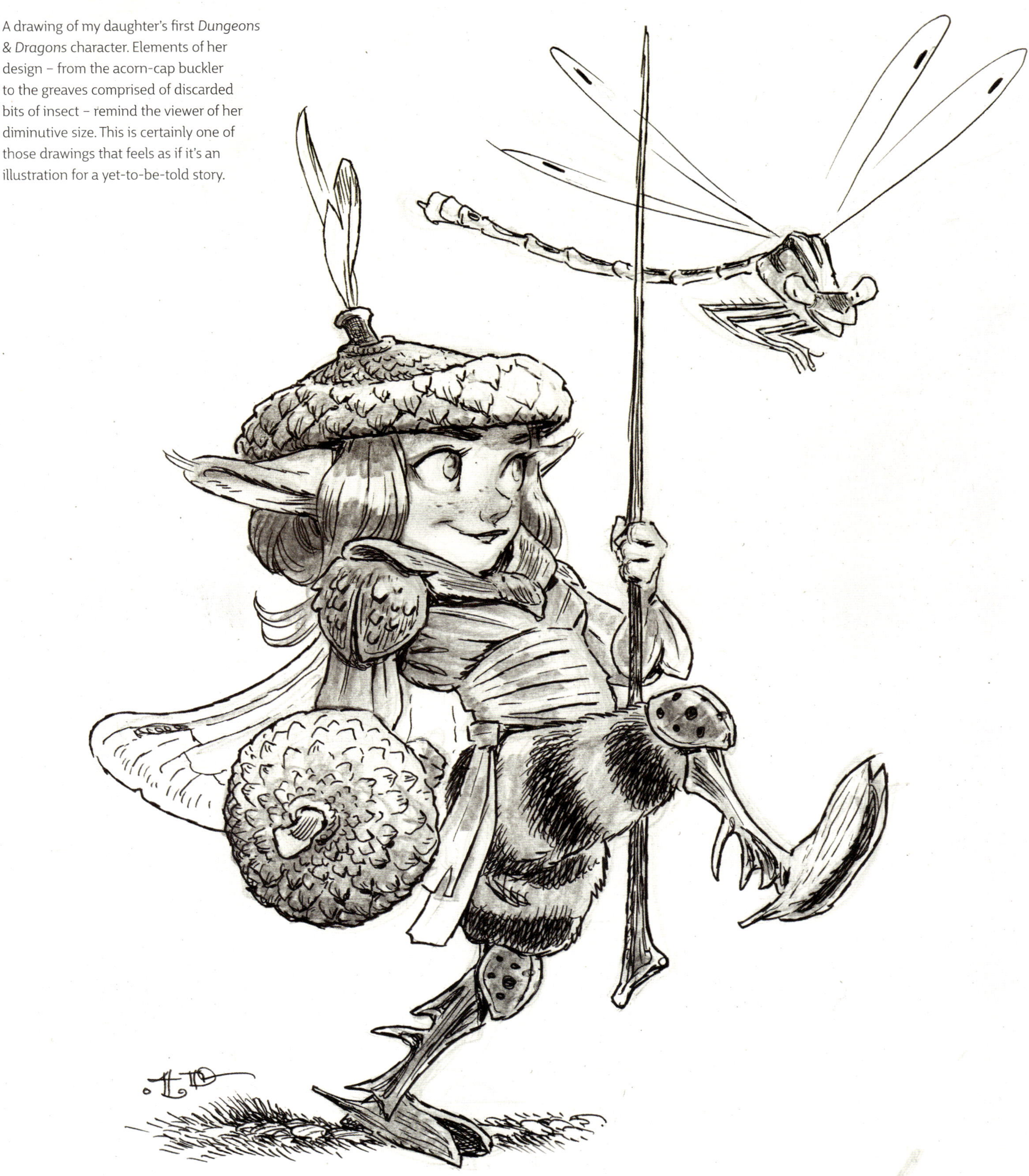

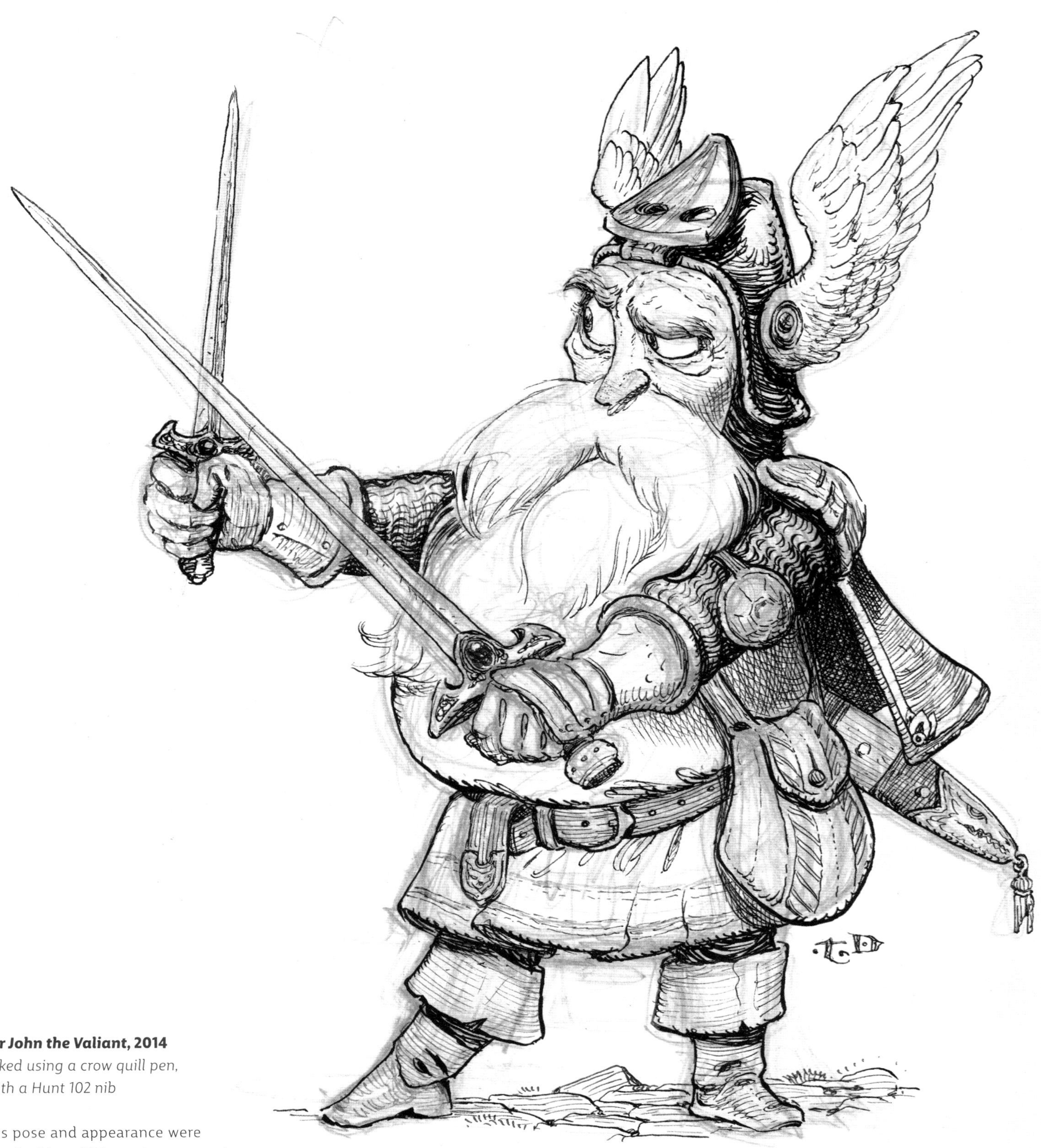

Sir John the Valiant, 2014
*Inked using a crow quill pen,
with a Hunt 102 nib*

His pose and appearance were
inspired by a 19th-century engraving
by legendary English illustrator,
Sir John Tenniel. The composition is
comprised of rounded triangles, from
the pointed faceplate on the helmet to
the tips of his tiny boots.

TWO TYPES OF SKETCHING

I sketch every day, but I realize that not every drawing needs to be amazing. Despite the artwork shared in this chapter, I do a lot of bad drawings before I get to the good ones.

For the most part, I do two types of sketching. The first is exercises to brush up on anatomy and perspective, often copying from a master artist I admire. While creating these types of sketches, I focus intensely on what I am drawing because I am learning. The second type of sketching is either for work or pleasure. For that, I don't think as much. I rely on my accrued knowledge, intuition, muscle memory, and the hunt for perfection.

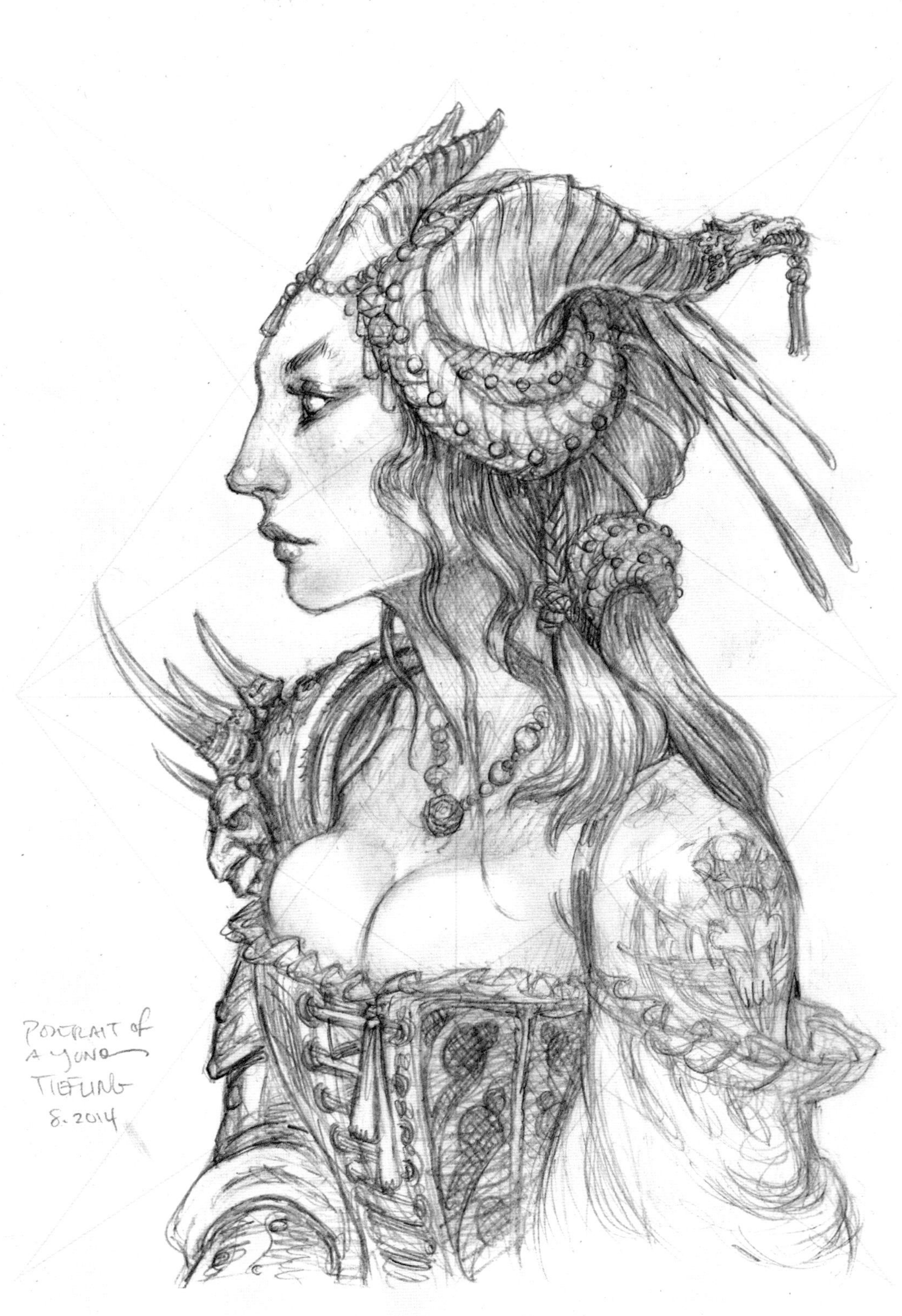

Study for Portrait of a Young Tiefling, 2014

Inspired by Raphael's 16th-century painting, *Young Woman with Unicorn*, the portrait is a revisit to my early years as Lead Artist for the *Dungeons & Dragons* campaign setting, *Planescape*. This race of half-fiend characters was one I helped define back in 1994 and I'm delighted to see they have remained a mainstay in the game ever since.

The Tiefling is TM & © 2025 Wizards

Opposite page | Study for Portrait of a Young Tiefling, 2014

After photographing a model for reference, I further developed the pose and drawing. The overlaid pattern is the sacred geometry often used by Renaissance painters. But unlike Raphael's unicorn, this gal is holding a Displacer Beast cub.

The Tiefling is TM & © 2025 Wizards

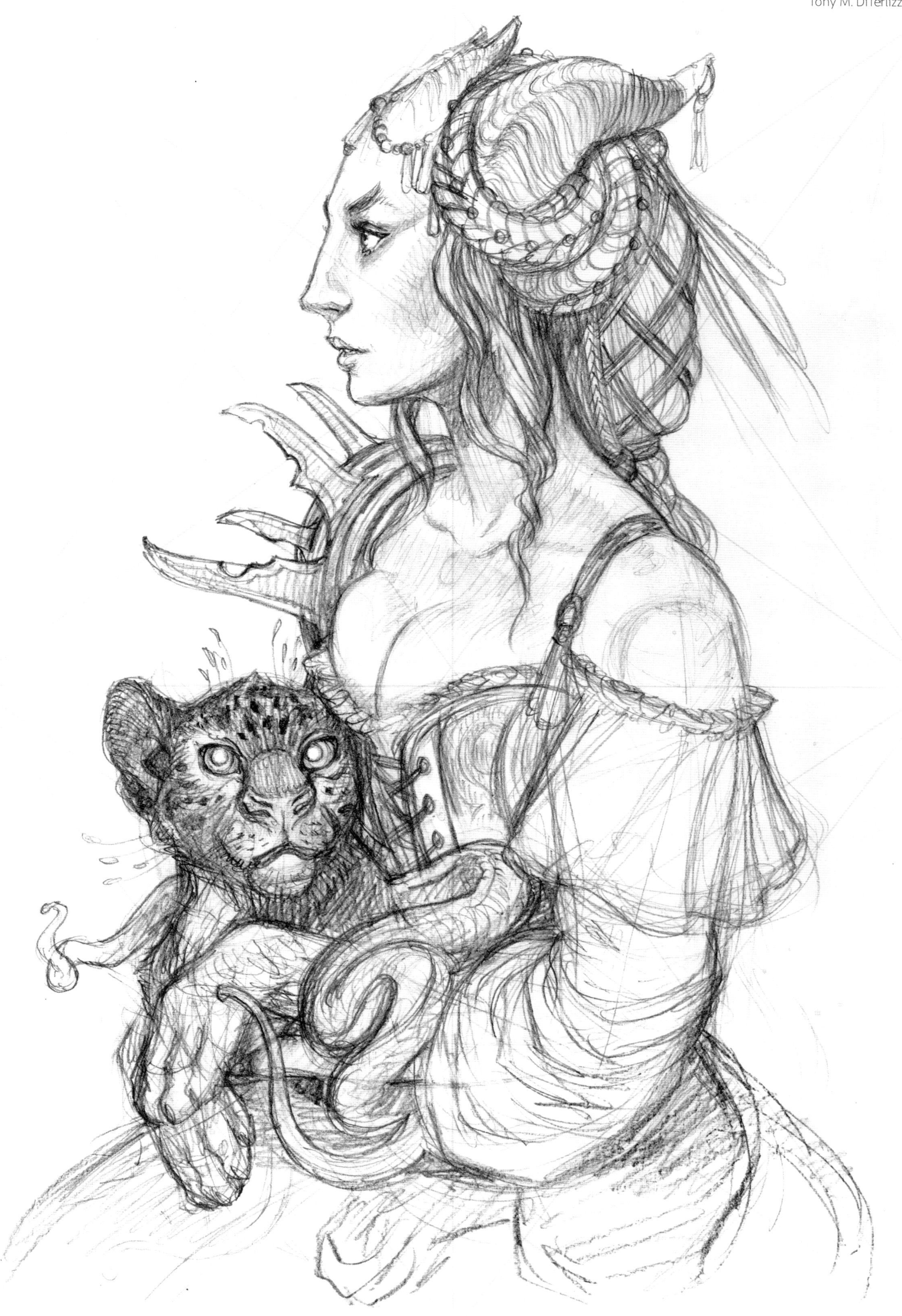

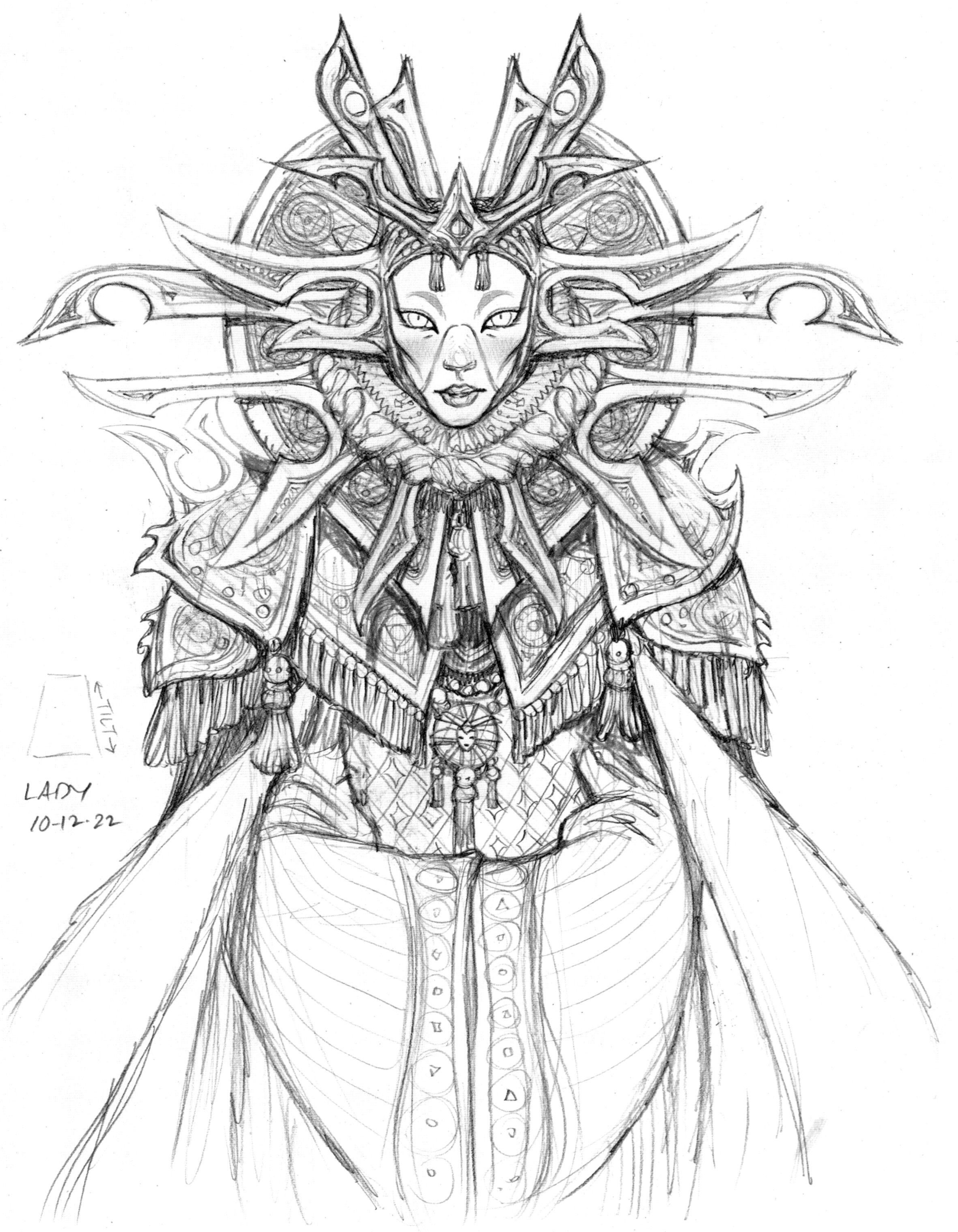
←TILT→
LADY
10-12-22

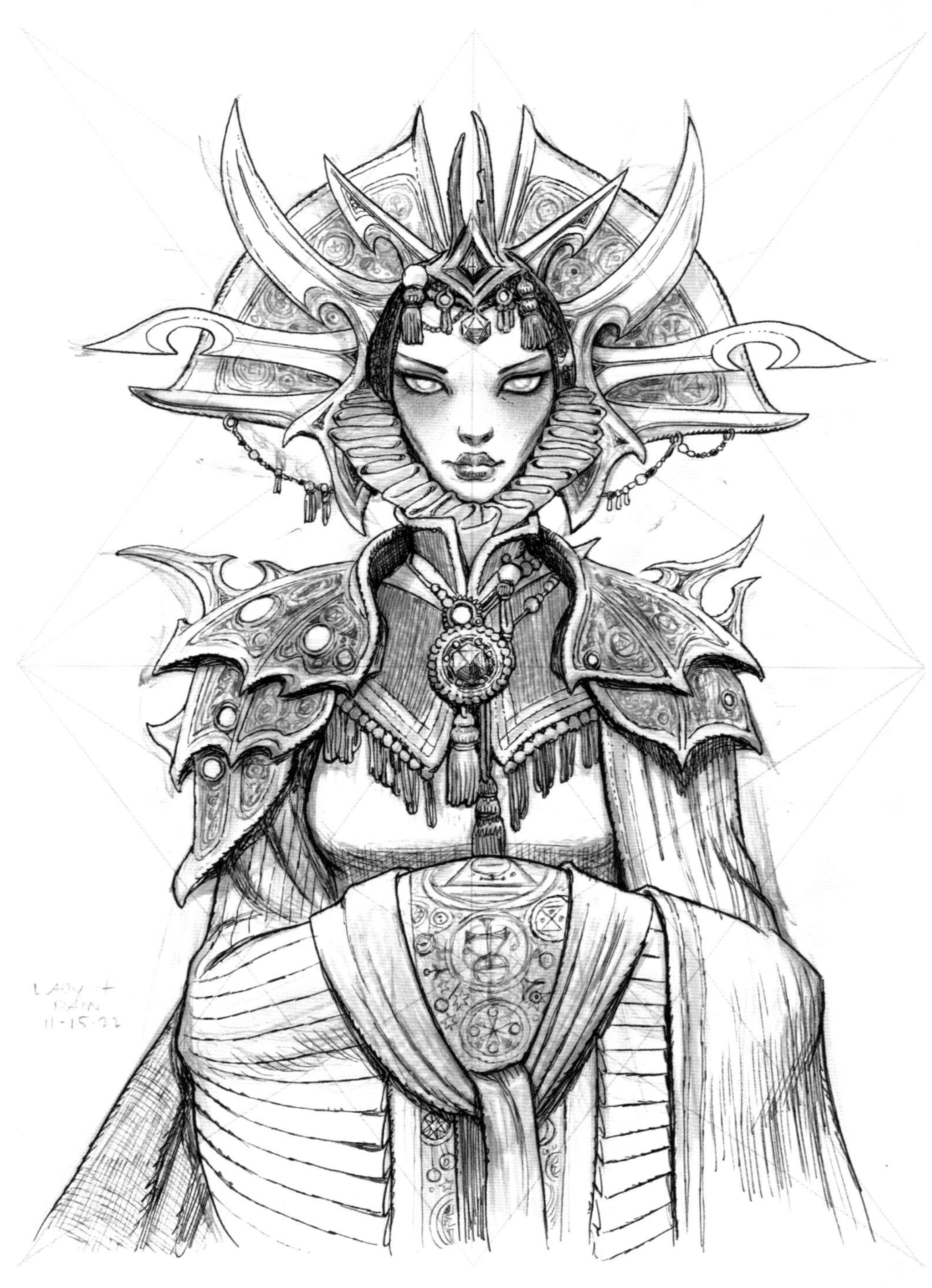

My final design of the Lady harks back to my original nineties illustration, while updating her look for a new audience. As with *Portrait of a Young Tiefling*, I used sacred geometry as a compositional guideline. Both the pendant and headdress feature the game's essential twenty-sided dice. This piece was inked using a crow quill pen, just as I'd done with the original artwork for *Planescape* back in 1994. Talk about a full-circle moment!

Opposite page | **Study for *The Lady of Pain*, 2022**

In 2022, I returned to the start of my career as a fantasy illustrator for the *Dungeons & Dragons* world, *Planescape*, for a new edition of the game. This offered an opportunity to update the iconic Lady of Pain, who I first illustrated back in 1994.

CREATIVE PROCESS

I keep two types of sketchbooks. One is a pocket, or travelling, sketchbook, which is purely for capturing ideas and brainstorms. The second, more thorough, is a story sketchbook that is reserved for the current story I'm developing. It has character designs, settings, maps, diagrams, and all sorts of visuals related to the narrative I'm conceiving. Inevitably, usually near the end of one of these assigned story sketchbooks, there will be a burst of imagination for a completely new, unrelated story. It's a creative pattern of mine that I've realized and now take advantage of while writing and drawing.

Each story I develop has its own dedicated sketchbook, though other ideas will often bubble up and sneak onto the pages during the creative process. I take care to label the content of each sketchbook so I can easily locate past ideas and ongoing story concepts.

When creating a story, I usually start by doodling and jotting down ideas in its assigned sketchbook. It begins with a sketch of the protagonist. I start there because I must first fully understand the main character. Otherwise, how can I expect a reader to care about them? I then continue exploring the physical traits of the character through repeated sketching. I add notes in the margins about personality and possible challenges they may deal with. A conversation between words and pictures sends me off and, if I'm lucky, I'll have a story to show for it.

The truth is, however, that though I use sketchbooks for the initial genesis, concepts, and notes for my stories, once I begin production, I draw on loose sheets of paper. This is mostly because a loose sheet of paper is less precious than a bound book. Plus, they're easier to scan.

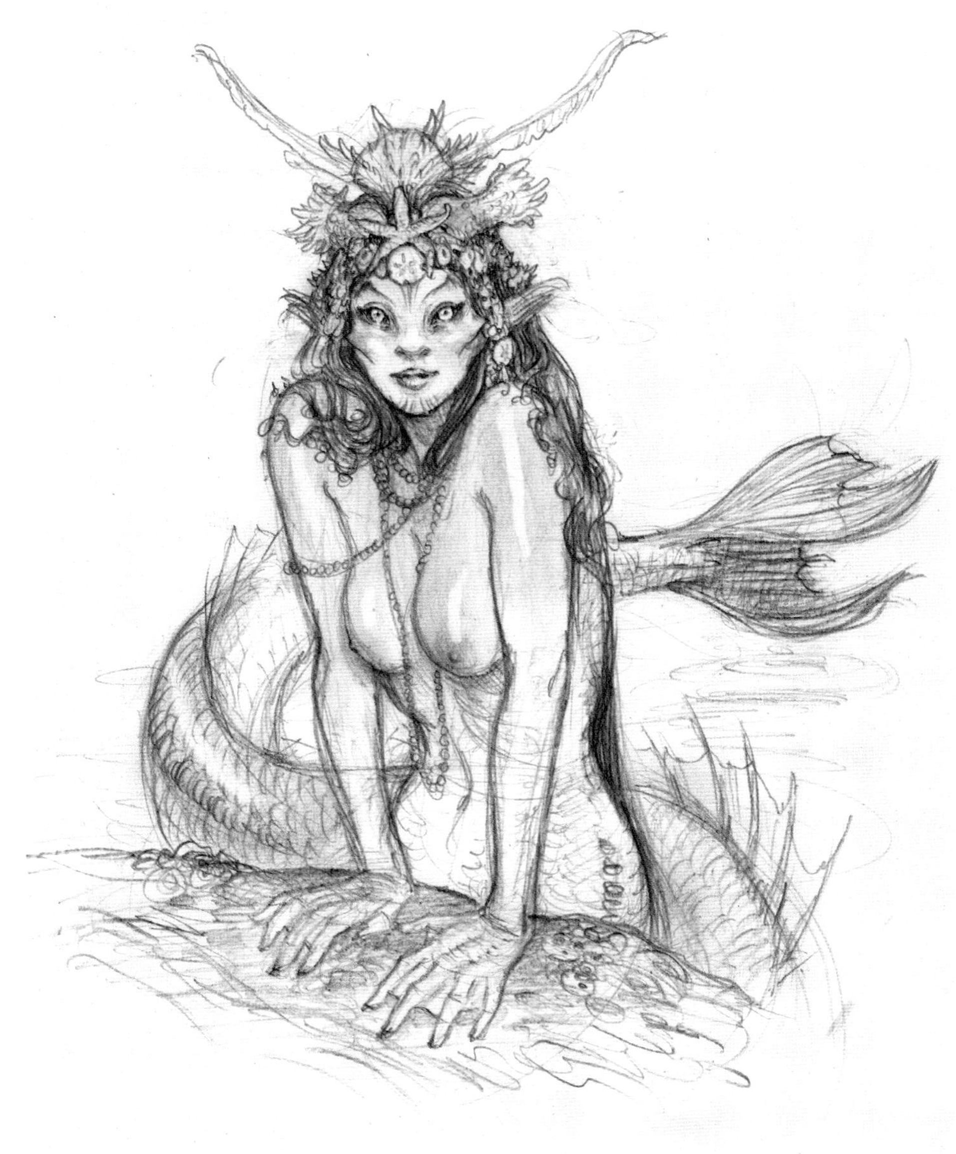

Siren, 2014
Pencil and eraser

My curiosity for the wonders of the ocean has remained a passion since my childhood days of living in a small beach town on the Florida coast. This sketch is a great example of using the other end of the pencil. The eraser is not just for removing mistakes!

Each story I develop has its own dedicated sketchbook, though other ideas will often bubble up and sneak onto the pages during the creative process

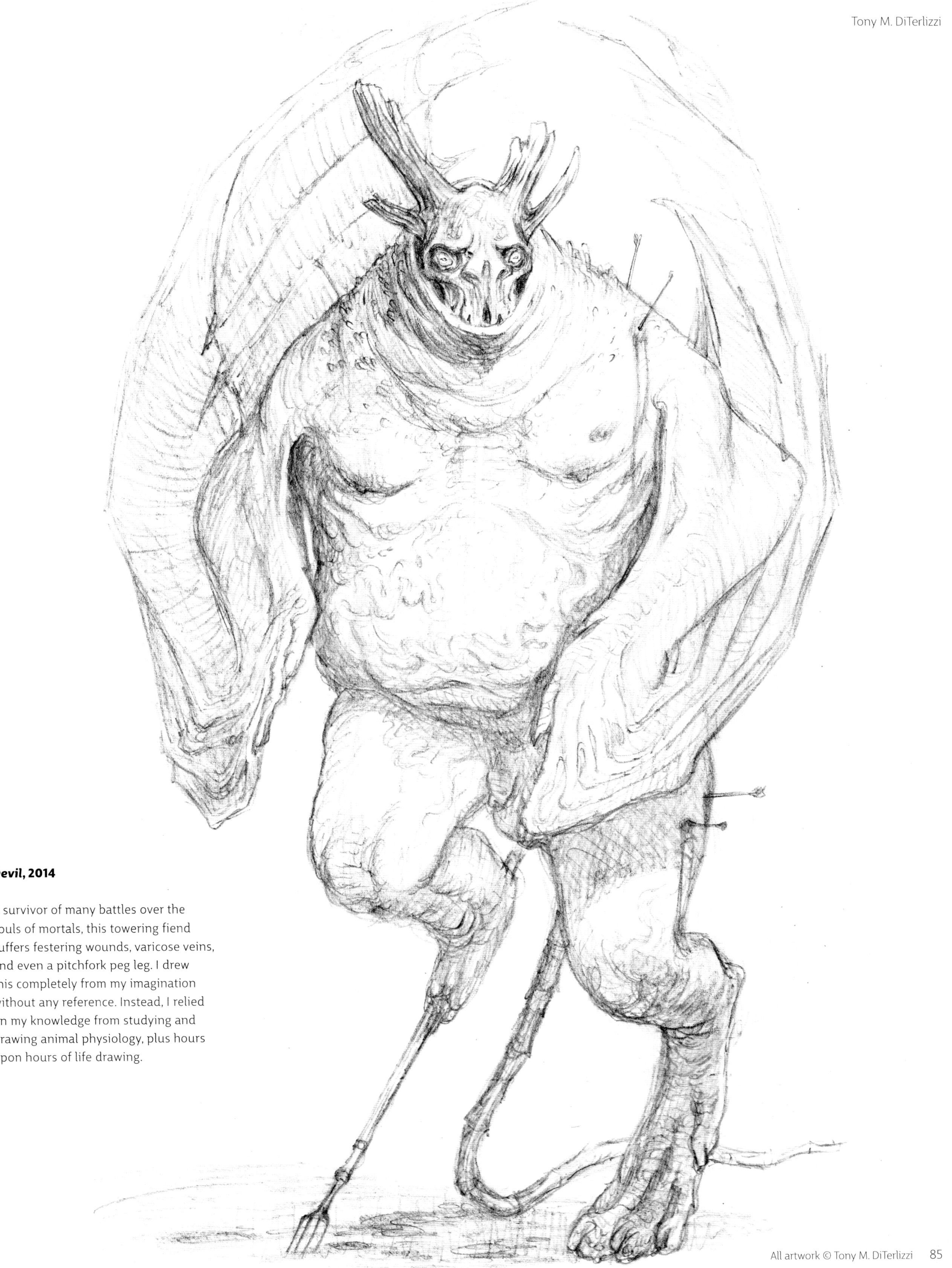

Devil, 2014

A survivor of many battles over the
souls of mortals, this towering fiend
suffers festering wounds, varicose veins,
and even a pitchfork peg leg. I drew
this completely from my imagination
without any reference. Instead, I relied
on my knowledge from studying and
drawing animal physiology, plus hours
upon hours of life drawing.

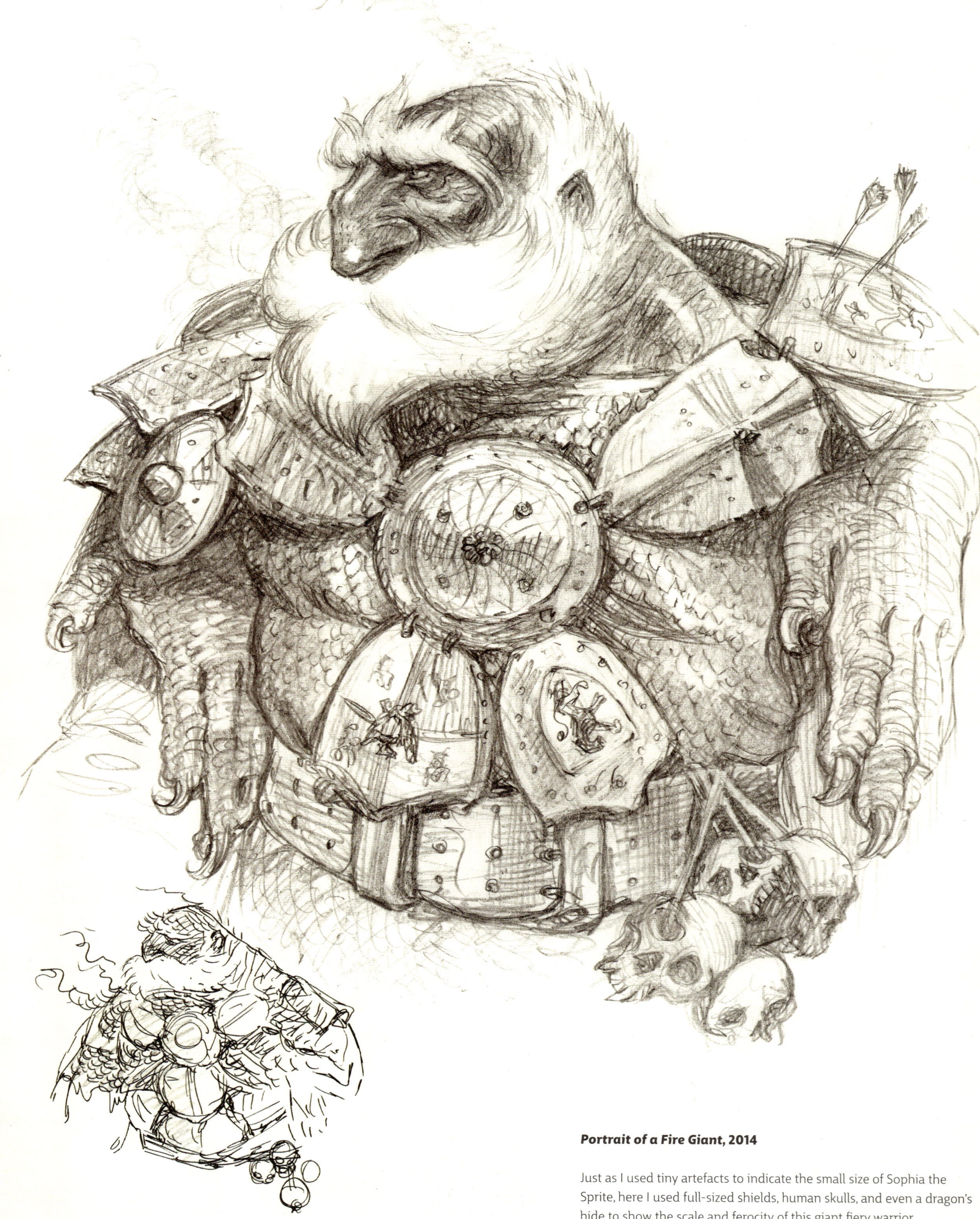

Portrait of a Fire Giant, 2014

Just as I used tiny artefacts to indicate the small size of Sophia the Sprite, here I used full-sized shields, human skulls, and even a dragon's hide to show the scale and ferocity of this giant fiery warrior.

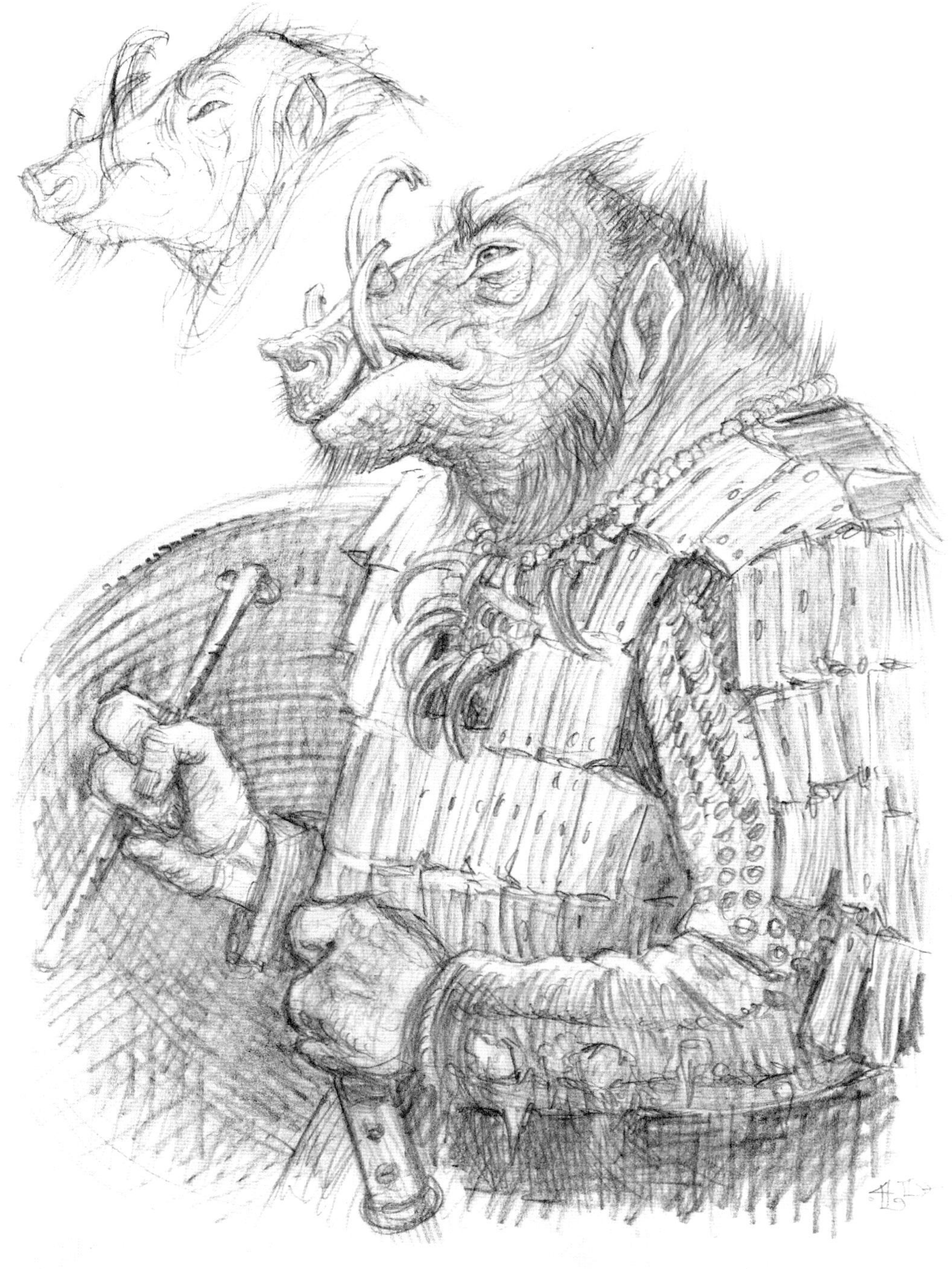

Portrait of an Orc, 2014

Though our modern depiction of orcs comes from the books of J. R. R. Tolkien, this design comes from the pig-faced brigands of early editions of *Dungeons & Dragons* that I often encountered as a young gamer. The head is inspired by the Malaysian boar, the babirusa, whose tusks continually grow, often puncturing the snout and skull.

This was a preliminary drawing for a painting I'd hoped to include in *REALMS: The Roleplaying Game Art of Tony DiTerlizzi*, but I ran out of time. It was later included in my self-published sketchbook, *Album per Schizzi*, in 2016.

PUTTING INK TO PAPER

I've been drawing with pencils and pens for as long as I can remember. I was never intimidated by the permanence of a black line when putting ink to paper, whether it be a steely crow quill or a worn-out Sharpie. Generally, in my sketchbooks, I use Pilot Precise V5 or V7 rollerball pens or a standard no. 2 Ticonderoga pencil with a cap eraser.

For story creation and planning, my preference is an 21 × 12.5 cm softcover Moleskine. I also have small, pocket-sized sketchbooks for travel and larger academic 21.5 × 28 cm hardbacks with toned tan paper. While they're a diverse crew, varying in height, colour, and even binding (some of the early ones are spiral-bound), they all sit amiably next to one another on my bookshelf. My life in imagination, rendered in pencil, pen, and paper.

As soon as I could afford it, I stopped selling my original artwork and started archiving it. All my art is stored in flat files with each finished piece protected by an archival polyester sleeve. My childhood and college work was stored in a facility in my old home town in Florida. When I finally retrieved it, I was delighted to find a cache of drawings from my elementary school days. When I think about it, the circumstances and chances of that stuff surviving are pretty slim, so I am thankful to have these artefacts from my early years as an aspiring artist.

Polypore, 2012

Though youthful in appearance, this fungal fairy is older than the forest she protects. Another piece that was intended for a finished painting but never made it past the sketch stage.

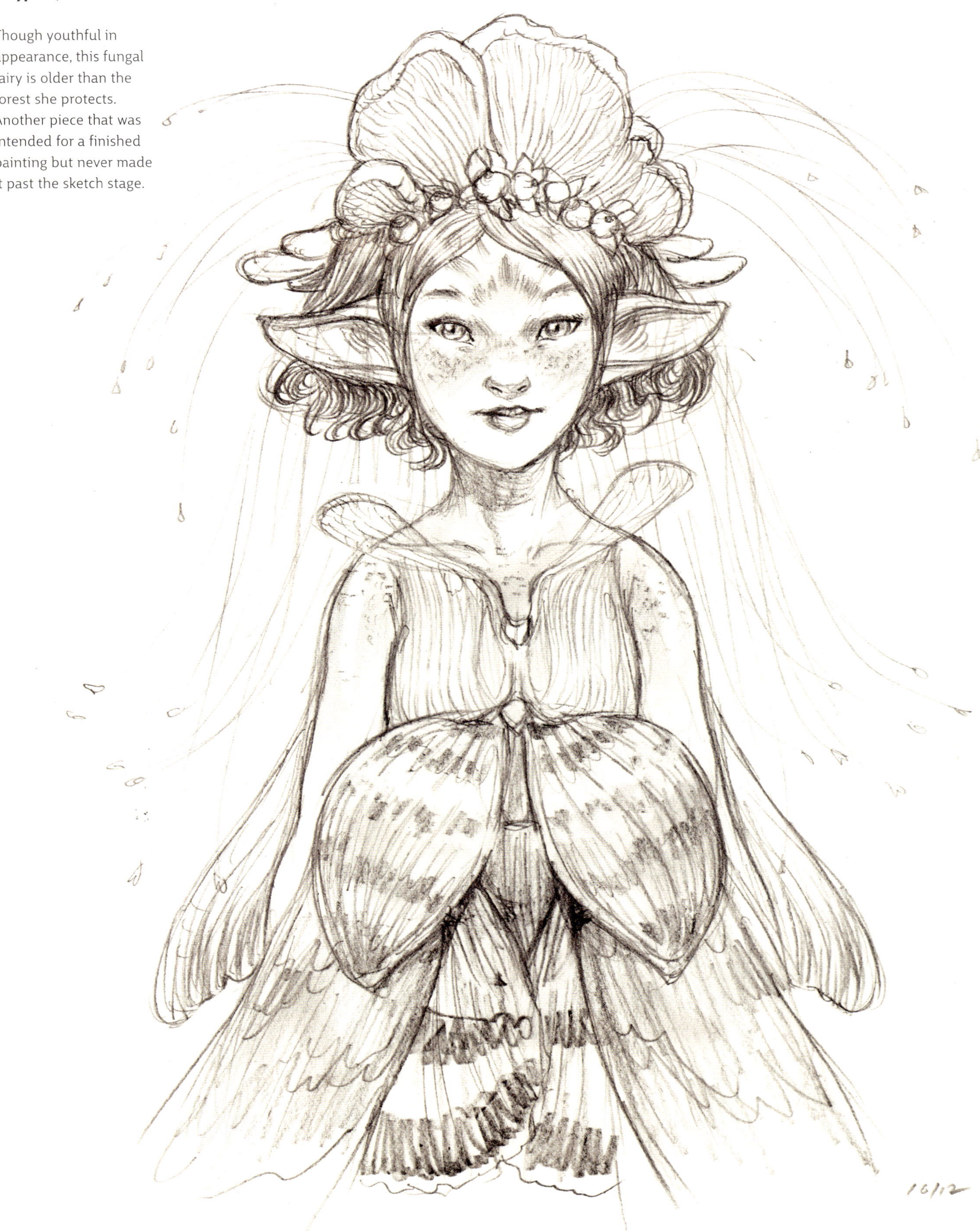

SKETCHBOOKS AS MEMOIRS

Sketchbooks have helped me improve my craft. It is constant practice and refinement of skill. I've filled numerous sketchbooks over the years, documenting the evolution of my style and growth as an artist. By revisiting my old sketchbooks, I can track my artistic progress, identify areas for improvement, and, frankly, appreciate how far I've come – especially when I redraw an old sketch from decades ago. Sketchbooks mark periods in my life. I am always at some stage of filling a sketchbook, either at home or while travelling. They have become, in part, my memoirs.

I've learned to capture every fleeting thought, daydream, and spark of an idea, because I never know what I can develop it into. When I start a new story, I often page through old sketchbooks for ideas. I am continually surprised by sketches for story concepts that I have no recollection of creating. As I do this, I often note the myriad of mistakes in my sketchbook drawings, but I still recall the joy I experienced in rendering each one. That exciting feeling of opening my sketchpad and uncapping my pen to conjure up fantastic new scenes, creatures, and characters hasn't diminished since I was a kid. I hope it never does.

Dryad, 2011

A drawing of my daughter at four years old as the ancient protector of trees and forests. Some drawings so perfectly capture what I imagine that I feel no amount of refinement or painting will improve them.

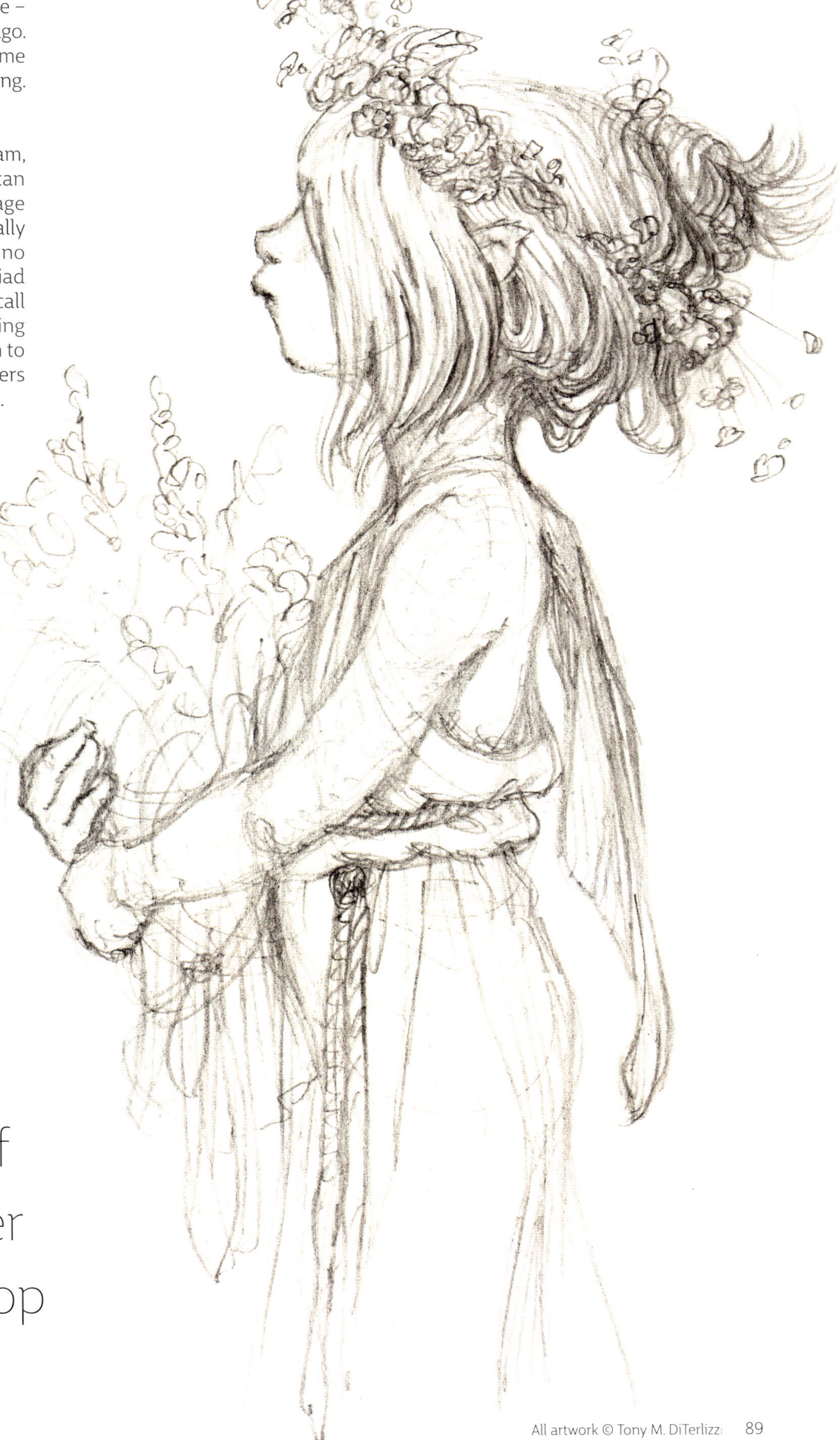

I've learned to capture every fleeting thought, daydream, and spark of an idea, because I never know what I can develop it into

NEVER GIVE UP

My advice to artists just starting out is: ever give up. It was always my dream to become a professional illustrator. In art school, there were artists who were faster than me and much better technically, but I did not give up. Ultimately, I persevered.

At a certain point I realized: *This is all I know how to do. This is what I am put on this Earth to do.* Every 'no' from an art director or publisher only pushed me to find that person who would say 'yes'. And there were a lot of 'no's before I received that 'yes'. I think that's the way it's supposed to be though, because when I heard that 'yes, we want to publish you', it was an amazing feeling. I felt victorious, and it encouraged me to keep going. That drive has never left me.

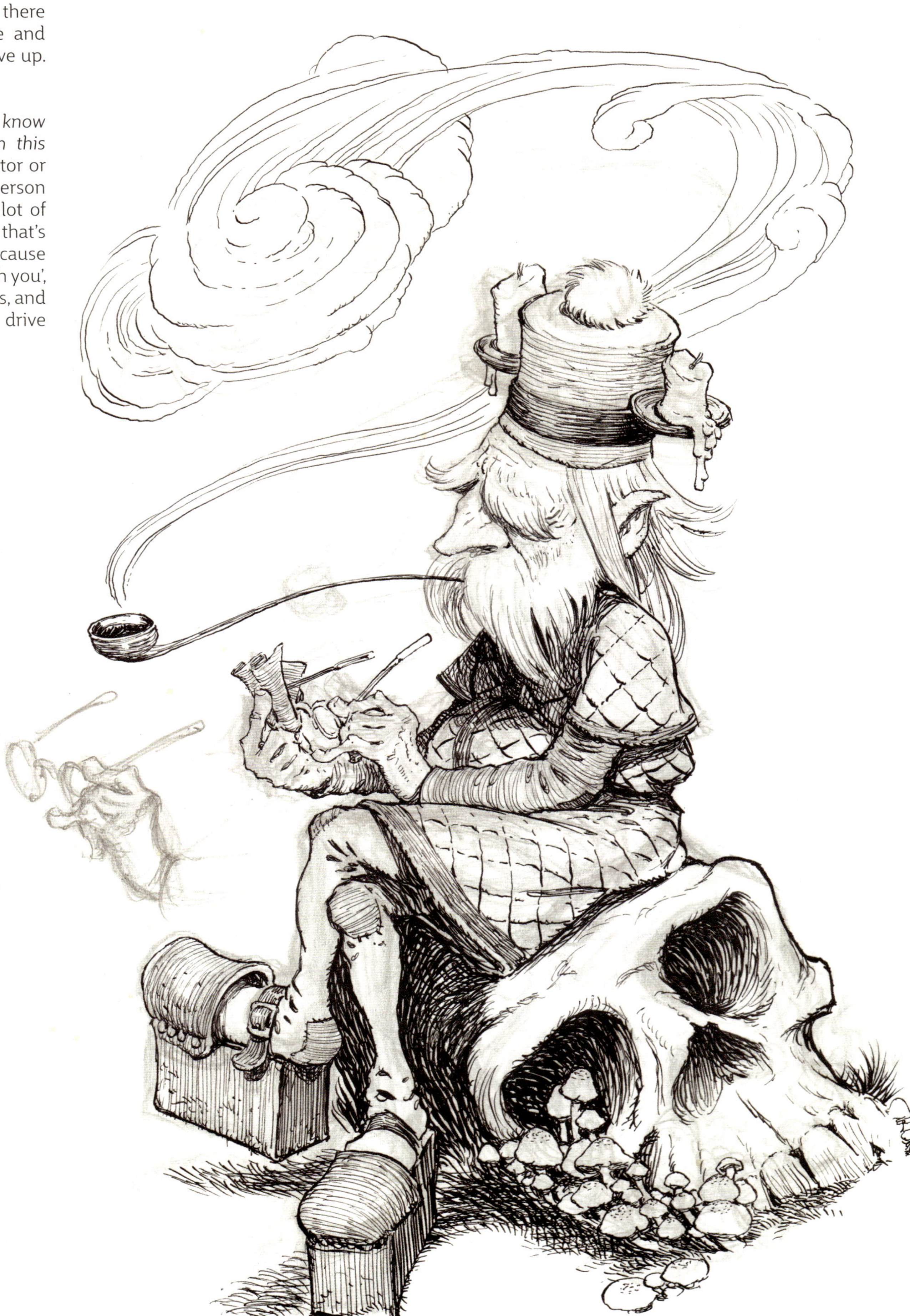

Gnome Illusionist, 2013
Finished with crow quill pen,
using a Hunt 102 nib

There's a bit of W. Heath Robinson in the inking style here – especially his early book illustration work.

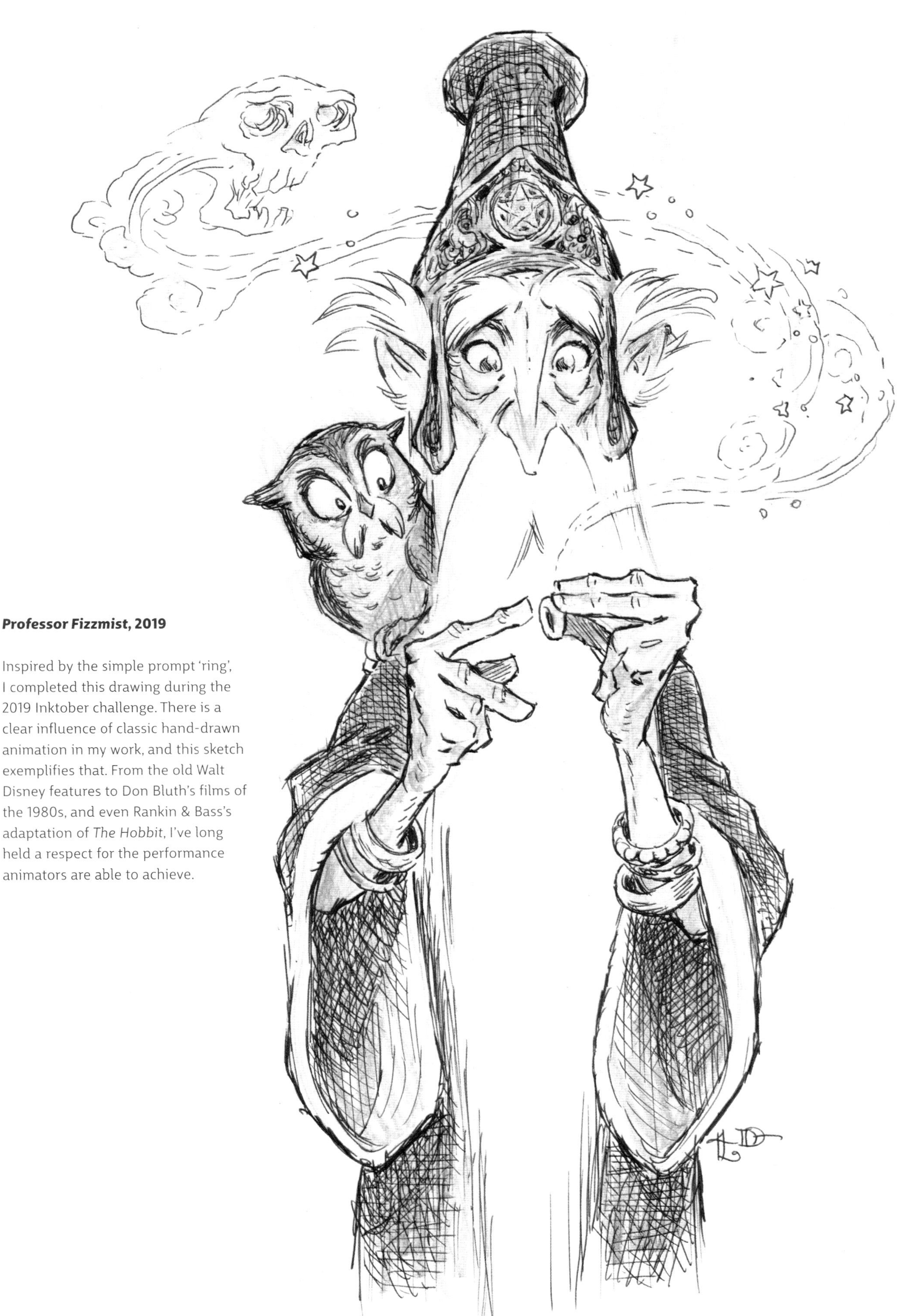

Professor Fizzmist, 2019

Inspired by the simple prompt 'ring', I completed this drawing during the 2019 Inktober challenge. There is a clear influence of classic hand-drawn animation in my work, and this sketch exemplifies that. From the old Walt Disney features to Don Bluth's films of the 1980s, and even Rankin & Bass's adaptation of *The Hobbit*, I've long held a respect for the performance animators are able to achieve.

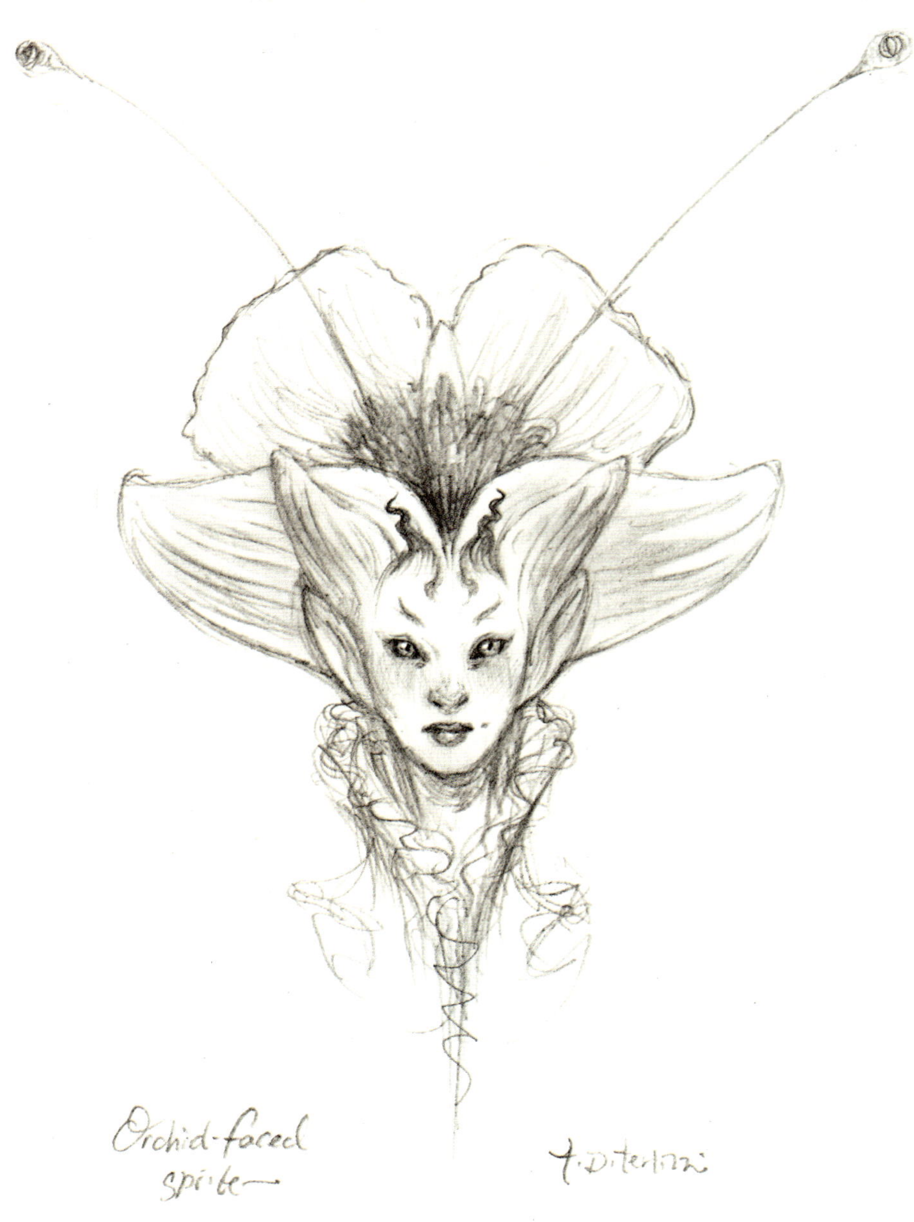

Orchid-Faced Sprite, 2014

My fairy designs incorporate elements from exotic plants and insects, inspired by the works of the Victorian painter, John Anster Fitzgerald. Though I later inked and coloured this sketch, the final artwork lacks the warmth and spontaneity of this initial sketch. This is an ongoing challenge for me – trying to capture the energy of the drawing in paint without it feeling traced or overworked.

Self-portrait

Preliminary layout for the exhibition poster of my retrospective at the Norman Rockwell Museum, 2017. This was my initial idea for the poster, but I ultimately opted for a horizontal layout instead before transferring the drawing to Bristol board for the final painting.

A fairly accurate depiction of the inside of my mind, crammed full of characters from various books I've written or illustrated. What you can't see are the other characters patiently waiting for their story to be told…

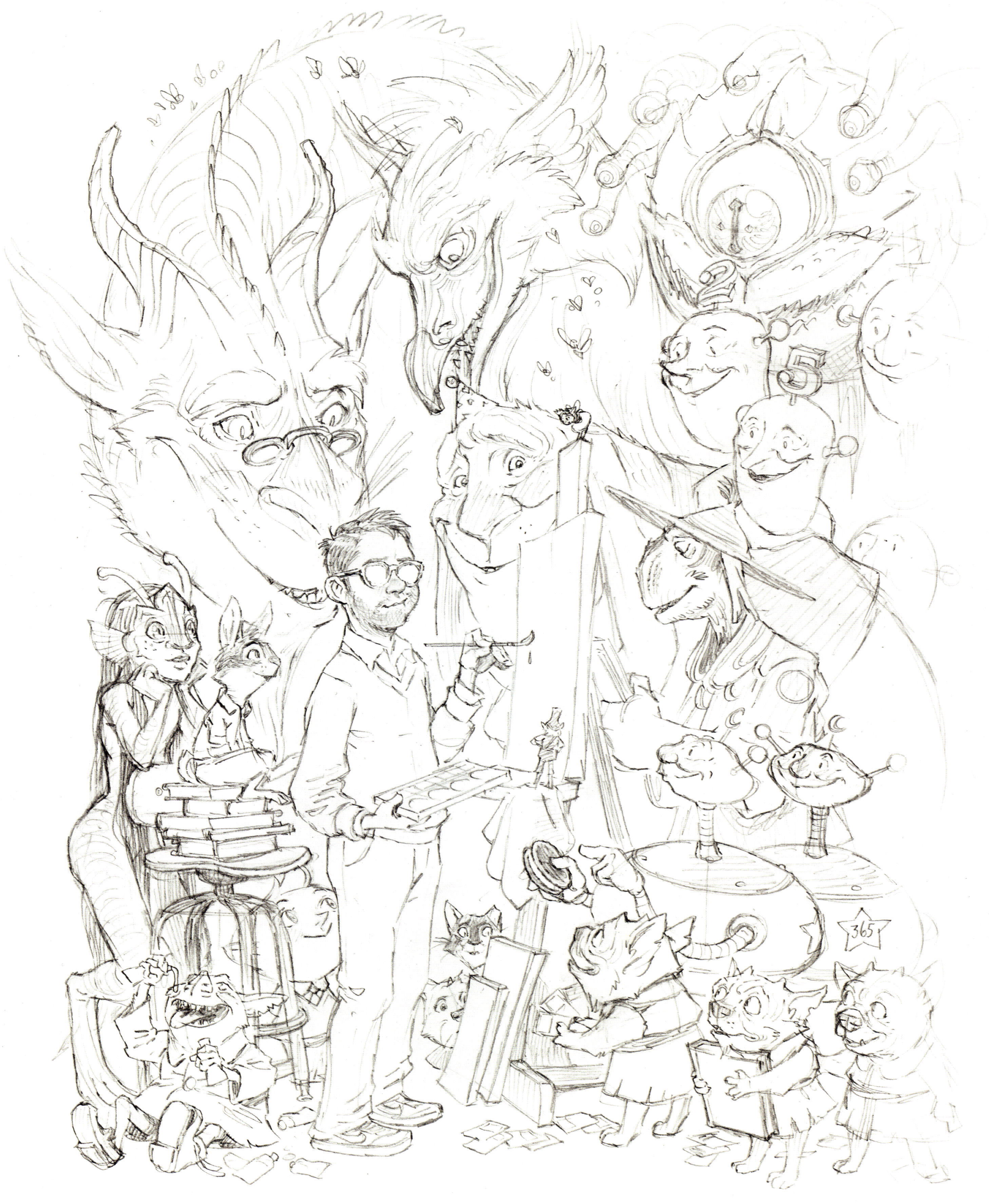

Dave McKean

ILLUSTRATION ORIGINS

When I left art school in 1986, I'd already been working professionally for a year, making illustrations for bank brochures and record covers. I'd also put together four issues of a comic called *Meanwhile...* with four like-minded students. This work was noticed by editors in London and led to my meeting other young creators.

My first professional comic was a three-page *Mr X* story I wrote and illustrated, colours on spec, which was bought and published by editor Bill Marks at Vortex. Since then I've illustrated over ninety books and graphic novels, collaborating with authors including Ray Bradbury, David Almond, and John Cale, as well as creating the self-penned *Cages* and *Black Dog: The Dreams of Paul Nash*.

I don't really dwell on feeling proud about things. That said, I directed a film called *The Gospel of Us*, which was a record of a three-day live theatrical contemporary passion play that actor Michael Sheen created in Port Talbot, Wales. The project involved 1,000 locals, and various theatrical, art, and music groups were formed for it. The project changed the spirit in the town and a sense of social and political purpose returned to a pretty ignored corner of Wales. The project changed Michael's priorities; he became an activist first and actor second.

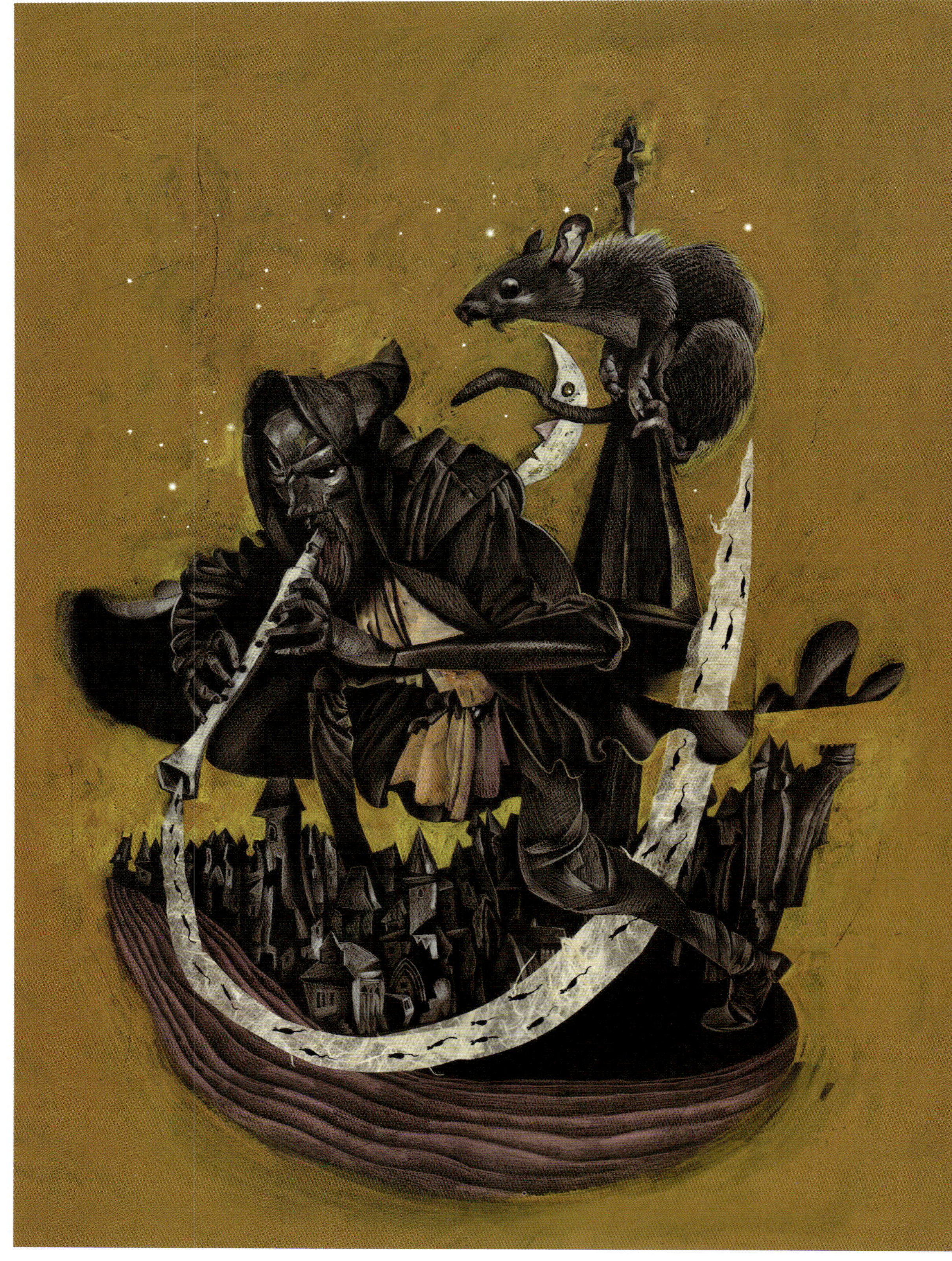

The Pied Piper Blu-ray cover
Deaf Crocodile Films Inc. 2023

This film poster and Blu-ray cover was created for the amazing puppet animation of the Pied Piper of Hamelin story by Jiri Barta. I played with various poses and compositions, all centred on the playing of the pipe and the music flowing around the town. The animation is created with roughly carved wooden puppets, so I used coloured pencils on black card to mimic the carved wood look of the film.

More detailed drawing for the rough stages before final artwork

Final rough visual for approval

Developing the figure

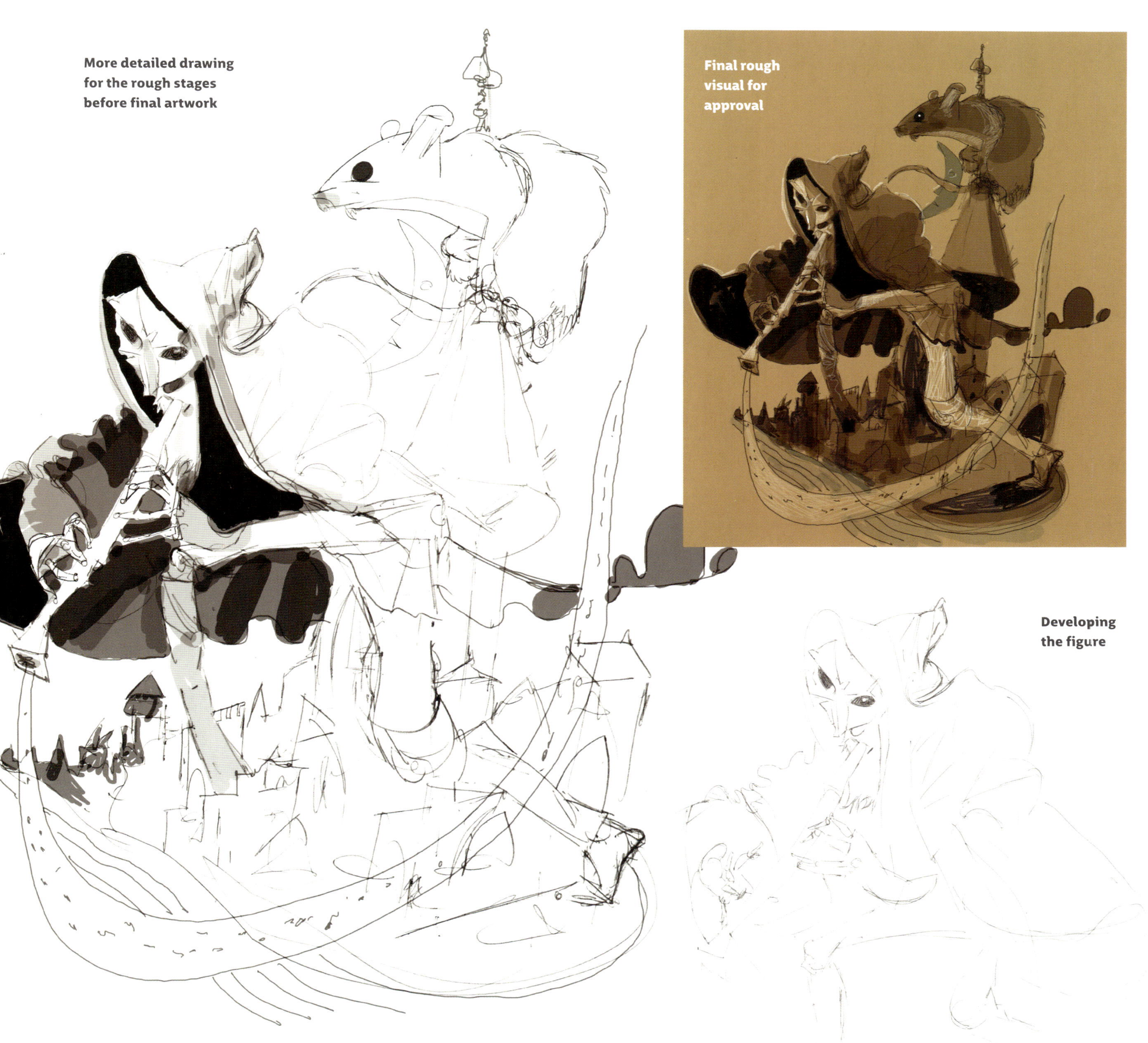

The Pied Piper Blu-ray was released by Deaf Crocodile Films

   95

**Working out the figure
in my sketchbook,
with various other
notes around**

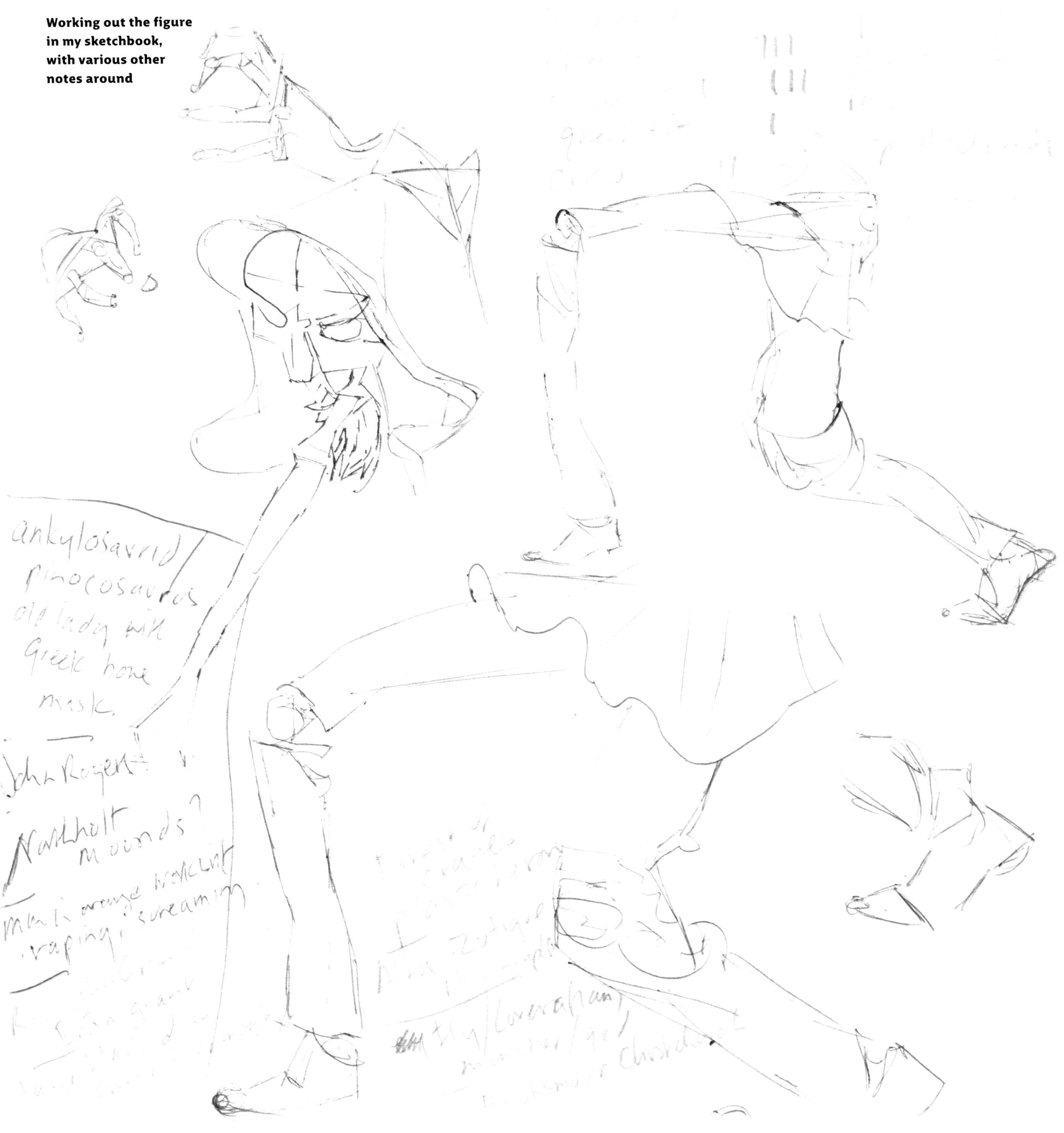

The Pied Piper Blu-ray was released by Deaf Crocodile Films

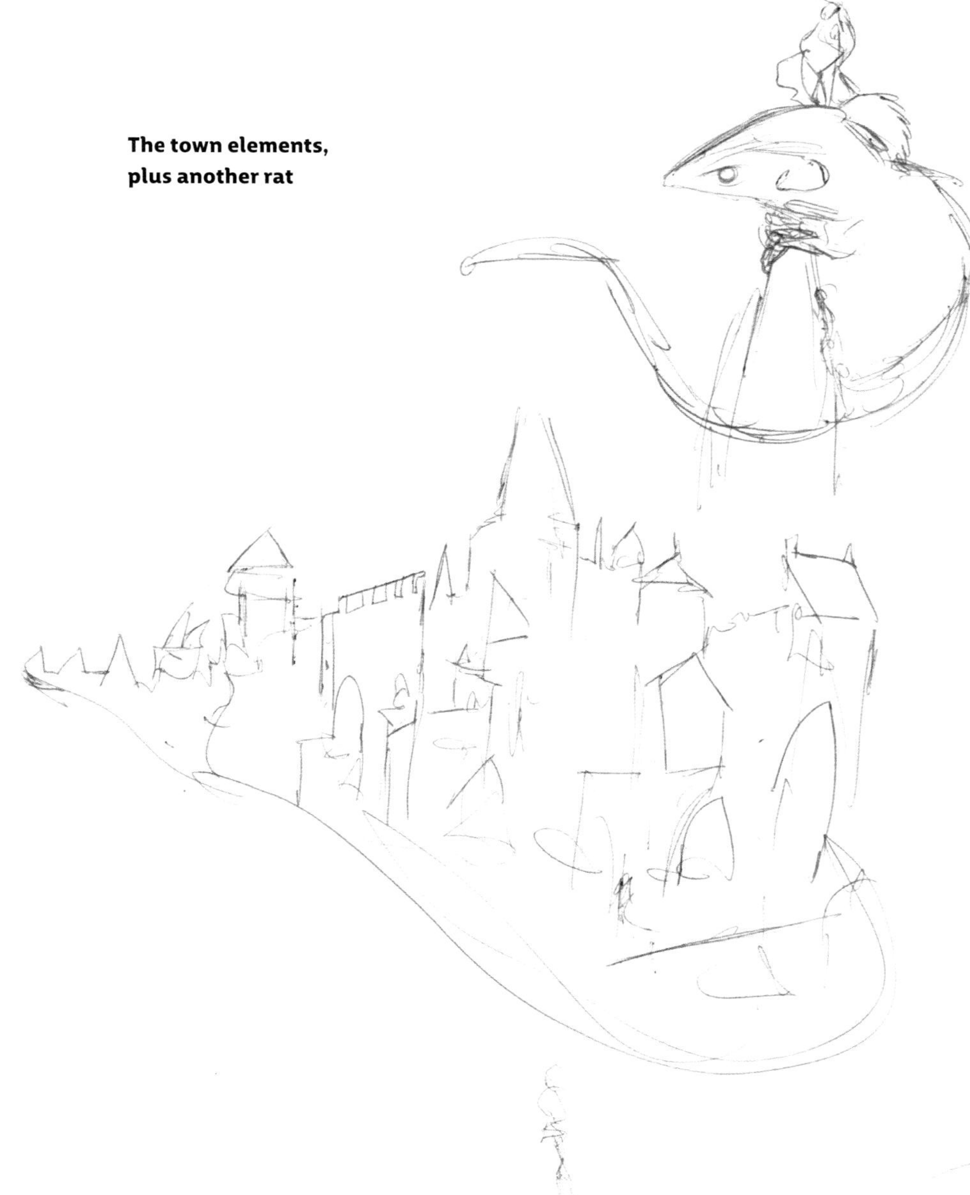

**The town elements,
plus another rat**

Dave McKean

I don't think of the
sketchbook as the
finished work in any
sense – they are just
part of the process
of developing ideas...
They are stepping
stones, rather than
telling a full story

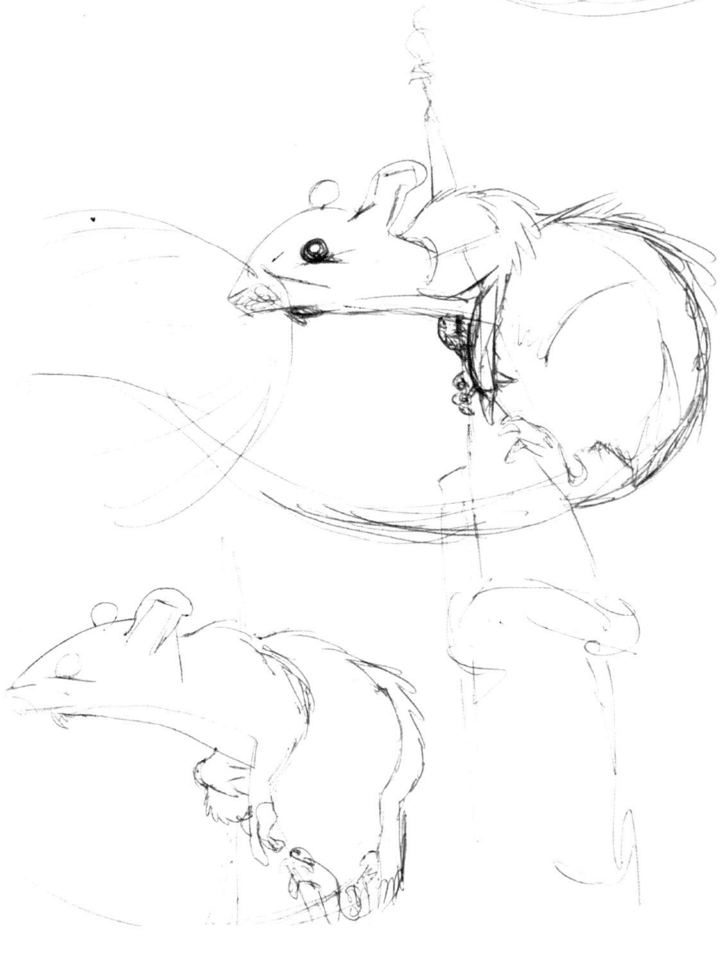

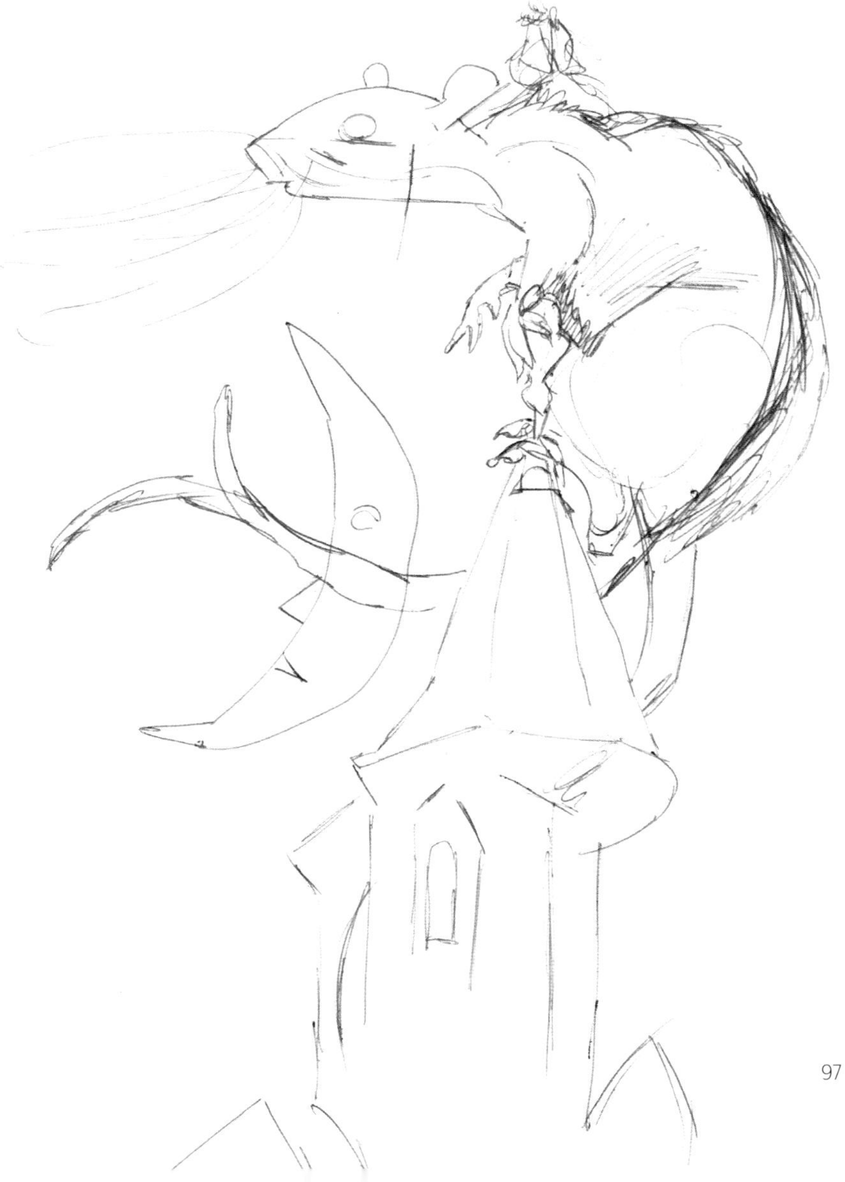

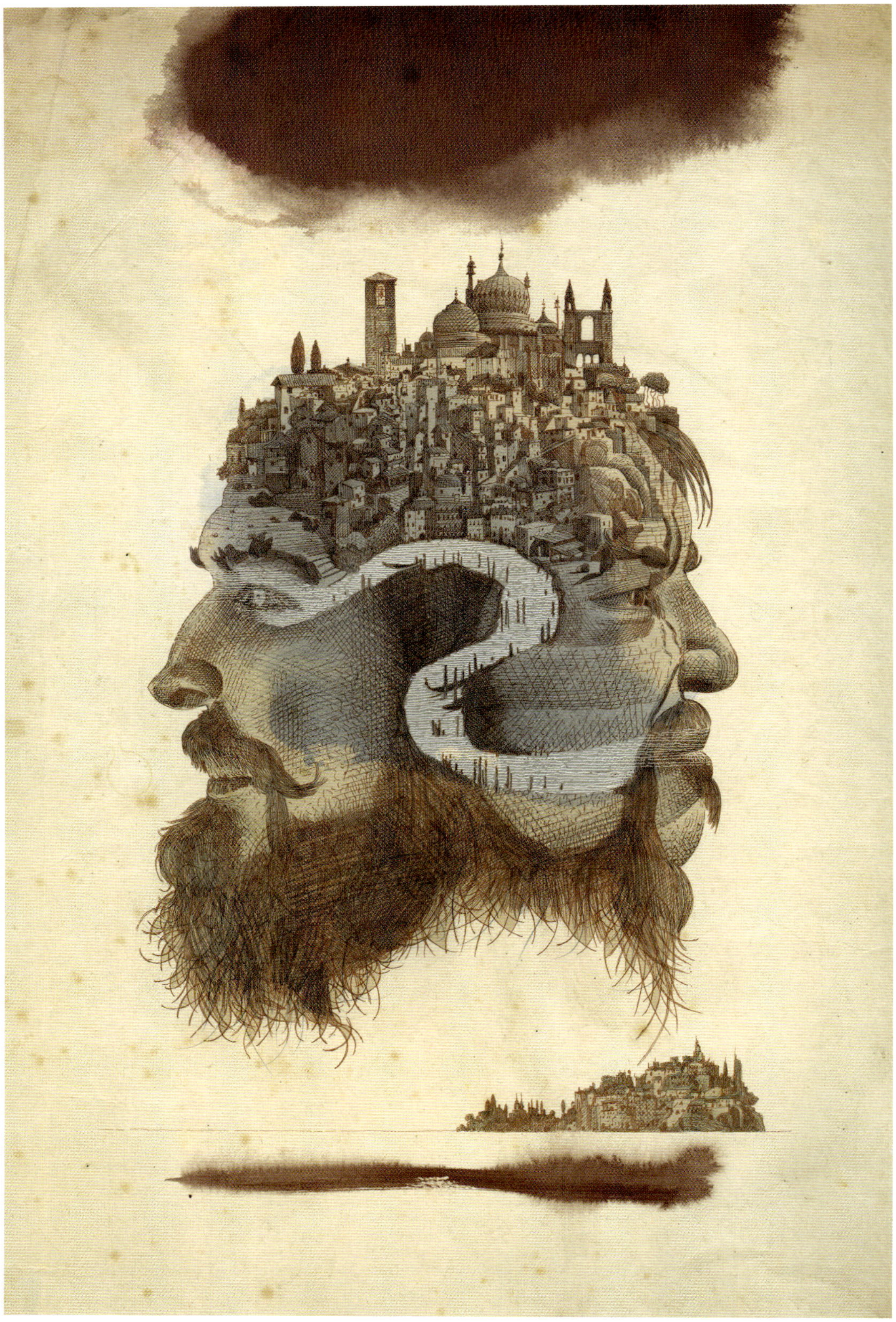

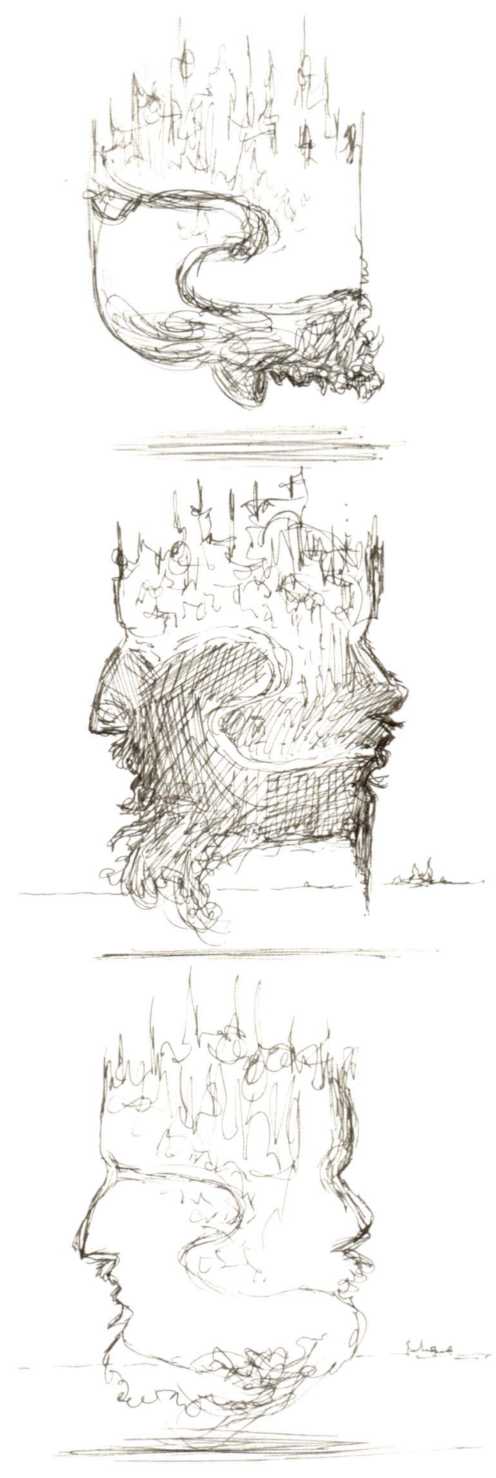

Invisible Cities by Italo Calvino, book cover
The Folio Society, 2023

I love this conversational book; a mental chess game between Kublai Khan and Marco Polo. The reader is never sure whether the cities described are real or versions of Polo's home city, so I thought the cover should be a series of sketches of impossible cities that have the feeling of old Venetian etchings. My sketchbook notes were all about trying to find the right way of portraying a floating island of surreal conversation.

Sketches working out the best orientation of the Janus head image

INFLUENCES

Milton Glaser's attitude to drawing and sketching was a big influence on me in art school. I saw a great documentary about him on TV. It's still a favourite. Barron Storey is the master sketchbook keeper and a rare example of someone for whom that medium is their main form of expression. Almost all the greats have kept visual notes in their books, offering a tantalizing idea of how they think – how they translate information from the eye to the brain to the hand.

Illustrations from The Folio Society edition of *Invisible Cities* by Italo Calvino
Artwork © Dave McKean [2023]. Exclusively available from foliosociety.com

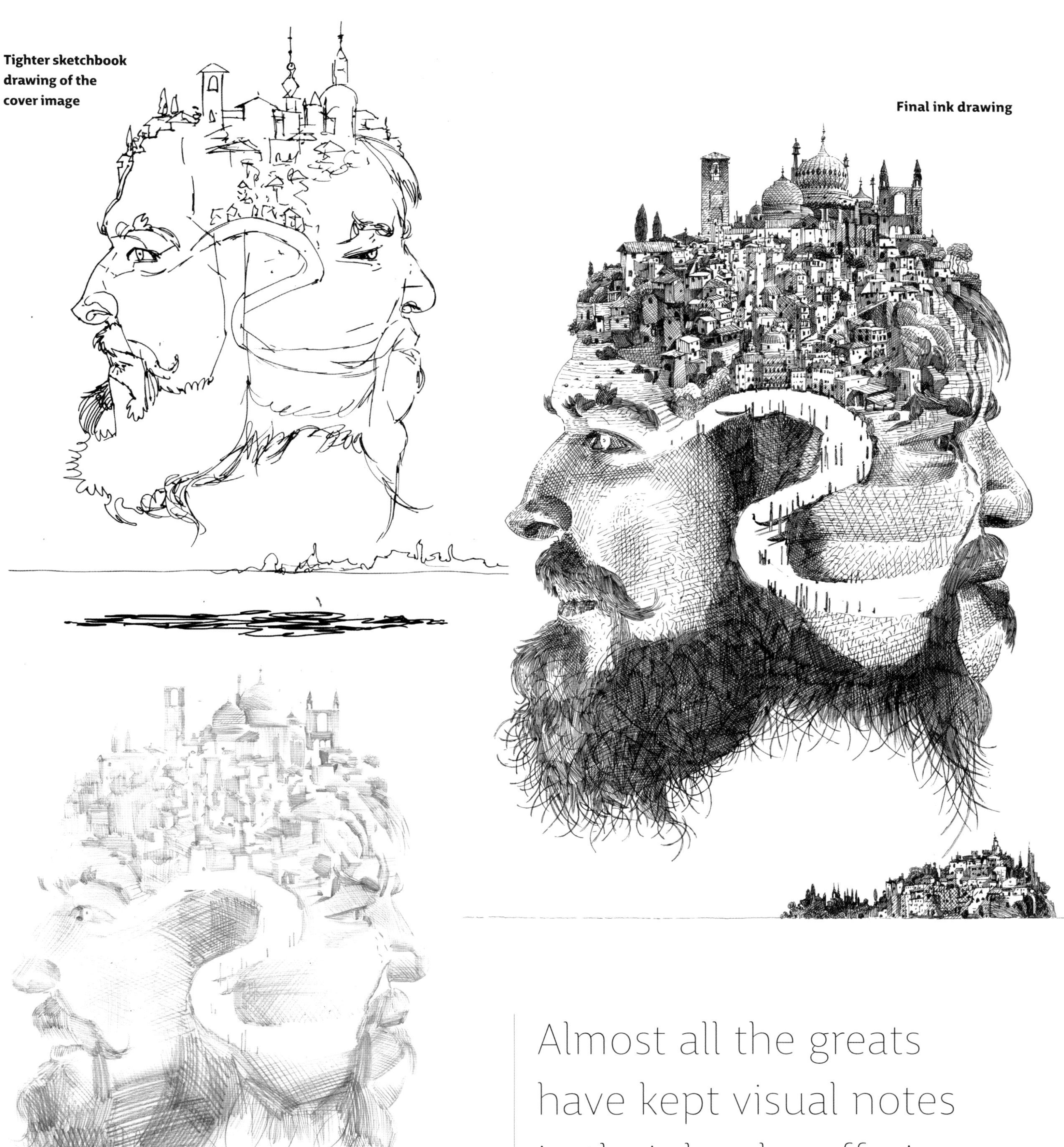

Tighter sketchbook drawing of the cover image

Final ink drawing

Pencil overlay image drawn on the back of the ink drawing

Almost all the greats have kept visual notes in their books, offering a tantalizing idea of how they think

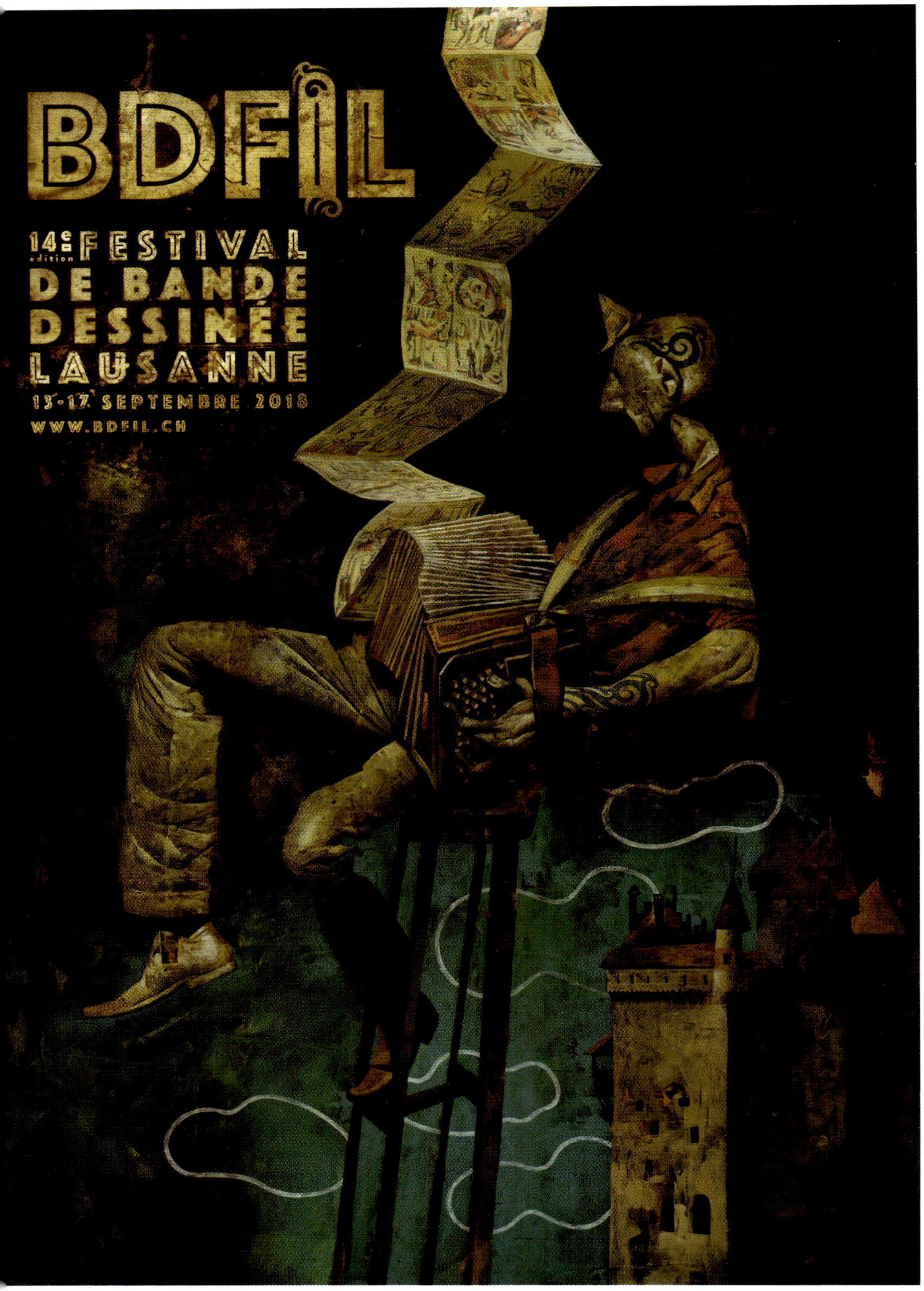

Lausanne BDFIL festival poster and catalogue cover

A poster for the comics festival in Lausanne, Switzerland. Lausanne is one of the world's great concert venues. One of my favourite composers, the nuevo tango bandoneon player Astor Piazzolla, recorded his seminal *The Lausanne Concert* there. So, tango and this Swiss town on Lake Geneva are linked in my mind. I got quite a long way down the road of a face-on clown image before deciding it was too busy. I started redrawing in my sketchbooks until I settled on this. It's sometimes useful to draw individual elements, and then bring them together in Photoshop, to push the conjunction of those elements to extremes. It can help to surprise yourself.

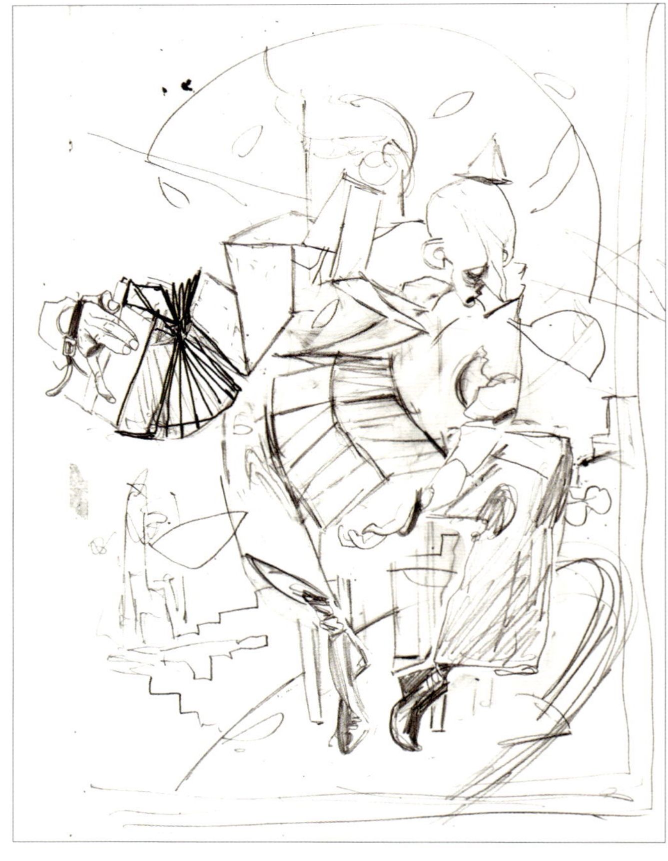

An initial idea for the figure; I redrew this several times before deciding it was all too fussy and I needed a simpler shape

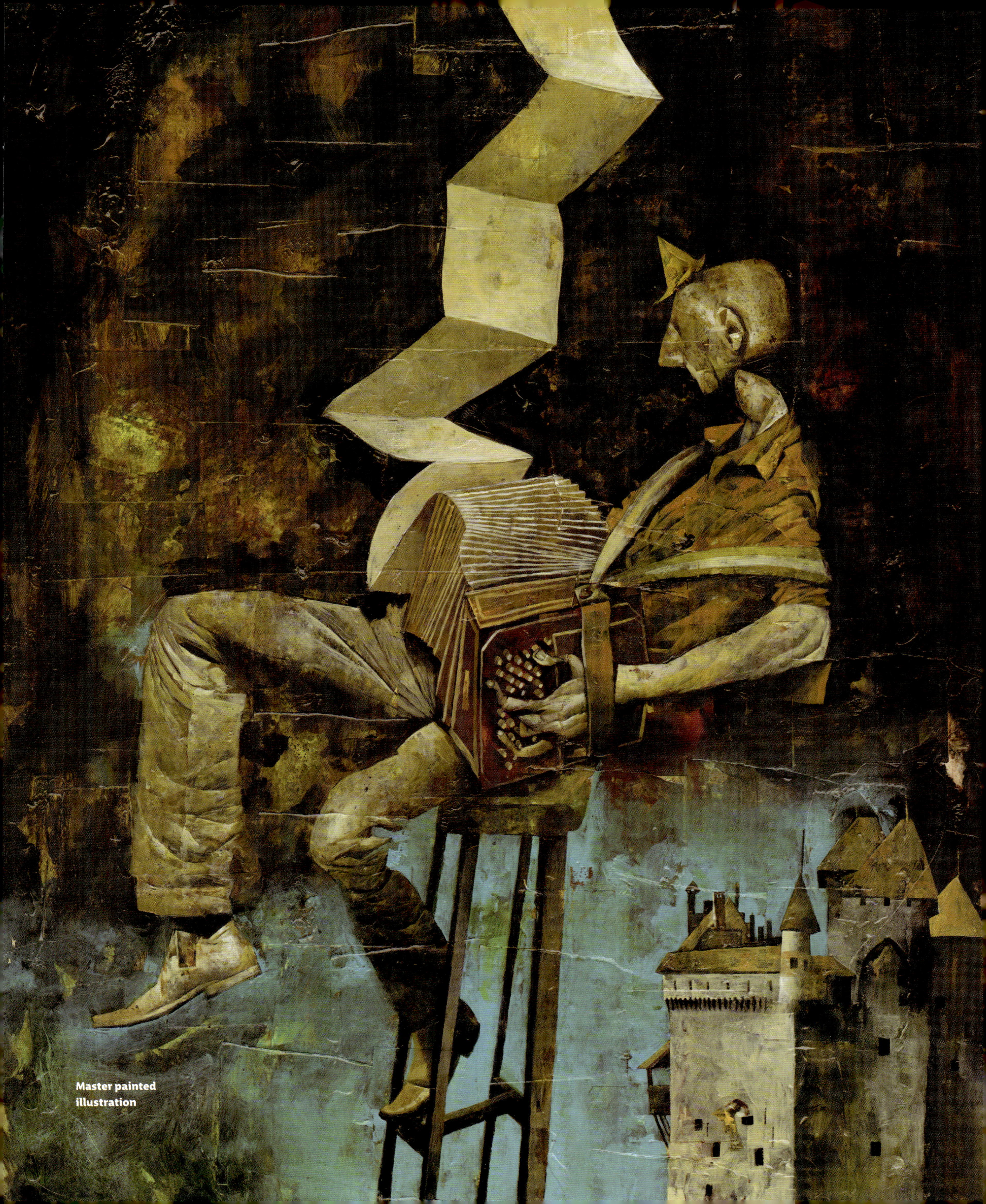

Master painted
illustration

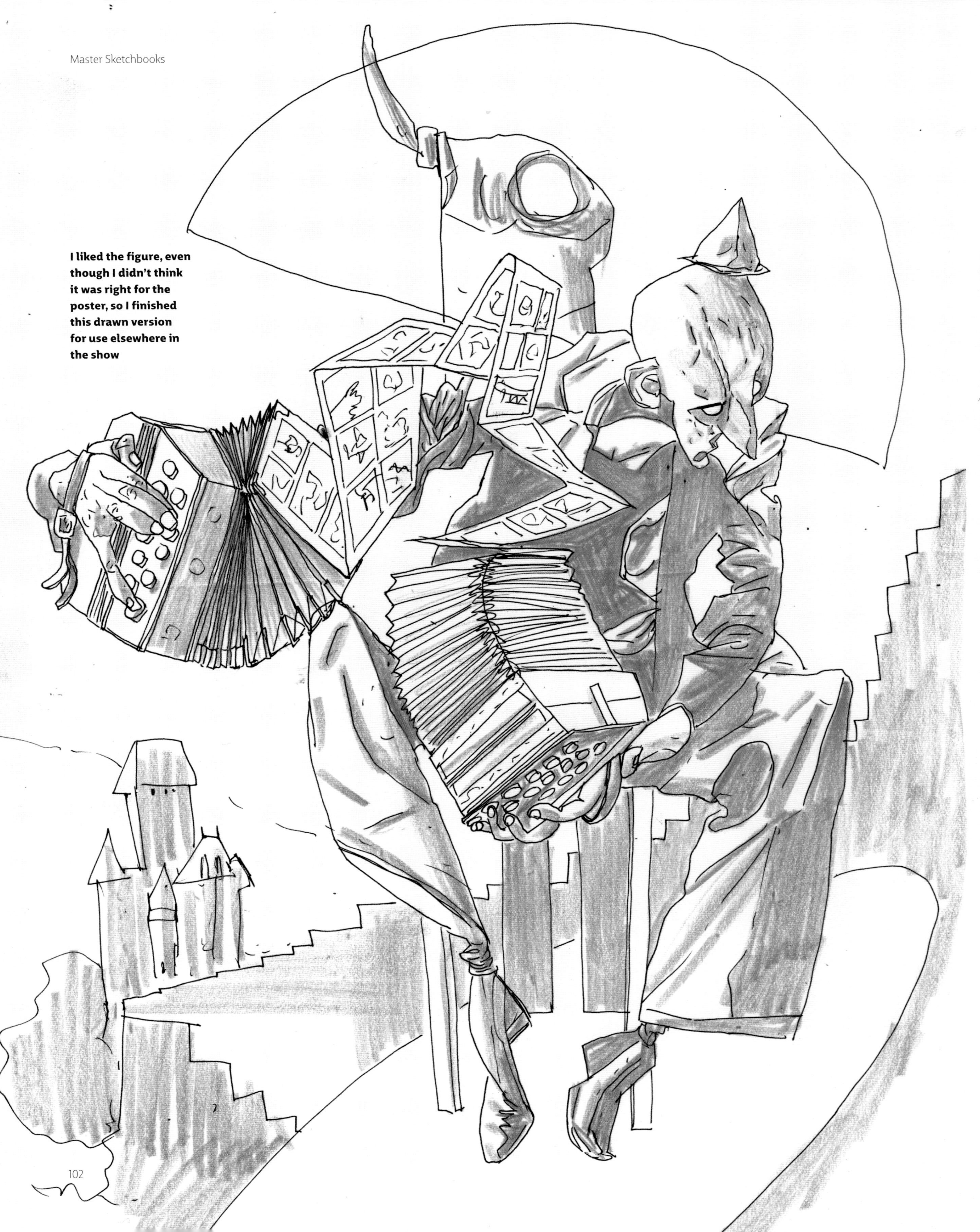

I liked the figure, even though I didn't think it was right for the poster, so I finished this drawn version for use elsewhere in the show

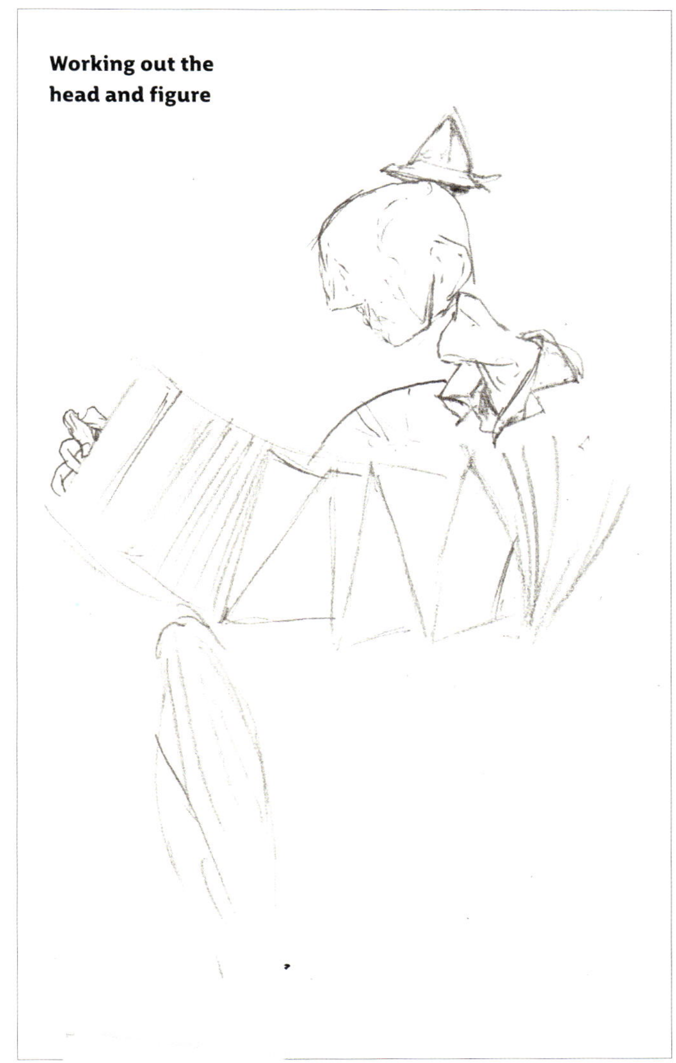

**Working out the
head and figure**

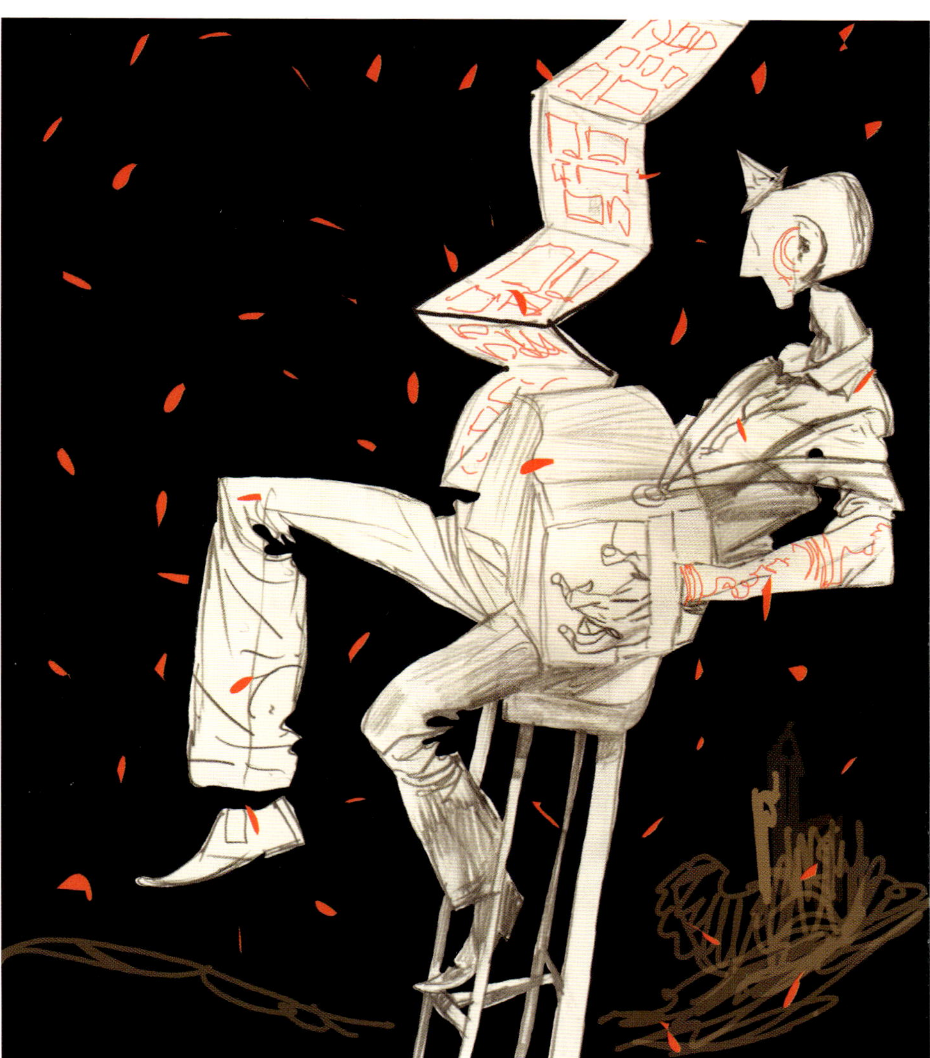

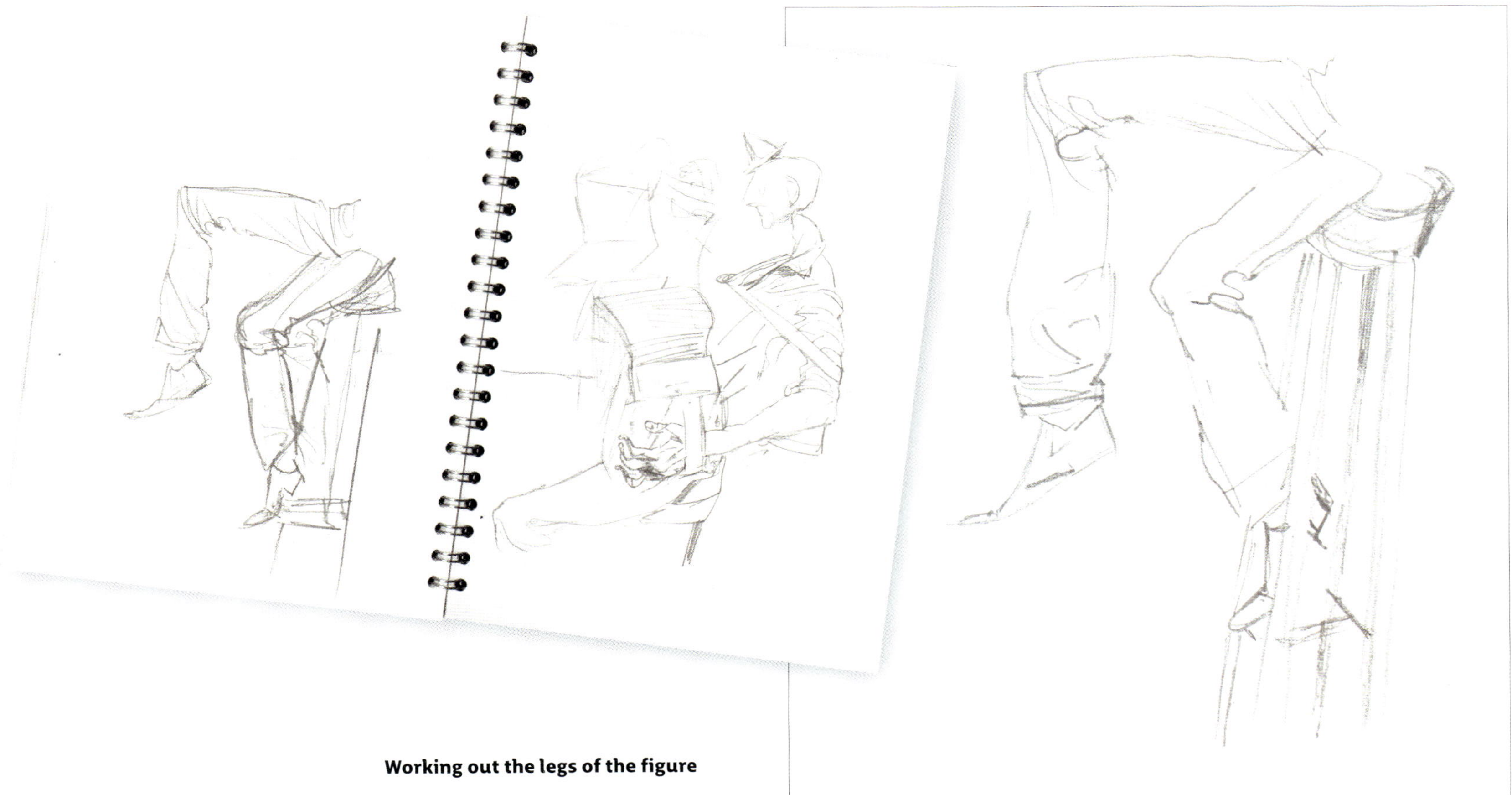

Working out the legs of the figure

Tyger by SF Said, book cover
David Fickling Books, 2022

This is my fourth book with SF Said. He takes several years to write each one – somewhere between ten and twenty drafts. During this process we keep in touch, and as the book draws close to completion, we start swapping ideas about imagery, styles, and other artists' work we like that could be appropriate.

As the story takes place in two worlds, I immediately thought how the tiger's stripes could represent that. Sitting in a concert hall, waiting for my wife's orchestra to play, I worked out the basic image of the tiger's face, with the white, black, and orange areas becoming textured landscapes, and the eye becoming the universe. It only took about twenty minutes to make note of this. I didn't have any other roughs or suggestions, but that was okay as everyone immediately liked this idea. This is the advantage of dealing directly with one author and one editor. The current system of marketing departments running the art direction of publishing has ruined the standard and variety of book covers.

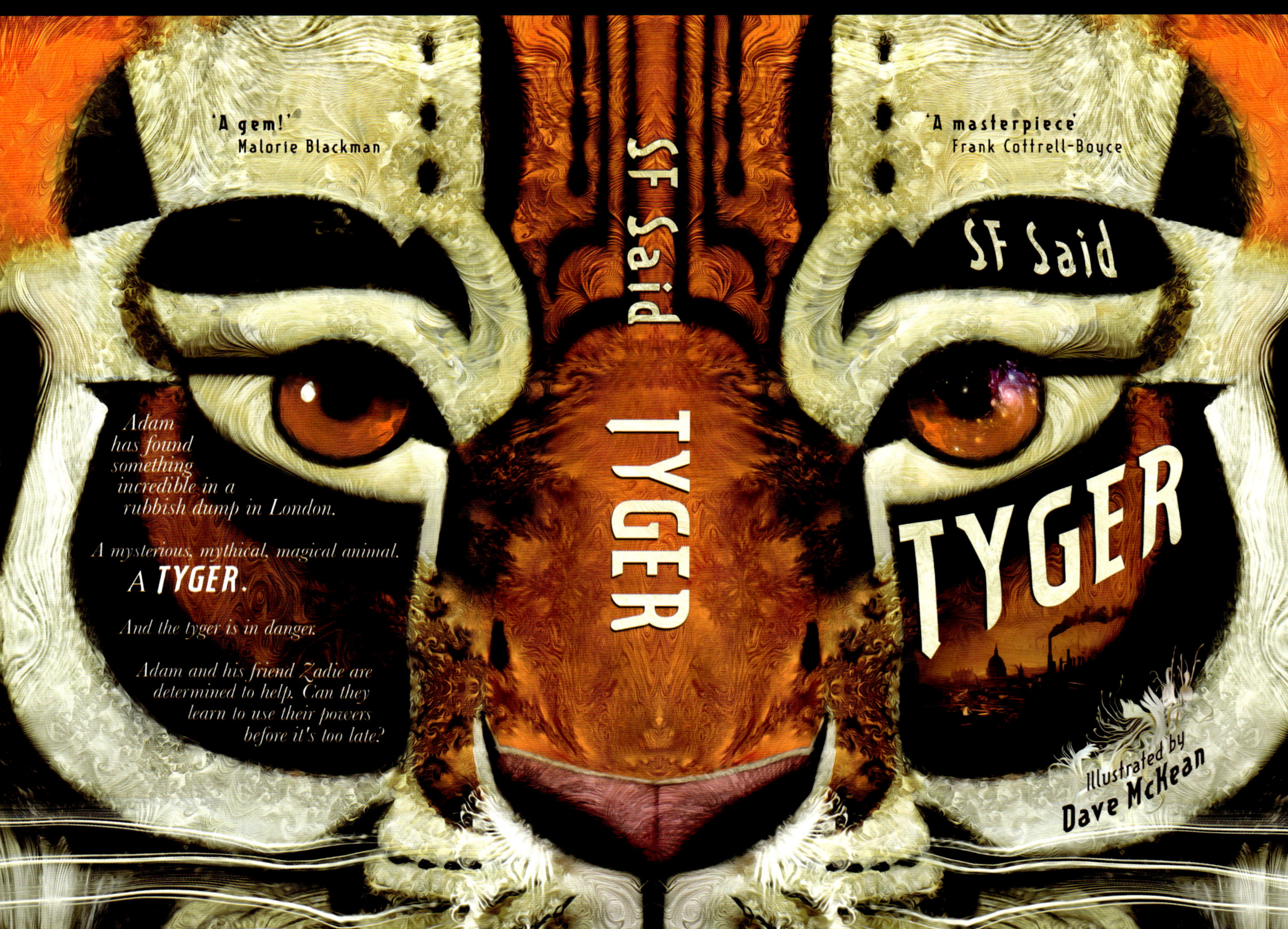

Final artwork

Dave McKean

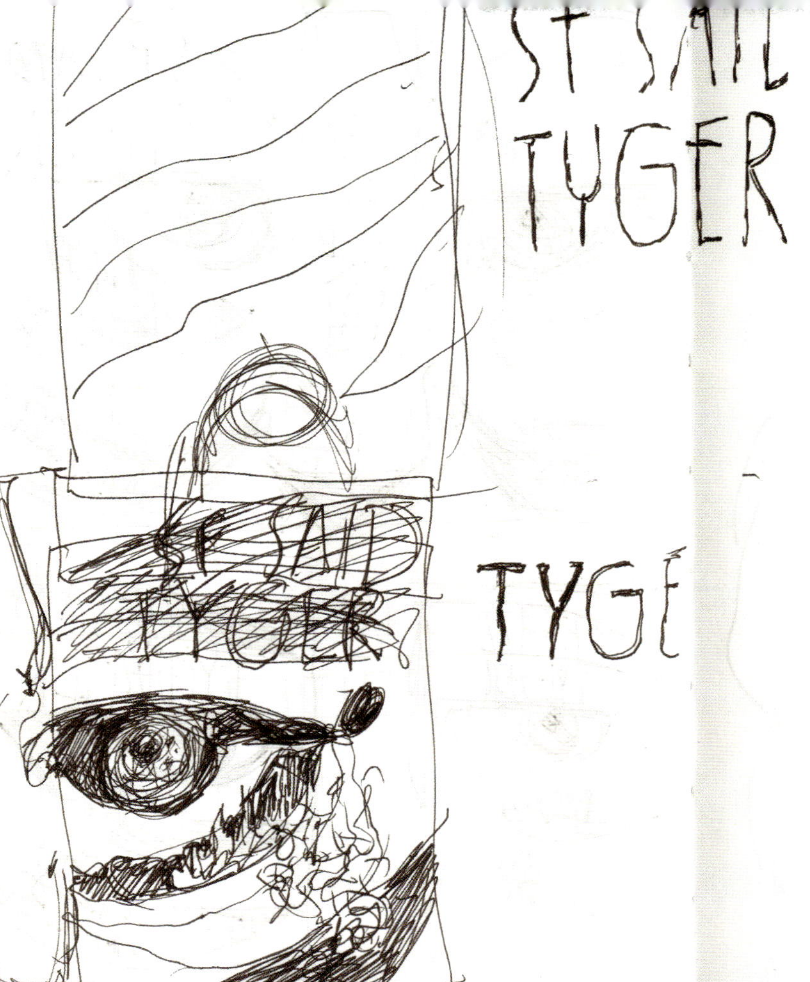

**First idea
noted in my
sketchbook**

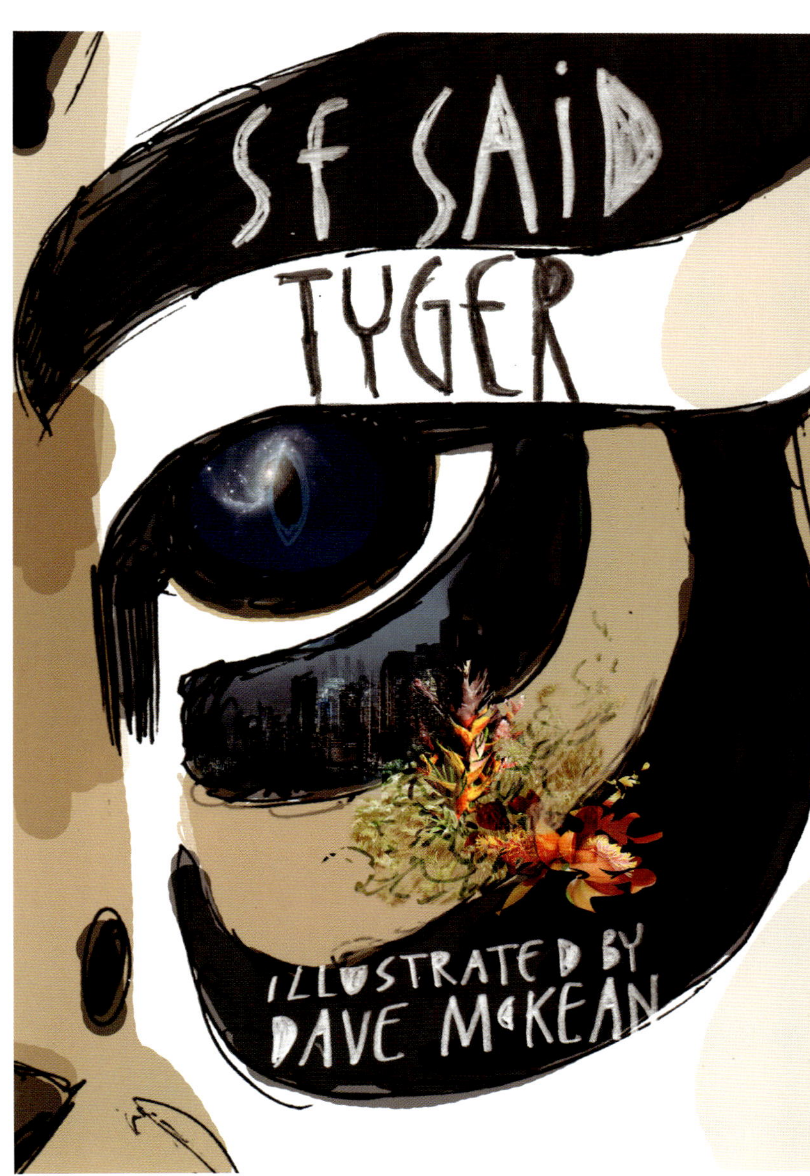

Colour rough

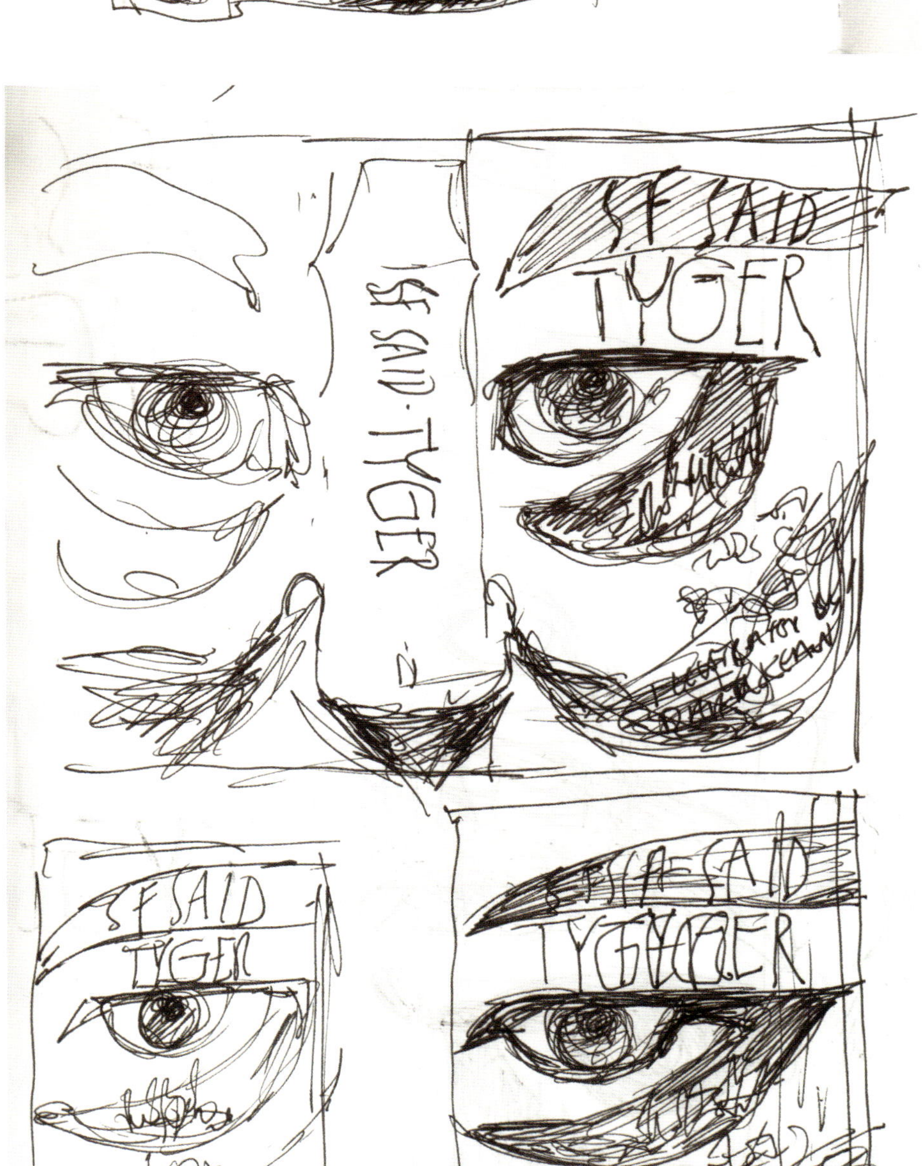

**Working on balance
of composition in
my sketchbook**

SHAPES, COMPOSITIONS & VISUAL IDEAS

I started keeping a sketchbook much more thoroughly in art school because the process of the work completed there was as important as the final piece. That's really where the creativity is: the journey, the trying different paths, the testing yourself. It is what is completely absent from the AI experience. I don't think of the sketchbook as the finished work in any sense – they are just part of the process of developing ideas. Projects jump around between books, or even loose paper. They are stepping stones, rather than telling a full story.

I mostly use sketchbooks for working out ideas and capturing trains of thought. I constantly make little calendar notes and plans. I jot down story notes, often with images attached. The start of a project usually involves a lot of reading and thinking, so my sketchbooks are the place where I try to put all that information into shapes, compositions, and visual ideas.

I don't like doing roughs, and certainly not pitching lots of ideas. I tend to focus down on one image very quickly and refine that to the point that I'm clear it's a good, hopefully the best, way of tackling that problem. You won't find hundreds of thumbnail workings out in my books, just a bit of compositional refinement, and then drawing and redrawing the main elements to find the best shapes.

Being free with my ideas is definitely part of the process of mulling over possibilities in doodles on paper. It is the most natural way for me to think. My travel sketchbooks have been a way of responding to what's around me, with no expectations. I've found new lines, marks, shapes, ways of thinking and drawing. Those little sketchbooks have probably taught me the most over the years, and I've taken those lessons on to much bigger jobs.

Keeping a sketchbook is like keeping a diary. I can remember instantly where I was when I made a drawing and what music I was listening to at the time. When you draw, you pay attention, and all that metadata is somehow part of the ink on the page. When I'm travelling, I use sketchbooks to make drawings as a record of each place. Many of these I've published in my *Postcard from…* series of travel notebooks. But I spend so much of my time drawing, I tend not to do too much of this when I'm taking a break on holiday.

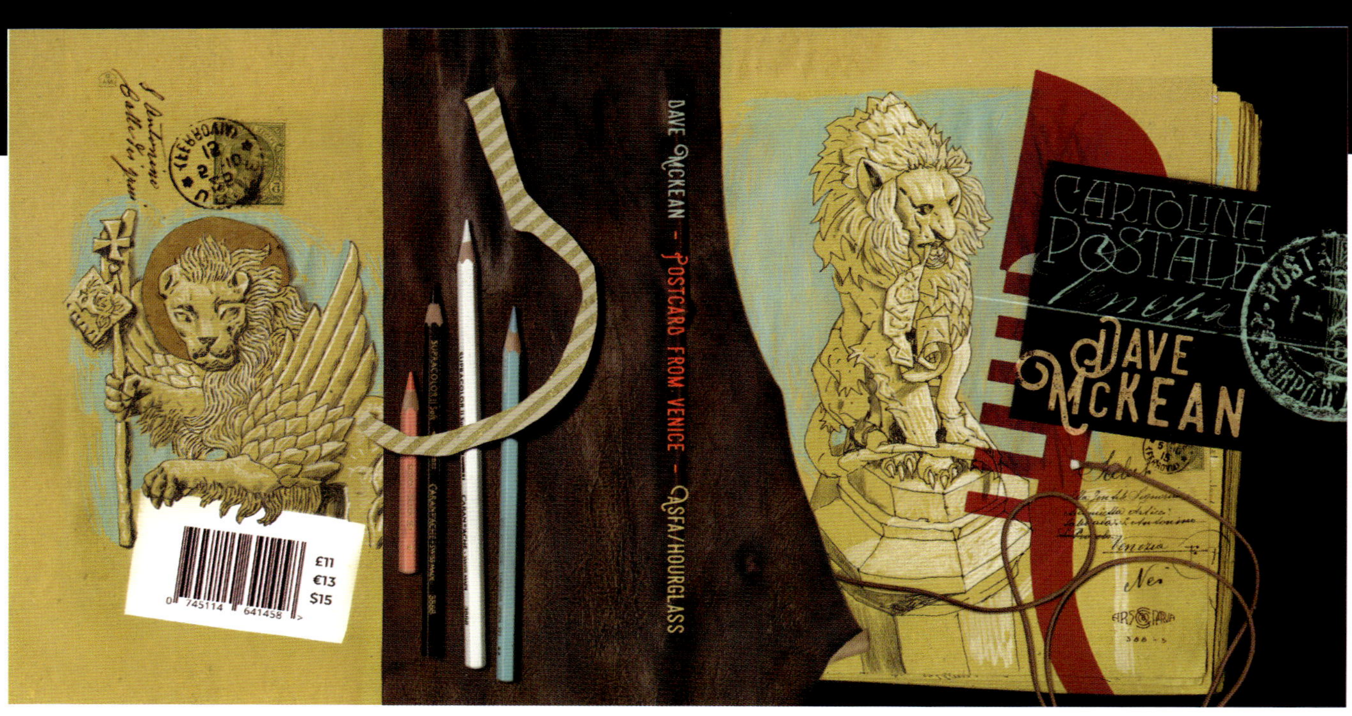

Final artwork for the cover made from two sketches, a photograph of the sketchbook cover, and pencils

***Postcard from Venice* book**
Hourglass, 2018

I've always carried a sketchbook around with me on my travels – a habit begun in art school. I mostly use them for making notes when ideas occur, working ideas out, planning my time, and capturing quick sketches of people and places. When on holiday in Vienna with my family, I bought us all little sketchbooks so we could make drawings based on our favourite Gustav Klimt and Egon Schiele paintings, along with whatever else we found. It meant that my kids remembered everything. When you draw, you really pay attention in a way you just don't when snapping a photo.

I started to publish my city sketchbooks, of which Vienna was the first. They usually comprise a percentage of drawings created during the visit, and then a few more considered drawings made at home based off photographs I took. I've learned a lot from creating these little books. Venice is my favourite city, so it was very hard to do her justice in fifty-six pages.

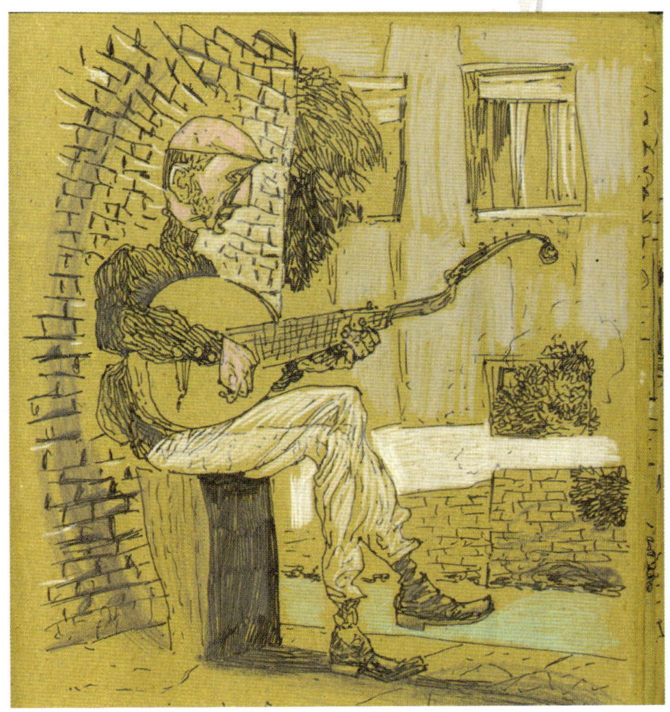

**Watercolour sketchbook: ink
and water sketches to try to
express the watery, ethereal
atmosphere of Venice**

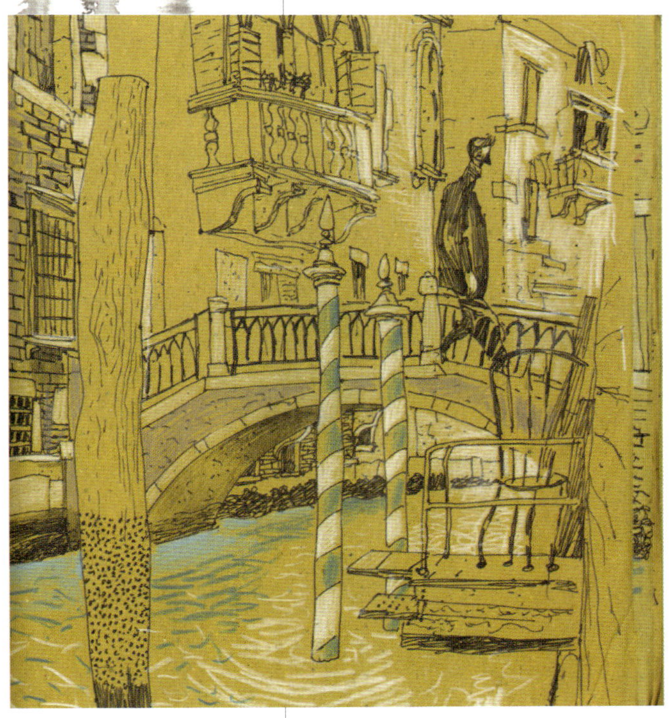

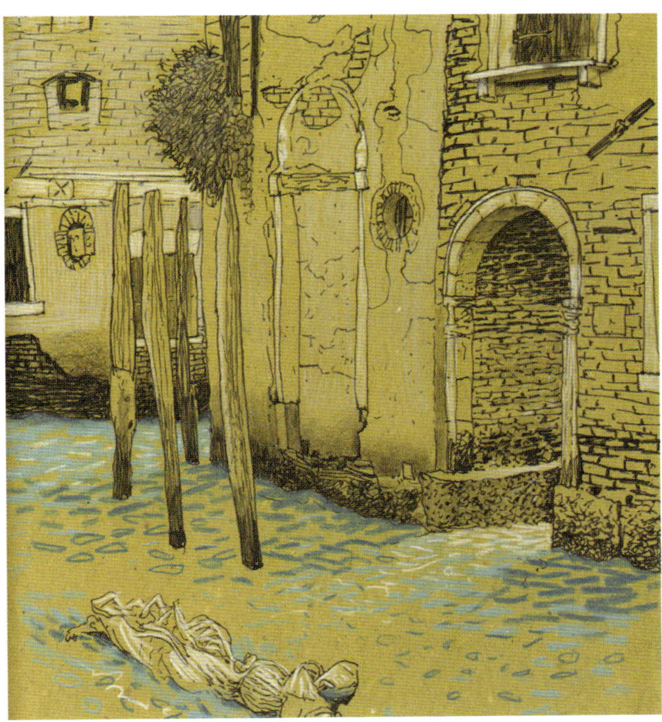

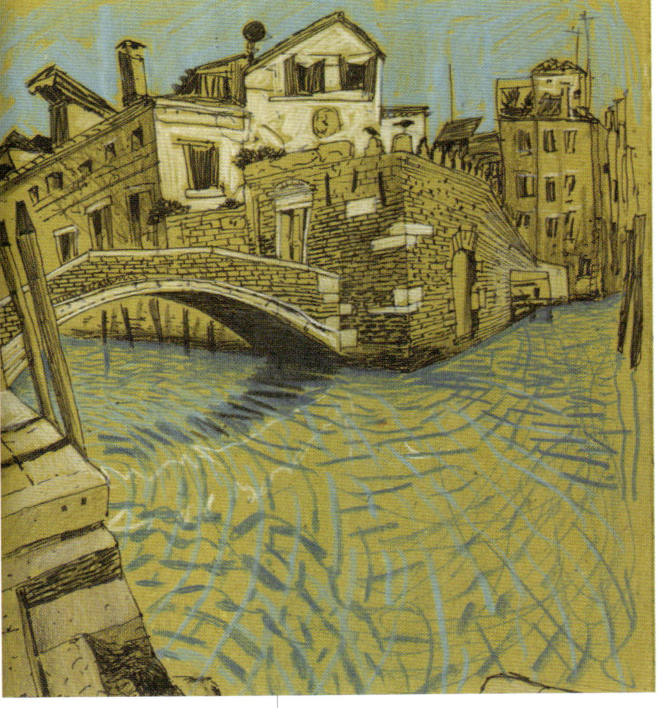

**Ink and coloured-pencil
sketches on brown paper**

COMMITTING SOMETHING TO PAPER

I don't have dedicated sketchbooks for different projects. Instead, I have small 15 × 15cm sketchbooks for working out ideas, and then larger 30 × 23 cm sketchbooks for developing tight drawings. All of my sketchbooks contain a mixture of text notation and diary workouts, through to finished drawings and paintings. I opt for hardback ring-bound sketchbooks, as these provide a flat surface when drawing. I prefer cartridge paper, although I do like watercolour and textured papers, and recently I've been drawing with white and grey off-black paper. I typically use black pen or pencil in my sketchbooks, as I'm just working out the basic ideas and compositional shapes. When drawing while travelling, however, I've used everything from paint and pastel to cut paper and stencils, mechanical devices, photographic elements, writing, bits of scrap material ... anything.

I like the uneven lines and angles created when using pen or pencil on paper, and how the speed of drawing represents the speed at which I can think. I like the phrase: committing something to paper. It feels positive and assertive, rather than an endlessly 'undo-able', 'save-able' digital space. I like that I can take a sketchbook on a train, to a beach, or on a walk in the woods. It can be a finished drawing, the simplest of notations, or even just text notes. It's a record of thought. Sketchbooks capture fleeting moments. Ideas, like dreams, can evaporate, but they are preserved in ink on paper.

I keep three digital archives of everything. The physical work is a mix. A lot of it sold at galleries and conventions. I keep examples of every project in my own archive. Some of it is framed, while other pieces are in job bags in plan chests. I've had to rescue some of it from mice, but we now have a very reliable trap.

Crime and Punishment by Fyodor Dostoevsky, book and slipcase cover
Beehive Books, 2020

I was given the chance to illustrate any classic book that was over 100 years old. I chose *Crime and Punishment* because of its exploration of the value of human life and, unlike many perennials, it has not been illustrated very often. It examines whether moral behaviour comes from within or from above, and if there isn't an above, how do we know what is moral, which seemed crucial to our time. Every moment in the book provoked ideas for illustrations, so I ended up creating many more drawings than the eight or so paintings the publisher asked for. The book also seemed to me to be bound to the history of early film; the expressionist era that I love so much. *Raskolnikov* is an early Robert Wiene film and one of only a handful of genuinely expressionistic films made in Germany in the 1920s. I wanted to evoke that era and push the idea of creating a psychological space of painted sets, distorted windows, and exaggerated perspective and proportions.

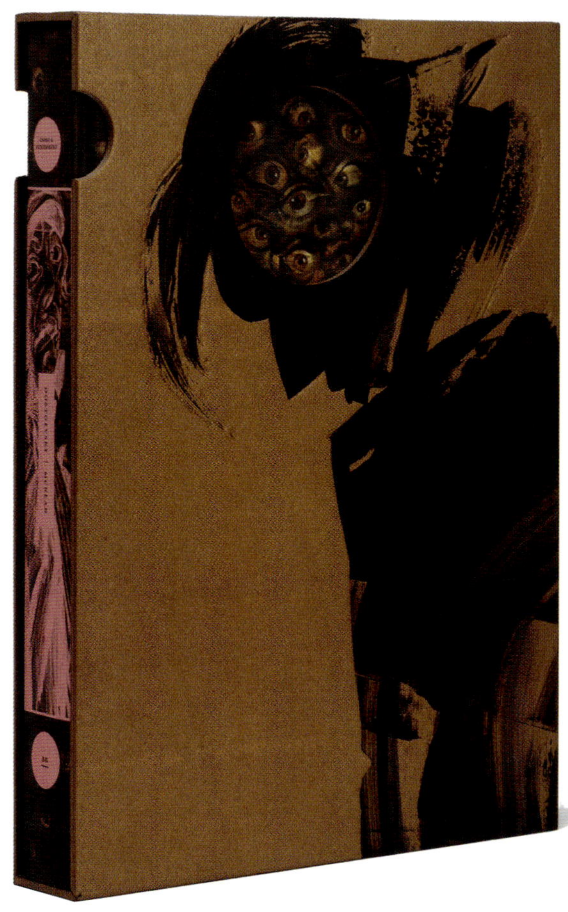

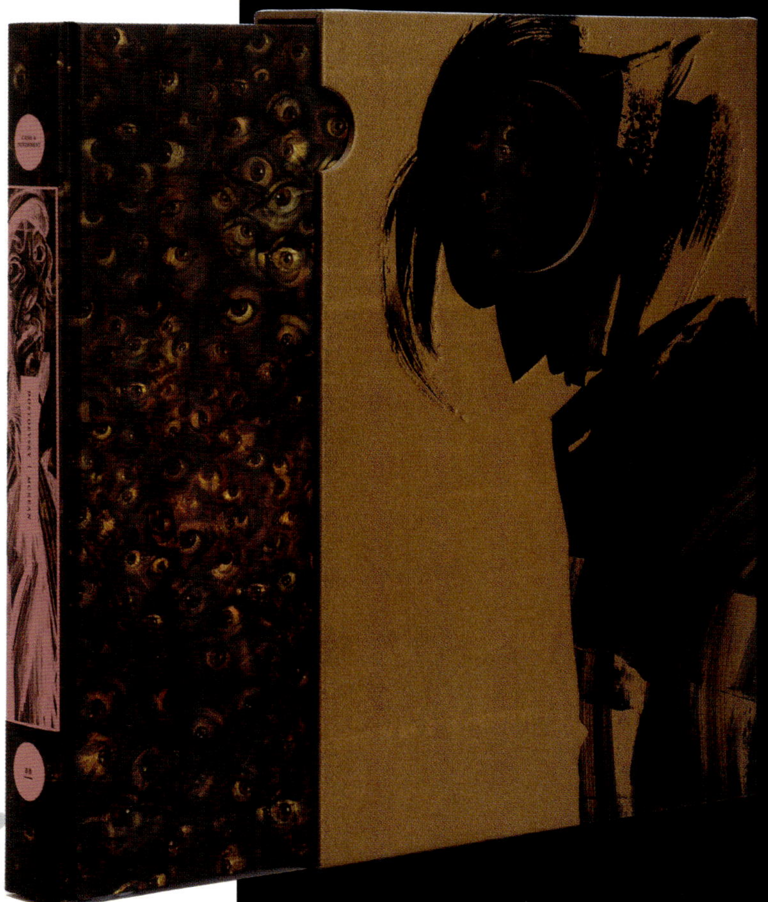

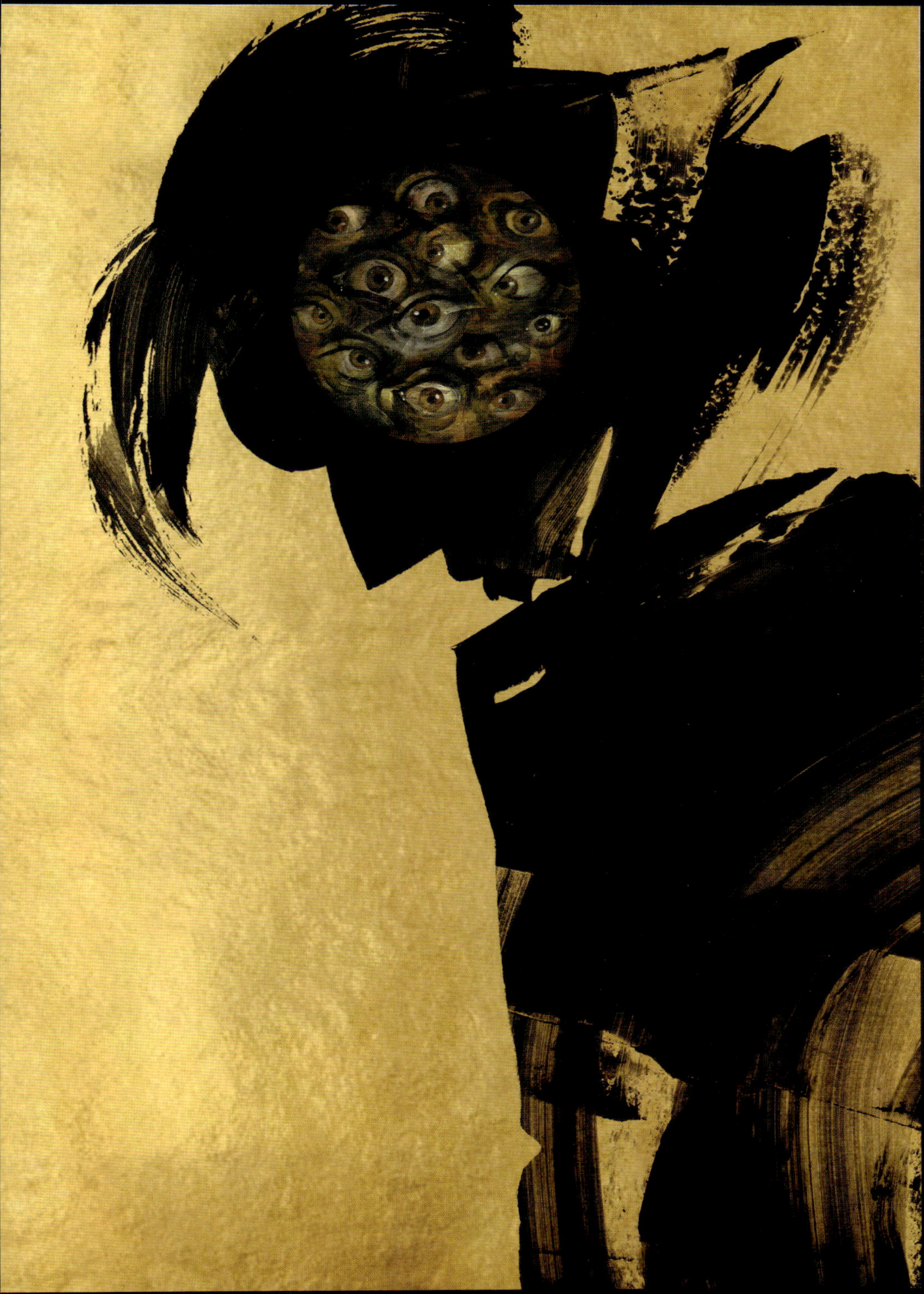

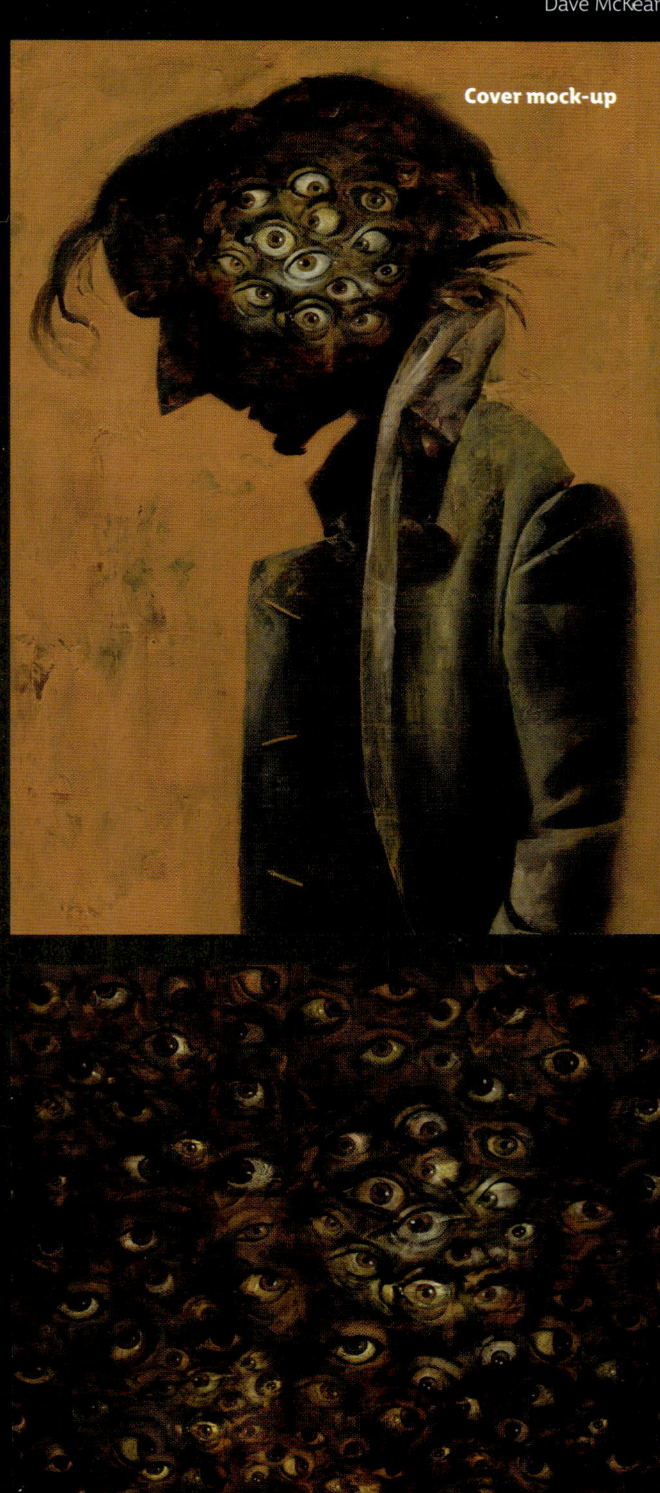

Slipcase and book final composite, with the eyes image visible in the circle die-cut of the slipcase

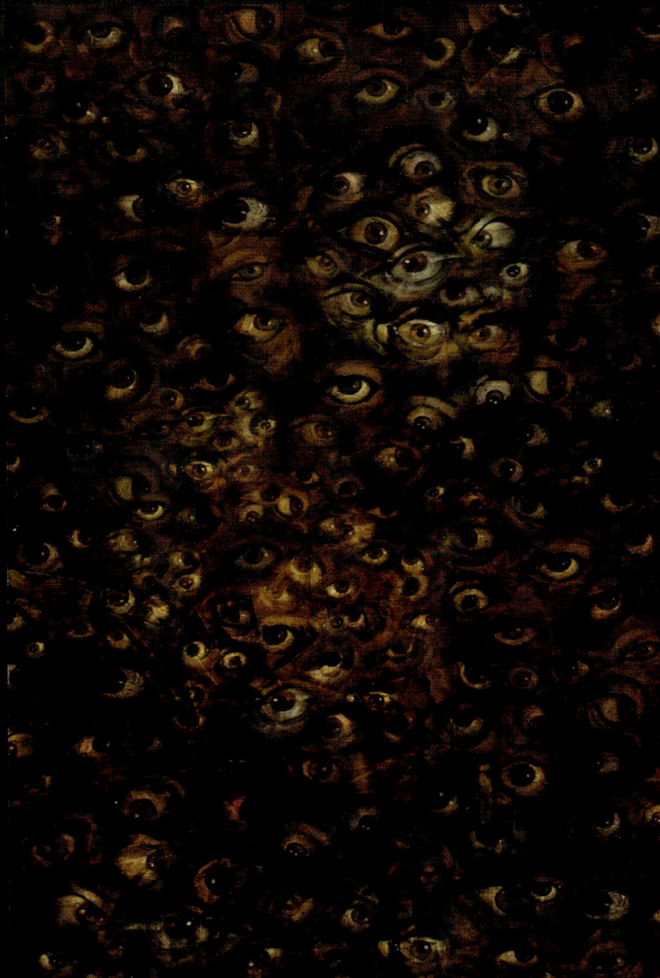

A painted version

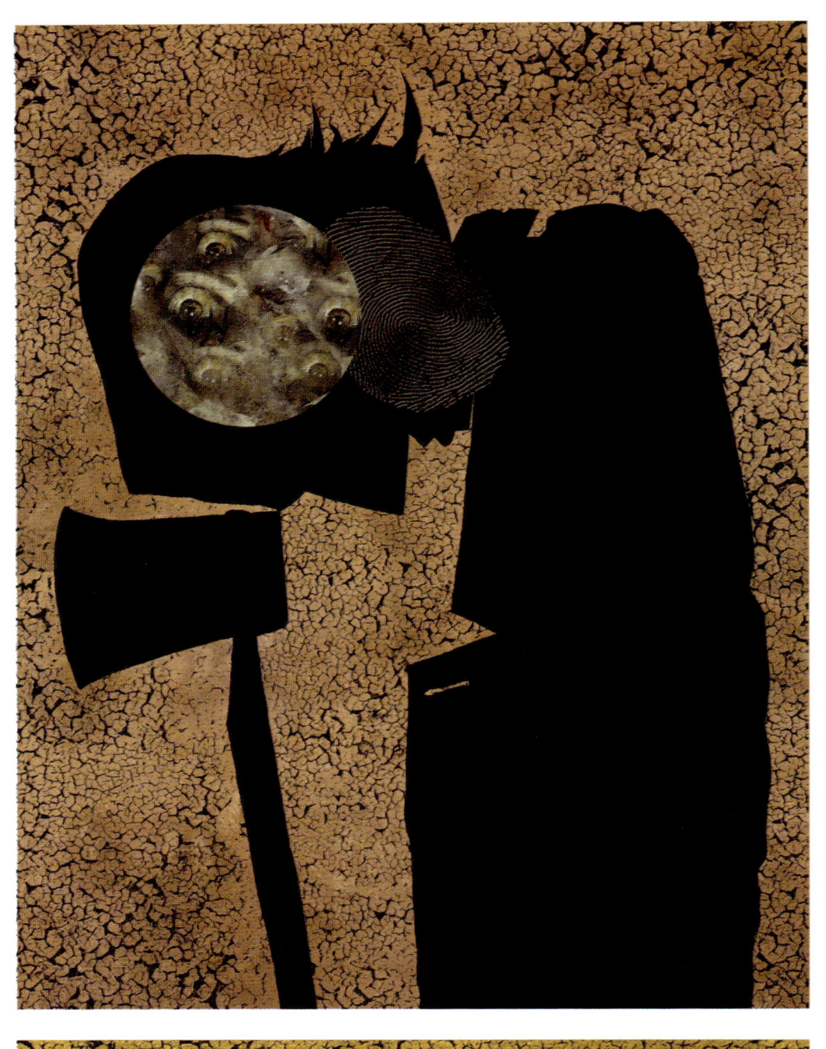

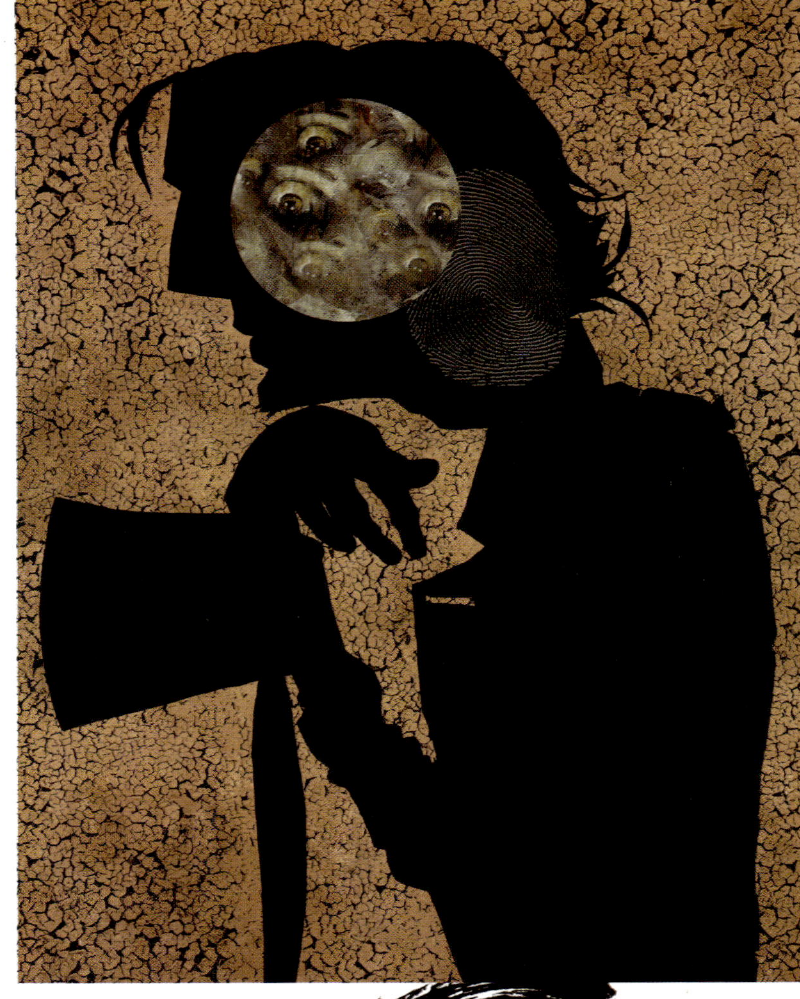

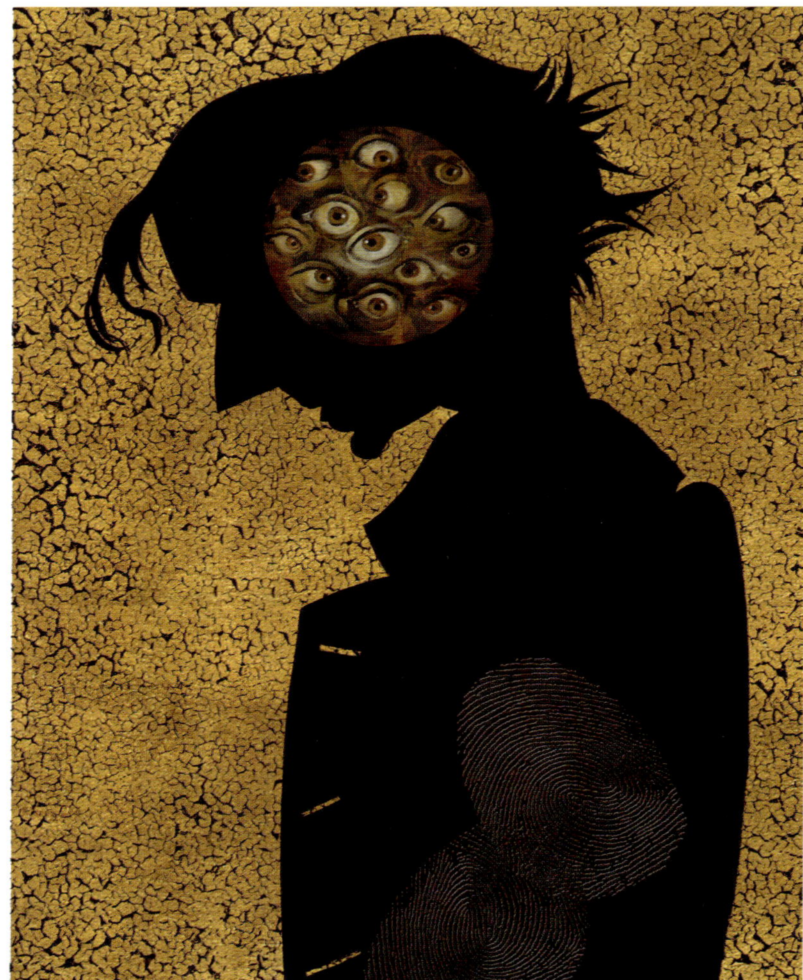

Cover visuals trying out additional elements

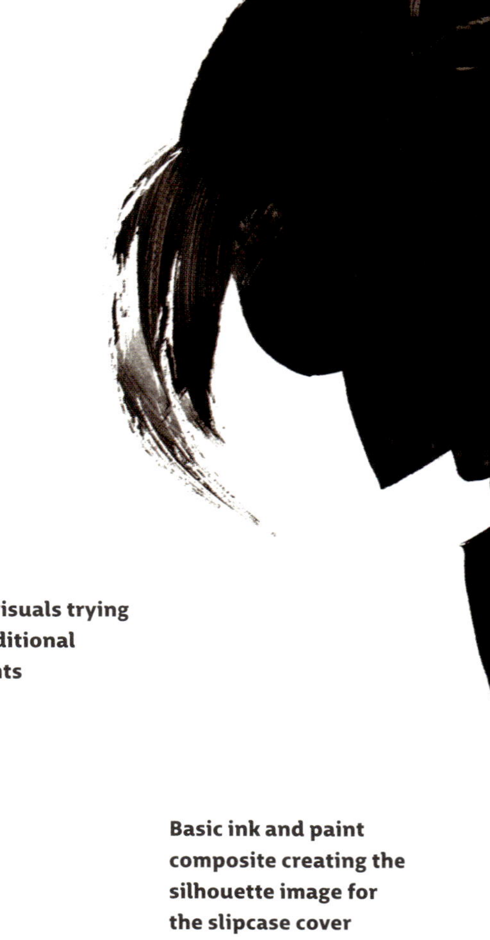

Basic ink and paint composite creating the silhouette image for the slipcase cover

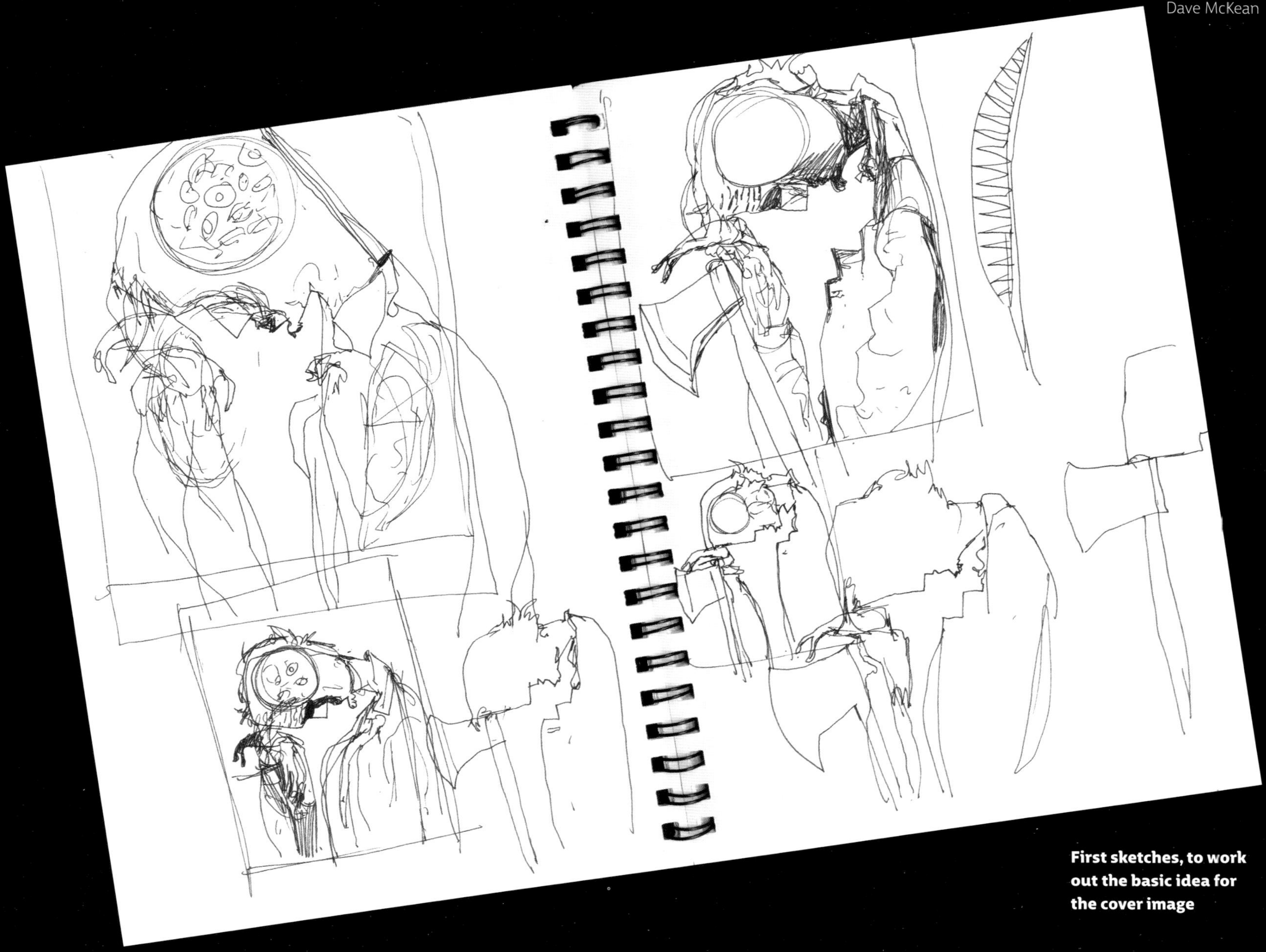

Dave McKean

**First sketches, to work
out the basic idea for
the cover image**

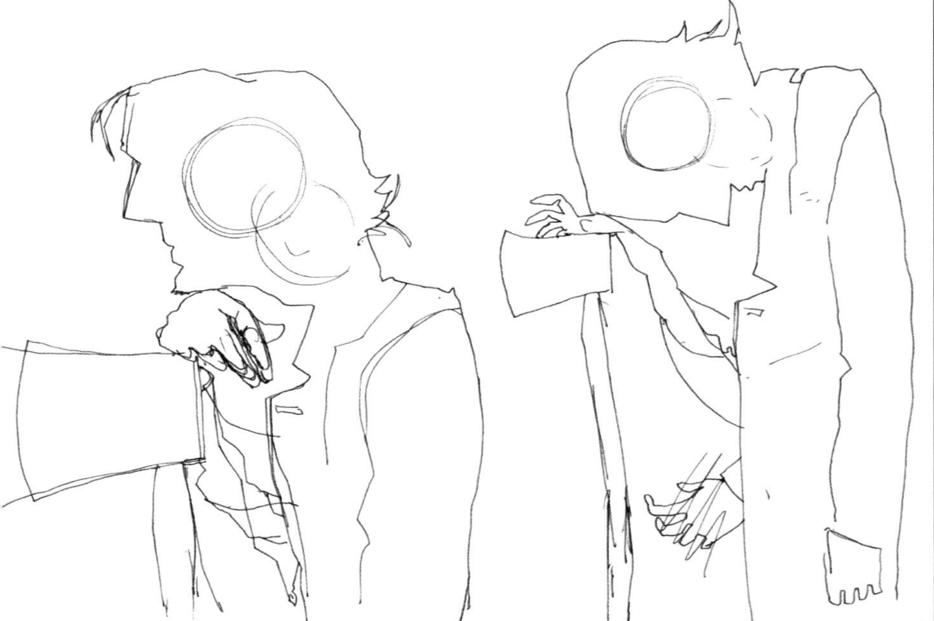

**Sketches trying out different versions of the
silhouette figure on the slipcase**

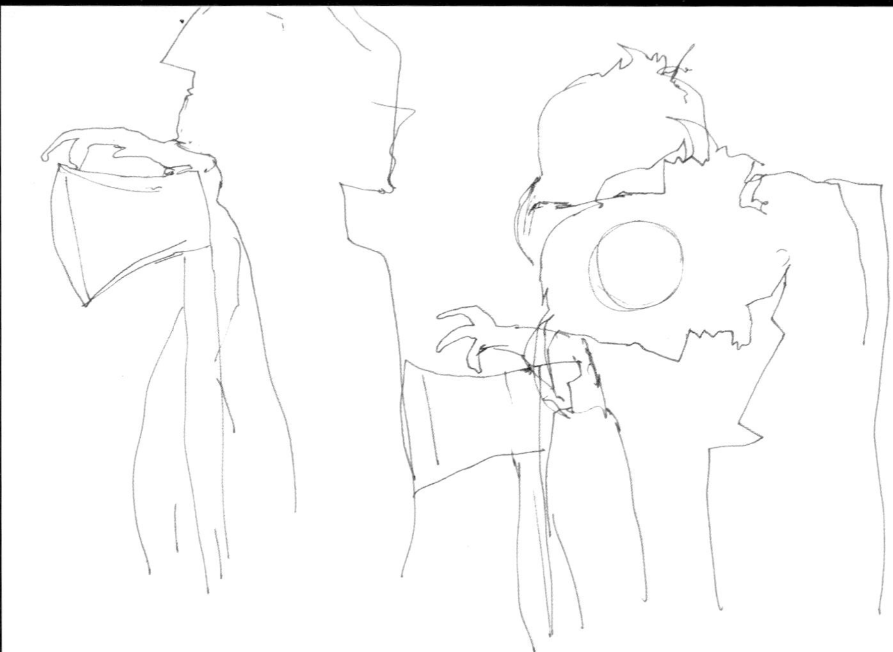

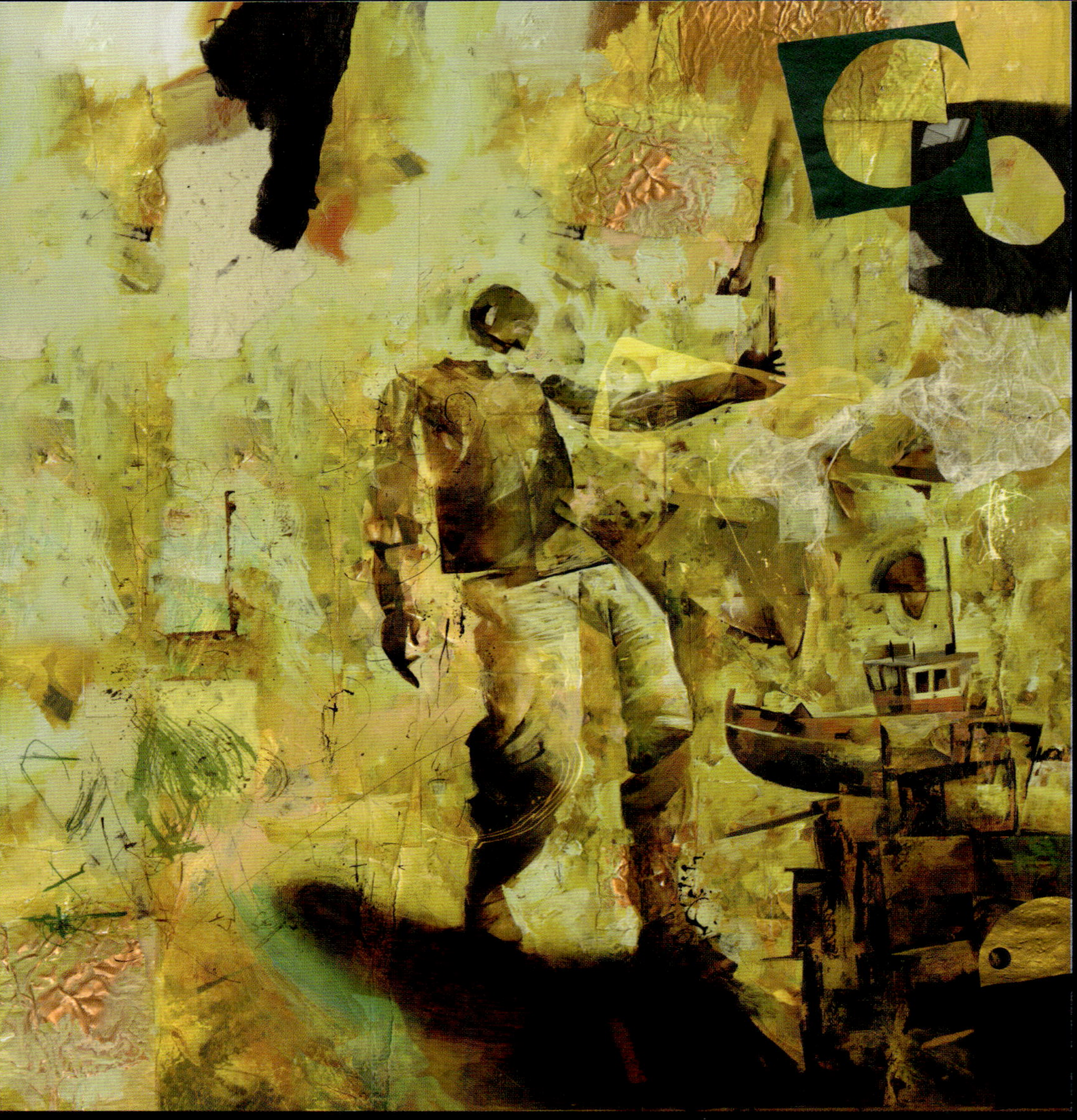

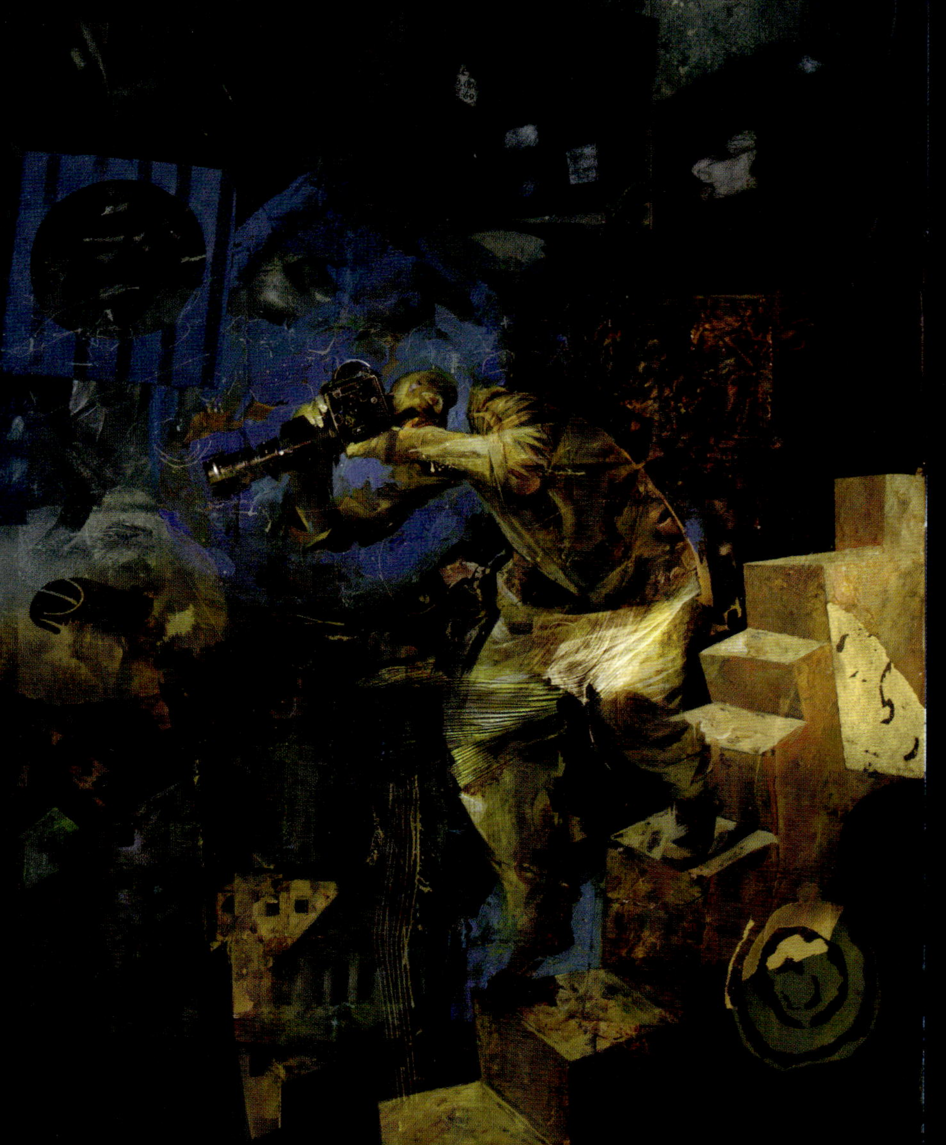

**Thalamus: The Art of Dave McKean,
two-volume set, covers**
Dark Horse Books, 2023

During the 2020 COVID-19 lockdown, I started working
on a retrospective book covering all the work I've
created over the past thirty-five years. It soon became
much bigger than the publishers initially suggested,
ending up totalling 600 pages over two slipcased
volumes. I wanted to create new images for the covers,
but trying to find something that would represent
everything in the book only led to countless little
doodles in my notebooks of possible ideas. In the end
it seemed impossible, so, since almost all my work is
about people and storytelling, I simply focused on
making an artwork of figures creating.

Most of my workings out from that point onwards
were about trying to find an expressive figure.
Something happens when you draw and redraw the
same thing over and over – you start to leave literal
accuracy behind and get to know the inner tensions
and shapes of the figure. It becomes more expressive.

Working out the figure in my sketchbook

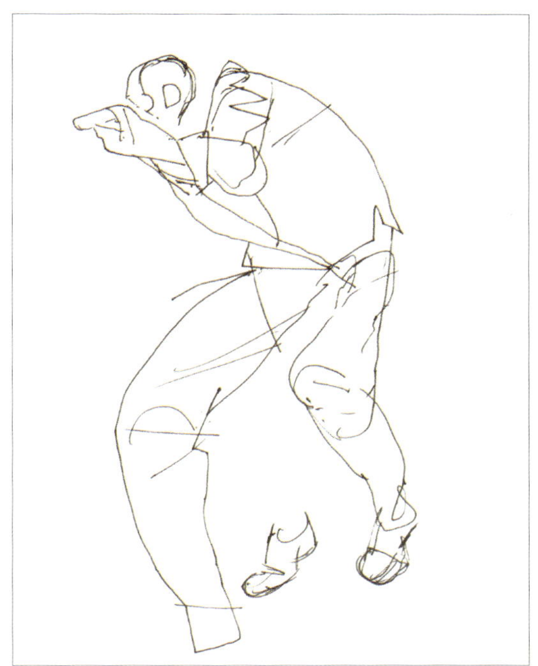

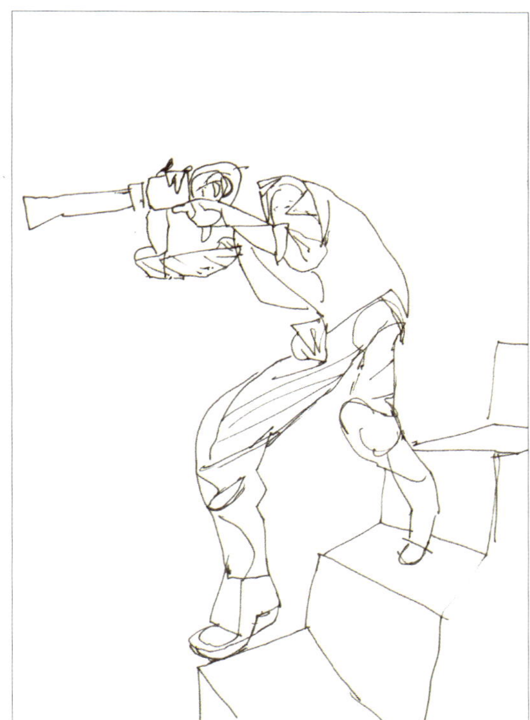

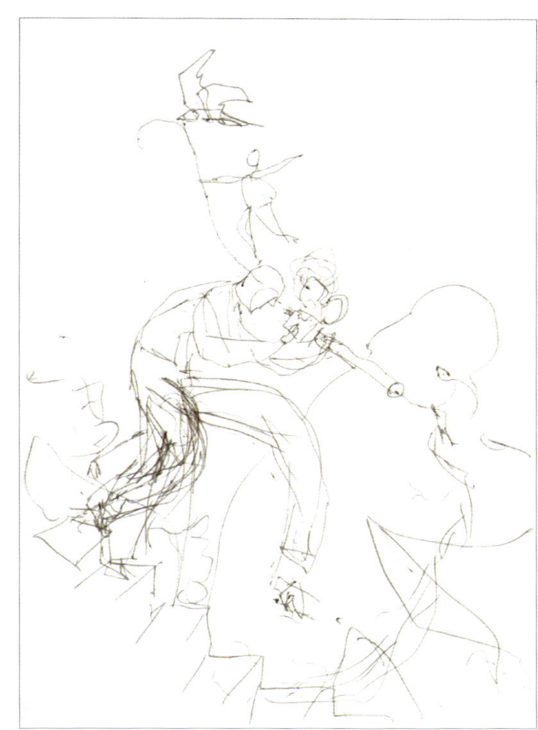

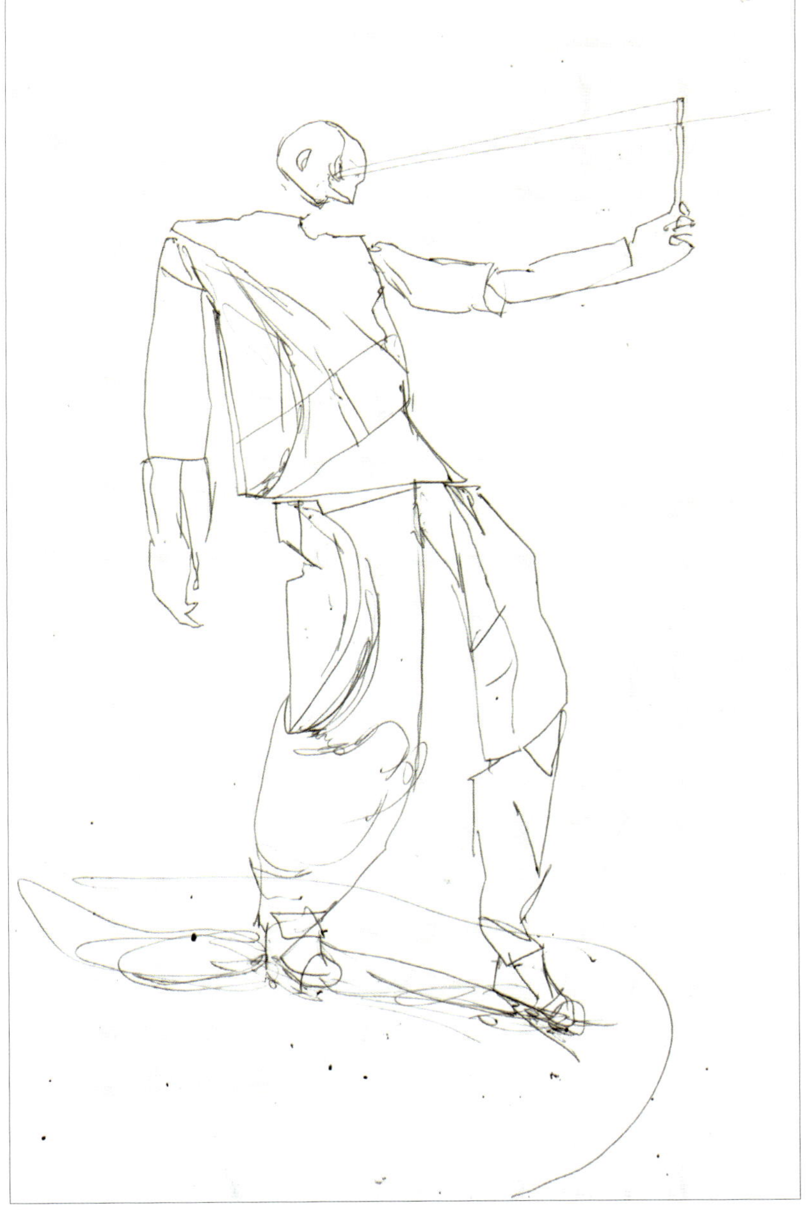

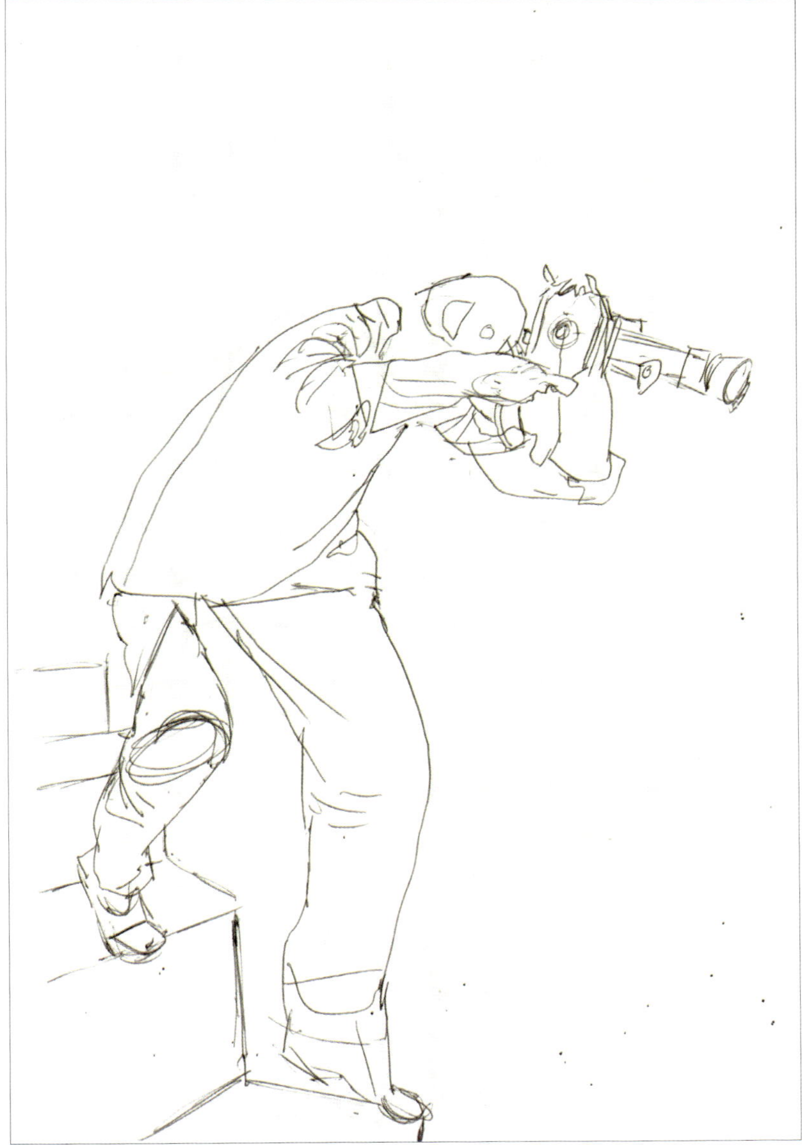

Tighter drawings of the figures

PRIORITIZE YOUR OWN WORK

It's very hard to give advice. The world has changed so much. I've lived through the transition from analogue to digital. The internet has completely transformed the creator's relationship with their audience. AI has not threatened to change the definition of creativity and art, so it's down to the current generation to work out their own ethical framework and just how far down the antisocial-media rabbit hole they want to travel. I think the only advice I've ever given that still holds, now more than ever maybe, is to prioritize your own work. It's very easy to get trapped on a hamster wheel of professional deadlines, meaning your own personal work slips down the schedule. It's much more important to prioritize that work; it's the only work that will really represent you and your view of the world, and on reflection, it will probably be the only work that really means anything to you in the end.

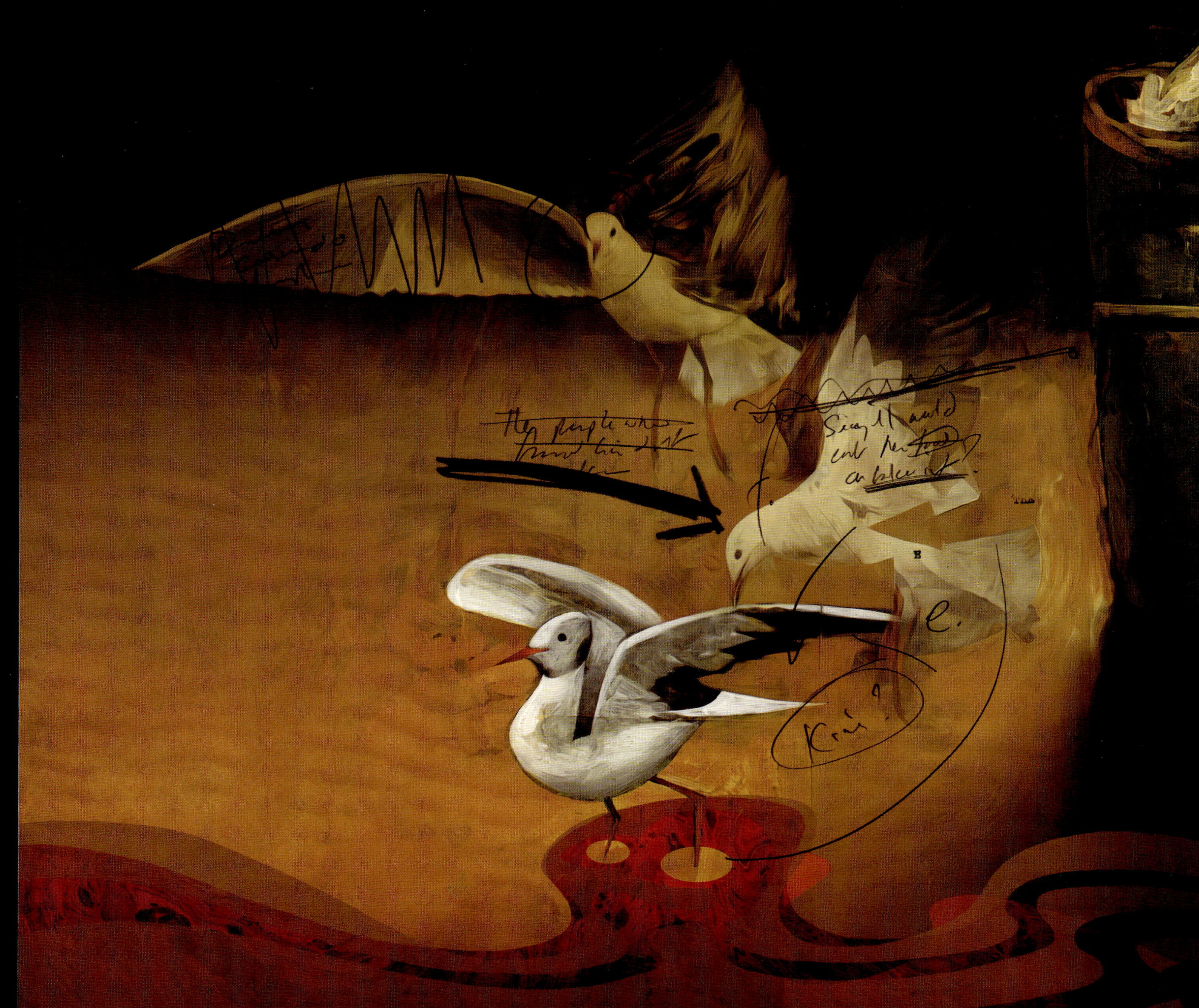

Colorado Kid by Stephen King, book and slipcase cover
PS Publishing, 2018

This Stephen King novella follows an investigation into the body of
an unidentified man found on a tiny island off the coast of Maine.
The idea of investigators taking notes, connecting events and
evidence, and circling clues became part of the imagery throughout,
as if the illustration elements were part of the process of piecing the
details together.

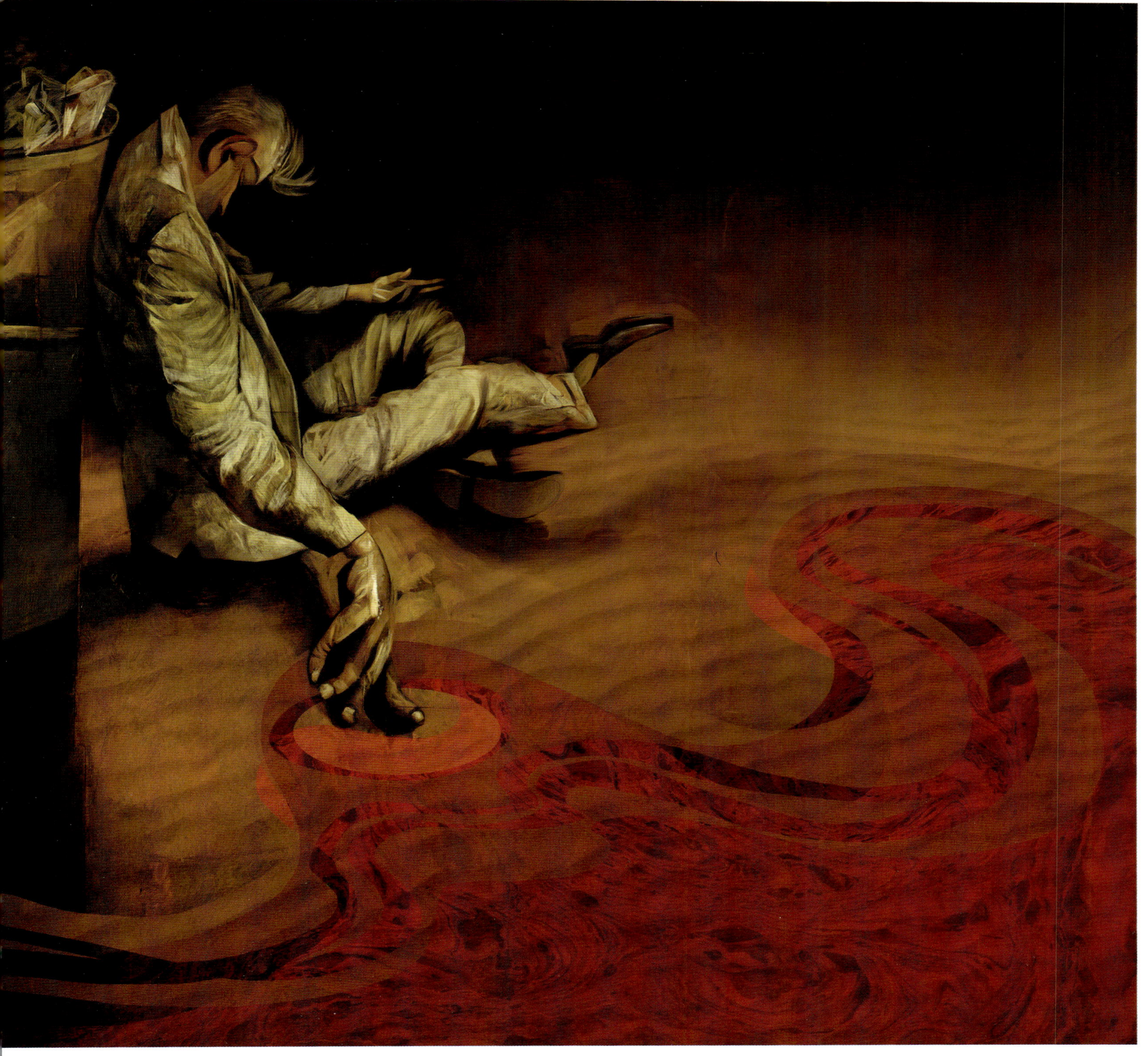

**A rough, ragged painting as a first
layer to work over in Photoshop**

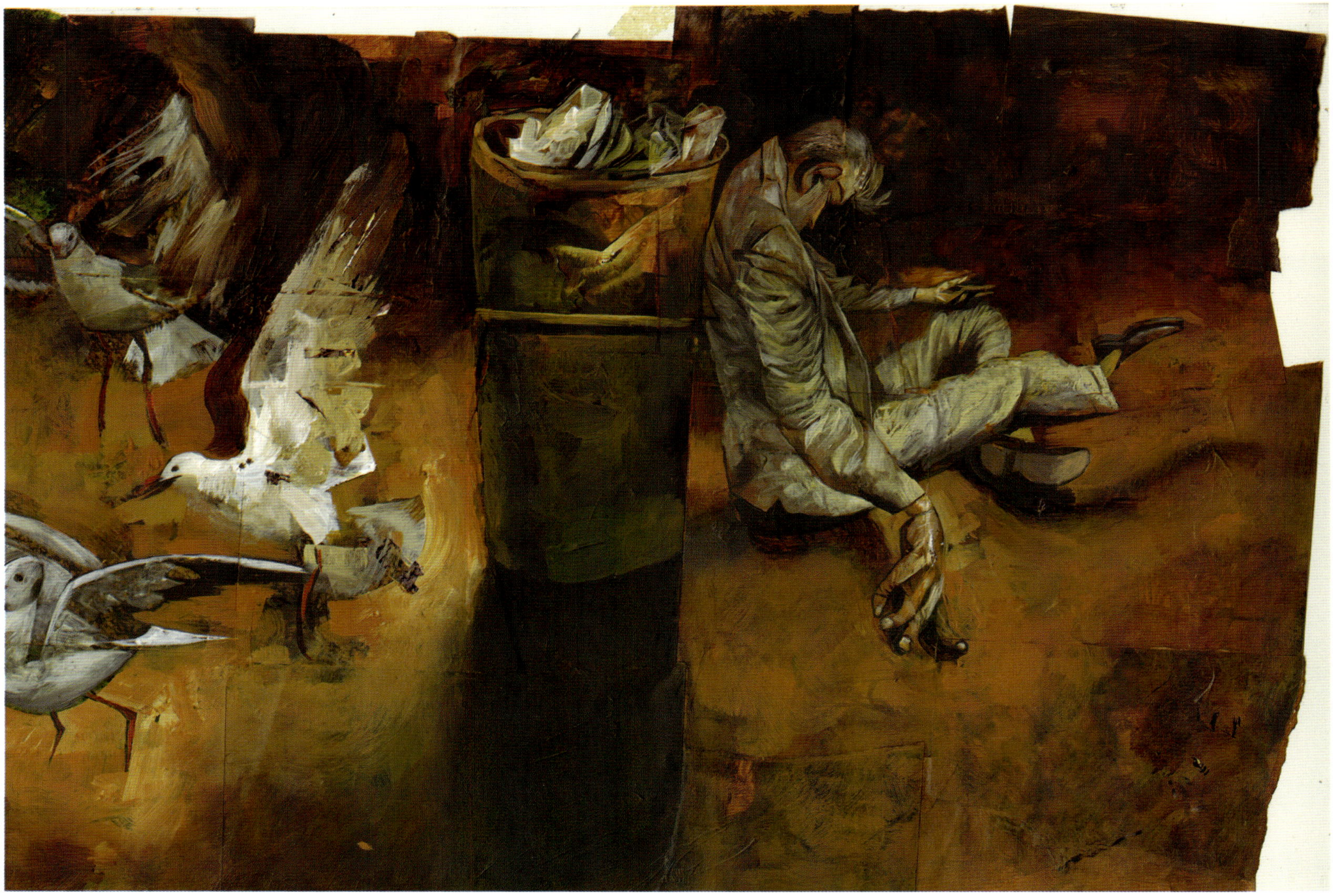

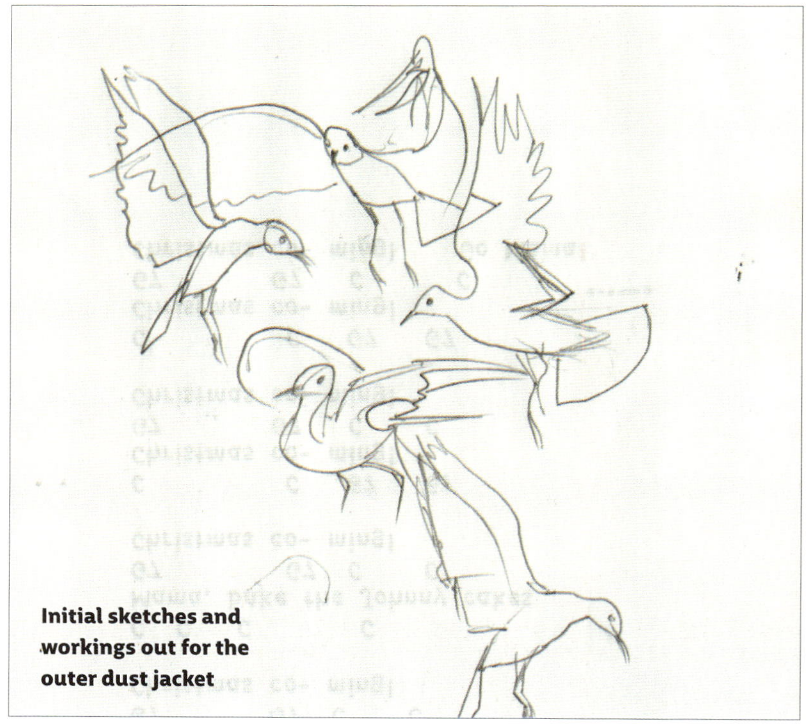

**Initial sketches and
workings out for the
outer dust jacket**

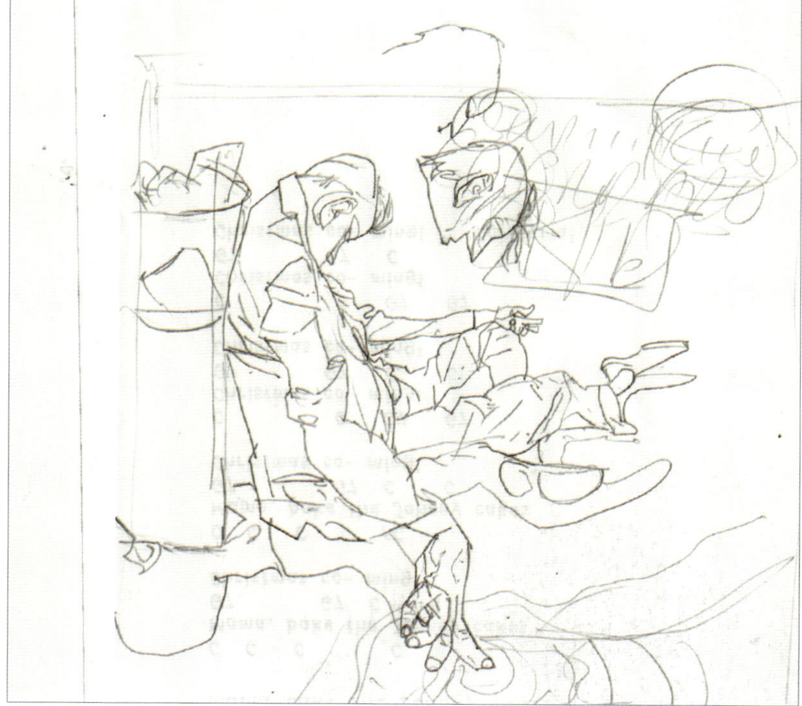

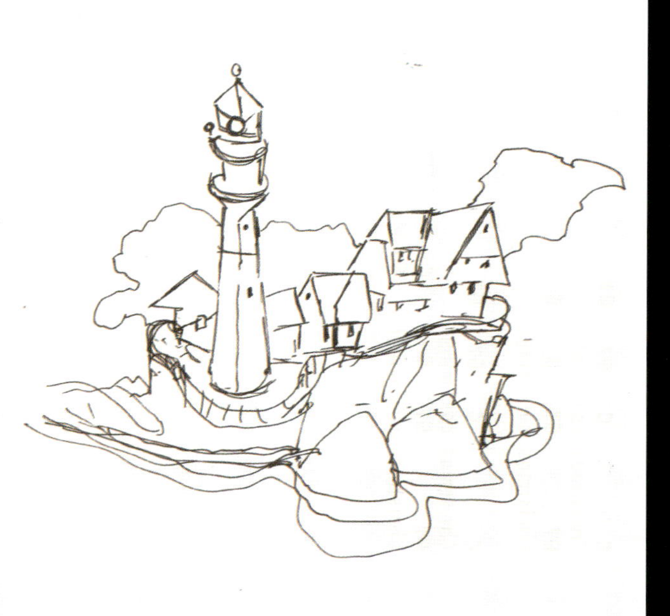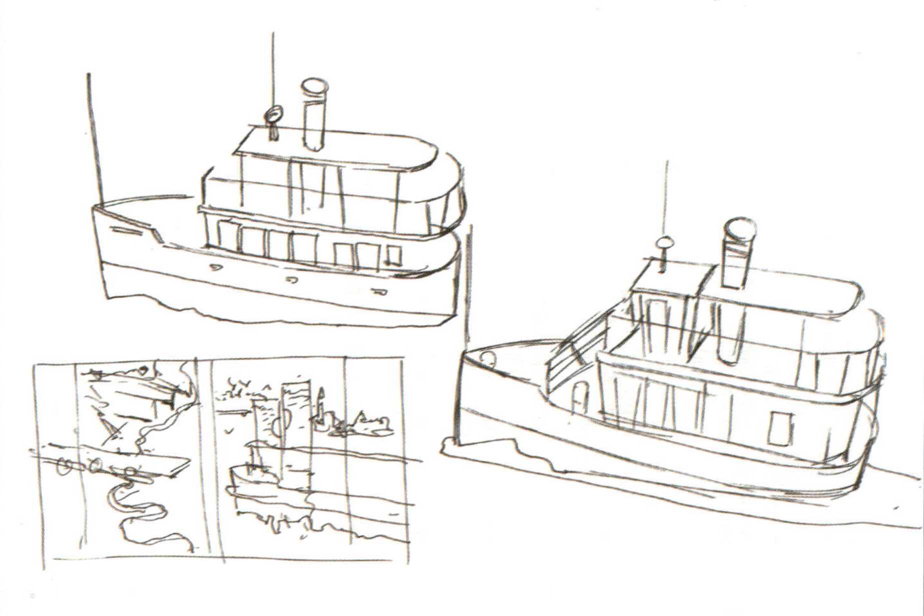

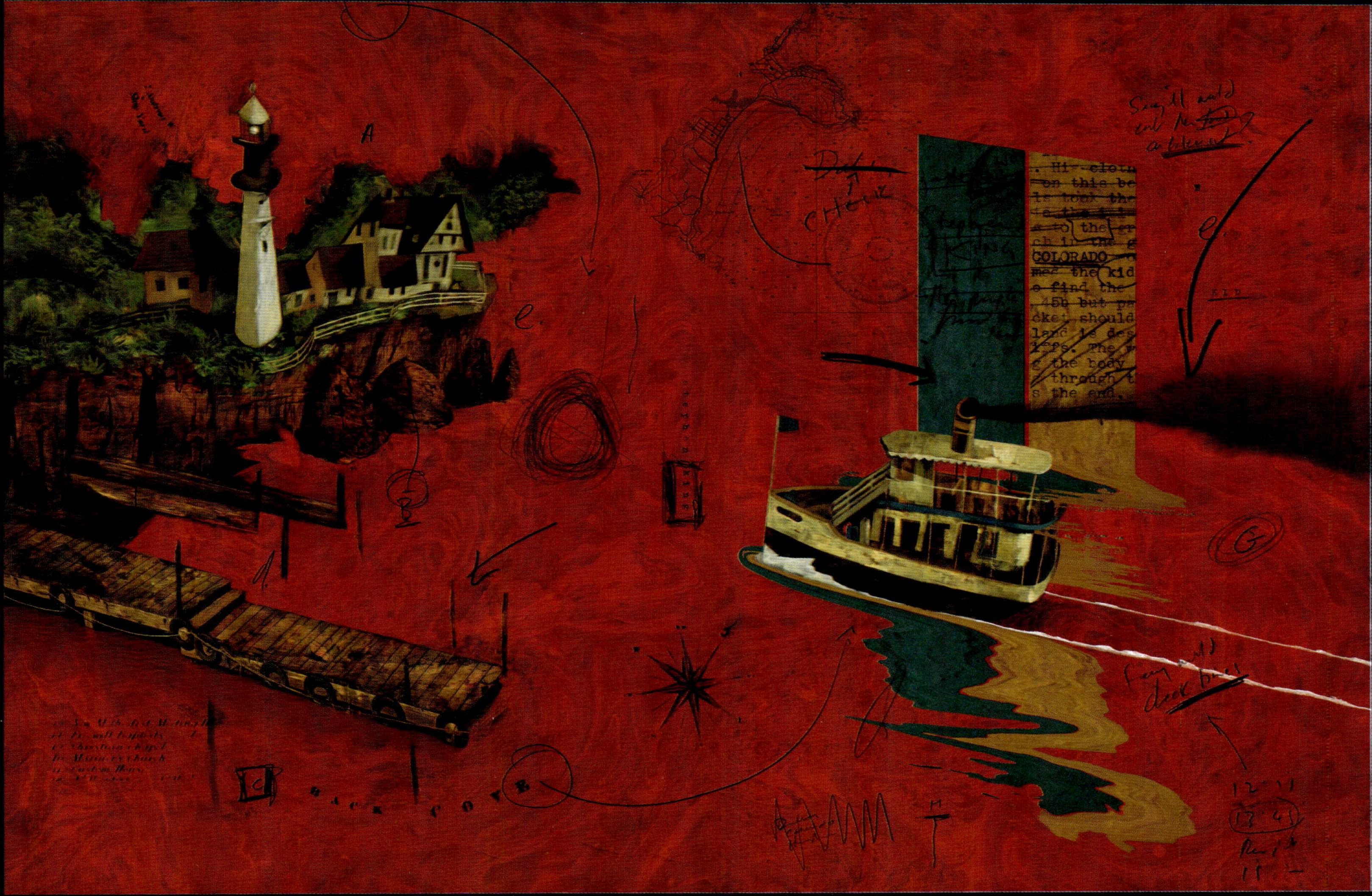

Tighter drawings for the dust-jacket image

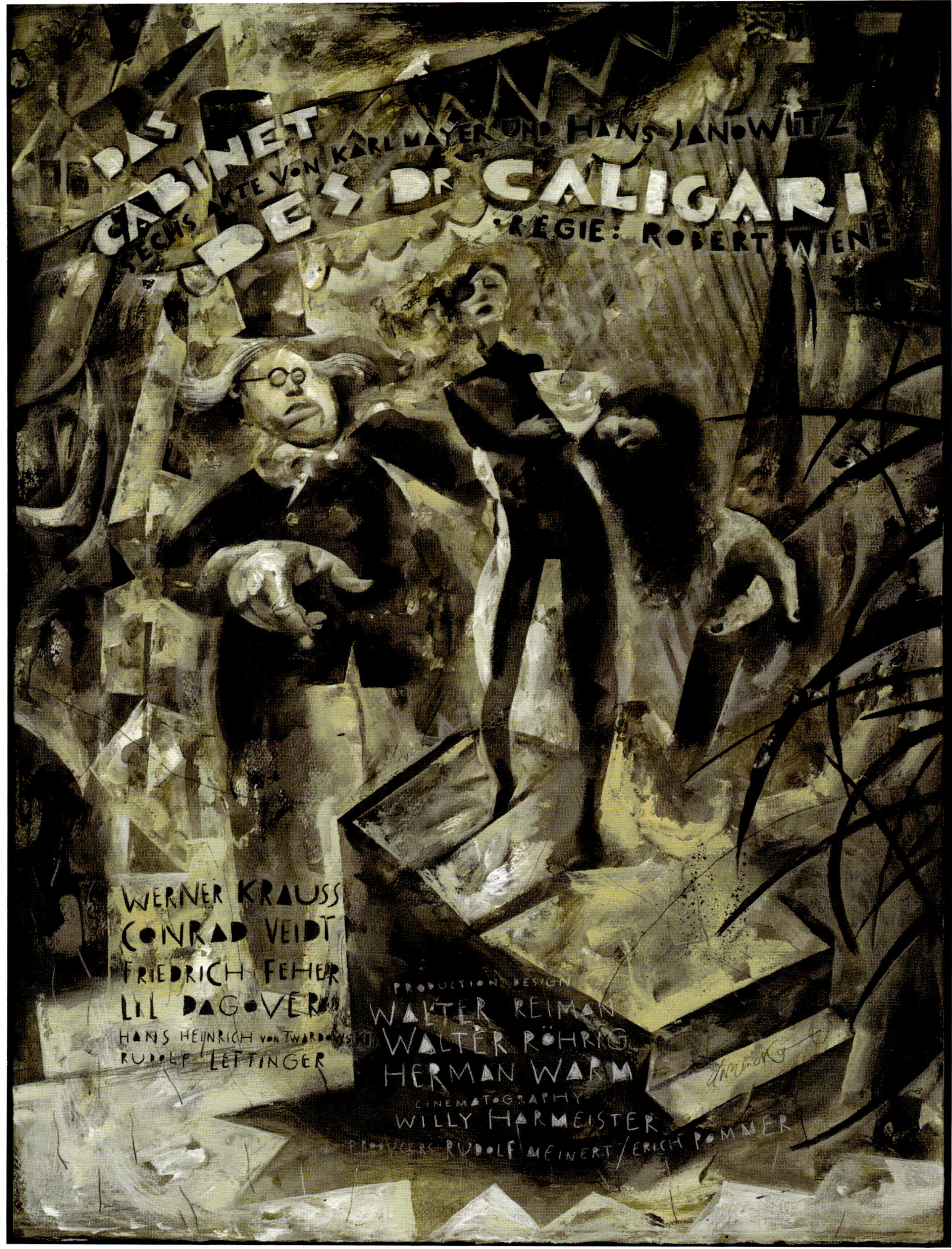

The Cabinet of Dr Caligari poster

An image created for a gallery exhibition of posters and artwork by numerous artists, all directly inspired by films. I've been working on a very long project of paintings and drawings inspired by silent cinema, so I used this opportunity to create a poster for the great UFA expressionist classic *The Cabinet of Dr Caligari*. I have already made a few images inspired by this film for my forthcoming book *Nitrate*, so my sketchbooks contain many notes of figures, angles, and ideas for images.

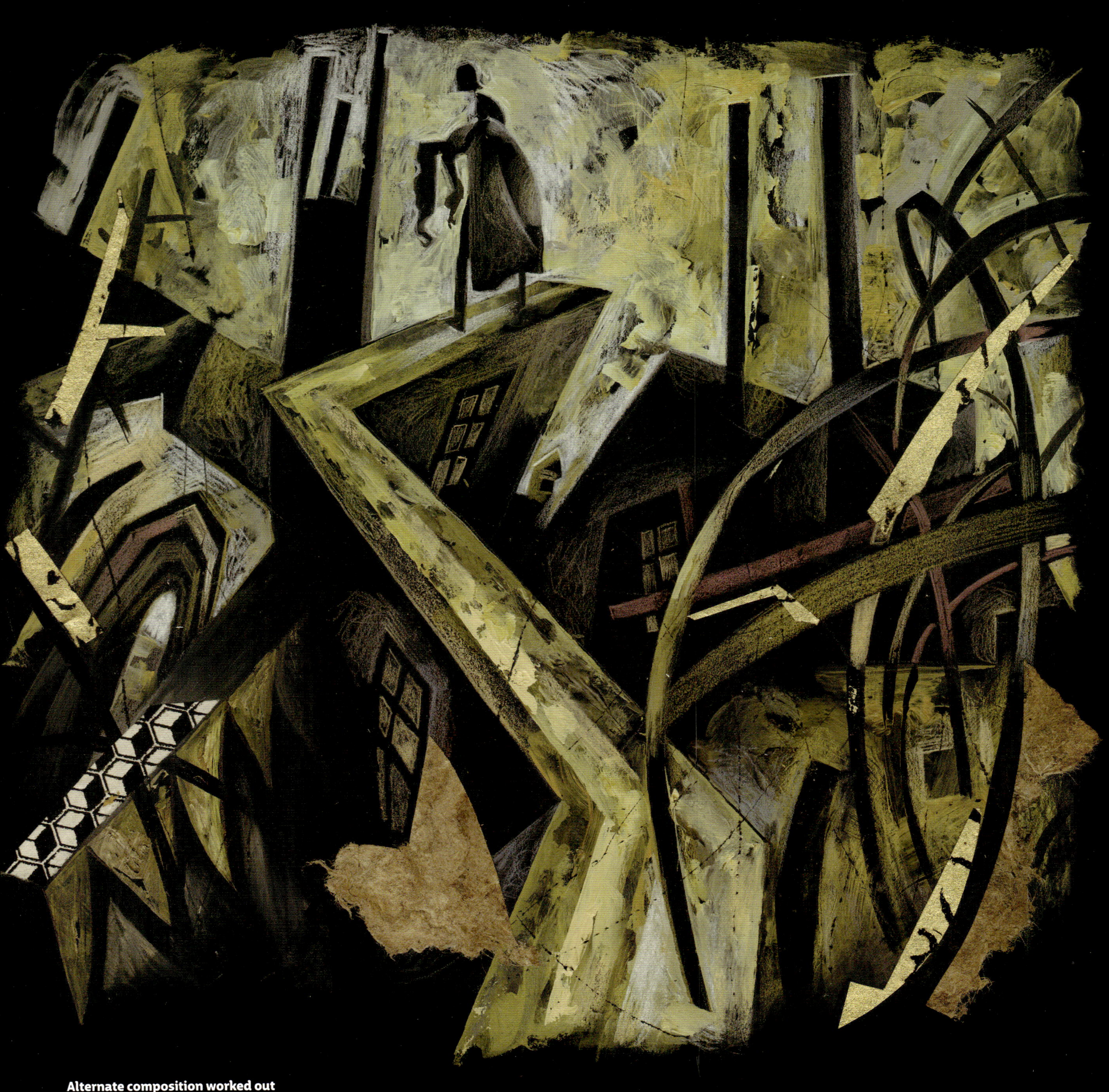

Alternate composition worked out
on black card with acrylic, coloured
pencil, and paper collage

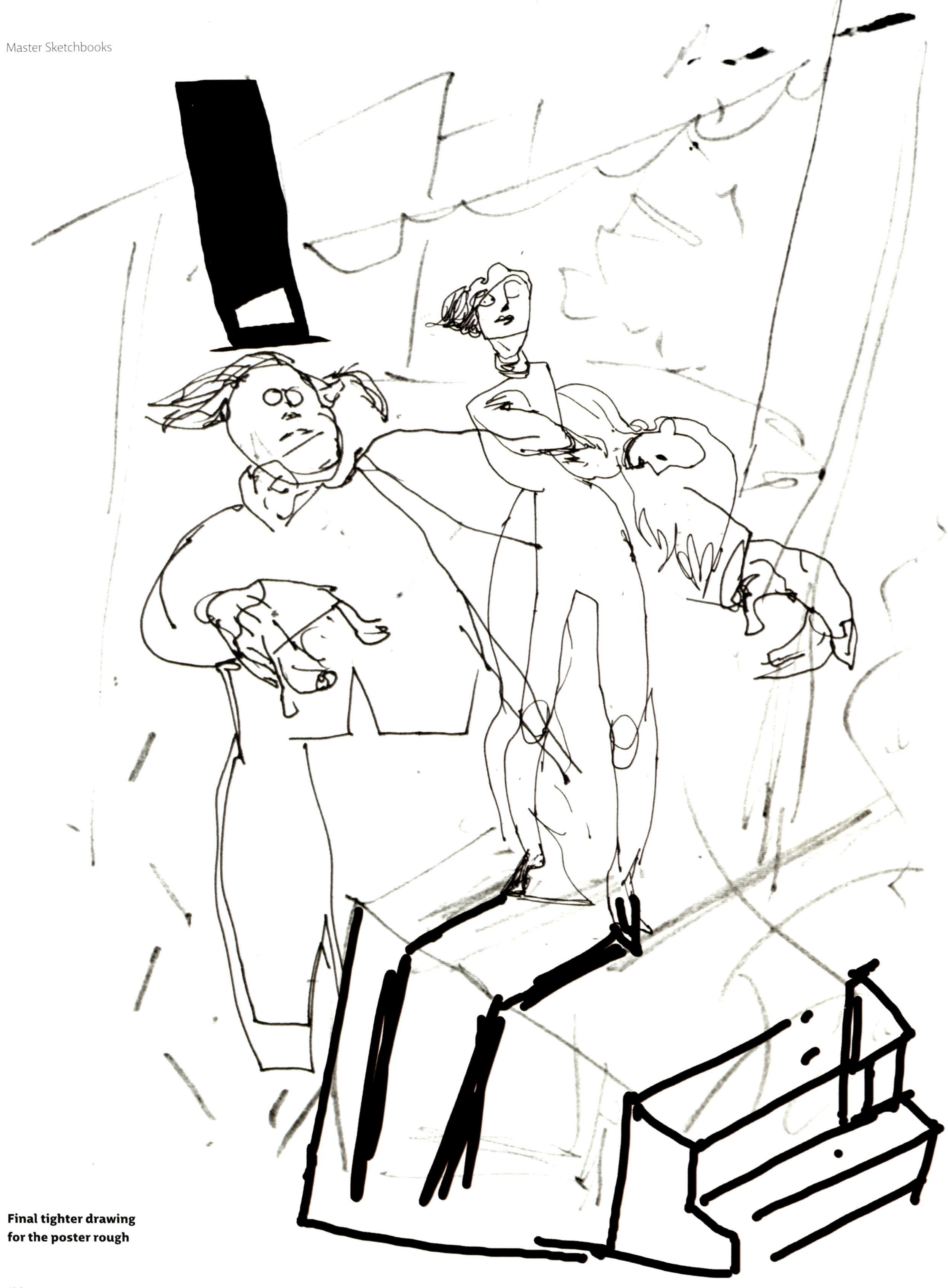

**Final tighter drawing
for the poster rough**

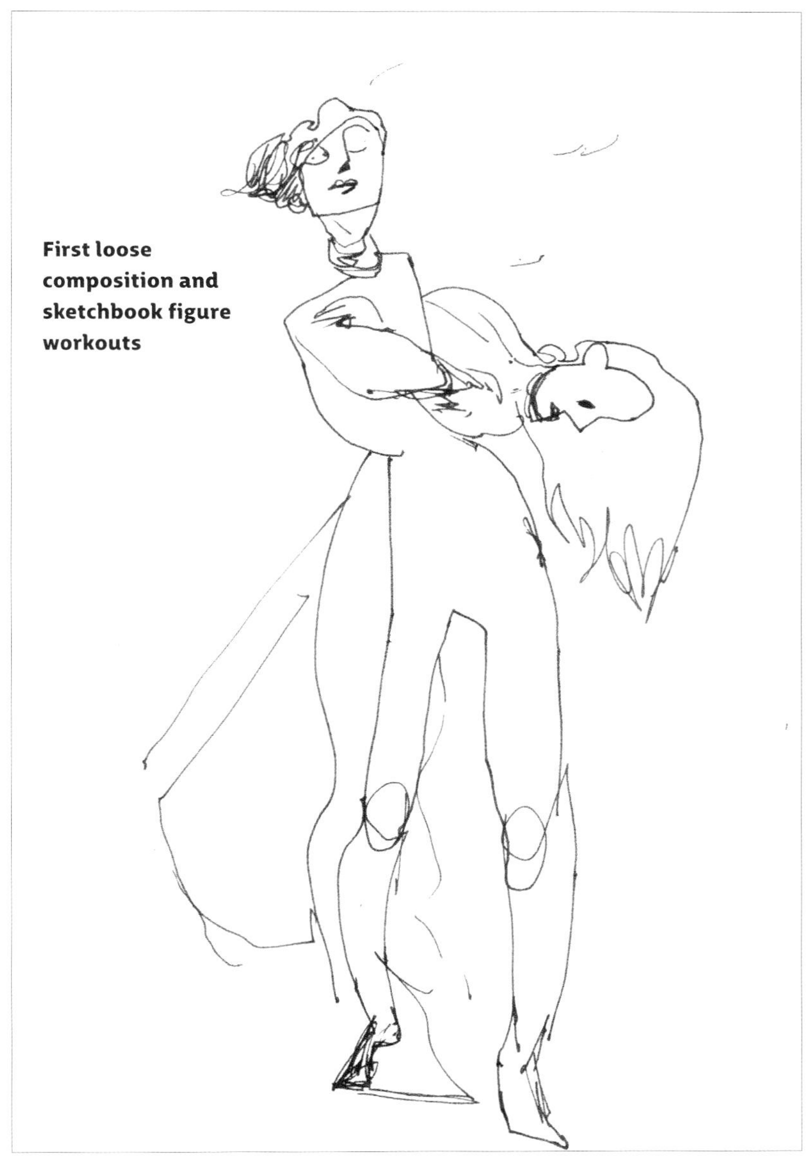

**First loose
composition and
sketchbook figure
workouts**

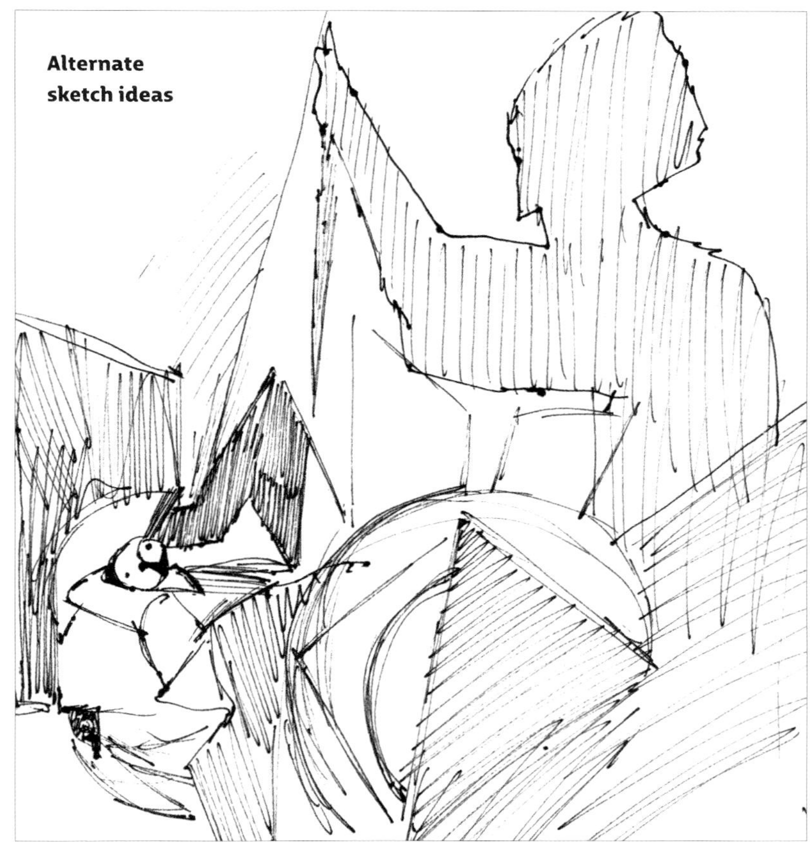

**Alternate
sketch ideas**

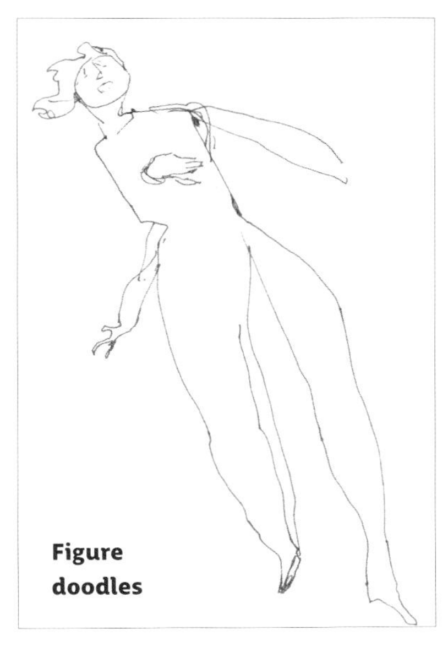

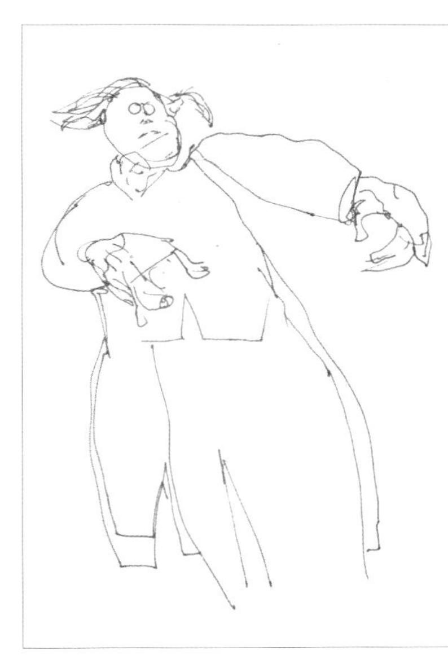

**Figure
doodles**

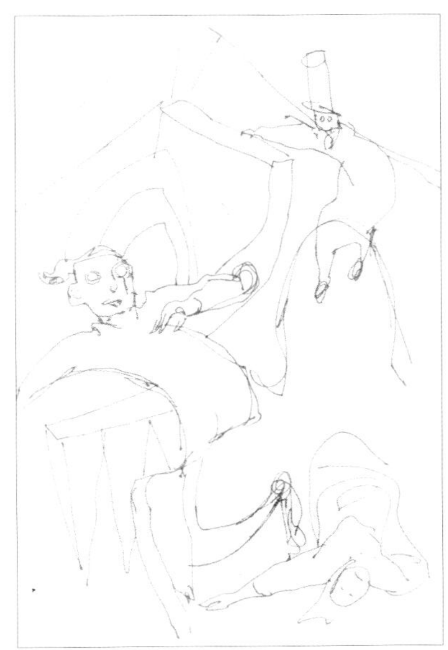

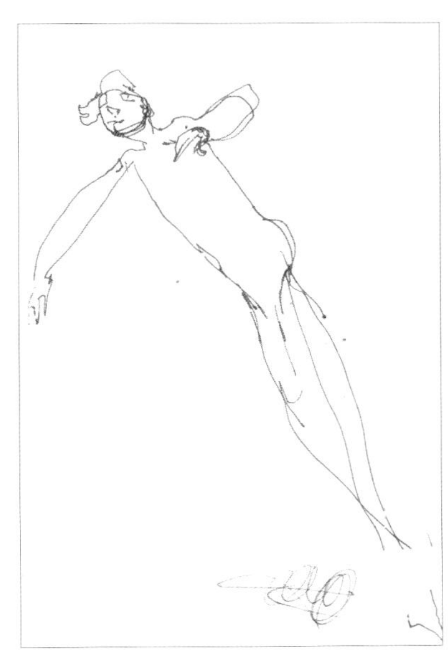

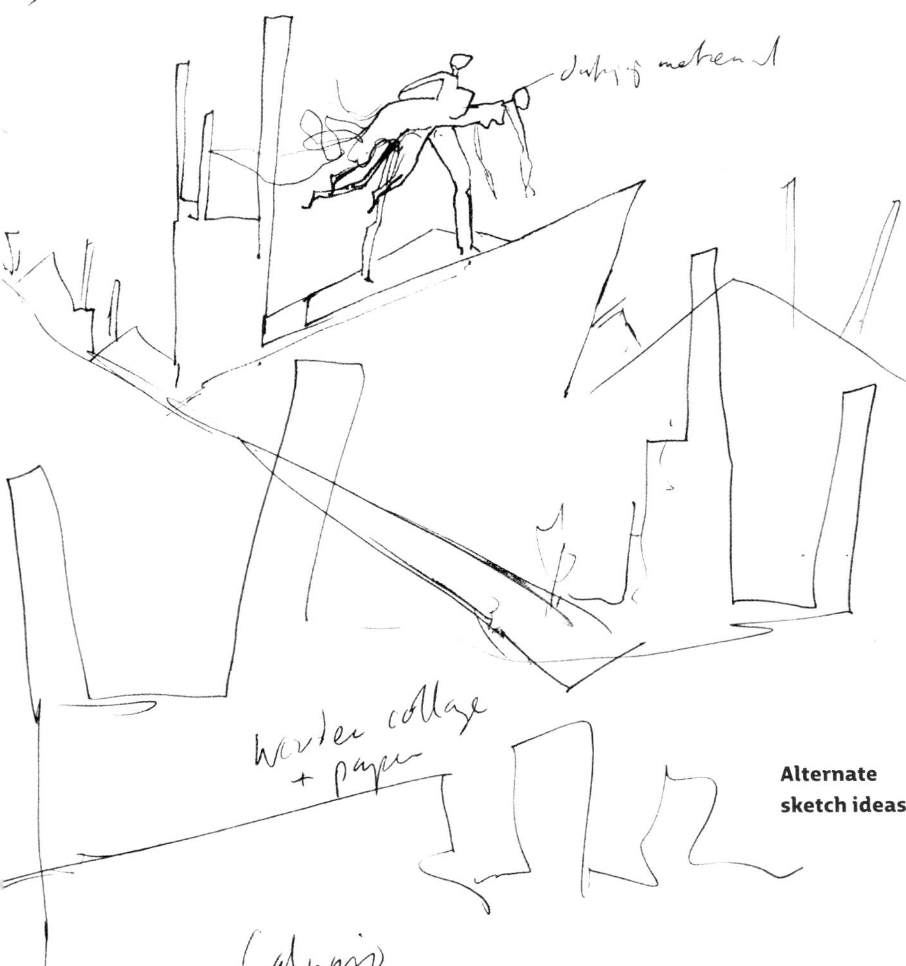

**Alternate
sketch ideas**

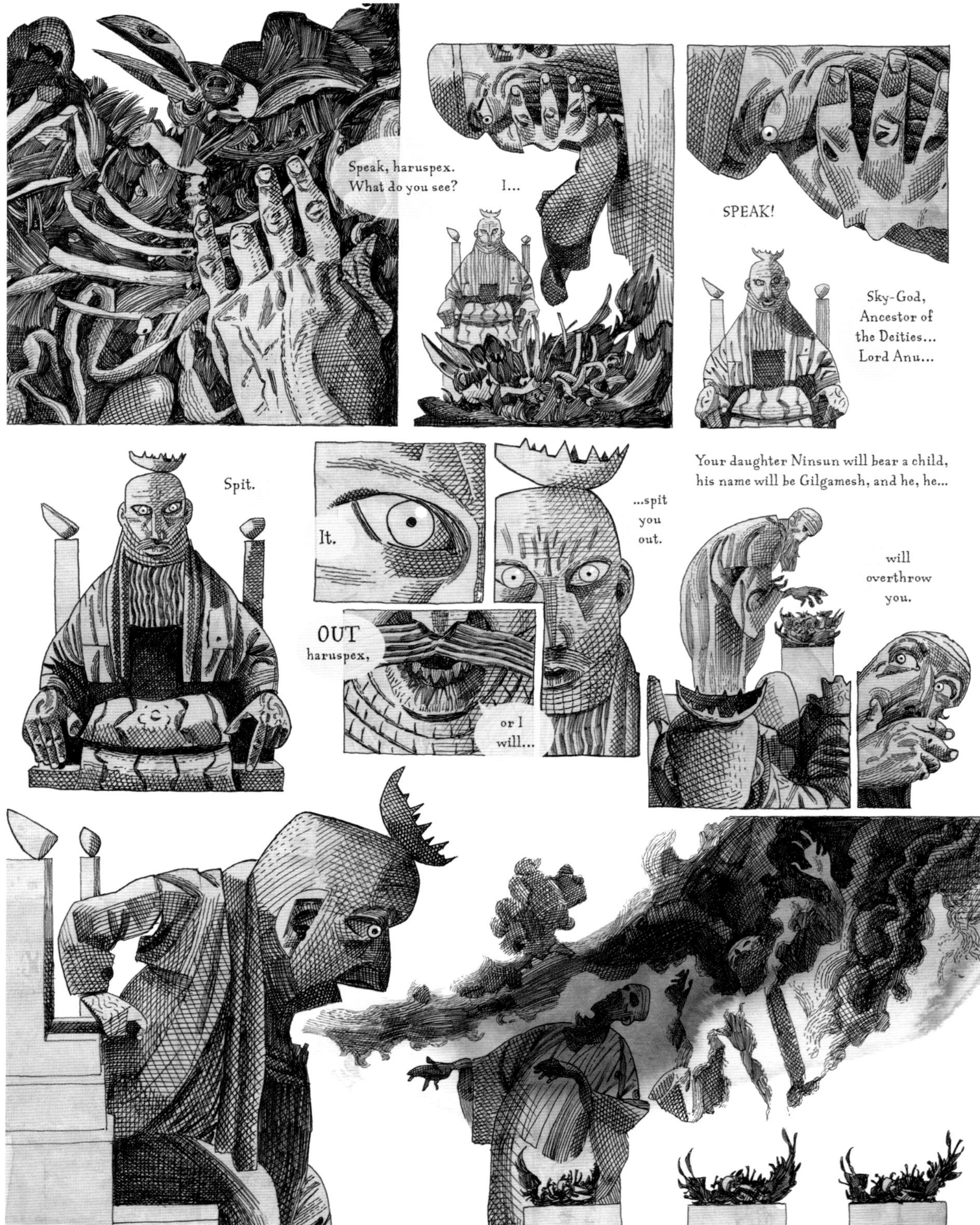

Gilgamesh book project, as yet untitled, written by Robert MacFarlane and Johnny Flynn

Penguin Random House and W. W. Norton,
to be published 2026

Robert and I have been looking for a project to work on together for a few years. During lockdown, he and his actor/musician friend Johnny Flynn created a song cycle and performance work called *Lost in the Cedar Wood*. When I saw it performed, I thought it could be expanded into a graphic novel. It involved a retelling of the Gilgamesh story – our oldest known fiction – the story of the story, and how it survived thousands of years underground, locked in the writing system of cuneiform before it was translated. It also involves the story of George Smith, the young untrained Assyriologist who unlocked the Flood tablet at the British Museum in the late 19th century. I've been trying to find the right tone of voice for each page of this interweaving narrative.

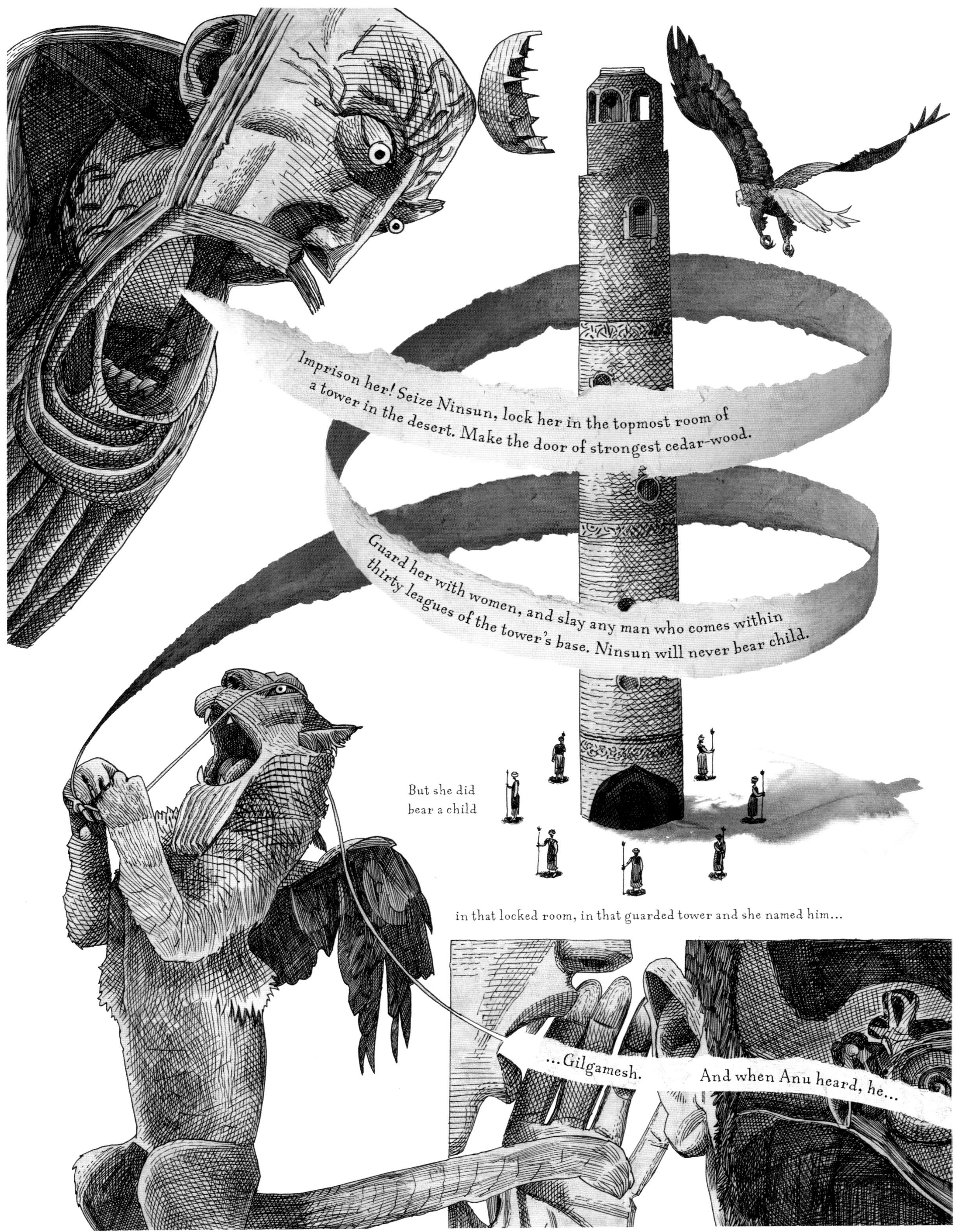
Imprison her! Seize Ninsun, lock her in the topmost room of a tower in the desert. Make the door of strongest cedar-wood.
Guard her with women, and slay any man who comes within thirty leagues of the tower's base. Ninsun will never bear child.
But she did bear a child
in that locked room, in that guarded tower and she named him...
...Gilgamesh.
And when Anu heard, he...

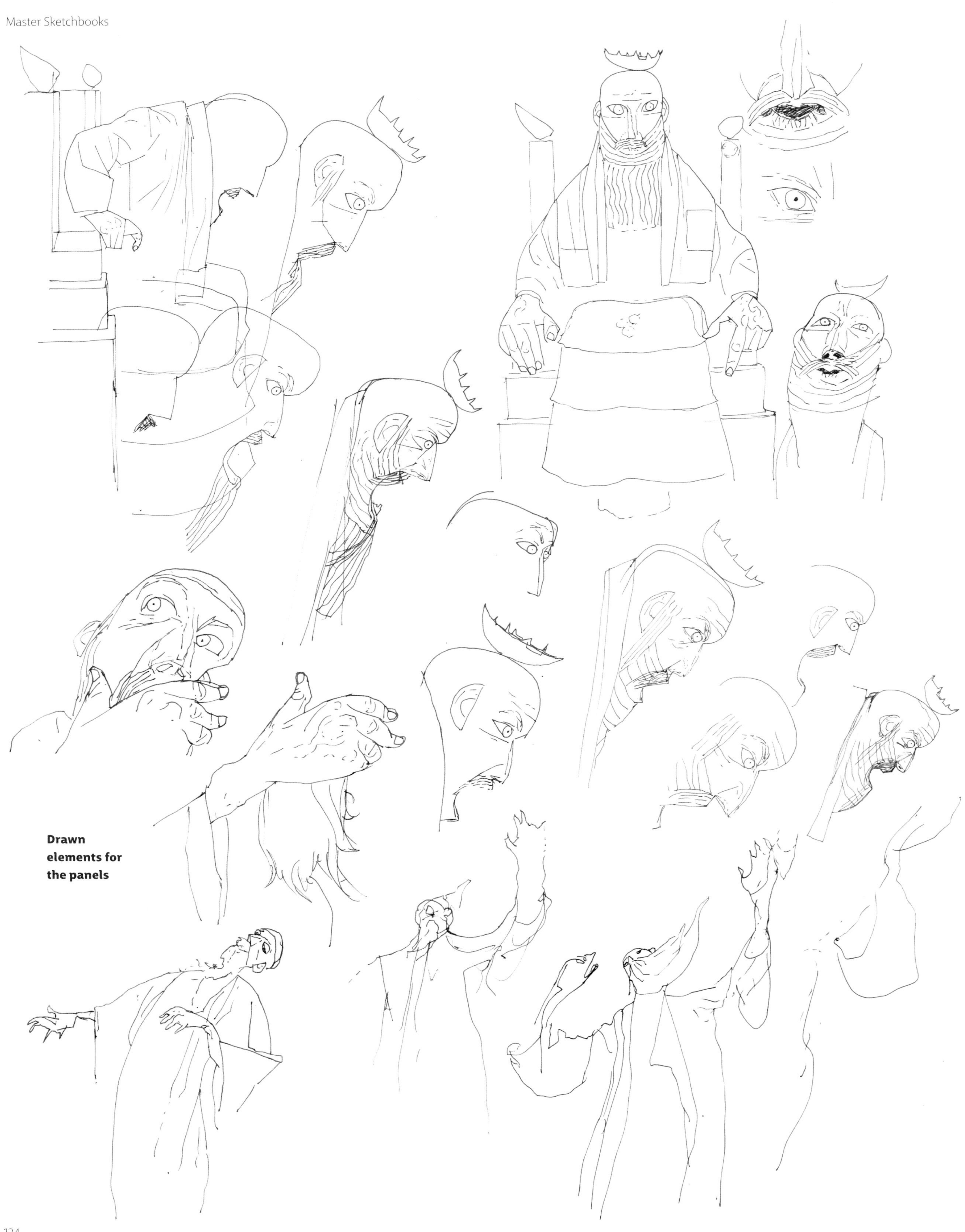

Drawn elements for the panels

Ink line-drawn page

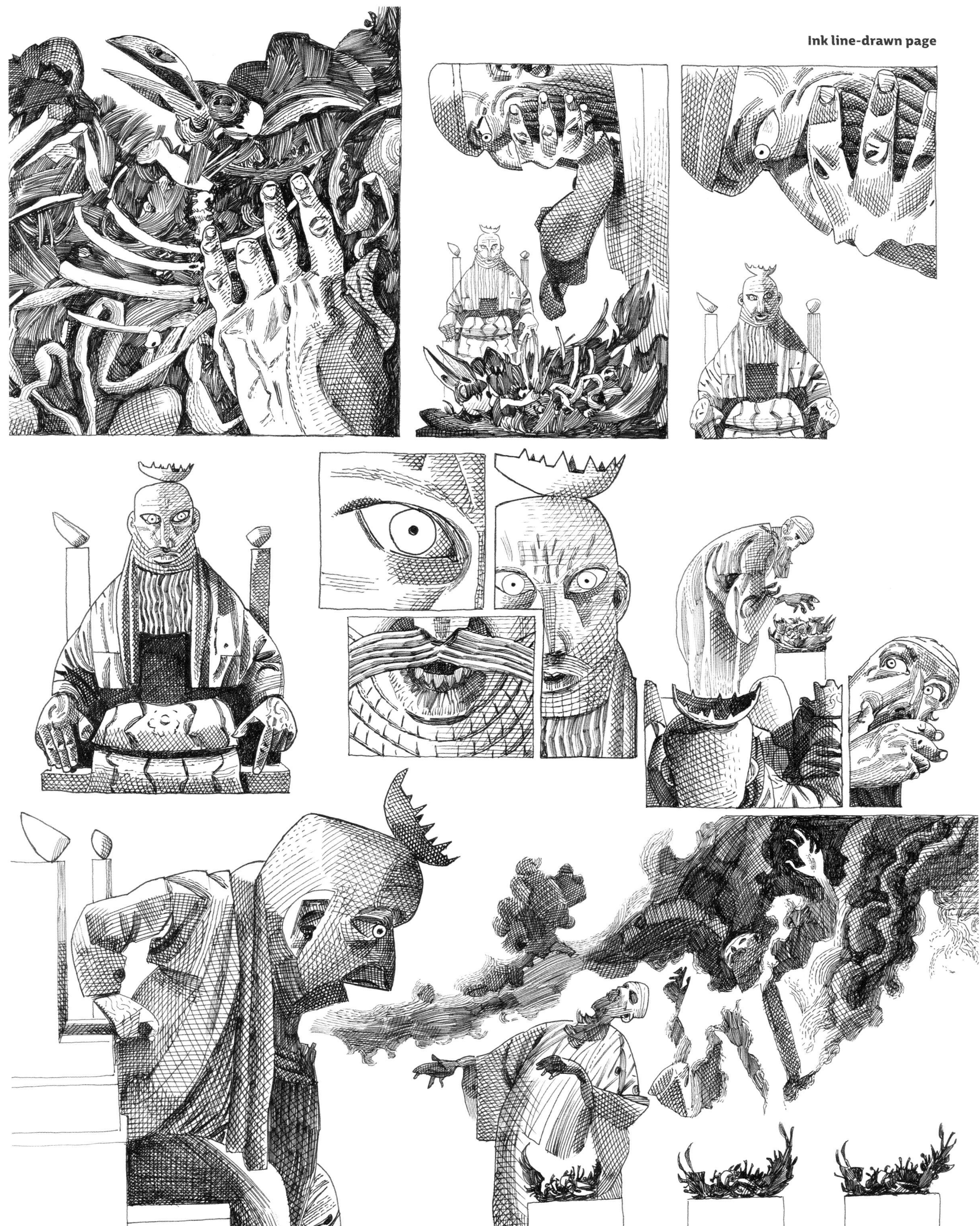

Gilgamesh (title tbc) to be published by Penguin Random House and W. W. Norton
Artwork © 2024 Dave McKean   125

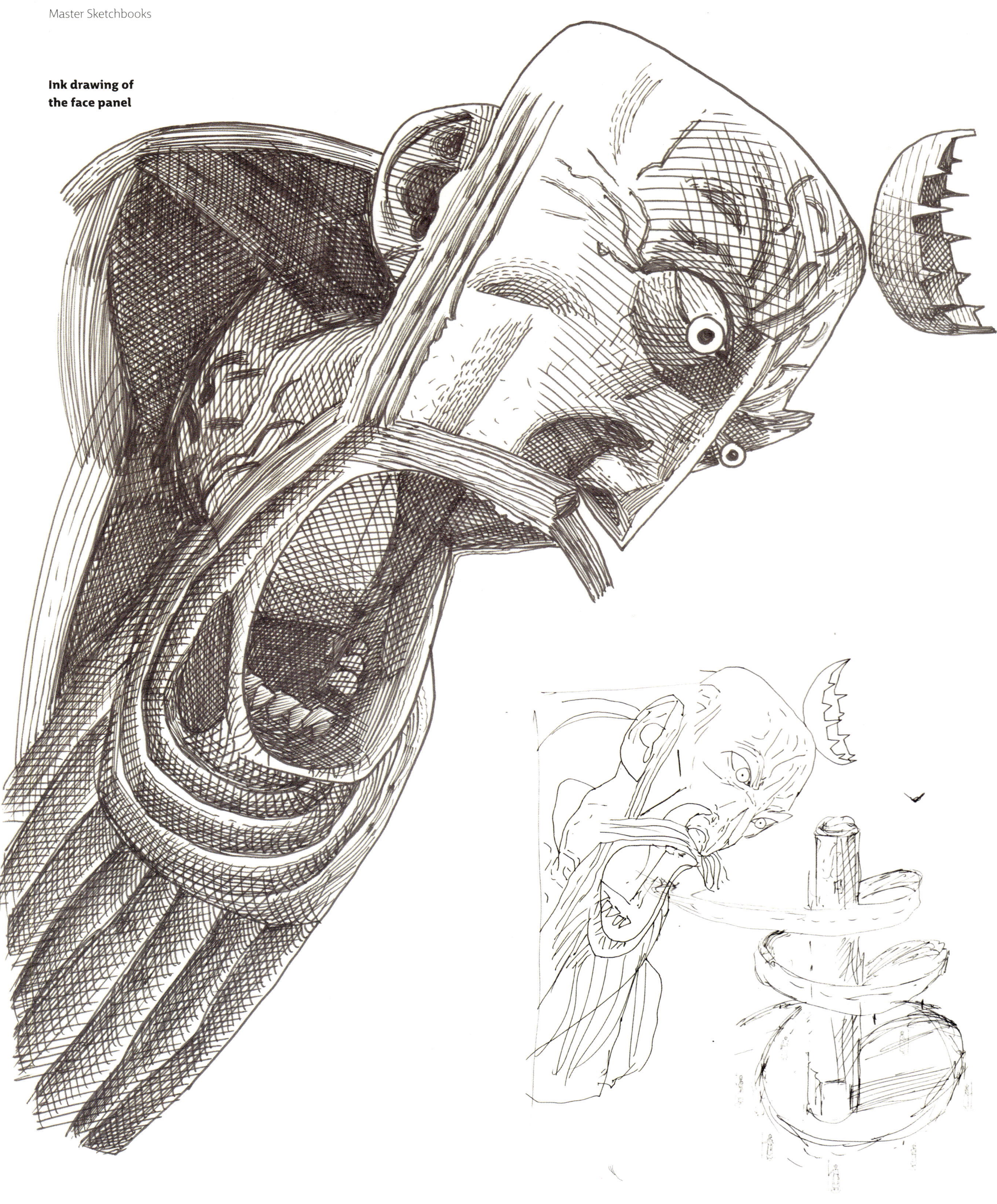

**Ink drawing of
the face panel**

Dave McKean

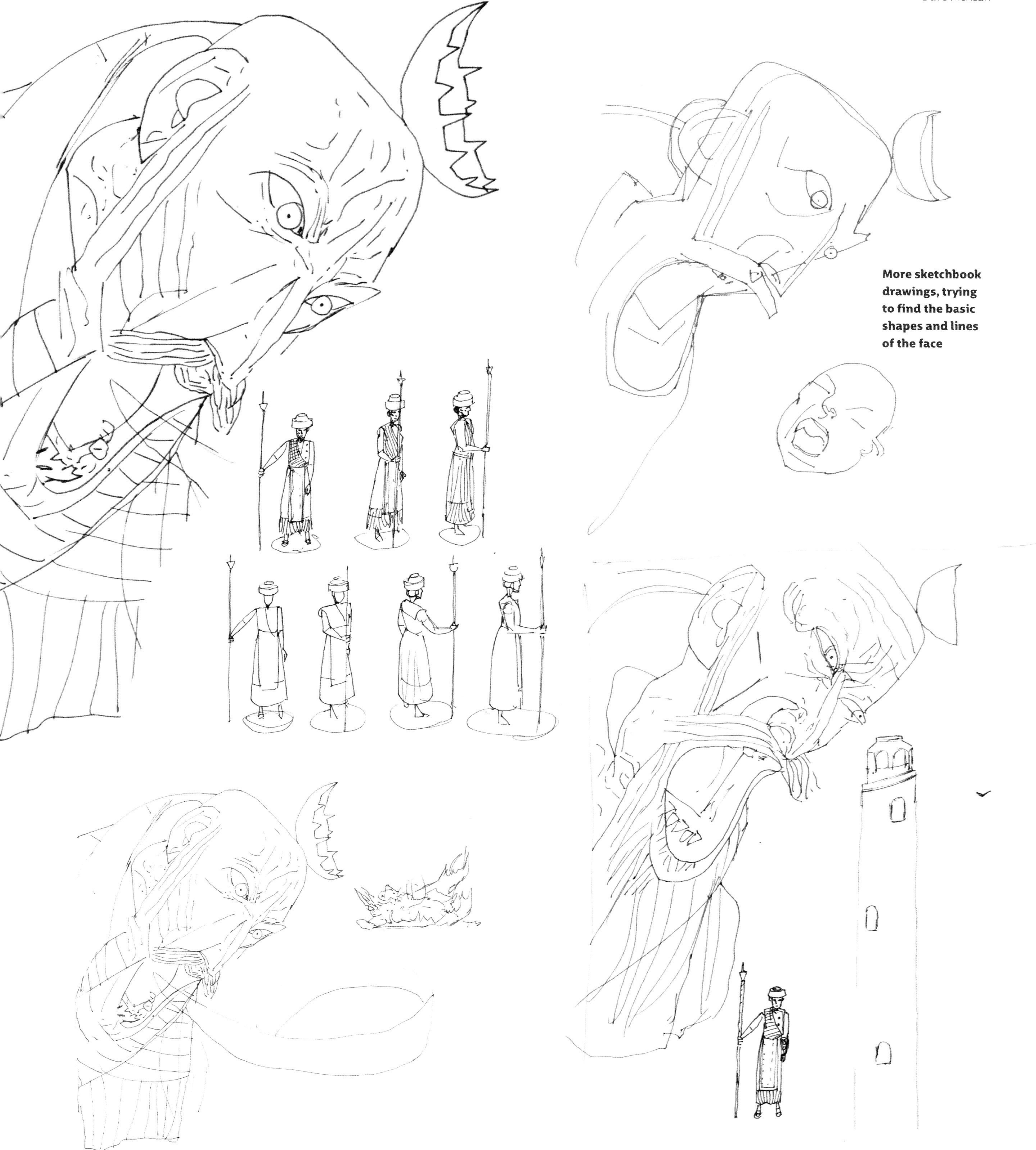

**More sketchbook
drawings, trying
to find the basic
shapes and lines
of the face**

Vincent Di Fate

CAREER HISTORY

I've been an illustrator for nearly sixty years, having begun my career while still in art school, around 1966 or 67. I'm an illustrator, not a fine artist. I do demanding and creative work, to specification and to deadline, which requires considerable discipline and skill. I've been active in my speciality for my entire career, which involves the creation of science-fiction, aerospace, astronomical, and, occasionally, fantasy art. I've worked for clients such as IBM, *Reader's Digest*, The National Geographic Society, and NASA.

In that post-World War II era when I was growing up, with all of its lofty hopes for peace and abundance, there was still that looming fear that the world might again be plunged into global war – only this time, with nuclear weapons and advanced technologies, there were likely to be no winners and no survivors. I've read science-fiction literature all my life and what I know is that the science-fiction story is a cautionary kind of literature. It isn't necessarily pro-science; it recognizes that scientific advancement disrupts and displaces. Anticipating cause and effect is essential to adapting and surviving. To my mind, this is an important piece of information and the genre is constantly asking, 'What if?' to suggest answers to where the future is headed.

While I've always found the making of art to be extremely challenging, I've been fortunate enough to have been recognized several times over the years. I'm a Hugo Award winner for Best Professional Artist (1979), have been inducted into the Science Fiction Hall of Fame (around 2011, I think) and, more recently, the Society of Illustrators' Hall of Fame (2019). Probably the most telling thing is that I've been busy throughout my sixty-year run, working exclusively in the science-fiction/fantasy field.

To do almost anything for that length of time – even rotating automobile tyres, for example – has to mean something. If you love making art, and know in your heart that you do, admit it to yourself, commit to it, and don't give up. But make sure that you're good at it before you give up your day job! The one sure way to determine that is to show your work. If assignments start coming your way, that's a sure form of validation.

Sketches
Ballpoint and gel pen on lined paper

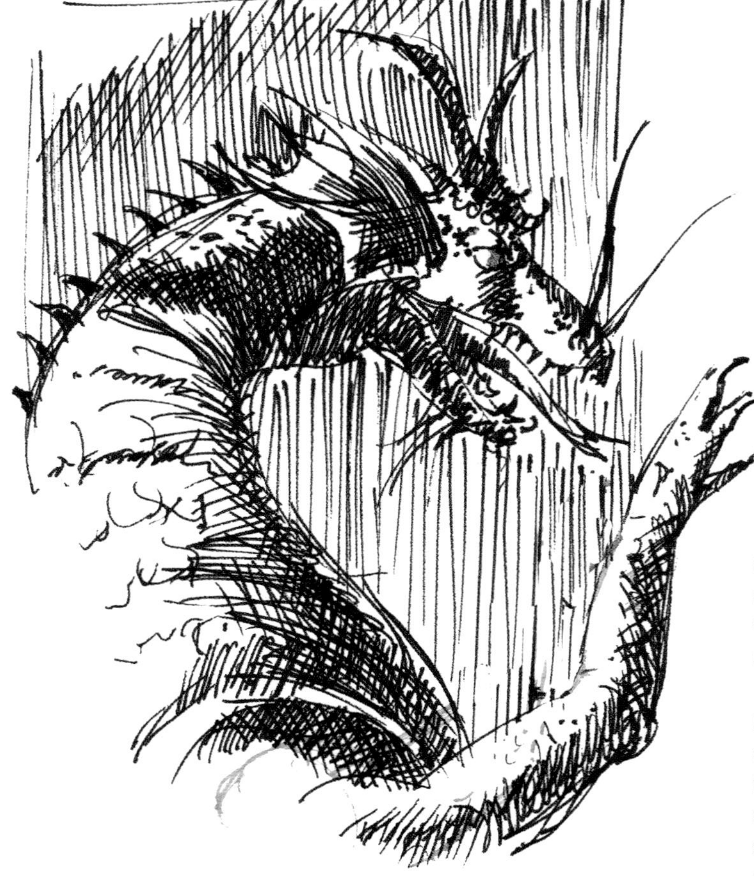

Opposite page | Magazine interiors drawing for Connie Hirsch's story 'Dragon-in-Law', 1996
Pen and ink on scratchboard

Dragons are easily made up and can feature a variety of interesting textures on a medium such as scratchboard, where the rendering is scratched away, rather than drawn on. An effective scratchboard drawing is typically an interplay between drawing and engraving.

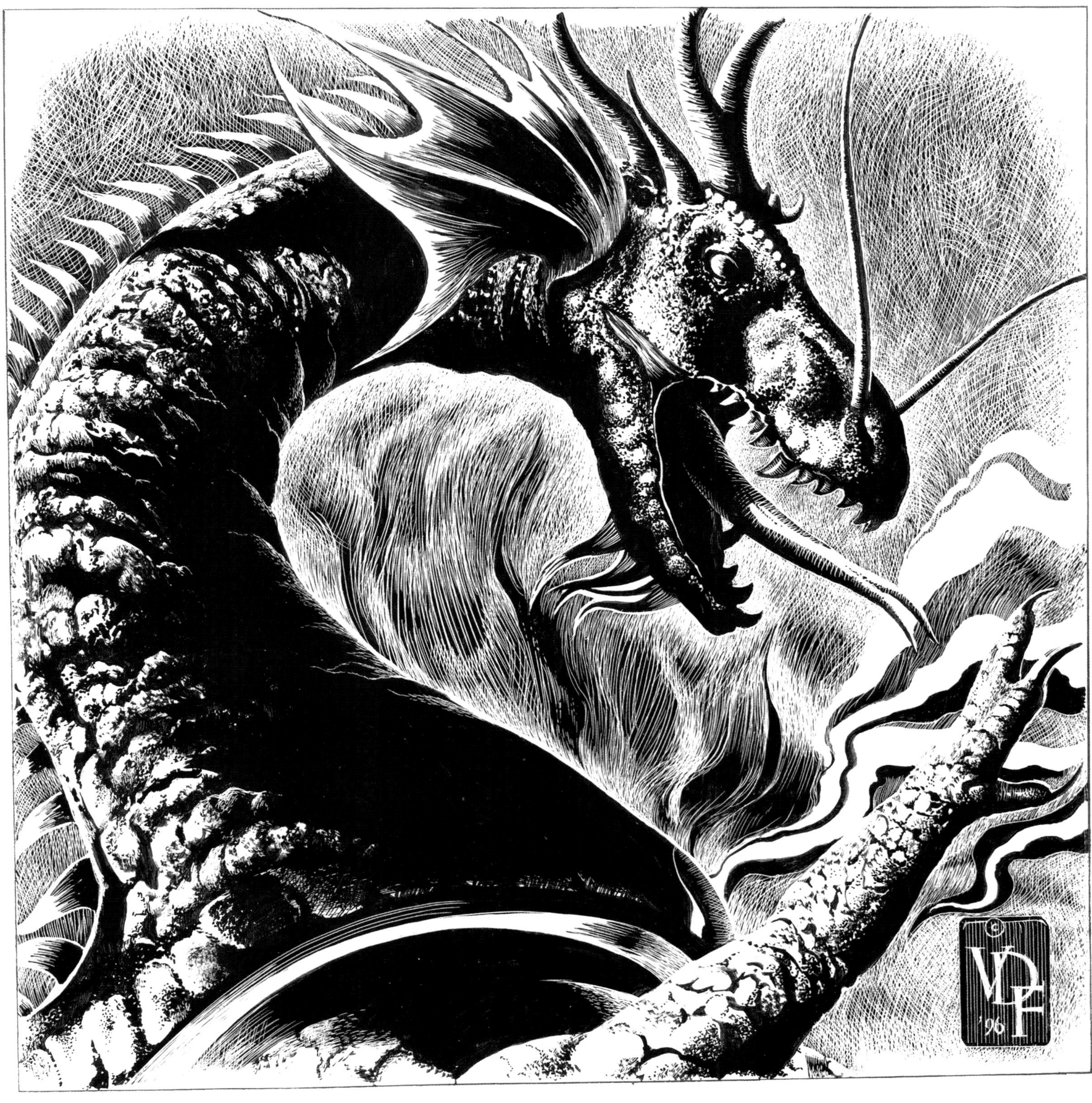

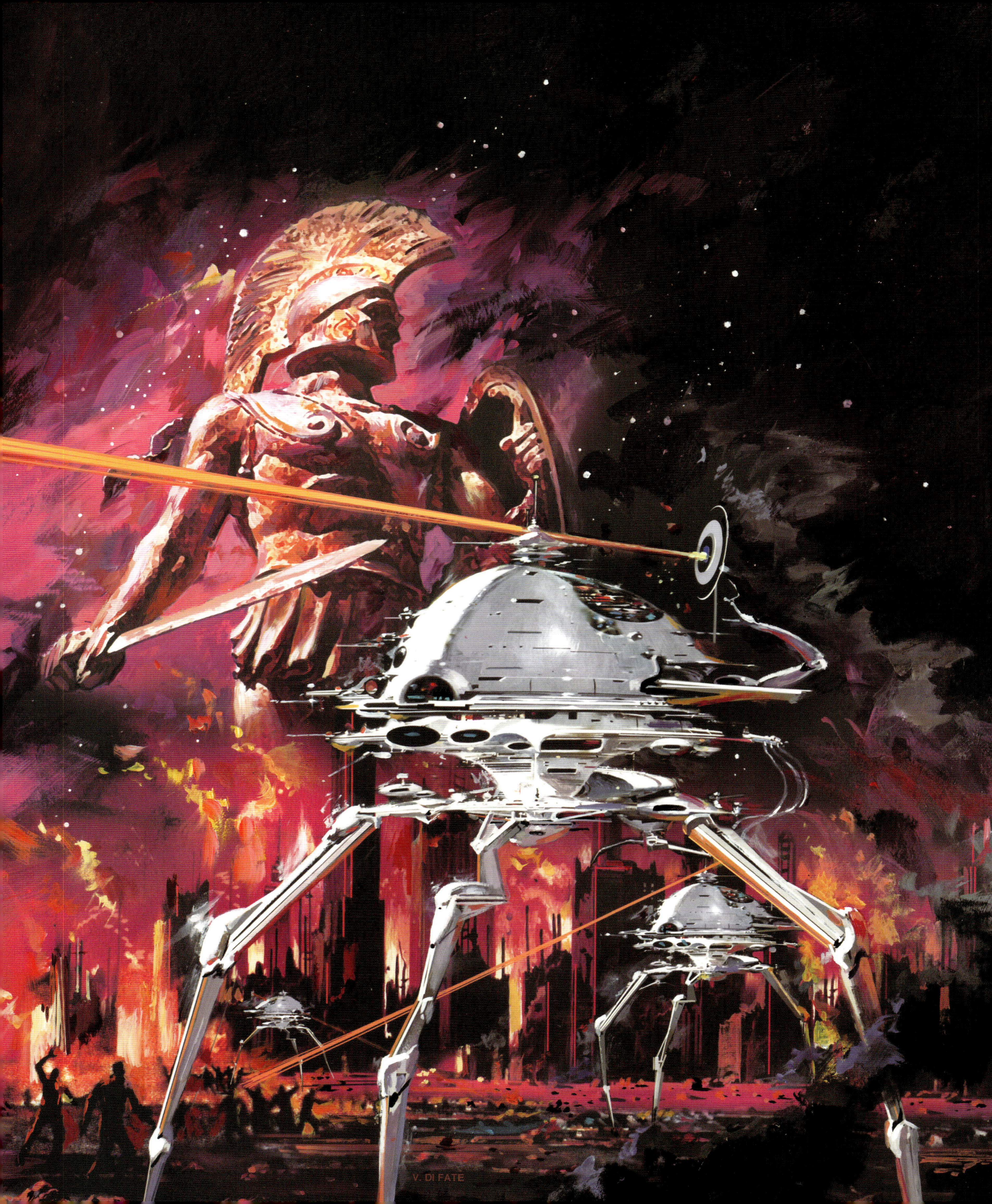
V. DI FATE

Opposite page | **Painting for the cover of *Reed Magazine*, March 2015**
Acrylic on board-mounted paper

Finished art for an essay on the use of classical mythological imagery in science-fiction literature.

Right | **A colour sketch incorporating the image of Ares, the God of War**
Acrylic on standard hardboard

The Greeks called him Ares; the Romans knew him as Mars. By whatever name, his image has long been associated with H. G. Wells' seminal novel of alien invasion, *The War of the Worlds*, which I think is what motivated the selection of this sketch for the finished painting.

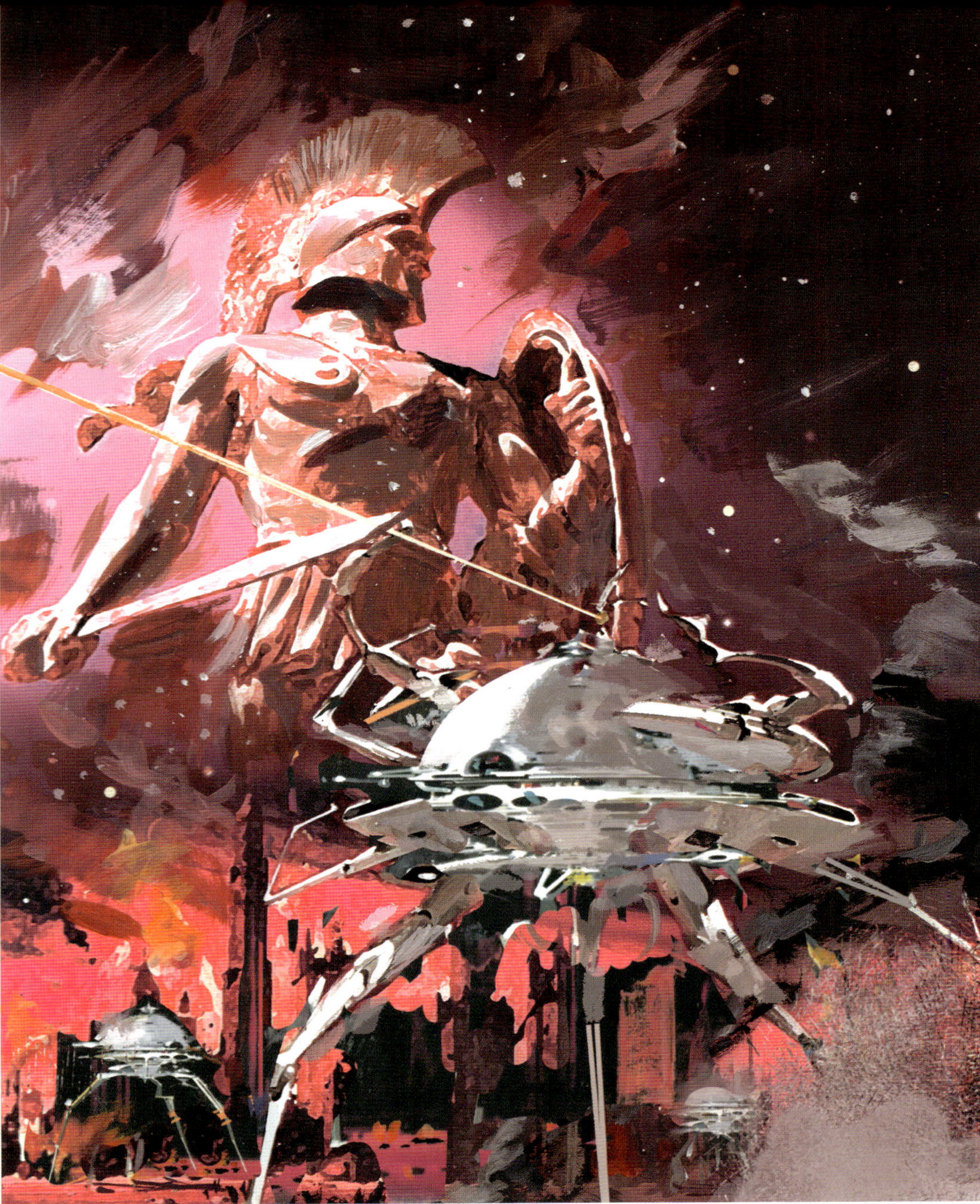

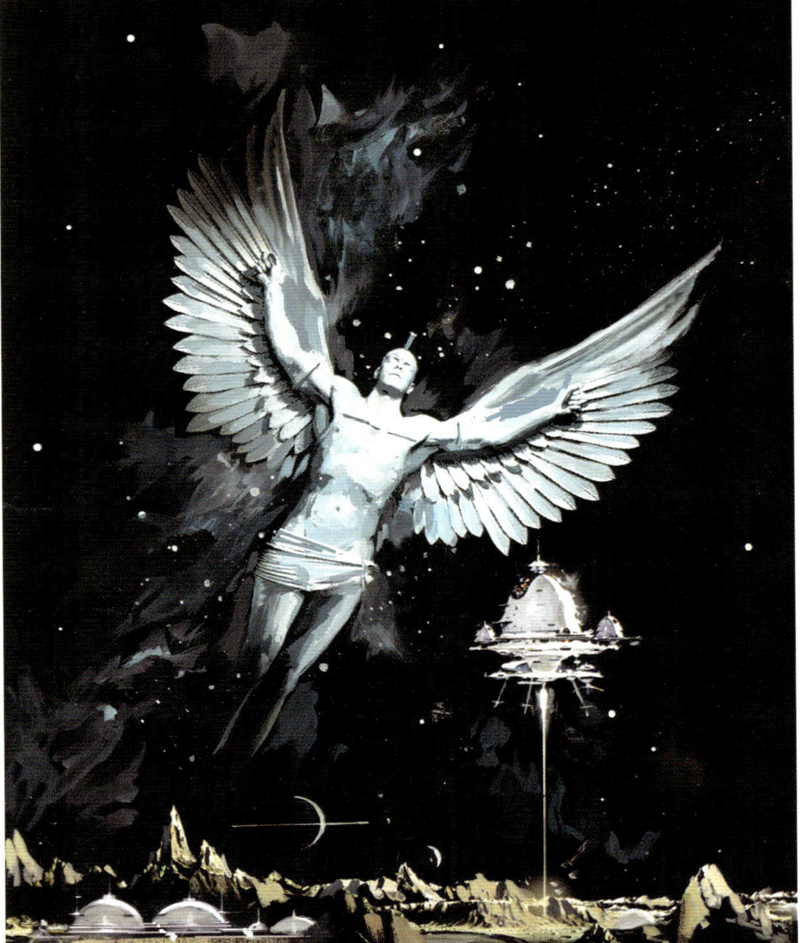

Left | **A colour sketch incorporating the image of Icarus**
Acrylics on standard hardboard and on board-mounted paper

The second image for *Reed Magazine* depicts the story of Icarus fearlessly spreading his wings against the sky, unmindful of the heat of the sun and how it will affect the tallow holding the wings to his arms. Both images were based on existing sculptures, but Icarus would require considerably more modification to work, and the ominous mood and colour palette of the 'war' theme of the Ares painting seemed to better suit the accompanying essay.

I try to avoid developing a personal preference when such alternatives exist so as not to be disappointed. Staying neutral is of course, an impossibility, but having thus deluded myself, I can then put my all into making the best of the final choice. This is one of many factors that differentiate the fine artist from the working illustrator. The illustrator does not work in service to the Muse – he must paint it red, rather than blue, include all that is required of him in the scope of the assignment, and hand it in by Friday. That may seem cynical at first, but there's something exhilarating in rising to the challenge and discovering that, with a bit of skill and discipline, you can successfully solve the visual problem, still make good art, and maybe even exceed your own expectations.

Originally published in *Reed Magazine*, 2015
 131

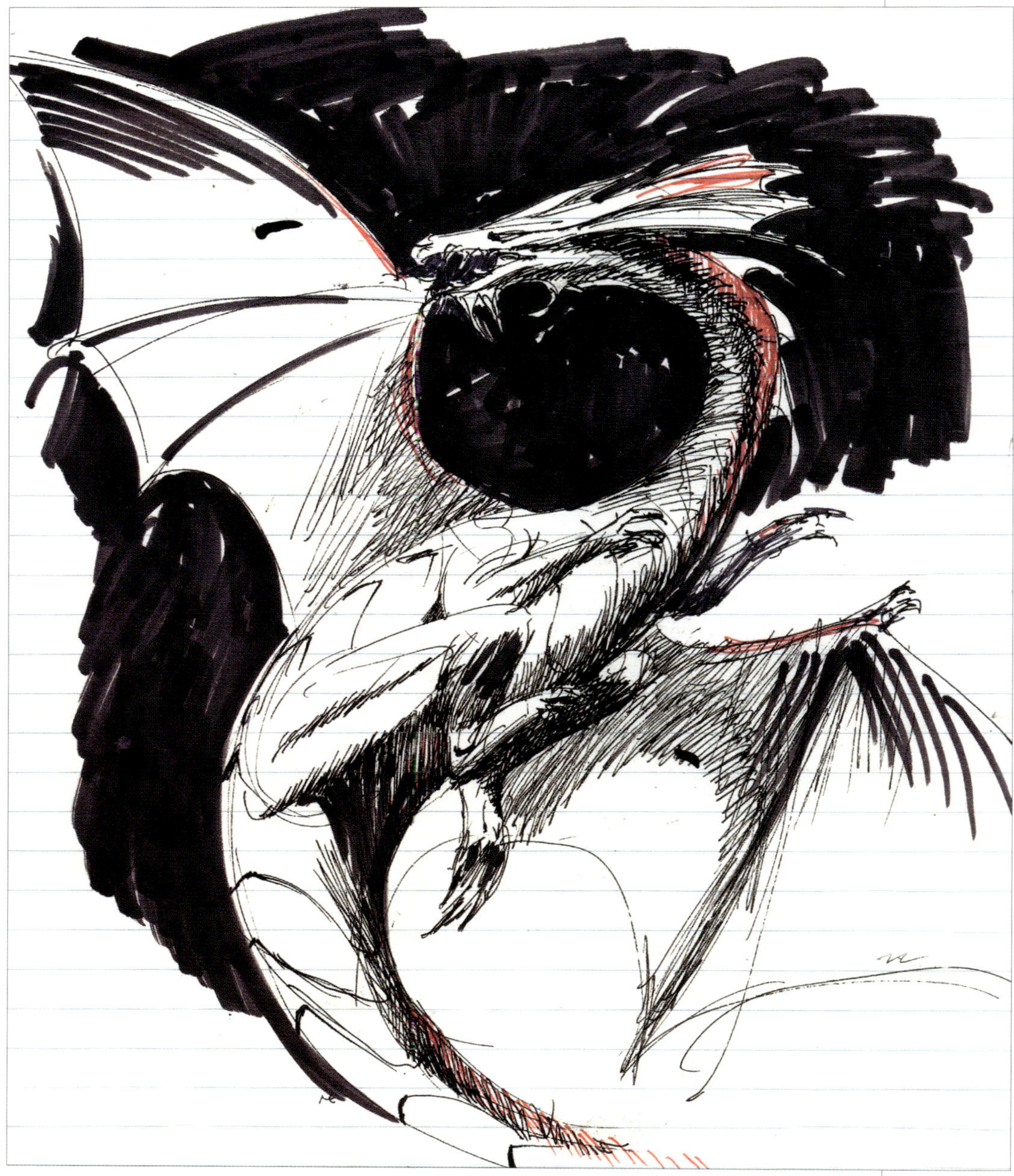

Two-colour sketch
Gel pen and black and red markers on lined notebook paper

I created the following drawing on my train ride into school one morning. While it's always desirable to work from life or from good picture reference, giving in to working exclusively from imagination can be effective in expanding and conditioning one's visual memory, and sharpening one's observational skills. These are essential skills needed in producing effective and original concept drawings. The challenge is always to make the finished drawing better than the sketch, while not losing the simplicity and energy of the original.

PROFESSIONAL SKETCHING

I mainly sketch when I've got an assignment to tackle, not just for the sheer joy of doing it. I scribble on the manuscripts – which are usually disposable – in the margins and on the blank sides of the pages. Once the job is finished, I typically toss the manuscript out. When I have maintained sketchbooks on film projects, I've usually had to surrender them at the end of the job.

As I tend to discard sketches once a project is finished, it was only through considerable effort that I was able to find what I could for this book. Except for a very few instances, I never think to hang on to these things. There's something about purging my studio at the end of an assignment that helps me to clear my mind for the next one. I never got the impression that I would ever run out of ideas, so hanging on to thoughts that I've had on other projects seemed less important.

I've always kept the number of paintings in my studio at a minimum, choosing instead to sell off work when I get it back, rather than to stockpile it. I keep roughly forty pieces on hand in the event I'm asked to contribute to a show somewhere, which happens from time to time.

There's something about purging my studio at the end of an assignment that helps me to clear my mind for the next one

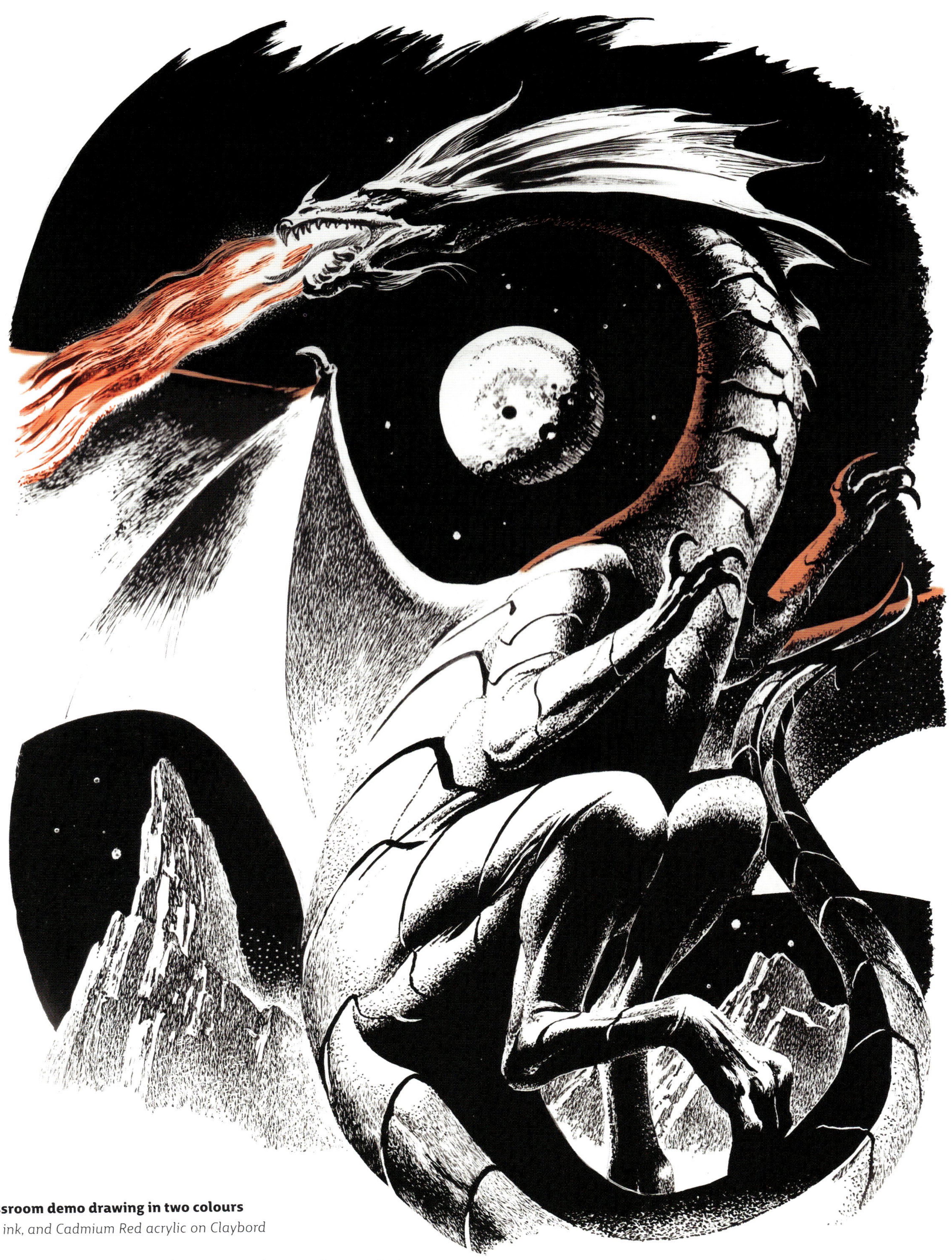

Classroom demo drawing in two colours
Pen, ink, and Cadmium Red acrylic on Claybord

This originated as a classroom demonstration for an assignment that would challenge students to create a two-colour fantasy drawing entirely from imagination. Another aspect of the challenge was to suggest a simple background through minimal detail.

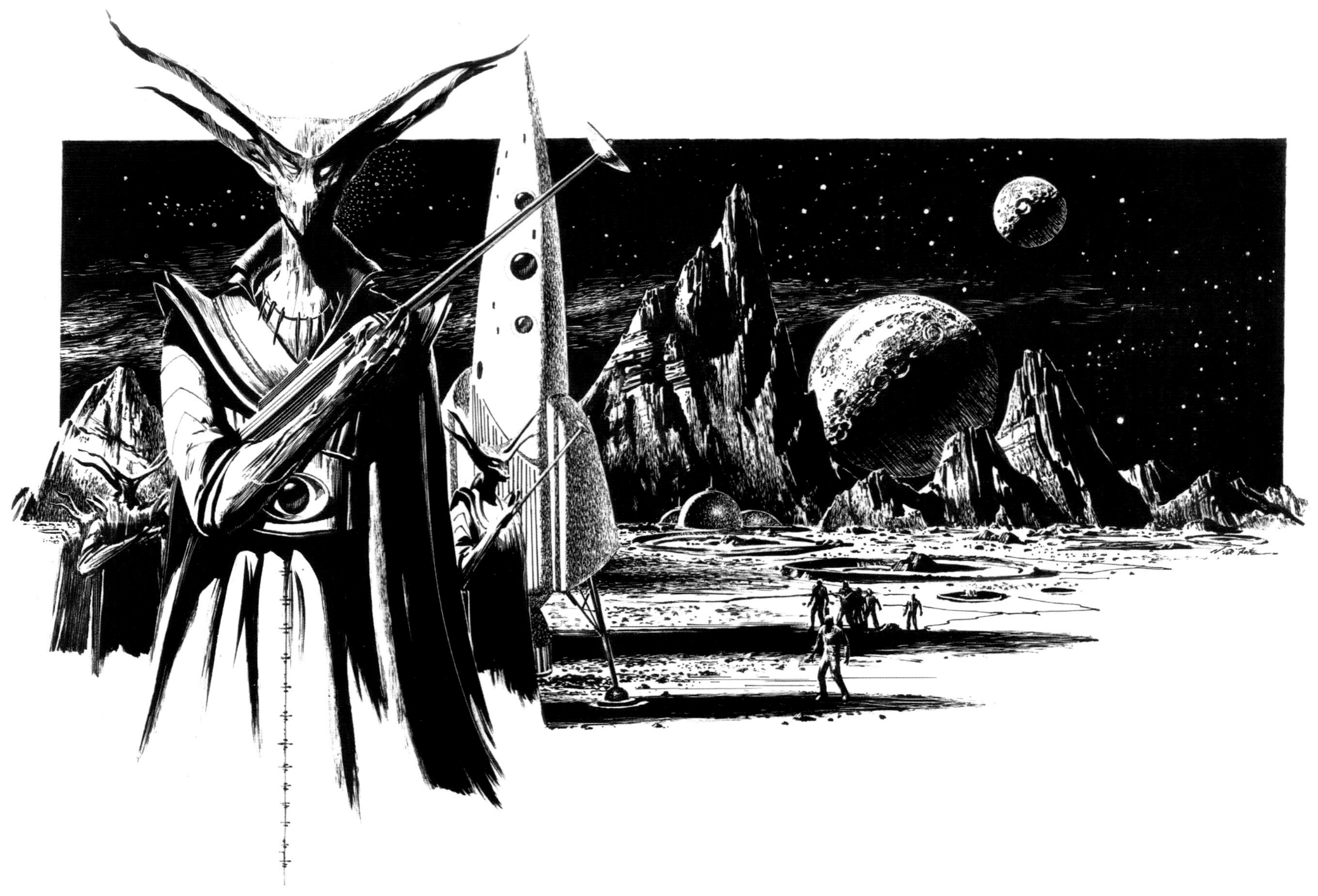

Questions and Answers
Pen and ink on Claybord

Here is a frontispiece drawing for a collection of
stories and essays written by Poul Anderson and
published by NESFA Press, circa 2015.

I've always been in awe of science-fiction writers.
I suffer from attacks of 'fan brain' every time I'm in their
presence and find myself unable to speak. I usually just
nod, smile, and try not to set myself on fire. Working in
the same field for decades, Poul Anderson and I crossed
paths many times over the years, and he was always
cordial. The last time I saw him, we ended up as
co-guests-of-honour at a science-fiction convention
in Phoenix, Arizona. During the banquet, Poul leaned
over and surprised me by saying: 'Vincent, it's been
one hell of a collaboration all these years, hasn't it?'
I wasn't expecting that, nor had I even realized that
I'd illustrated covers and interiors for over thirty of his
books. Small world ... I guess we're all just human under
the skin, no matter how well we try to conceal it.

Opposite page | **Sketches**
Fine-tipped gel pen on paper

What I attempted to achieve with these drawings
was to create a full visual representation of these
indigenous creatures as if viewed from all angles,
all the while refining their features as I went along.
I don't think I ever quite achieved all that I set out to
do, but this kind of exercise is essential in developing
credible-looking non-human characters.

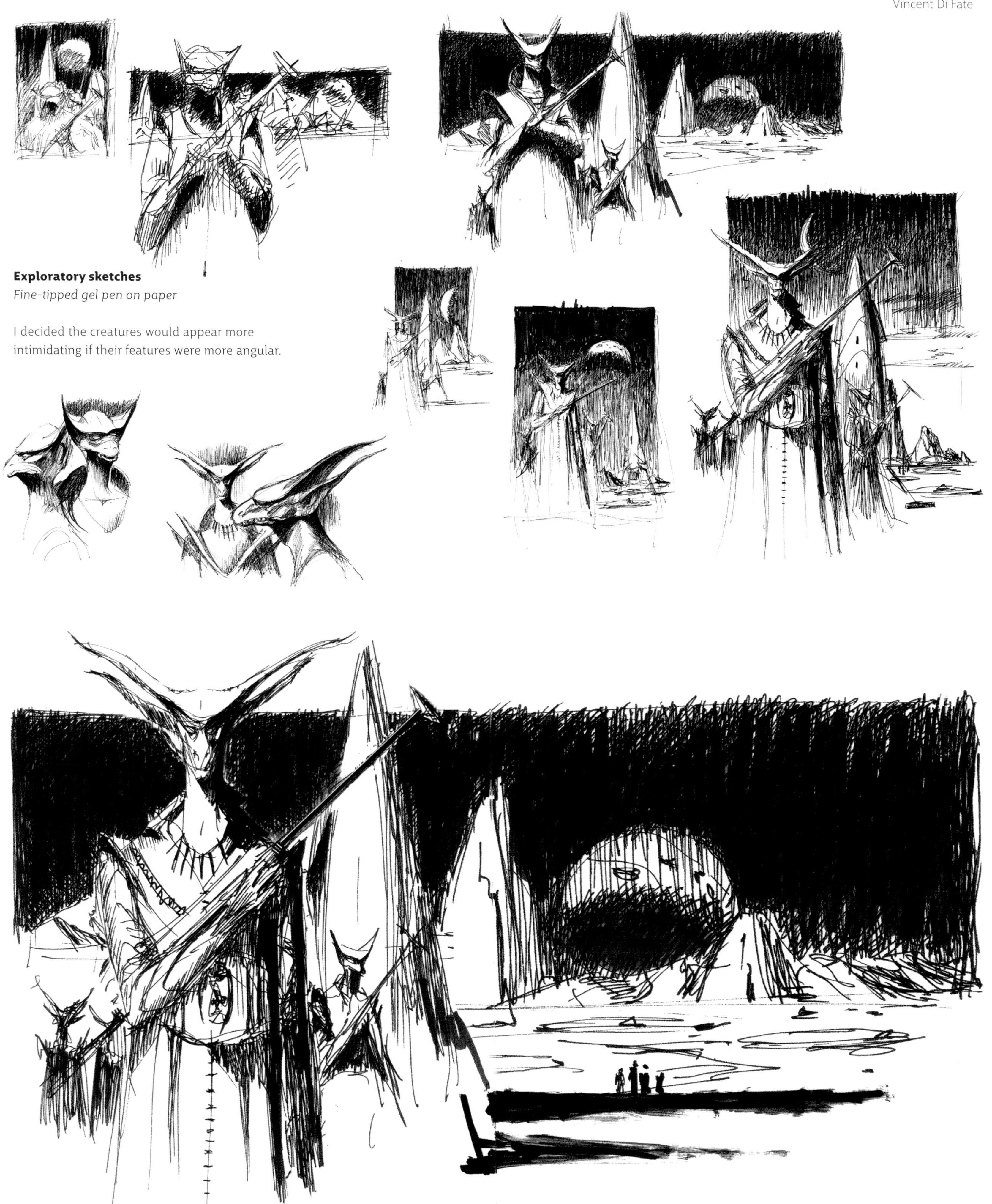

Exploratory sketches
Fine-tipped gel pen on paper

I decided the creatures would appear more intimidating if their features were more angular.

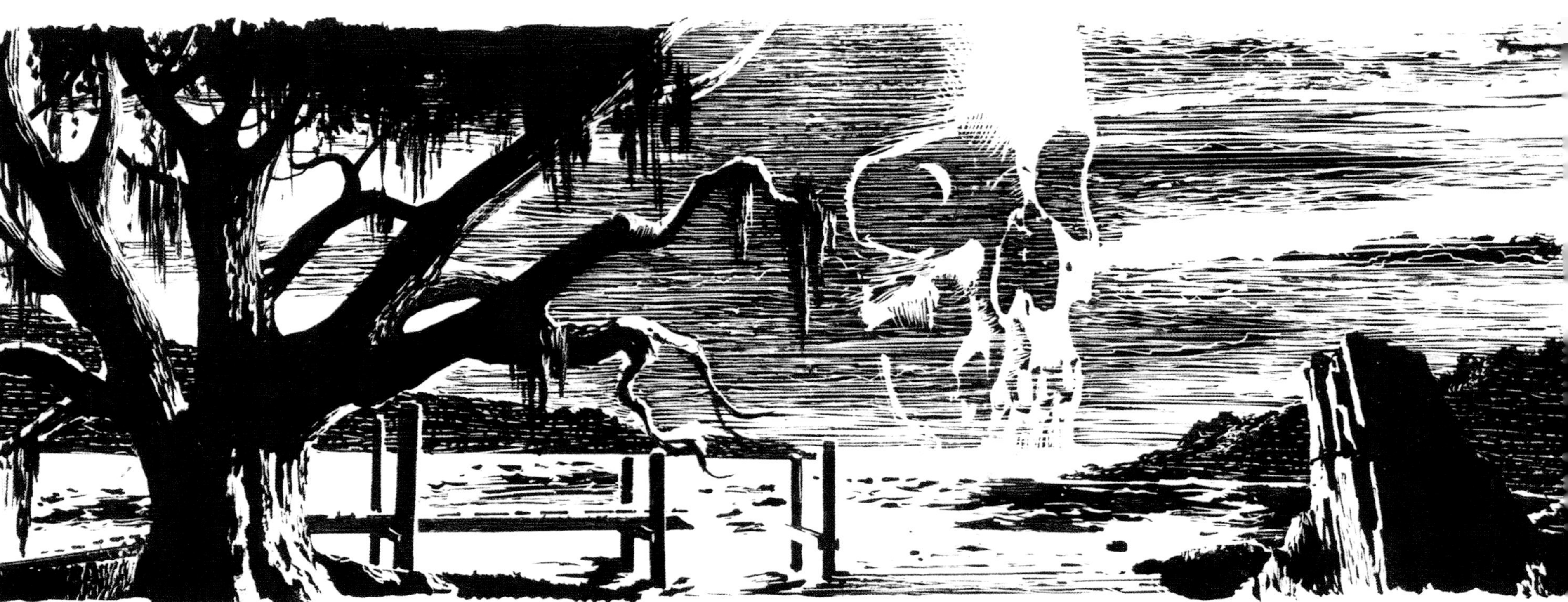

Opposite page | **Interior illustration for Frank Tuttle's short story, 'Passing the Narrows', which appeared in** *Weird Tales*, **2000**
Pen and ink on scratchboard

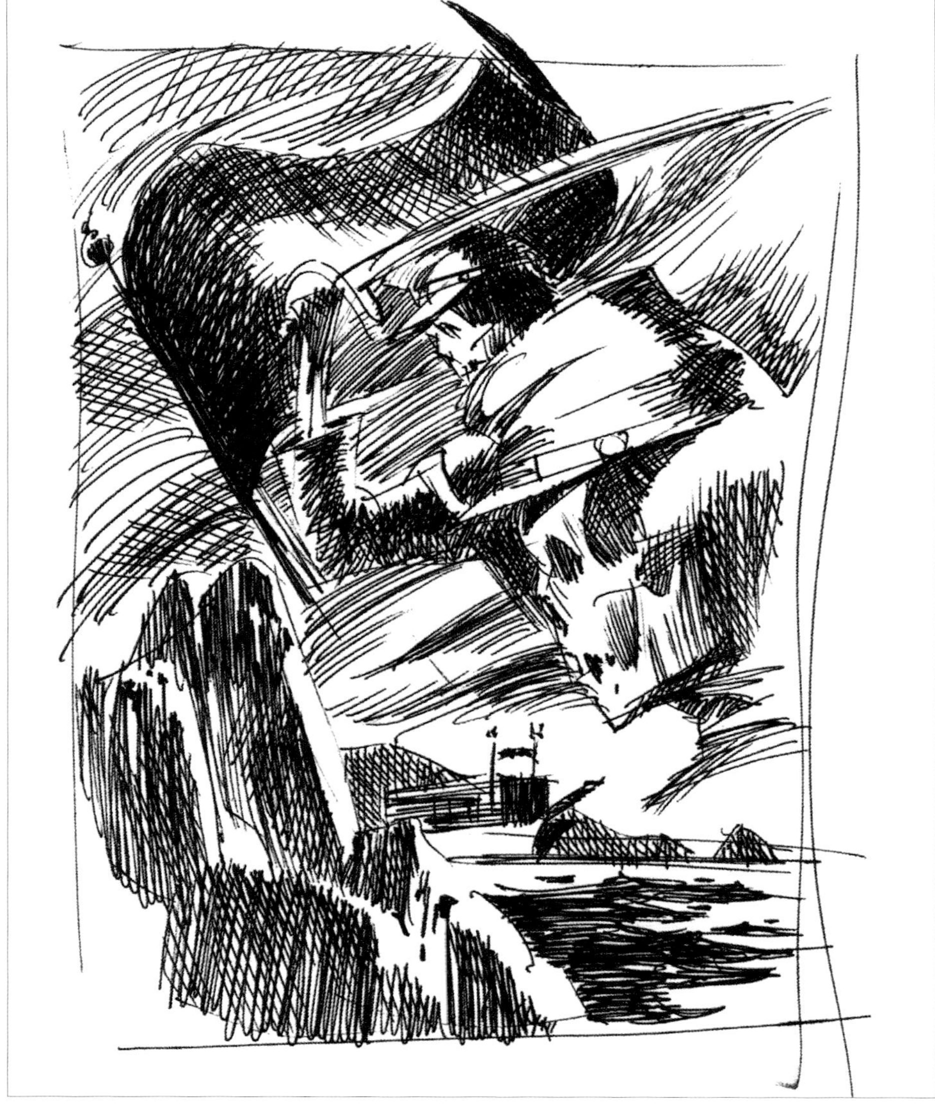

Sketches for opener and page-width spot
Fine-tipped gel pen on paper

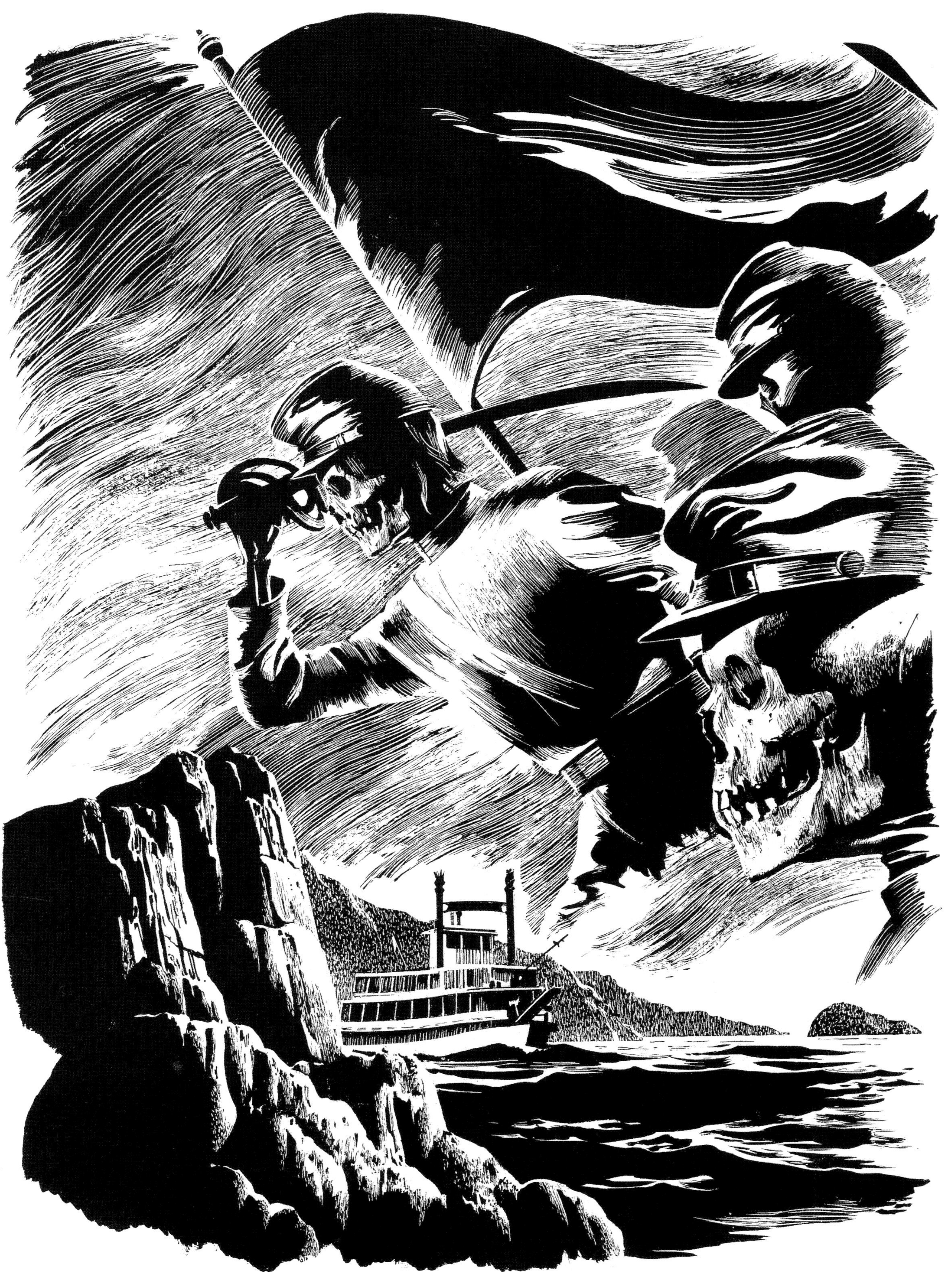

Vincent Di Fate

Originally published in *Weird Tales* magazine, 2000

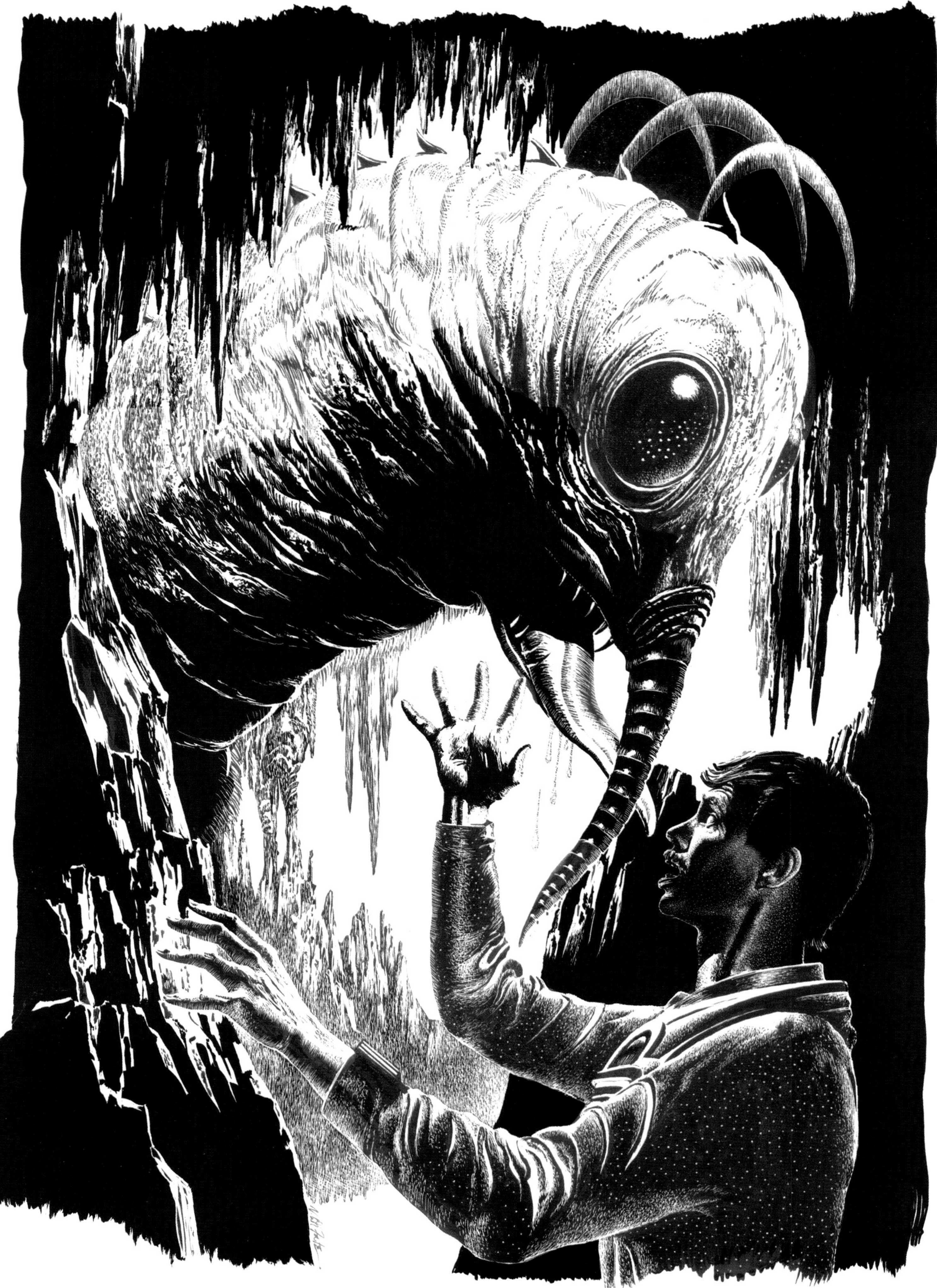

**Opposite page | Interior illustration for
M. Stern's short story 'Pharmakon, Pharmakon',
appearing in *Startling Stories*, 2022**
Pen and ink on Claybord

My typical process is to read through the manuscript
with a yellow highlighter in hand, highlighting any key
scenes and descriptions as I go. For the three or four
best scenes, I'll create a small abstract schematic with
just enough visual content to allow me to identify
the scenes quickly as I begin my review of the text.
Sometimes these schematics are meant to exaggerate
the image, as a reminder that there is an issue in need
of resolution...

Sketch for 'Pharmakon, Pharmakon'
Gel pen on paper

...Such was the case with the interior illustration
for 'Pharmakon, Pharmakon'. Its creature came
dangerously close in the author's description to
looking like a child's toy, rather than a fearsome
cave-dwelling monstrosity.

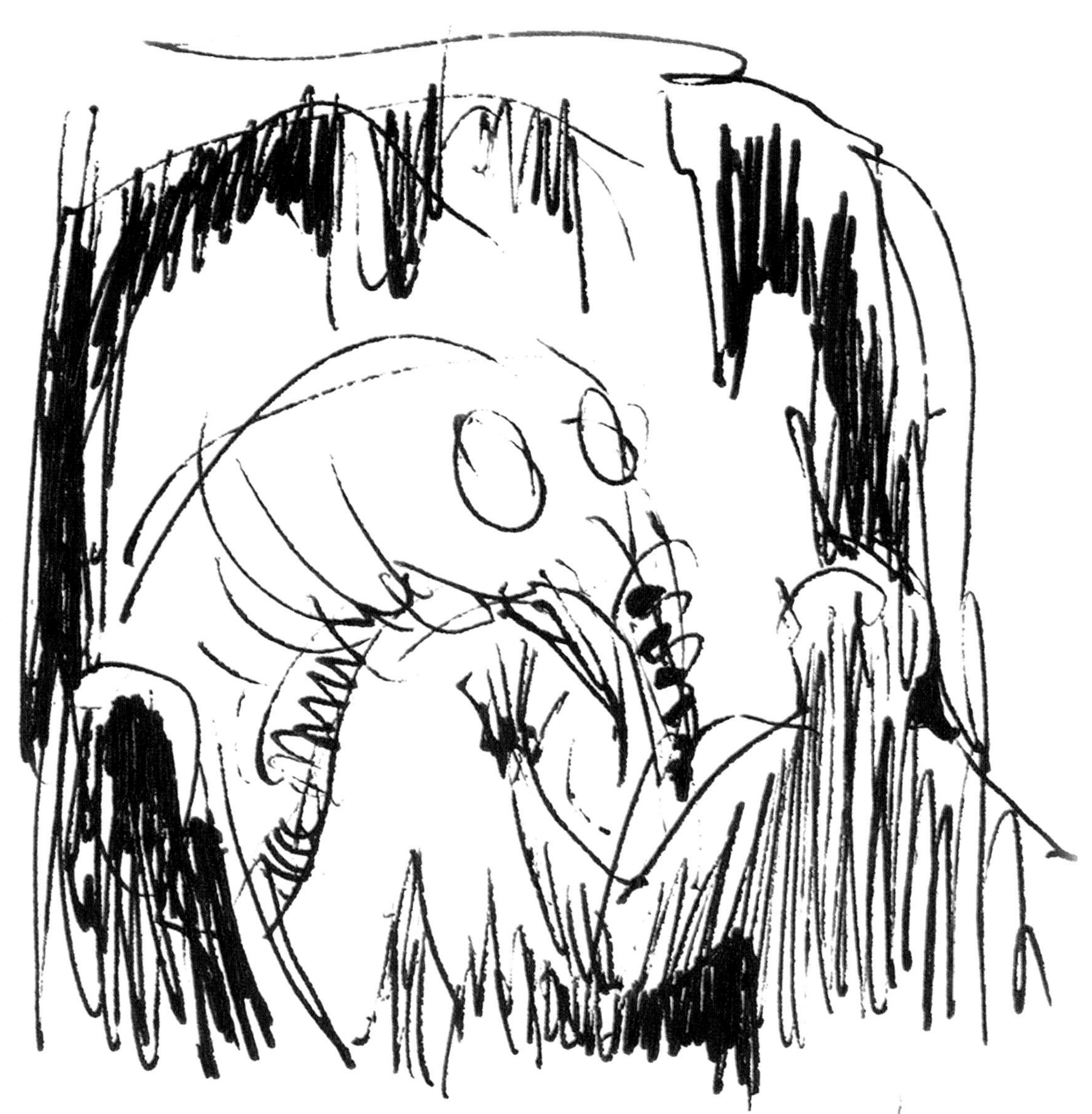

SKETCHING PRACTICE

If there are things that I see – a car, a bird, a woman in a dress – that attract my
attention, I'll make a quick sketch to record whatever it is that's caught my interest.
I don't sketch nearly enough and – truth be told – have never kept sketchbooks in
the usual sense. I should have, but never did, and am unlikely to do so in the future.
I advocate to my students the importance of maintaining sketchbooks, but I'm a
poor study myself. Keeping a personal sketchbook sounds quite wonderful, but film
work is exhausting and I don't know too many concept artists with much steam left
at the end of the workday.

The many advantages of keeping a sketchbook are obvious, but it can also risk leading
you to work in a visual shorthand that can at times be limiting, particularly in your
black-and-white work. When working in black and white, you're always interpreting and
working reductively to record what you see, since you're only using two real values.
In time you can develop a kind of visual shorthand that can narrow your range of
expression, rather than expand it.

When used well, sketchbooks can act as a quick source of reference when you're trying
to problem solve. Sometimes an older idea, that once didn't seem to work, may suddenly
spring to life. Because I don't listen to my own advice, I usually have to reinvent the
wheel every time I need to visualize something new. I comfort myself with the colossal
lie that I'm better at inventing from scratch.

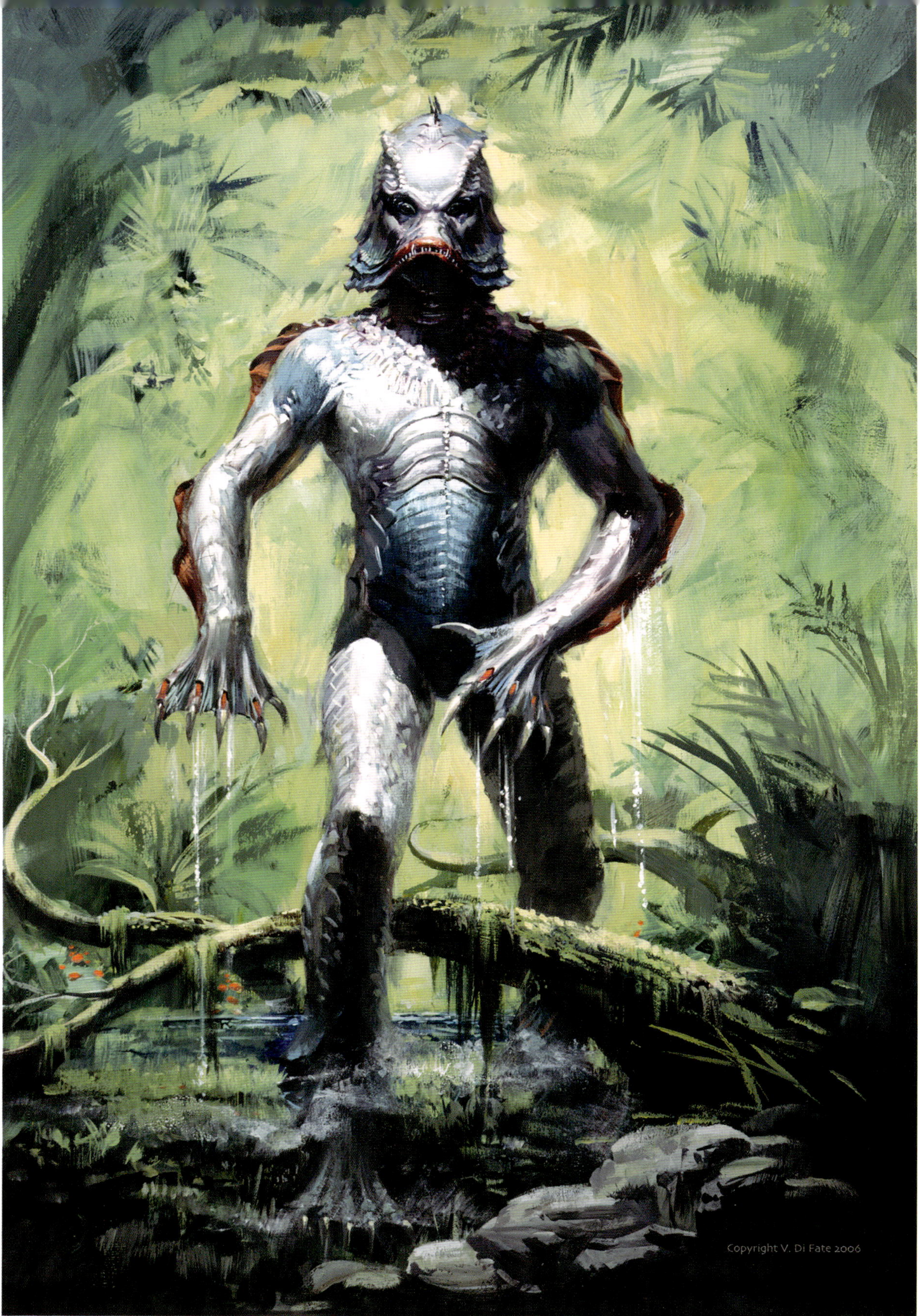

Initial concept painting for the redesigning of the *Creature from the Black Lagoon*
Acrylics on standard hardboard

In 2004, I took it upon myself to try writing a screen treatment for the classic Universal film *Creature from the Black Lagoon*. Originally released in 1954, the Creature was now a half-century old and he seemed long overdue for a reboot. A year or two later, Ricou Browning, the gentleman who'd played the Gill Man in the underwater scenes in all three of the original films, joined me and we began a collaboration that culminated in the registration of a statutory copyright for a new creature property in 2007. Ricou was more than just the Gill Man – he was a producer and director, and was for many years the VP in charge of project development for Ivan Tors Productions. He, for example, co-created the original films and later the TV series for *Flipper*. This was my initial take on a Gill Man redesign.

Concept drawings for additional creature designs
Graphite on paper

In the midst of all of this, and by sheer coincidence, it became known that producer Gary Ross, son of Arthur Ross, the original screenwriter for *Creature from the Black Lagoon*, had purchased the licensing for a remake sometime around 2005. Greg Nicotero, a friend and a co-founder of KNB EFX Group, a well-known movie make-up effects company, called and asked if I'd care to collaborate on the Gill Man redesign. This was not in any official capacity, but Greg felt that if anyone should be pitching to work the Creature redesign for the proposed new film, it should be KNB EFX.

Early in the development process, Greg made an important observation: the original Gill Man – ingenious though the design was for its time – had limited facial mobility. Modern make-up techniques and new technology had radically expanded what could be done, and it was now possible to create a Gill Man with many more points of articulation and greater physical flexibility. And whatever couldn't be achieved with an actor in a suit could be supplemented through computer-generated imagery. To my utter disappointment, however, we never got much beyond this point of new pencil drawings, when Greg's attentions were refocused on what was to become the wildly successful *The Walking Dead* TV properties for AMC. Now, far more than just a highly talented make-up artist, Greg is busy creating and directing for *The Walking Dead*, *Creepshow*, and beyond.

In my years as a professional illustrator, I've been involved in seventy or more similar false starts on film projects. There's always a pay cheque in there somewhere, but the meagre handful of films that actually get made pales in comparison to the number that are proposed, and even funded, but that never make it to the screen.

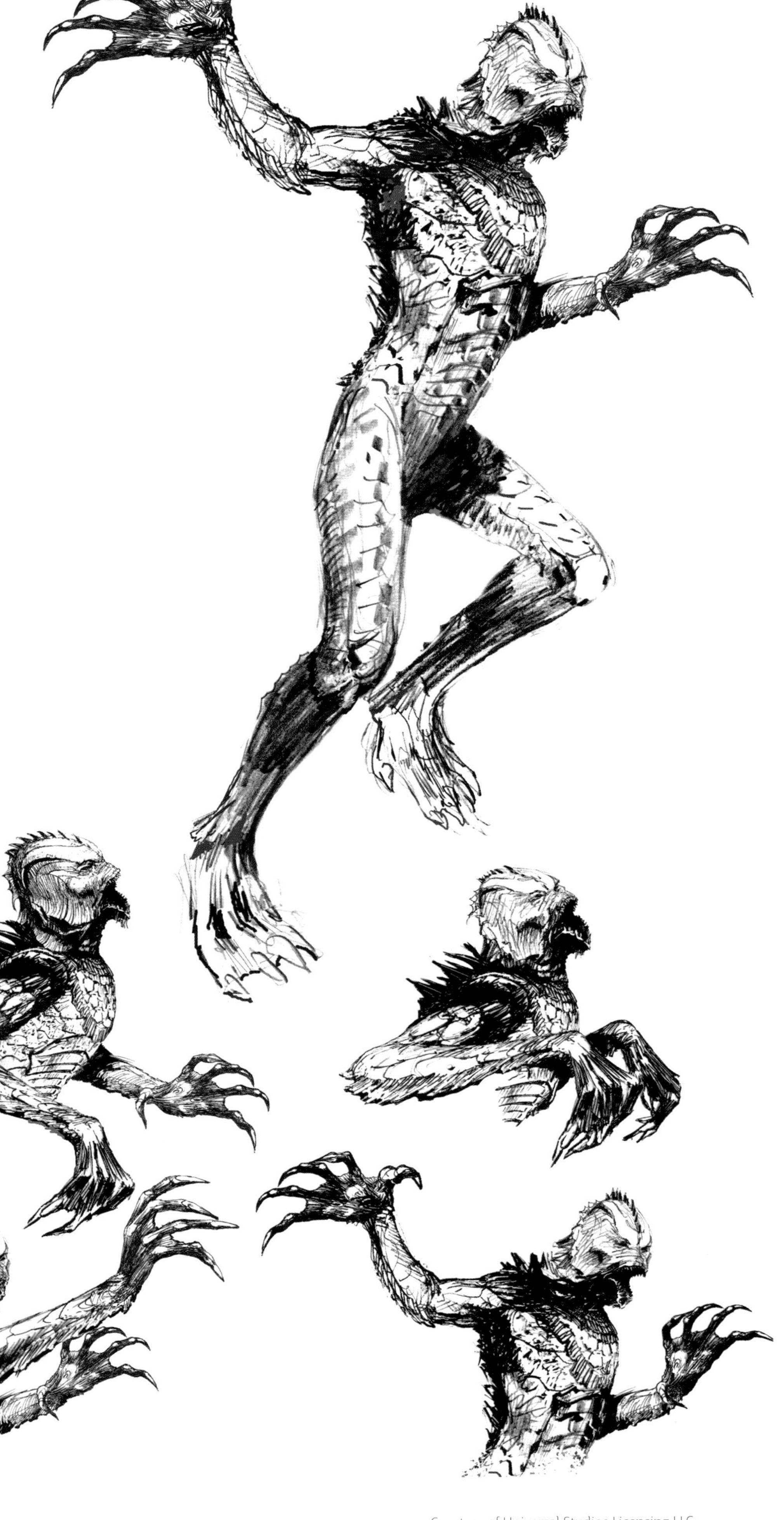

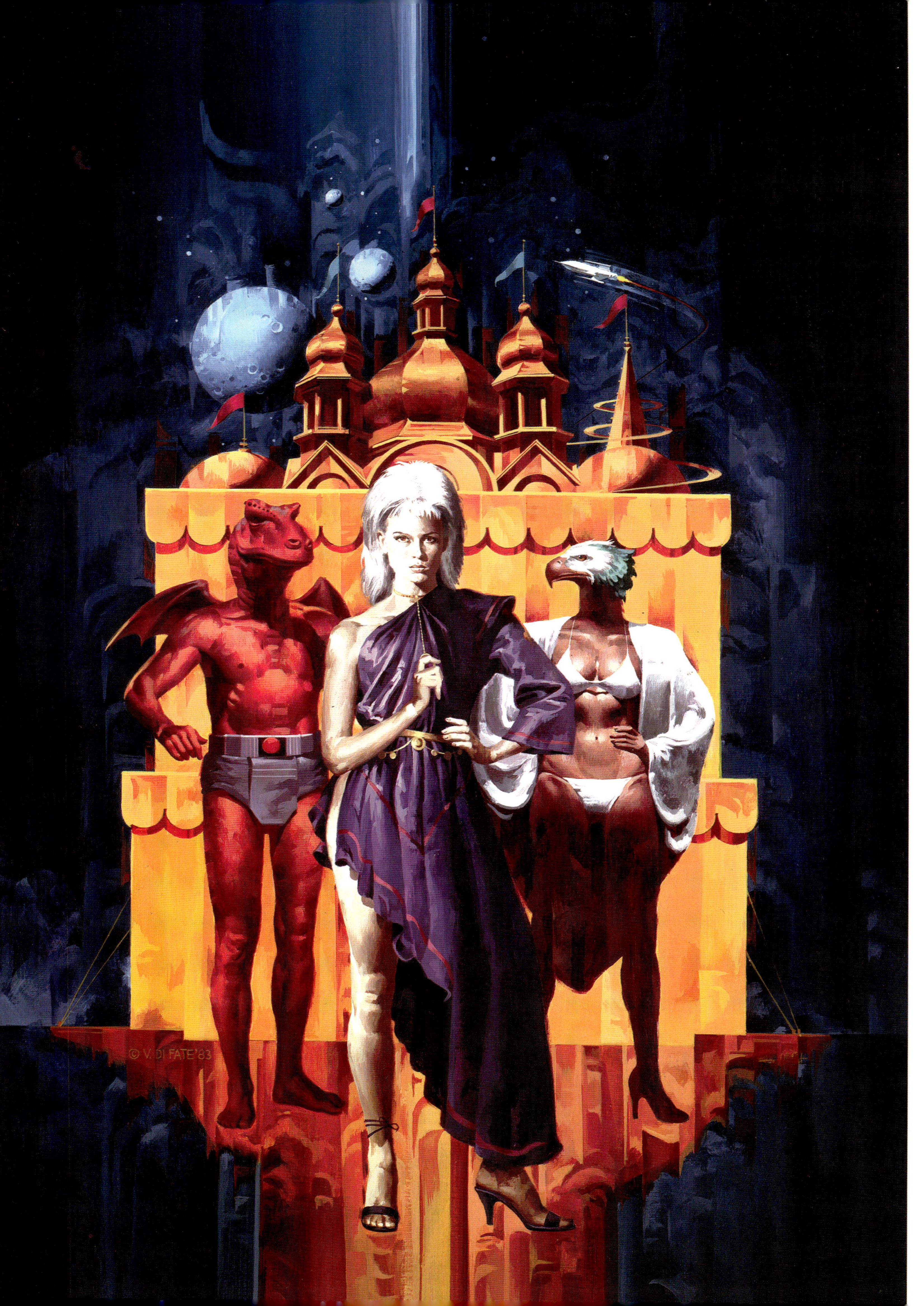

**Opposite page | Cover painting for the 1983
Daw Books paperback edition of the novel
Melome by E. C. Tubb**
Acrylics on standard hardboard

Here is my cover painting for a novel in Tubb's *Dumarest
of Terra* book series. The protagonist, like Odysseus on
his return from the Trojan War in Homer's poem *The
Odyssey*, is lost in his efforts to return home. In this
adventure, Dumarest crosses paths with the seductive
Melome, a young woman possessed of psychic powers
who performs in a travelling interplanetary circus made
up of a menagerie of curious creatures from all over the
cosmos. Having been typecast at this time in my career
as a 'gadget' artist, I leapt at the opportunity to finally
paint a pretty girl.

Right | Comprehensive colour sketch
Acrylics on standard hardboard

Since my abilities as a figure painter were largely unknown to
members of the science-fiction publishing community at the time,
I produced this small comprehensive sketch in order to clarify what
I had in mind. In doing so, I uncovered an important fact about the
process by which art is often commissioned: in certain circumstances,
the sketch can be everything. If the sketch works, there's no reason
to believe that the finish shouldn't, too. And the sketch is the perfect
roadmap to creating the finish. At the sketch stage, even though you
are preparing something to be seen by others, there's a fearlessness
about its execution, because there's always an assumption that there
are refinements yet to be made as the art develops to the finish.
Also, if the client requests changes, it's always best to test them
out by altering the sketch to make sure that the requested changes
will work.

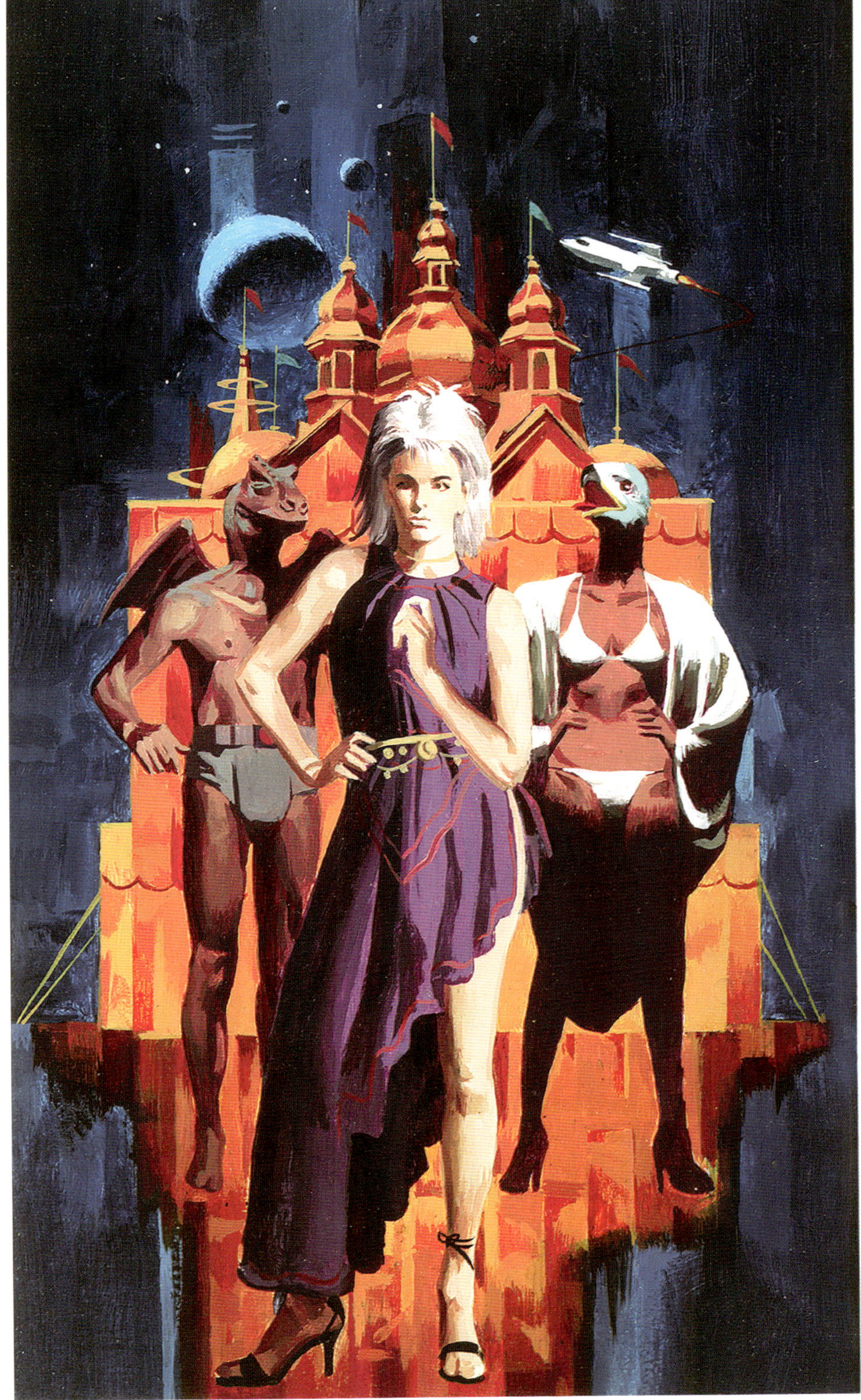

The 1983 Daw Books paperback edition of the novel *Melome* by E. C. Tubb

David Colman

BEGINNINGS

I've had a very successful career and an interesting path thus far. I didn't go to art college. In high school, I gave up art for sports and the other interests you have as a teenager. I didn't want to be a 'comic-book nerd', or so I felt at the time – there's no slander meant there at all! Instead I went to the University of California, Santa Barbara, and figured I would use my art background and creativity to go into advertising. I started studying communication, then fell in love with drawing again and ended up double-majoring in art. But I never finished. The programme was more like liberal arts – 'draw what you feel', 'paint and make a statement', or 'make a boat out of paper and float in it'. When I left, I still didn't know that animation or film were careers I could actually pursue.

Some people had looked at my work and said, 'You're very good at capturing characters – a good character designer,' but I never even knew that was a thing! I didn't grow up loving animation and film. I drew like everyone else, but it wasn't a big dream of mine. Falling in love with this art form has been my journey.

When people said I could be a good character designer, I thought, 'Do I have to go to art school?' I was told I could just take some classes at the local animators' union, so I talked my way into some classes there, and even into some classes at Disney. I worked for my dad's law firm during the day, then went to the classes at night. On the weekends I would go to the zoo and study animals from life. My animal artwork is now my 'brand' and what I'm known for, more than anything else. I've self-published seven art books and have a whole line of animal-art apparel and prints. Animals became my thing – I fell in love with them along the way.

Thumbnail exploration for book cover design
Tuscan Red Col-Erase pencil and white Prismacolor pencil on toned sketchbook paper

Here is a sketchbook page where I was exploring an idea for the second-edition cover of my book, *Art of Animal Character Design*. You can see some scribbles I abandoned early because I knew they were the wrong direction. And that's what a sketchbook is for: exploring, finding what works and what doesn't. It's not about perfection, but informing your process.

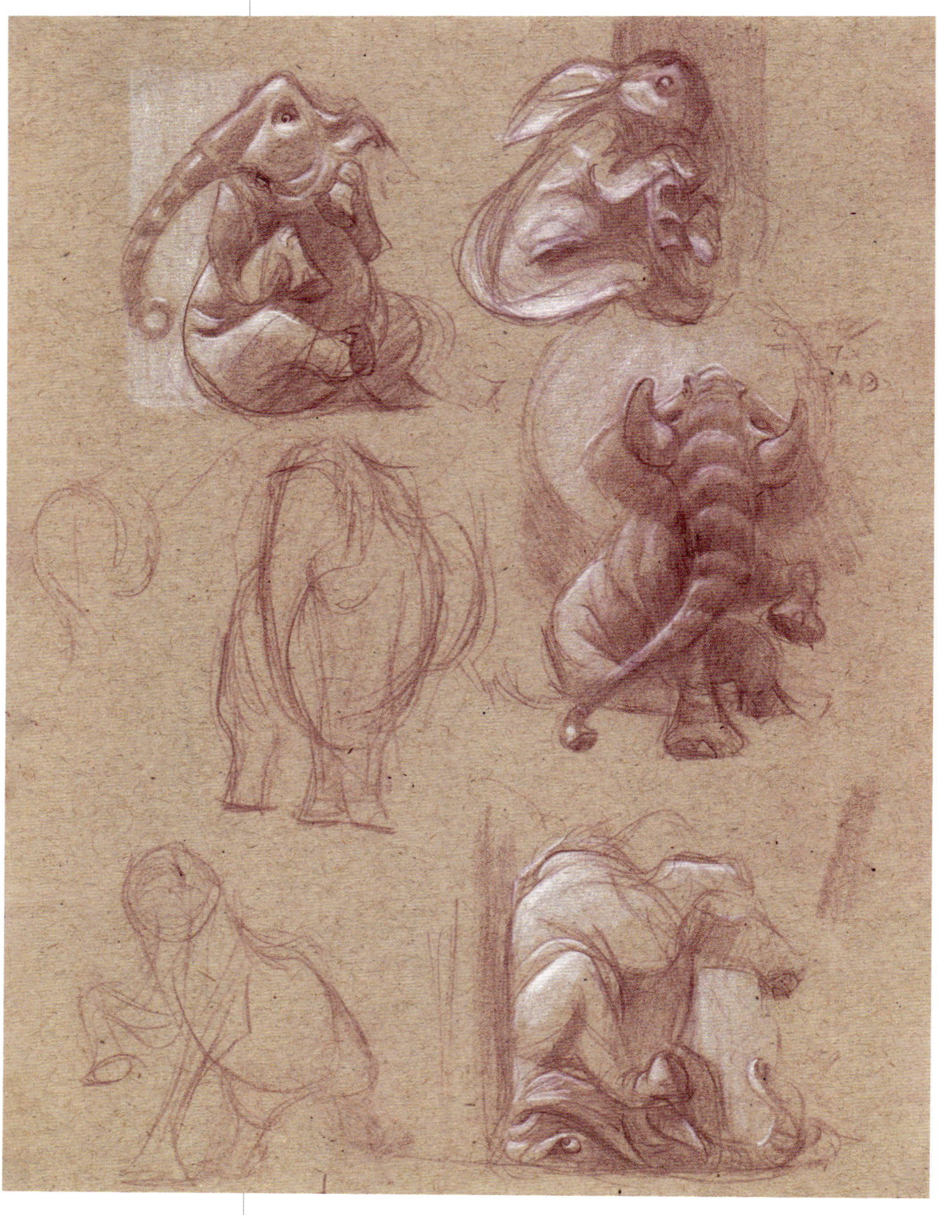

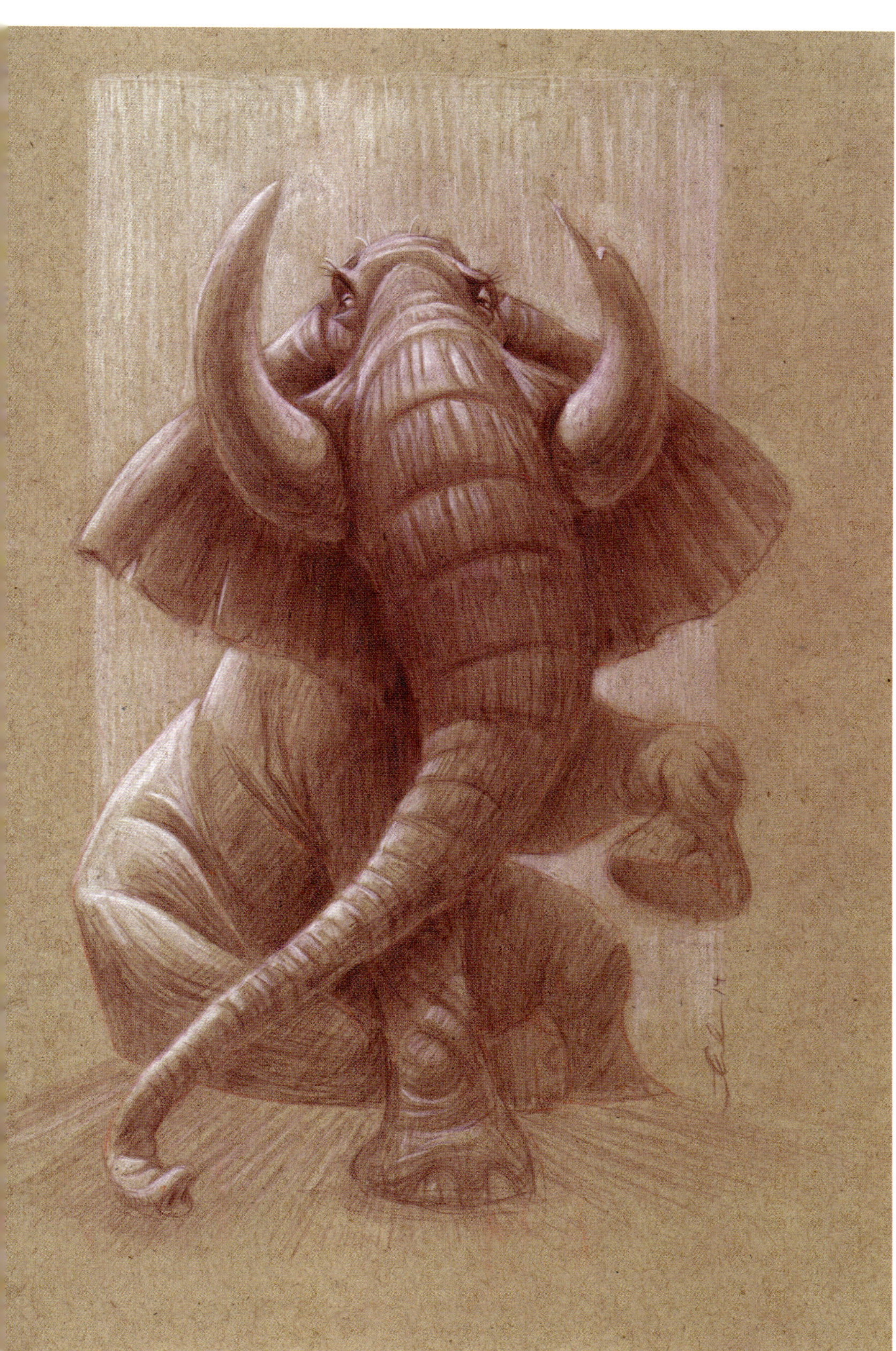

Final illustration for book cover
Col-Erase Tuscan Red coloured pencil and white Prismacolor pencil on rose-toned paper

You can see how the thumbnail exploration led to this final image for the book cover. Exploring it in my sketchbook first led to a more efficient process and a successful final illustration.

Oddly enough, I got into the business by delivering mail at Disney. It sounds like a fairy tale, but I'm not lying! I left my dad's firm and placed myself at a temp agency that I knew filled positions at Disney. I got a job working in the mailroom, then got hired for shipping full time, then I worked in the copy room, then I became a production assistant. When I worked in the copy room, I would make little signs on the walls with my drawings, trying to advertise my art. When I dropped mail off on people's desks, I'd drop off drawings to some of those big-time artists. I talked my way into life-drawing classes. I took a free class with the amazing Paul Felix, a top production designer at Disney, and showed him my work. He was very impressed and asked, 'What do you do here?' and I said, 'I work in shipping.' He had a good laugh at that!

Working as a production assistant on *Pooh's Heffalump Movie*, it was good to have a job and be immersed in all the goings-on of production, and to get all the free classes. I would go into the park and paint on my lunch breaks, just taking it all in like a sponge. But having been rejected everywhere, I was also very frustrated.

I was a shameless self-promoter, but I couldn't get a job as an artist no matter how hard I tried. I was either told I wasn't in the union or I didn't have enough experience – but how could I get in the union if I couldn't get any experience? I was just getting the run-around and felt jaded by the business before I'd even been hired. I still drew a lot on my own and became very driven, motivated, and self-taught, but it was at a time when Disney wasn't really hiring. This was probably the early 2000s, after *Tarzan* had been released, and things were starting to steer more towards 3D animation. There was no way they would give a chance to an artist who didn't have any experience and hadn't even gone to an art school.

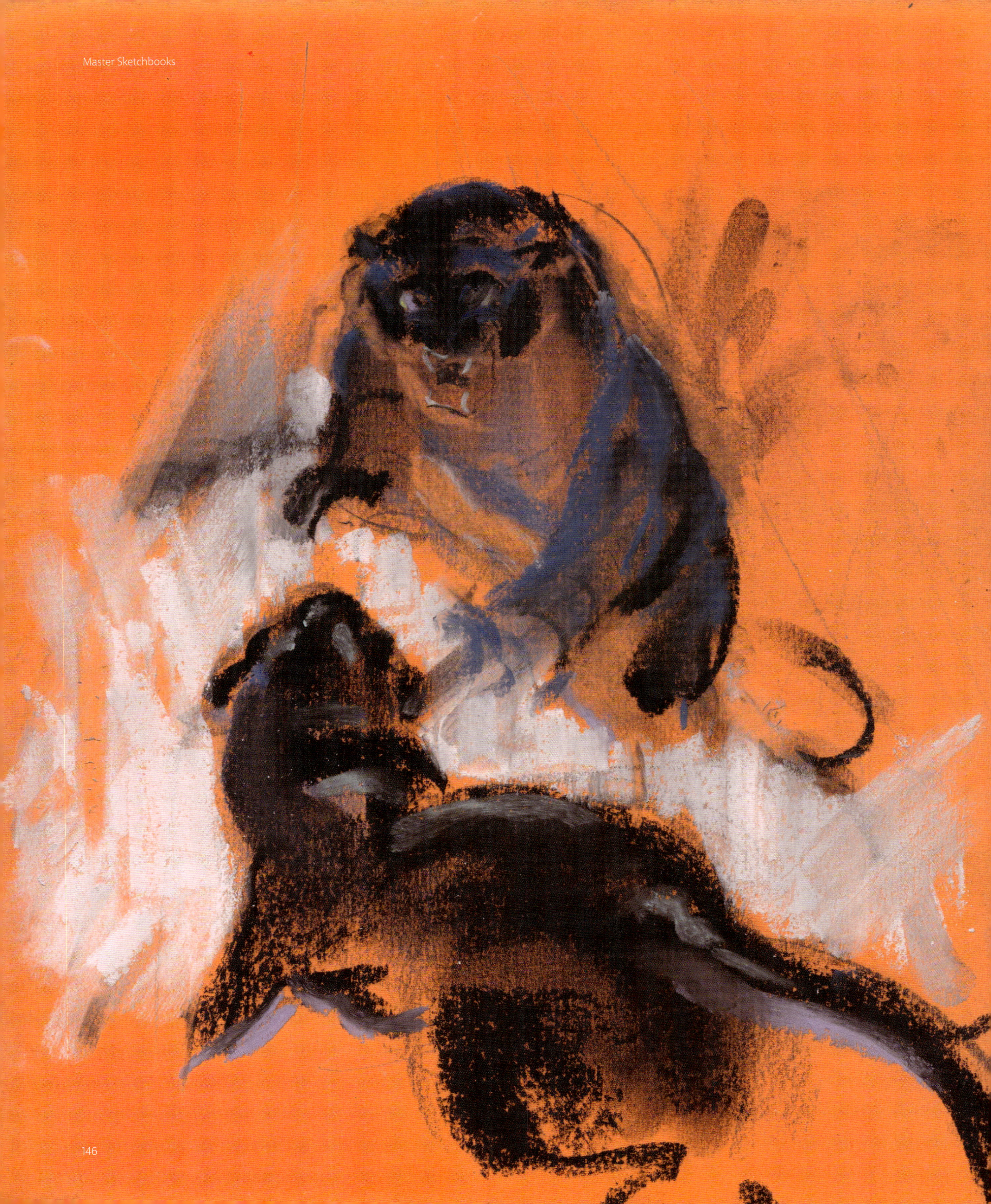

A PHONE CALL FROM SONY

When Sony started up their animation department, I sent them my work. The internet was only just starting and emails weren't a big thing yet, so I was coming up at a time when it wasn't easy to have online visibility. People had AOL and dial-up modems, and there was no such thing as social media. When I got a phone call from Sony, I was already so jaded, I thought they must want my address to send my portfolio back. But they said they wanted to talk to me.

The voice on the end of the phone said, 'It says here you're a production assistant on *Pooh's Heffalump Movie*.'

I replied, 'That is correct.'

'But your artwork is beautiful. Why aren't you working?'

I gave them my whole spiel and they said they really wanted to meet me. They were starting a new animation division with Sandy Rabins and Penney Finkelman Cox. Two titans of the industry, powerful women in the business – and they were interested in me!

'Could you bring in your portfolio?'

'I sent you my portfolio.'

'No, no. We want to see your originals.'

I thought that was a little weird and Paul Felix advised me to not leave my originals there. I spent the weekend with drawings all over the floor of my apartment, sorting through folders of character designs, life drawings, animal drawings, layouts, paintings, and stacks of sketchbooks.

When I went to meet Sony, it wasn't just a small office but an actual conference room. As I set out my originals, they said, 'You had all this raw talent but no experience. We thought you were stealing art from others and passing it off as your own.' It felt like a backhanded compliment!

'We had to see it. There was no way you were this talented and hadn't worked yet.' They'd wanted to call me out on it but, sure enough, those were my original drawings.

Sandy said to me, 'How come you're not working?'

'Well, I'm not in the union, and I don't have any experience.'

'Does Disney know you're here right now?'

'No, they think I'm at a dentist appointment.'

'When can you start?'

Even just reliving this story, I get the chills again!

Sony put me to work on *The Polar Express*. I was one of the first traditional artists on the project. They started teaching me 3D, I worked on lots of animals, and I even got to work briefly with Tom Hanks. Overnight, I became a professional. When that project finished, I moved on to *Open Season* and *Surf's Up*, and ended up being trained by the great Marcelo Vignali.

Now I've worked all the way up to being Head of Story at DreamWorks on a movie called *Gabby's Dollhouse*. It's a live-action/animation hybrid movie based on the very successful streaming series of the same name. It's a perfect fit because I've now worked in both the live-action and animation fields. Funnily enough, the production designer on it is Marcelo Vignali, my mentor at Sony all those years ago. We've got to work together again, this time as peers leading our own departments.

I've taken a very interesting, different path to get to where I am today. You can still gain a lot by going to art school, but it is possible to make it without going through the traditional routes. All it takes is that fiery passion and you can make your dreams come true.

Panther scuffle
Pastel on Canson orange-toned paper

In this exploration I was inspired by Bob Peak's rough sketchbook studies. I took that same approach, using pastel and just going for it. I love the bold clarity amidst the loose energetic strokes.

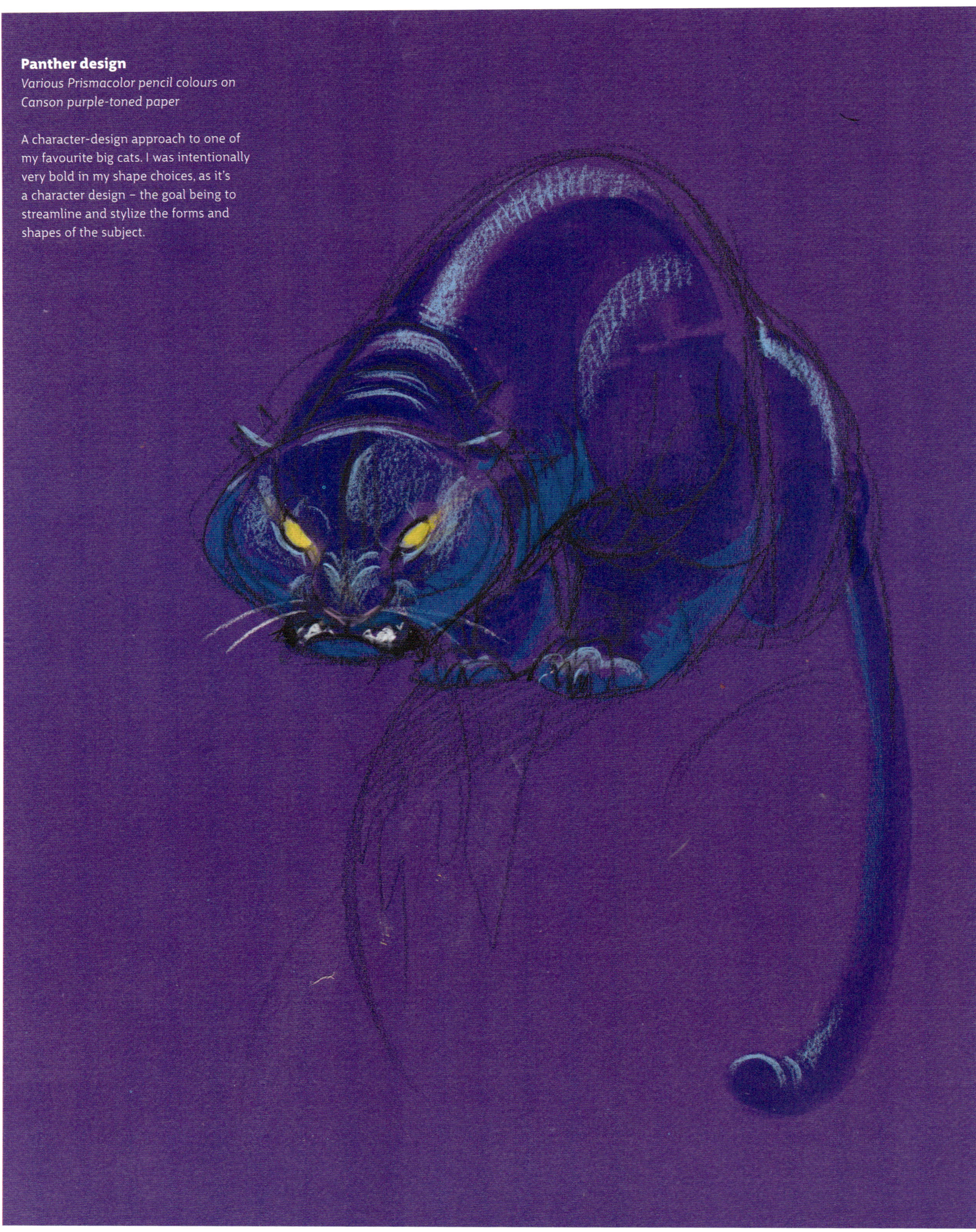

Panther design
Various Prismacolor pencil colours on Canson purple-toned paper

A character-design approach to one of my favourite big cats. I was intentionally very bold in my shape choices, as it's a character design – the goal being to streamline and stylize the forms and shapes of the subject.

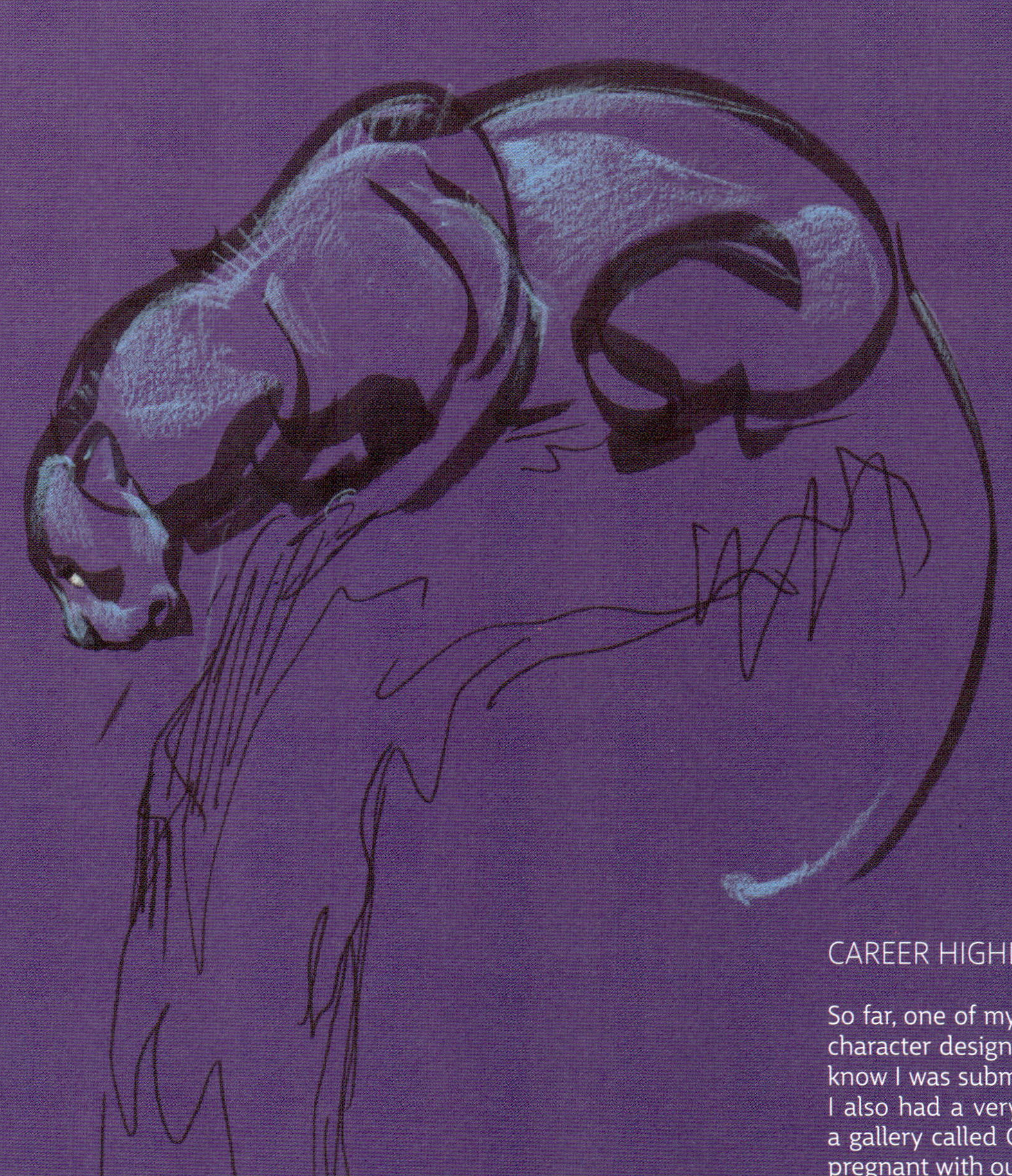

The thing I'm proudest of is that I am able to support my family with my passion

CAREER HIGHLIGHTS

So far, one of my proudest moments is winning an Emmy in 2008 for character design on *Class of 3000* for Cartoon Network. I didn't even know I was submitted – I just got a phone call telling me that I'd won! I also had a very successful art show in Paris – my first art show at a gallery called Galerie Daniel Maghen, near the Louvre. My wife was pregnant with our first daughter at the time and I got a trip for us both there, all expenses paid, plus I sold forty paintings and illustrations. That was another pretty awesome accomplishment.

It's really hard to get into the Art Directors Guild Local 800 to be able to work on live-action boarding, but I willed my way in. I made it happen! The great Robert Rodriguez called me to storyboard *We Can Be Heroes* and that helped me get my hours. Before I knew it, I was flying to Atlanta to work on set with Chris McKay for *The Tomorrow War*. It was pretty cool to hang out with Chris Pratt and get to see him act out the scenes I'd boarded, as well as see a whole set built based on those scenes. Since then I've worked on big movies with visionary filmmaker Barry Jenkins on *Mufasa: The Lion King* and the uber-talented Joachim Rønning on *Tron: Ares*. I have worked my way up through many different disciplines, from design to story, building up to a leadership role. I've been an Art Director twice, Character-Design Supervisor once, and now I'm officially a Head of Story on a big, live-action/animated movie.

However, the thing I'm proudest of is that I am able to support my family with my passion. I am able to take care of, feed, and clothe my kids and put a roof over our heads doing something I love, which is not something many people can say they can do. If ninety per cent of the job force hates their job, I am one of the ten per cent that loves what I do, and I do not take one day of that for granted. Despite all the ups and downs and strikes in this roller coaster of an industry, I have stayed employed for about twenty-five years – I've only been unemployed for three months out of that whole time. That's something I am grateful for.

Panther on a tree
Black Tombow brush pen on Canson purple-toned paper

Experimenting with various media, starting with pen and adding blue pencil to bring out the form. This was a fun one.

Standing black bear
Non-photo blue, black, and cream Prismacolor pencils on Canson red-toned paper

Another illustrative doodle where I used bold colour choices with my loose energetic style. I liked this one so much that I made shirt designs of it.

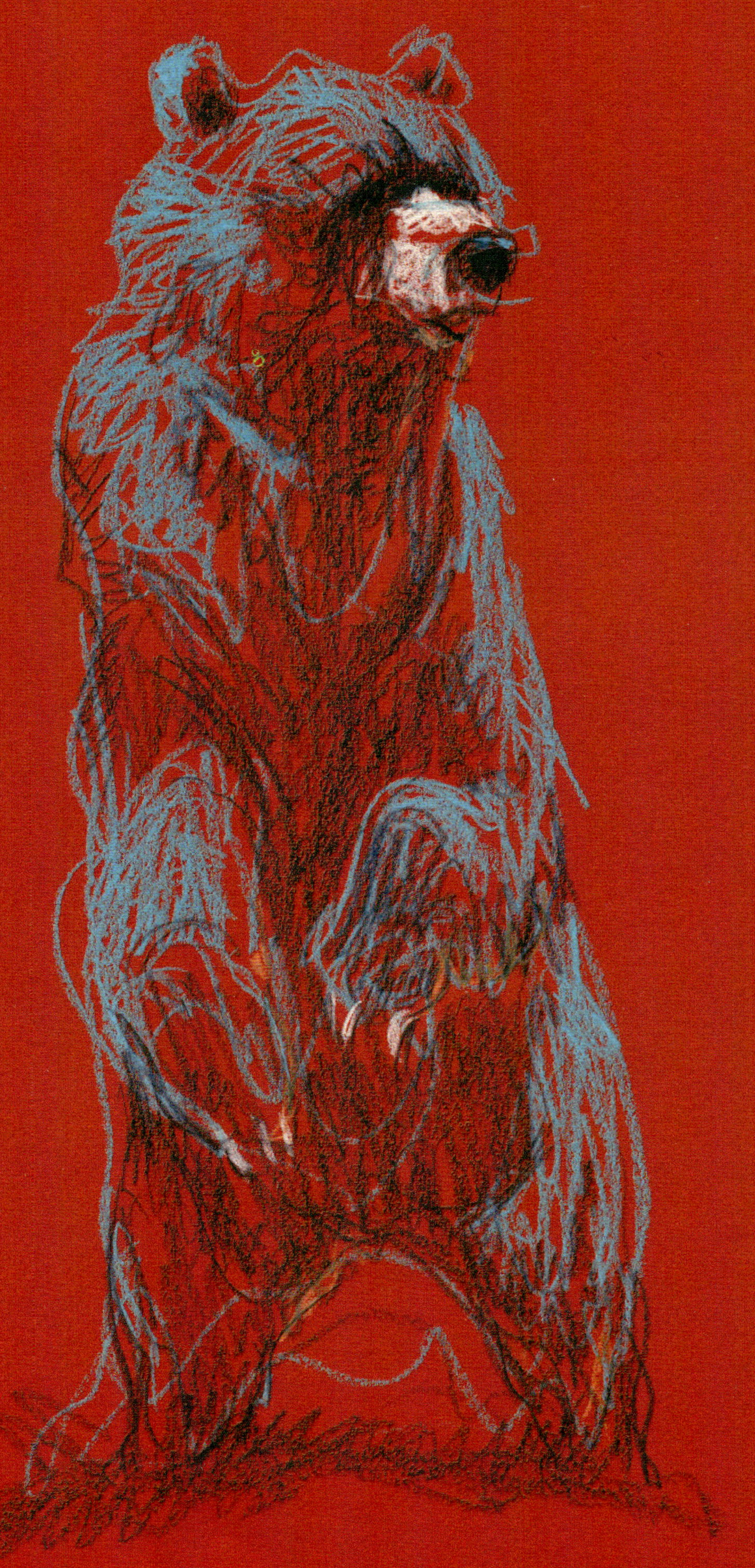

KEEPING A SKETCHBOOK

I didn't always keep a sketchbook. When I was about twenty-two and began studying academically, I took art classes with Glenn Vilppu, Karl Gnass, and Paul Wee. All three beat us around the head about the importance of keeping a sketchbook. I still keep one today. I also now use other disciplines and different platforms for exploring ideas – but the same idea is still there and has remained with me throughout my career.

There's no wrong or right way to use a sketchbook, but the best thing I can suggest is that your sketchbook is a place for *you*. It's where you can explore your own ideas and it's okay to make mistakes. Your sketchbook is not for public consumption but is your own private diary. Use it often. When I get a new sketchbook, sometimes I won't draw on the first page, as it feels like there's all this pressure. Instead I open it up in the middle and just draw anywhere. There's less pressure when you start drawing from the middle of the book.

We are born with 10,000 bad drawings in us. With me, I feel like it's even more and it'll take a lifetime to get them out! The sketchbook is a good place for that. If you were to look at my sketchbook, you might find two or three pages of what almost looks like the same drawing. That's because I was trying to find the right iteration of something I saw in my head. For some reason, in a sketchbook, it doesn't feel final. You're not afraid to mess up or try new things. You can keep drawing the same thing over and over again, and you won't get frustrated because it's just for you. It's all in this little book that's not going to be on display. It's not going to be put up in a museum or in a frame. It's an area for you to trip and fall and then get back up.

Find yourself a small sketchbook and a pen, carry them with you all the time, and sketch if you're standing in a long queue or waiting for a coffee. I'm working on a storyboard book at the time of writing this and so I take my iPad wherever I go, as that's my sketchbook. I've got notes, panels, frames, and tutorial materials for the book in there. If I'm at my daughter's track meet and I'm waiting between races, or waiting at my other daughter's gymnastic meets, I've got my iPad with me. You can always be studying and learning, even if you're not in a focused mode but are just passing the time.

I tend to use my sketchbooks for early explorations – the 'blue sky' stage of the process. Sometimes this is just a matter of note-taking. If I have an idea, I can just write it down or do a little scribble. Sometimes those spontaneous scribbles are better than sitting down in front of a blank canvas to do a giant illustration. At this stage you're more at ease because you're really exploring, using sketching as a journey, an exploration for your first ideas for a job, a film you're working on, or a personal painting you're just thinking about. That first image you have in your head may not be the final one, so it's good to set out and try to find the best way to execute your idea, both narratively and technically.

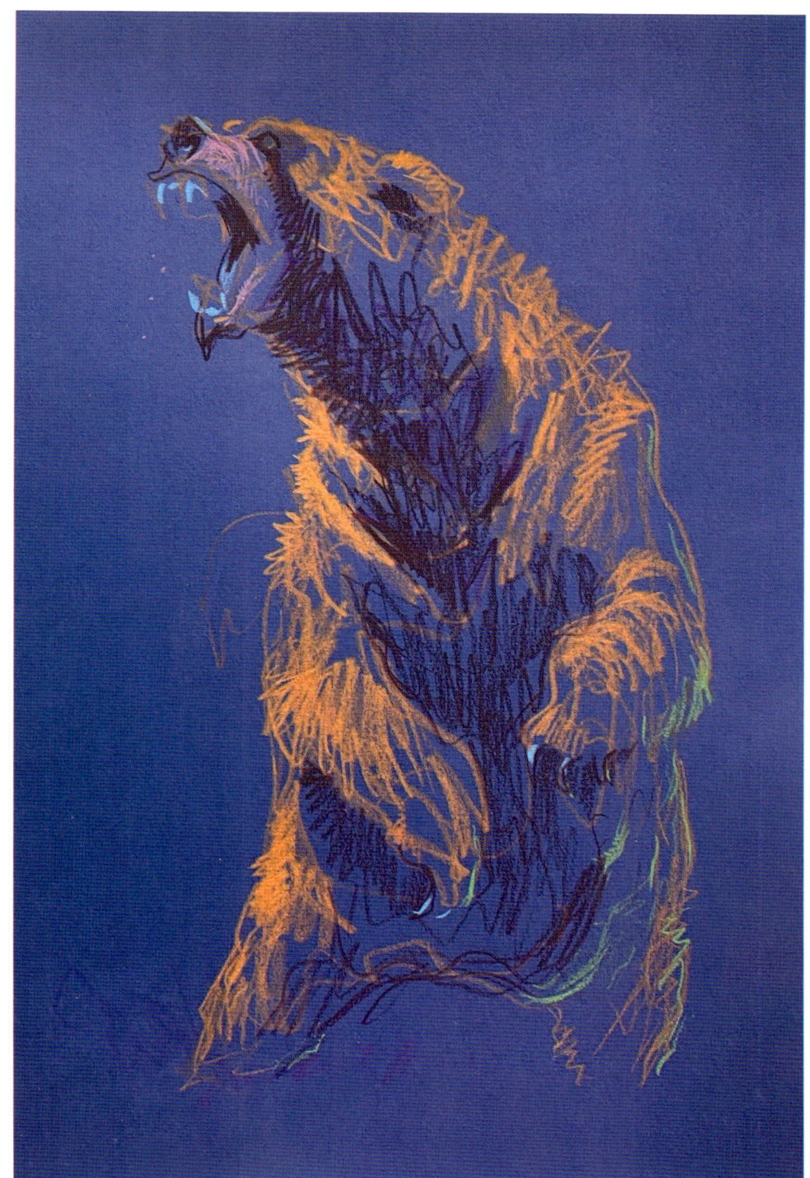

Grizzly growl
*Prismacolor pencil on Canson
blue-toned paper*

Here is a style I recently got into: making bold colour choices with no under-drawing, just going for it and enjoying the journey.

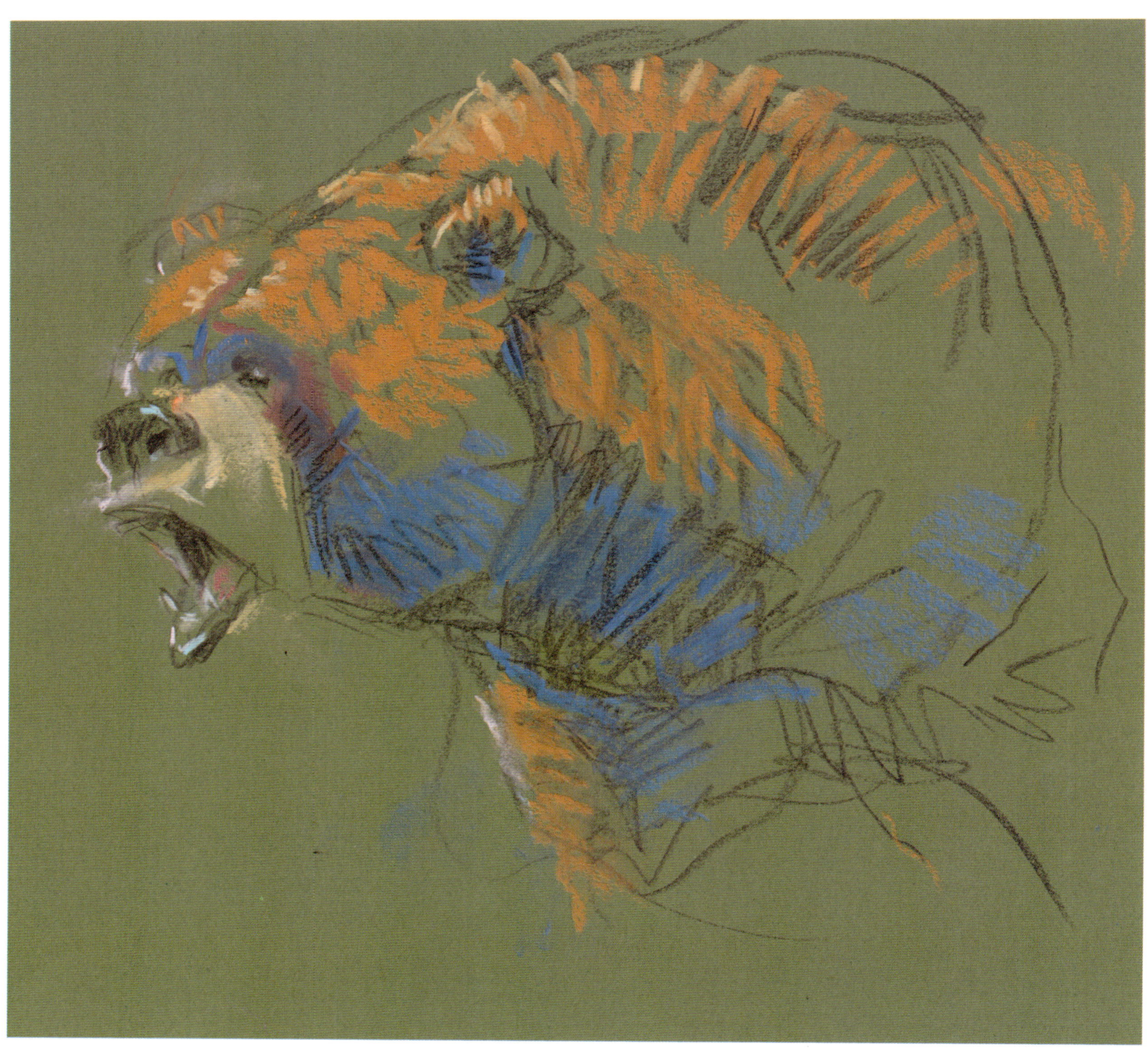

Bear pastel
Pastel and Prismacolor pencil on green-toned paper

More of the 'bold colour choice' approach. For this
one I scribbled an under-drawing in black pencil and
then added bold strokes in pastel over it to give it that
colour and gravitas.

Grizzly bear
*Terra Cotta Prismacolor pencil on
textured resume paper*

Here I was trying to be more efficient
and painterly in terms of my approach.
I don't mean painterly in terms of style,
but in how a painter would approach
the line-drawing phase of a painting,
with very efficient contour and big
shadow-shape design.

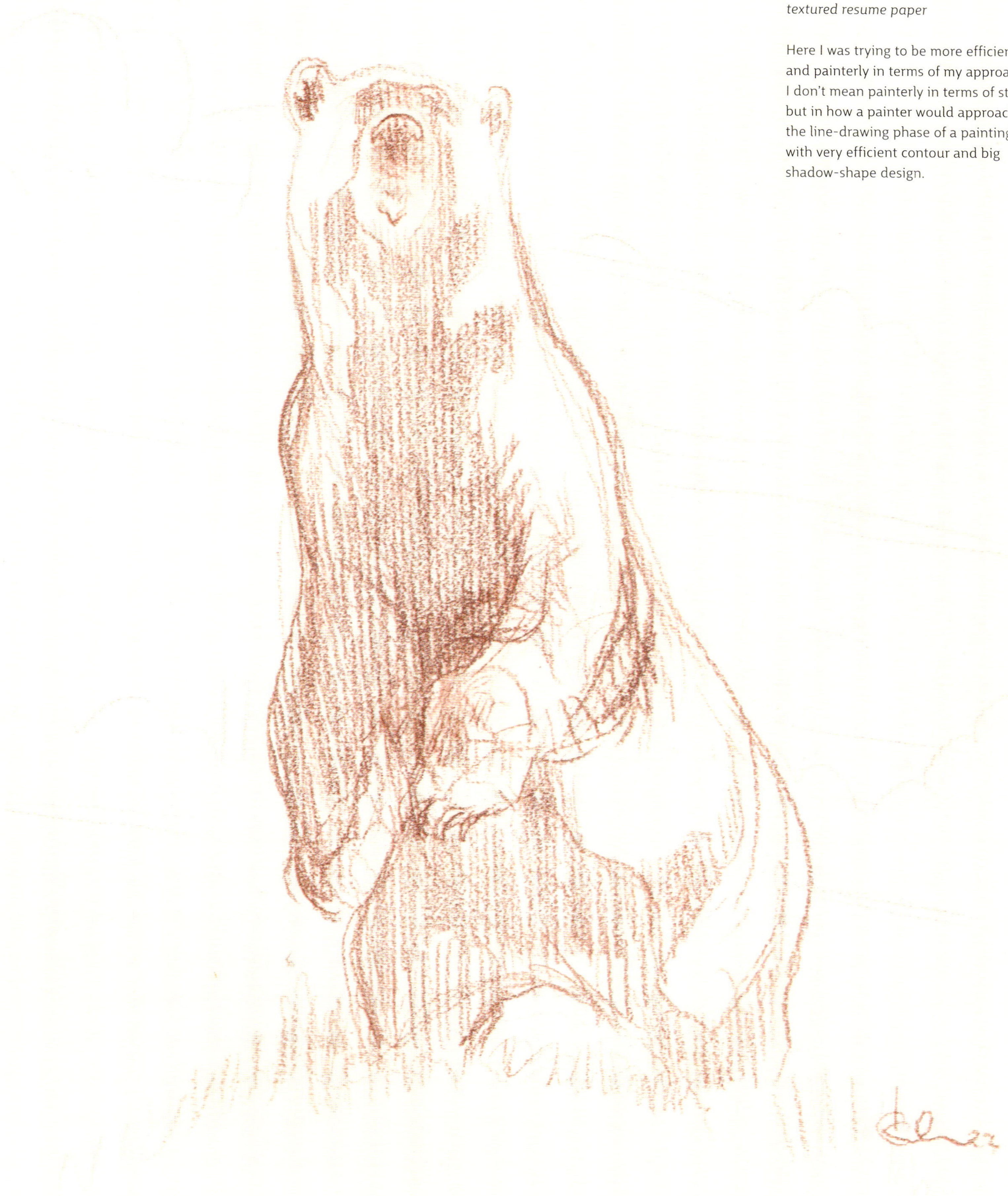

Looking back at older sketchbooks is a reminder that you will always continue to improve

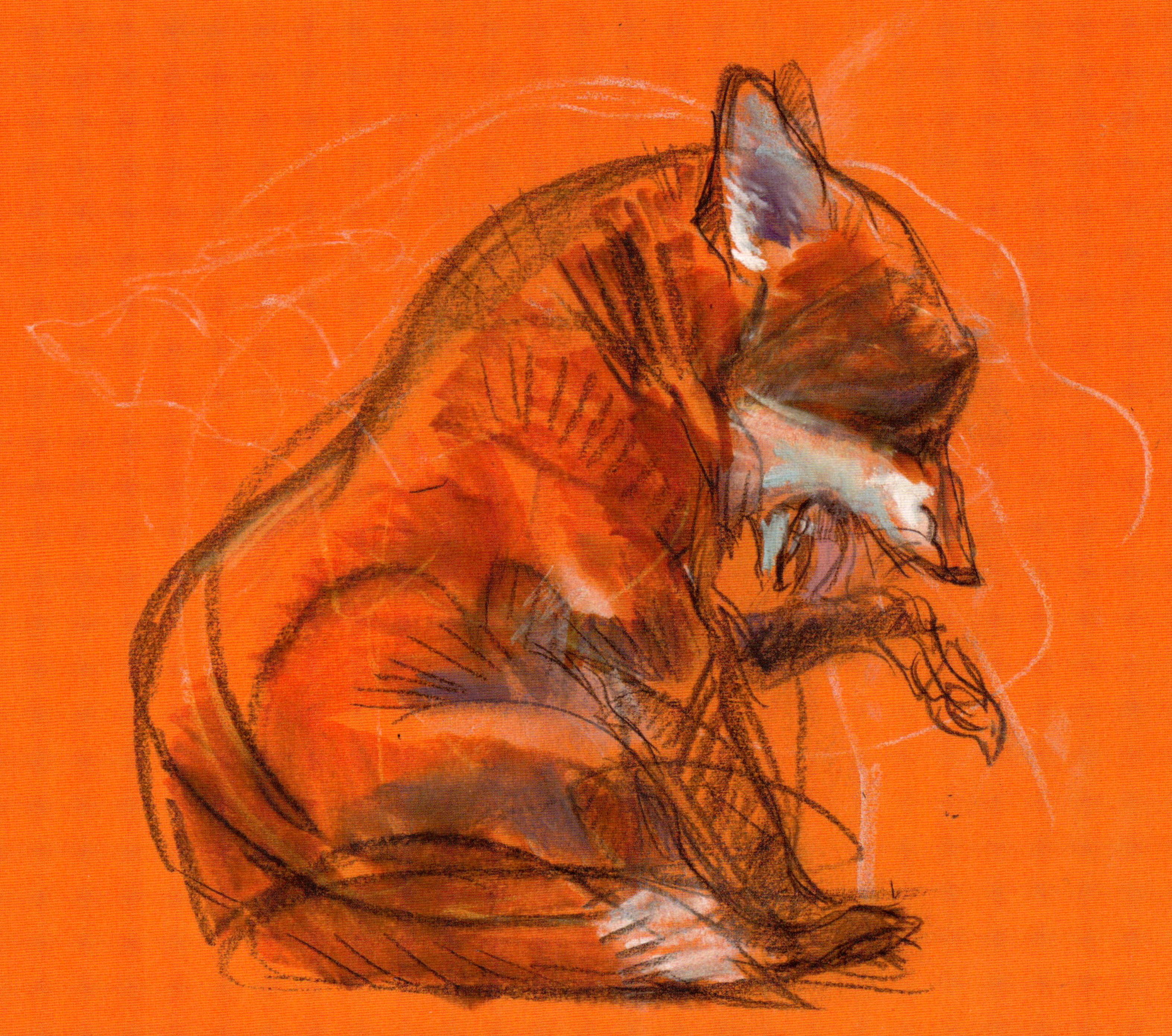

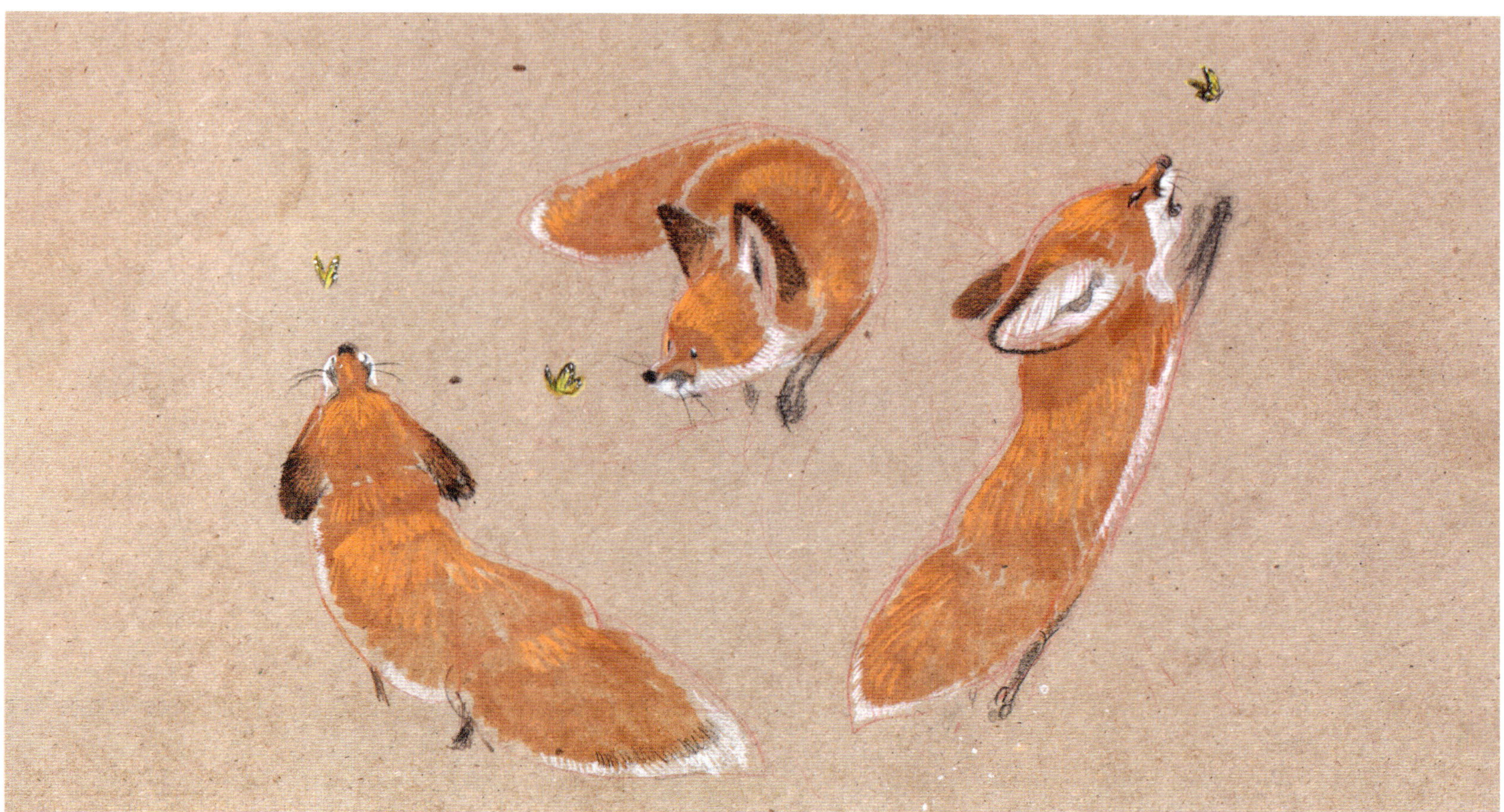

Above | *Fox and friend*
Prismacolor marker, pencil, and white gel pen on chipboard

I had fun playing with full yet simplified shapes and forms for one of my favourite animals. It's a common practice of mine to put two subjects together for both narrative and scale purposes.

Opposite page | *Bath time*
Black, blue, and white Prismacolor pencil and orange Prismacolor marker on Canson orange-toned paper

Expressive poses are one thing, but the subtlety and challenge of a natural pose are something else, and so appealing to me. I wanted to capture an animal in a natural routine moment, completely drawn from my head, no reference (as just about all my artwork is in this chapter). Because I've spent so much time drawing from life in my sketchbooks, I have a very extensive visual vocabulary for animals. I draw exclusively from my head unless I'm in the field, or checking references for specific colour patterns.

CREATING SOMETHING FROM NOTHING

At one time I was struggling to find my next job; I was never out of work, but I was becoming frustrated going from job to job. It's just the way it is – we love our jobs, we get paid well, but the trade-off is the lack of job security. I remember talking to a friend who worked in finance and he said, 'Yeah, but you create something from nothing.' And I thought, 'Holy crud. He's right!' Just let that resonate. *We create something from nothing.* We can take a blank piece of paper and make something, even if it's just a doodle. There was nothing there until we touched it.

Don't take for granted how amazing and cathartic your craft is. When I have my sketchbook with me, if I'm having a bad day and I just start drawing, it's like nirvana. Make sure you have access to your sketchbook all the time, draw often, and remember it's for you. It's fine to share it, but keep in mind that it's your own private journey – that will make you feel more at ease and less worried about making mistakes. It's where you're going to do most of your growing. Keeping a sketchbook makes you a little more courageous. You can be bolder in your sketchbook because it's for you and your own progress. You become braver about drawing from life in public too.

A TIMELINE OF GROWTH

What I've learned the most through keeping sketchbooks is that they act as a timeline. Looking at my shelves, there is spine after spine of big sketchbooks, small sketchbooks, collectable ones, sketchbooks that I've been given as gifts. It's all a timeline of my growth. This is why you should date your sketchbooks, so you can return and look back at your progress. I can also date mine by my signature, which I changed midway through my young career. You can really see that 'before' stage, when I hadn't yet become the artist I am today.

Looking back at older sketchbooks is a reminder that you will always continue to improve. As good as you are now, where are you going to be in three months, six months, or two years? It's an amazing experience to look back at some of your first sketchbooks, see where you are now, and get excited about what the future holds for your artistic growth.

Breast Cancer Research tiger
Pen and Prismacolor marker on white animation paper

My wife is a breast cancer survivor – seven years, at the time of writing this. Every October I would doodle animals with breast cancer ribbons, sell them, and donate half the proceeds to the Breast Cancer Research Foundation. Sadly, I haven't kept up on this in the last few years, but I hope to get back to it one day. I have probably done over fifty of these doodles.

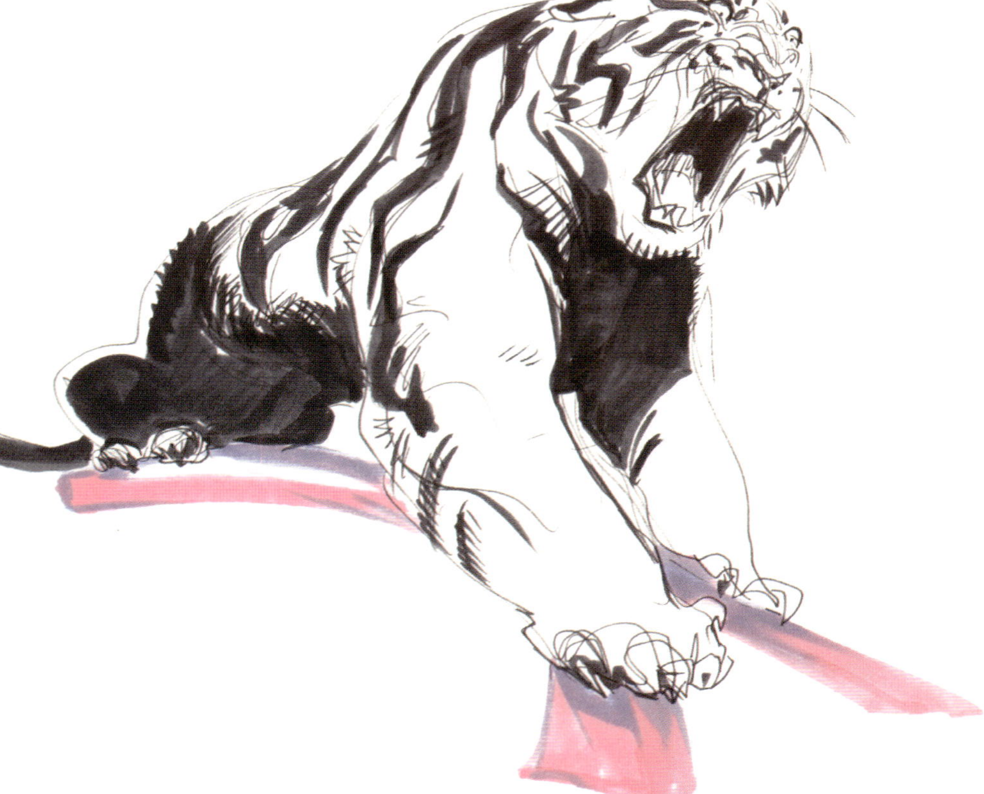

DRAW FOR YOURSELF

I am a big believer in drawing for yourself every day. It allows you to warm up or wind down. (I like to do a warm-up sketch before the day starts.) It's also the idea of not giving everything to the paid project – not giving everything to 'The Man', as they say. It's important to draw for yourself because it reminds you why you do what you do for a living.

When taking a tour of Disney years ago, before I got my mailroom job, I asked a character designer there if he had any advice. He said, 'Listen, just remember to keep drawing for yourself even after you get a job in this industry. I used to draw monsters all the time and now I just draw Mickey Mouse all day and I hate my job.'

He had stopped drawing for himself and had lost that reminder of why he'd chosen this career path. He had ultimately lost touch with his passion and the love of his craft. Keeping a sketchbook allows you to stay connected to the passion that drove you to this career path. He was the one who got that into my head early on.

Panther playing with Breast Cancer Research ribbons
Prismacolor marker and coloured pencil on white paper

More drawings with the same mission. These are very tiny doodles, no bigger than my thumbnail. I really enjoy exploring doodles at this scale because it forces me to be more abstract. I have sketchbooks filled with tons of these colour thumbnail doodles.

Breast Cancer Research hyena
Graphite pencil and Prismacolor
marker on white paper

Another donation image. I really
like the expression on this guy –
it's appealing and funny.

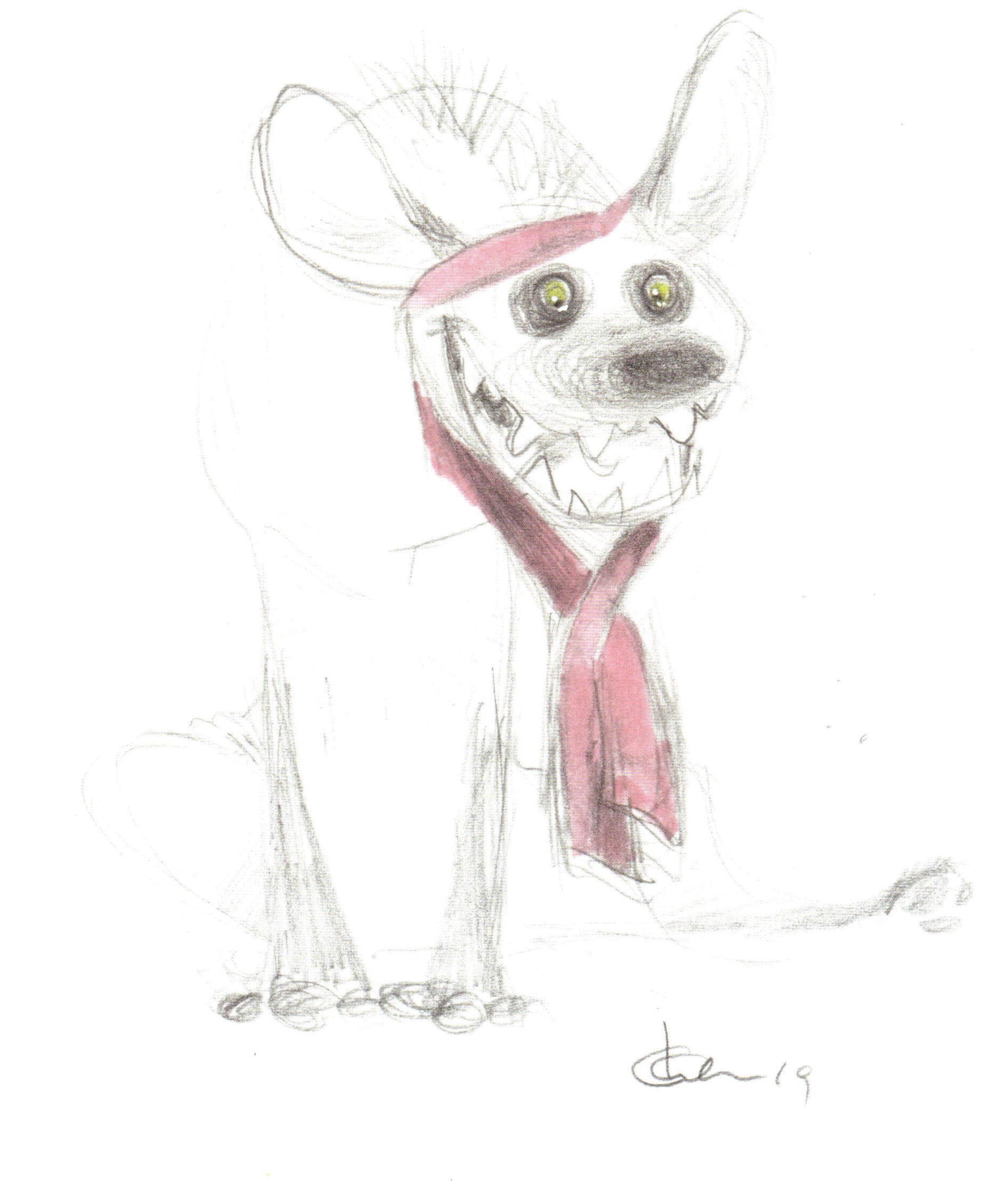

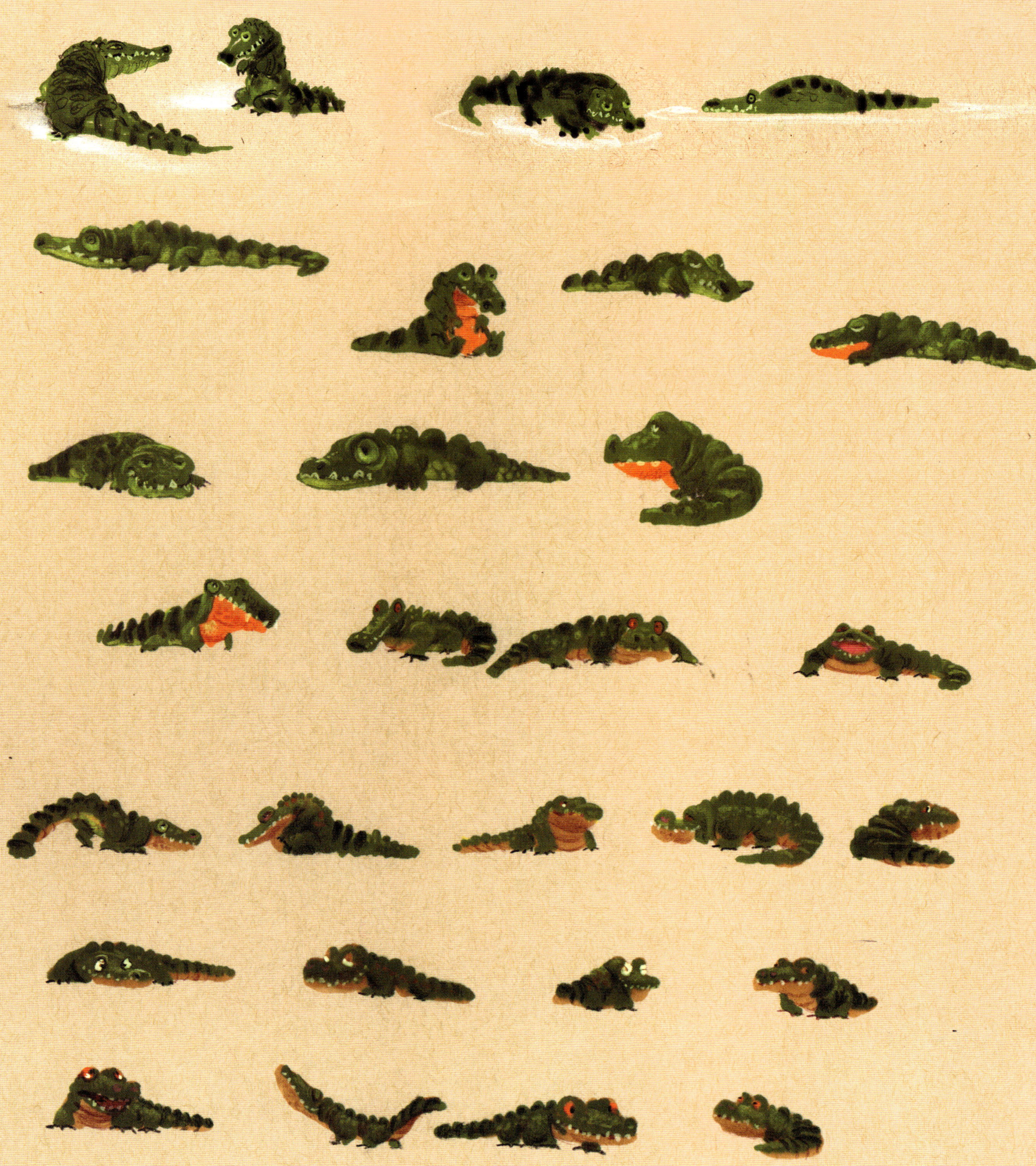

SKETCHING TOOLS

Karl Gnass taught me early on not to fall in love with any one medium. In life-drawing classes I was encouraged to try charcoal, marker, Conté crayon, pen, graphite dust, China marker – all these different materials. If you follow my work today, you'll see ballpoint pen, Prismacolor pencil, Sharpie, brush pen, watercolour, and pastel.

I love to draw very loosely and use a lot of energy in my sketches, which pastel really brings out. It adds these beautiful blocks of colour, and is so visceral and seductive, which I really gravitate towards. I also love coloured pencil. The black Prismacolor pencil is a good go-to. When I'm on the go, I carry travel watercolour kits by Winsor & Newton and Rembrandt. I use them with waterbrush pens that have a little brush at one end and can be filled with water. These are what I use for watercolour sketches in smaller books.

It's very important not to become a slave to one choice of media. You will box yourself in, cut down your growth, and actually close off your mind. You want to keep that mind open to using many different materials in your sketchbook process. This way you will continue to grow and you won't be stuck in one corner with one type of pencil.

I'm constantly asked, 'David, I love your work. What pencil are you using?' As if that's the magic – like if I tell you what pencil I'm using, you're going to become an amazing artist overnight. Not true! It makes me want to do a drawing using only a stick and mud, to show people that materials don't matter. It's the skill. It's all about versatility and continuing to grow on your own journey. Be open to drawing with different materials in your sketchbook, as it will grow your skill and allow you to reach your full potential.

That said, pen is still my favourite medium, especially when I'm out and about. Ballpoint, Sharpie, brush pen. I love a brush pen when it's dried out and produces really nice soft and hard edges. I recommend drawing with pen, as it will help you to work on your line efficiency. You'll learn that drawing is more thinking than actual drawing. A lot of drawing is done in your head, and you'll become a lot more efficient if you use a medium that's permanent. I found that if I was using pencil, I relied too much on erasing, and I was more hesitant. When I started to draw much more with Sharpie and brush pen, I learned line efficiency very quickly.

Opposite page | ***Tiny crocs***
Prismacolor marker and colour pencil on toned paper

A full page of tiny thumbnail crocs from my toned paper sketchbook. Each one is no bigger than my thumbnail. I love how abstract this process forces me to be – I find interesting new shapes for my subjects every time. I would love to do an alphabet book in this style, with the crocodiles arranged to make a large letter C, and so on!

Alligator, creeping...
Pastel and Prismacolor pencil on toned paper

This was a time when I really enjoyed exploring mixed media, specifically the boldness of pastel with coloured pencil. No real intention, just enjoying the journey.

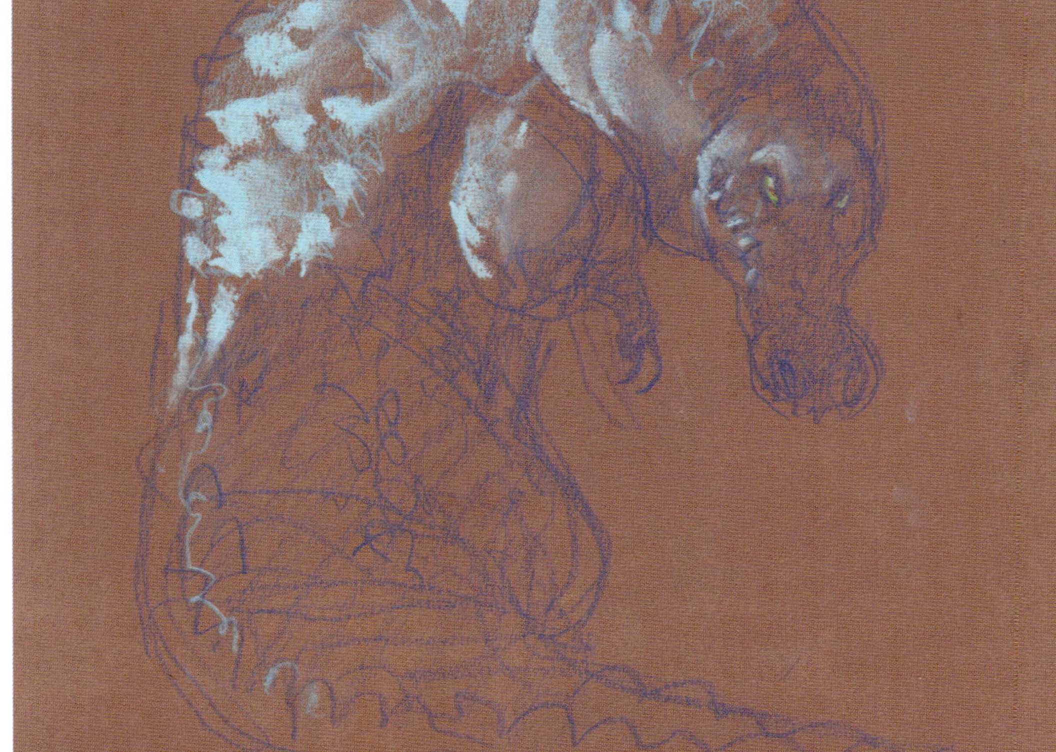

SKETCHBOOK FORMATS

I use sketchbooks of all shapes and sizes. I have sketchbooks as small as 7.5 × 12.5 cm that can fit in my back pocket, and as large as 36 × 43 cm for when I'm using a big paintbrush with watercolours. But my average size, the one I take everywhere, is roughly 15 × 23 cm. That size fits into my backpack, which I carry most of the time when I'm going to and from the studio, or when I'm travelling. I like to always have one with me. When I'm at home, I can just grab it out of my backpack or off the shelf.

I prefer a hardback sketchbook as it's more durable – it can be stuffed in a bag, suitcase, or back pocket. You can sit on it and you're not going to damage anything. When you're sketching at the zoo, you can rest a good-sized sketchbook against the fence and use its hard surface for support. I used to do that a lot, but over the years my sketchbooks have become smaller and smaller.

When you're first starting out, you tend to carry your sketchbook everywhere – a whole big book and all these different pencils. After deciding I didn't want to carry all that around, I started to carry pocket-sized Moleskines instead, and simply grab one of my favourite pens.

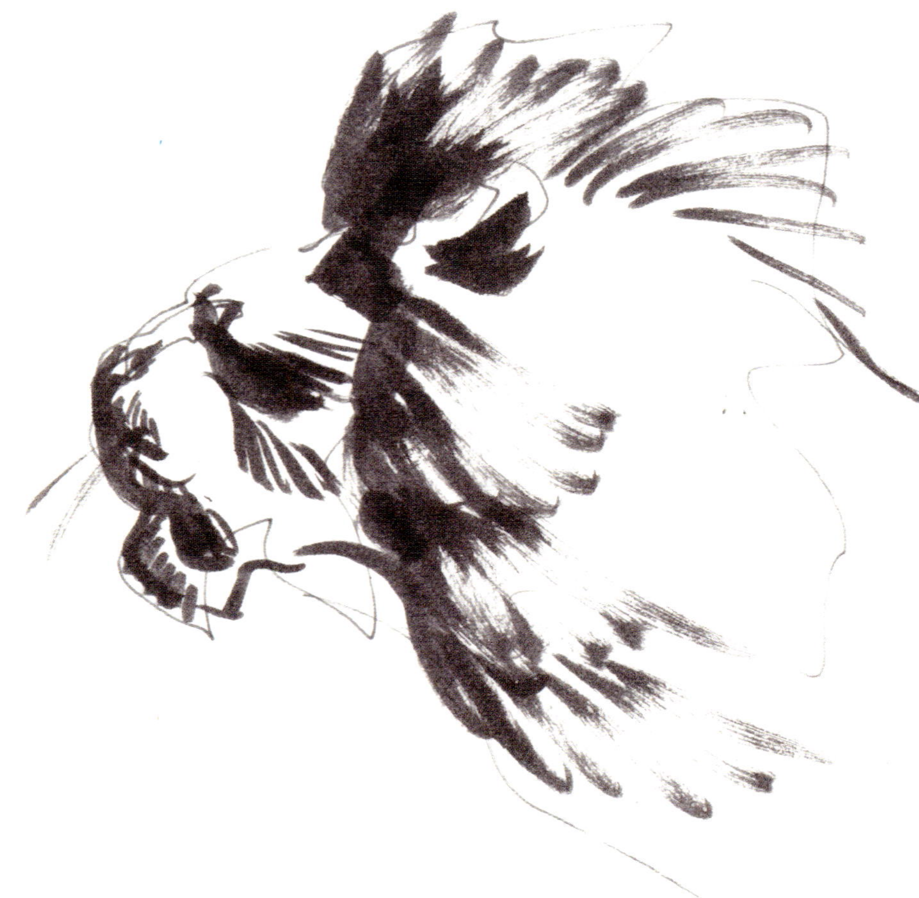

Big cat doodles

*Pentel fountain pen and Tombow brush
pen on white paper*

Small, square pen images from my
sketchbook. Relatively quick, but clear
and impactful.

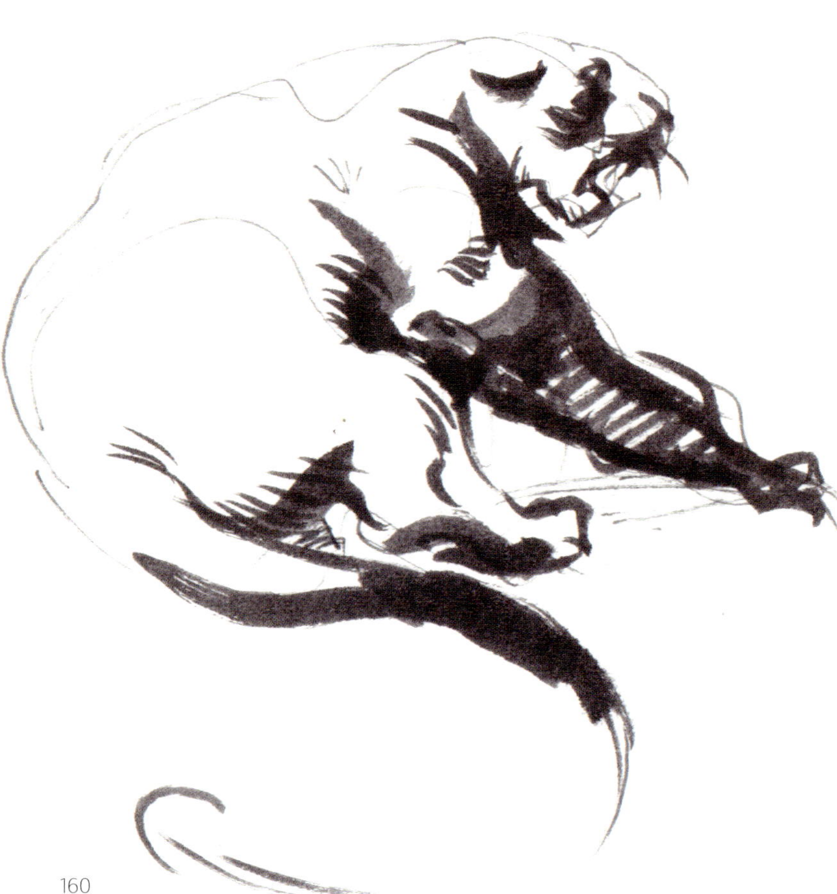

Nowadays I care more about the quality of the paper I'm using. I've got a ton of free sketchbooks that are absolute garbage – it's the nicest way to put it! Those stay up on a shelf for my daughters to use, or I donate them to a school so others can make better use of them. I love Moleskine and the quality of their paper. I've got watercolour sketchbooks and toned sketchbooks. I love Cottonwood Arts, which is run by fellow industry artists, for their toned, recycled paper.

I enjoy drawing on toned paper because the tone acts as a keyed canvas. You've already got your medium tone, and you can then use white and darks to sculpt the subject. If you make a quick ballpoint sketch on toned paper, you can use a white pencil to bring out the highlights. It gives a bit more gravitas to something that could have just been a doodle. I also draw on chipboard (the stuff that's used for the back of legal pads and notepads) because it's so much fun to draw on. There's often serial numbers on it, which I work into the actual drawing.

I used to make my own sketchbooks, but I'm not that ambitious any more. I would get different types of paper – Canson paper, toned paper, tracing paper, animation paper – and I would go to Kinko's and get it bound. So one sketchbook would have all these different papers that I could use with different materials. To reiterate a point I made earlier: using a book of mixed paper forced me to be versatile. In those homemade sketchbooks, I'd be at the mercy of whatever the next page was, instead of getting used to just one medium or one texture of paper. That was cool and something I definitely recommend you try.

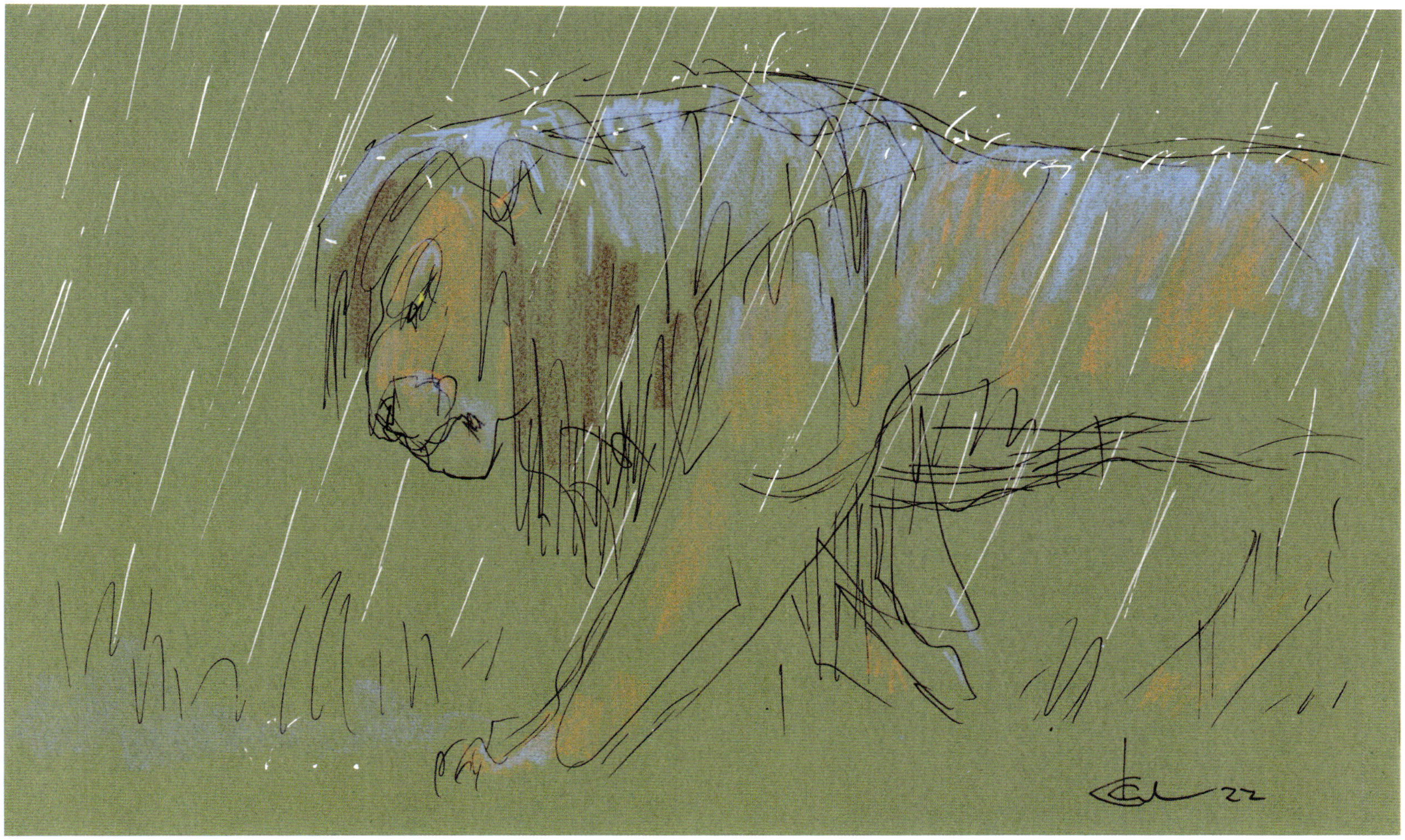

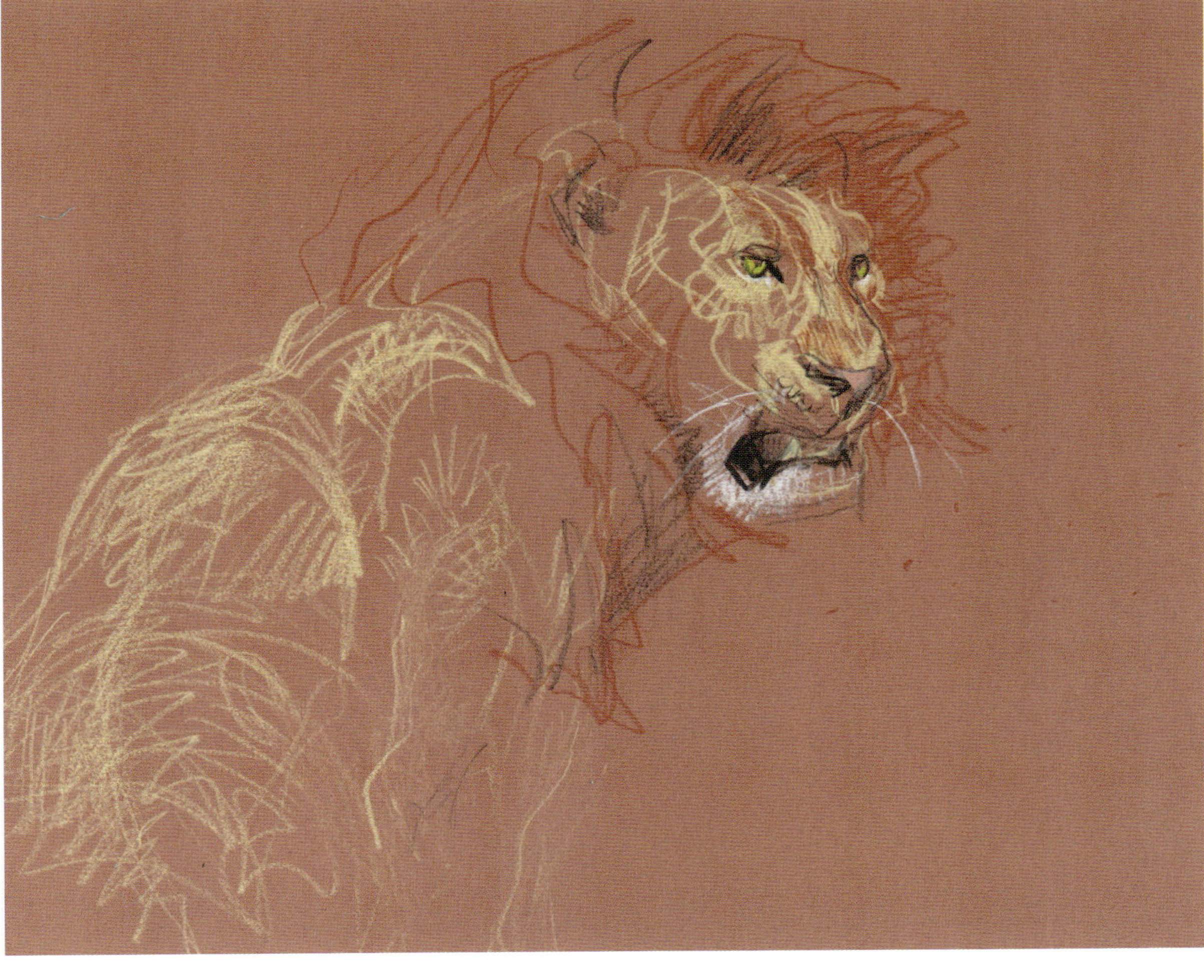

Above | *Walk in the rain*
Pentel fountain pen, Prismacolor pencil, and white gel pen

Experimenting with mixed media again, all about mood: the pose, the blue colour reflected from a dark rainy sky, the stark white raindrops, the expression, and limited line work merging the giant paws with the negative space of the ground below ... I was working on *Mufasa* at the time, so I was doodling *a lot* of lions in my sketchbook and warm-up doodles.

Lion scribble
Prismacolor pencil on Canson toned paper

I really enjoy just building up the form with this colour-scribble approach. I've kept this sketch in my flat files and intend to frame it one day.

　　

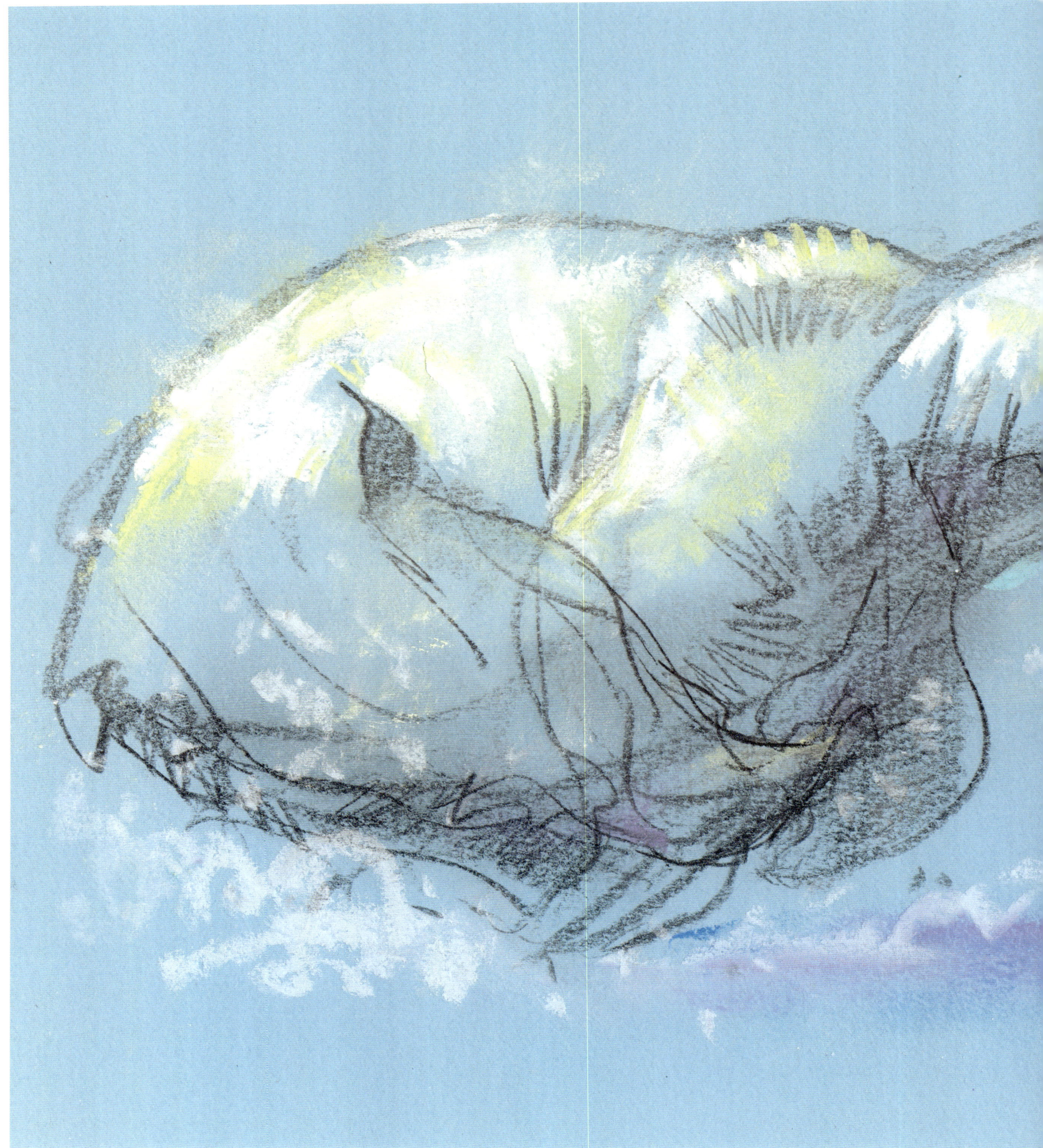

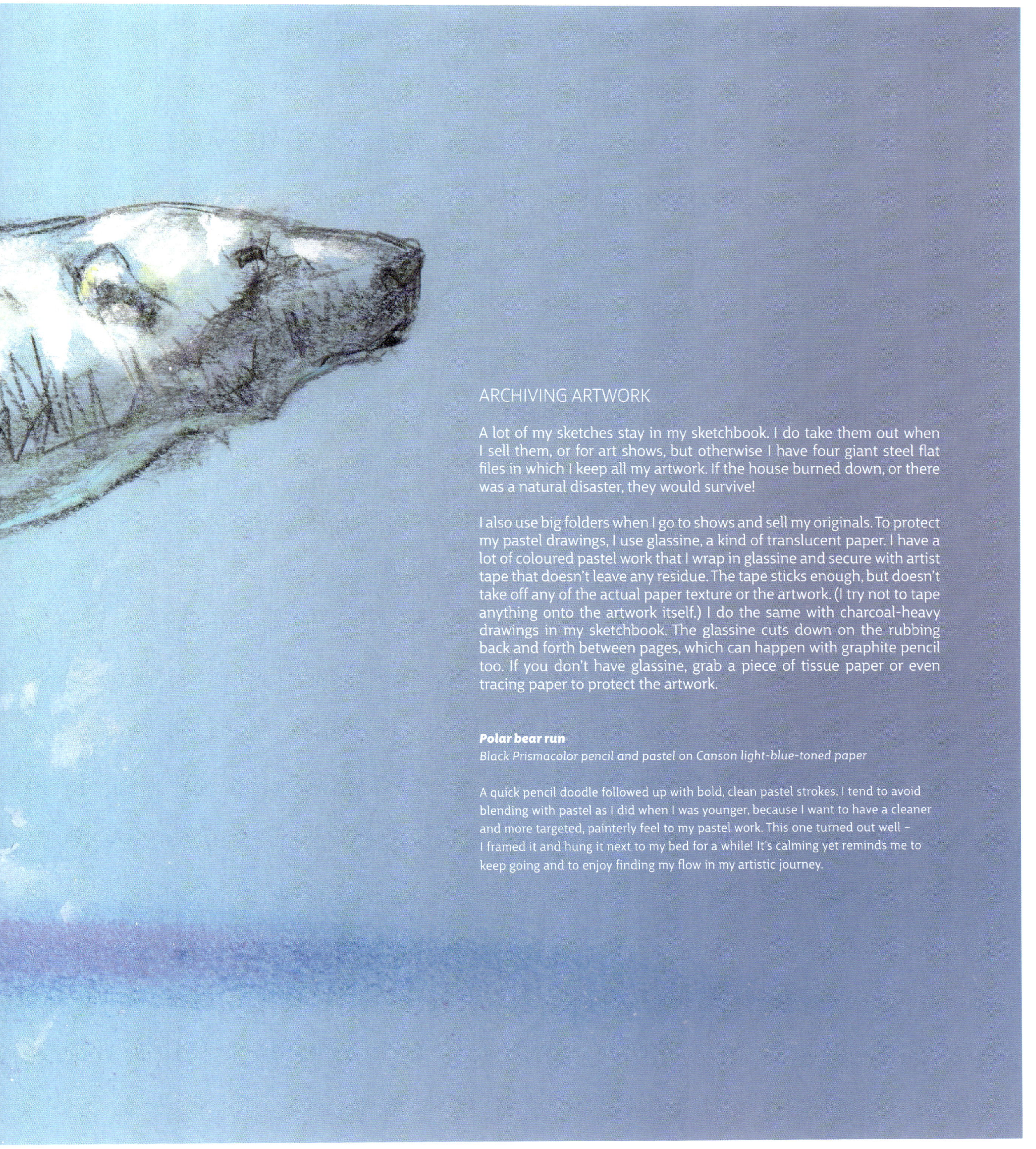

ARCHIVING ARTWORK

A lot of my sketches stay in my sketchbook. I do take them out when I sell them, or for art shows, but otherwise I have four giant steel flat files in which I keep all my artwork. If the house burned down, or there was a natural disaster, they would survive!

I also use big folders when I go to shows and sell my originals. To protect my pastel drawings, I use glassine, a kind of translucent paper. I have a lot of coloured pastel work that I wrap in glassine and secure with artist tape that doesn't leave any residue. The tape sticks enough, but doesn't take off any of the actual paper texture or the artwork. (I try not to tape anything onto the artwork itself.) I do the same with charcoal-heavy drawings in my sketchbook. The glassine cuts down on the rubbing back and forth between pages, which can happen with graphite pencil too. If you don't have glassine, grab a piece of tissue paper or even tracing paper to protect the artwork.

Polar bear run
Black Prismacolor pencil and pastel on Canson light-blue-toned paper

A quick pencil doodle followed up with bold, clean pastel strokes. I tend to avoid blending with pastel as I did when I was younger, because I want to have a cleaner and more targeted, painterly feel to my pastel work. This one turned out well – I framed it and hung it next to my bed for a while! It's calming yet reminds me to keep going and to enjoy finding my flow in my artistic journey.

Gorilla charge I

Prismacolor pencil and pastel on Canson blue-toned paper

This was the first 'charging gorilla' sketch I experimented with, showing my sketchbook process for the idea. I wanted to make him more immersive, so my later front-on version has him coming right at the camera. Your first take might spawn something new and send you in a different direction. Embrace that process!

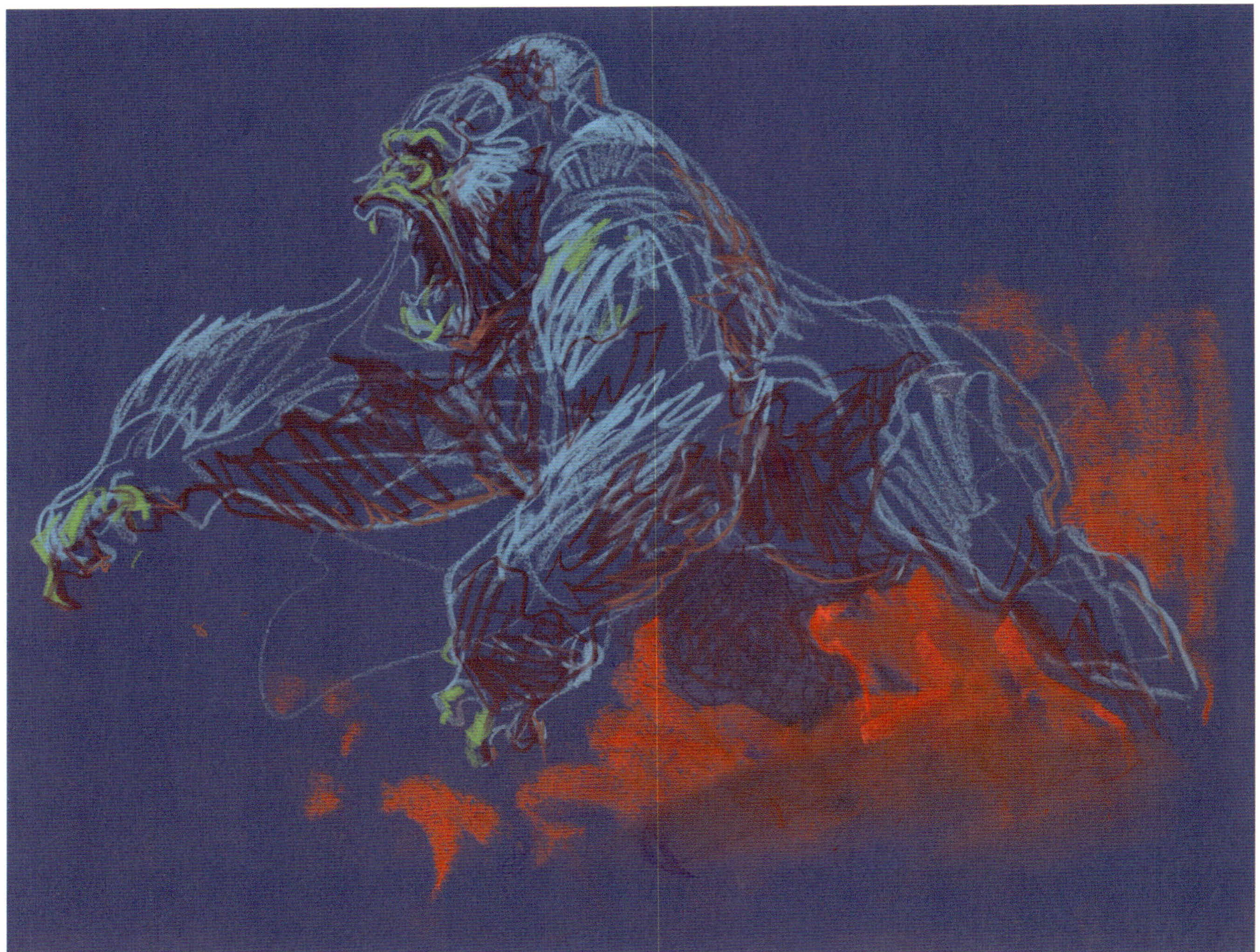

A SPACE FOR YOUR IDEAS

Another benefit of keeping a sketchbook is it keeps everything in one place, as opposed to lots of loose pages. Even though I draw a lot on individual pieces of paper, because I tend to sell a lot of my pieces at shows or on social media, having your own private thoughts and ideas scribbled in one space can be useful.

For a while I had a sketchbook that was just for animal drawing, another that was just for life drawing, another that was just for studying perspective and cityscapes, and *another* that was just for projects, which had more notes in it. I gradually bailed on this approach. Now it's whatever book I grab first. It's too hard to have different sketchbooks for all the things I do, which is why I just have catch-all sketchbooks now. When I'm on the go and working on so many different things at once – I'm Head of Story on a DreamWorks project, I'm working on my own new book, and I'm still trying to draw for myself as much as possible – it's easier to just have one sketchbook on the go.

For my DreamWorks project, a lot of my sketchbook work is edit notes or little ideas that I have to direct my artists through. Sometimes I'll be blocking out a sequence in my head while going for a run or a swim. Then I'll go back and jot it down in my actual sketchbook, the one that's in my backpack – just a quick little doodle as a reminder of what I was thinking about.

My sketchbooks don't just tell the story of my own growth as an artist, but the story of an idea as it develops. For example, I'm working on a children's book idea, which is always ongoing in the background. I started it when my kids were young and, by the time I get it right, maybe it'll be ready for *their* kids! You can see where I'd started a new sketchbook and thought, 'I'm gonna make this sketchbook just for the children's book!' and then abandoned that idea, with the sketchbook becoming all-inclusive for whatever I was working on at the time.

My superpower is multitasking on many projects at the same time. My brain is firing on all synapses at once, and that's why I have the energy I do. It's evident in my sketchbook process, as I will have lots of different ideas going on in one book. Some artists might be more disciplined than I am, with a clearer process and more structure in how things are labelled. But this is just who I am as a person! I'm very spontaneous and like to get my work done. You can see in my drawings, I kind of just go for it. It's the same in my sketchbook process – I just grab whatever's there, get it down, use a few pages for one project or another, and move on.

Gorilla charge II

Prismacolor pencil and pastel on Canson blue-toned paper

More of that colour-scribble approach, using bold colours right away with no real under-drawing. This one was turned into a shirt design.

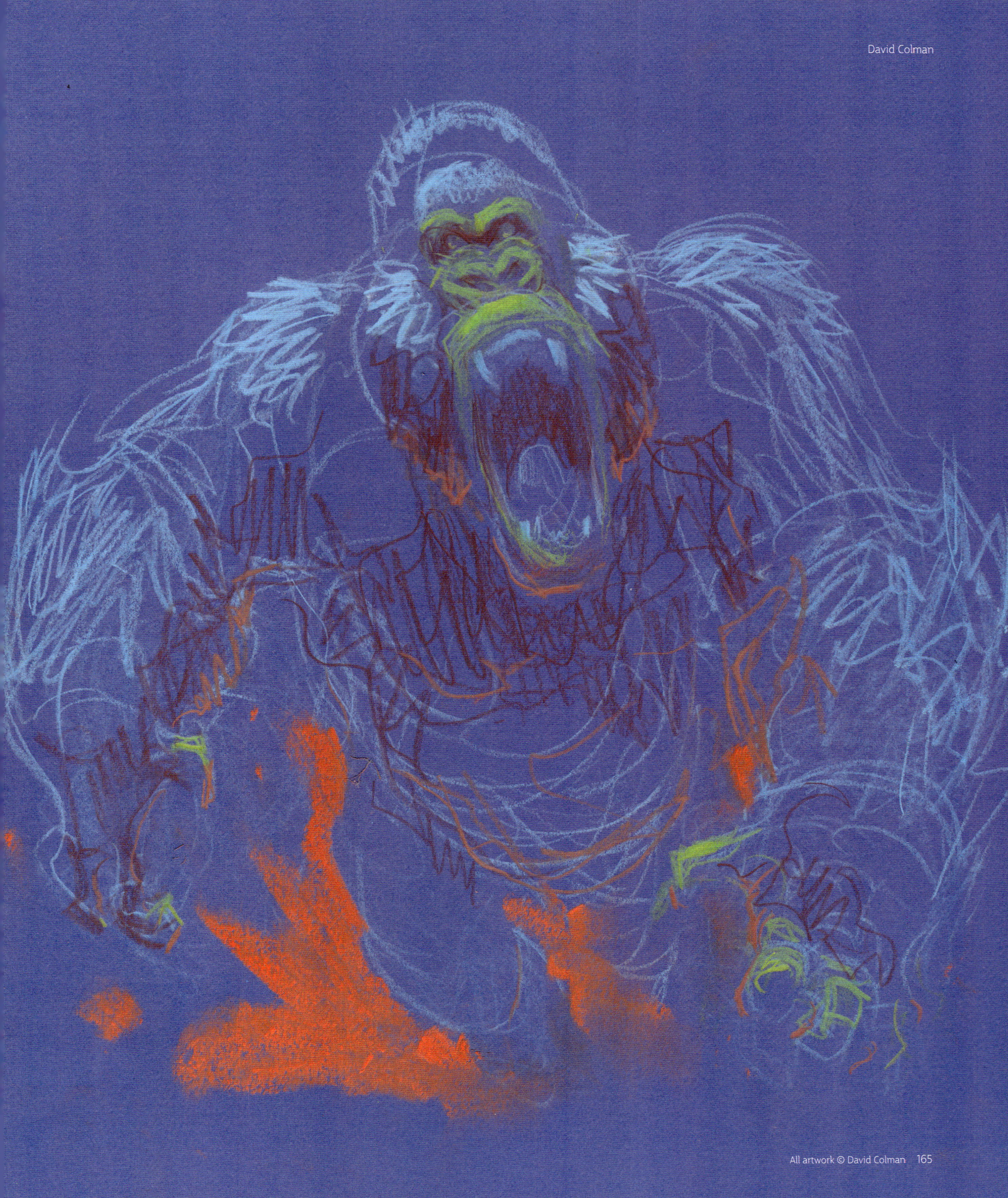

Girl and big cat
*Pentel fountain pen on
animation paper*

Inspired by my number-one influence,
Frank Frazetta: loose, energetic,
narrative, a feminine character with
a large feline.

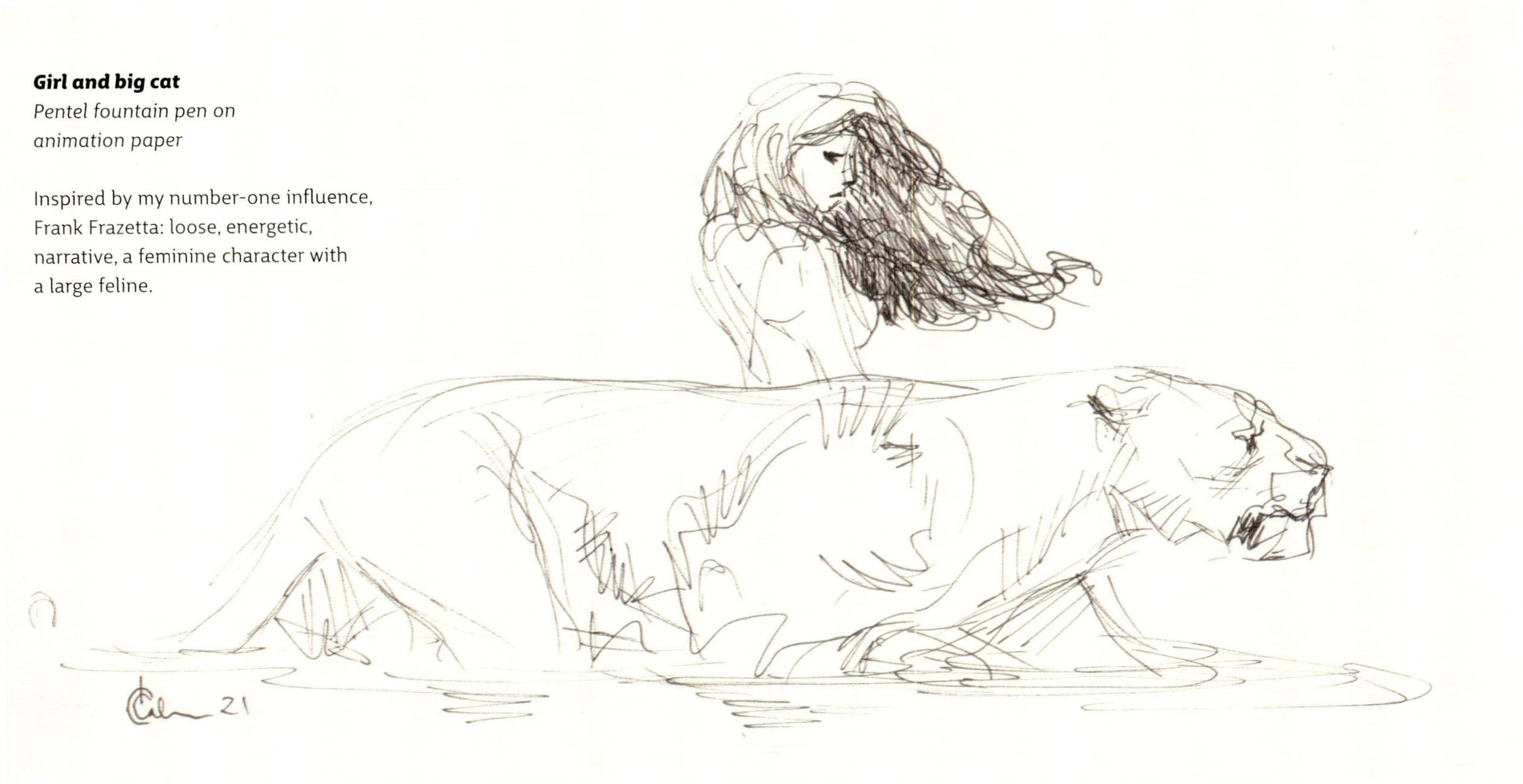

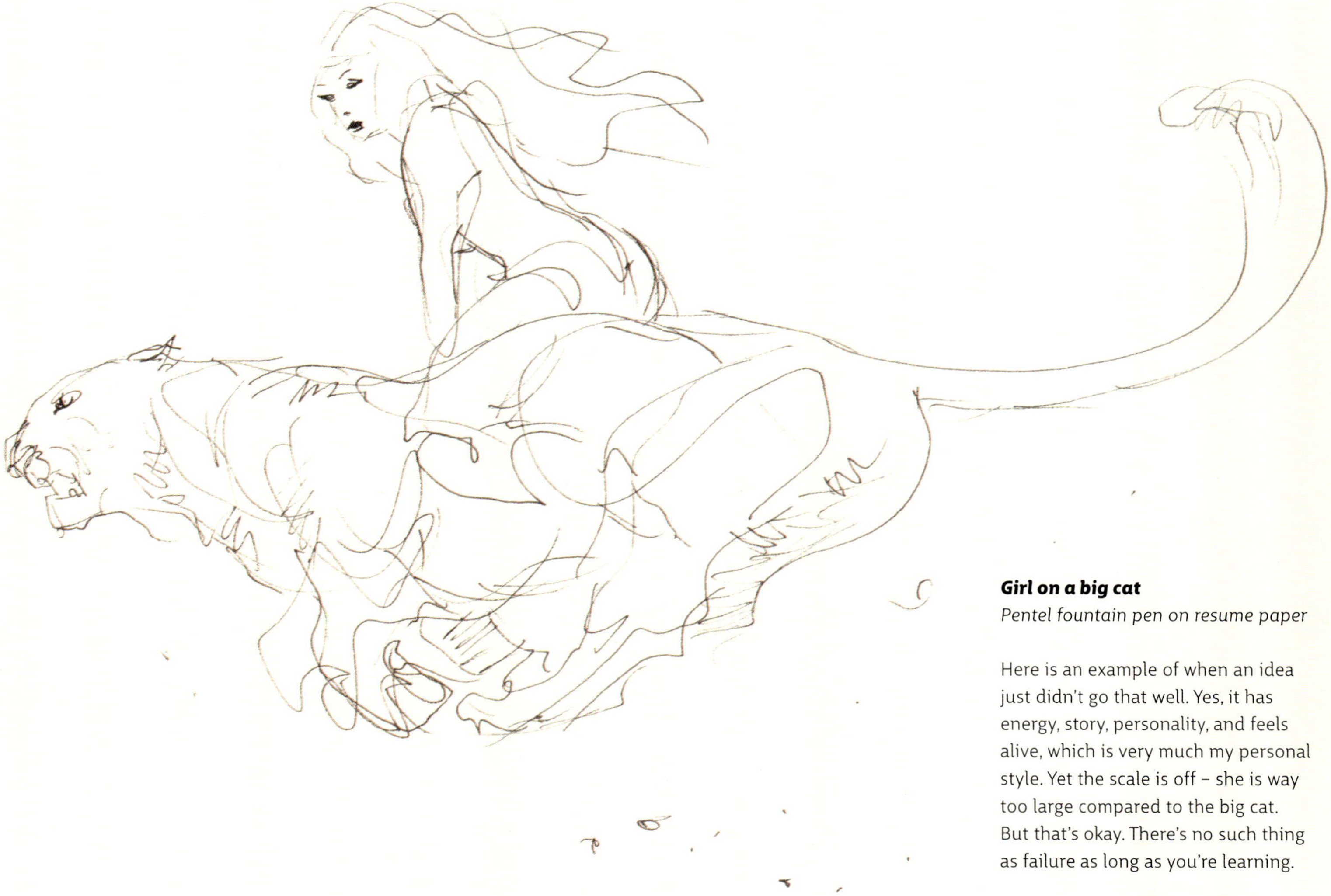

Girl on a big cat
Pentel fountain pen on resume paper

Here is an example of when an idea
just didn't go that well. Yes, it has
energy, story, personality, and feels
alive, which is very much my personal
style. Yet the scale is off – she is way
too large compared to the big cat.
But that's okay. There's no such thing
as failure as long as you're learning.

SKETCH INSPIRATIONS

My sketching inspirations are multifaceted. The early teachers in my career, the ones that I took night courses with, they made it a big part of the process to carry a sketchbook everywhere we went. Glenn Vilppu was a big believer in that; Karl Gnass as well. Stephen Silver was another – we would sketch together at lunch. When I worked delivering mail for Disney, and he was designing on *Clerks: The Animated Series*, I'd meet him at the commissary and we would draw people.

Marcelo Vignali was another inspiration. He started Sketch Club. The first rule of Sketch Club is you don't talk about Sketch Club. We would draw together at Sony, out at cafés and other places, just drawing different people and things.

When I took an animal-drawing class with Joe Weatherly, we drew at La Brea Tar Pits in Los Angeles. It's like a natural history museum, but smaller. I remember he saw my first drawing of the mammoth skeleton, looked over his shoulder to make sure no one was around, and then said to me, 'You are by far the best natural artist I've ever had. You just have to work at it.' That inspired me and I started drawing in my sketchbook all the time, especially animals.

To take it up a step further: Frank Frazetta. He is one of the reasons I started drawing when I was younger. He's by far my number-one influence, which I think you can tell if you look at my energetic artwork. I have many of his books, but the *Frazetta Sketchbook* is what inspires me the most – it's great to see all his ideas and thumbnails. That book has continued to inspire me to keep drawing in my own sketchbook, even up until recent years.

The feeling of catharsis is also what keeps me in my sketching practice: the mood it puts me in when I actually draw in my sketchbook and draw for myself. I become happy, because it's just for me. It reminds me why I do what I do for a living. I love my craft. This is what really does inspire me to keep sketching for my own personal growth in my own sketchbooks. When I'm at the zoo, even with my kids (because I don't get to go and draw that much anymore), just getting a quick little doodle of a zebra is something that makes my heart smile. I love being able to capture life, to observe something in reality and quickly sketch it down. Then to try to capture what I see in my mind's eye, with all the gravitas, perspective, personality, or soul the animal has. These are all things that I love being able to capture in my sketchbook.

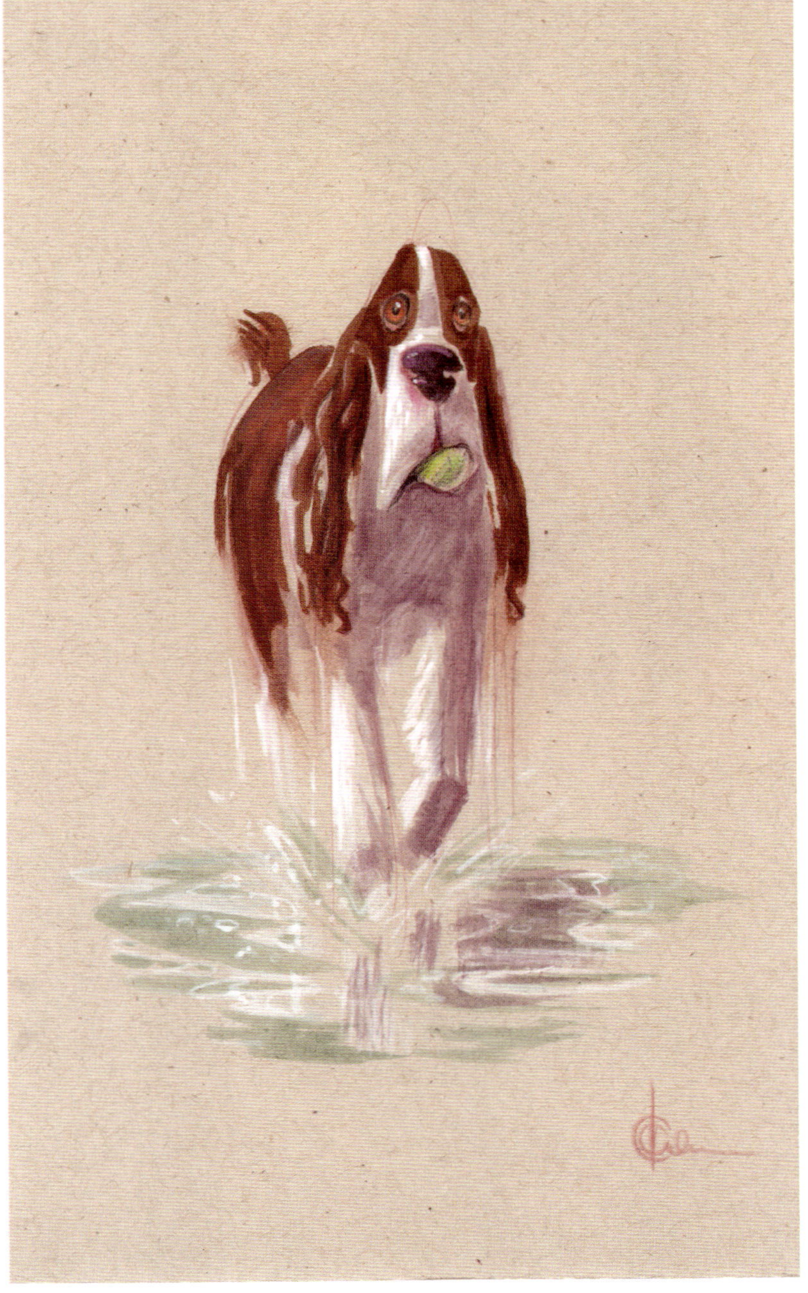

Henry

Tombow brush pen, watercolour, and coloured pencil in a toned sketchbook

We took our springer spaniel, Henry, to the dog beach, where he loves playing fetch in the water. I wanted to capture that day in a sketch, so I proceeded to draw this in my sketchbook as soon as we got home. I really pushed the character design and wet feel. Once finished, I removed it from my sketchbook and framed it for our house.

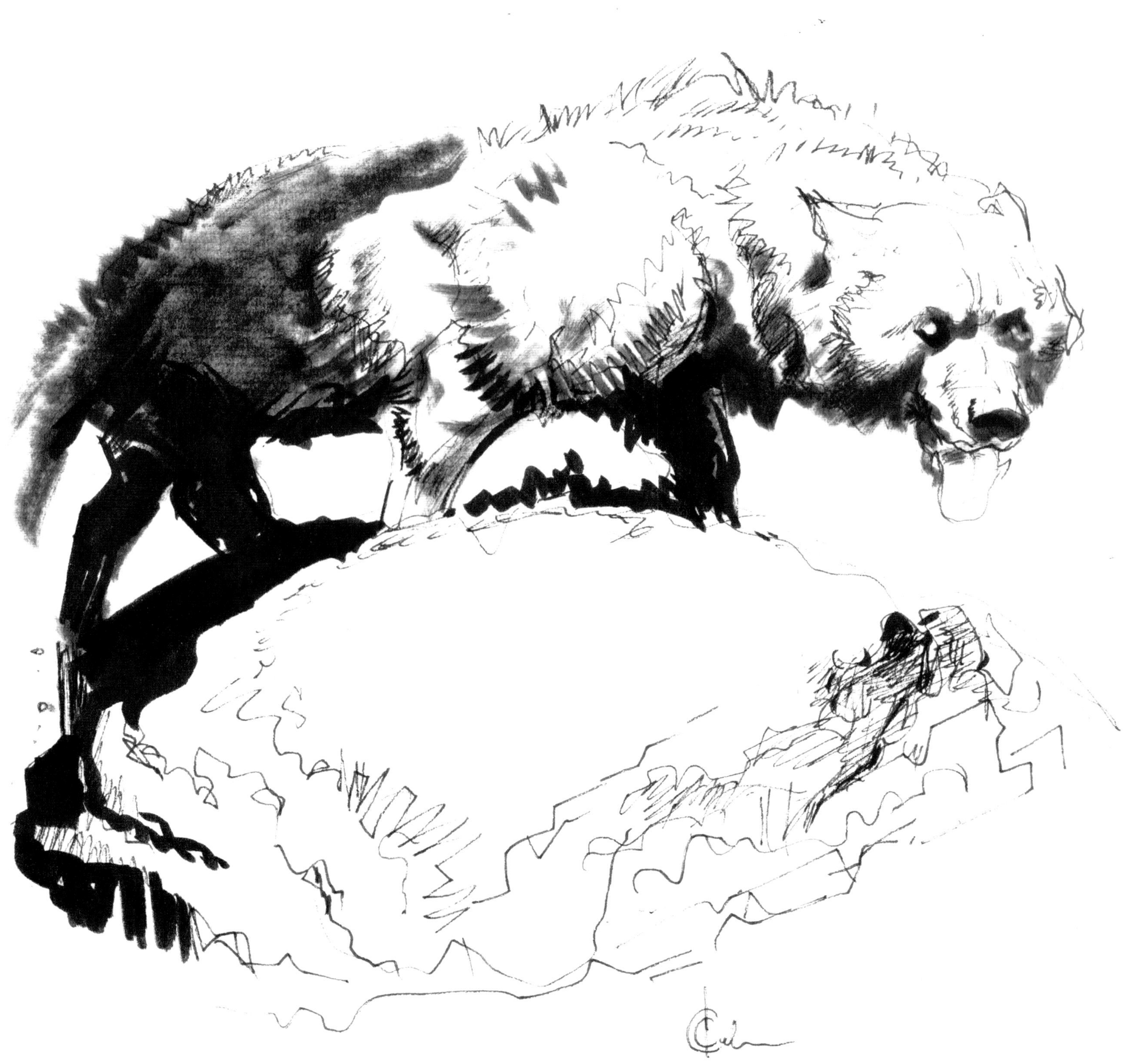

Frazetta wolf
*Pentel fountain pen and Kuretake Zig
brush pen*

This was directly inspired by Frazetta's
pen work. I feel I did a good job with it,
as well as capturing distinct character
in the body pose and facial expression.
This is still in my personal archives.

Grizzly bear with power
Tombow brush pen and Pentel fountain pen on animation paper

There was a time in recent years when I started leaning heavily into black-ink doodles: big, bold shadow shapes allowing for a clean silhouette in the shadow, combined with energetic line work in the light. This is now something I do regularly and it all started with exploring in my sketchbooks.

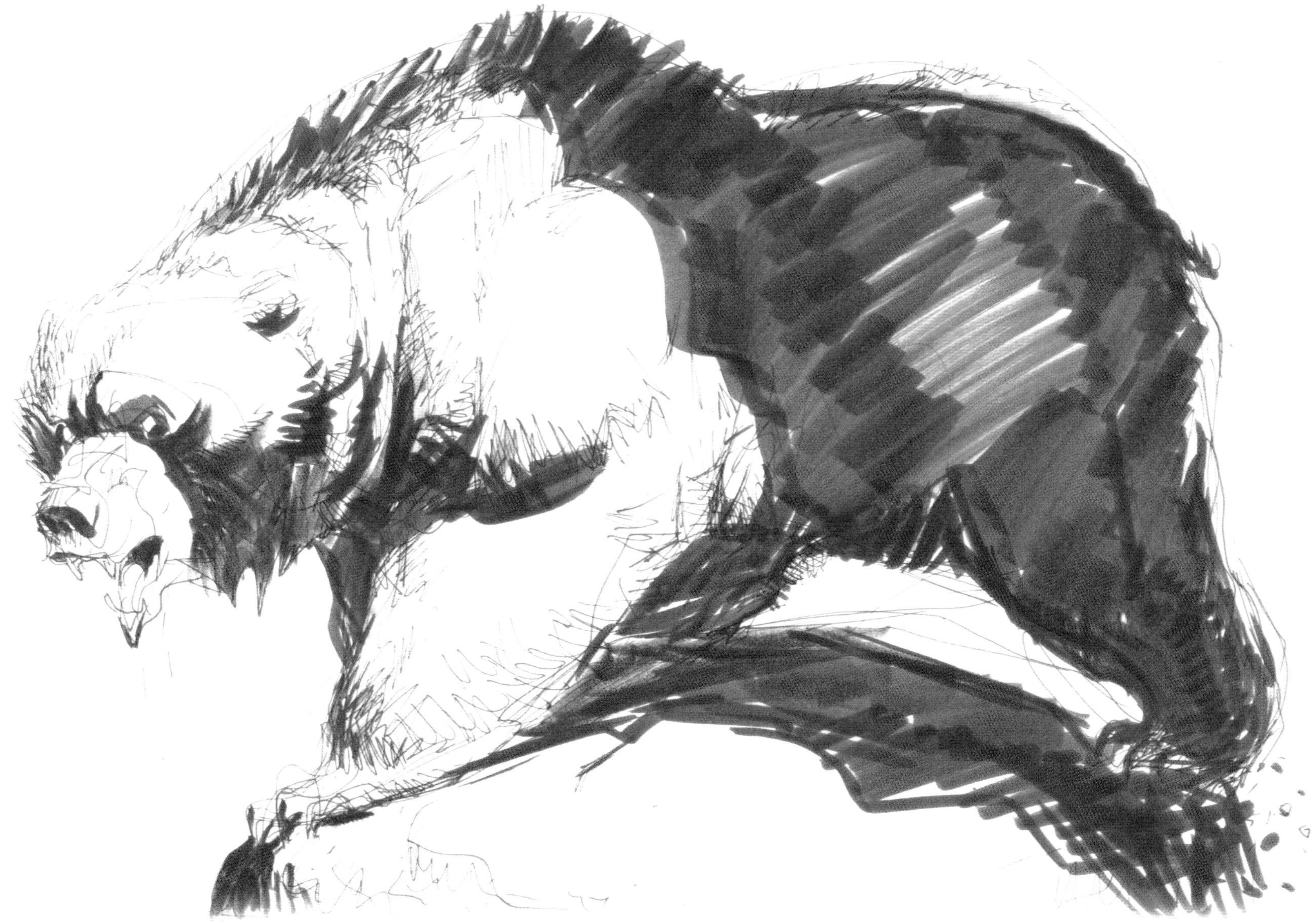

ADVICE FOR ARTISTS

Don't take anything personally. It's hard not to when our art is so personal to us. We're emotionally attached to it. We love it. It's who we are. It's in our DNA. It's hard not to take things personally. But when you're in a profession, especially in production, if your design is not approved, or you have to redo a sequence, or some of your art isn't being used – whatever the reason – you can't take it personally. The project is about the bigger picture and you've got to see the forest for the trees.

You've also got to want it more than the next guy. You have to constantly be feeding the beast, being a sponge, soaking it all up, practising, growing, wanting it more than everyone else. If you're not getting better, the person next to you is going to surpass you. Early on, when I was working on *Stuart Little 3: Call of the Wild*, I was trained by a top artist. He was really impressed with how I took his notes and advice. He said he'd met so many young artists who think they know everything: 'They think, I've gone to school, I'm really good now. I draw better than this guy, I paint better than that guy, I animate better than this person, I sculpt better than them, I model better than so-and-so...' And that's very closed off. Whatever discipline you're passionate about, you're never going to grow as an artist with that mindset.

Keep an open mind, because you never know where it's going to take you. Be willing to learn something new and that growth will never end. It is *awesome* when you get to learn a new skill, or all of a sudden you notice, 'Oh, I actually know how to draw a hand better now than I did ten years ago, even though I *technically* knew everything then. But now it just flows!' It's such a great feeling. There is no end point. There is only a journey.

Be willing to learn something new and that growth will never end

Phantom tiger

Prismacolor marker and brush pen on yellow paper

I think I chose this title because of the tiger's eyes. This was a quick sketch with no real intention and became one of my personal favourites by happy accident. It's the earnest narrative pose, the personality, the expression even without much facial detail, the strokes of the marker, and the cool blue shadow amidst the complementary warm orange on his back. Plus the texture of the brush pen for the stripes. Explore in your sketchbooks and don't get too fussy – it will only hold you back.

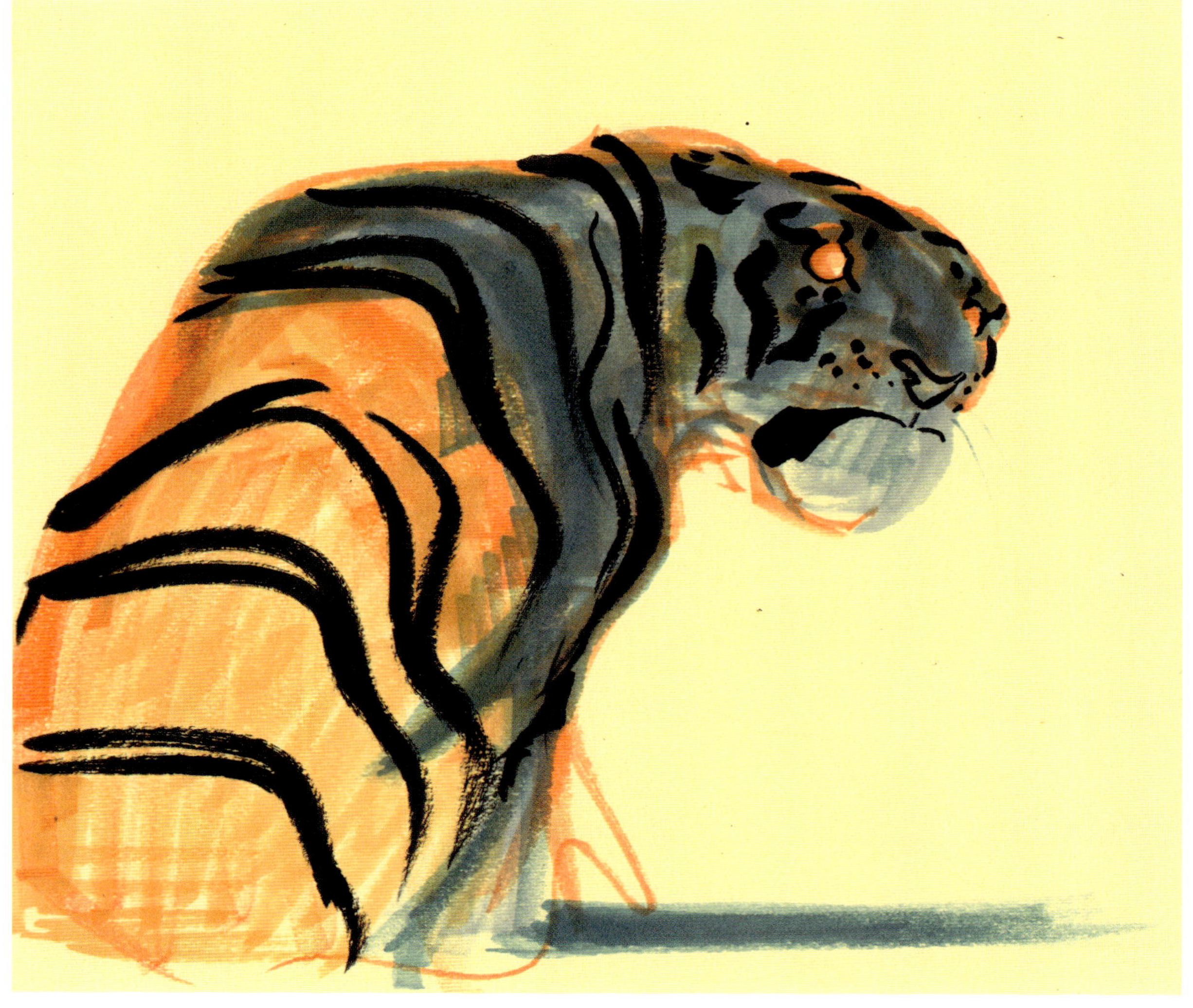

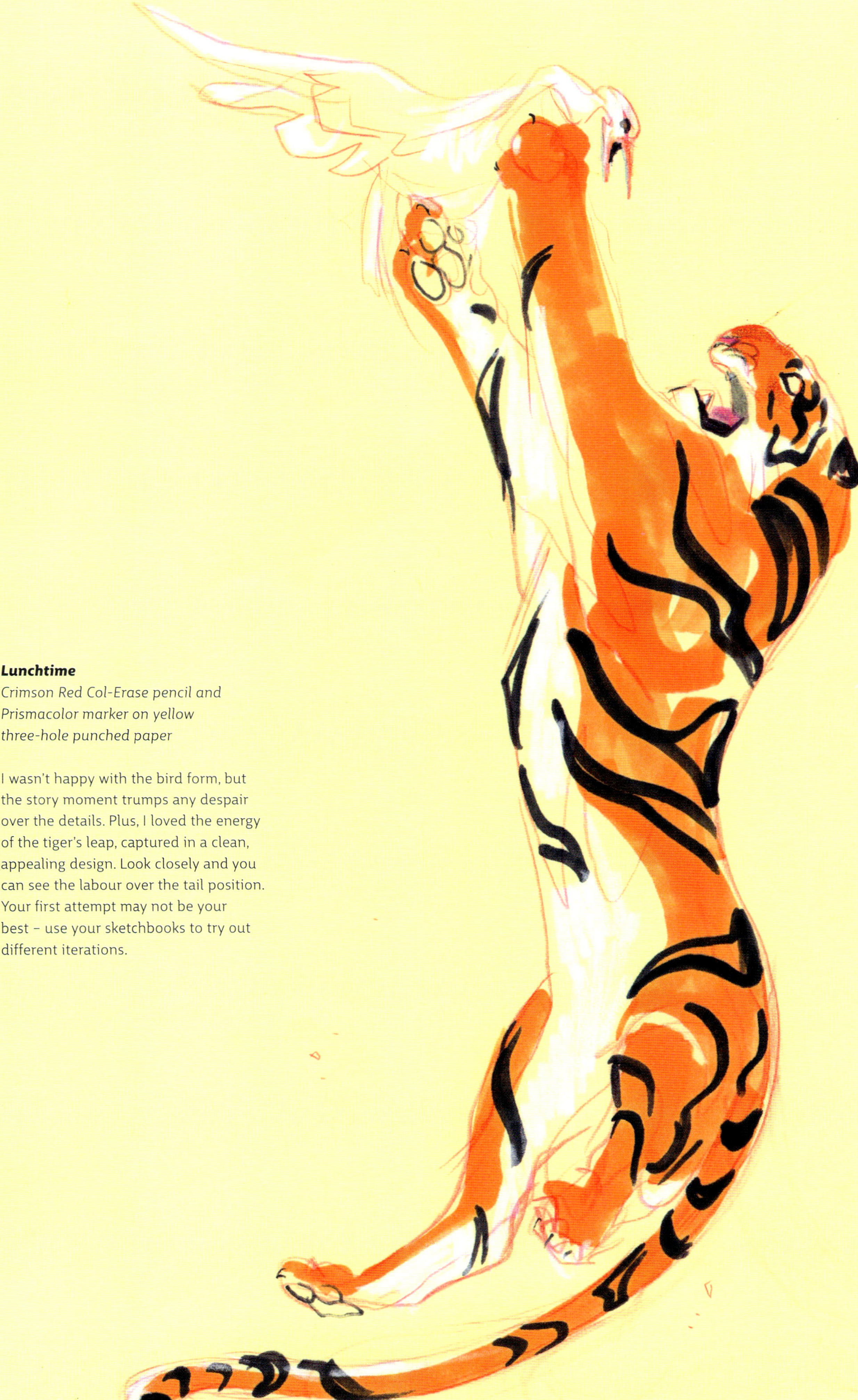

Lunchtime

Crimson Red Col-Erase pencil and
Prismacolor marker on yellow
three-hole punched paper

I wasn't happy with the bird form, but
the story moment trumps any despair
over the details. Plus, I loved the energy
of the tiger's leap, captured in a clean,
appealing design. Look closely and you
can see the labour over the tail position.
Your first attempt may not be your
best – use your sketchbooks to try out
different iterations.

Terryl Whitlatch

ANIMAL ANATOMY EXPERTISE

Most of my education is in the sciences – vertebrate zoology – rather than art. My goal was to become a natural history illustrator for zoos, museums, and scientific publications like *National Geographic*. Lucasfilm hired me straight out of school because of my expertise in animal anatomy – this was something they could use for creature design. I worked as Principal Creature Designer for *Star Wars: Episode I – The Phantom Menace*, before going on to work for countless other studios in the entertainment industry. My work has also appeared in science publications, such as *Scientific American*, as well as in documentaries such as *Prehistoric Planet*. My book, *The Katurran Odyssey*, is one of the proudest moments of my career, as are the friendships I've made and solidified along the way.

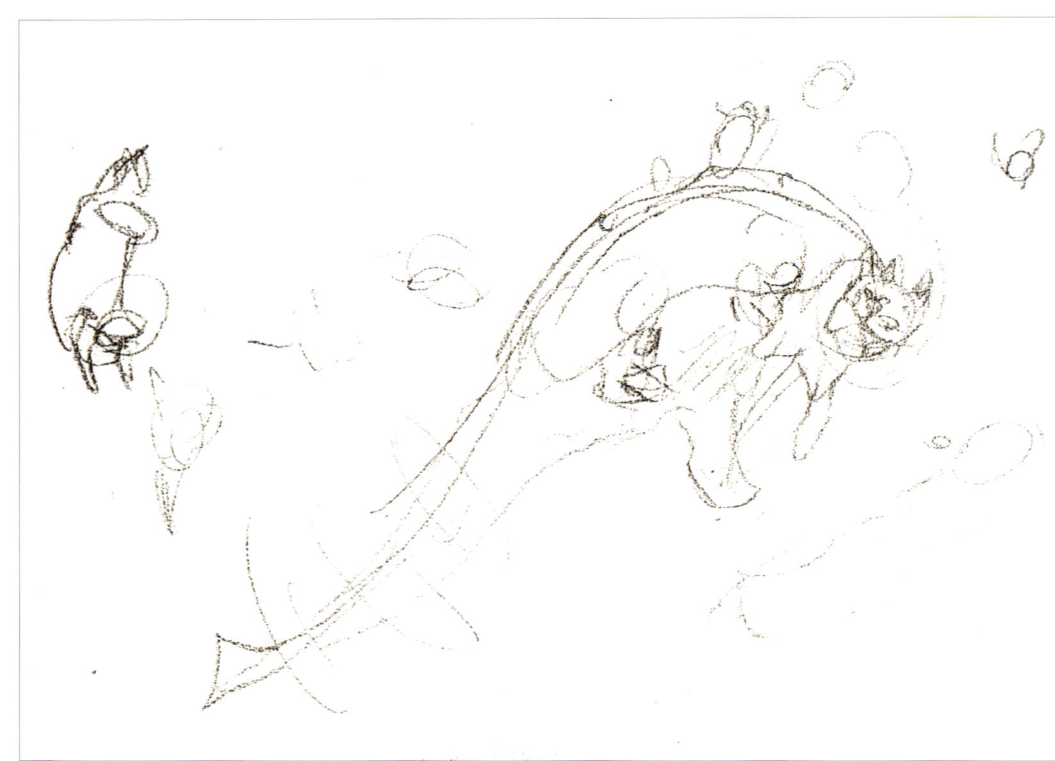

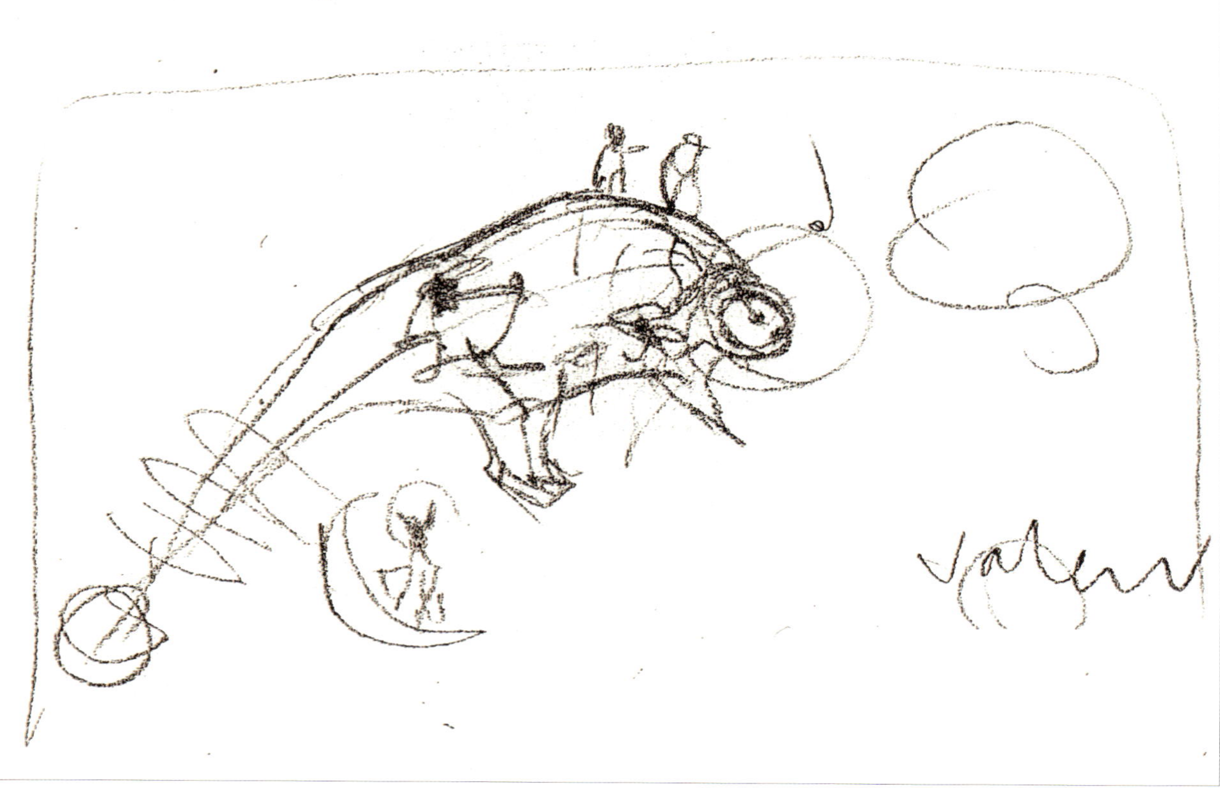

Initial ideas for retro mid-century-style illustration of giant glowing prehistoric armadillos (glyptodonts) in outer space

As soon as I get an idea, I scribble it down on whatever is available; usually tracing-paper pads (as in this case), but just as often – gasp! – on spiral-bound lined notebook paper. These are what comprise my 'sketchbooks'; they psychologically allow me to ideate and feel free to mess around as much as I like. Lovely Moleskin sketchbooks feel constraining – the nice paper is inhibiting, too nice to mess up. I like to draw on tracing paper with HB pencil, or newsprint with charcoal, or on lined paper using ballpoint pen when at the zoo or museums. My earliest roughs can be incomprehensible except to me, but hopefully in this example you can make out the animal forms, bounding through space. These are tiny pencil drawings, about 5cm long. I chose to develop the second image.

ANIMAL CONCEPT ILLUSTRATOR & CREATURE ARTIST
artstation.com/terrylwhitlatch

Playing with poses and exploration

On more tracing paper, I quickly roughed out various ideas for the poses of the glyptodonts and their travelling companions: a quartet of fairy armadillos. At this stage I'm not at all concerned about finesse, only line of action. All these little roughs were drawn from having seen photos or videos of them, as well as from my memory of previously drawing glyptodonts in my book, *The Katurran Odyssey*. For the fairy armadillos, I had seen armadillos at the zoo. These roughs also helped me to gauge how much research and reference gathering I would need to do.

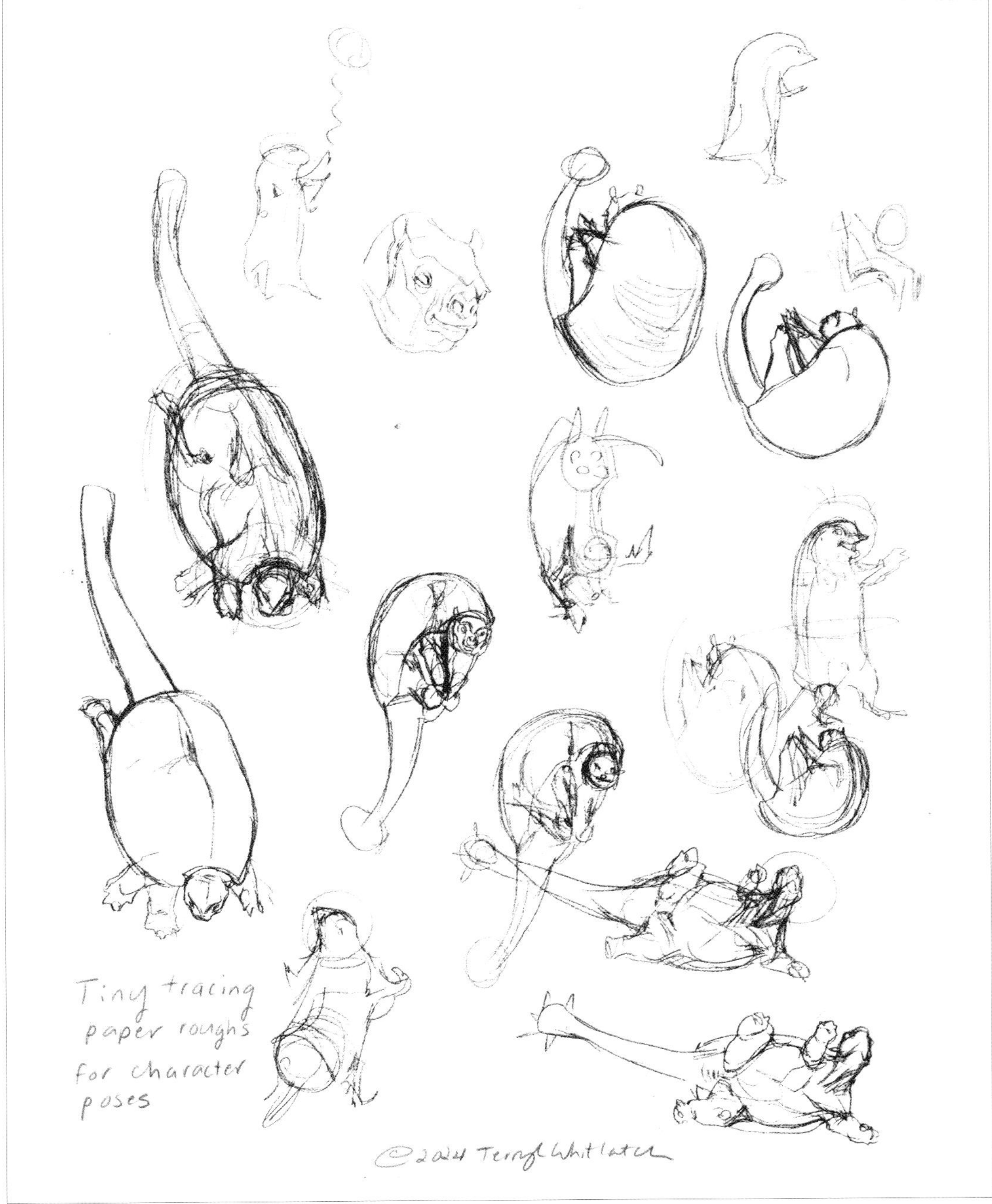

DESIRE TO UNDERSTAND

My sketchbook practice is inspired by animals and my intense desire to understand them. I seek to describe their beauty and personality, to attempt to capture and decipher these qualities, and to share with others how special and priceless animals are, in all their aspects. There is usually always a germ of a story involved. My drawings are very intentional. I have an idea, and then I explore, which includes practising techniques along the way. I don't draw an animal just to draw an animal. I want to explore the 'why' of the animal. There are all kinds of story implications in this.

My favourite artists are all wildlife artists, including Bob Kuhn, Jay Matternes, Paul Bransom, and William D. Berry. They capture the animal like no other artists I am aware of. When I run into a challenge, I ask myself, 'How would they handle it?' and that helps.

Working out the anatomy

After researching and gathering anatomical references, I reconstructed the glyptodont by drawing the iconic side/length/longitudinal view of its skeleton, from which I could gauge most other views. If I can't find a top view for width/lateral reference, I estimate it by examining the top-view anatomy of its closest living relatives. In this case, modern armadillos. I drew the side view of the skeleton on tracing paper, made a digital photocopy to get nice crisp lines, and scanned this into Photoshop. Using this copy and a combination of photo references (the actual skeletal specimen, plus the three-banded armadillo), I roughed out the front skeletal view and played around with facial possibilities.

Using multiple layers and the Symmetry feature, I reconstructed the various skeletal views and layered the muscular anatomy on top, being mindful of the origin and insertion points of the muscles on the skeleton. Glyptodonts are mammals, and all mammals share the same basic anatomy. Since I didn't have any armadillo muscular anatomy available to me, I used the top muscular view of a dog.

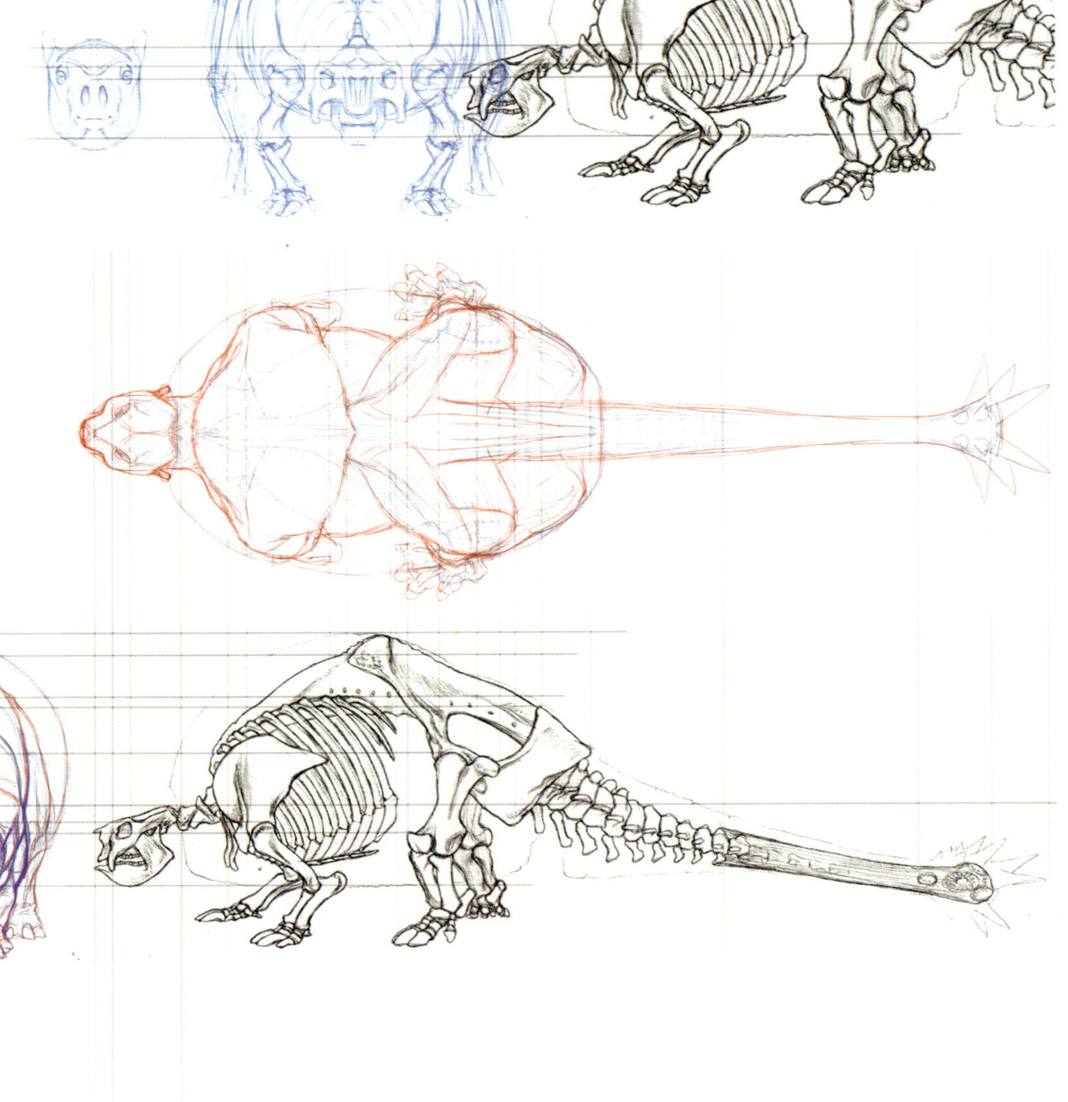

SKETCHBOOK PRACTICE

My sketchbooks are very informal. They aren't the traditional bound kind. Rather, they are of the same nature as my commissioned illustration work – collections of tracing-paper pads, spiral-bound lined notebooks, and loose reams of copier paper kept organized together. Even paper napkins on an airline flight! When the drawing surface is unbound or inexpensive, I feel free, like I can crumple up and toss a drawing that I'm dissatisfied with, because after all, it's *only* tracing paper, for example.

The sketchbook is there to capture ideas, followed by development and study. It is a means to an end. If the sketches themselves turn out to be something special, then that's serendipity. My sketchbook practice has taught me to be free with my ideas, learn from my mistakes, and the importance of exploration.

I begin with lots of doodles and gestures to get the gist of an idea down. Using a ballpoint pen is ideal at this stage. Goof ups and mistakes and smudges – bring it on! Eventually something exciting will happen that I can work with, usually sooner rather than later. This is especially useful when sketching moving targets, such as animals at the zoo. Charcoal on newsprint works similarly well. Then, back to the studio to gather reference and refine my sketches. More practice and exploration; trying out different line techniques, adding colour with markers, figuring out an elephant's scapula in a three-quarter view. I might add colour to both tracing paper and lined notebook paper. The lines create an interesting graphic effect and I've always been fascinated by the juxtaposition of natural (animals and people) forms and graphic elements. The great Art Nouveau artists, such as Mucha and Klimt, were experts at this.

I don't have different sketchbooks dedicated to specific projects or types of drawing. For me, it's definitely a catch-all approach. My sketchbooks are part and parcel of my professional work. They're relaxing, but in an intense, exciting way. The artwork displayed in this chapter shows this natural progress from initial scribbly pencil rough to the final drawings, to a full-colour completed illustration, all created using the same traditional media as those first sketchy idea thumbnails. From start to finish, I guess you could say it's all one big sketchbook, with only the last two stages digitally enhanced.

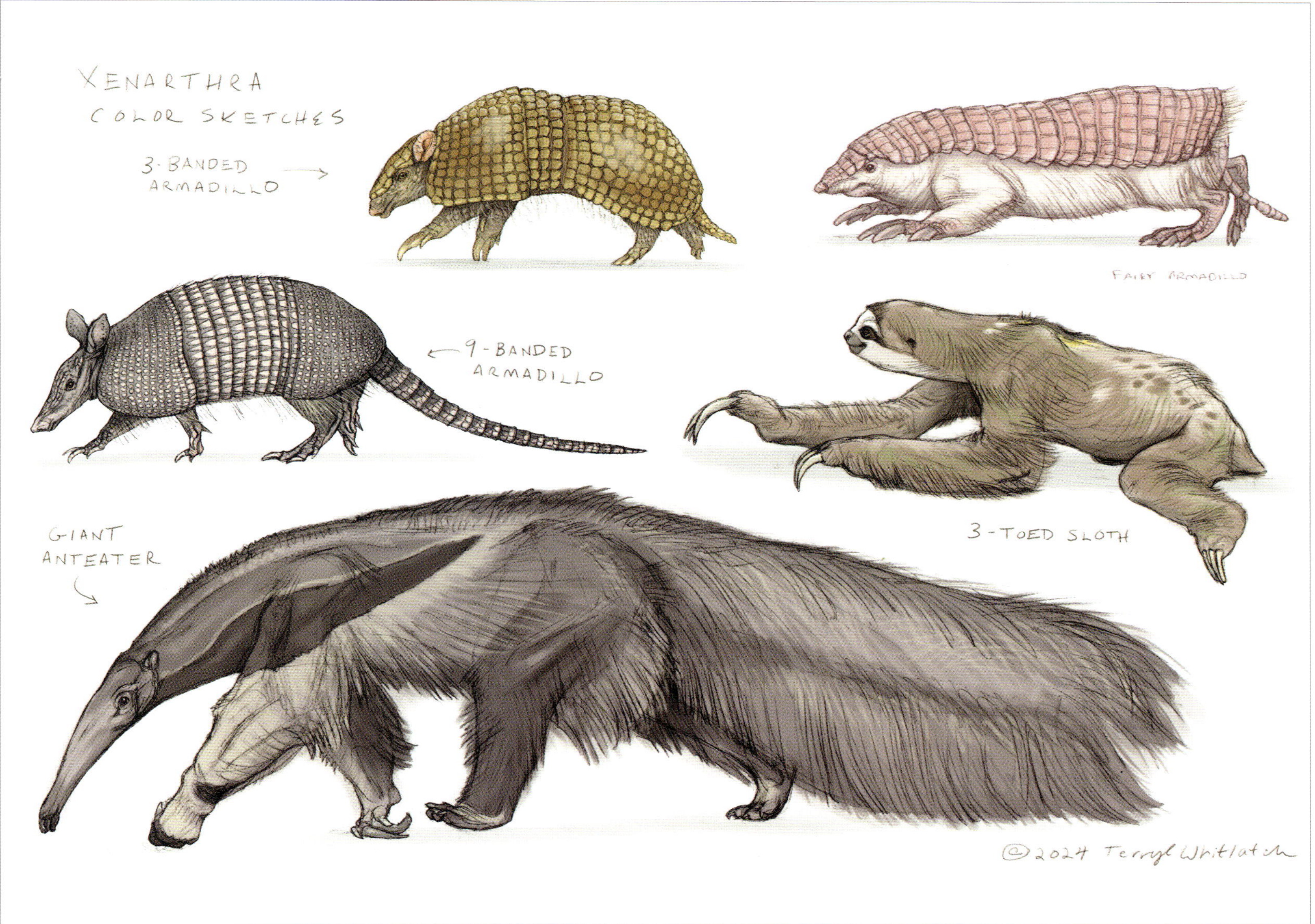

My sketchbook practice has taught me to be free with my ideas, learn from my mistakes, and the importance of exploration

Real animal study sketches

Glyptodonts belong to a zoological animal group called Xenarthra (literally, alien joint), which includes armadillos, anteaters, and sloths. So, it sort of makes sense to put them into outer space! They have all got big claws, extra articulations in their spines, and hefty pelvises that are fused to their sacrums. Crazy, weird alien Earth animals indeed! The particular glyptodont I chose to illustrate is Doedicurus, which is huge – about the same size and shape as a Volkswagen Beetle.

I wanted to familiarize myself with these creatures some more before going any further with the reconstructions. Plus, the giant anteater is one of my favourite animals, so any excuse to draw one is welcome.

I drew these sketches on tracing paper using a 2H technical pencil, copied them on the digital photocopier, and scanned them into Photoshop. I then used a combination of hard round and rough round bristle Photoshop brushes to apply loosely layered colour under the drawings, before softening the line work itself by creating colour channels. I liked the golden colour of the three-banded armadillo and decided to use it on the glyptodont. The animals aren't drawn to scale here – in reality, the fairy armadillo fits neatly into the palm of your hand. And yes, its carapace (shell) really is pink!

Glyptodont, surface, side view

In this side-view surface reconstruction, I paid great attention to the detail of the carapace. I borrowed the golden hue from the three-banded armadillo, because I thought it would create a nice glow effect in the final illustration. I love how the spines of the mace-like tail radiate outward and star-like, like mid-century atomic star motifs.

Glyptodont, hypothetical profile, side view

This hypothetical view of the animal without the carapace shows the profile of the body and how the legs articulate for positional and animation purposes.

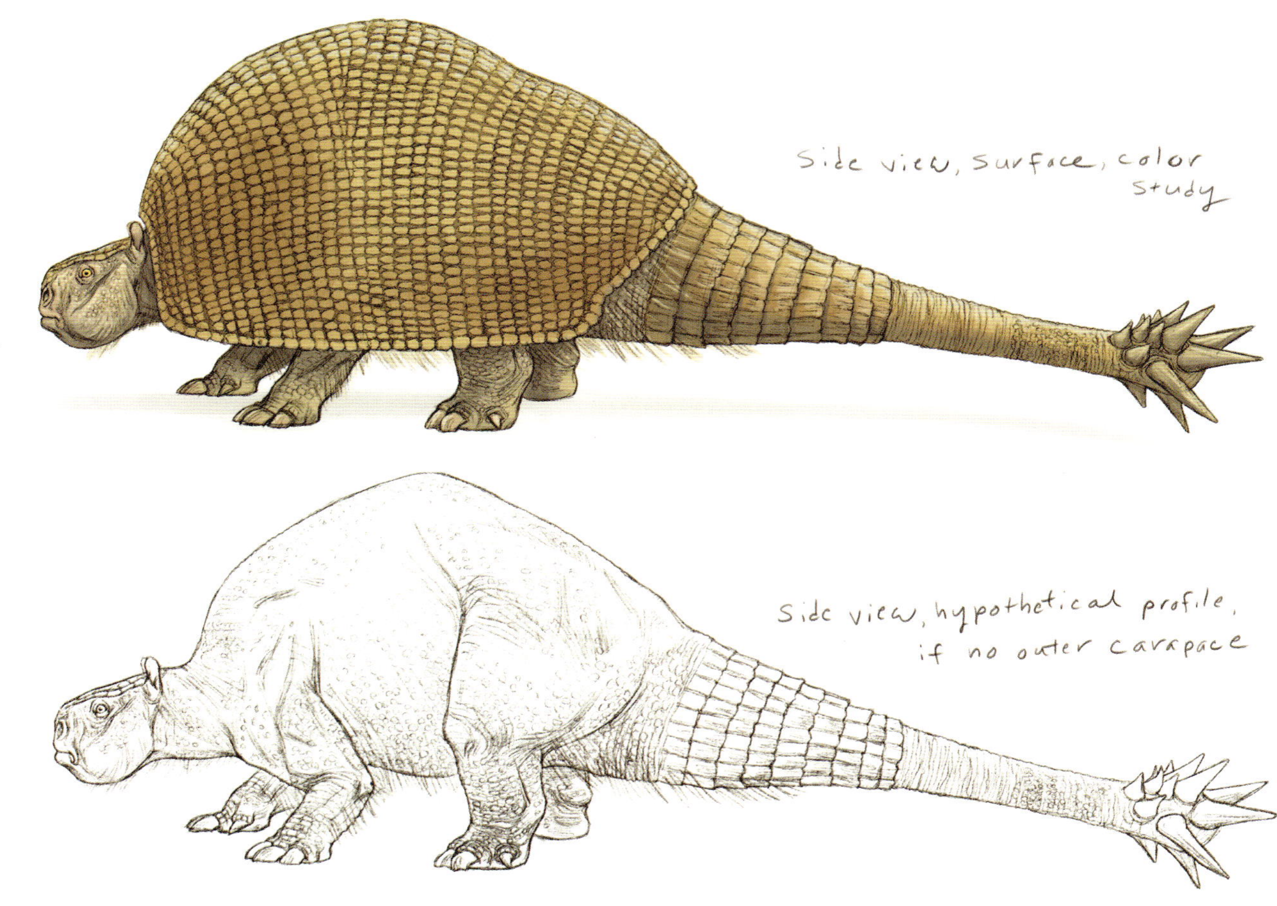

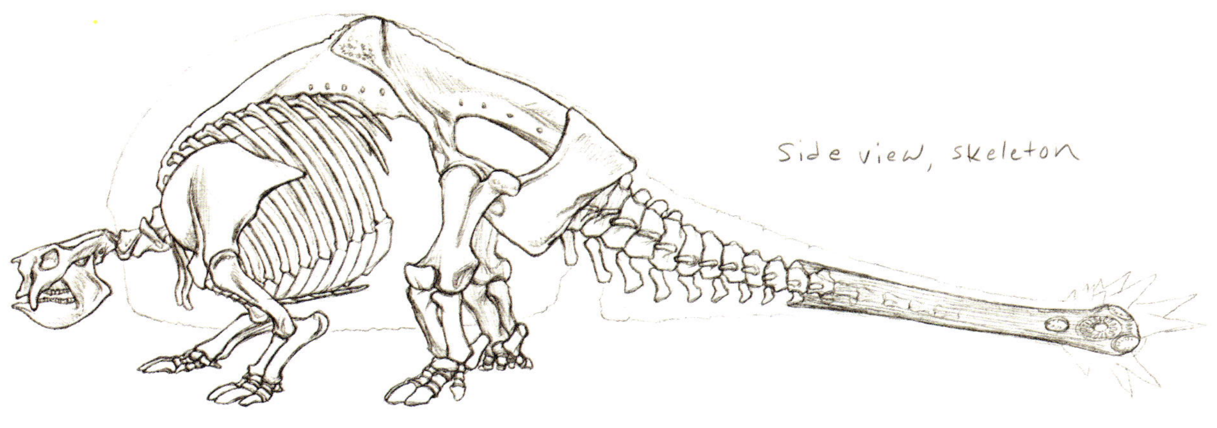

Glyptodont, skeleton, side view

Note the extraordinarily huge pelvis that is fused to the sacrum of the spine. The zoological term for this sort of pelvis-sacrum fusion is called a synsacrum. Birds have this feature too! Note also the prominent cheek flanges extending from the cheek bones – this gives an appealing round-faced look. In addition, you can see the collar bones hanging downwards.

Glyptodont, musculature, side view

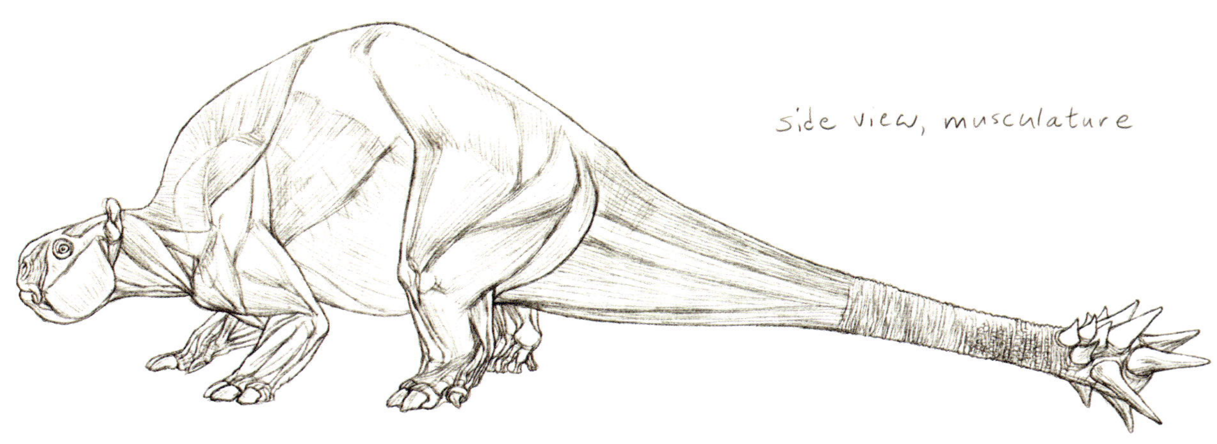

The musculature is straightforward, following the general mammalian pattern.

Right | **Glyptodont, skeleton, rear view**

The rear view of the huge synsacrum/pelvis. It's got a lot of weight to support – about as much as a small car.

Far right | **Glyptodont, skeleton, front view**

The front view of the skeleton – you can really see those cheek flanges. I moved the collar bones upwards, to their proper place, articulating with the spines of the shoulder blades (the same as in humans).

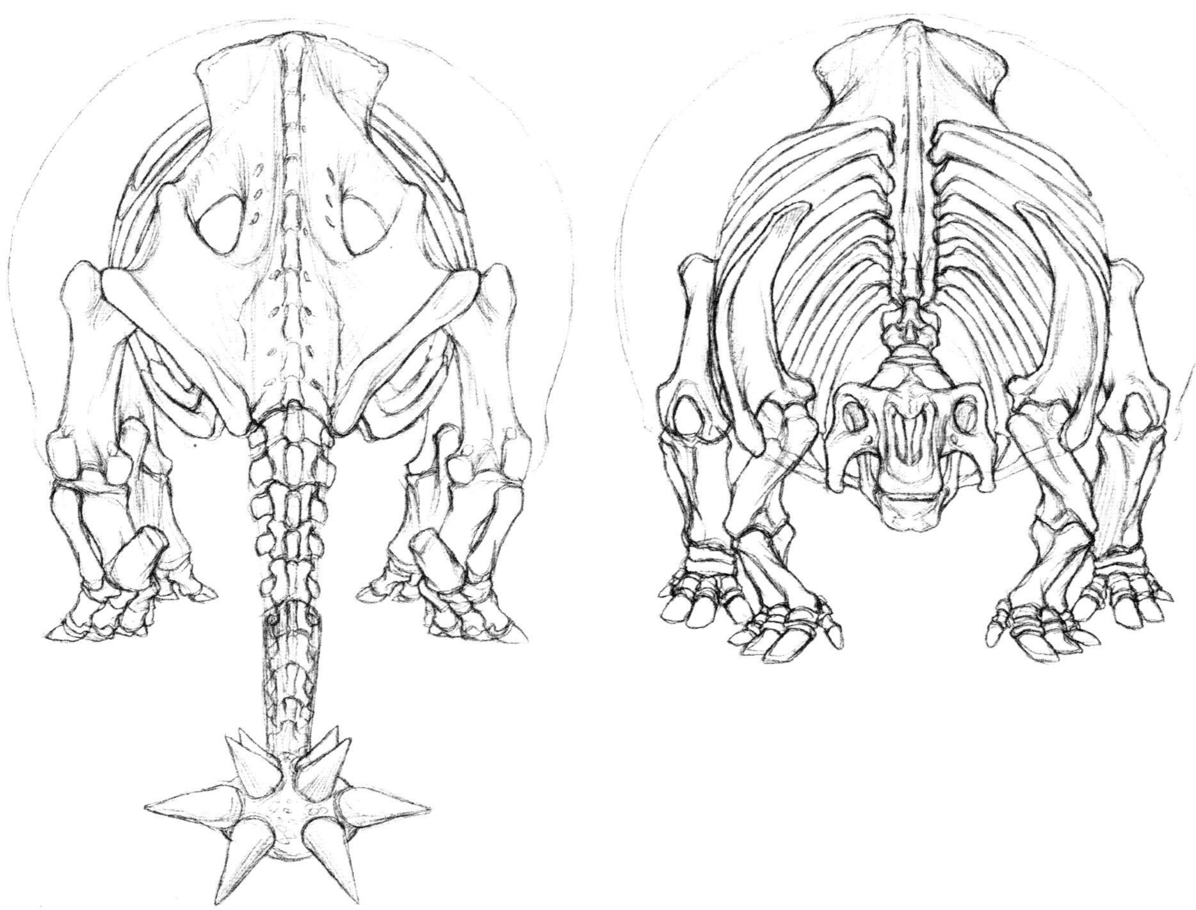

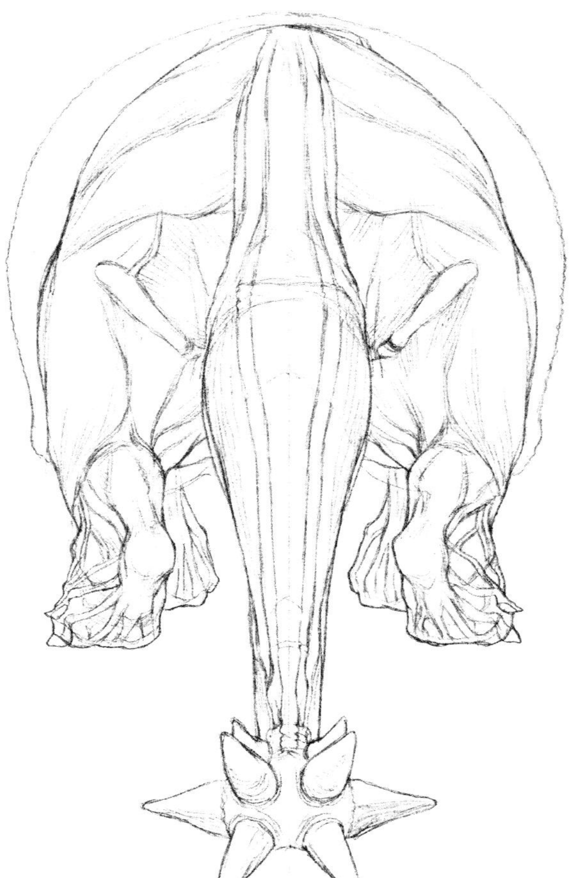

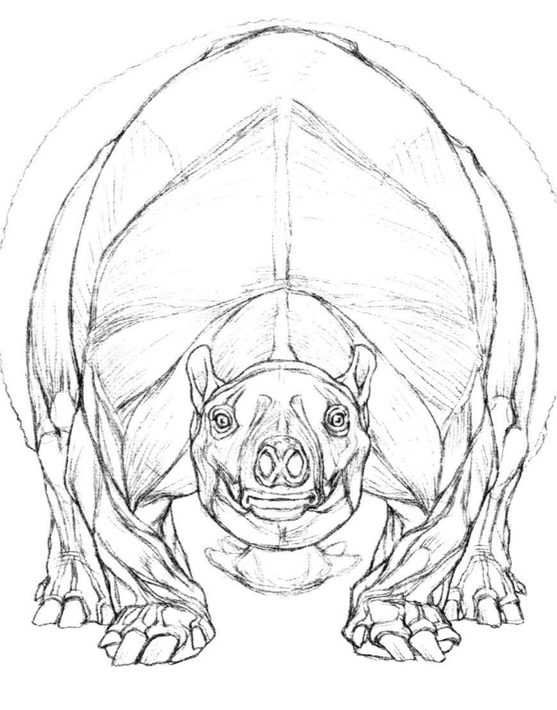

Far left | **Glyptodont, musculature, rear view**

The rear view of the musculature. Notice the sitting bones (the ischial tuberosities) poking through at a slant to one another. In life, these would be covered by protective fascia and fat.

Left | **Glyptodont, musculature, front view**

The front view of the musculature. The structure visible under the chin is the tip of the long tail in perspective.

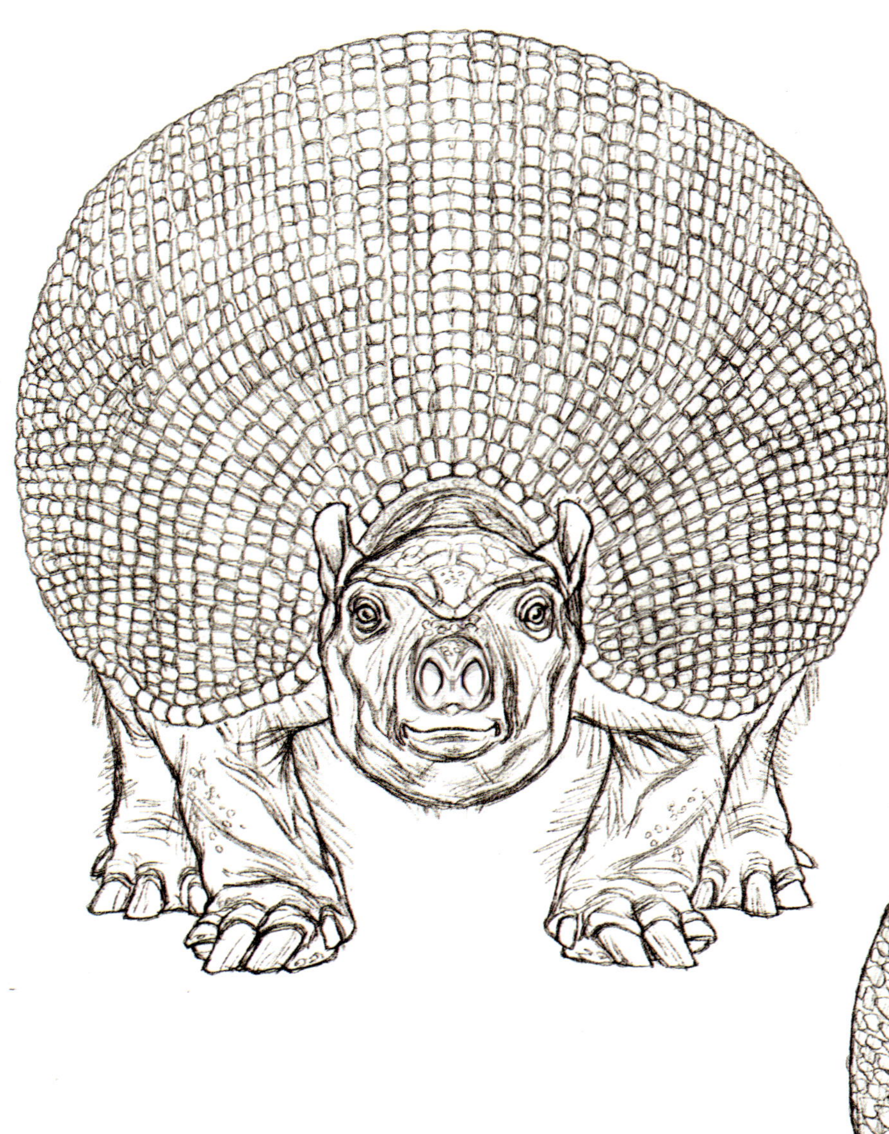

Left | **Glyptodont, surface, front view**

In the front view, I experimented with facial possibilities. All living armadillos have fairly long, pointed snouts with downward-facing nostrils. Glyptodonts have much shorter faces, not dissimilar to the skulls of giant sloths, which are just a bit more distantly related. I looked at the nostrils and skulls of the short-faced three-toed and two-toed sloths for inspiration. It was once thought that glyptodonts had short trunks, like those of tapirs, due to the short nasal bones (rostral bones).

Below | **Glyptodont, surface, rear view**

The rear view shows the mace-like tail to its advantage. Scientists postulate that it was used as a weapon against predators, such as sabre-toothed cats, or to settle territorial or mating disputes. Not all glyptodont species had these maces – these were peculiar to Doedicurus.

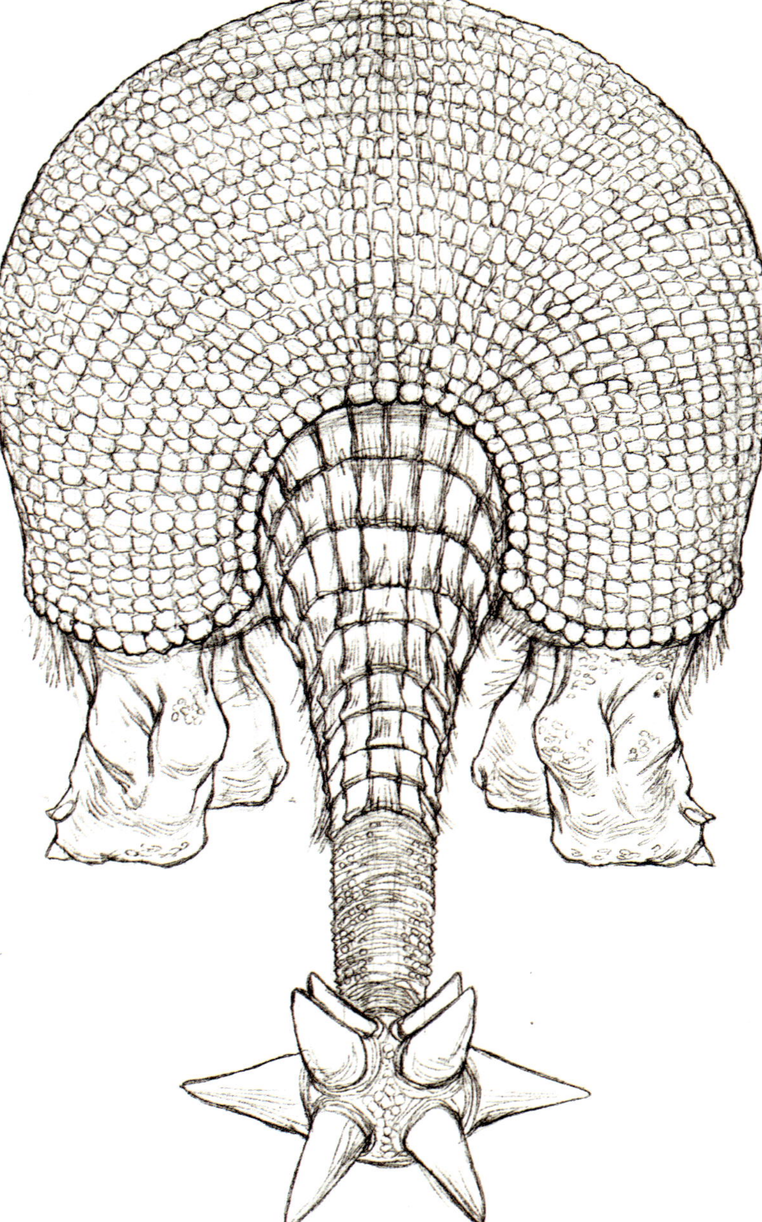

TRADITIONAL MATERIALS

I like using technical pencil on tracing paper, indigo blue Col-Erase pencils on copier paper, markers on digital photocopies, and charcoal on newsprint. The copies made off a digital copier aren't themselves digital – they are composed of graphite, laid down in the density I desire. So these are traditional as well.

My working format ranges from 23 × 30 cm to around 28 × 43 cm (conveniently the same size as copier paper). For newsprint, around 36 × 43 cm to 46 × 61 cm, and for tracing paper, 36 × 43 cm. Nothing too big.

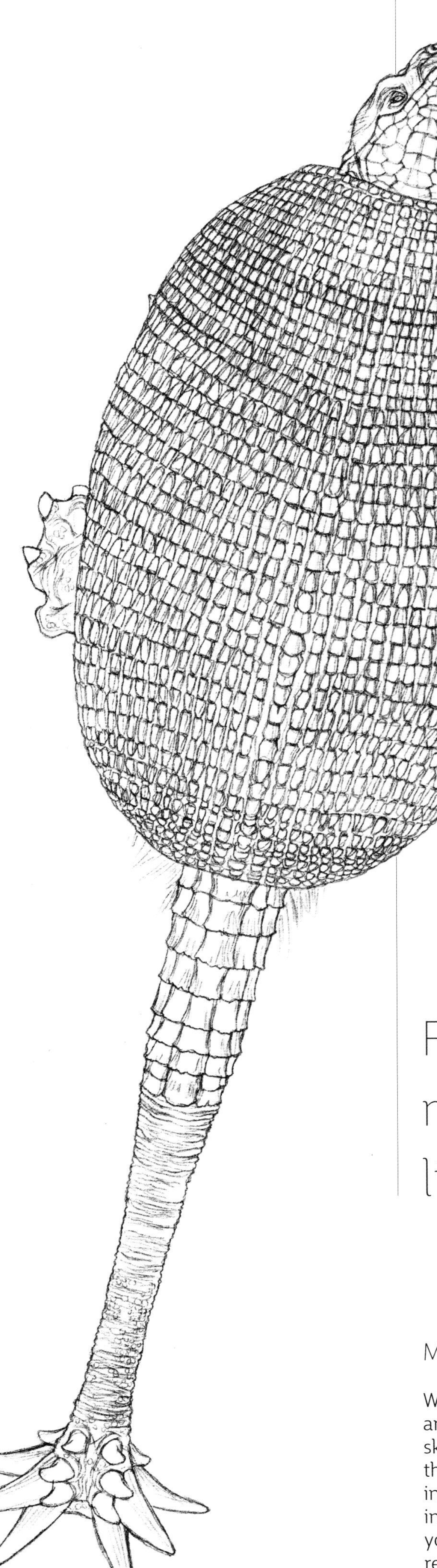

Glyptodont, surface, top view

The carapace is dermal, an adaptation of the skin. Due to the presence of keratin, the carapace would have been semi-flexible in the living animal, even though it's infused with bone. It took much longer to draw than the rest of the anatomy. There would be no bottom carapace, or plastron, as in turtles. Instead, the underside would be like the bellies of modern armadillos, covered with wrinkly, somewhat scaly, skin and some wiry hair.

Feel free to mess around and make as many 'mistakes' as you like. Your sketchbook is for you

MAKE MANY MISTAKES

When it comes to your sketchbook, feel free to mess around and make as many 'mistakes' as you like. Your sketchbook is for you. The freer and less inhibited you are, the more efficient, creative, and less stressed you will be in the long run. In contrast, make sure all of the artwork in your portfolio is your very best, while also realizing that your portfolio will never be perfect – it is only the very best representation of what you can do at any given time.

Right | Glyptodont, skeleton, top view

The top view of a skeleton makes clear how wide the animal is. Together with the side view, a prehistoric animal can be reconstructed with a fair degree of accuracy.

The fusion of the pelvis to the central sacrum can be clearly seen here. The second half of the tail is enclosed and stiffened with bone-infused keratin.

Far right | Glyptodont, skeleton, belly view

The belly view shows the structure and articulations of the clavicles. Mammals that are climbers, diggers, burrowers, flyers, or hold items in their paws, tend to have clavicles (collar bones). Mammals that are primarily runners and leapers don't typically have them.

Drawing the skeleton of the legs in this perspective is a great exercise!

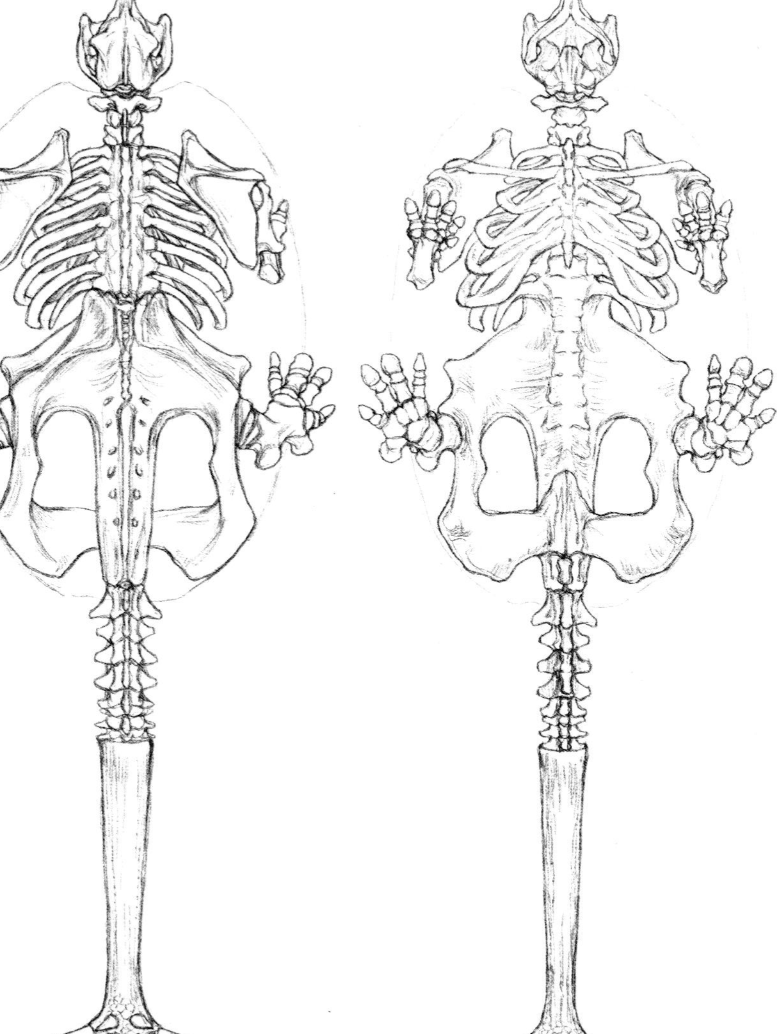

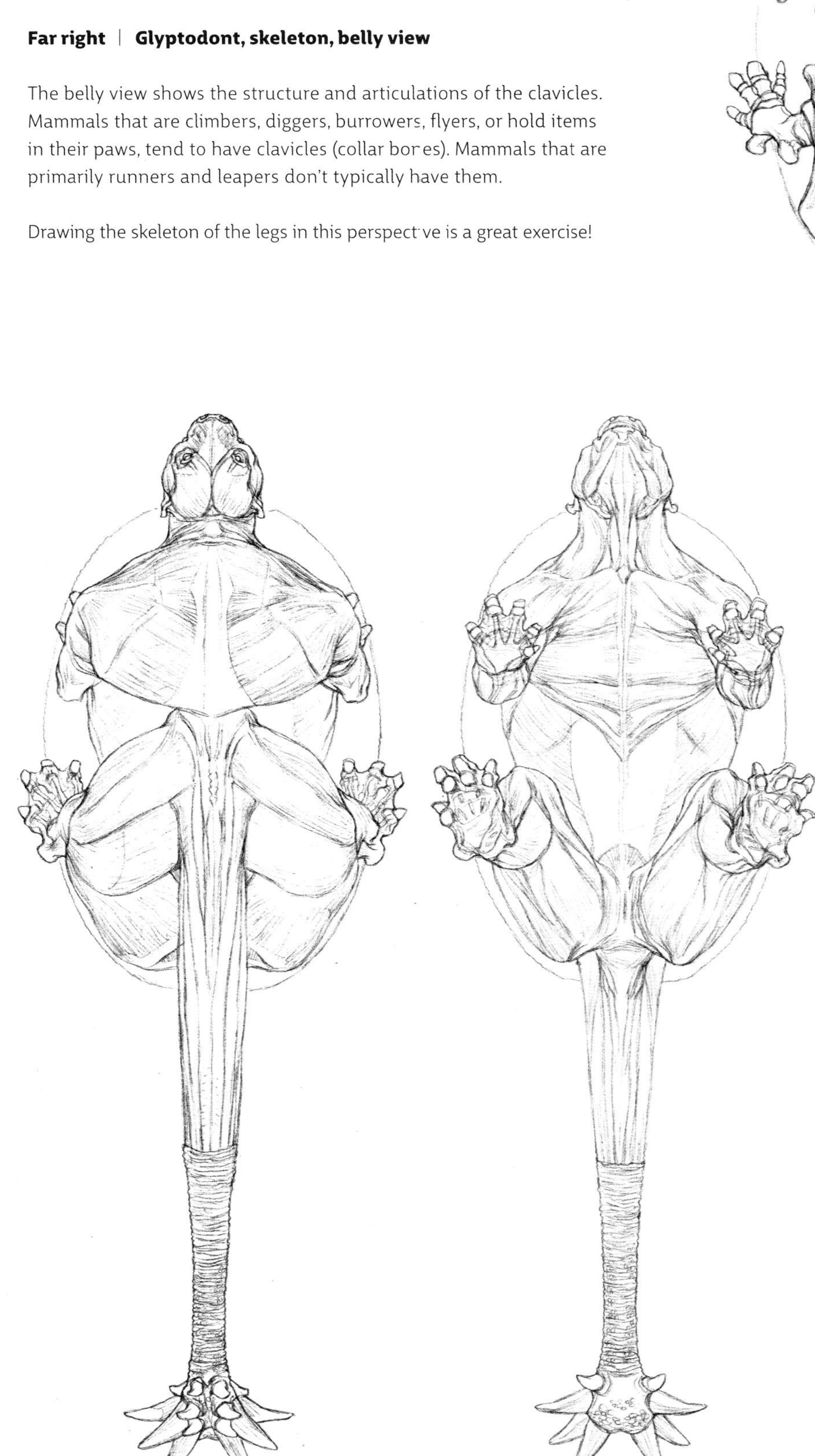

Far left | Glyptodont, musculature, top view

Based on the muscle scars on the skeleton that denote the origin and insertion points of the muscles, and how this works in living mammals, I attached the muscles. The 'blank' area in the musculature of the back indicates protective layers of tissue called fasciae.

Left | Glyptodont, musculature, belly view

I took the opportunity to establish the pectoral muscles and abdominal muscles, especially since I planned to draw a belly view of one of the glyptodonts in the illustration.

From my research, I wasn't sure if glyptodonts had five fingers on their hands, as this varies across the different members of the Xenarthra family. I decided that I could always eliminate the thumbs if necessary. The Xenarthra is one of the earliest orders of placental mammals, and while it is typical for the earlier orders to retain the full five digits, it's not always the case. Here I've only shown four digits. I need to consult a vertebrate palaeontologist on this one!

SAYING 'HELLO' TO OLD FRIENDS

I keep my sketches, drawings, and marker work organized in labelled, oversized manila envelopes and stored in architectural drawers/flat files. Paintings on illustration board and Masonite are stored in zipped portfolio cases. These are mostly acrylic paintings. Some favourites are framed and on my walls. So far, I've been fortunate not to have had any accidents or disasters, but whenever I've moved, and have had occasion to reorganize the drawers, I do revisit art from various jobs from decades ago. It's like saying 'hello' to old friends.

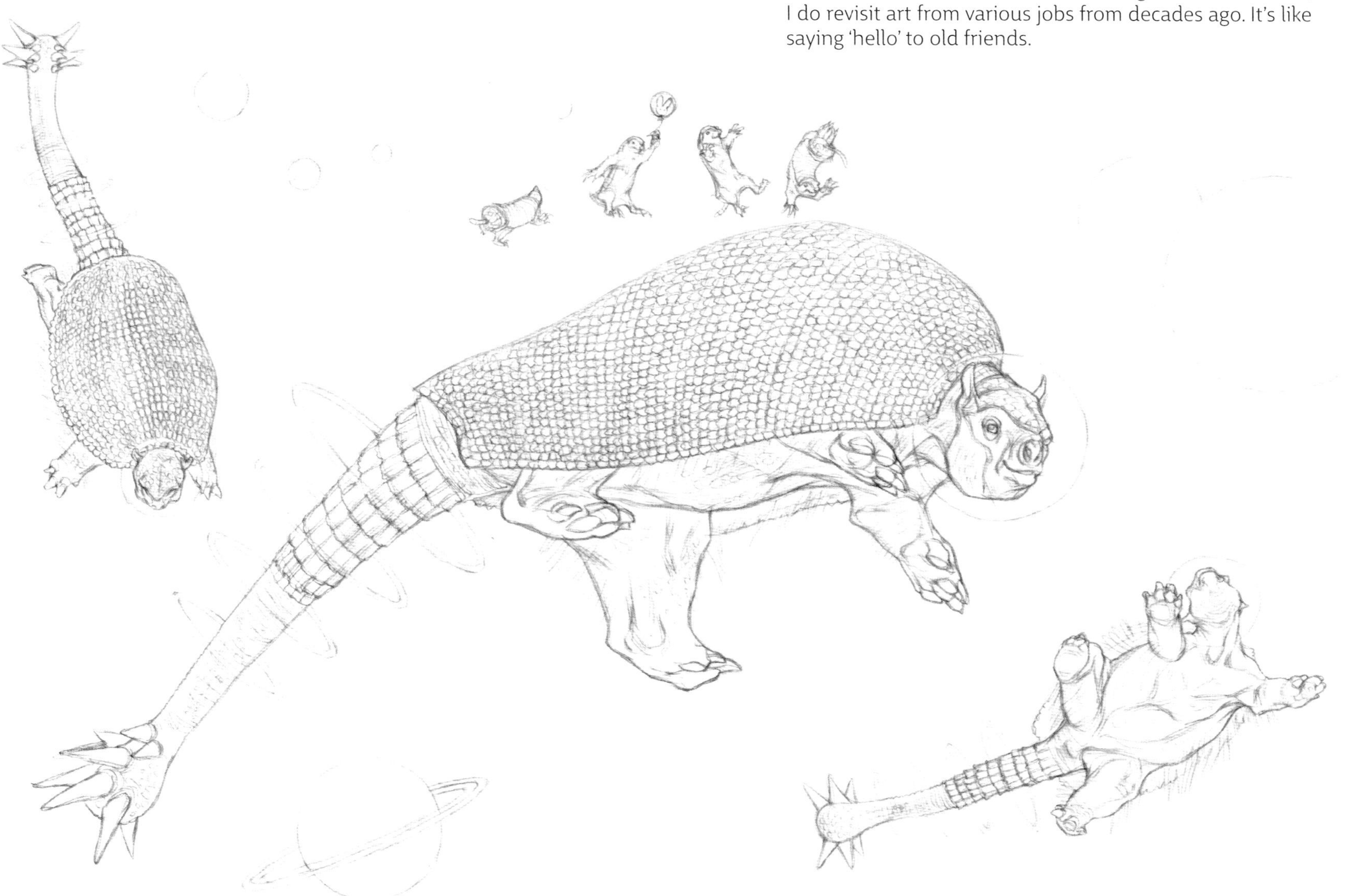

Glyptos a Glow-Glow, rough working drawing on tracing paper

Once I had a greater understanding of the glyptodont in all the essential views of its anatomy, as well as practising drawing its modern relatives, I could proceed with more confidence to the first working rough drawing and general layout using a mechanical pencil with 5 mm 2H lead. Free to be as messy as I wanted at this stage, I was able to explore anthropomorphism in the expression while still retaining accurate anatomy for the most part.

Next, I added the fairy armadillo astronauts. They would actually be much smaller than pictured (about the size of pet rats), but then you wouldn't be able to see them very well.

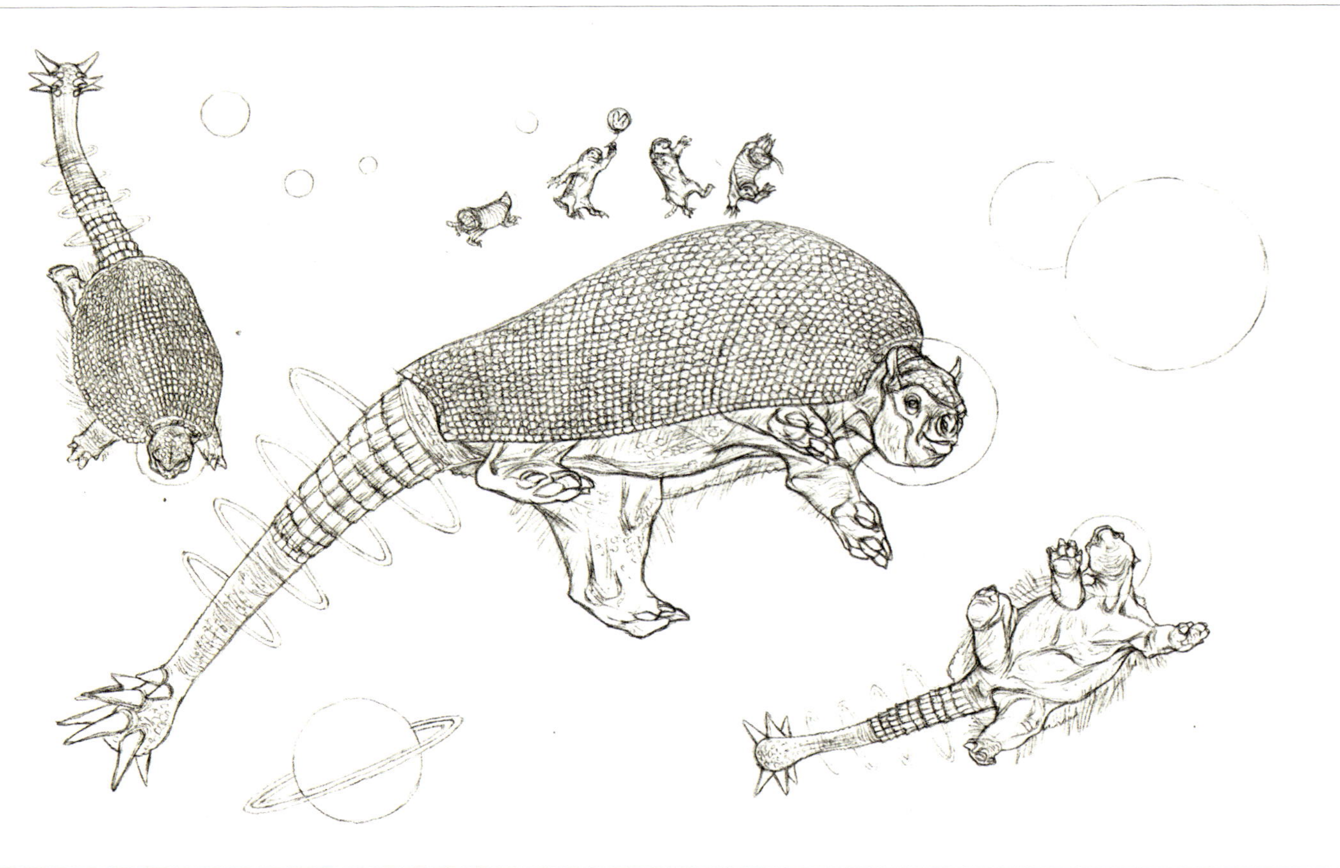

Glyptos a Glow-Glow, rough working drawing, digital photocopy

For the next stage, I made a digital photocopy to allow me to clean up and refine the drawing. I hand-traced over the photocopy using another layer of tracing paper to achieve the final working drawing. The more traditional layers, the more chaos factor is added in. Chaos inherent in traditional media adds energy to a drawing (and confounds AI somewhat).

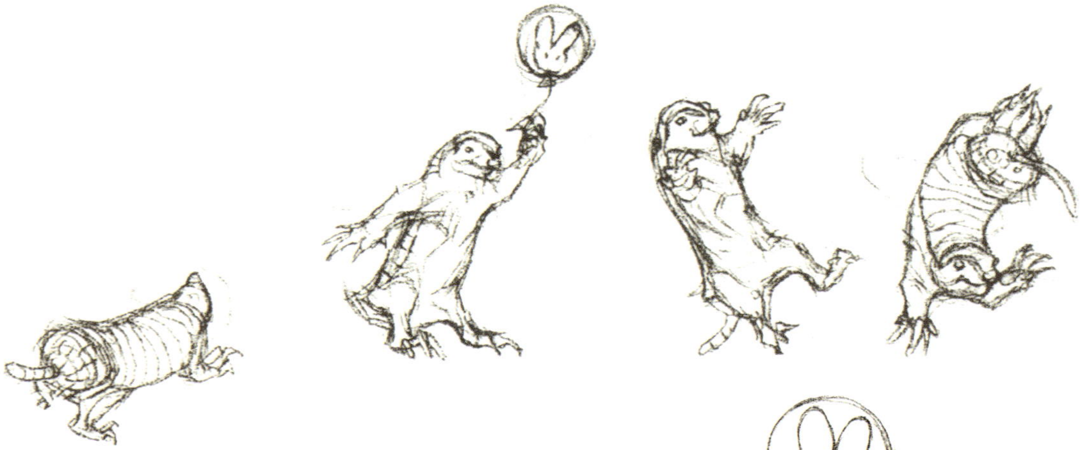

Fairy armadillos astronaut roughs, close-up

Note the round armoured rump disc – they're very funny, endearing creatures. I'm glad I drew the actual animal in my sketches. Reality gives you wings to exaggerate believably, regardless of aesthetic. Nature has all the best creature designs!

Fairy armadillo astronauts, refined

Once I understand the animal, I can put it into any pose I like. They will still be small in the final illustration, but larger than they would be in real life, relative to the glyptodont, so you can see them better. It is a fantasy illustration, after all.

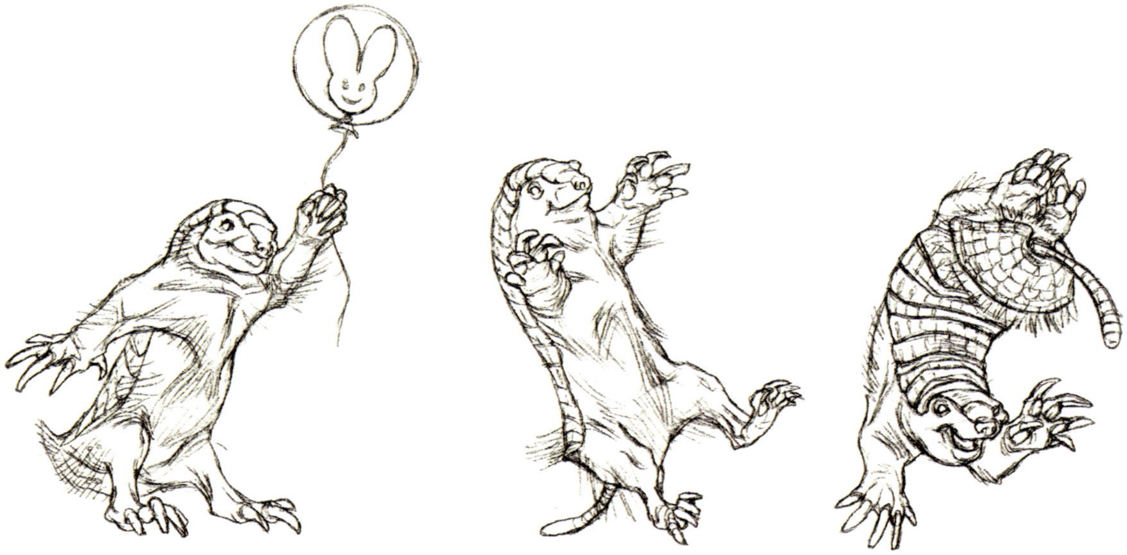

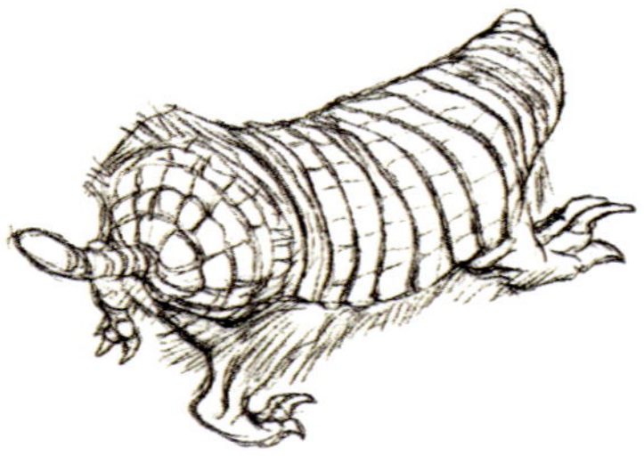

Primary glyptodon image, refined

The refined, reworked main glyptodon on tracing paper.
I concentrated mainly on the face and facial expression,
cleaned up and clarified the neck anatomy, plus other details.
I feel it has more authority and less exploration at this point,
which is what I wanted.

Anthropomorphism of animals in art is fun. Here I am
walking that fine line between the real and the cartoonlike.
Studios like Disney and DreamWorks do this all the time.

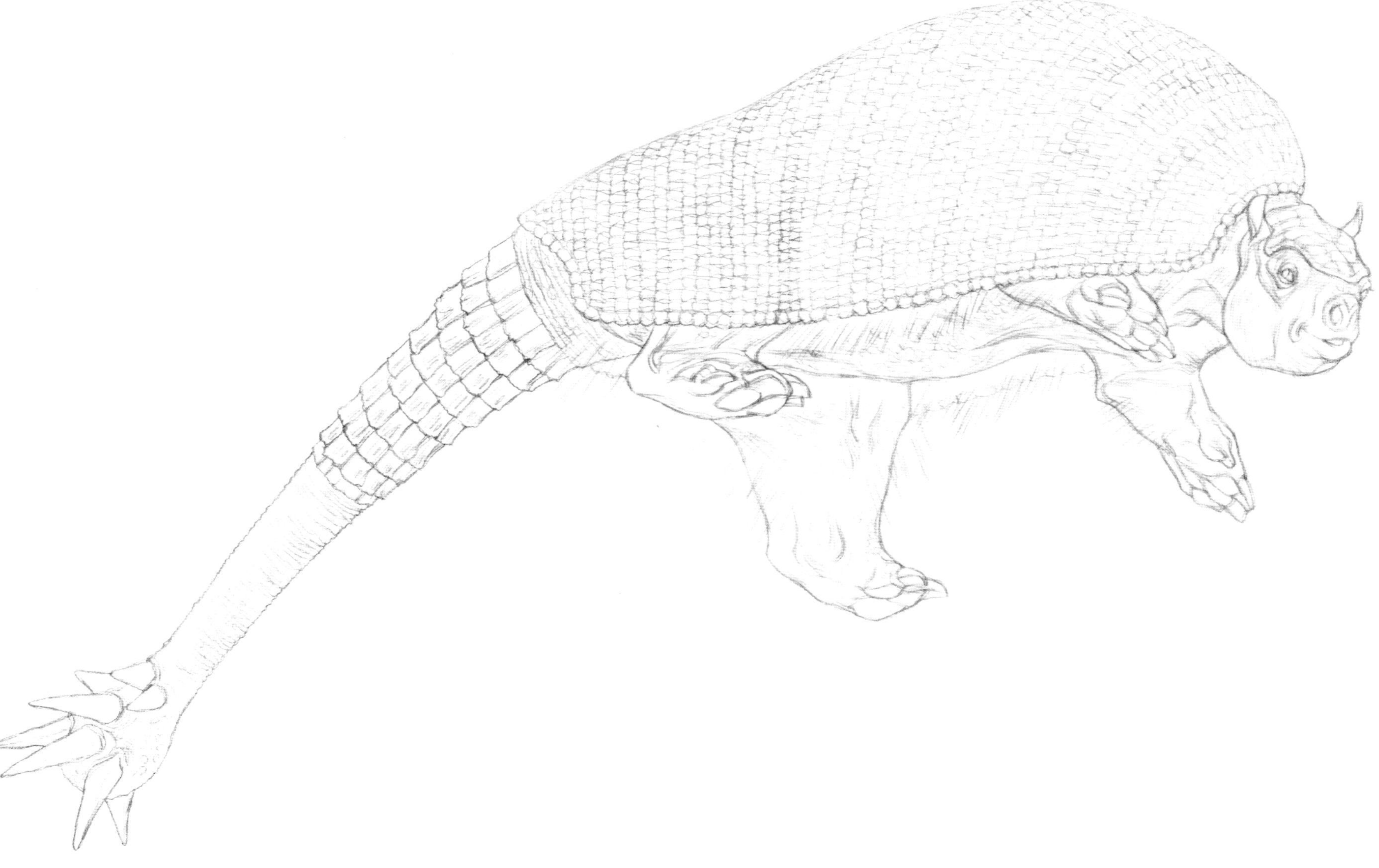

**Glyptos a Glow-Glow,
final working drawing**

I made digital photocopies of all the
animal characters, which were drawn
separately, and imported them into
Photoshop. Each glyptodont has its
own layer, and the fairy armadillo
astronauts share a layer. I then created
the graphic elements of the planets
and orbital 'energy' ellipses, and
imported copyright-free 'twinkle stars',
a common mid-century design motif,
from Shutterstock.

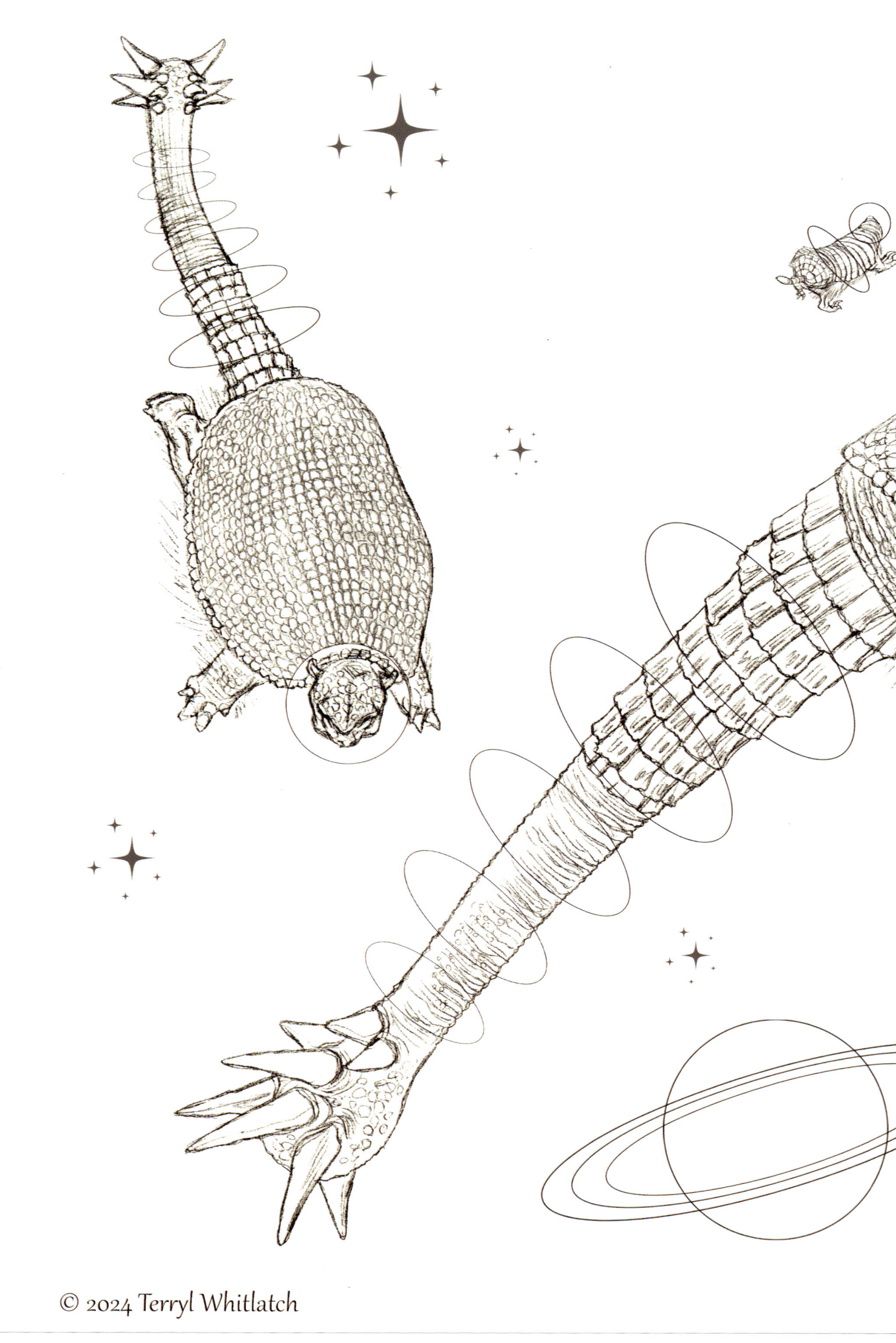

© 2024 Terryl Whitlatch

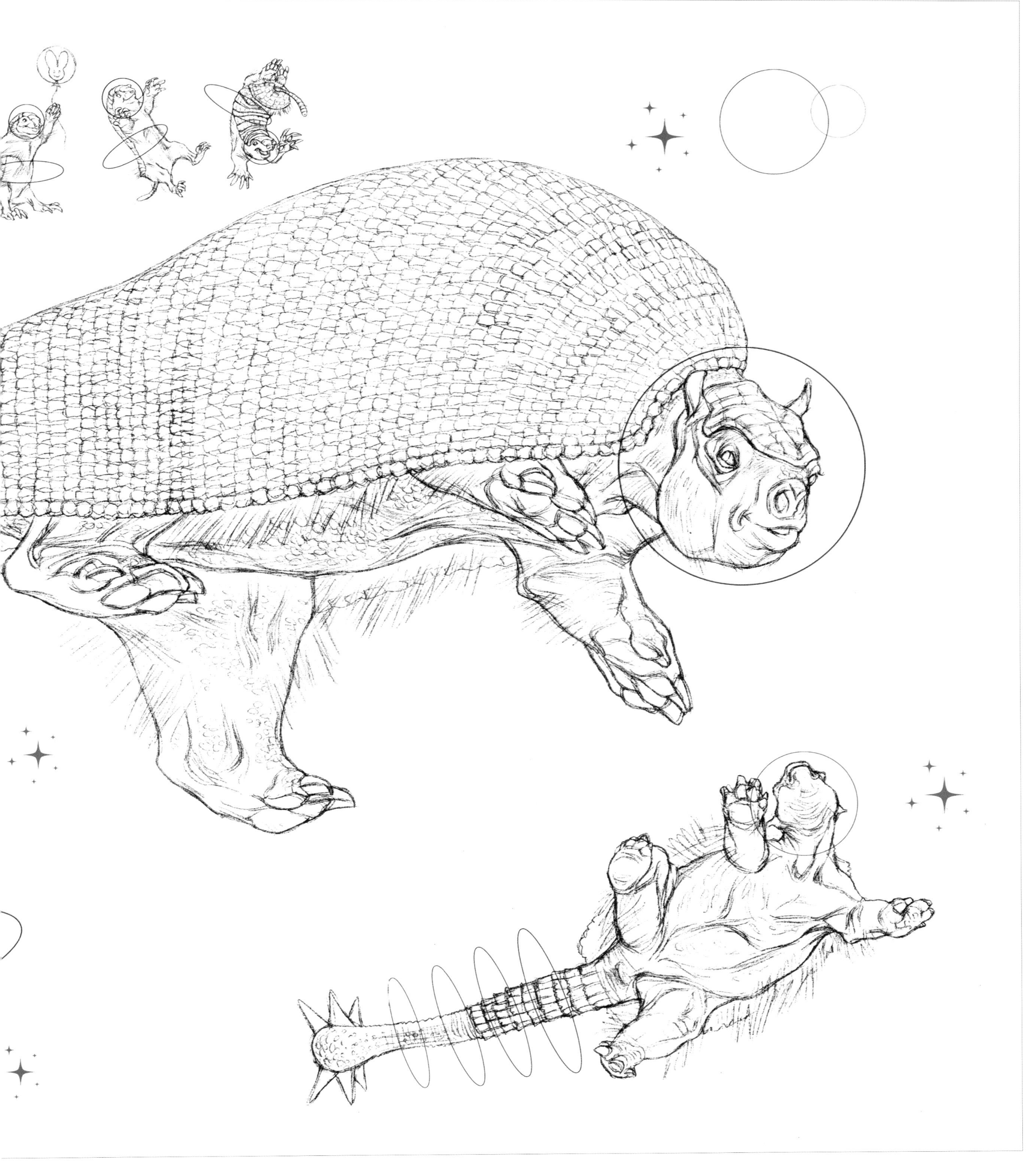

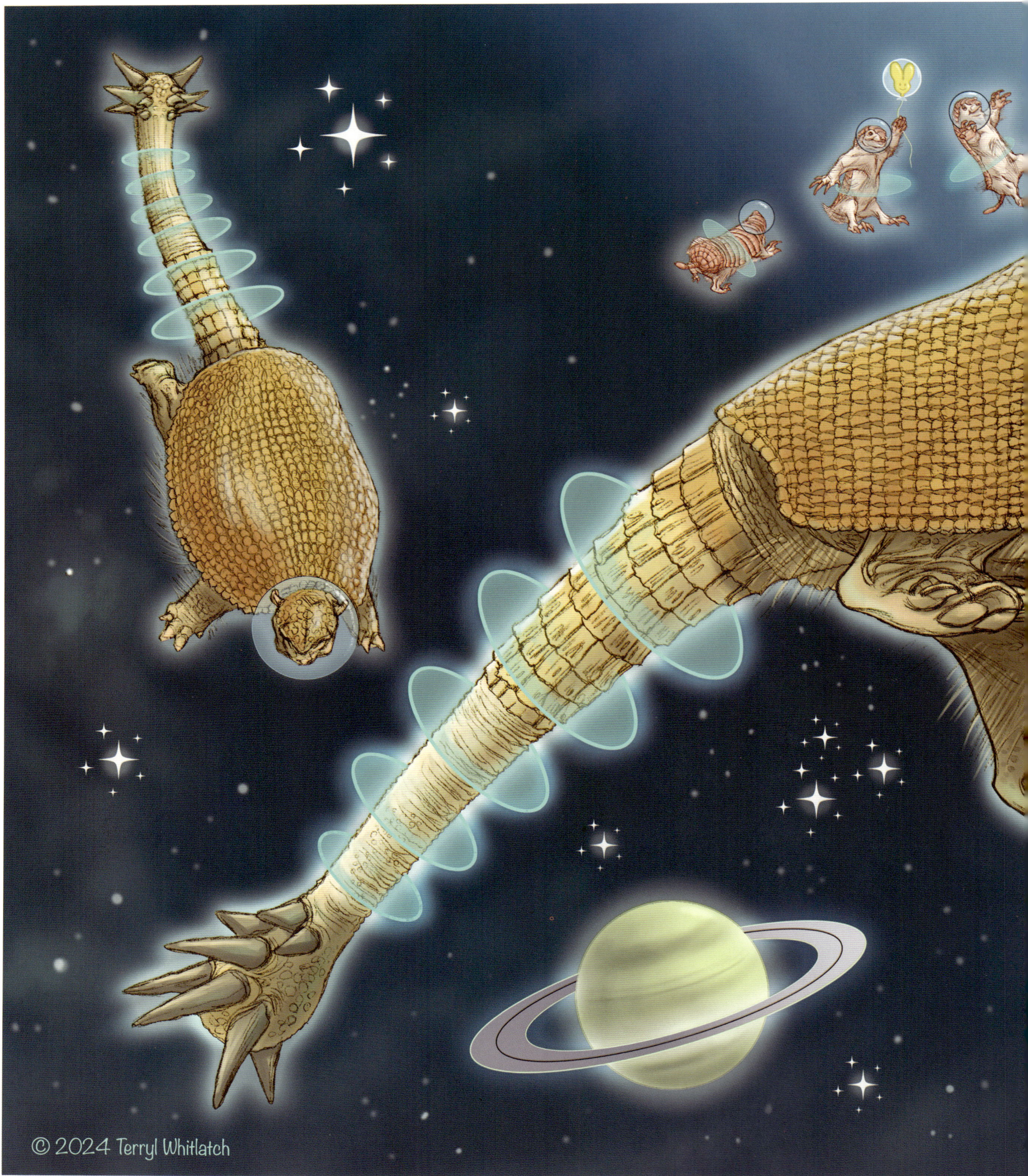

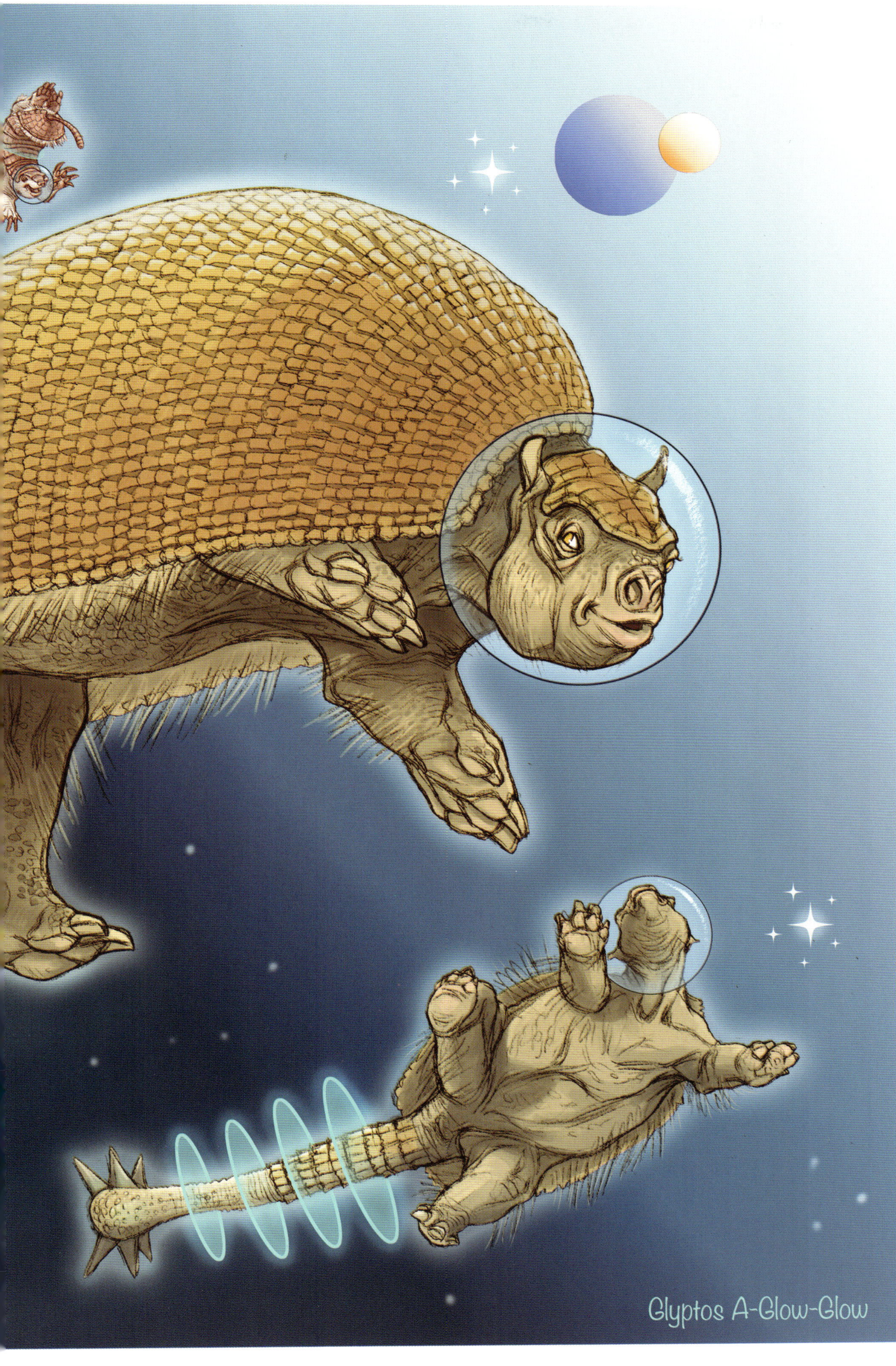

**Glyptos a Glow-Glow,
final colour illustration**

The completed illustration of happy,
glowing armadillos, large and small,
bounding through outer space on a
journey to who knows where. It must be
a very nice destination, because they all
seem very cheerful.

My goal was to achieve the space-
age design feel of late-1950s *Looney
Tunes* and mid-1960s *The Jetsons*, with
relatively flat graphic elements and the
more anatomically dimensional animals
juxtaposed against them. A quirky
surreality, which nonetheless hopefully
makes one smile.

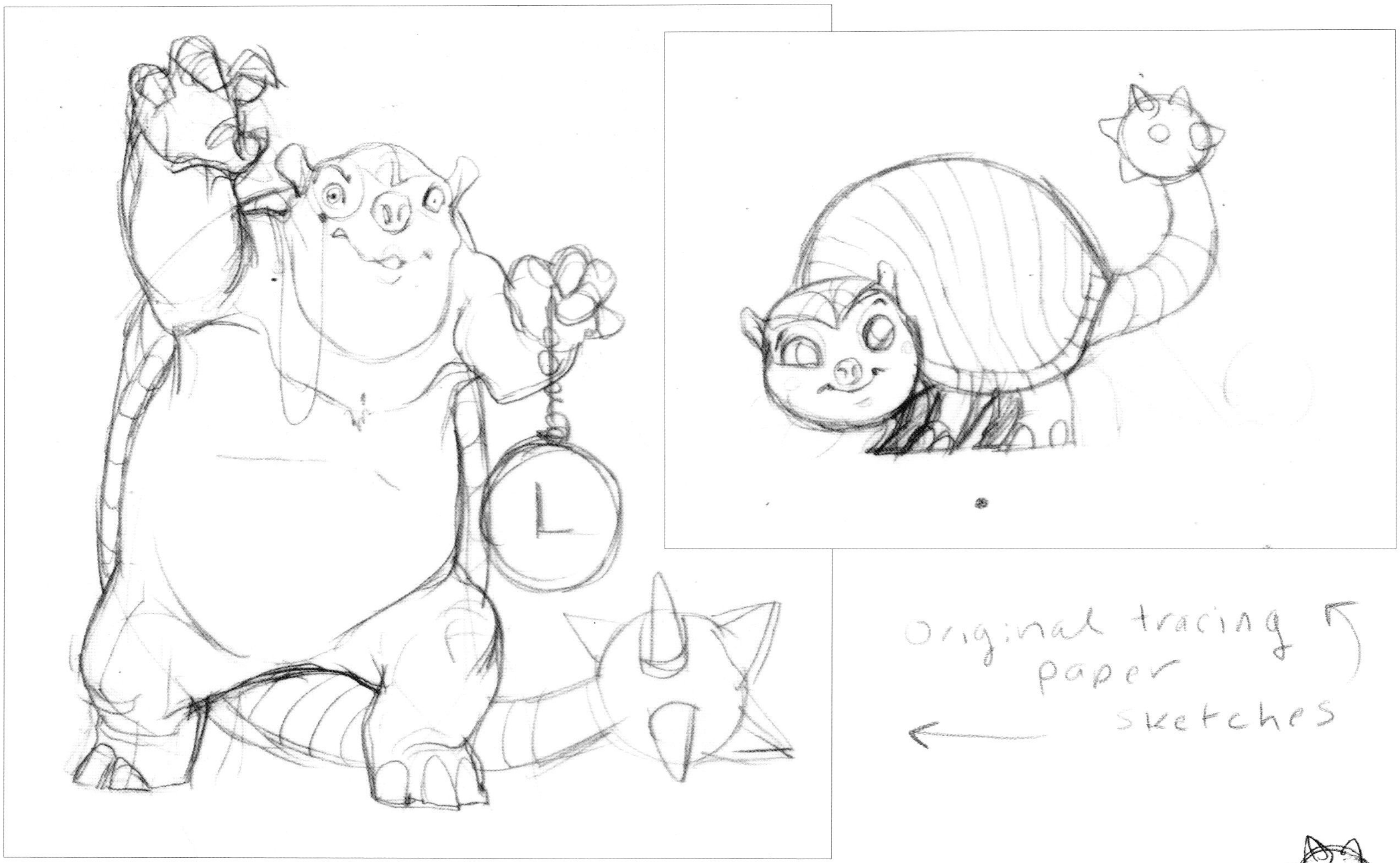

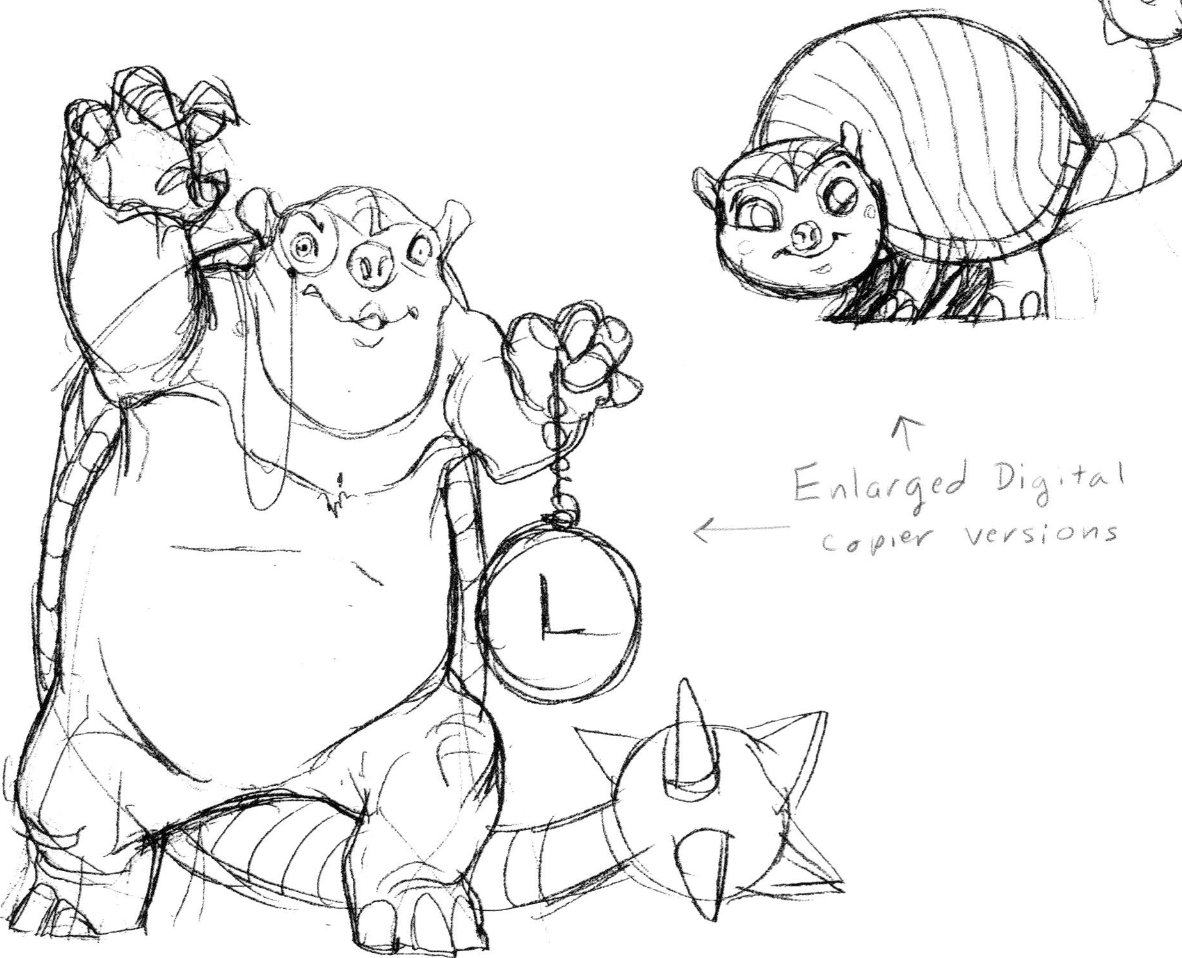

Simplified character roughs

As a character and creature designer, I need to be versatile in a variety of styles, depending on the aesthetics of the production. Here are examples of glyptodont characters in a couple of different more streamlined ('edited') styles suitable for episodic television productions.

These originated as sketches in my tracing-paper pad 'sketchbook', from which I made enlarged digital photocopies. One is a 'glypnotist' (a glyptodont hypnotist), and the other is simply a very cute 'glyptadorable'. Tip: when making a photocopy of a tracing paper drawing, put a piece of blank white paper behind it.

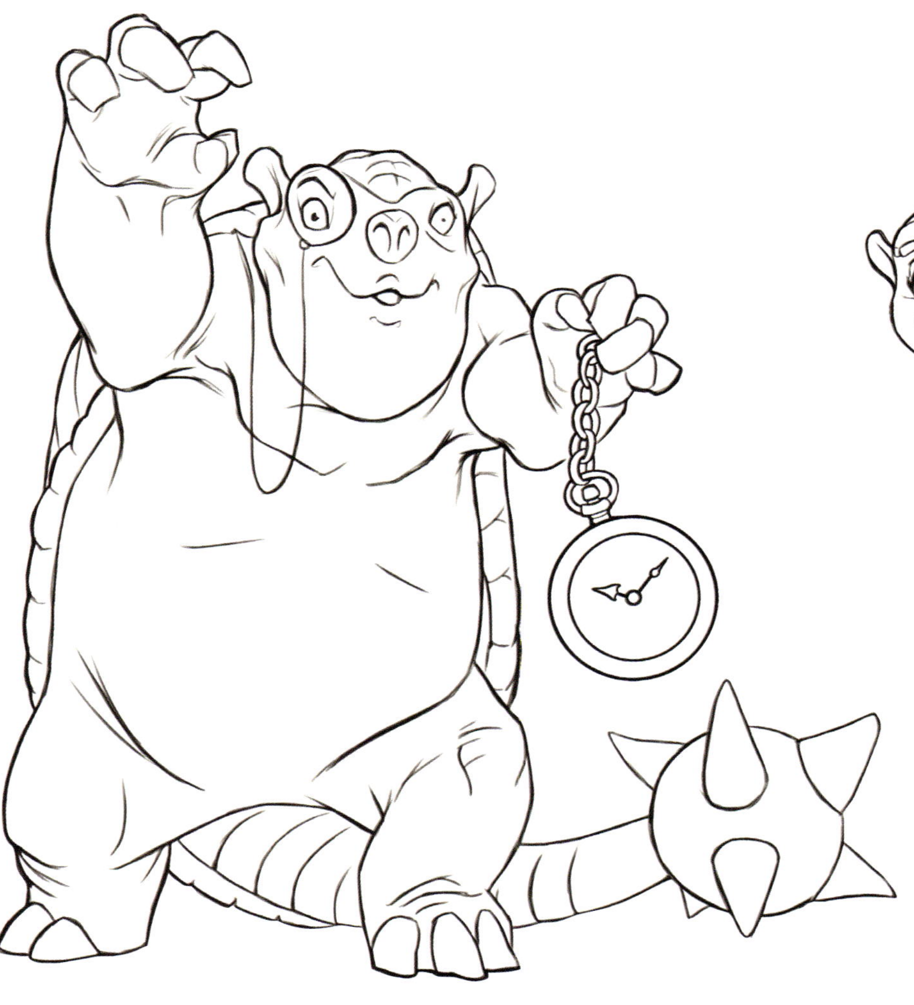

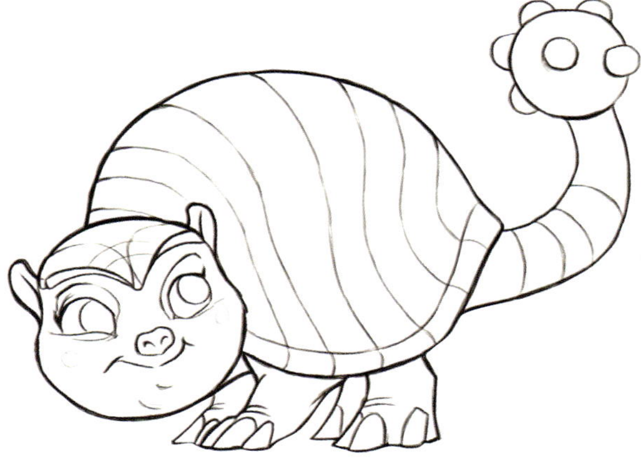

'Inked' characters

I imported these sketches into Photoshop, then traced them on another layer using a hard round pressure brush to simulate inking with a traditional brush. I created the giant pocket watch using the Elliptical Marquee tool.

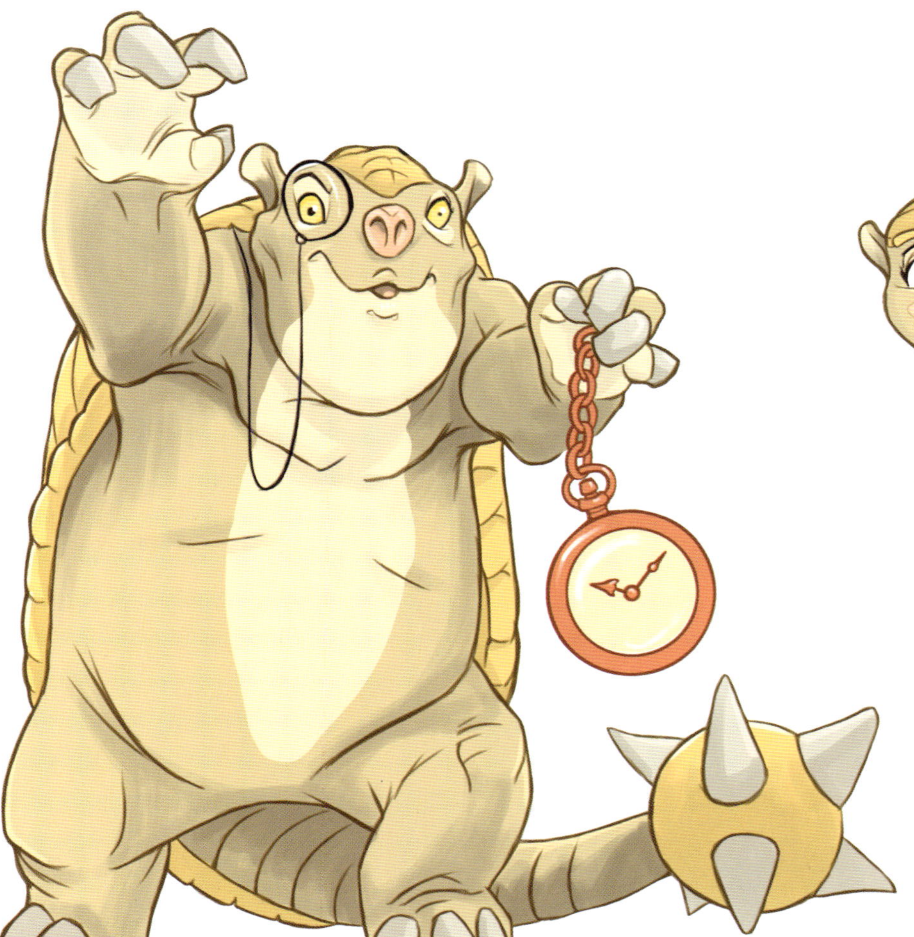

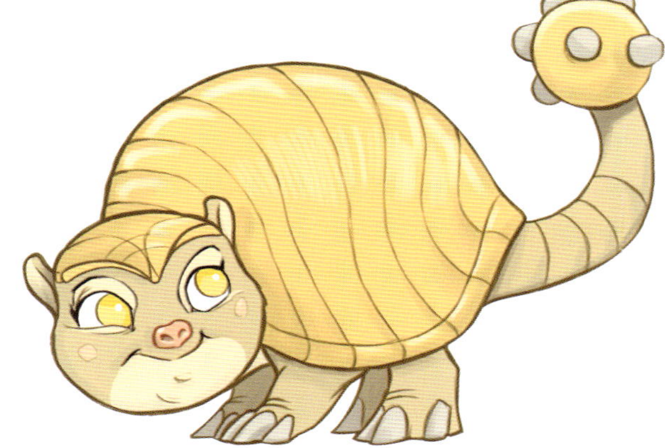

Finished inked and coloured characters

I changed the inked line art colour from black to dark brown on the glyptodonts, and to a red on the watch, by creating a channel. Underneath this ink layer, I applied colour using a hard round brush, with a dry brush on the monocle and watch face to suggest shine on a glassy surface.

So, there you have it. I've used the traditionally created sketches and drawings from my tracing-paper pad sketchbook with their inherent chaos factor, alternating back and forth between traditional and digital media to create a 'tradigital' illustration. Sort of like mixing practical and digital effects in a movie to achieve a compelling result.

Sandro Cleuzo

STARTING OUT

Born in Sao Paulo, Brazil, I've drawn since I was a young kid. My mother told me that I would ask family members to pose for me. As far back as I can remember, I loved comic books and watching cartoons on TV. In the late seventies and early eighties, there was a channel that would show cartoons all afternoon. Arriving home after a morning at school, I would eat lunch and then rush to the TV set in the living room to watch the various animated shows. I made sure to have paper, pencil, and crayons ready so I could copy the characters as I watched. I became good at drawing Woody Woodpecker, one of my favourite characters. I also had many Disney comic books and would copy the characters from the pages.

When I was about thirteen, I started to design my own characters and create my own comic books with them. This was usually cartoon pigs, chickens, and other animals. One day at school, I had finished my geography test earlier than my peers and while I waited for them to finish, I took out my comics and started to draw. When the teacher passed by and saw me drawing, she asked if she could borrow them. Without asking why, I handed them over. She didn't tell me, but she sent my drawings and comics to one of the most famous comic-book artists and creators of popular characters in Brazil. His name was Mauricio de Sousa and he was like the Brazilian version of Walt Disney. He had an

A boy and his animal friends

I love to draw interactions between kids and animals. This drawing is from a short story I was developing about a kid who brings home animals he finds, much to the despair of his parents!

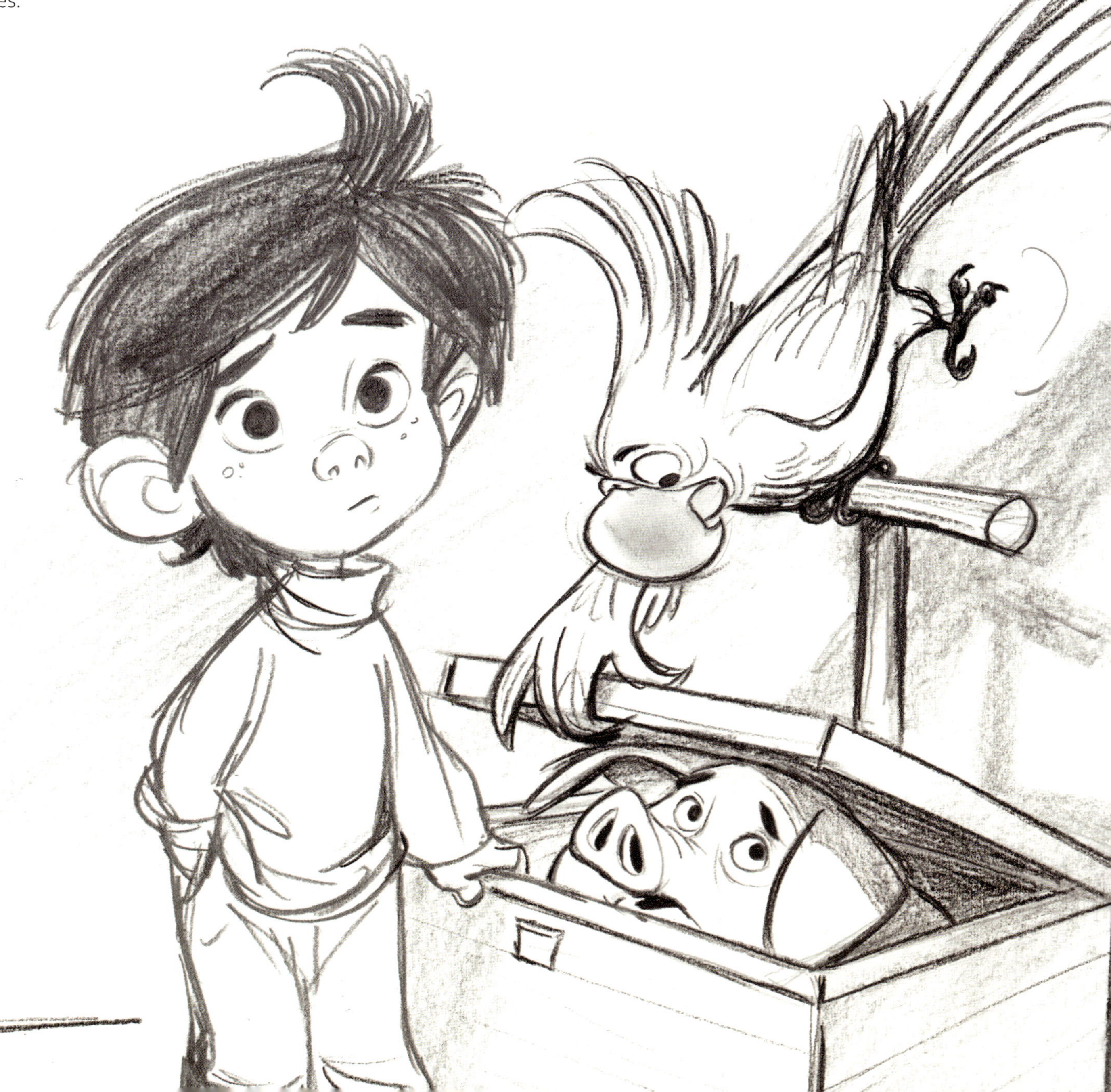

CHARACTER DESIGNER & ANIMATOR
instagram.com/sandrocleuzo

Get off!

When this scene popped into my mind, I quickly sketched it on paper. Anything can be expanded and turned into a story...

empire – his characters could be found on merchandise, in books, TV animation, theme parks, and more. He liked my drawings enough to offer me an internship at his company. At fourteen years old, it was my first contact with a prestigious studio and professional artists.

After a few weeks there, things were going well, but it all changed when I met an artist who worked as an animator for the studio's animation department. It was in another building and at lunchtime she took me to visit. The desks all had a lightbox and a disc with peg bars where they fitted the paper with the peg-bar holes... The whole set up was incredible! She took a stack of paper and began flipping through it, and I watched as the drawn character started to move. It was alive! There and then, I decided that I wanted to do animation, not comics.

The supervisor of the comics department was furious with me when she found out about my decision and I was fired. She happened to be the owner's wife and the comic-book department was her domain. Can you imagine how it felt as a fourteen-year-old boy to be fired from your first job in the arts? I was so ashamed and didn't tell my parents for a couple of days. I thought I had ruined what my teacher had so kindly secured for me. The funny thing was, being fired from that company was the best thing that could have happened to me, even though it was the most famous studio in Brazil. After hearing the studio had let me go, another artist there took pity on me and gave me a card with a studio name and phone number on it. She said it was one of the best animation studios in Brazil and told me to call them. This was Briquet Films, a small but important TV commercial studio that produced hundreds of animated commercials for big clients.

One thing many people don't know about me is that I never went to art or animation school. Instead, I learned on the job. Briquet Films became my school, teaching me all aspects of animation. I truly learned my craft and worked with the best animators in the country. At fifteen, within a month of my internship, I was hired full time.

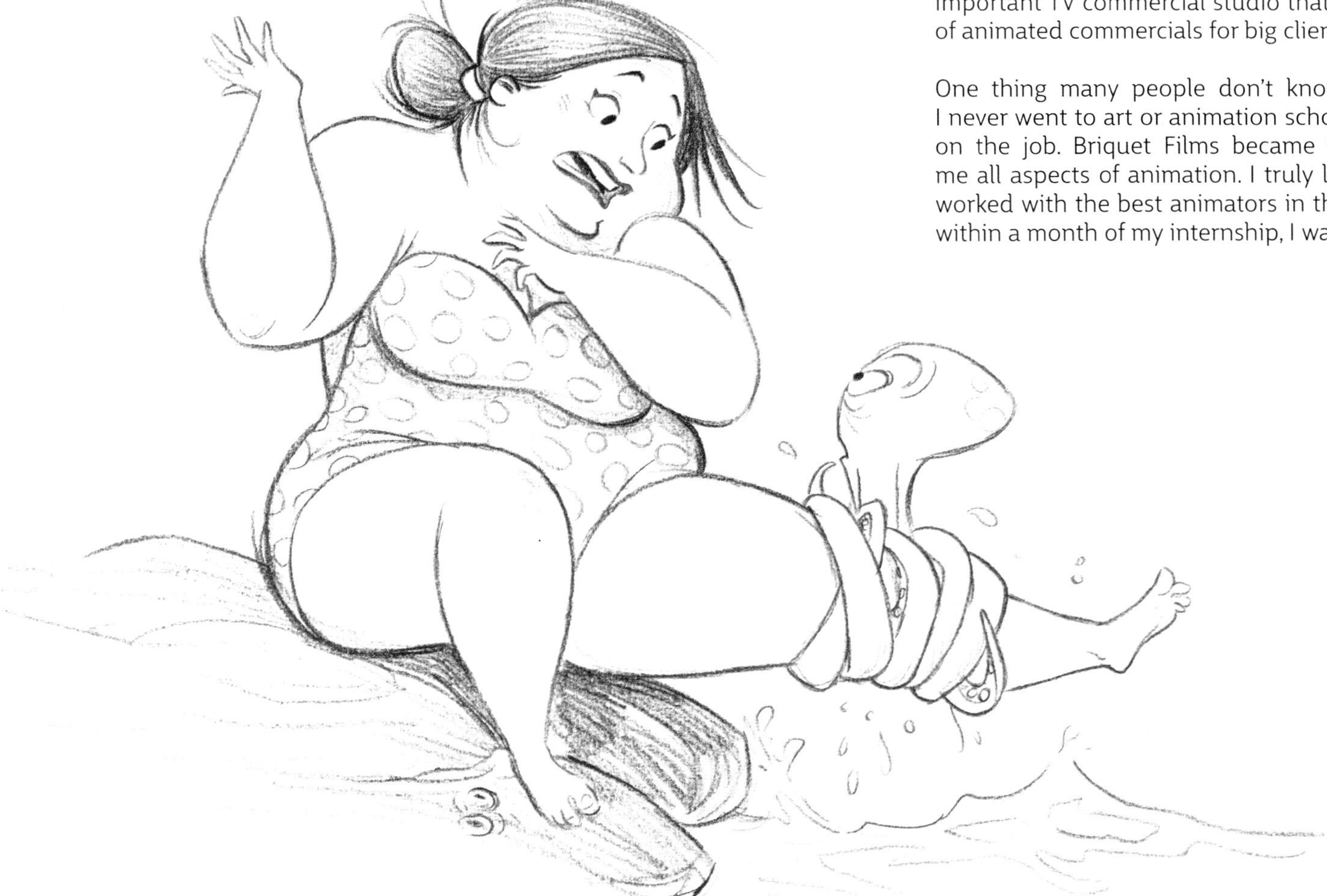

FEATURE FILM

After four years spent learning the basics of animation, I moved to Dublin, Ireland, to work with Don Bluth on feature films. This is one of the greatest moments of my career. I was a big fan of Don's films after falling in love with his first feature, *The Secret of Nimh*. I really wanted to work for him, so I prepared a portfolio, found the address for his studio in Dublin, saved some money, and flew there. At nineteen, it was my first time leaving home and travelling abroad.

When I arrived in Dublin, I took a taxi straight to Don's studio and told the receptionist that I wanted to work for them. At first, she asked me to leave my portfolio and go home to Brazil. I refused, telling her I'd flown all the way there to meet Don and show him my work. Despite my begging, they kept telling me it didn't work that way and said they would call me if they liked my portfolio. The next day I returned to the studio and begged some more. Finally, they took my portfolio to Don himself and he hired me on the spot as an animator. I started on my first feature film with Don and I will always be grateful for the trust and the chance he took on me.

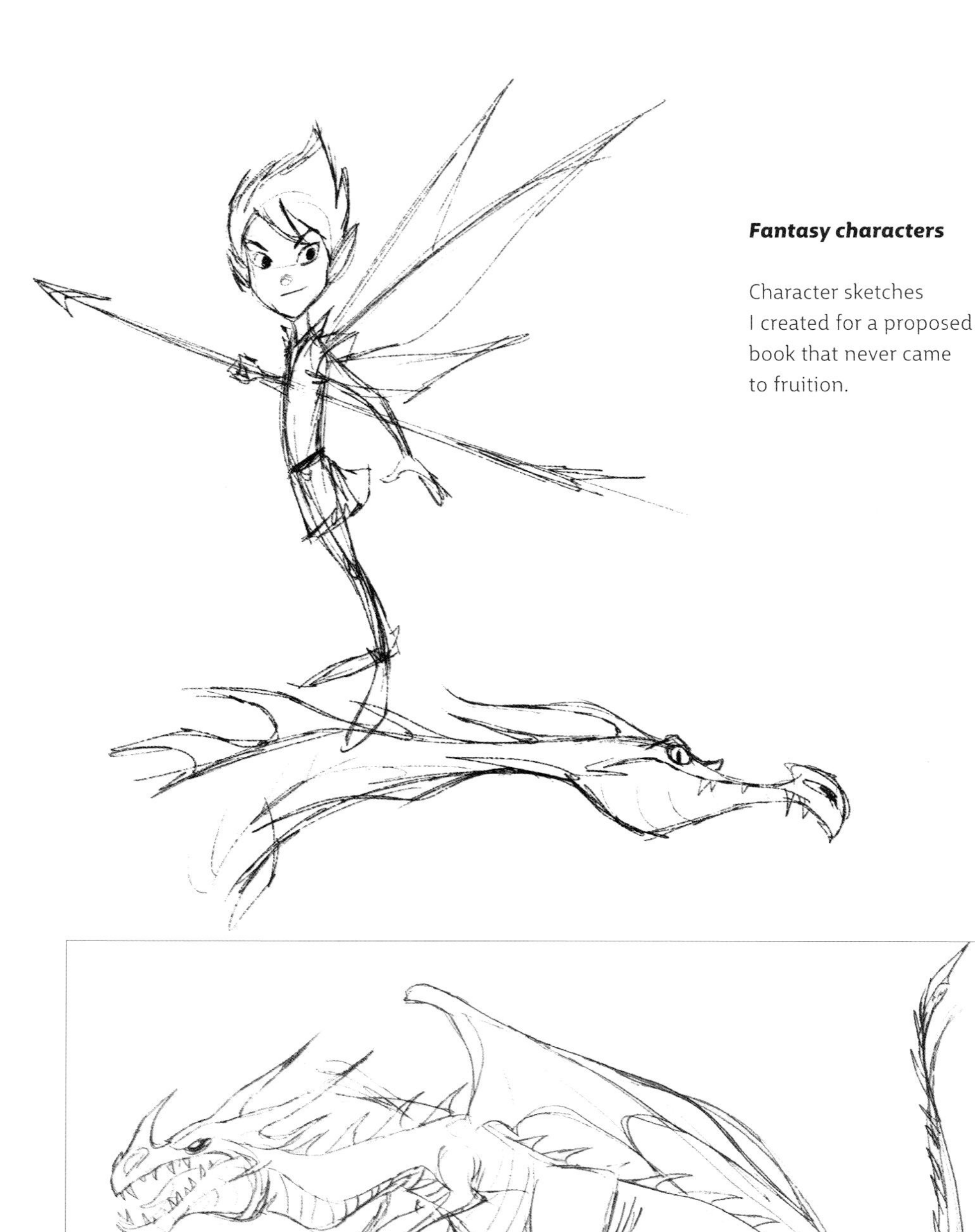

Fantasy characters

Character sketches I created for a proposed book that never came to fruition.

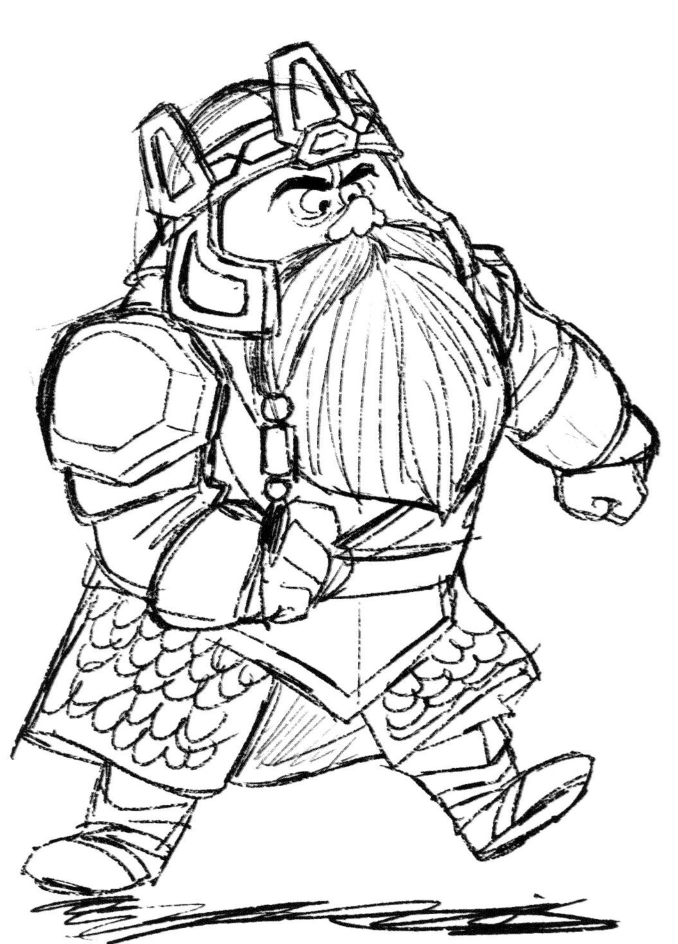

Dragon sketches

I also like drawing dragons. This page has a couple of quick sketches to explore proportions; for example, how the wings are related to the body.

Sympathy from the villain

A sketch based on a concept for an animated fantasy film I was developing. I love fantasy and what you can do with it, creating characters that are part human, animal, fairy, and elf.

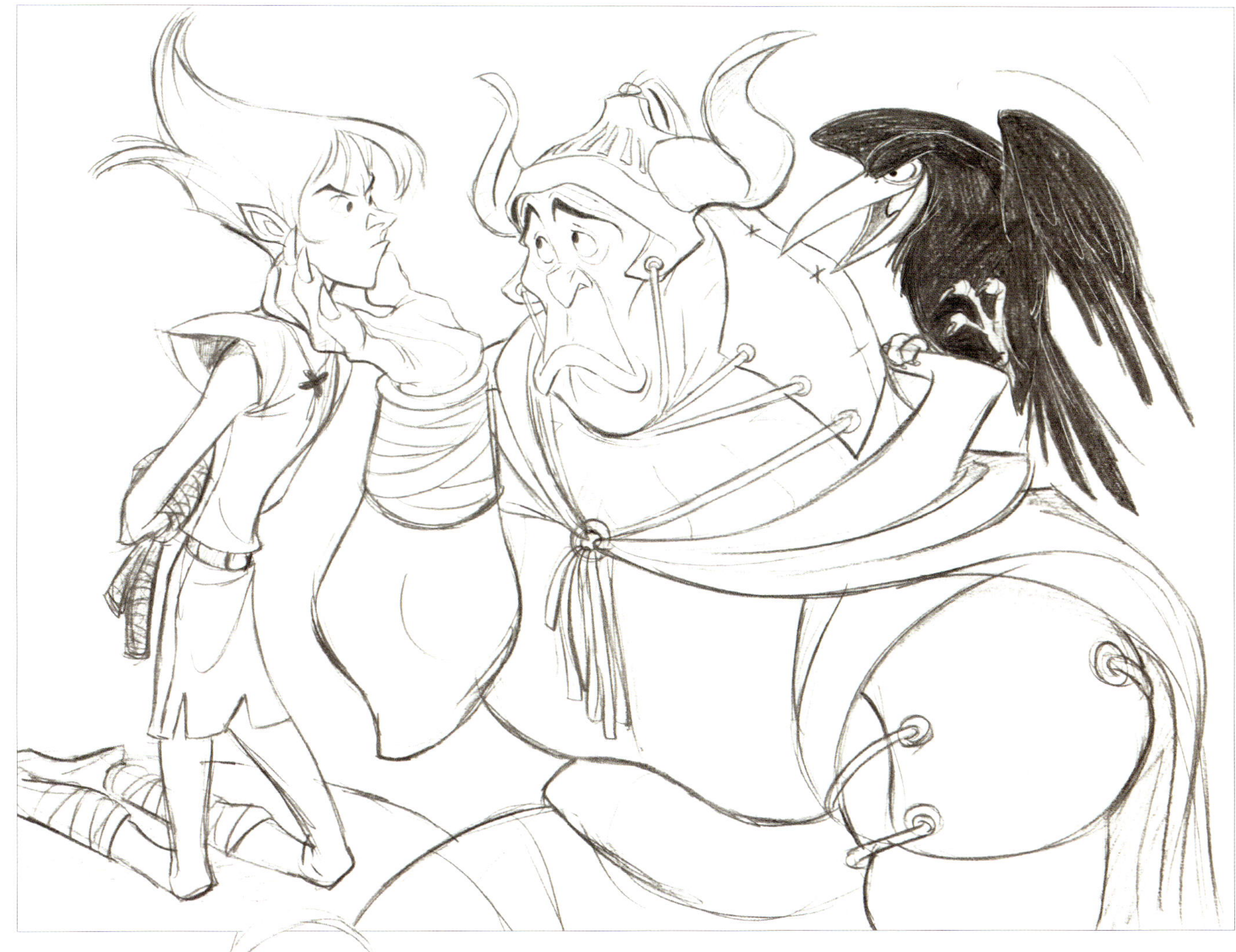

After working with Don Bluth for almost seven years, I applied to work as an animator at Disney. My first project was *Fantasia 2000*. Following that, I worked on a film that started out being called *The Kingdom in the Sun*. After several screenings, they decided to change the movie completely and it became the now cult classic *The Emperor's New Groove*, for which I was Lead Animator. I was then promoted to Supervising Animator and my next film was *Home on the Range*.

Being Supervising Animator at Disney Feature is another of my proudest achievements. I'd always loved Disney's animated films and to work there had long been a dream of mine. Growing up, I'd recognized that their films were better in quality. The characters moved better than what I was used to seeing on TV and the visuals, design, and music were always my favourite.

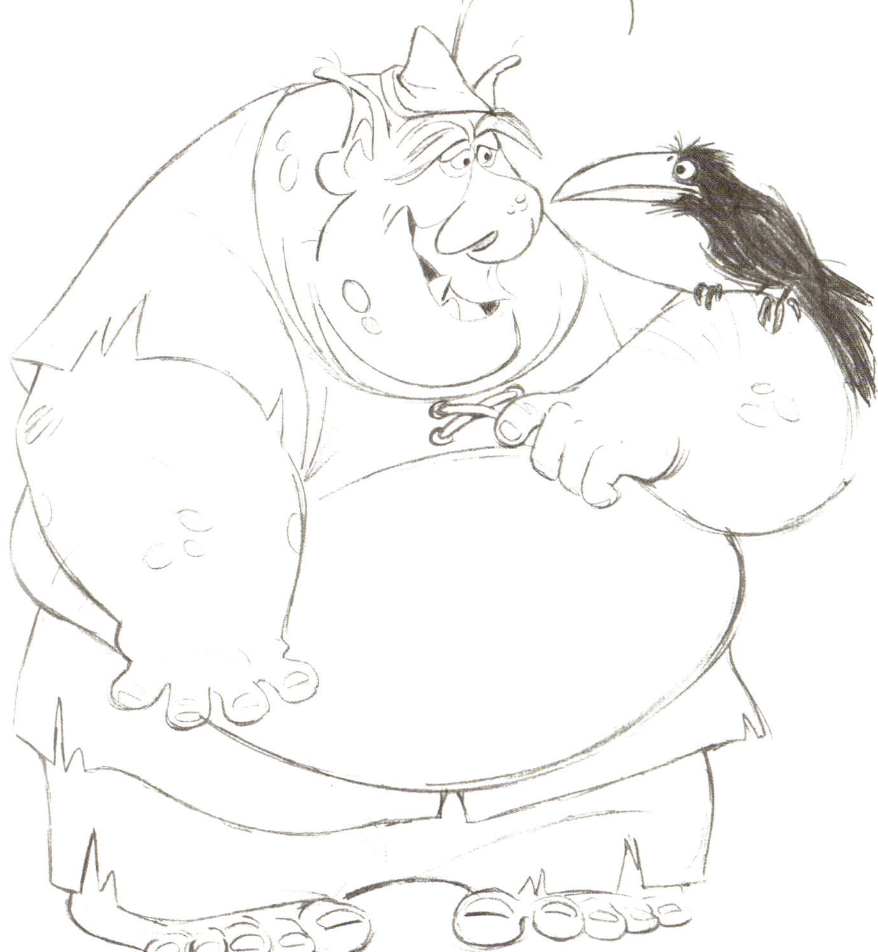

You are my friend now!

Ogres are usually portrayed as bad and evil, so I thought, what if one was actually good? I came up with this sketch and thought it could be developed into something bigger, perhaps a short film or a book. I like the idea that he is hideous while also seeming friendly and caring.

GOLDEN-AGE INFLUENCES

I am influenced and inspired by so many artists. It's funny that the artist I love most never carried a sketchbook or drew outside his paying job. Milt Kahl was one of the Nine Old Men from Disney's golden age. He started at the time Walt was beginning work on *Snow White and the Seven Dwarfs* and stayed until 1977. He was considered the best draftsman at the studio and responsible for at least eighty per cent of all the final designs for Disney features up to *The Rescuers*. And yet he never had a habit of sketching outside of his day job.

Another animator at the time who did carry a sketchbook was Marc Davis, the creator of characters such as Maleficent and Cruella de Vil. Known to carry sketchbooks when he travelled, he regularly drew outside of his day job at Disney. He had beautiful sketchbooks of animal drawings from the zoo and also from his trips to Europe and Africa, plus other sketchbooks containing cartoon characters.

Another artist I'm inspired by is Ken Anderson, who was also very influential for Disney animation. He was a concept artist, designer, story artist, and layout man who worked at Disney from the golden age until the late seventies. He had hundreds of sketchbooks from his travels abroad, including detailed drawings of locales, costumes, and people.

I will kill you!

Villains are always fun to design. Here I tried to push myself further than the ordinary villain stereotype, exaggerating the shapes to the extreme. Sometimes you need to break free of your usual way of drawing and push yourself out of your comfort zone.

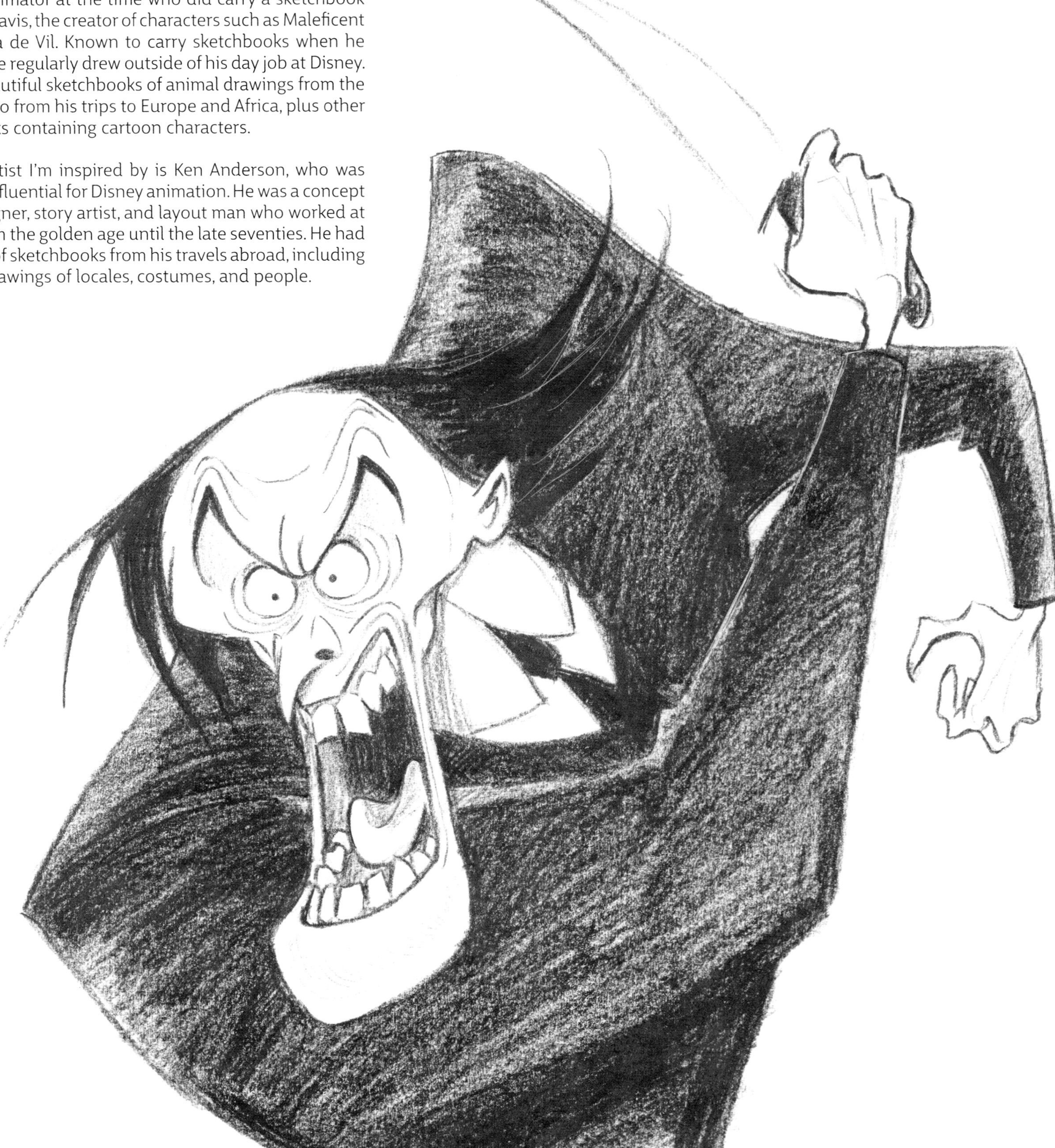

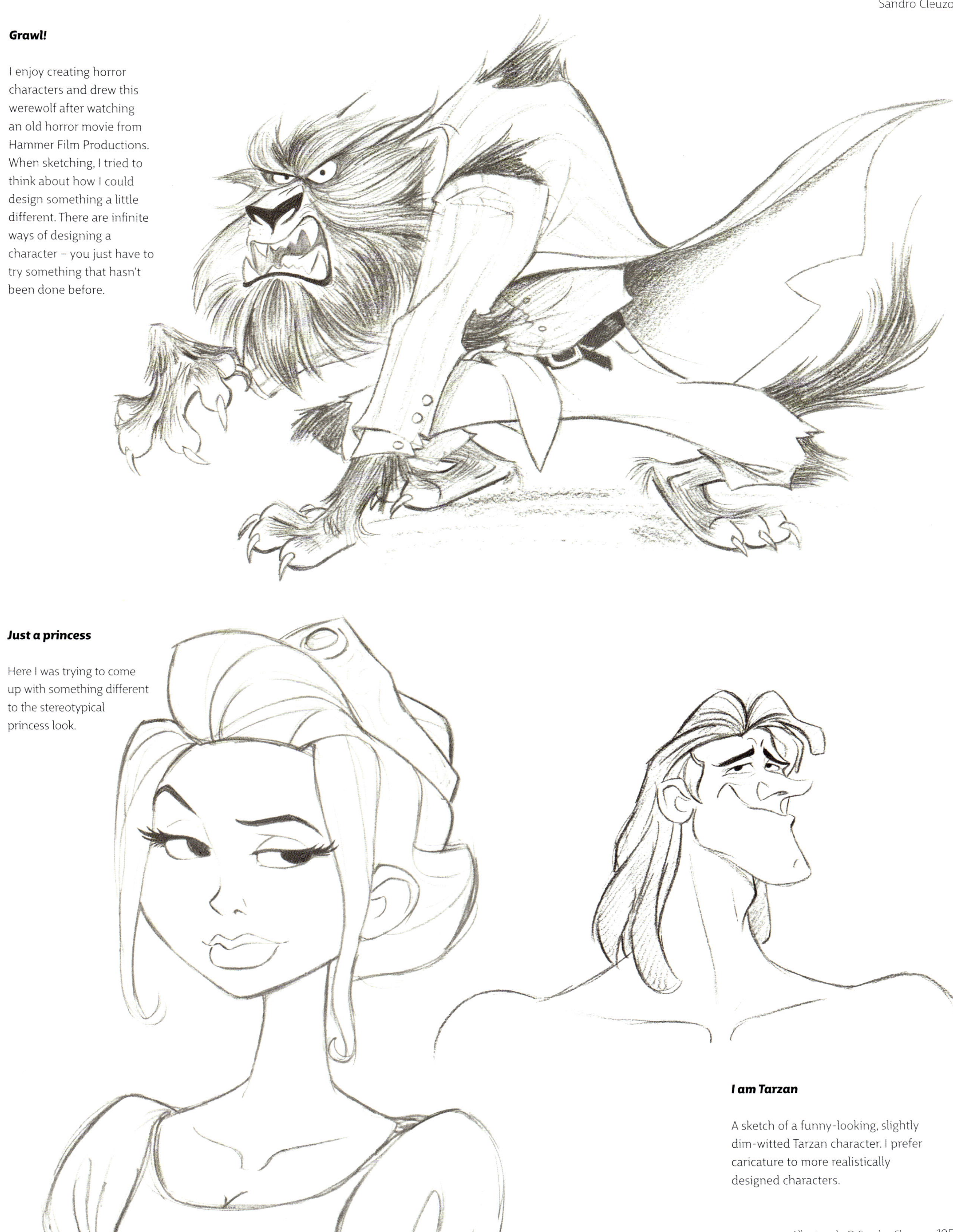

Grawl!

I enjoy creating horror characters and drew this werewolf after watching an old horror movie from Hammer Film Productions. When sketching, I tried to think about how I could design something a little different. There are infinite ways of designing a character – you just have to try something that hasn't been done before.

Just a princess

Here I was trying to come up with something different to the stereotypical princess look.

I am Tarzan

A sketch of a funny-looking, slightly dim-witted Tarzan character. I prefer caricature to more realistically designed characters.

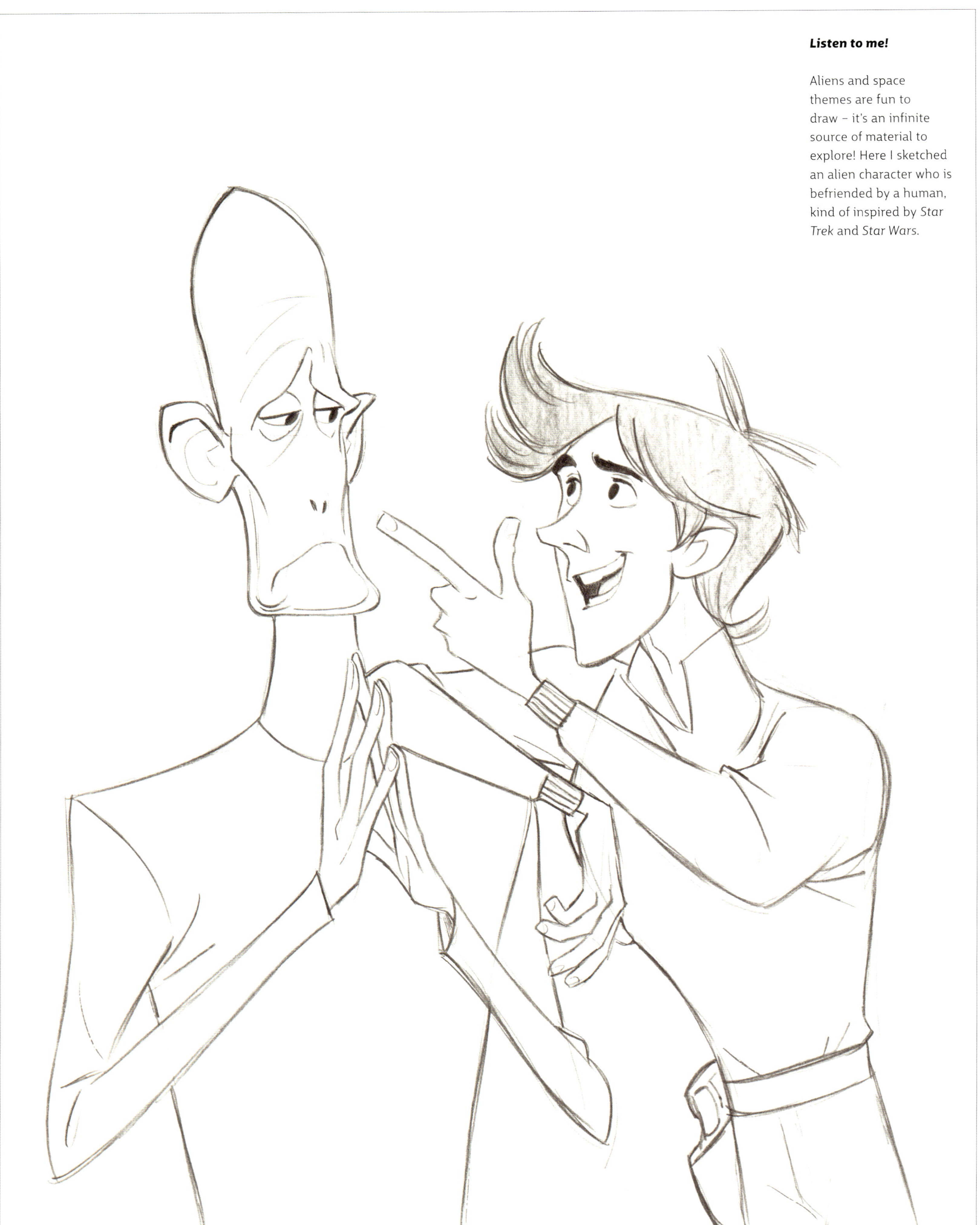

Listen to me!

Aliens and space themes are fun to draw – it's an infinite source of material to explore! Here I sketched an alien character who is befriended by a human, kind of inspired by *Star Trek* and *Star Wars*.

Hero

This page of sketches was dedicated to coming up with a hero-type character. I didn't want them to be too straight-laced and was leaning towards more of a comedy style.

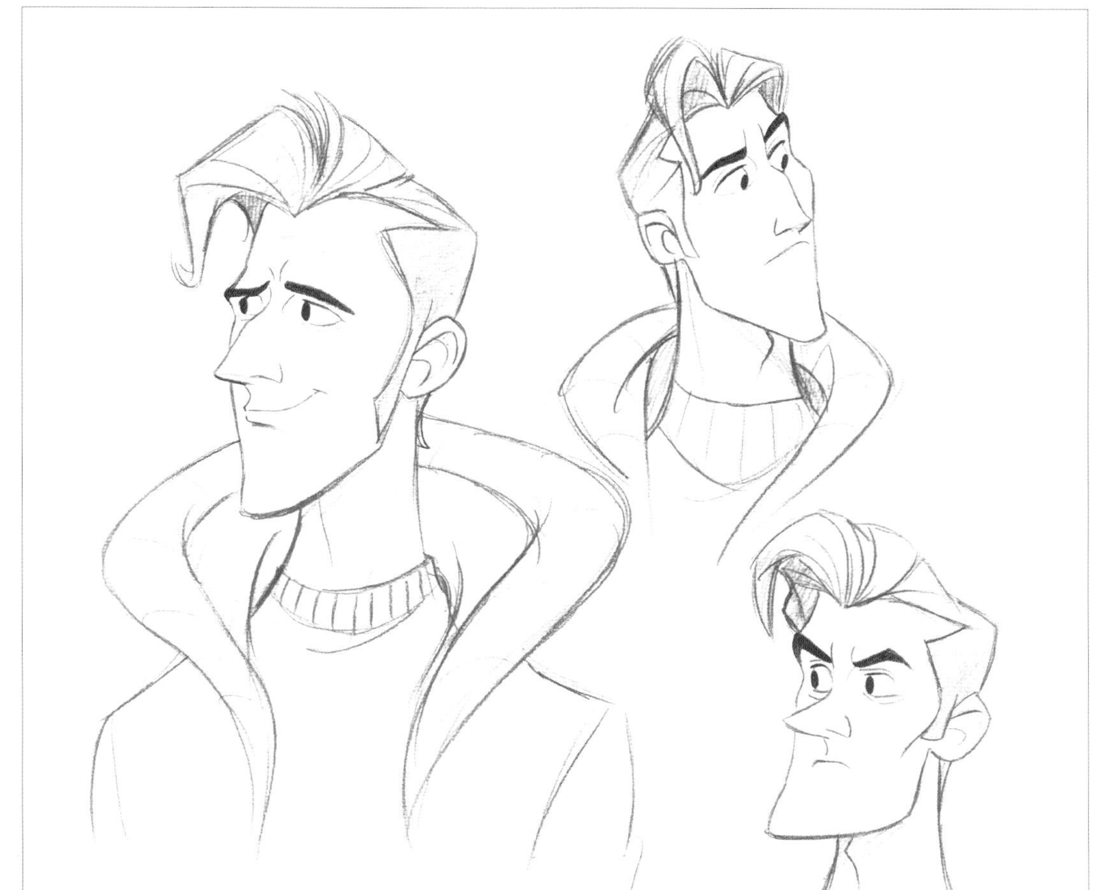

Space team

Another space-themed drawing. I came up with an idea for a crew consisting of a human and two aliens.

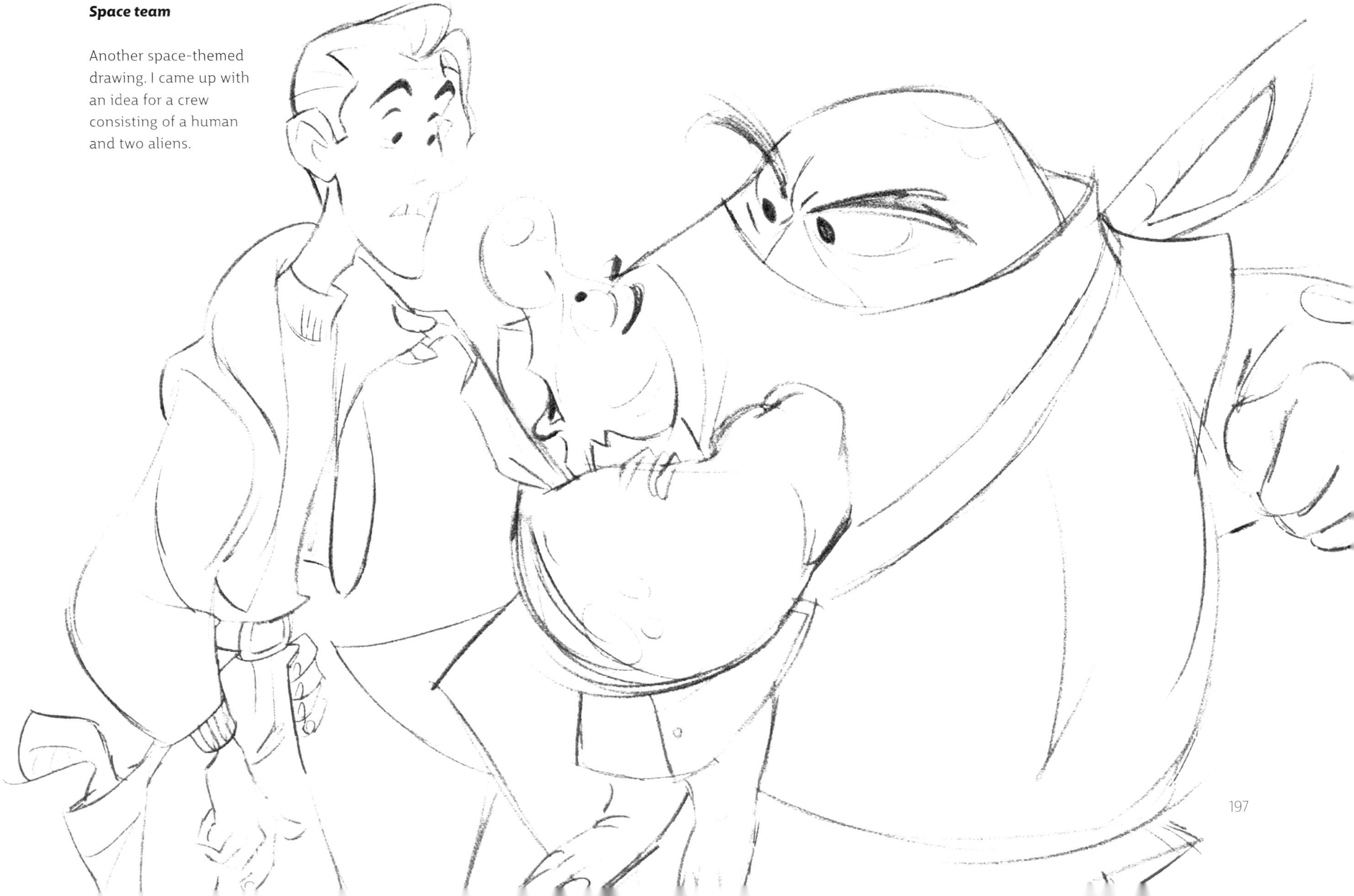

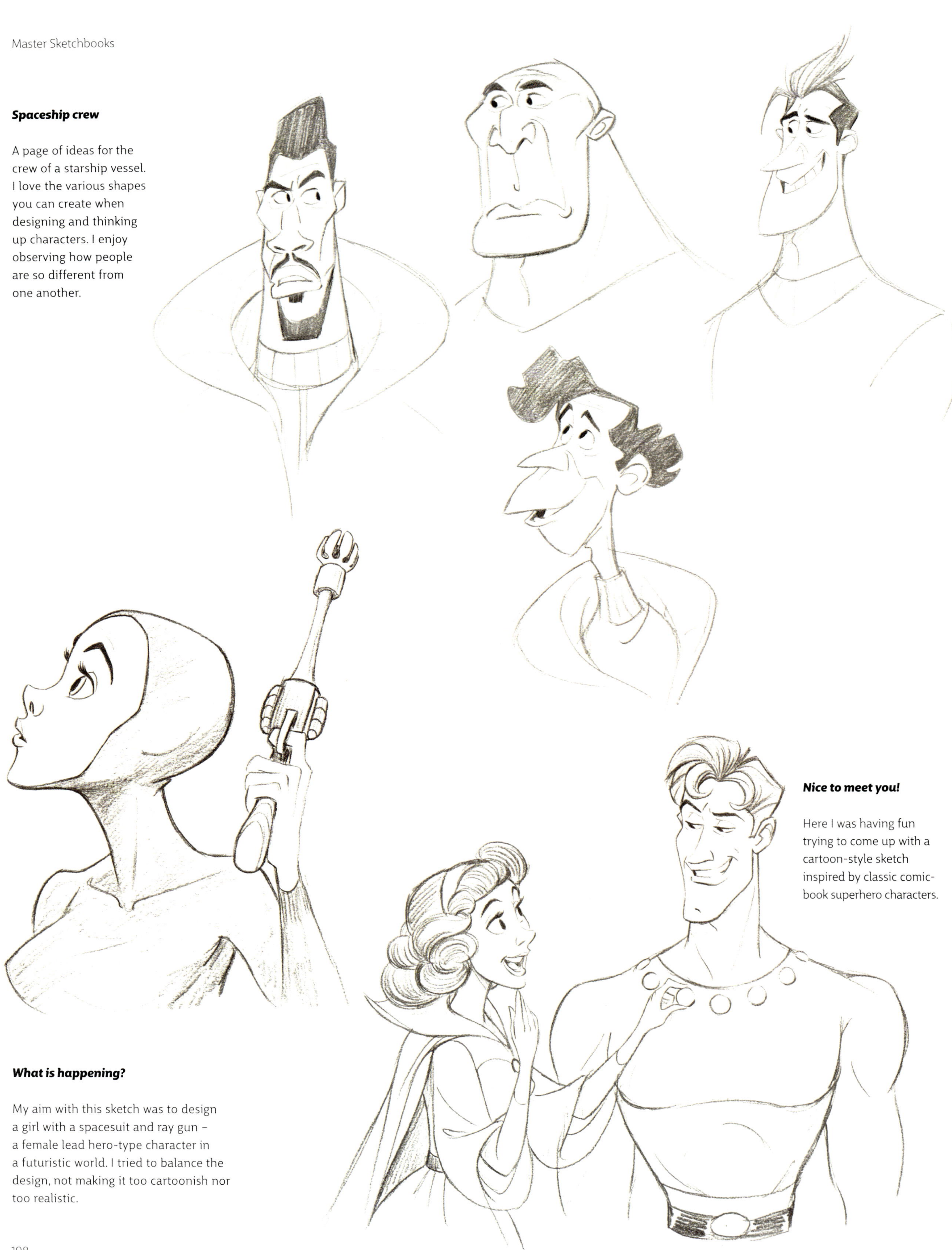

Spaceship crew

A page of ideas for the crew of a starship vessel. I love the various shapes you can create when designing and thinking up characters. I enjoy observing how people are so different from one another.

Nice to meet you!

Here I was having fun trying to come up with a cartoon-style sketch inspired by classic comic-book superhero characters.

What is happening?

My aim with this sketch was to design a girl with a spacesuit and ray gun – a female lead hero-type character in a futuristic world. I tried to balance the design, not making it too cartoonish nor too realistic.

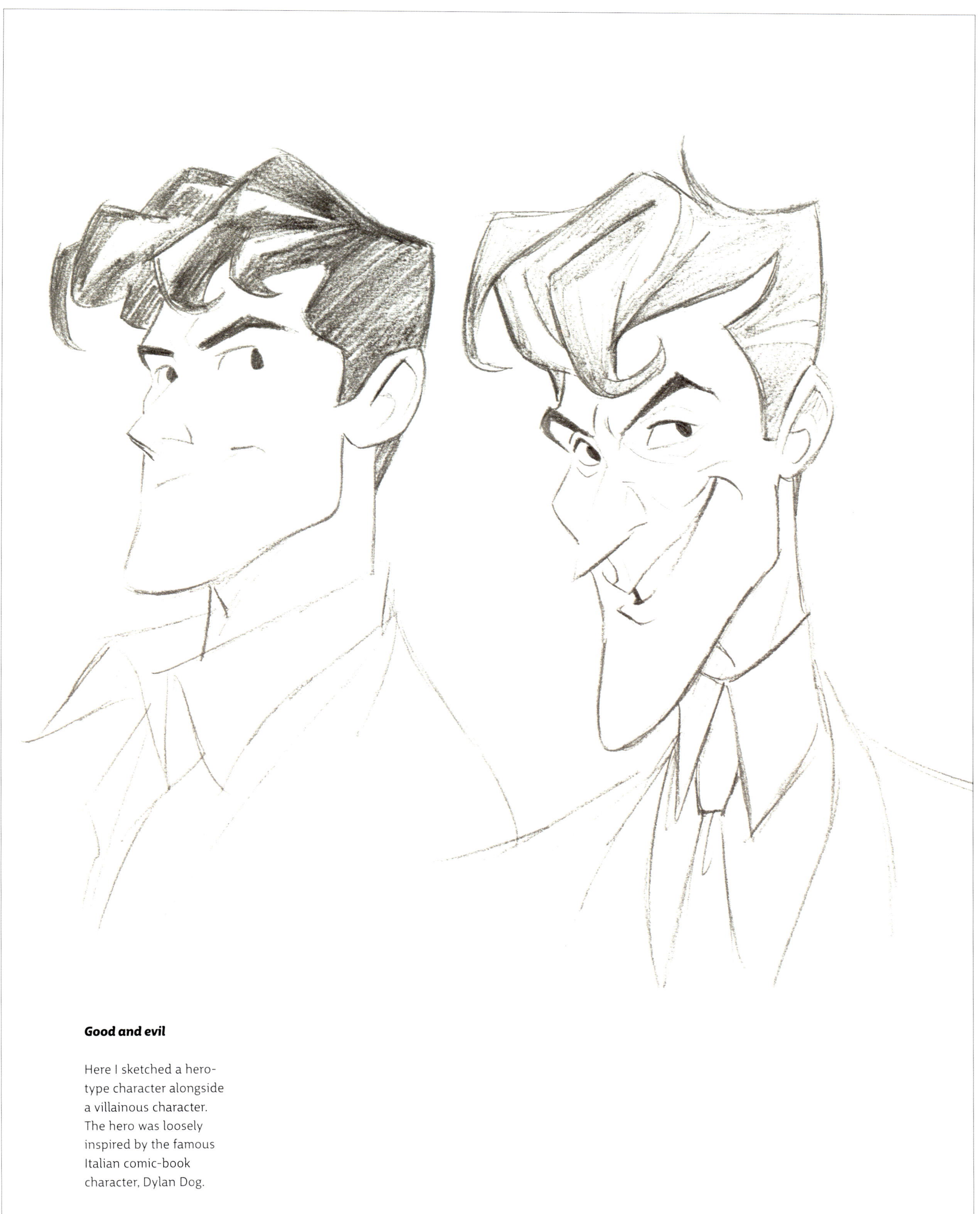

Good and evil

Here I sketched a hero-type character alongside a villainous character. The hero was loosely inspired by the famous Italian comic-book character, Dylan Dog.

Authority

In this sketch I wanted to capture the essence of a very authoritarian older lady, perhaps from a strict school or similar institution.

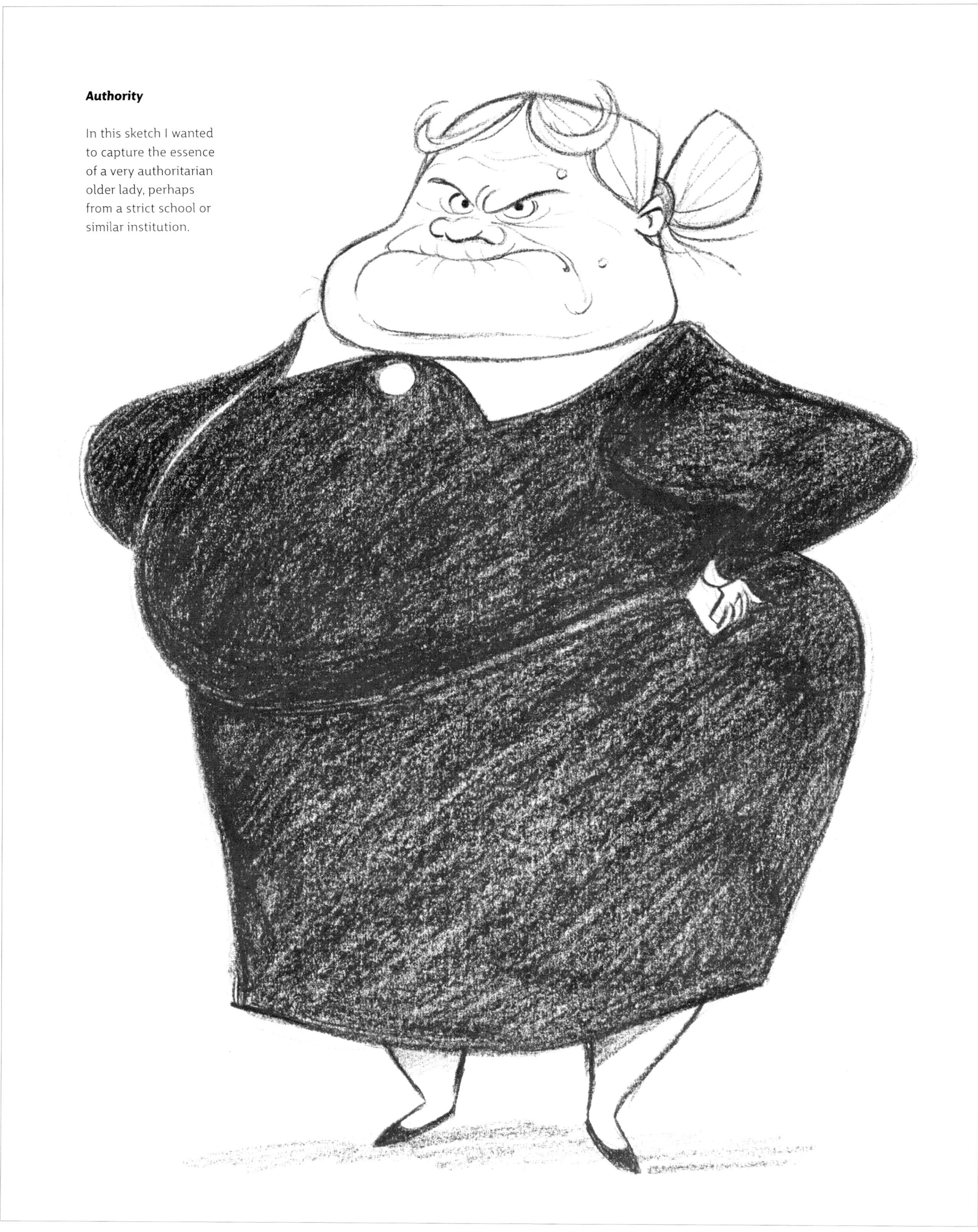

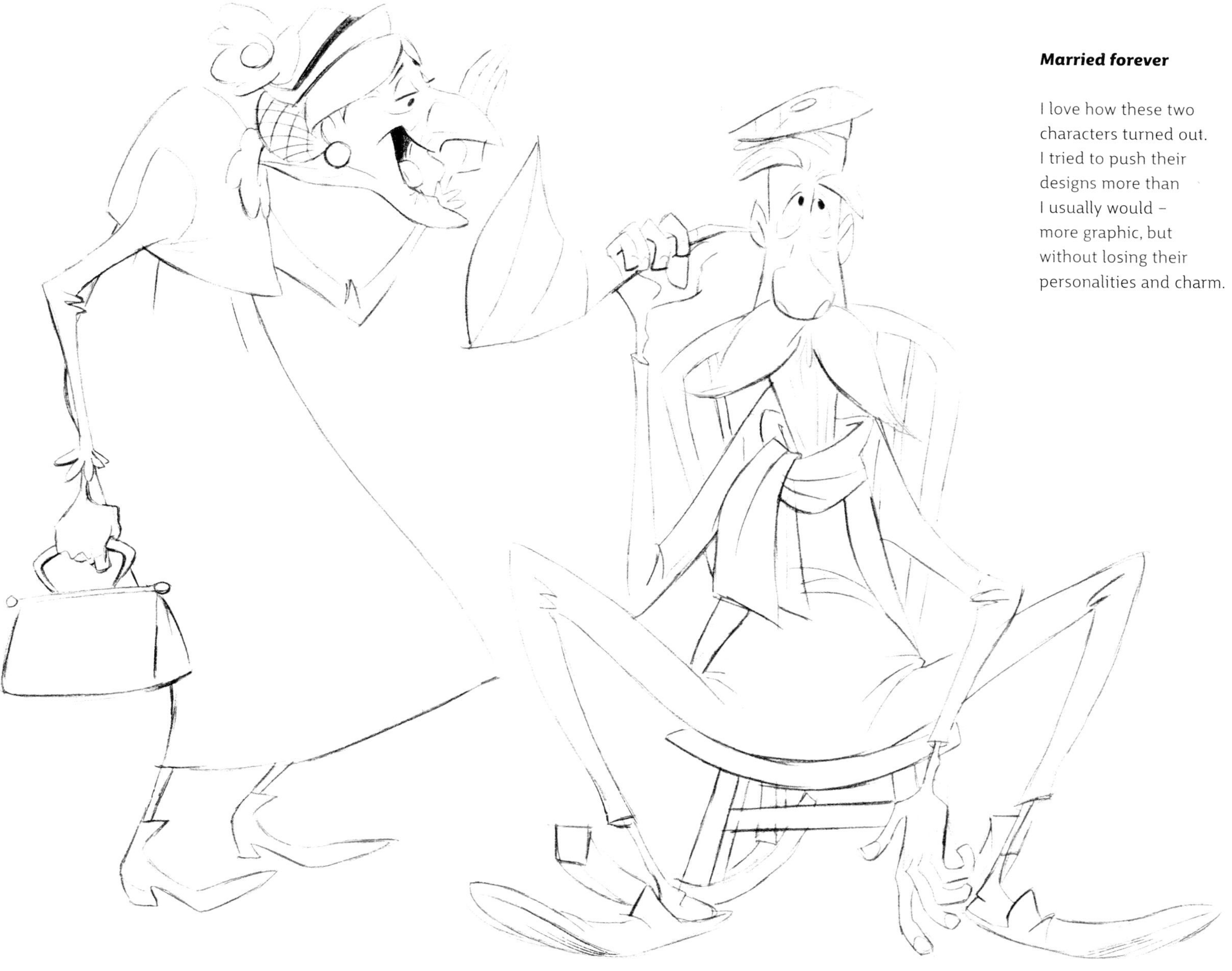

MATERIALS

When working as an animator for film studios, we always drew on paper. We had several different sizes to draw the characters, depending on the shots; sometimes a close-up, sometimes a medium shot, or a very tiny size if the character was in the distance. Because of this, I'm comfortable working on any size paper or sketchbook. If I had to choose, I like to draw big. At home I have a big sketchbook that I can spread out on a table. This allows me to draw on a large scale and use various materials, such as pastel or watercolour. When out and about, however, I like smaller sketchbooks that fit in my backpack. I prefer sketchbooks with a hardback cover and paper with a bit of texture that's not too thin.

I like using a nice 4B pencil when drawing in my sketchbooks. Sometimes I use pens and once in a while I'll add markers. I occasionally try pastels, but not that often. I like using a combination of pencil, pastel, and pen when creating concepts for backgrounds and locales. For characters, I prefer pencil and pen. When I'm outside or travelling, I typically use a 9mm mechanical pencil with a 2B lead, or sometimes a thin Sharpie pen, as it's more practical.

After working a full day on a studio job, I usually do some of my own personal sketching on paper or in my sketchbooks. Today, most of my work for studios is delivered digitally, but I still enjoy drawing on paper with traditional materials and try to do as much as I can in my spare time. For a freelance job that requires digital delivery, I might occasionally start the first drawings on paper. I then scan the rough drawings and finish them digitally, which can work very well.

I have never been too careful with storing my drawings, though I should. I just put them in drawers or boxes. In a few cases I've had drawings ruined as the paper has become yellowed with time and humidity. I'm trying to be more careful with my collection of original drawings from the Disney old masters. I have collected a great deal of original animation art from my favourite animators; some I have framed, but many are still in drawers.

You must first
know the 'real'
to be able to
caricature it

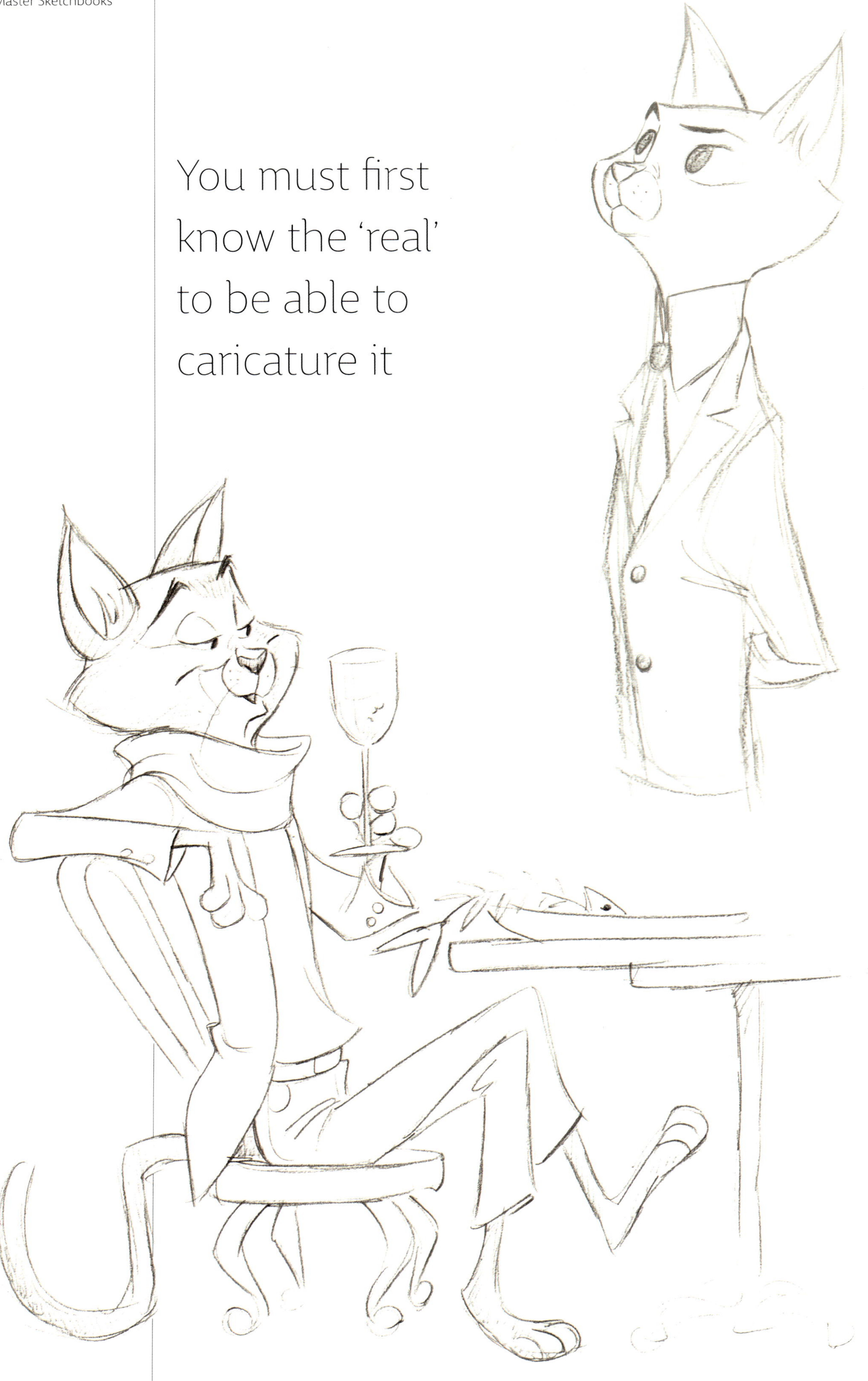

**My name is Bond,
Cat Bond**

A quick sketch from
when I had an idea for
a James Bond kind of
character – a cat in an
anthropomorphic style,
like Disney's *Robin Hood*.

La bella vita!

I love drawing cats!
Without too much
thought, I sketched an
anthropomorphic cat
sitting in a restaurant,
enjoying a glass of wine
with his meal. The way
I clothed him felt very
sophisticated and Italian.

A lady and her cat

This sketch was inspired
by another illustration
I never caught the name
of. I redrew the woman
in my style and added
a pet cat for her to
interact with.

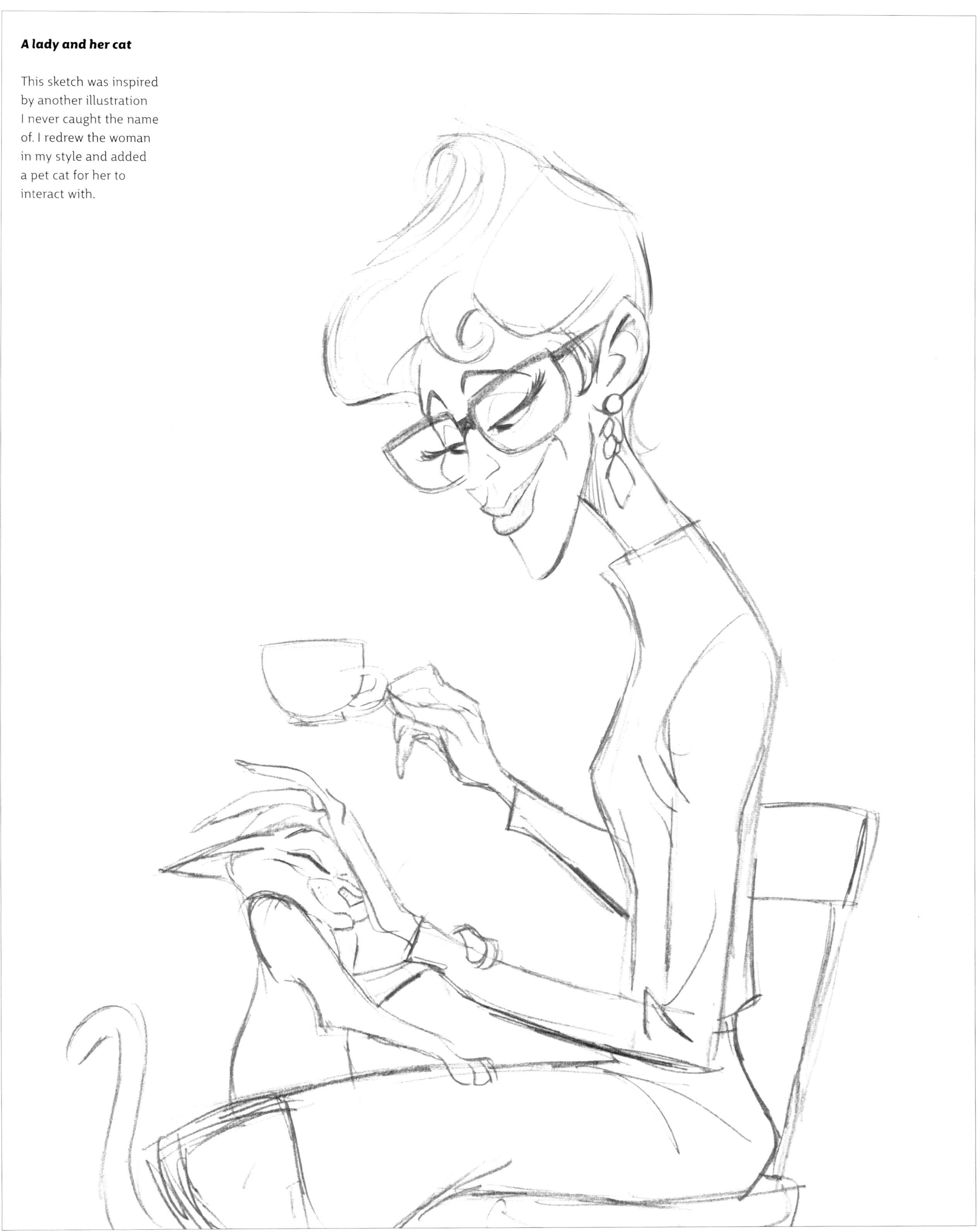

SKETCHBOOK PRACTICE

I've never had a mentor or teacher, so at the beginning of my career I didn't have anyone to tell me to get into the habit of carrying a sketchbook around with me to draw my surroundings. This came later in my career, when I was working at Bluth Studios. Since I started young and didn't go to art school, I only drew cartoon characters that I'd learned by copying or studying animation. I wished I'd had someone telling me to go out and sketch people and practise life drawing. I had to catch up later.

I remember my first life-drawing class when I was working at Bluth Studios. I realized I could not draw the model very well. What saved me was the little knowledge I'd picked up from copying superheroes, such as Spider-Man, from comics. I drew the life model in that style. After that I bought several anatomy books, including one on Michelangelo,

and started to learn basic classical drawing. I also learned by reading or listening to interviews with top artists in the animation field talking about how important it is to know how to draw people and animals. You must first know the 'real' to be able to caricature it.

I like to draw randomly in my sketchbooks, sketching characters based on people or animals I can see if I'm sat outside, or from TV or film. Most of the time I draw characters as soon as I think of them to get the idea down on paper so I won't forget it later. It's like when you are writing stories; if you think of something interesting but don't write it down, you might not be able to remember it later. Sometimes I have a subject in mind and will draw around the theme. For example, if I'm thinking of characters in space, I will draw spacesuits, aliens, or creatures.

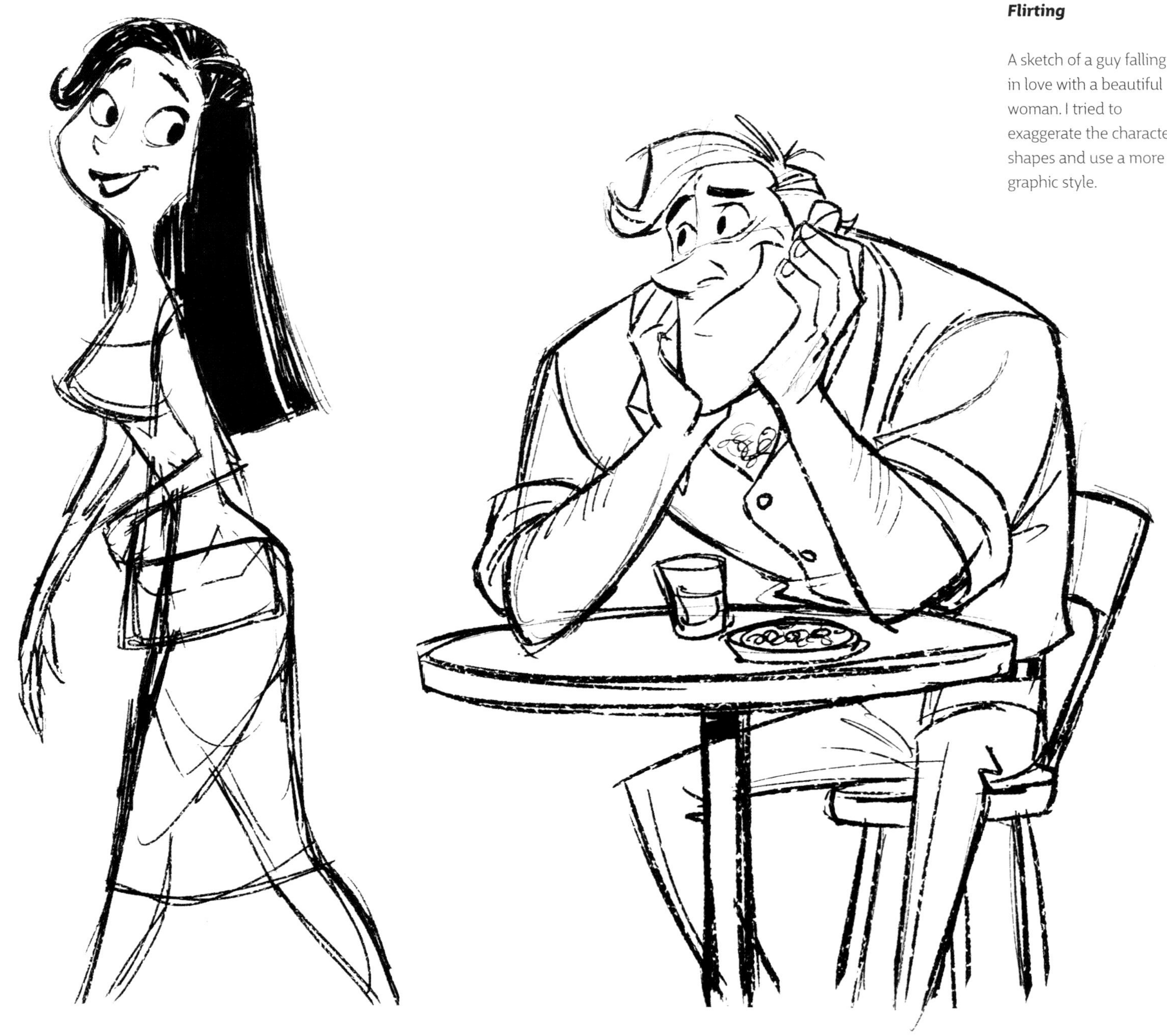

Flirting

A sketch of a guy falling in love with a beautiful woman. I tried to exaggerate the characters' shapes and use a more graphic style.

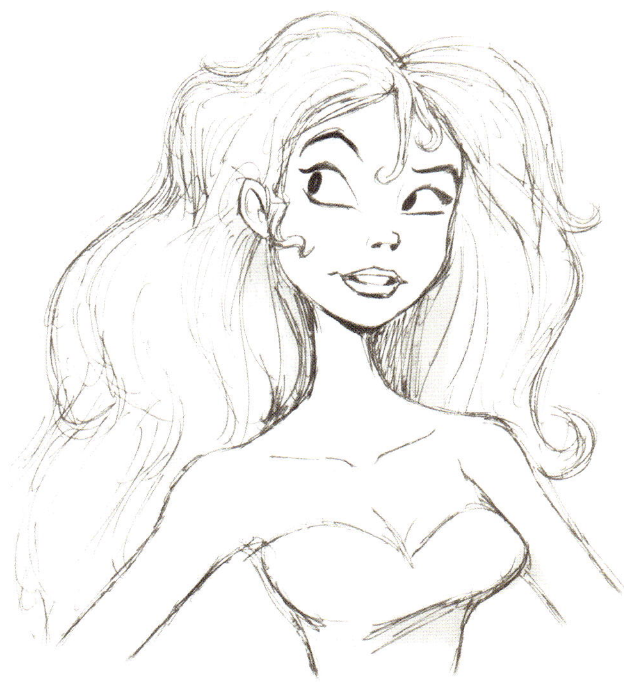

Wonder Woman

Here I wanted to try a new design for a Wonder-Woman-type character in my style and purely for fun. Created using a thin pen.

When drawing freely in your sketchbook without any pressure, you will find you can produce really interesting results, quite different than if you were making something specific and more self-conscious

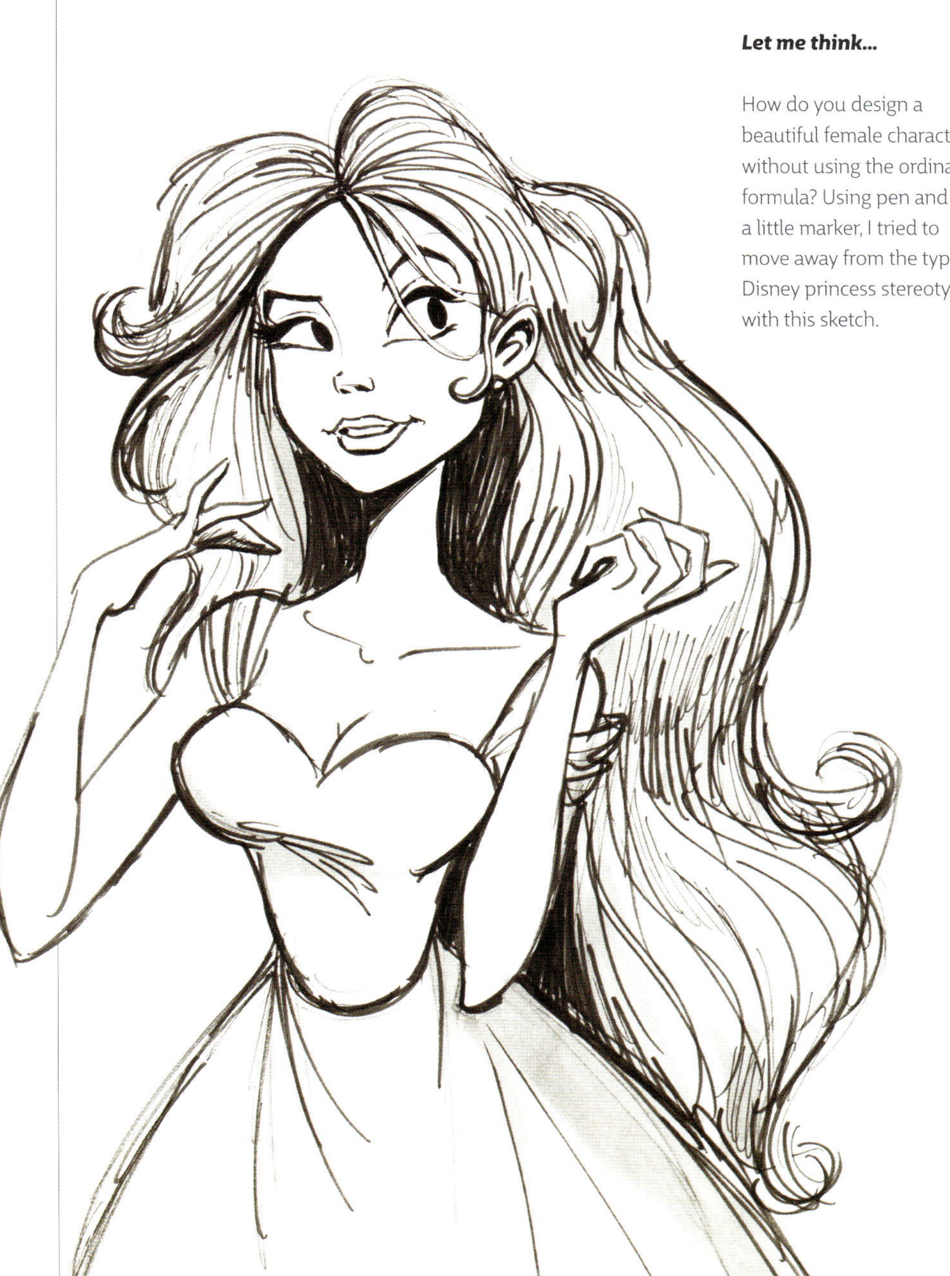

Let me think...

How do you design a beautiful female character without using the ordinary formula? Using pen and a little marker, I tried to move away from the typical Disney princess stereotype with this sketch.

I start by putting down the essence of the character's pose or shapes, rather than trying to create a perfect drawing to begin with. I don't worry if it's not a particularly appealing drawing at first. At this stage, I just want the ideas. I will finesse the rough drawings, add more details, and flesh them out later on. You should feel free when you are sketching, without any pressure to make perfect drawings.

My sketchbooks are a combination of everything: cartoons, sketches of people, ideas, locales, and more. Maybe it's a good idea to have separate sketchbooks for specific things; for example, one just for film ideas, and another for sketching freely. Though I tend to mix everything in one sketchbook, I do sometimes write little notes explaining things.

I usually try to capture ideas I have, plus interesting things and people I see. If I have specific ideas for a story, I might set aside a page or two with sketches specifically for that idea. I quickly put down the drawings that come to mind, plus anything interesting that might be useful for the story. My sketchbooks don't usually follow an order; the pages capture each moment and idea. For example, if I am watching the news and there's an intriguing or unusual person, I will try to capture their essence on the page, which could then be turned into a character in a story in the future.

When drawing in your sketchbooks, you don't always need to be precise; you can be loose and explore and push designs, perhaps more than what you are used to for paying jobs. When drawing freely in your sketchbook without any pressure, you will find you can produce really interesting results, quite different than if you were making something specific and more self-conscious. By drawing in a way that's markedly different than you would usually for studio jobs, your sketchbook practice can allow you to develop a totally different style.

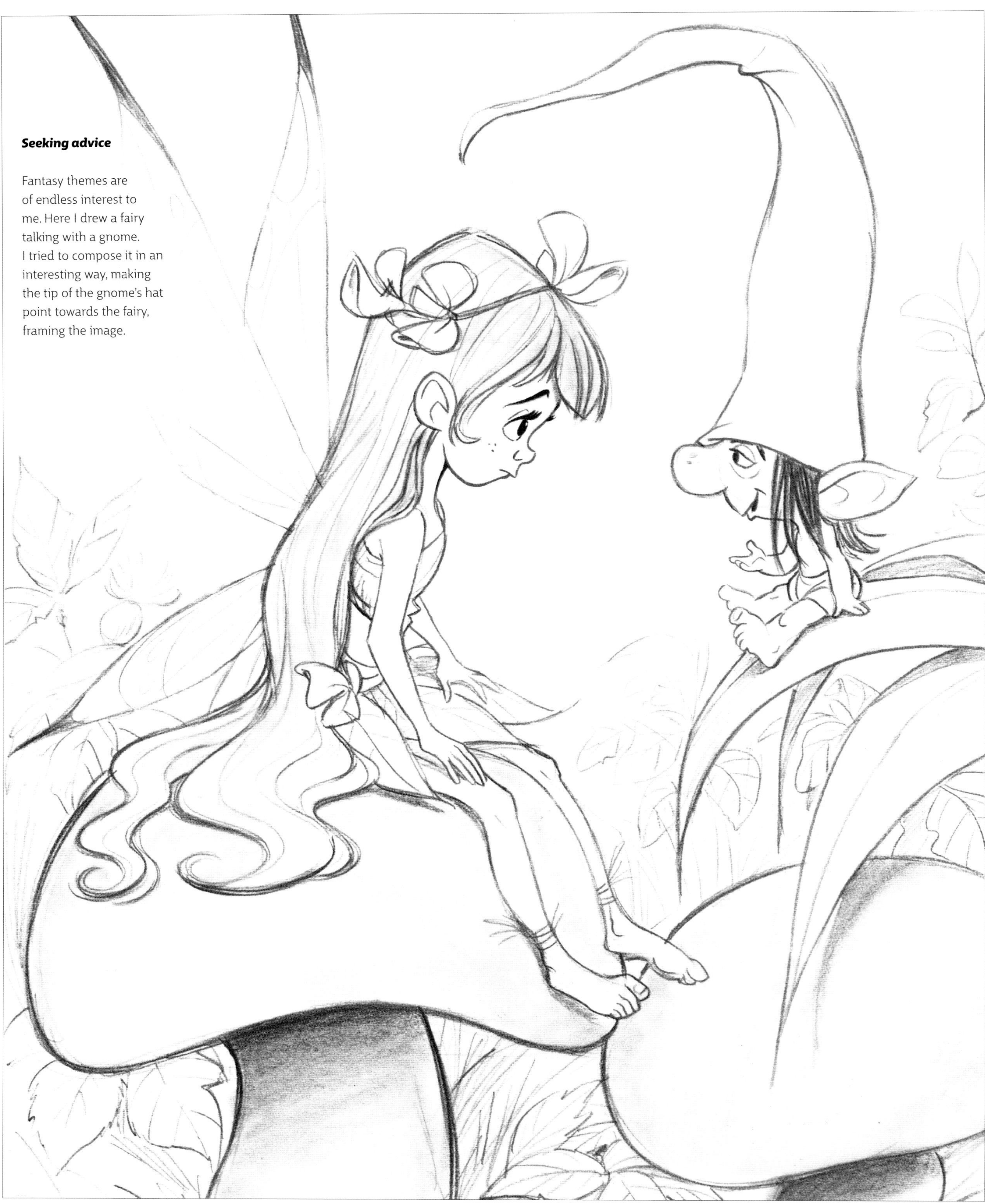

Seeking advice

Fantasy themes are of endless interest to me. Here I drew a fairy talking with a gnome. I tried to compose it in an interesting way, making the tip of the gnome's hat point towards the fairy, framing the image.

ALWAYS BE LEARNING

My number-one piece of advice to artists just starting out is: draw! As well as regular drawing practice, you also need to study drawing by analysing the work of other artists. This is so much easier to learn today than it was for me when I was starting out in the early eighties. Other than a few books and magazines, there weren't many art publications or resources. Today, besides the internet, there are hundreds of great books on animation that are essentially short art courses within themselves. Take advantage of this! I buy everything related to animation, comics, illustration, and art. I own lots of books and specialized magazines, plus a big collection of movies, both animated and live action. I learned a lot about animation by studying scenes frame by frame and analysing the movements, drawings, poses, timing, and so on. You must always be learning.

Set some time aside to learn the basics of drawing humans and animals. Get into the habit of sketching people when you're out and about, as well as family and pets you live with. Sketching all the time will improve your skill and make you draw faster, which is useful for being able to capture a pose quickly. Be curious about artistic styles different to your own and absorb everything. Take an interest in theatre, opera, museums, and more...

SKETCHING HABITS

Carry your sketchbooks everywhere you go and draw people and animals with quick sketches. Don't try to create beautifully perfect drawings – just aim to capture the essence of the person's pose or features in a few seconds or minutes. Also, make a habit of drawing from TV and movies. Great movies can teach you a lot about composition – try sketching out the composition of a shot on paper. It's also good to come up with designs of your own, such as your own characters based on people you know or actors you like. Caricature can be a great way to develop personality for your character designs.

Sketchbooks are not only great for practising drawing, but also for keeping a record of your ideas. They allow you to sketch an idea you have right away, instead of waiting to draw it later and perhaps forgetting. You can track your progress by comparing your current sketchbook to previous ones. Making sketching a regular habit will lead to quicker improvement. Try to remember to date each page as you draw. This will allow you to track how you progress from month to month, and year to year.

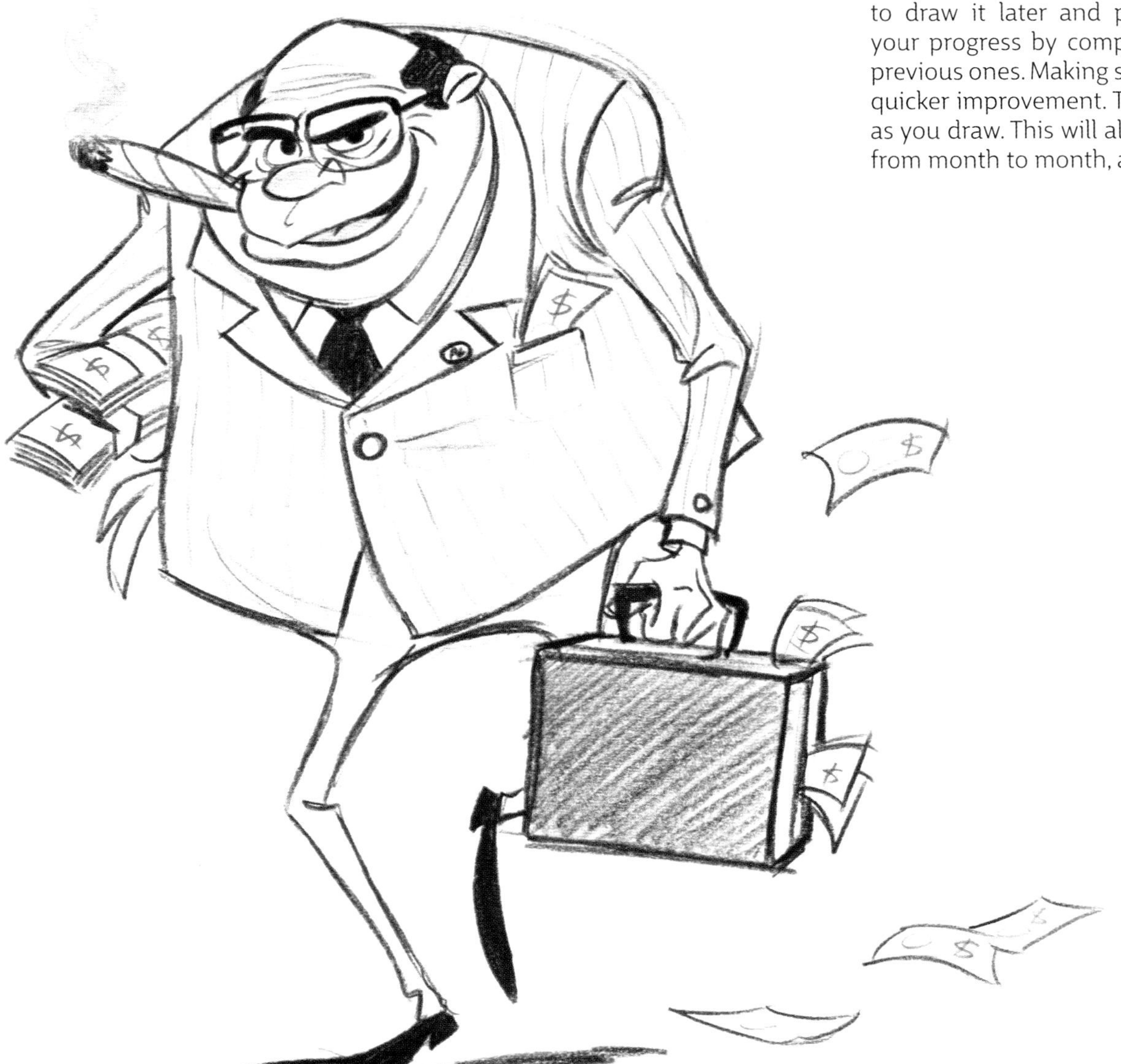

Thanks for your money, suckers!

Watching the news about the corruption scandals in my country, I drew this politician character escaping with money stolen from his people. They usually have a face that says it all...

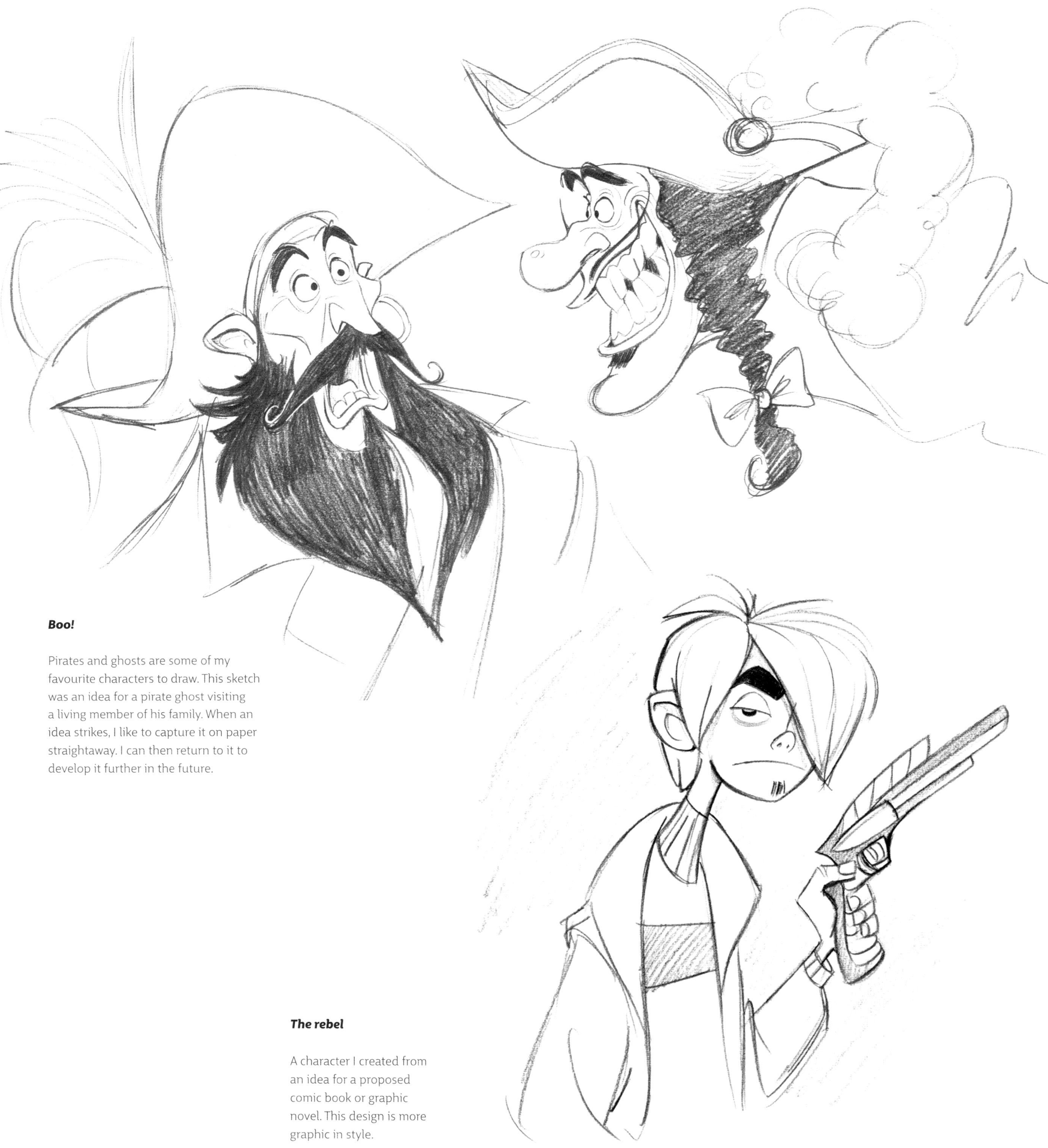

Boo!

Pirates and ghosts are some of my
favourite characters to draw. This sketch
was an idea for a pirate ghost visiting
a living member of his family. When an
idea strikes, I like to capture it on paper
straightaway. I can then return to it to
develop it further in the future.

The rebel

A character I created from
an idea for a proposed
comic book or graphic
novel. This design is more
graphic in style.

Sancho Panza

I was thinking about how the novel *Don Quixote* by Miguel de Cervantes could be turned into an animated film, maybe through the eyes of the animals. This is one of my sketches of Don Quixote's companion, Sancho Panza.

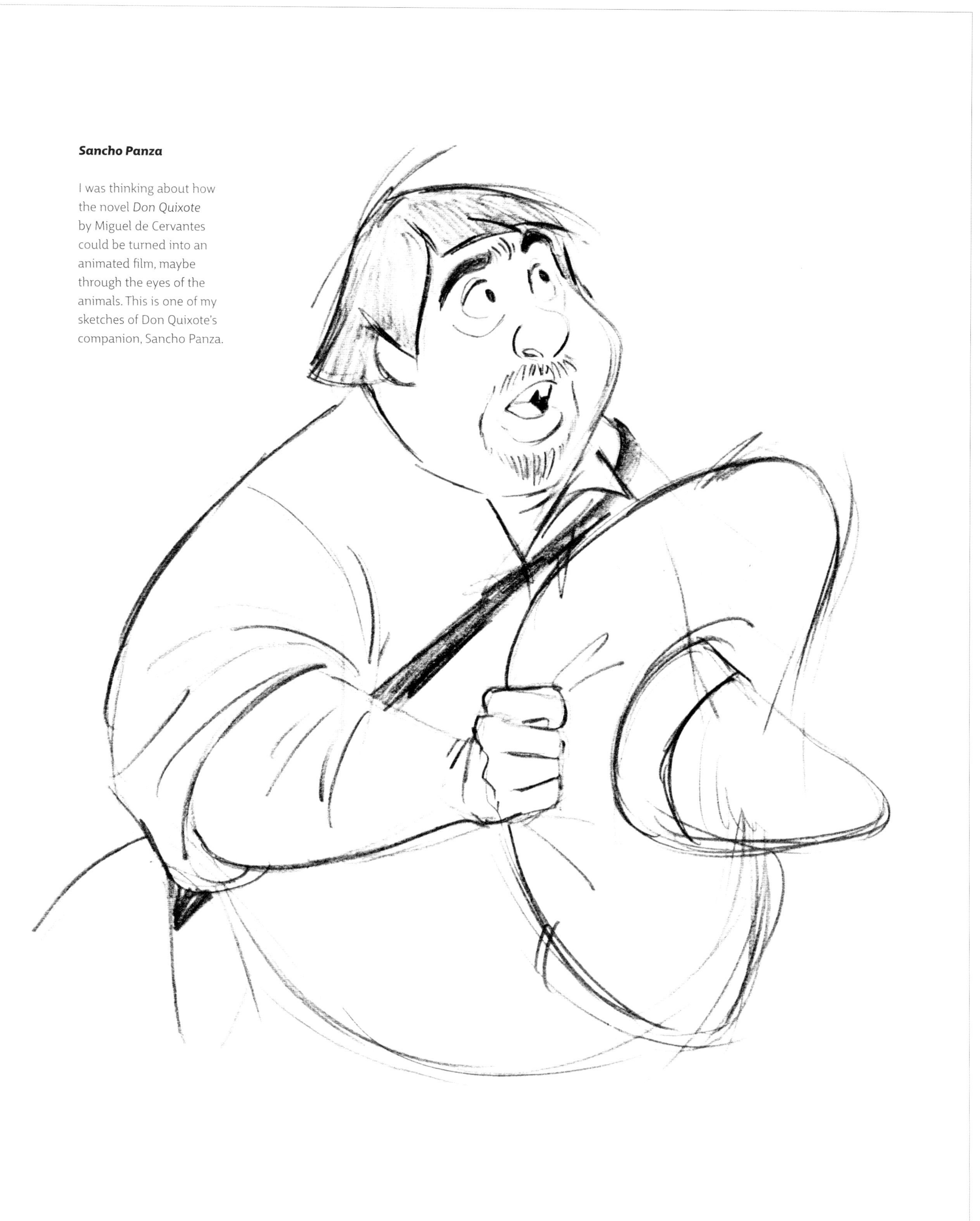

Wayne Barlowe

LOOKING BACK

Art has been a part of my life since childhood. My best education came in the form of simply watching my nature-illustrator parents at work. By osmosis they taught me the basics of creating marketable artwork. That said, they never sat me down for formal instruction. I spent two years at Cooper Union in NYC where I rounded out my education learning a few small things about picture making.

Out of everything I've created, oddly I'm probably most proud of the publication of my first novel, *God's Demon*. It was the hardest thing I'd ever done up until that point. Despite my tone-deaf publisher asking me whom I might want to do the cover for it, I created the cover too, so it wasn't just a writing achievement.

INSPIRATION

Peter Beard's notebooks are, in my mind, the aspirational, platonic ideal. Crammed with art, photos, and tiny, crabbed, stream-of-consciousness notes, nothing can touch them in terms of manic self-indulgence and creativity. They are monuments to the art of the notebook. Masterful and irreproducible, they are an unobtainable goal!

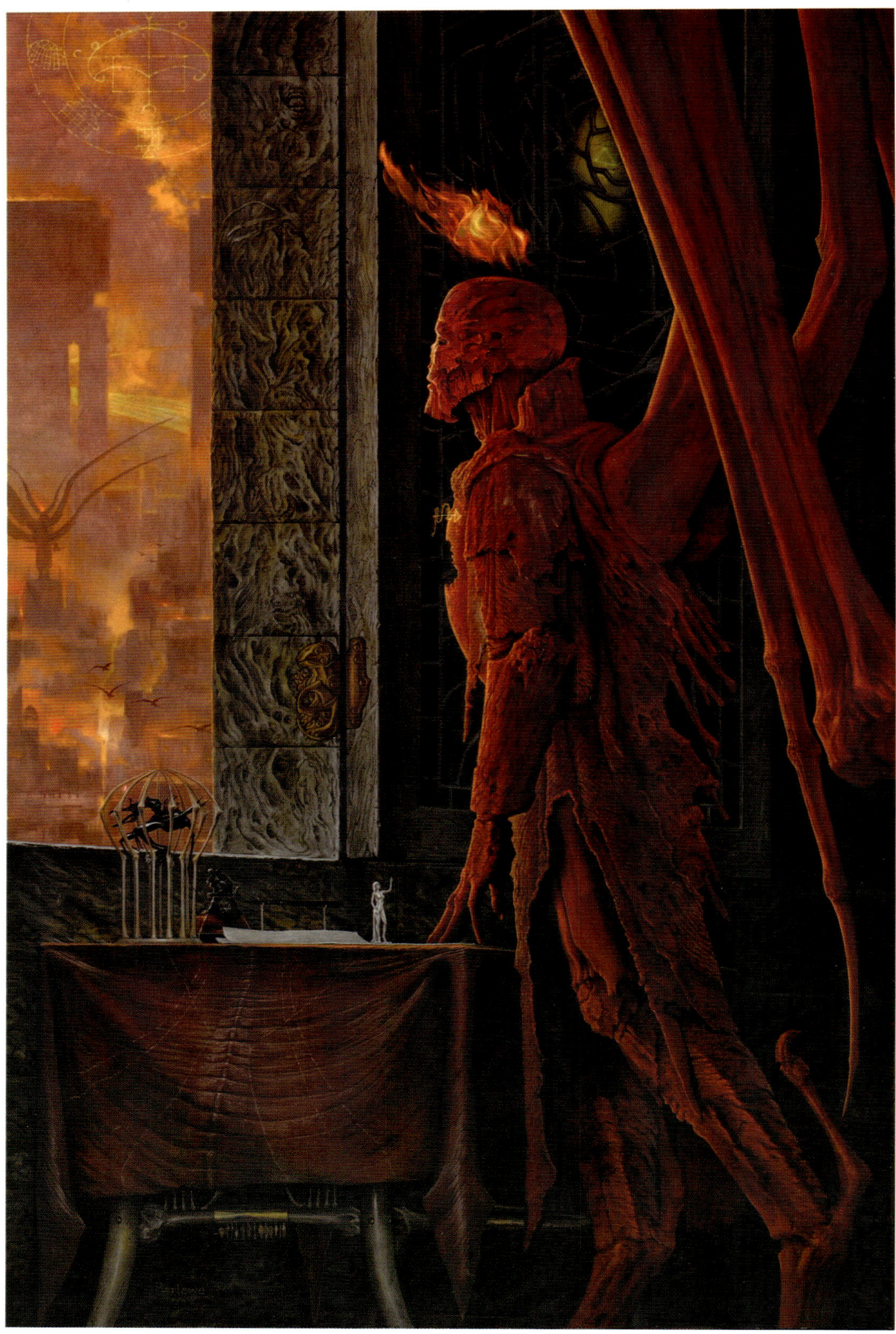

God's Demon

SKETCHBOOK PRACTICE

I used to keep various notebooks and almost always used a fine-point pen, either a Micron or ballpoint, to do my sketches. Sadly, I have the unfortunate habit of never finishing them. Most only have a few pages of sketches and notes. Only one, a hell-themed sketchbook, has been used consistently since I started that journey, but I put it aside when I went digital. My advice for aspiring artists keeping a sketchbook is don't be a slave to your sketch. Your sketch and your finished painting will and should have their own lives.

It's strange but, despite having worked on a number of films, I've never kept an art notebook for any of them. The days are, for me, too exhausting to want to do even more drawing in a hotel. I've had a lot of ideas for both book and film projects myself. I always felt compelled to start a new notebook for each one with the unrealistically optimistic notion that I would fill it up with great ideas. Of course, this never happened, and to this day the notebooks sit there, grim, defiant reminders of unfulfilled promise. Such is life.

I don't have that many stored originals. I've sold a number of older paintings and am now running out of things I've painted traditionally over the years. What I do still have are kept wrapped in boxes, up off the floor in my basement to avoid the risk of flood damage. There have been a few floods in the past where I lost some older paperback-cover illustrations. That event was sobering and has since made me take precautions.

My number-one piece
of advice is: be original...
It's ok to be consciously
inspired by other artists.
It's not ok to be
consciously derivative

TRANSITION TO DIGITAL

About five years ago I picked up my iPad and downloaded Procreate. At the time, I had no idea how much of a seismic shift that app would make in terms of both my work approach and my output. I've generated more work because of working digitally than I could ever have done using traditional paint. Unfortunately, one of the casualties was my dependence on sketchbooks. I now do all of my thinking on a digital layer that gets folded into the finished piece.

Apart from occasional experiments, I always have a notion of what I'm going to do in terms of picture making. I start with a background colour, do a rough sketch on a separate layer, and then proceed to flesh out the composition over multiple layers. Working digitally affords me the option of trying things out with little risk, which I love. That said, my approach is not all that different than my approach using acrylics, which may explain why I found it easy to make the transition to digital.

DRAWING DAILY

Though I'm not really the right person to give notebook advice, I do acknowledge the benefits of drawing daily. Working digitally is not the same as holding a pencil and it's easy to fall out of the practice of drawing traditionally. The absent Undo button can be frustrating and an eraser just seems pathetic by contrast, but I'd always advocate keeping a pencil and pad nearby. My number-one piece of advice is: be original. I know, it's hard. It's okay to be consciously inspired by other artists. It's not okay to be consciously derivative.

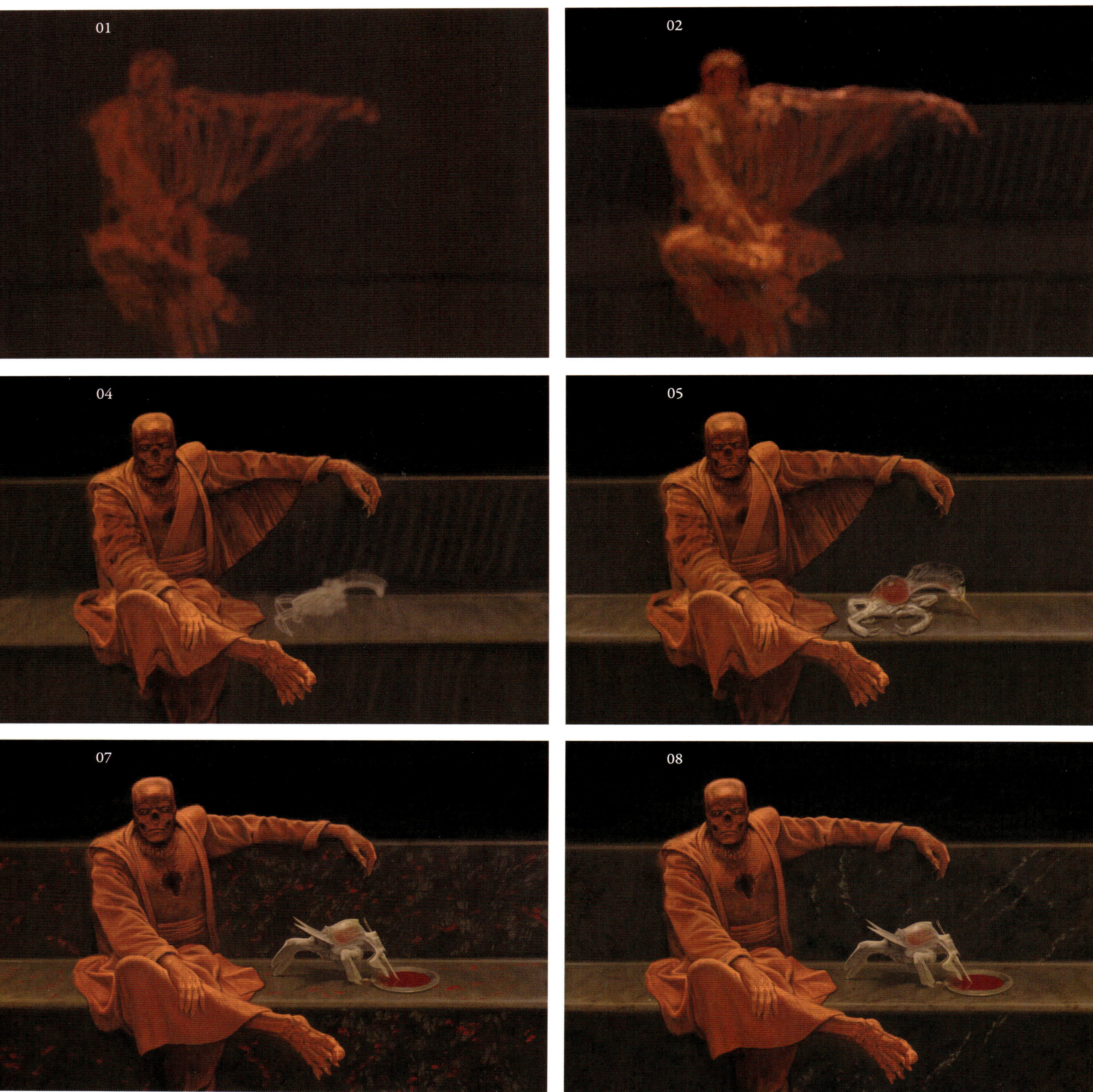

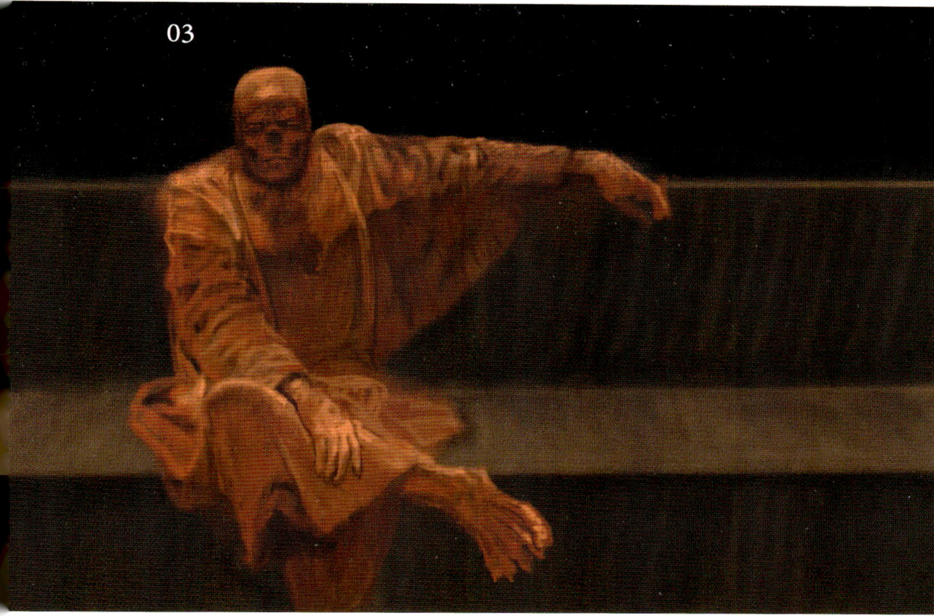

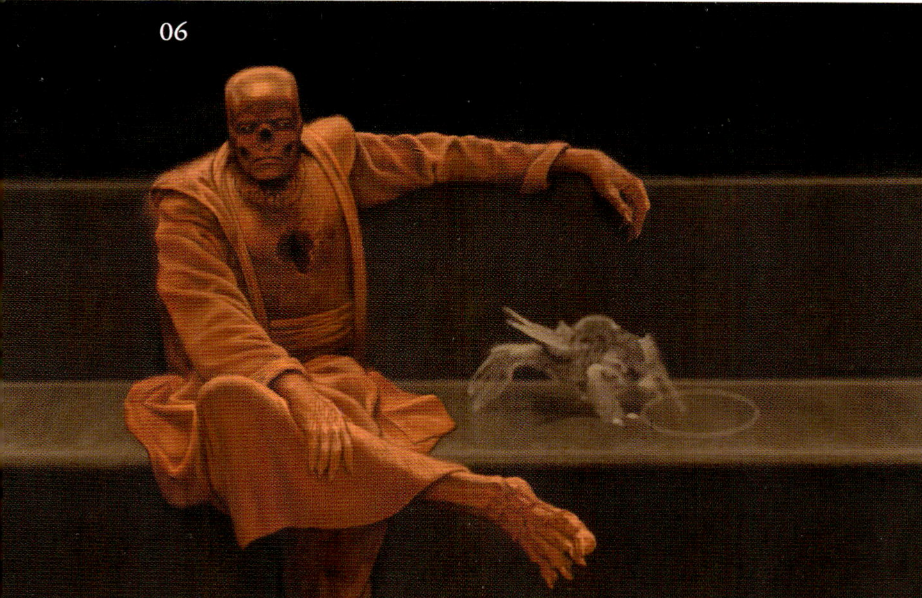

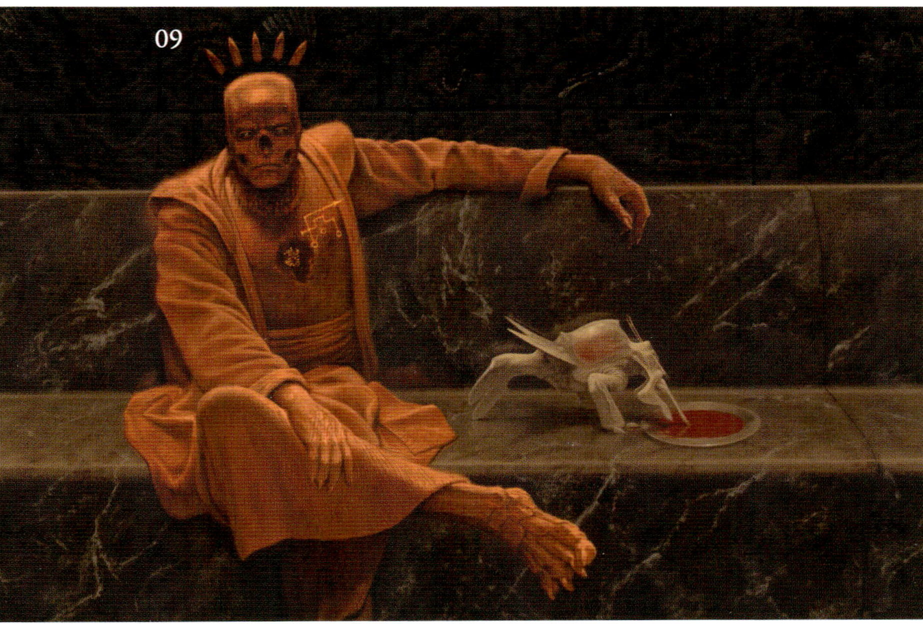

01 Using Procreate's Bonobo Chalk brush, I began by blocking in the rough figure against a simple background. The background is a flat colour, which I laid in using the Round brush set to maximum.

02 I indicated the light source and roughly laid in the bench. I then further refined the lighting and the figure's form, as well as the bench.

03 Paying more attention to the light source, I used the Bonobo Chalk brush to refine the main figure's form with sharper detail.

04 I added various elements to the figure and drew in a rough first attempt at the small abyssal pet next to the demon on a separate layer.

05 After refining the bench's polished texture, I added detail to the abyssal. That said, the design of the creature wasn't working for me.

06 I introduced much finer detail to the demon and completely changed the design of the abyssal. Next, I used Procreate's Ellipse tool to block in the plate. I then removed the draped cape for the sake of simplicity and extended the leg.

07 After using the Artist Crayon brush for a first attempt at applying stone texture on the bench, I finished the abyssal drinking from the plate.

08 I didn't feel the bench looked enough like marble, so I used the Bonobo Chalk brush to modify its texture on a separate layer.

09 Using the Artist Crayon brush and Bonobo Chalk brush, I finished the soul brick wall behind the demon. I worked out final details – such as the hornlets, sigils, and chest fire – and added these to the figure on separate layers.

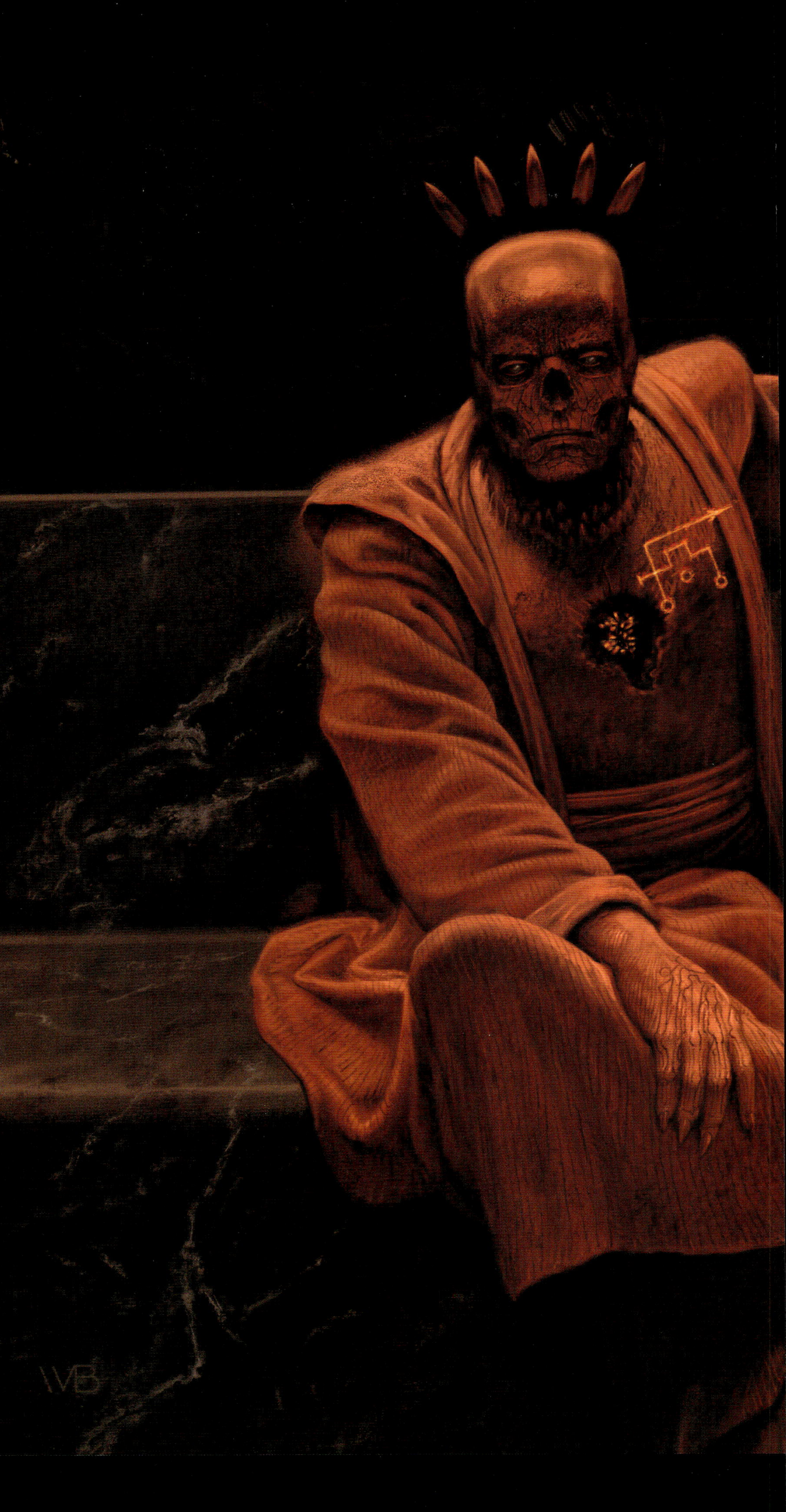

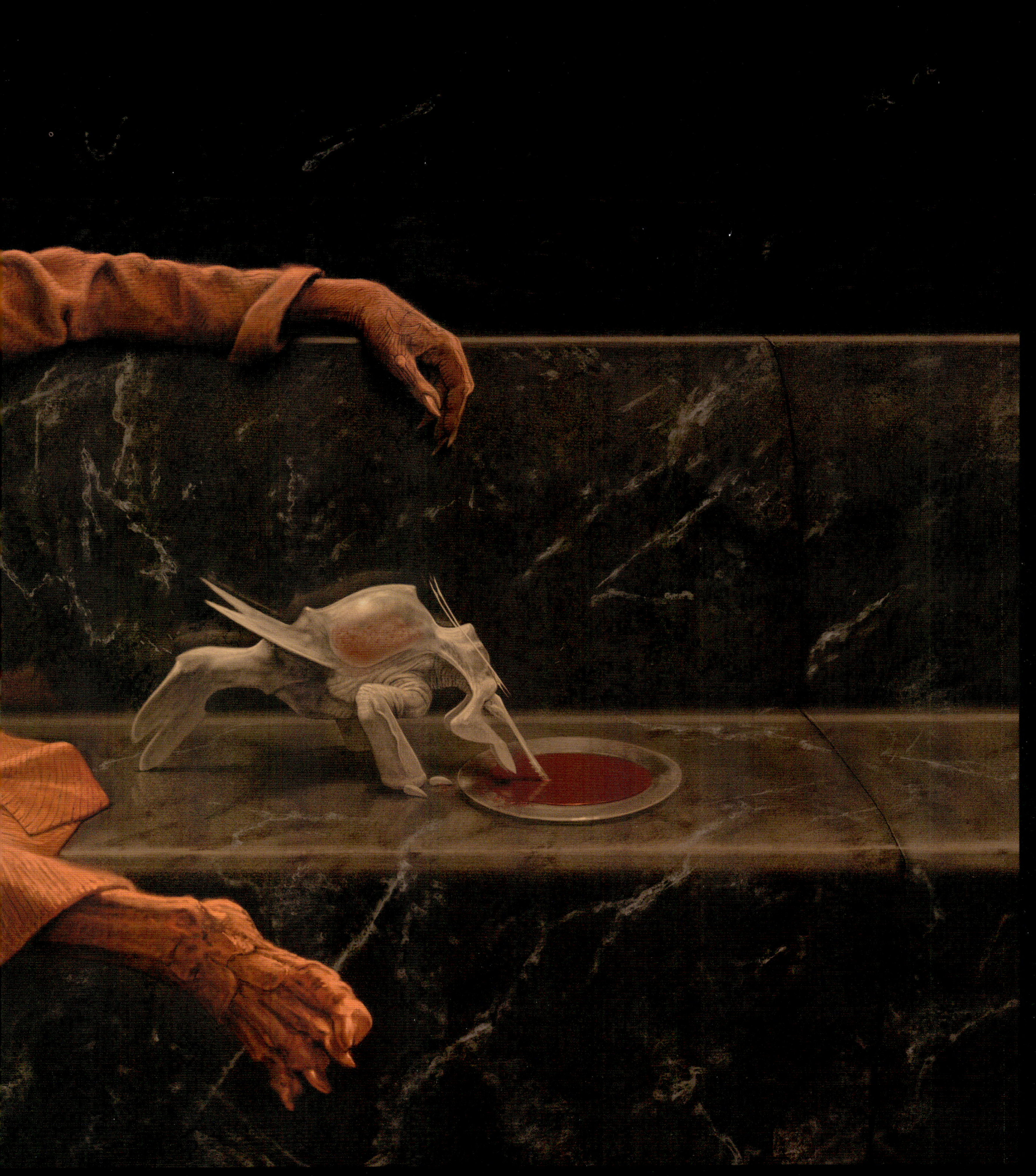

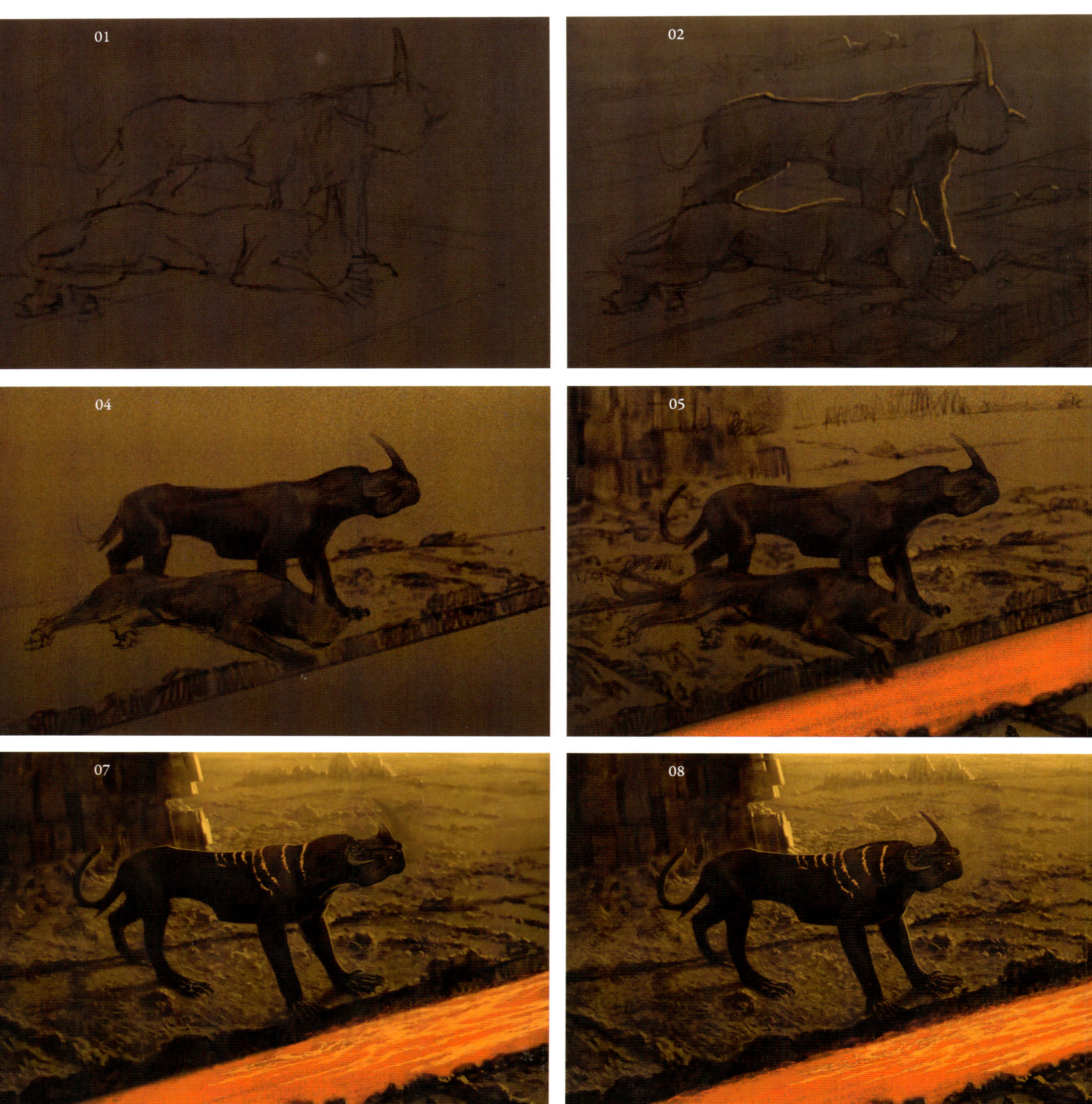

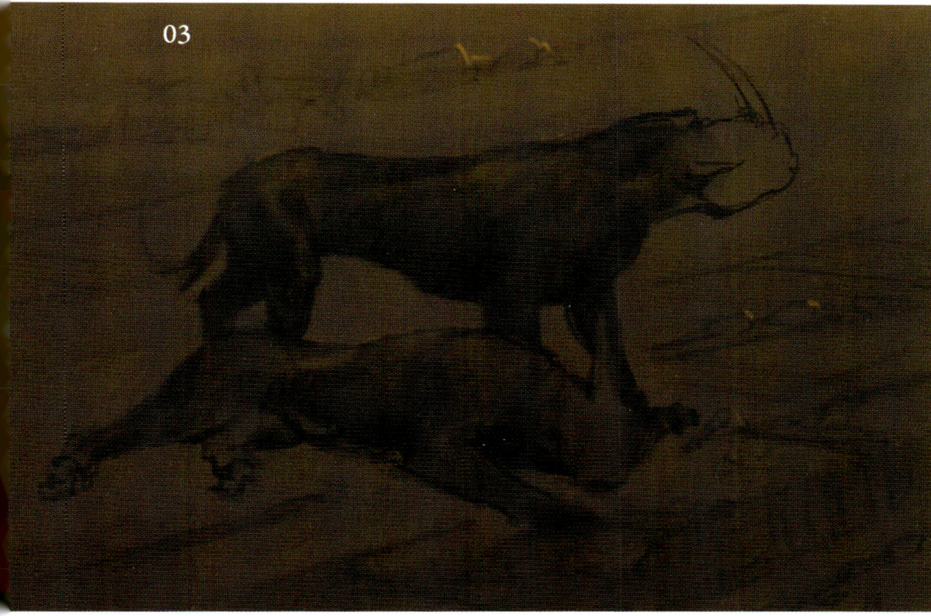

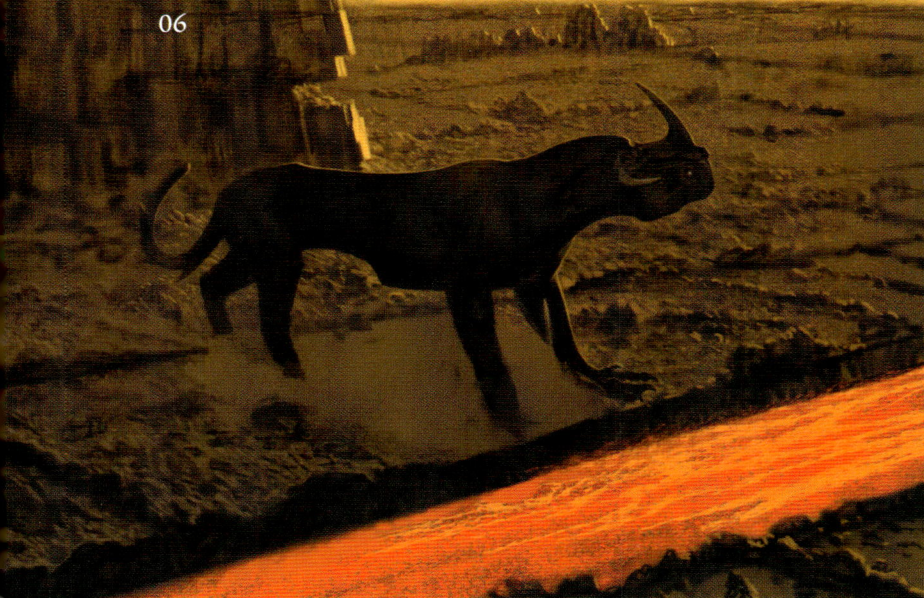

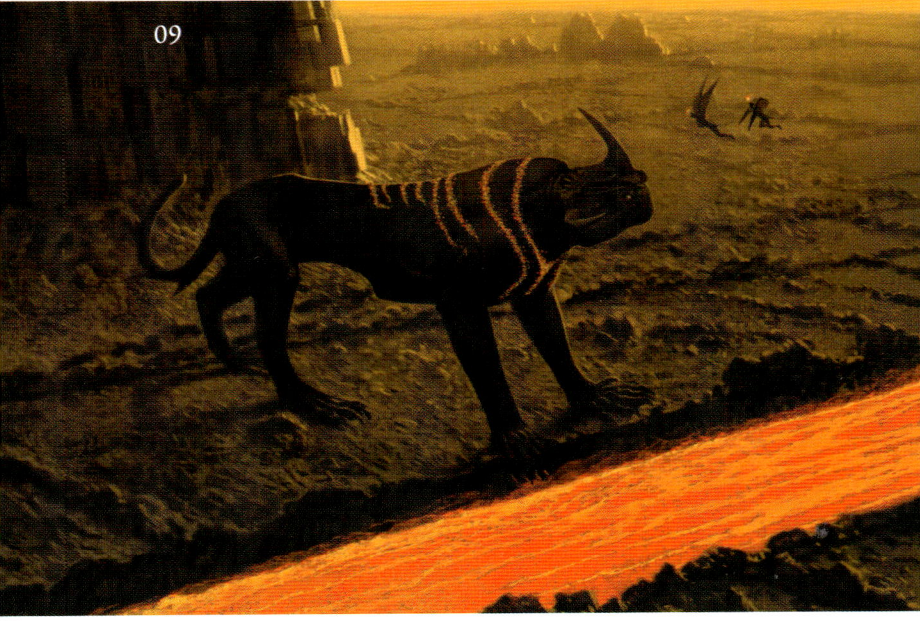

01 With the base background colour laid in, I began to sketch in two creatures. The original concept was to depict these animals straightforwardly as a wildlife piece. This would change.

02 I applied form-defining light and shadows, as well as a rough layout for the ruined buildings on the ground.

03 Here I added strong darks to the creatures to determine whether the composition worked.

04 Using the Airbrush, I introduced ambient light on an under-layer. I then used the Transform tool to make the creature grouping smaller.

05 Using the Bonobo Chalk brush, I painted in the lava river and blocked in the rubble and building foundations. I also established the horizon.

06 I modified the horizon, which affected the overall landscape. I decided to remove the recumbent beast because once shadows were added, its form was less clear. As it wasn't on a separate layer, I painted it out. Next, I introduced luminous detail to the lava river.

07 After repainting the ground next to the remaining beast, I used the Airbrush to add more atmosphere. Next, I shortened the beast's neck by duplicating the beast layer, erasing the body, and utilizing the Transform tool. I then painted stripes on its body.

08 I further modified the creature's head by erasing the original head and repainting a new one, leaving the background in need of repainting.

09 I drew a new perspective line because I felt the original was incorrect. I then finished painting the lava river and added flying demons. What started as a wildlife painting ended up as something of a narrative piece.

Beast Taunting

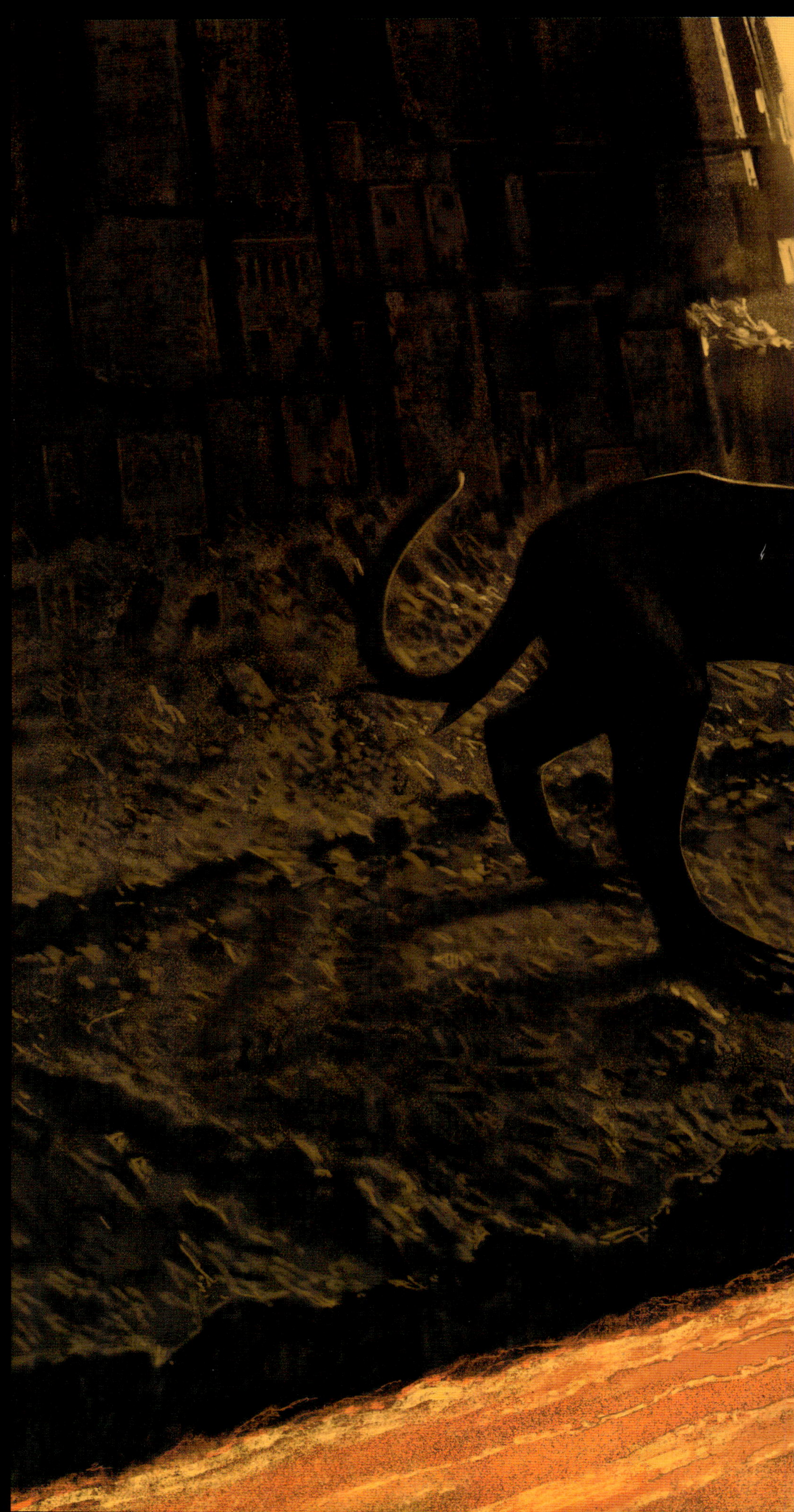

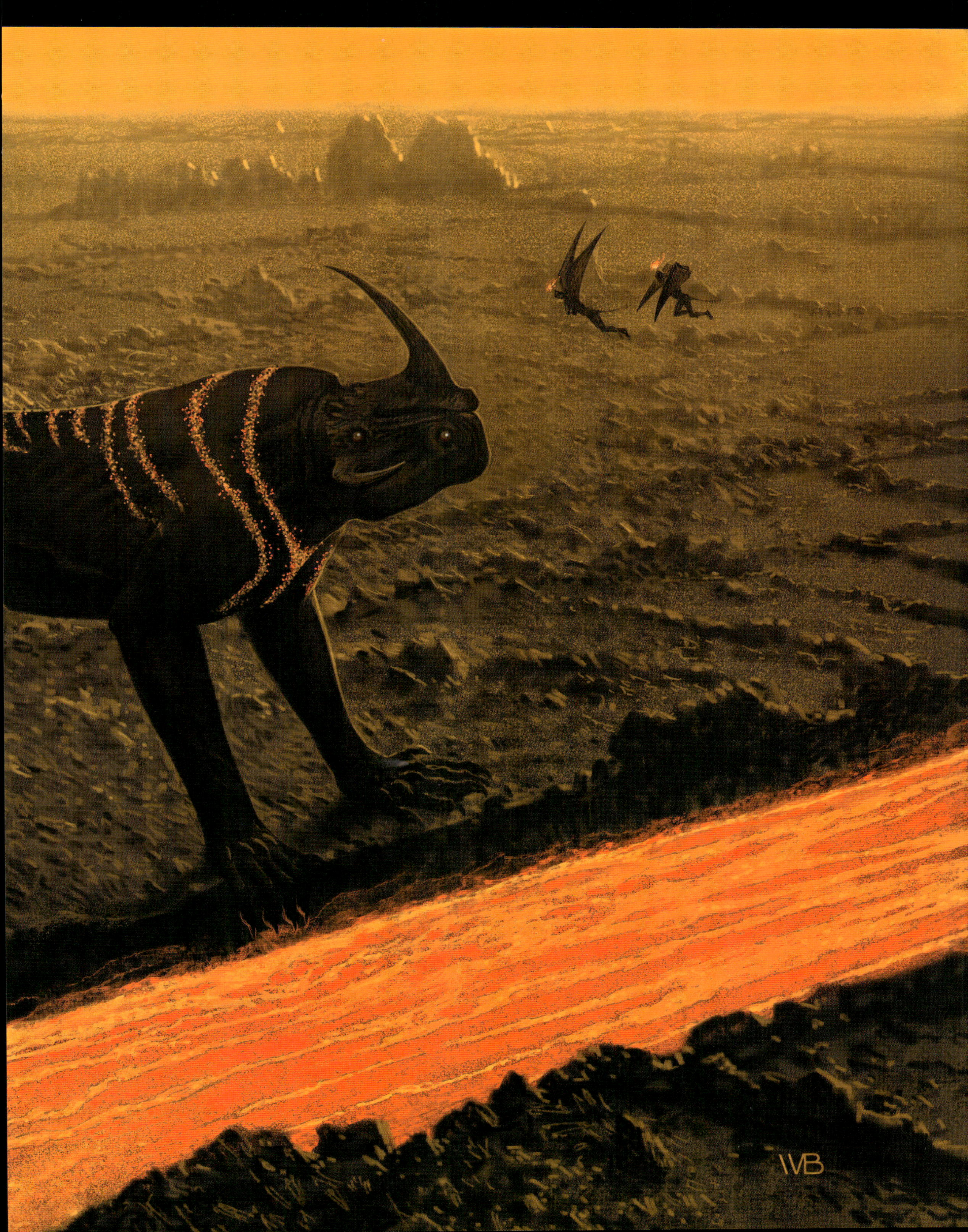

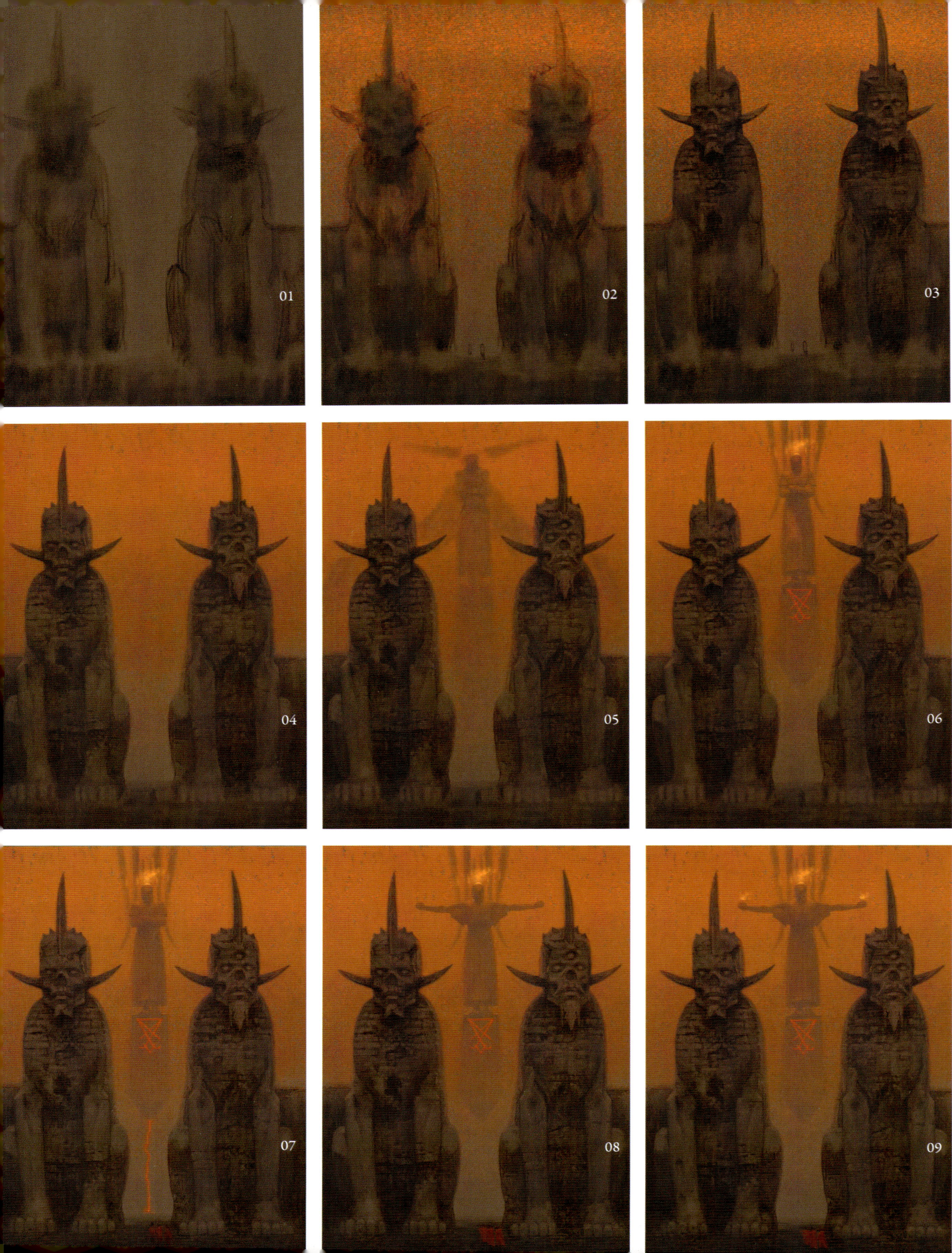

01
02
03
04
05
06
07
08
09

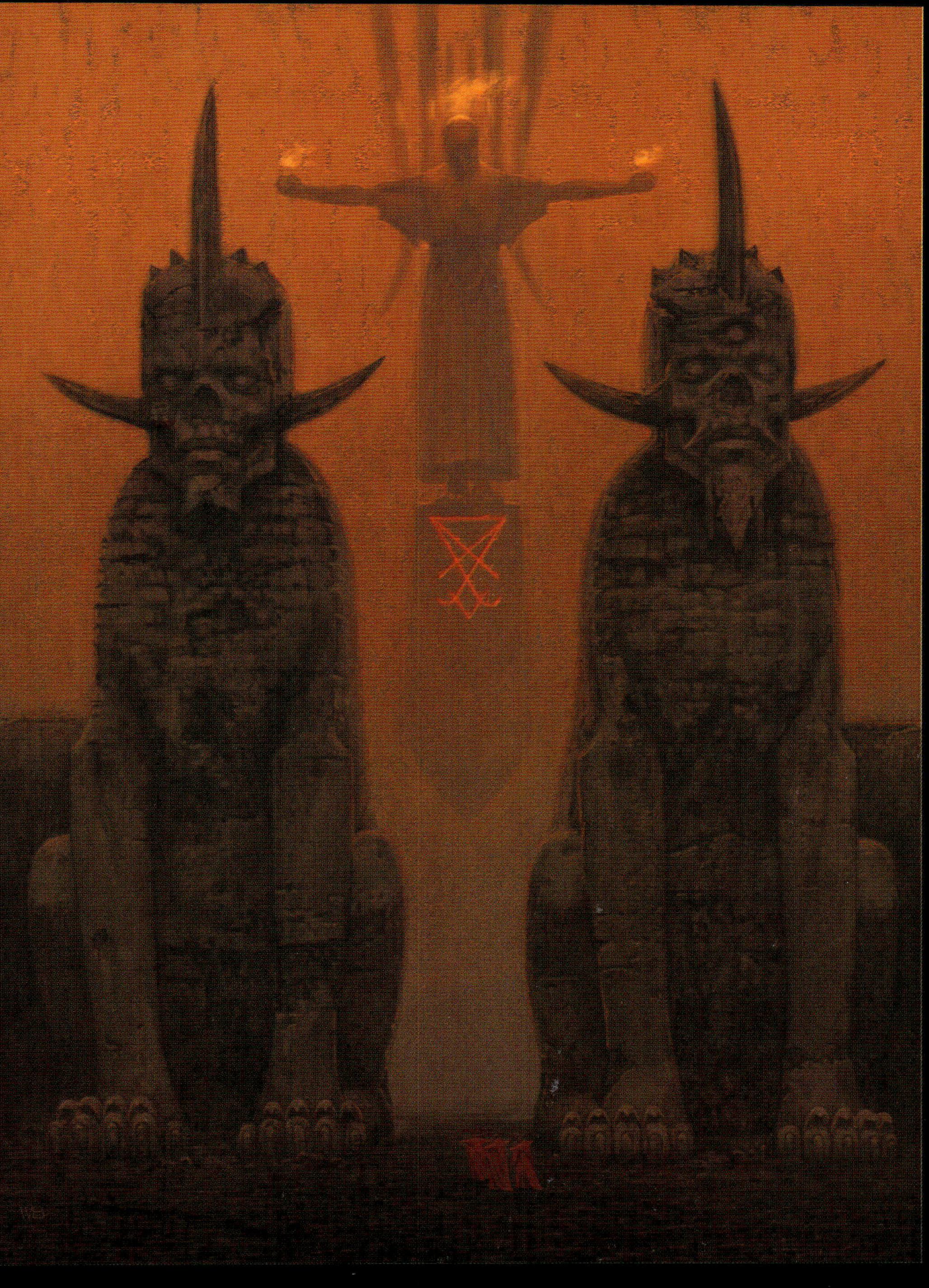

Cenotaph to Lucifer

01 To begin, I roughly blocked in two statues using the Bonobo Chalk brush. Beneath this layer is the original toned ground I laid in using the Painting Round brush.

02 Using the Bonobo Chalk brush, I added a light colo[u]r pass on the background sky to establish the mood and atmosphere, then began the process of modelling the two sphinxes.

03 Next, I started to refine the forms of the statues.

04 Further refinement of the statues also brought a heightening of contrast. After adding tiny figures to establish a sense of scale in my mind, I used the Impasto brush to create a more painterly sky.

05 Here I added a basic silhouette of the floating cenotaph itself.

06 I applied the second in a series of design explorations to the cenotaph, bringing in the fiery element as well as the magenta sigil. Each element was worked into a separate layer for flexibility.

07 I refined the ground, as well as the now red-clad demon-monks on their pilgrimage. A single bolt of levitating lightning was added as a possible concept...

08 ...but was discarded as it felt too obvious. Instead, I added details to the sphinxes.

09 To finish, I finalized the statue upon the cenotaph, with its arms outstretched.

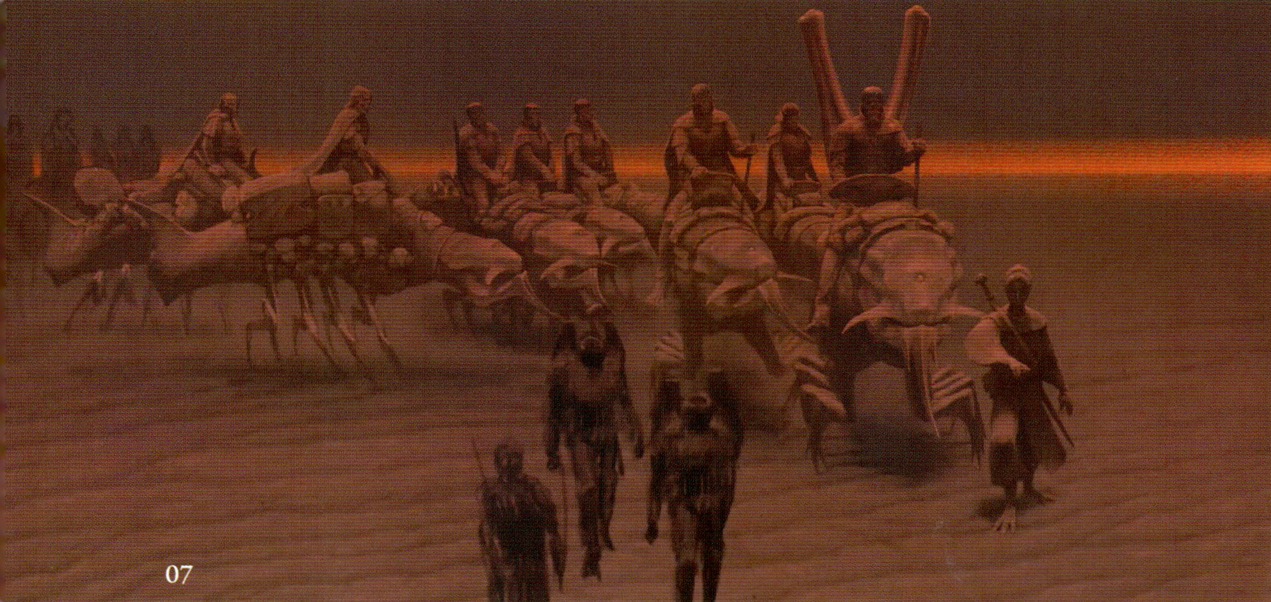

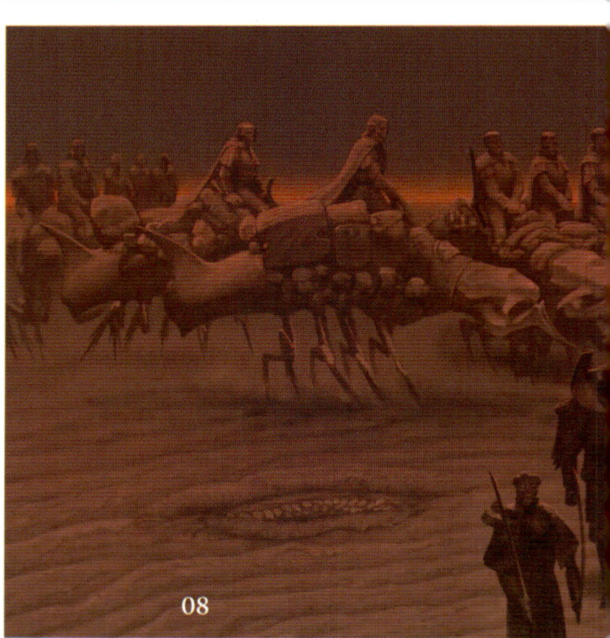

01 Using the Bonobo Chalk brush, I sketched in the basic composition on a layer separate from the background tone.

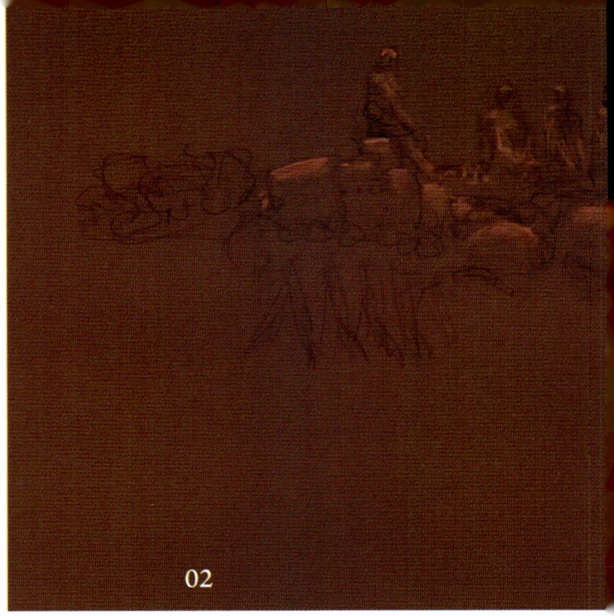

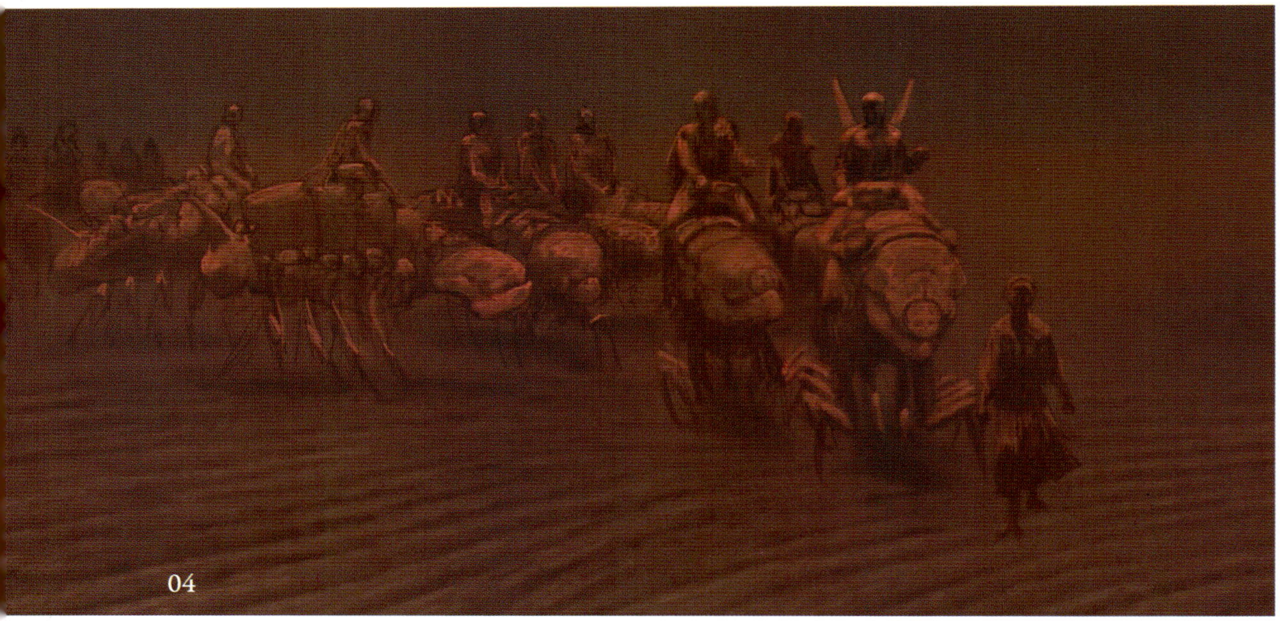

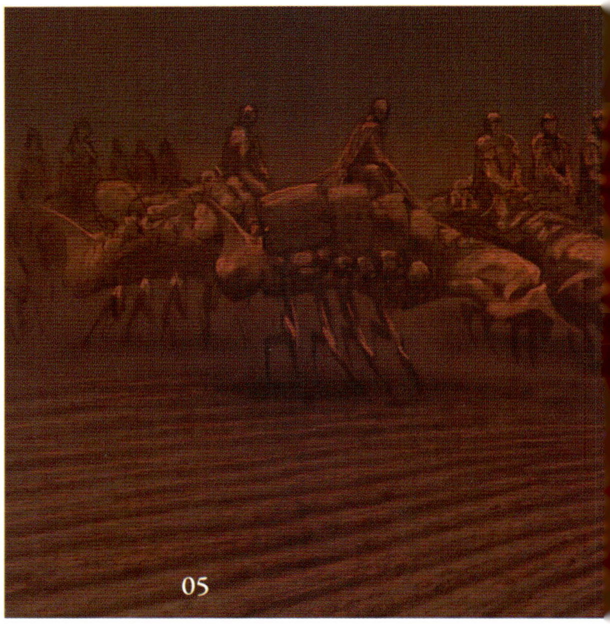

02 I indicated the basic forms of the caravan and a light source with broadly painted lighter tones.

03 I added the horizon, plus deeper darks to the figures and steeds.

04 Next, I introduced ground texture and modified the horizon. I positioned an additional figure on a separate layer and introduced shadows.

05 After heightening the light tones and solidifying design elements, such as the forms of the riders and steeds, I added detail to the various figures.

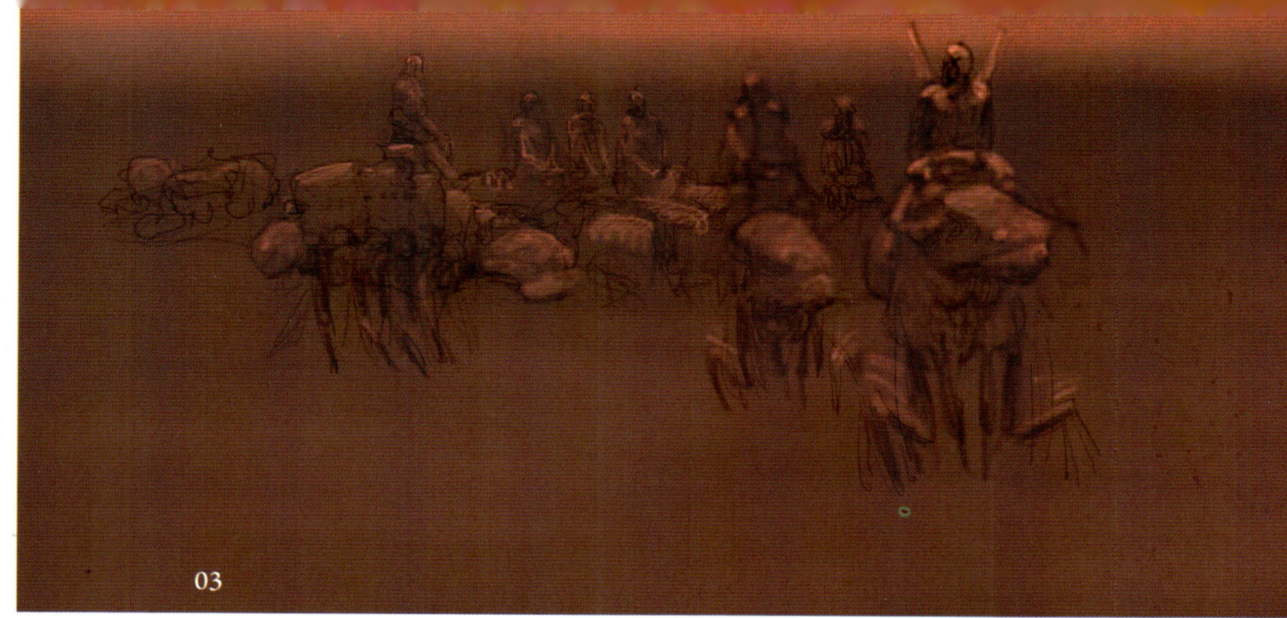

03

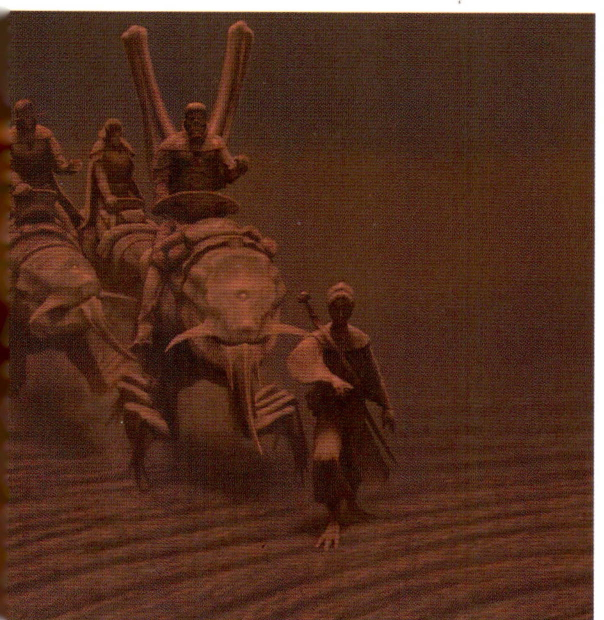

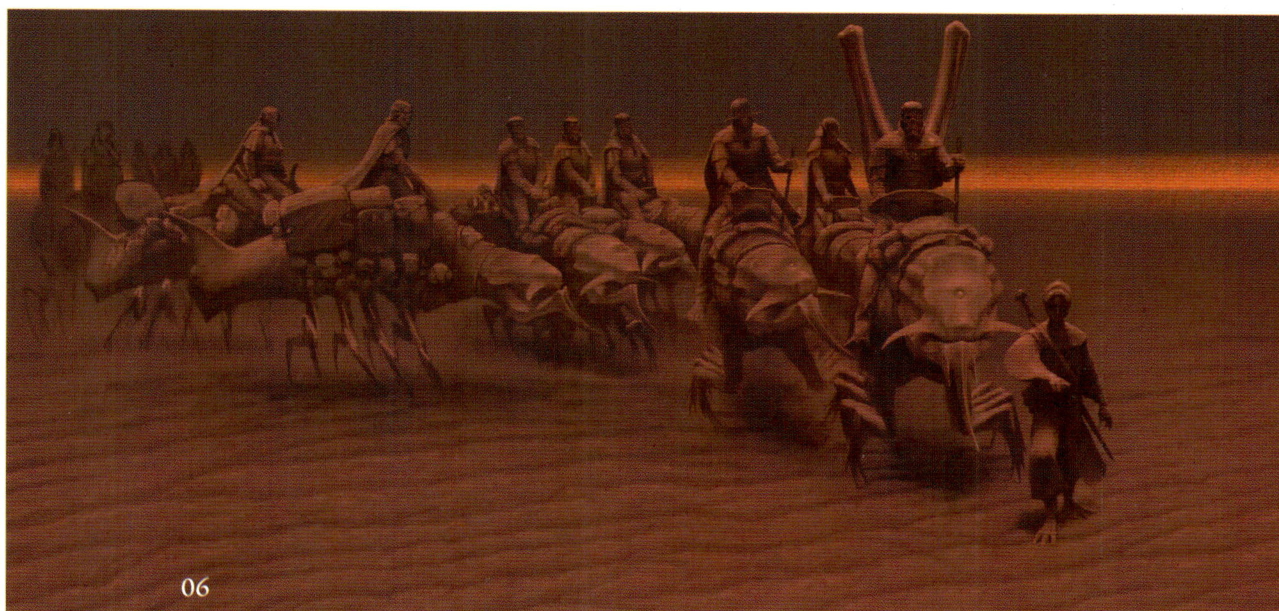

06

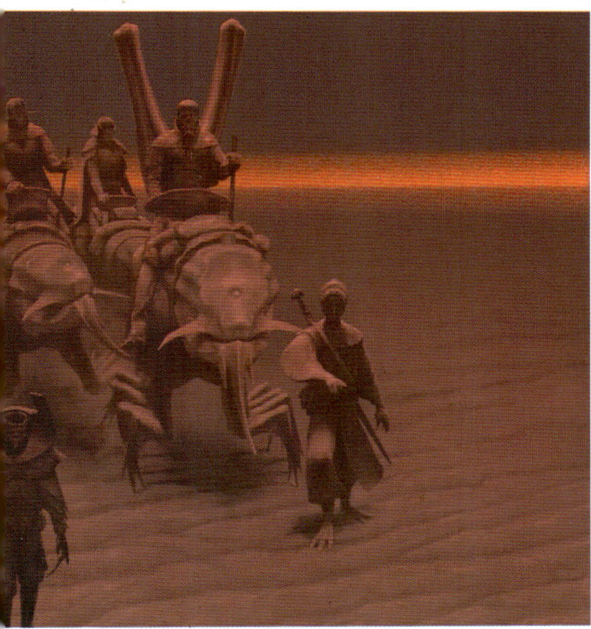

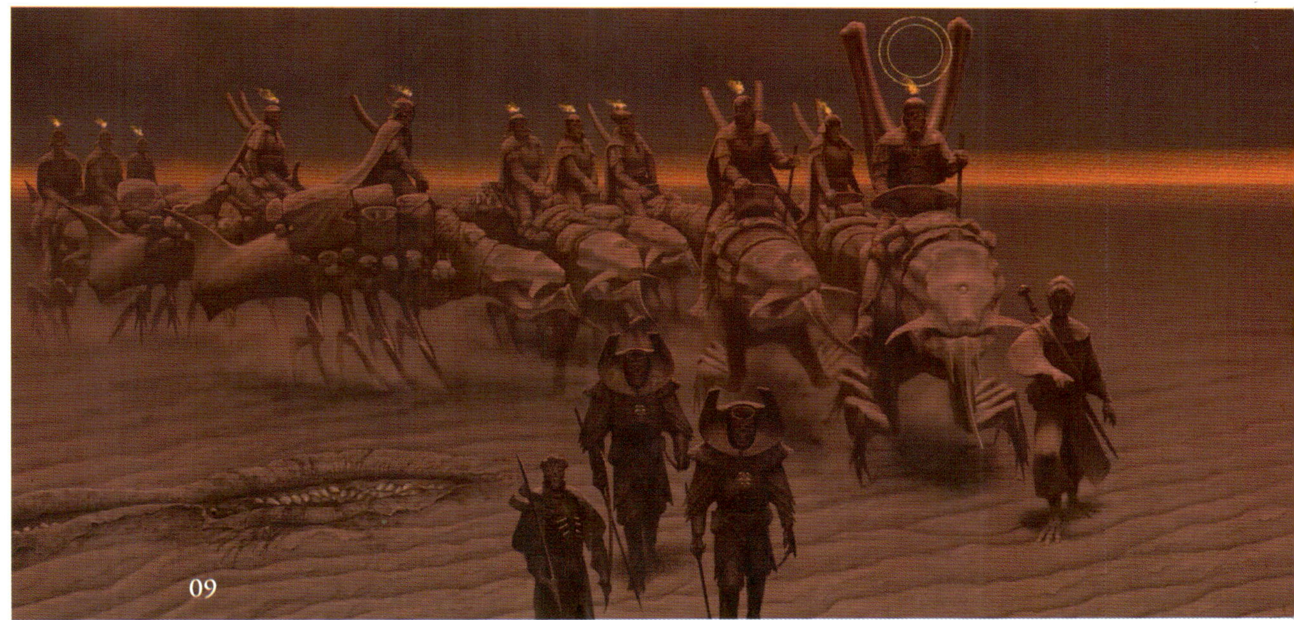

09

06 I made the ground firmer and created the final horizon line.

07 Positioning sketchy foreground figures on a separate layer allowed for possible repositioning.

08 I laid in the rough hellmouth, then refined the rear figures of the caravan.

09 After finishing the hellmouth, I added dust clouds to the finalized steeds. I painted flames above the demons' heads on a separate layer.

To finish the image, I lit the sigil above the principal demon and added the mounted figure on the far right.

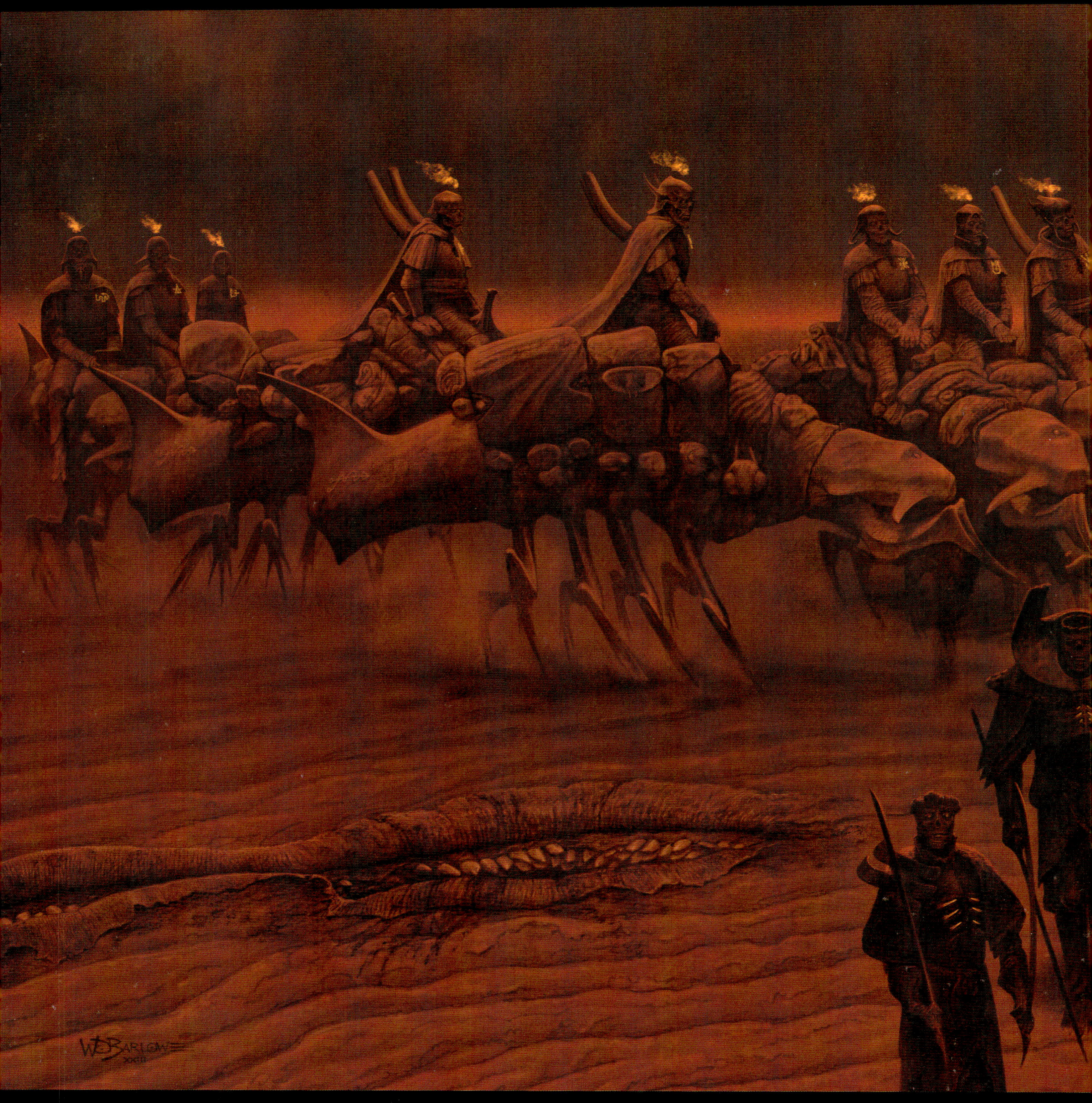

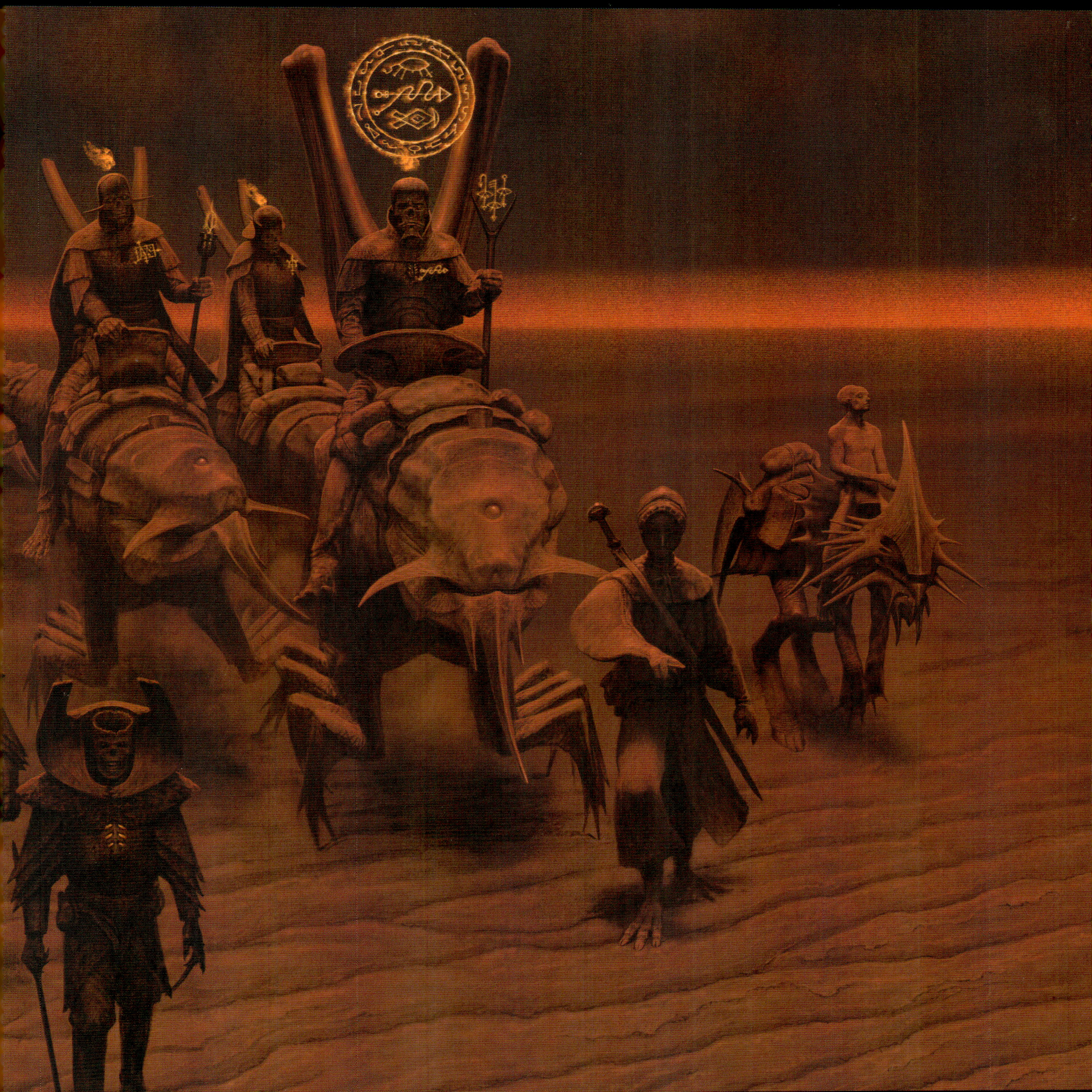

Eligor's Expedition

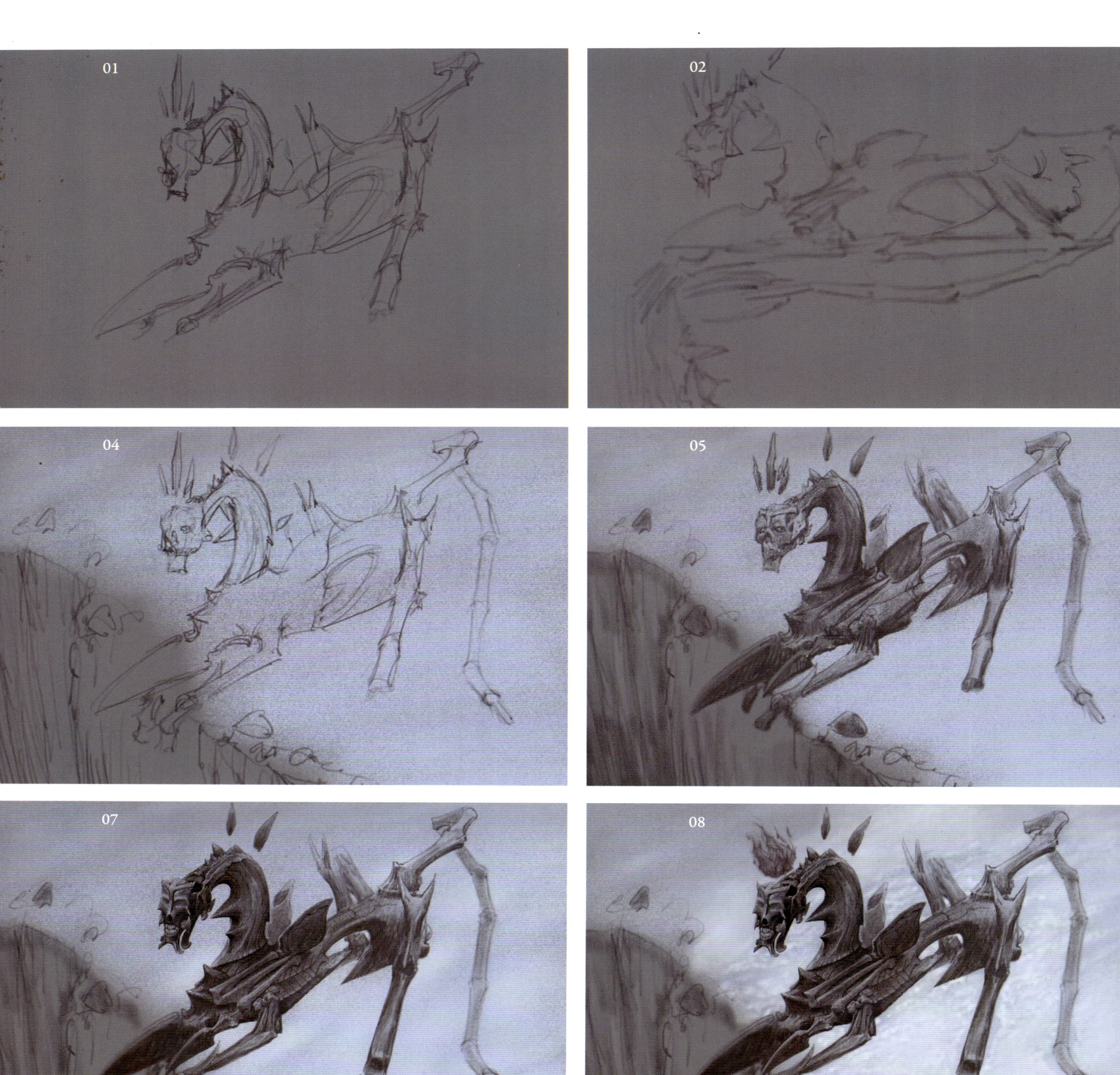

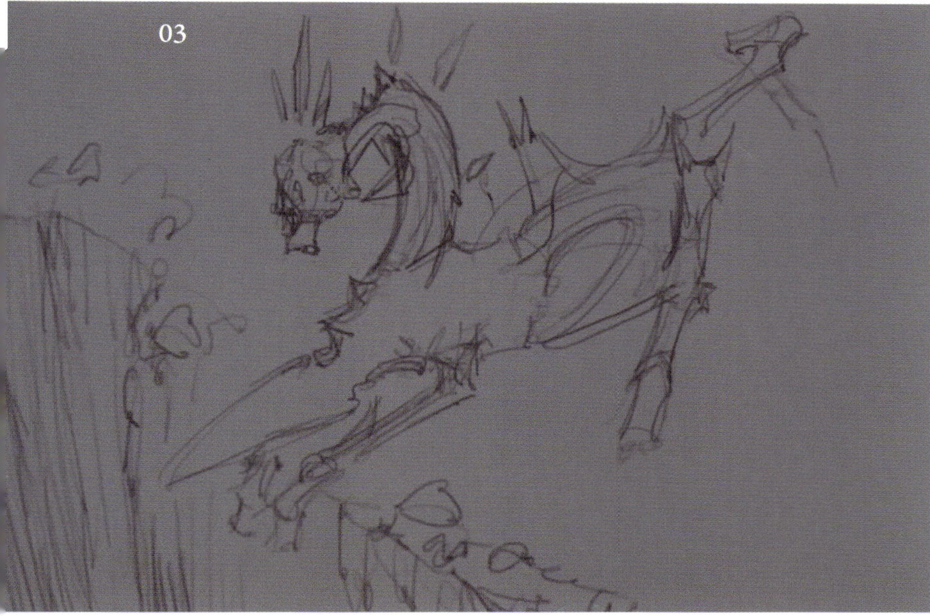

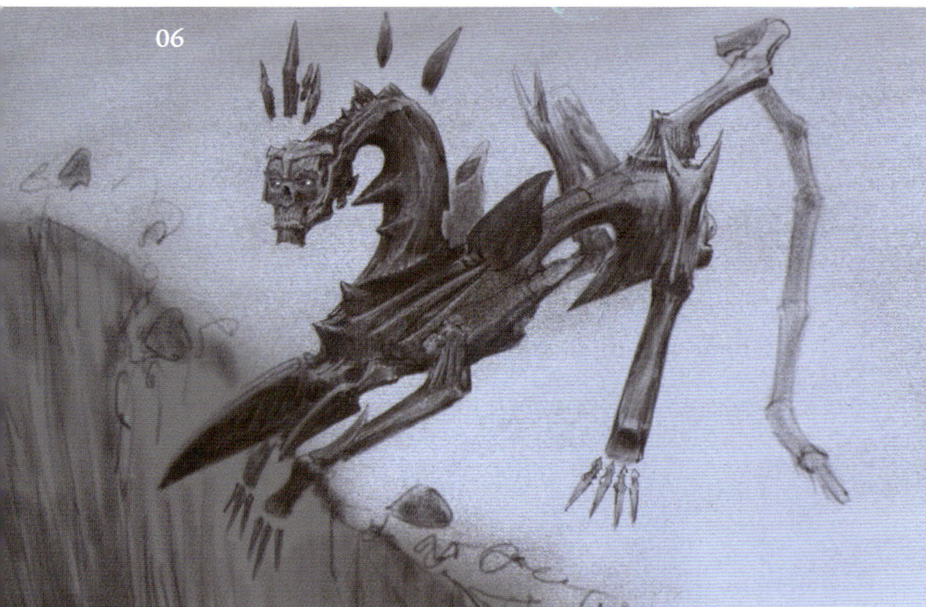

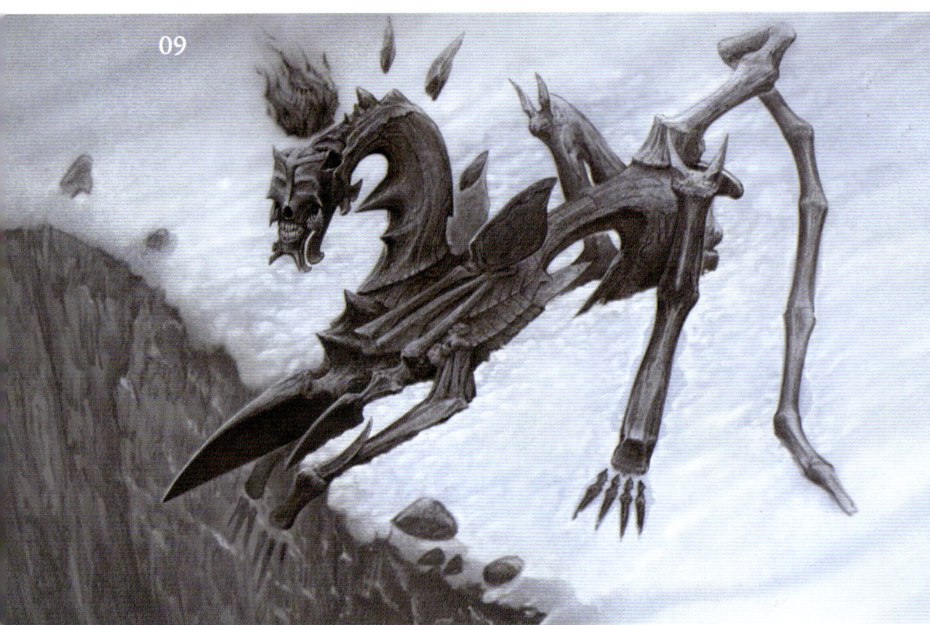

01 I began by sketching the creature on a separate layer from the background.

02 I took a very different approach with the second sketch, laying it on a different layer for thoughtful consideration.

03 As the second, more dynamic sketch better suited my idea, I began to define the creature with some sketchy additions and indicated the receding cliff side.

04 I added a light dusting of snow to create the plane the creature sits upon. I then drew in a tail, as per an original drawing I'd done some time before.

05 I used darker grey shading to begin to add form to the creature, as well as the cliff side. The creature's complex shapes started to resolve through my use of darks and lights, plus finer detail.

06 Stronger contrasting tones gave the creature solidity. I also added elongated nails.

07 Feeling unsatisfied with its initial design, I gave the head some serious attention. After many iterations, I finally arrived at something I liked. Early highlights began to add texture to the snow.

08 On a separate layer, I painted dark fire above the creature's head. As it was separate, I tried a few variations before arriving, finally, at black flames. I then added churned-up snow around where the creature would have disturbed it.

09 I finished painting the snow using a combination of the Airbrush and Bonobo Chalk brushes. The finest setting on the Bonobo Chalk brush allowed me to address the details on the creature and cliff.

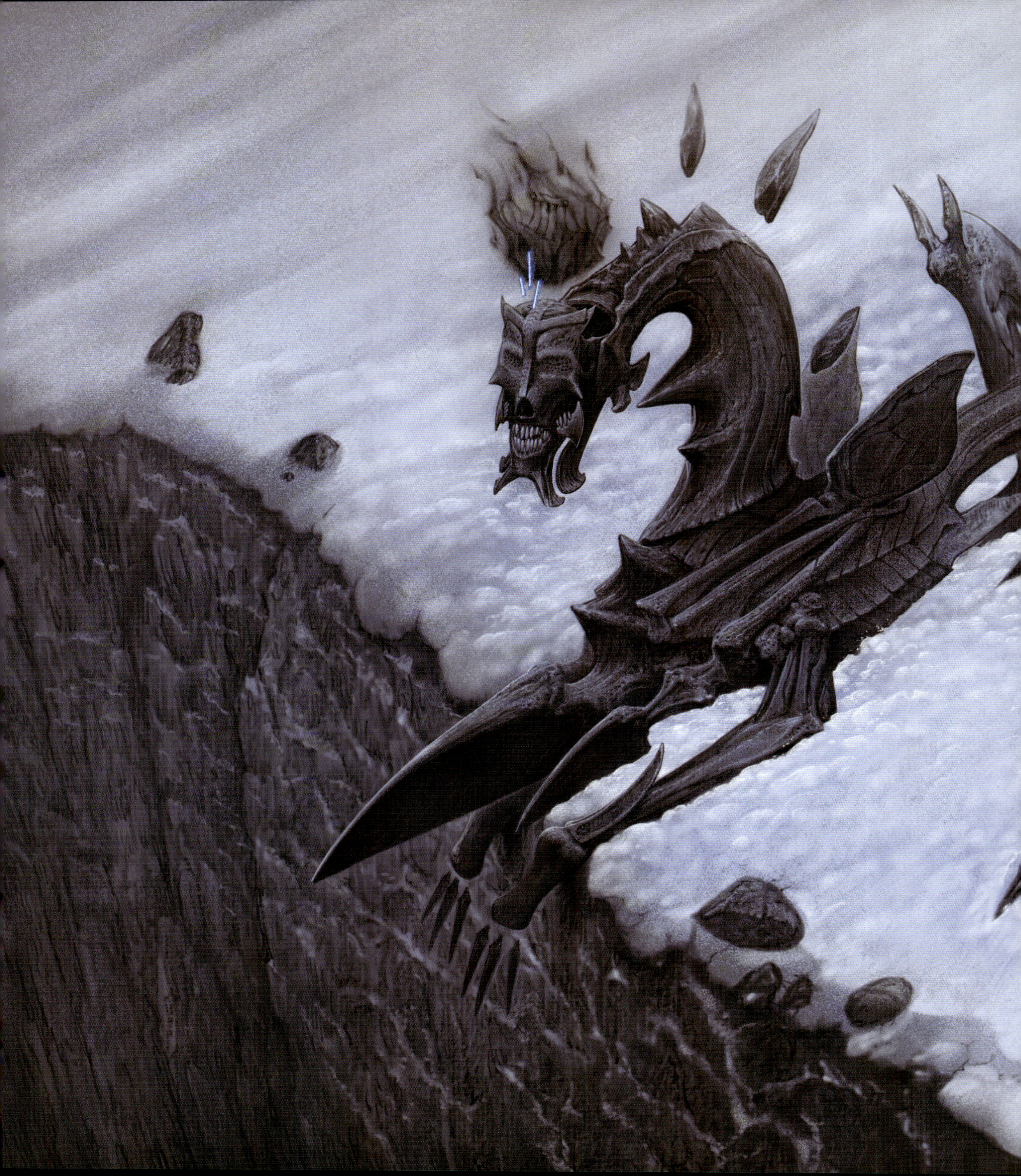

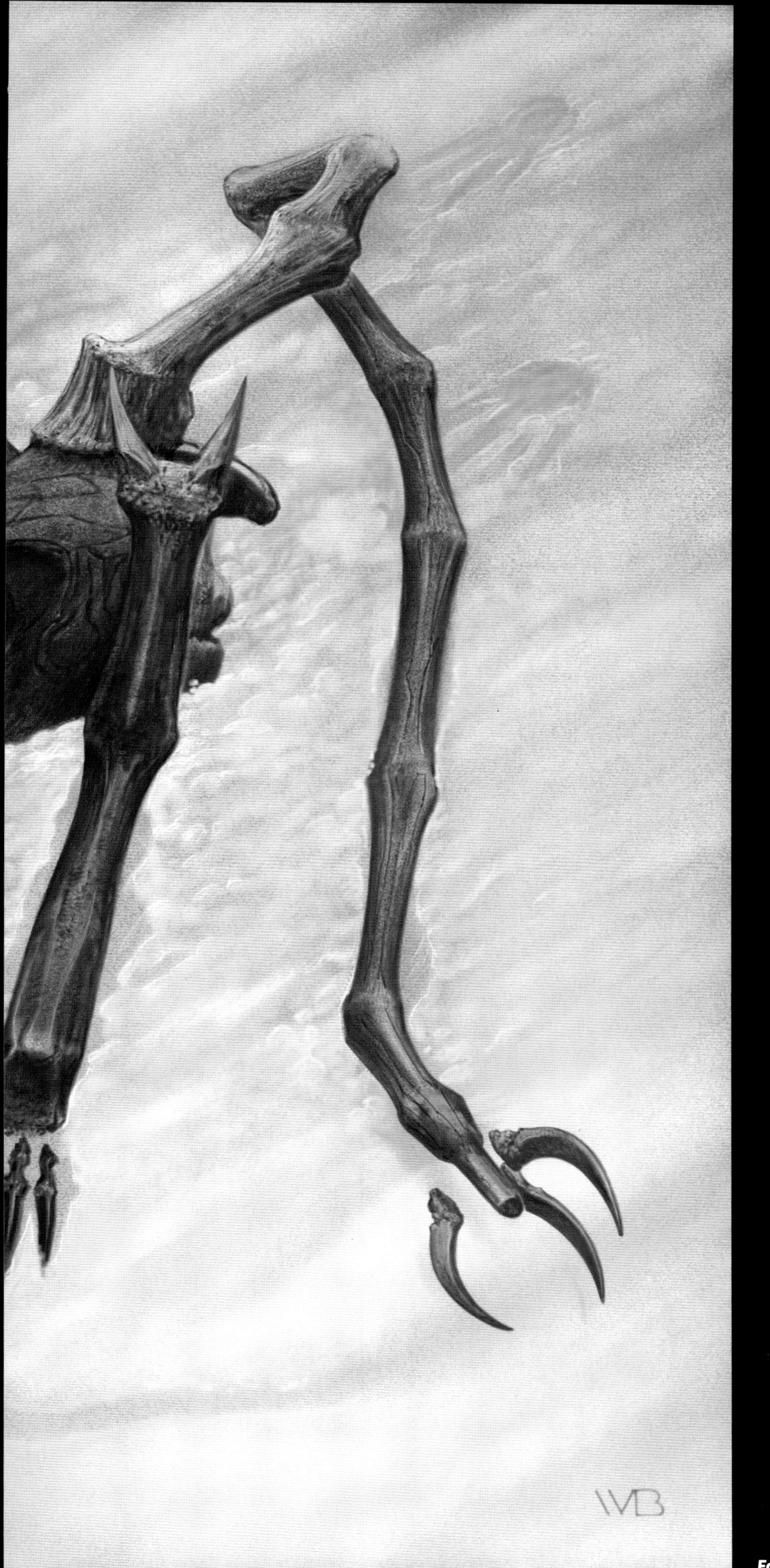

Faraii Abaddonicus

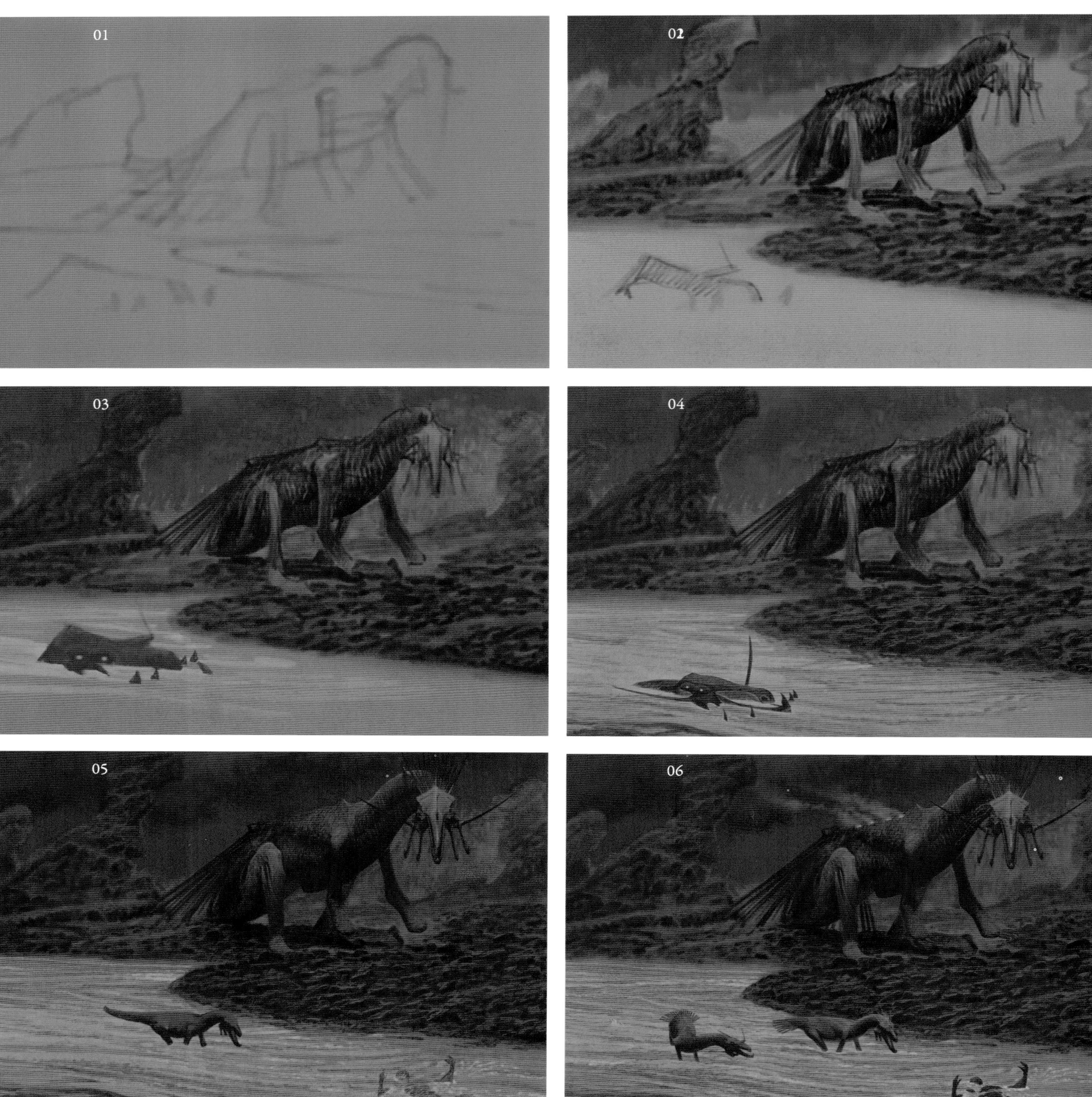

01 On a layer above the flat background colours, I began to sketch out the composition. The original concept was to have a submerged gouger accompanying the one on the shore.

02 After adding darks all around, I blocked in the shapes of the landscape and sky. I then increased the contrast and further refined the form of the principal gouger.

03 I enhanced the intensity of the sky, then clarified the submerged gouger on a separate layer. I also worked on the lava to convey its flow.

04 Once I'd moved the submerged head to a more pleasing location, I began working on the rocks and lava in earnest, adding hardened skeins and deeper tones.

05 I removed the submerged head altogether; it had broken down in its forms to become unreadable. Instead, with a new narrative in mind, I added a floating soul, before sharpening the forms of the gouger. I then sharpened both the background and the gouger. On another layer, I added a young gouger wading in the lava and peering at the soul.

06 I moved the same young gouger and added another curious baby. Next, I applied fiery nostrils and smoke to the torso of the gouger. Once again, I moved one of the young gougers, then finished the floating soul, rocks, and small details on the gouger.

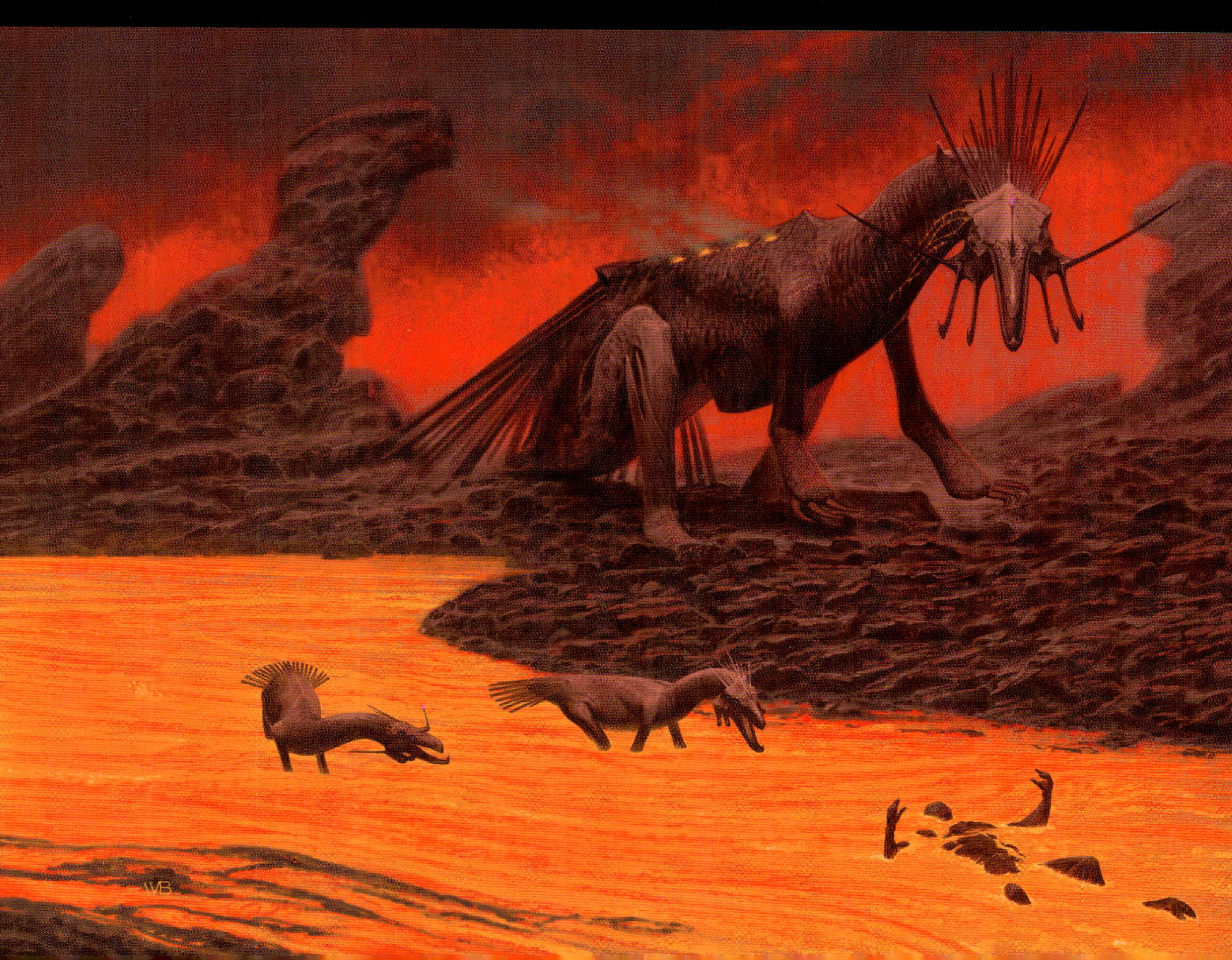

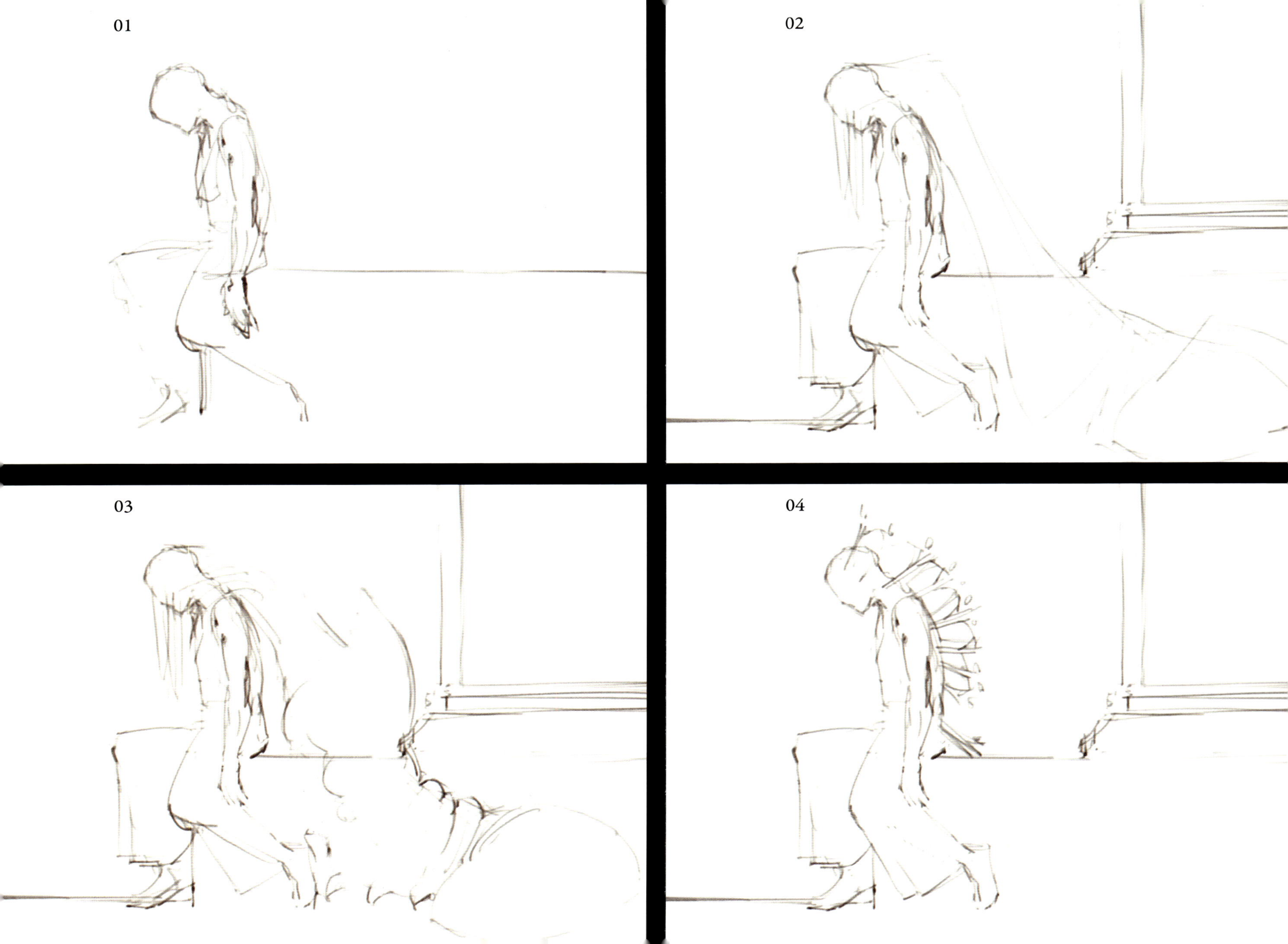
01
02
03
04

01 I laid in the first concept sketch using the Bonobo Chalk brush.

02 I then introduced another compositional element, before adding a first attempt at a parasitic creature to the figure.

03 A second, more baroque attempt. But something still wasn't working.

04 Further exploration in a different direction, before I took a break from solving the parasite problem...

05 ...and, on a layer below the drawing, I laid in the low-contrast background tone. I then added highlights on the figure and column, as well as the newly added floating winglets. The addition of the wings imposed new compositional constraints and started the gears grinding.

06 I enhanced the shading and highlights, then lightly sketched in what was to become the final parasite design.

07 Once I was happy with the parasite's silhouette, I began to refine it.

08 Next, I turned my attention to the wall and the floor, beginning to address the textures of both. I then brought the figure and its drapery, as well as all the background textures, up to the proper degree, all accomplished with Procreate's Bonobo Chalk brush.

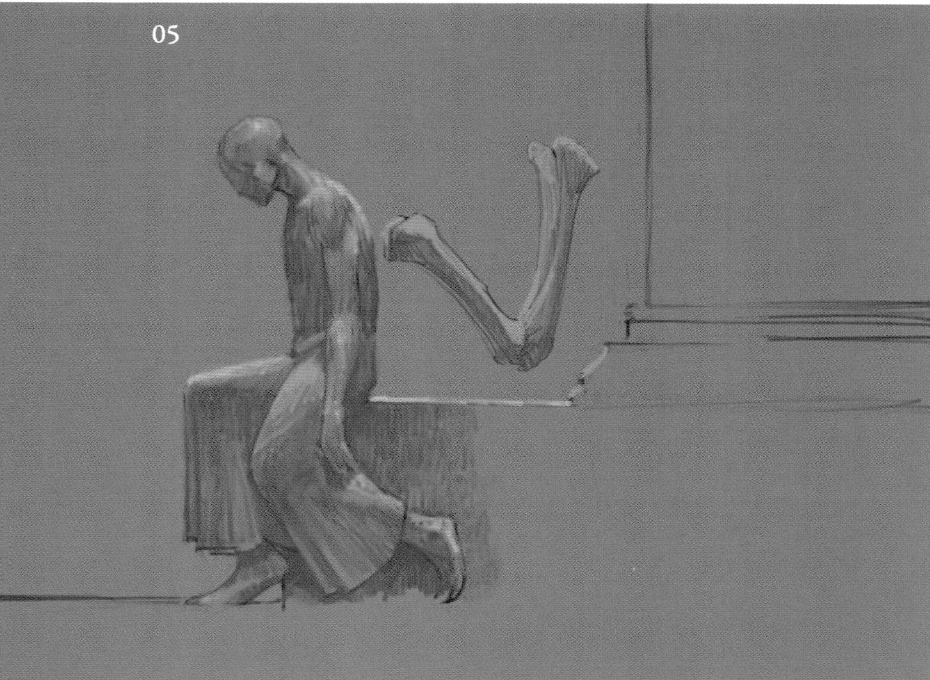

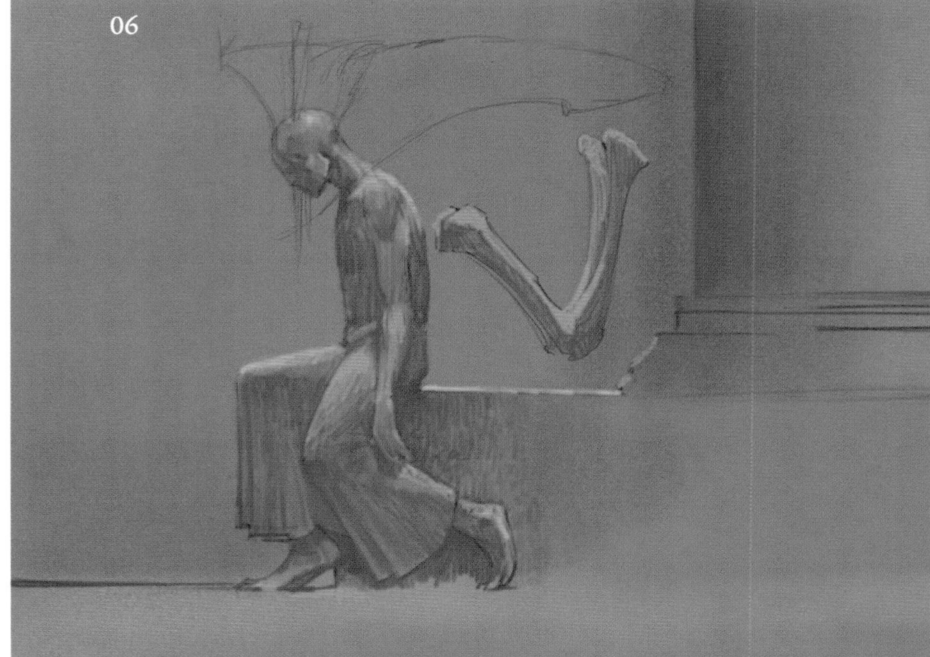

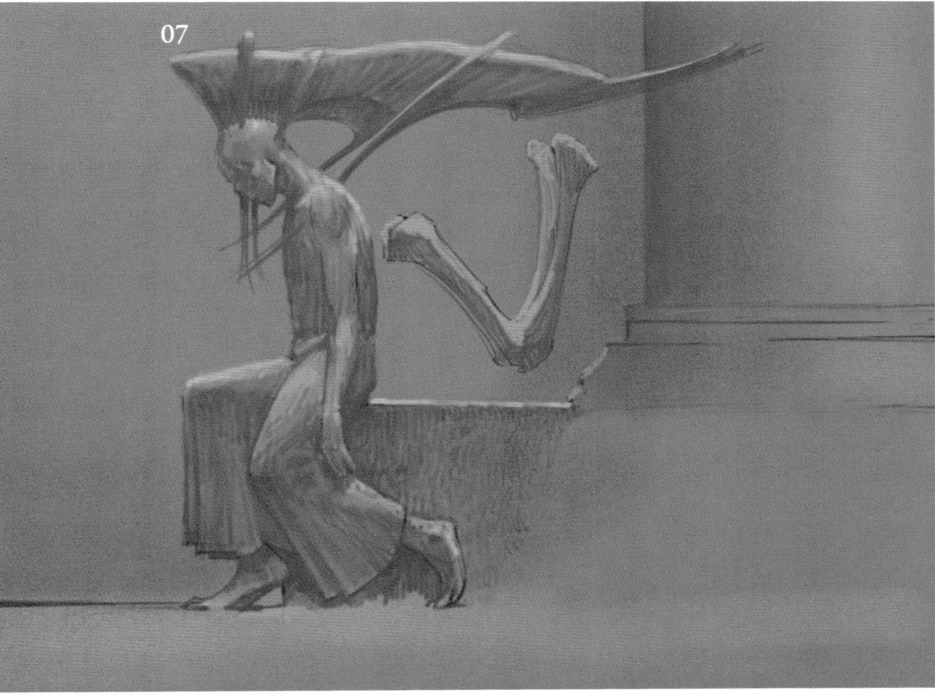

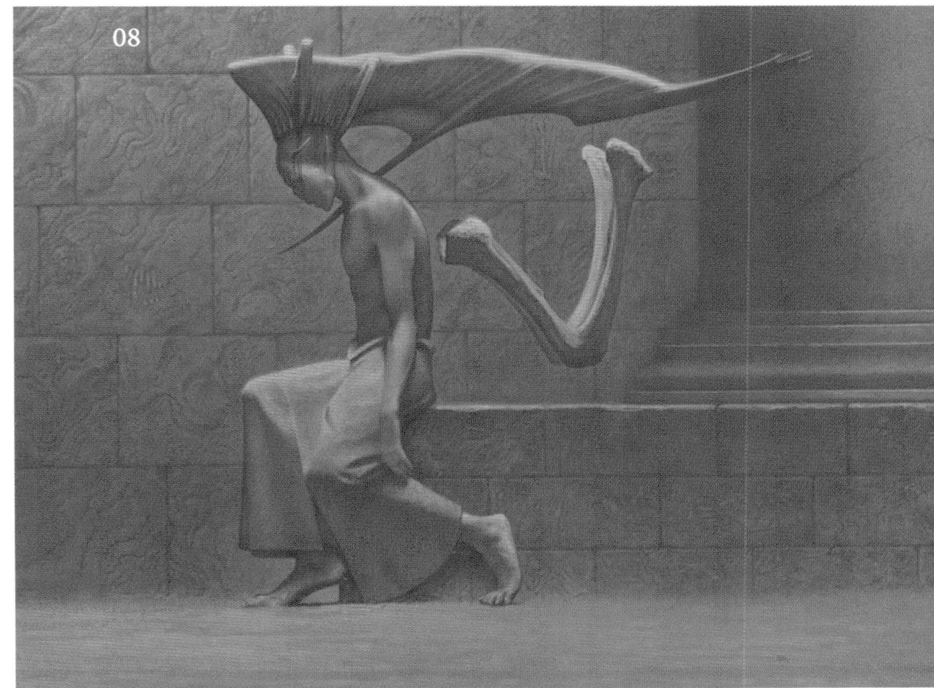

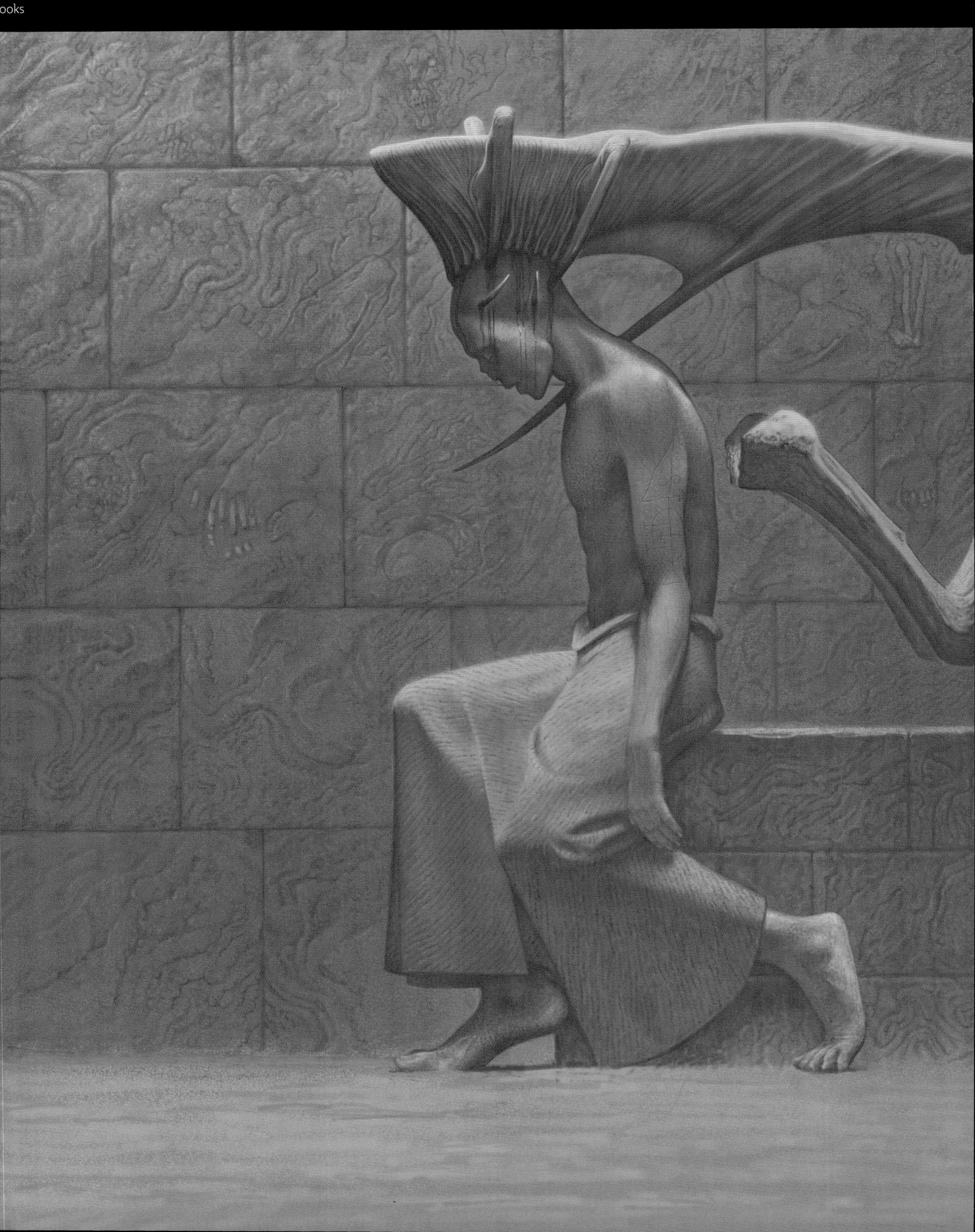

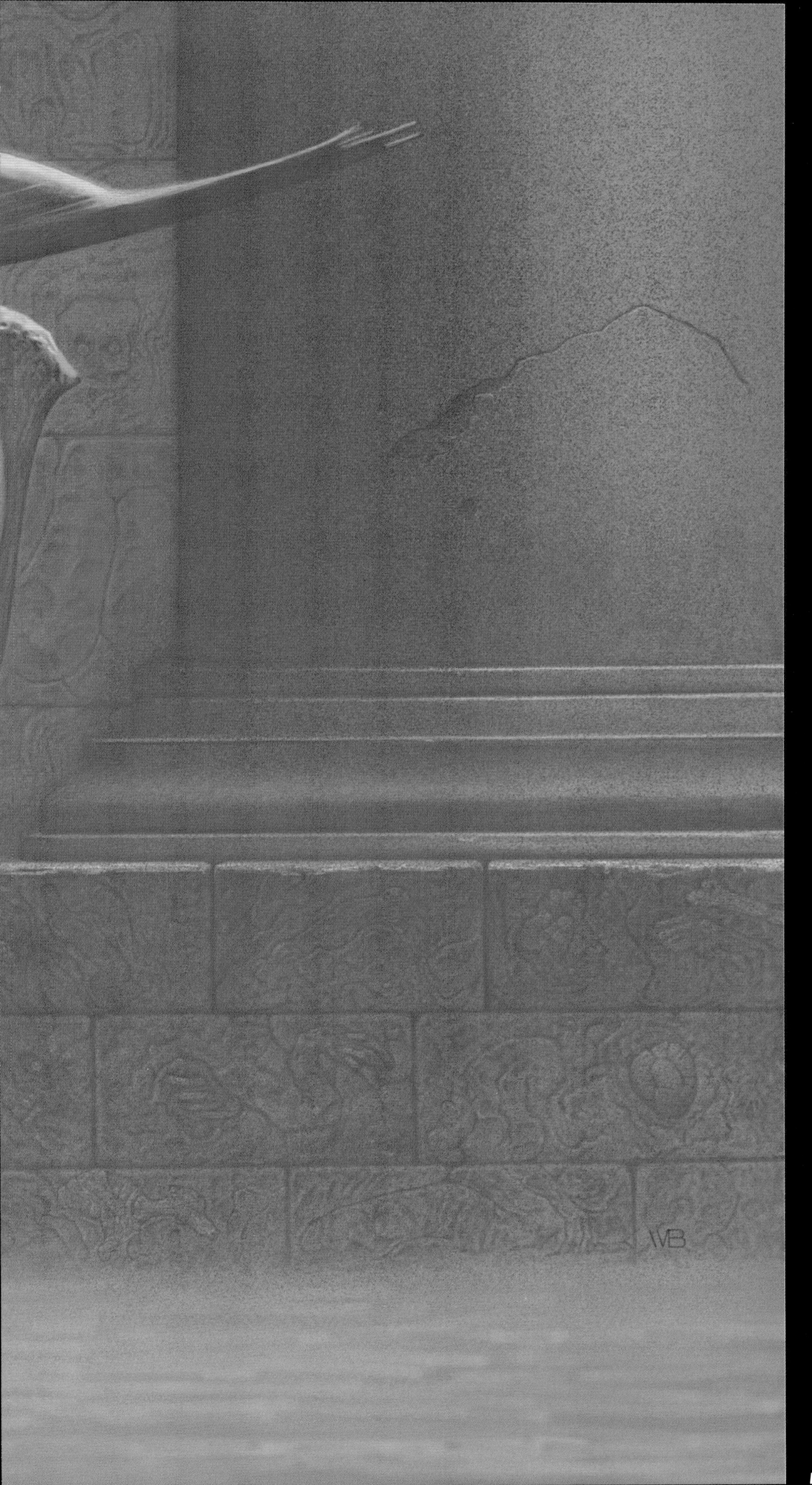
Parasite

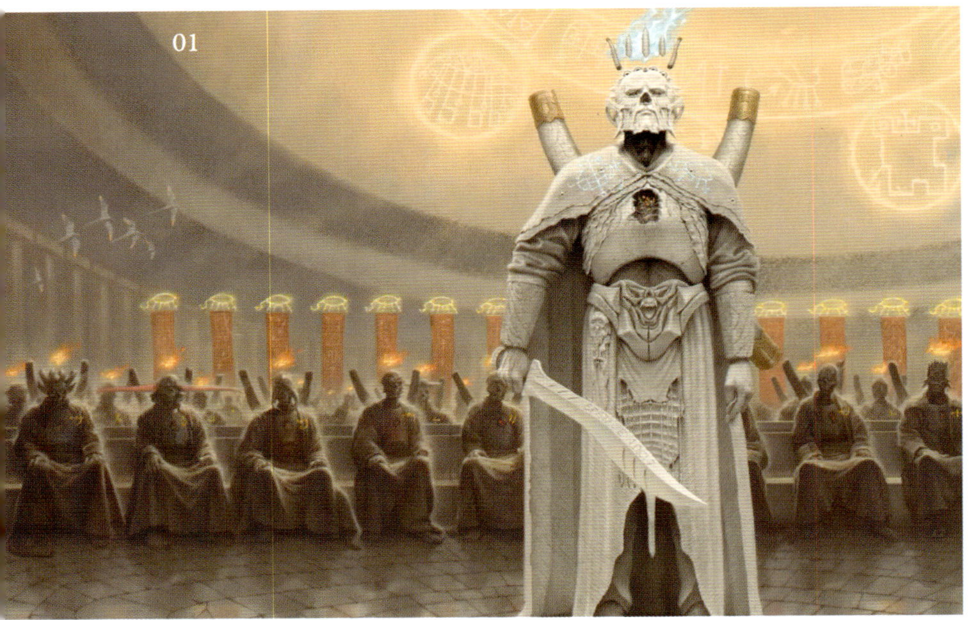

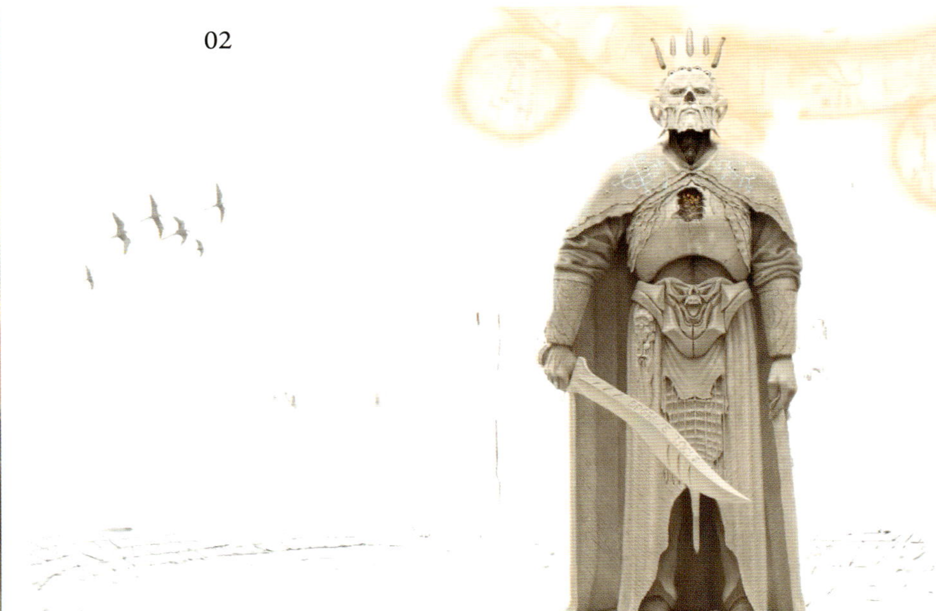

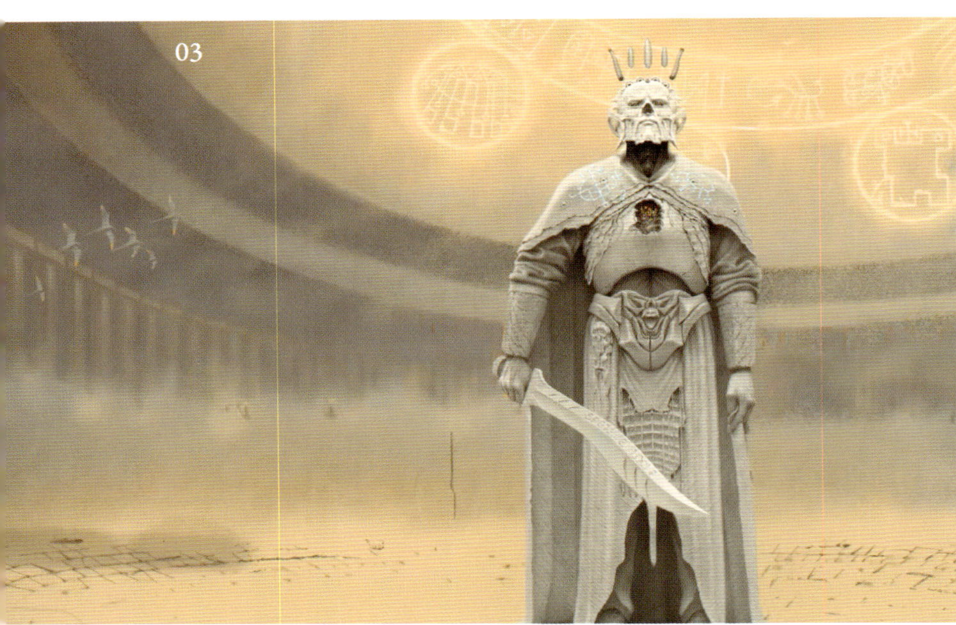

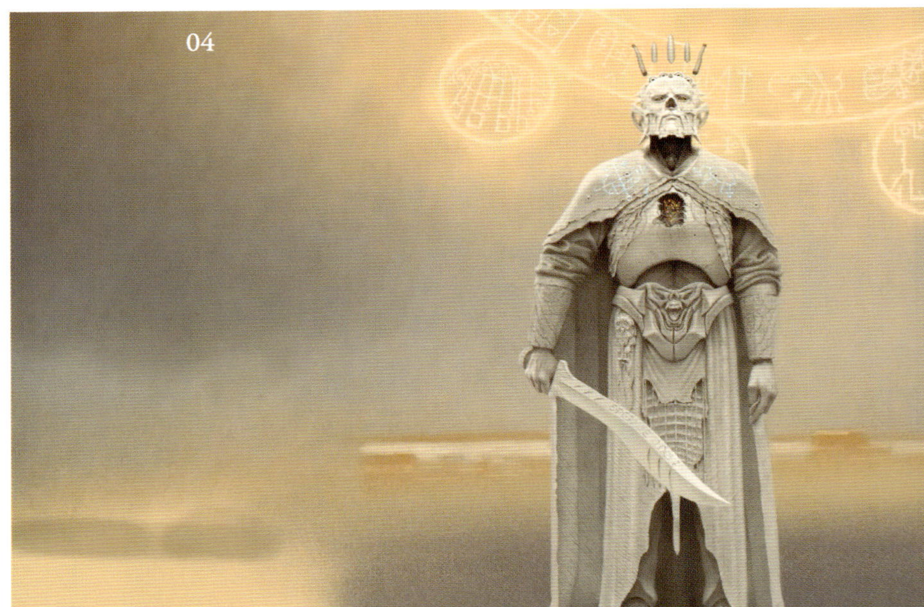

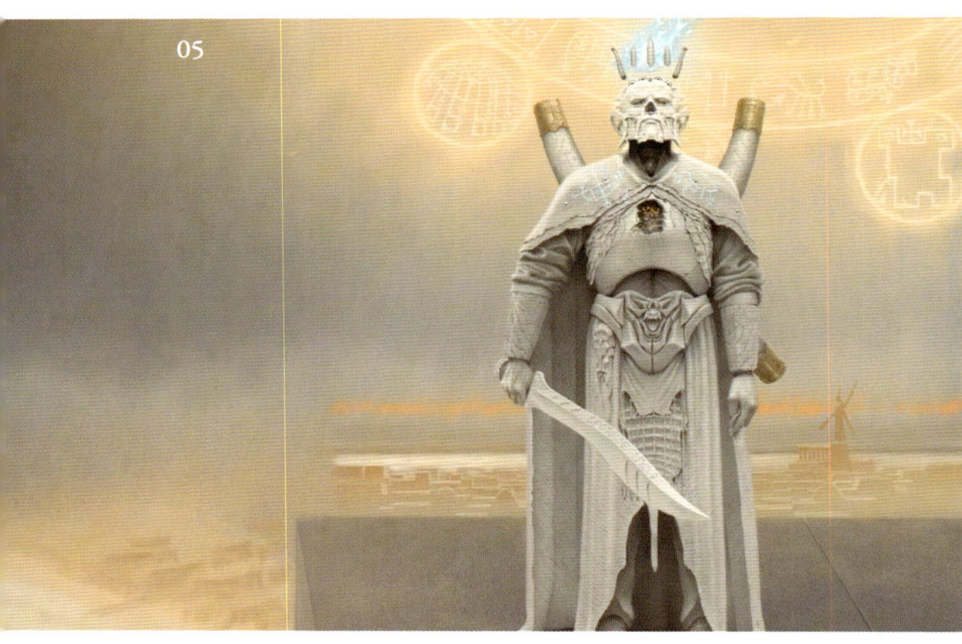

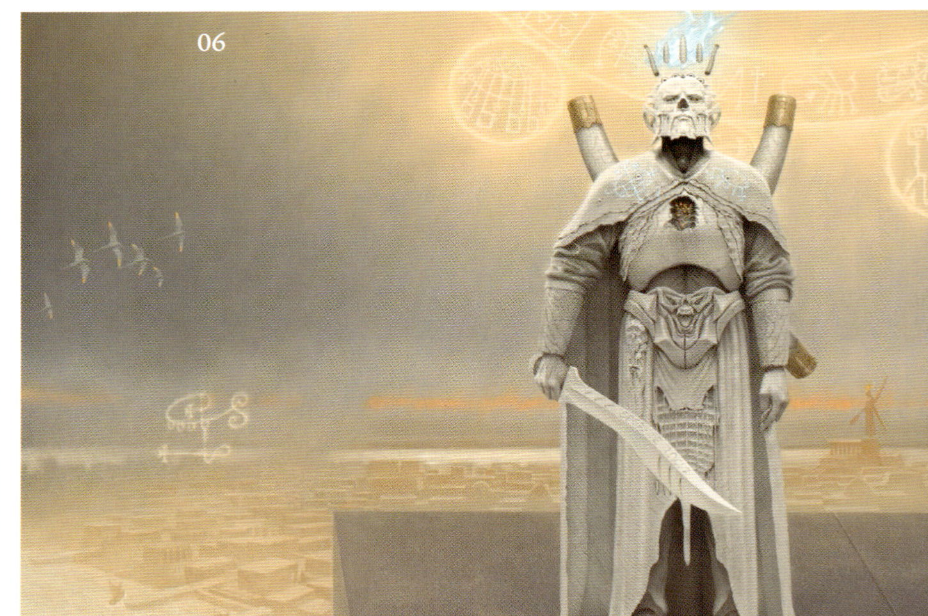

01 On rare occasions, I decide to completely revise a pre-existing painting. Here, the original did not work for me for various reasons.

02 Because the main figure was mostly completed on a separate layer, I decided to remove most of the underlying layers, leaving certain elements – the flying abyssals and the huge floating sigil – for future work. The blue flame and wings stumps were also on separate layers.

03 At first, I thought I might simplify the background, leaving the vast domed ceiling intact.

04 But I decided to completely revise the concept, leaving only the main figure from the original painting. Instead of an interior setting, I decided upon a huge panorama.

05 I began to lay out the distant city and even more distant river, before painting in the platform the main figure is standing upon and wrapping the river around the city.

06 I added the flying abyssals from the older iteration, along with the floating sigils, then refined the buildings of the city.

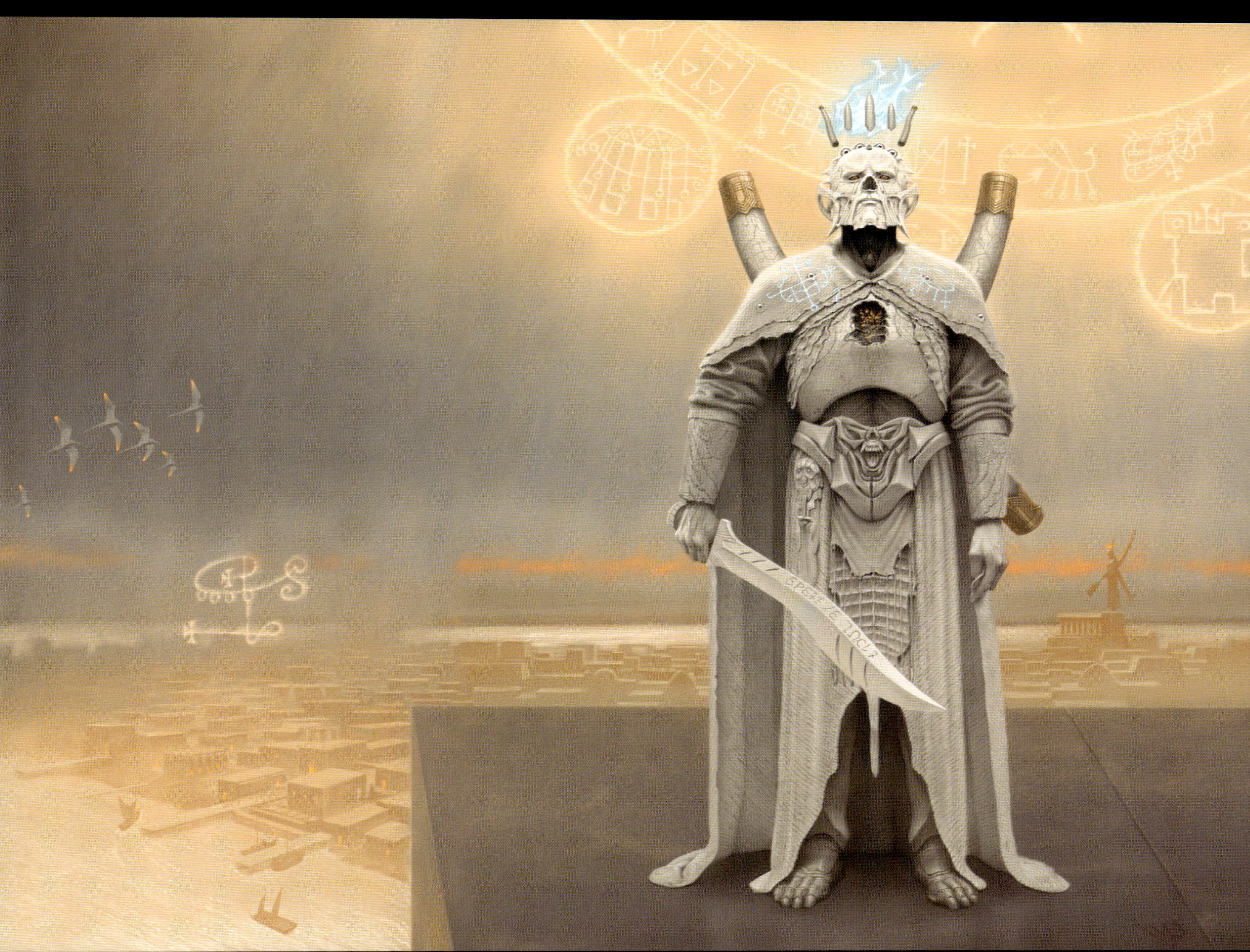

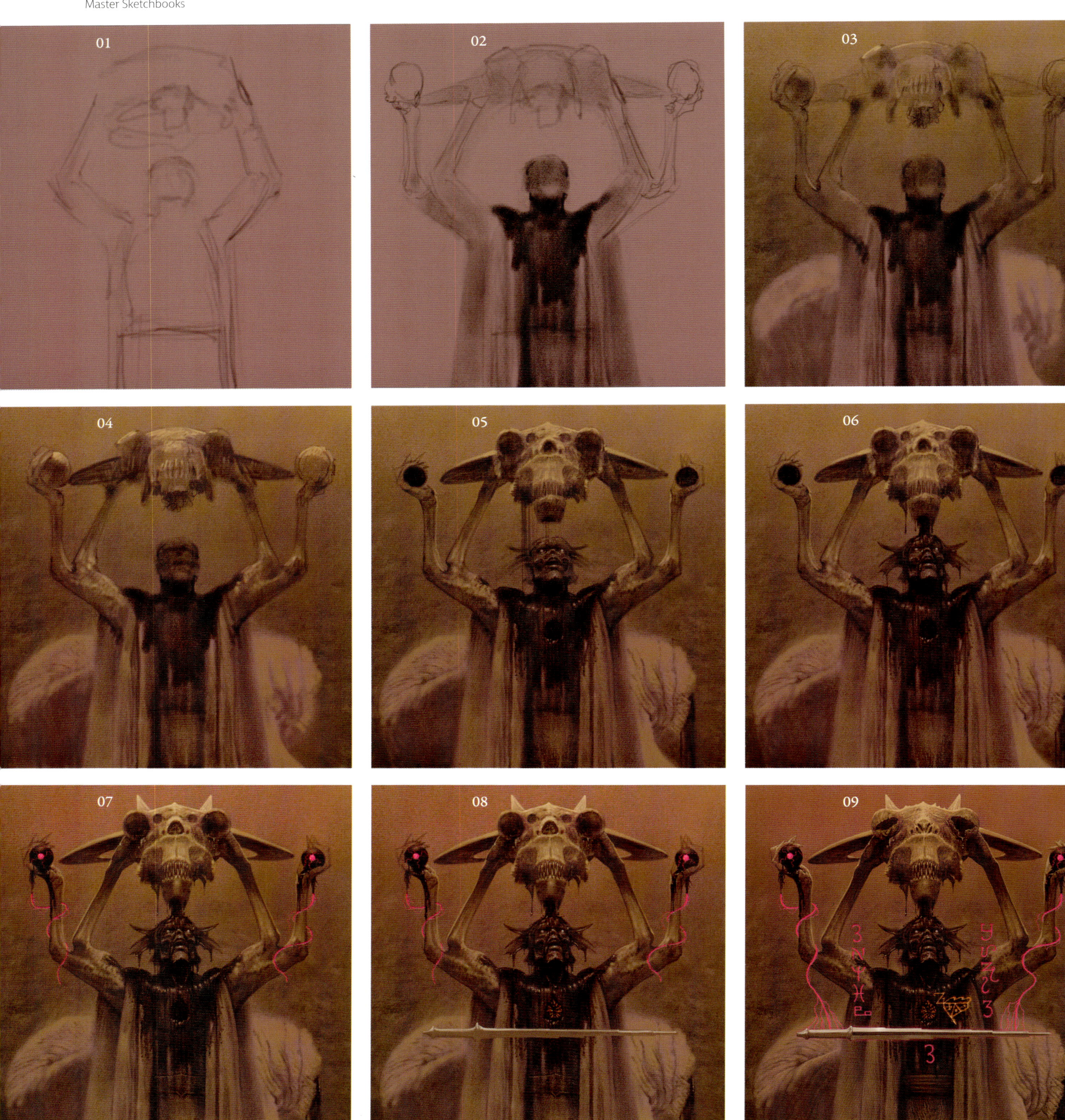

01 On a layer above the background tone, I began by sketching the main figure.

02 I added more ideas – additional arms, skull, and orbs – to the figure as the first indication of the figure's blood-covered torso.

03 After roughly applying the background, I added the form of the kneeling creature behind the figure.

04 I then solidified the forms using lights and darks on a separate layer.

05 Next, I sharpened concepts and elements, before exploring the skull's form on multiple layers. I then drew in various details.

06 Here I focused on resolving the demon's head.

07 Finally, I arrived at the design of the skull. I then worked on detail throughout the figure and the background creature, before lighting the eye-orbs and adding lightning in magenta.

08 I designed the sword on a separate layer.

09 I refined the hands, eyes, and skull. On another layer, I finished the painting by adding the floating glyphs in magenta.

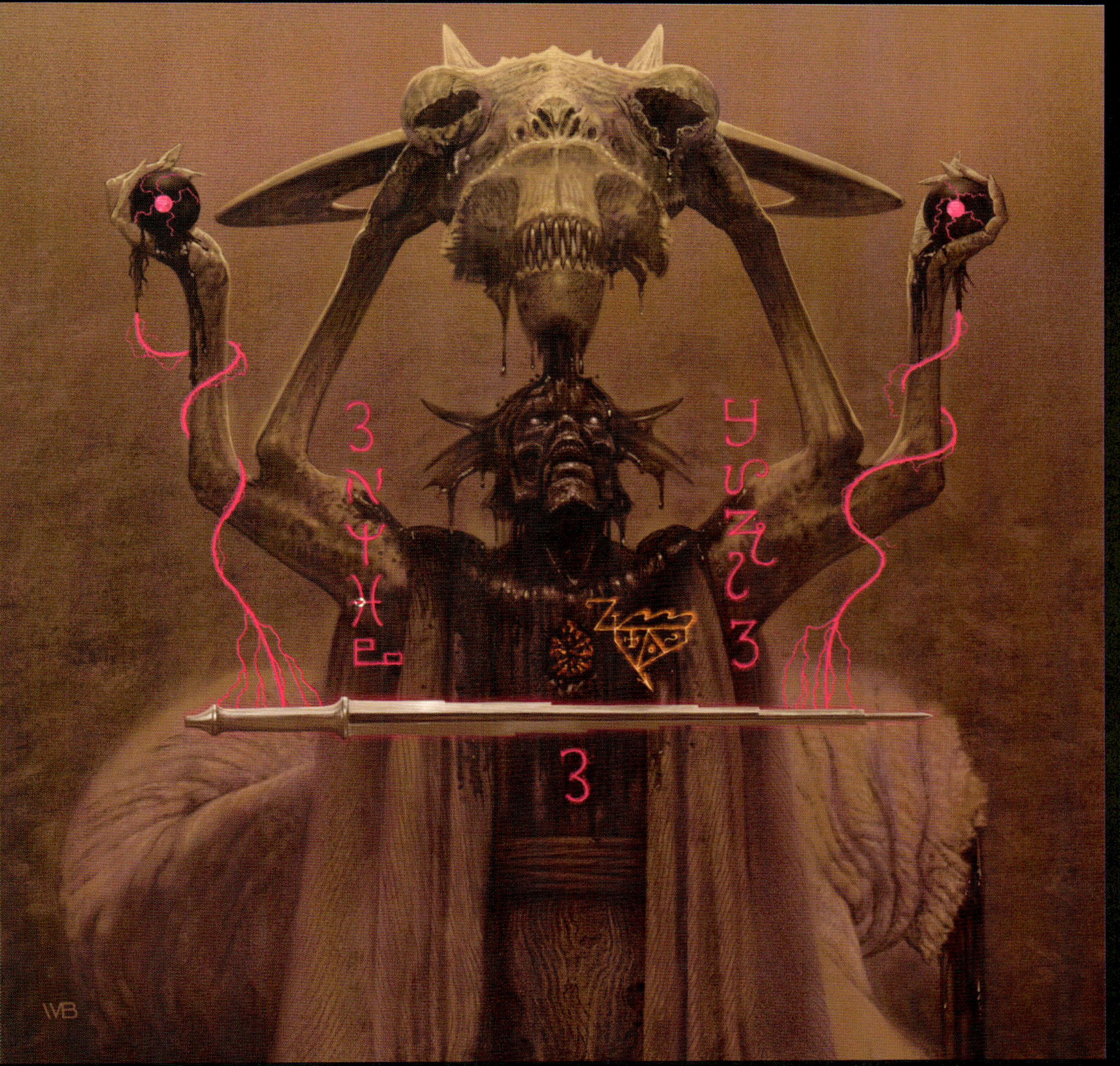

Transmuting the Sword

Darrell Warner

Agnetta, working drawing

Young fairies are a mischievous bunch and are sworn to wear bells about their neck to warn elders of their presence. This is a stage two development drawing exploring the notion of what a mischievous fairy might look like. I decided to imbue a little narrative and backstory... Agnetta appears rather miffed and sore at the prospect of being grounded after falling foul of a broken wing. Hence her sullen expression and attitude.

Part of my process is to make an initial drawing and then photocopy it multiple times to explore variants on a theme. By doing so I can iron out any design, costume, or character issues going forward. I tend to develop ideas organically according to brief and my design instructions.

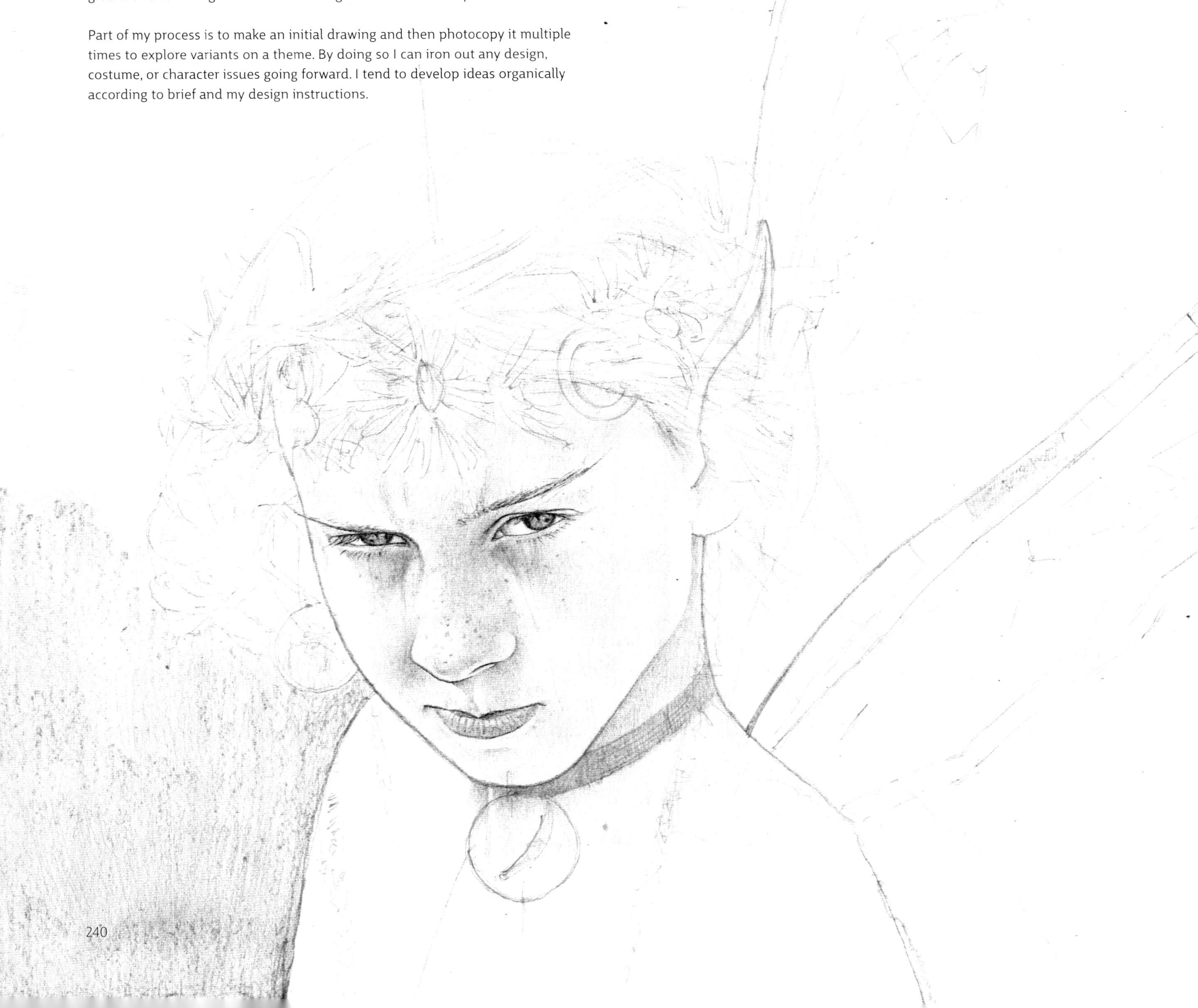

CHARACTER/COSTUME CONCEPT ARTIST & ILLUSTRATOR
darrellwarner.co.uk

FROM ILLUSTRATION TO FILM

I'm a traditional artist who specializes in both figurative watercolour and pencil, with a major focus on costume concept art for the film industry. Upon graduating from art school in 1984, I jointly began a co-operative illustration studio in the Cotswolds, England, and proceeded to spend the first sixteen years of my freelance career producing high-end quality prescriptive illustration for the advertising, publishing, and editorial markets. My client base was wide and varied, including Porsche, Williams F1, British Airways, and Intel. Following six very successful years, in the early 1990s I struck out and established my own studio. Here I began to traverse into other areas of the illustration profession, from publishing and editorial to privately commissioned fine art. I illustrated titles from *Frankenstein* to *Jekyll and Hyde*, *Wuthering Heights* to the *Bible*.

In the late 1990s I stepped very tentatively into the film industry. After a few smaller projects, my first big recognition came from my work on *Pirates of the Caribbean: The Curse of the Black Pearl*. I have remained true to what I believe in and stuck to traditional media throughout. It appears I'm an anomaly in an industry that celebrates technology and, as such, have since become known as 'the bloke that draws' and seemingly named 'the graphite gangster'. My main area of focus within film is centred around costume and character development, with a good deal of costume illustration along the way. Time has flown by and, with some fifty-plus major film titles under my belt and an amazing array of talented costume designers worked for, I have found myself to be reasonably established and highly thought of in the industry.

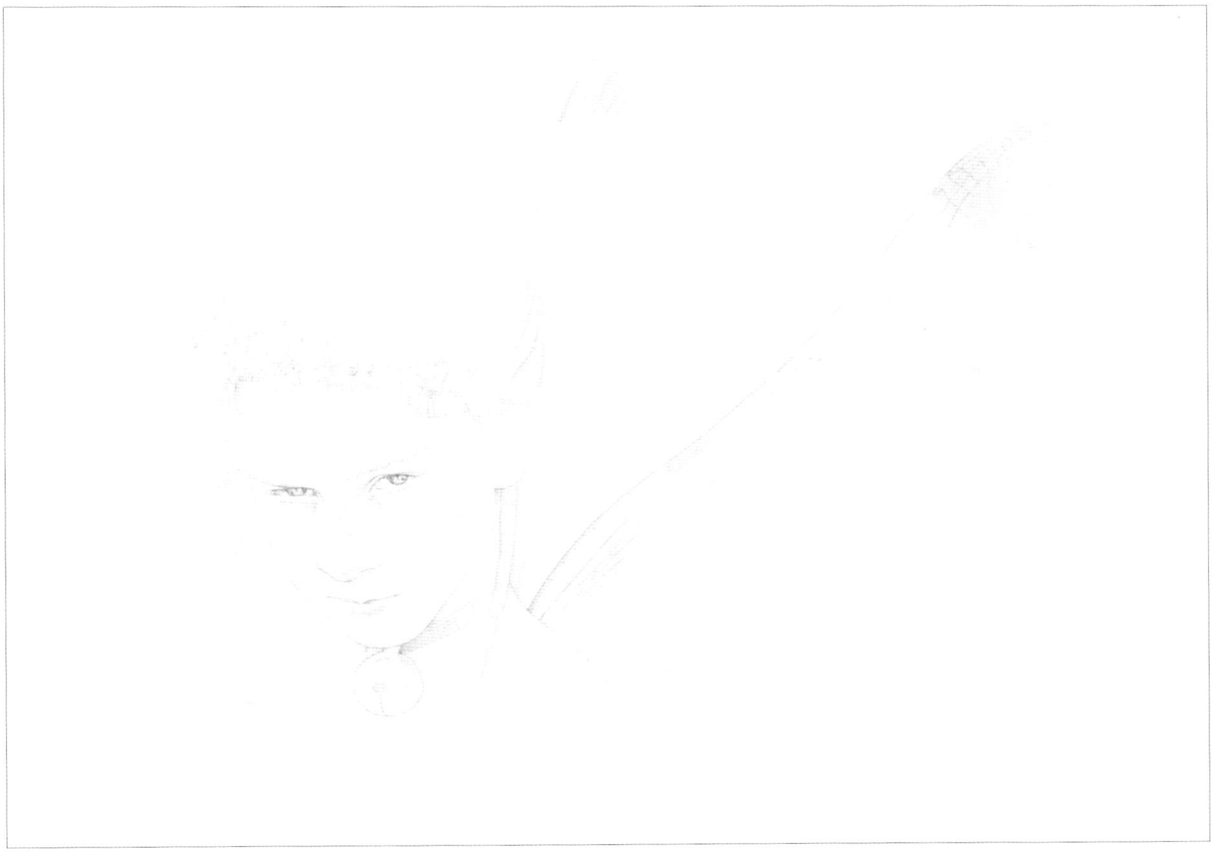

Agnetta, final drawing

A slightly more refined and accurate drawing. After working through the previous iteration, I ended up with an image ready for presentation. At this stage, if approved, this would likely go forward to being a form of blueprint, giving the entire department an idea as to where and how the character should look. For the best part, it is often only a flavour, and any number of visual decisions will have to be made by the various costume artisans employed to bring this to life along the way.

PERSONAL PROJECTS

As well as the commercial side of my artistic practice, I also continue to pursue my own painting projects. Although all my initial training and early painting was in oils, for the past forty-plus years I've focused on pushing the preconceived perception of what watercolour is. I featured in the first series of Sky Arts Portrait Artist of the Year in 2013 and have won a number of British Art Society Awards for various paintings. I've also become a semi-regular exhibitor at various Federation of British Artists society shows, when time allows.

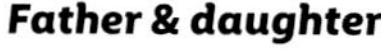

Father & daughter

I wanted to explore the idea of a double portrait by way of playing with composition. This is a sketch that I developed over the course of a number of evenings, embracing shape and some aspect of pattern. The sense of weight of line is critical in making this work.

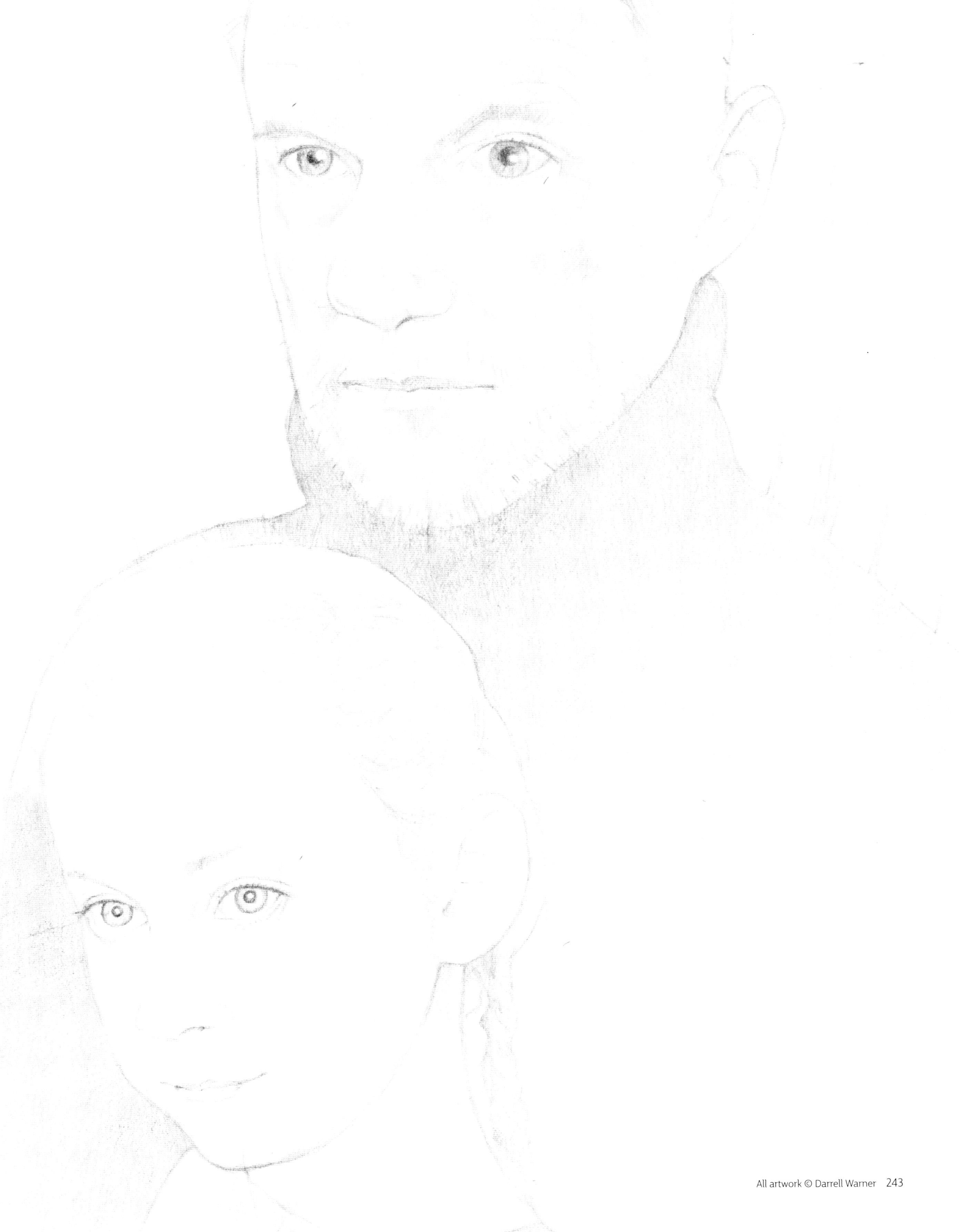

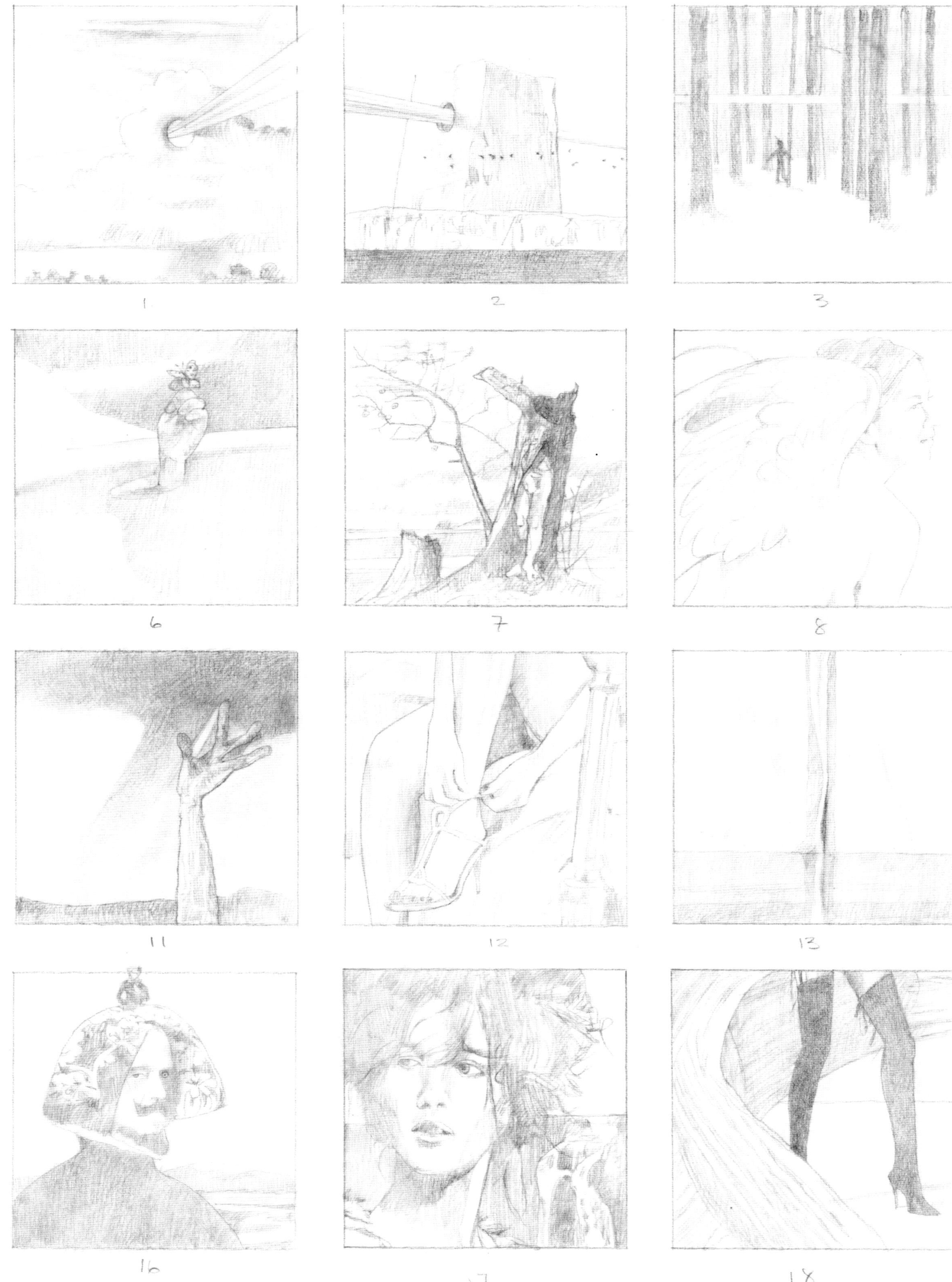

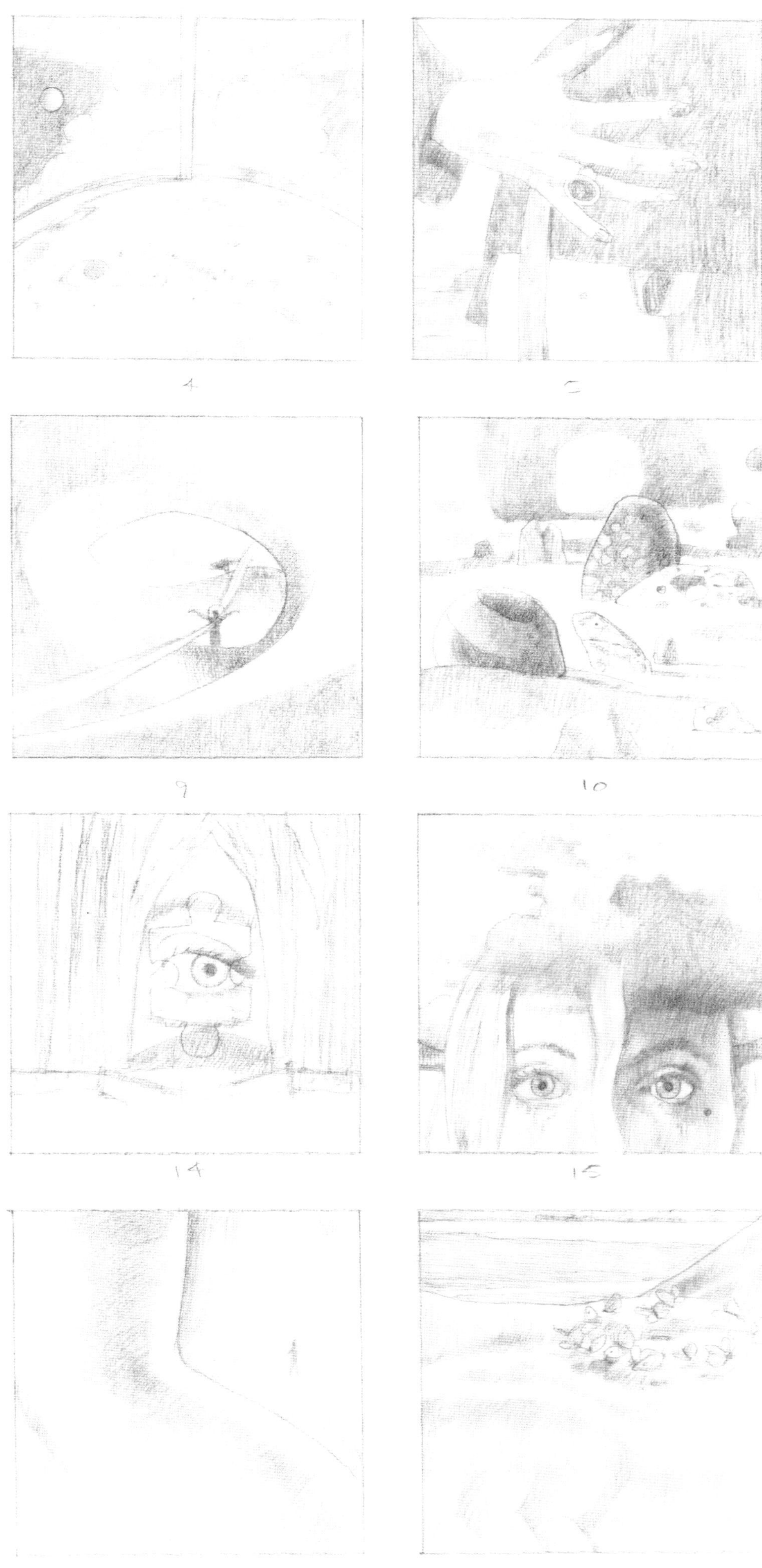

Surrealist thumbnails

Gridded and massed exploration of surrealist ideas. I'll often draw 30–40 mm grids, photocopy them multiple times, then simply construct or sketch down thoughts. In this case, the concepts are fairly well worked through.

Valvehead, exploratory sketch

I wanted to explore the notion of a future cyborg subculture, loosely based on present-day Japanese subcultures. (The fact that there are young people who continue to dress and emulate Elvis Presley fascinates me). Therefore I thought, what if cyborgs, or similar futuristic beings, were captivated with 'analogue tech', hence the notion of 'valveheads'. They openly exhibit that old tech, which becomes inherently part of who and what they are. Given their fascination with the past and being alienated from the natural world, 'educational pop-up charging stations' can be found about the cities, which cyborgs can visit to recharge, while also being exposed to some form of past alien (to them!) lifeforms. Insect-based charge stations prove popular and intriguing.

This is a second-stage working drawing, exploring shapes and sense of style. I referred to a mood board of references I thought would enhance the story I was attempting to tell. For the most part I rarely set about drawing any form of background or location, simply because my job is to sell the character and costume. By imbuing some form of narrative, I can engage the viewer. Plus, it makes it a little more interesting to execute on my part, rather than a simple flat-on diagrammatic illustration. In doing so, I attempt to make the whole design very naturalistic in balance.

CAREER HIGHS

Working on the first _Pirates of the Caribbean_ film was an amazing experience and one I hold dear to my heart, for little was I to know how extraordinary that project would be. It subsequently became great exposure for me going forward. The fact that I have now worked on all five films in the _Pirates of the Caribbean_ franchise to date seems surreal, and honouring giants of the illustration world, such as Howard Pyle and N. C. Wyeth, along the way has been an absolute pleasure. Working on the recent _Wicked_ film has been a similar experience, if not more so. Once again, working within a costume department with visionary costume designer Paul Tazewell and an array of sublime artisans has been another career highlight.

With regards to personal painting, a number of pieces have heralded new landmarks over the years. For example, watercolour paintings that have become slightly out-of-body experiences simply because of the affect the images have had on people, and seeing them subsequently go on to have this other life beyond my mind and hand that created them. As paintings, they go on to have an aura of their own; something one often strives for as a painter.

I began to enter painting competitions in earnest back in 2013 while balancing commercial and personal work, often failing to complete even one personal painting in any given year. The pieces I did complete and enter, however, have had moderate success. Although not many have achieved recognition over the years, winning the Best in Show at the Society of Equestrian Artists (2013) and the Award for Excellence in Watercolour from the Royal Society of Painters (2023) were amazing moments. My painting _Crucifixion_ being accepted for the Leigh Yawkey Woodson 'Birds in Art' that same year was the icing on the cake. I have also been awarded an Art Directors Guild Award for my work on Marvel's _Black Panther_.

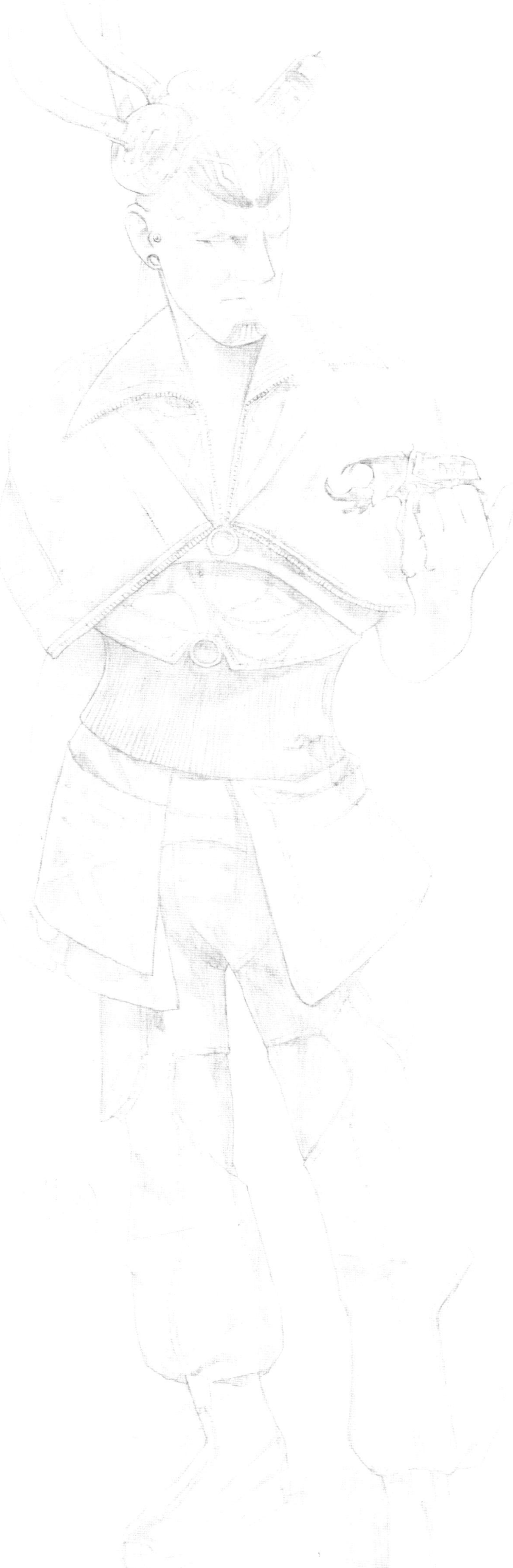

Valvehead, final drawing

Final refined drawing, adding tone, shadows, and much more detail. With this type of image, line weight becomes a focus and remains an important way for me to make the figure appear more three-dimensional. I rarely conjure the correct attitude, stance, and posture for the figure directly out of my head and straight onto paper. Once I have an idea or vision in my mind that I'd like to achieve and know will sell the character, I simply ask someone to pose, directing them accordingly. I then use those photographs as reference. This practice is very important, as it saves time attempting to figure out and draw the underlying figure from scratch. Plus, the photographs provide an exactness upon which I can focus on the job in hand. Much of what we do as concept artists is about efficiency. At the end of the day, time costs money, so the quickest route to a finished image should always be paramount.

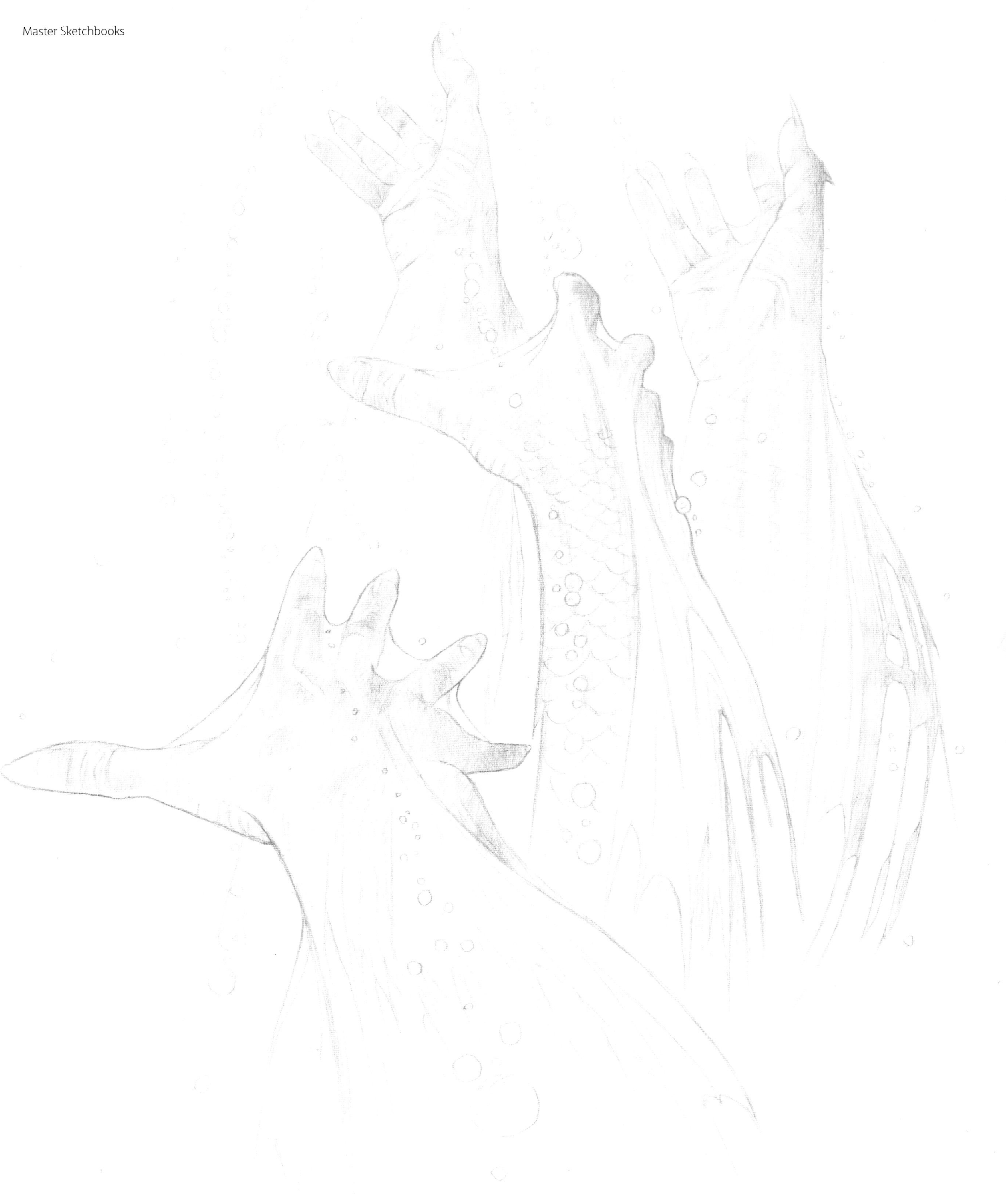

Mermaid arms and Pirate, sketches

Mermaid arms stretching up towards
the sea's surface, alongside a piratical
sea dog. In this instance I sought to
create both a presence and boldness
of stance, while employing a dramatic
angle and attitude to sell his character.
In addition, I added drama with his
windblown cape and scudding gulls.

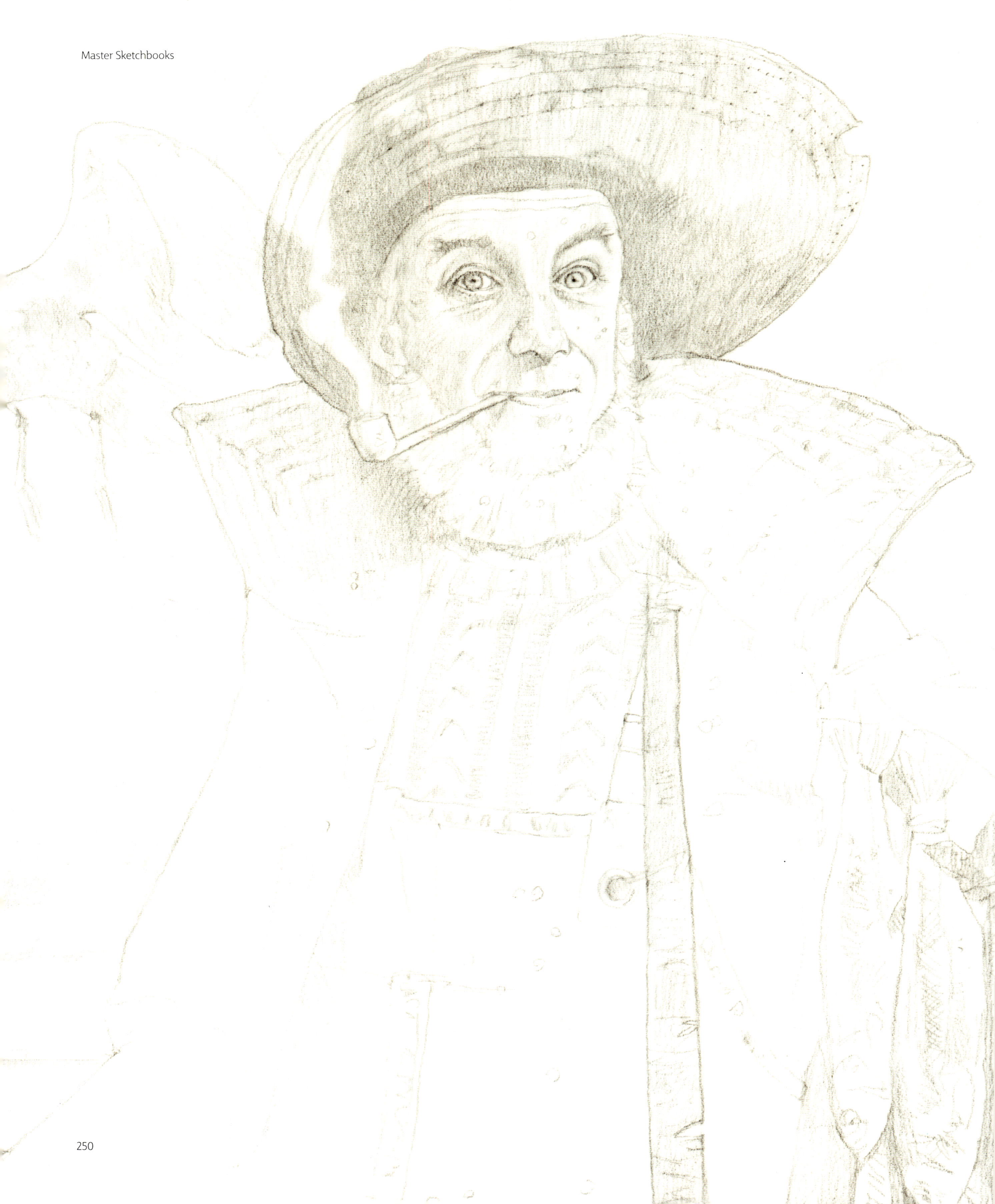

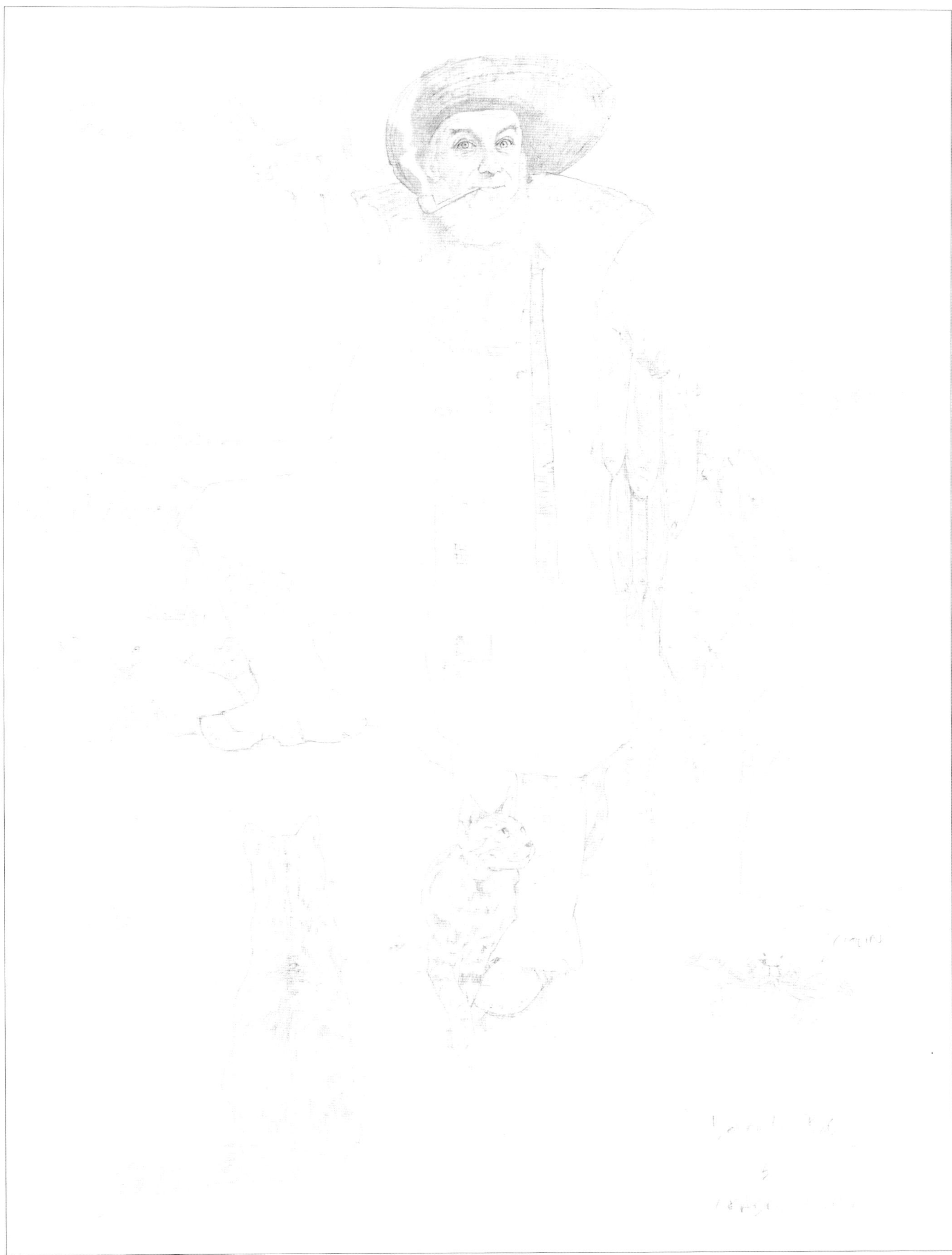

Barnacle Bob, working drawing

An explorational drawing, attempting to work out how to best tell the story. I wanted to project this notion of Bob as a slightly 'out of the back of a boat' seller of pilfered fish. I'm a big Norman Rockwell fan, so to create a humorous element, I developed the drawing by introducing cats and vying seagulls. Crabby Colin was sketched in soon after.

REMAINING TRUE TO TRADITIONAL MEDIUMS

My sketchbooks vary from leather-bound A4 and A3 cartridge pads to handy A5-sized pads and scraps of paper. I draw a lot on photocopy paper too, as I often photocopy multiple basic figure silhouettes and proceed to make working drawings so as to configure garments, while continually assessing whether what I am sketching will work. I particularly like recycled photocopy paper as it has a good deal of tooth and, being cheap, has no preciousness attached. As a rule, I don't like textured or weighty paper in a sketchbook and typically veer towards smooth surfaces. I use tracing paper a good deal, as it affords me the opportunity to view ideas like layers. Much of my work is museum-grade archived, with both drawings and paintings placed in acid-free sleeves and then stored in archive boxes by project.

Generally speaking, seventy to eighty per cent of my work for film is hand-drawn graphite. I use graphite (4–9B), chalks, charcoal, pen and ink, fineliners, and Biro. My desire to remain true to traditional mediums makes me an anomaly in the industry these days.

I use tracing paper
a good deal, as
it affords me
the opportunity
to view ideas
like layers

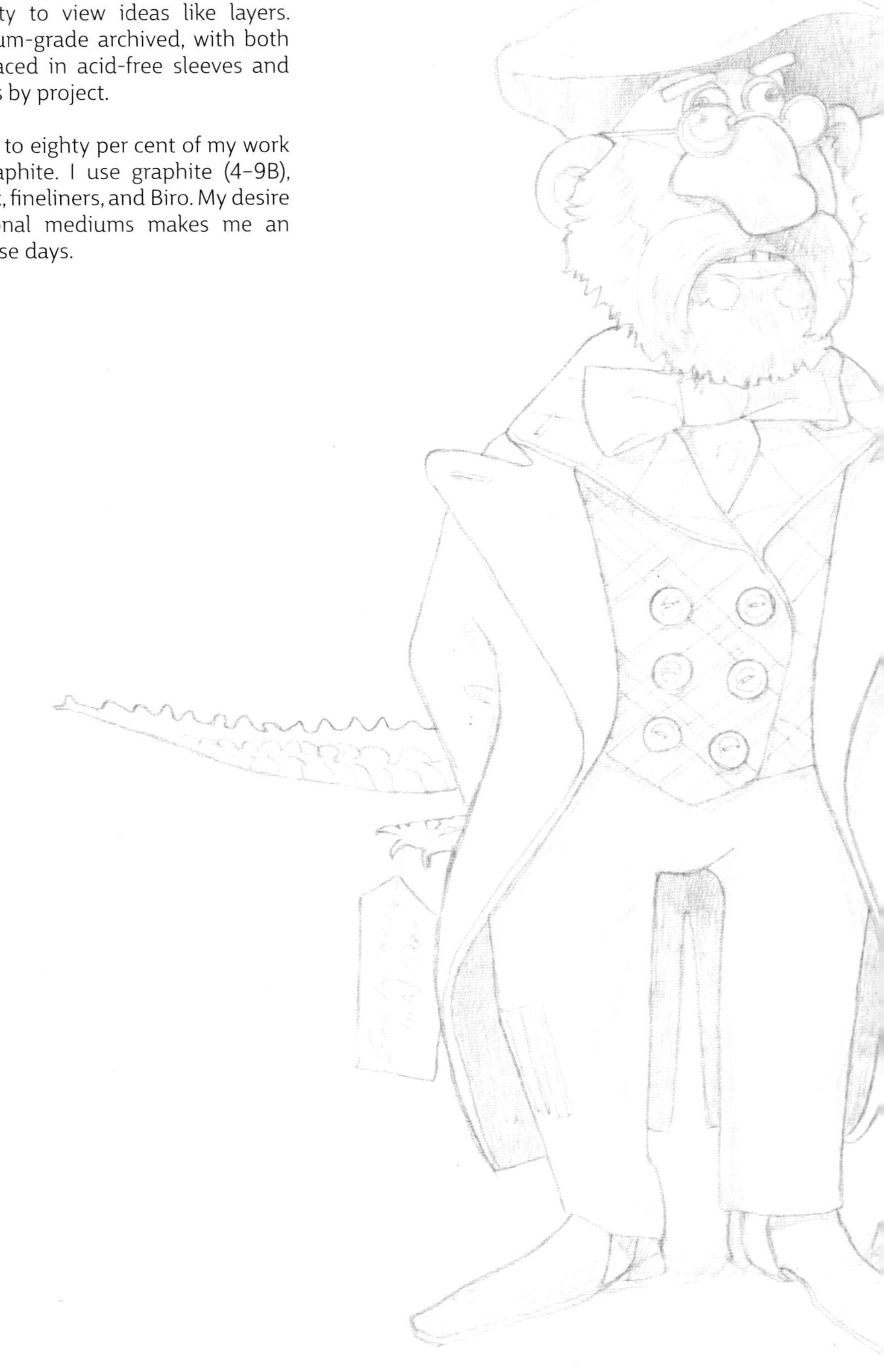

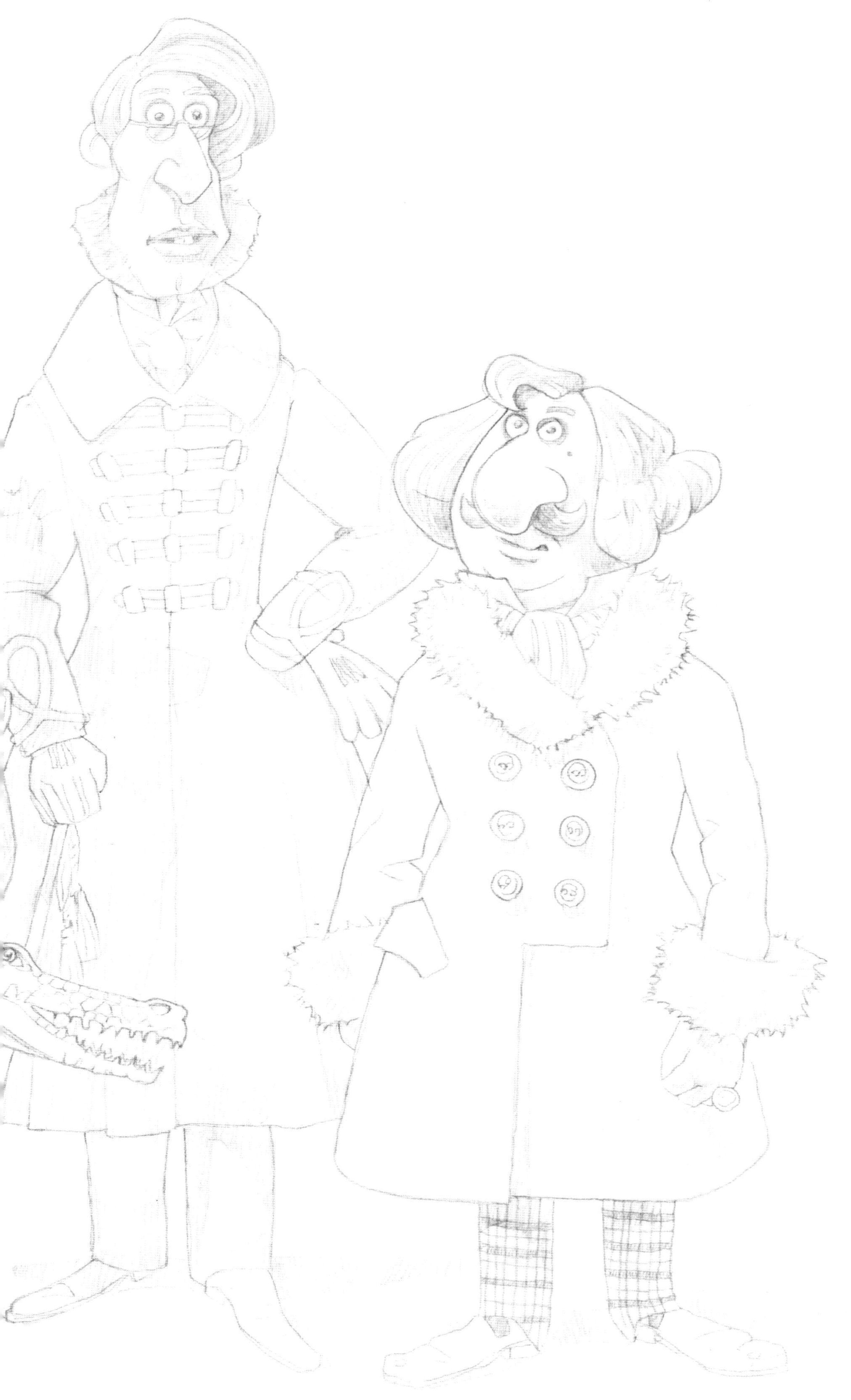

The Victorian Scientists, sketch

A stylized development drawing
exploring profile and character.
By adding in the stuffed alligator prop,
I was able to hint at the Victorians need
to both collect and stuff animals.

 253

Hendricks, pencil study I

A proposed portrait for a client some
years ago.

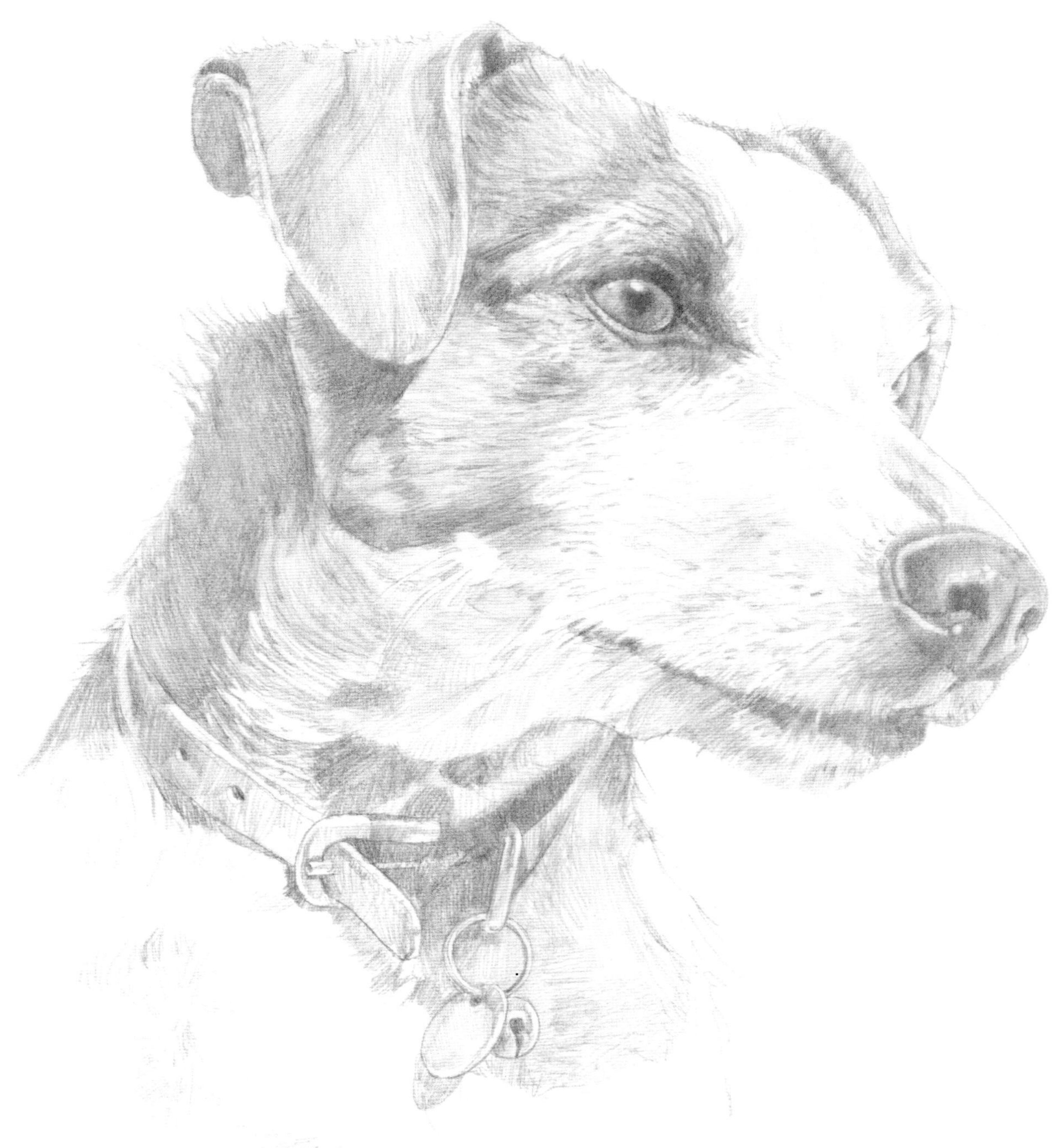

HOW TO VISUALLY SOLVE A PROBLEM

I used sketchbooks in my youth and throughout art school as it was compulsory, but that practice tailed off as soon as I became a freelancer. Much of my early career was spent as a journeyman illustrator, initially based out of a collective illustration studio. The jobs were very prescriptive for the most part, orchestrated by an art director from an ad agency or publishing house. I was employed because my style of illustrating was what they required. As it was the client's vision I was being commissioned to illustrate, my ideas were not usually called for. I got back into sketchbooks in the late eighties when I felt I needed to re-engage my own thoughts in order to find solutions.

I draw initial thumbnails through to finished drawings in my sketchbooks. It's about working out and analysing how best to sell or visually solve a problem. It's imperative to work out what sells a concept or idea and what I need to do to get that across – whether that's a simple pose in pencil, focused costume vernacular, or a fairly concise and finished drawing.

My paid jobs do and don't inform my sketchbook practice. My brain works in many compartmental ways, so projects often facilitate a certain way of thinking and drawing. I'll go from horribly loose, often nonsensical mark-making that only I can understand, to highly finished drawings, often with notations. As I draw all day for work, I very rarely sketch outside of my work hours, as I have no desire to further tax my brain.

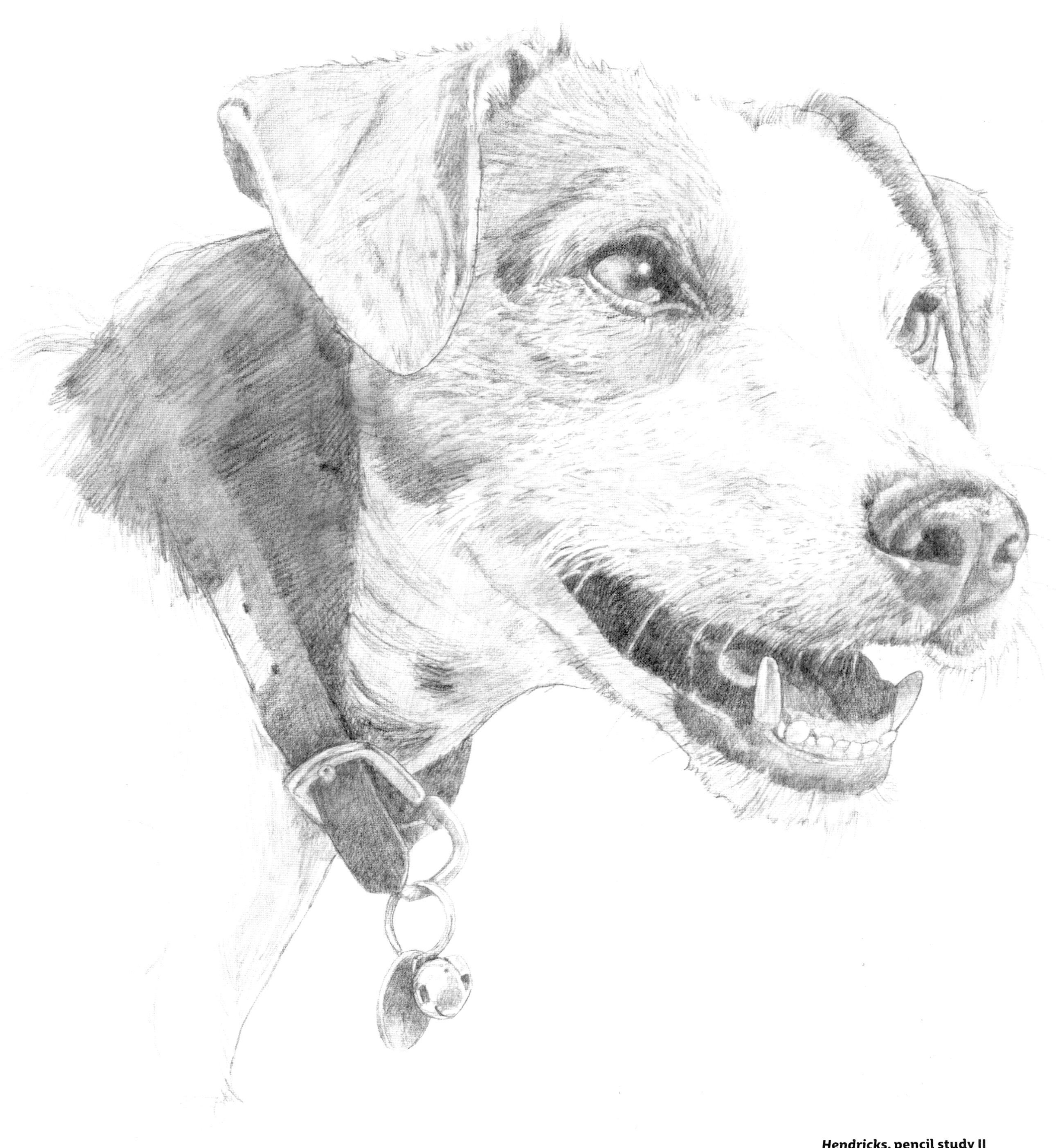

Hendricks, pencil study II

Here I was attempting to capture the
character of the dog.

WORKING MANUALS OF SELF

Keeping sketchbooks is a good barometer of one's creativity and ideas. I may go months not sketching, but then, out of the blue, tap into some creative thought that will deliver endless ideas, filling numerous pages with sketches. If you looked at all my sketchbooks over time, you would see the maturing and development of ideas, giving an insight into what it takes to be an artist. I certainly don't use sketchbooks just to practise. Nor am I one for sitting in a cafe and capturing people about their daily lives. If anything, I may take a photo with my phone or make a note to work from later. I work a lot from such notes.

I find the best aspect of keeping sketchbooks is the ability to review ideas, whether from yesterday, four days ago, or four years since. Nothing is wasted when an idea sketched long ago provides a solution to a present problem you're attempting to solve. I also love the fact that sketchbooks are working manuals of self. For the best part, my sketchbooks are functional volumes of potential ideas – a maelstrom of everything. Letters to friends, ideas, sketches, my present bank balance, garden design ideas, studio ideas, home extension ideas, promotional ideas, lists...

> Keeping sketchbooks is a good barometer of one's creativity and ideas

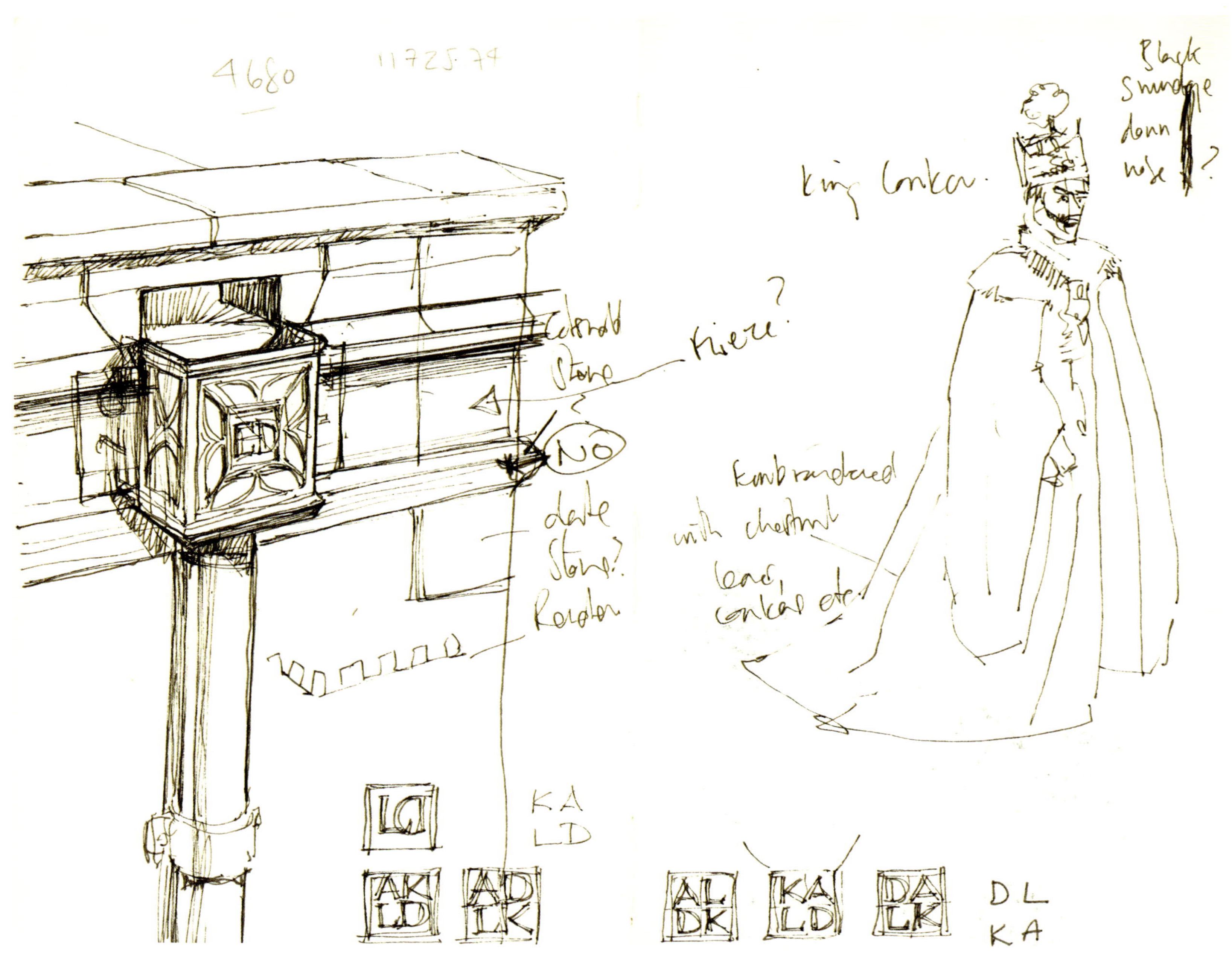

***King Conker,* exploratory sketches**
Brief 0.5mm fineliner sketches based on a self-initiated story in one of many Moleskins.

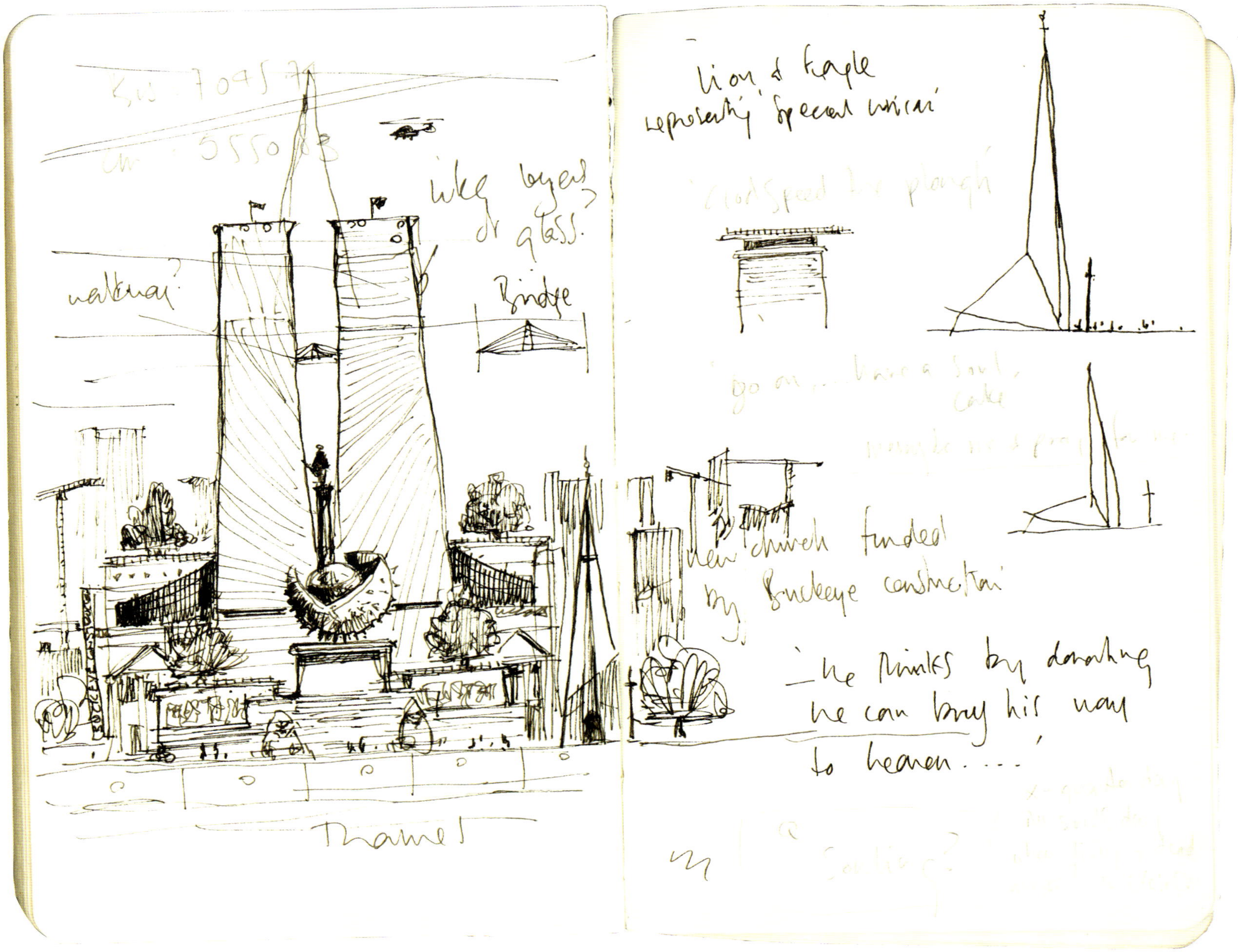

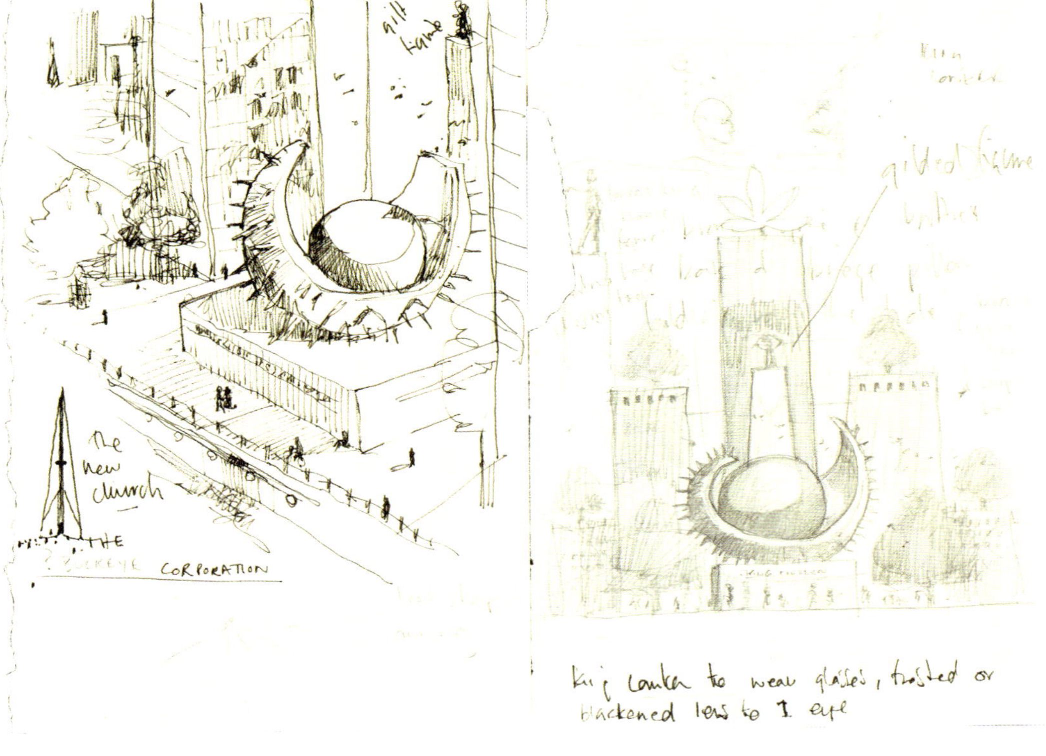

King Conker, environment sketches
Exploring a more cohesive vernacular
and scale of visual elements.

King Conker, world-building sketches
Further sketches in fineliner and pencil,
pushing ideas of architecture, scale, and
environment design.

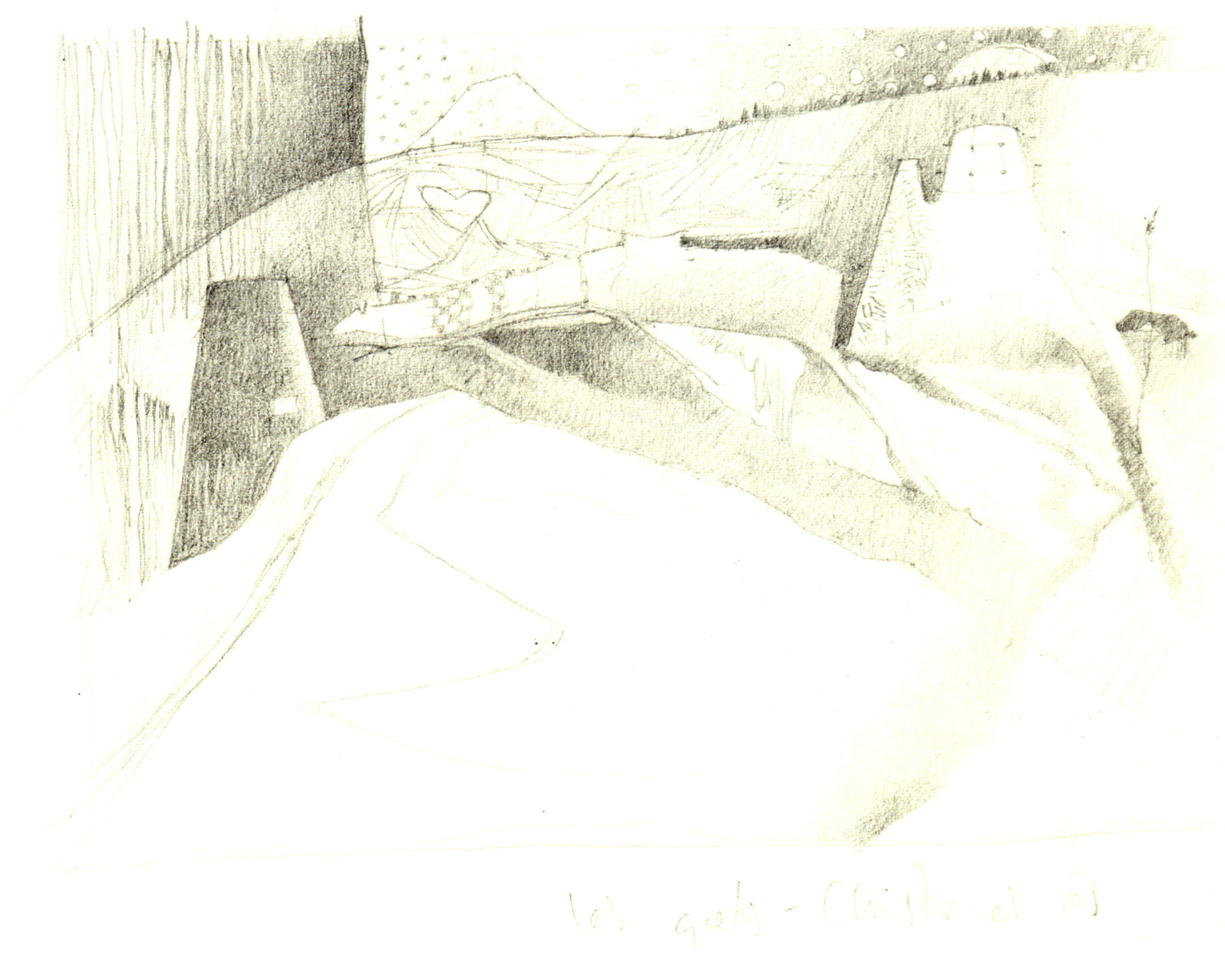

Les Gets

A heavily stylized development sketch
for a proposed painting or pastel, drawn
one evening while away for Christmas
in the Alps.

Nothing is wasted when
an idea sketched long ago
provides a solution to a
present problem you're
attempting to solve

The Enclosure

This is a roughing out of an idea based on or around caged birds. The focus here is a rook, a member of the corvid family often viewed as an open farmland/grassland bird common in the UK. Simply playing with design and composition, while notations remind and steer me towards further possible notions.

White Squaw of the Blackfoot Indians, under-drawing

An under-drawing of a silhouetted figure, with measurement and axis lines. By starting each costumed figure drawing in this way, I can address critical measurements and anatomical axes in order to dress the figure as I proceed.

White Squaw of the Blackfoot Indians, working drawing

Much of what I do as a costume concept artist is to propose and explore interesting profiles. Here I analysed costume shape and vernacular, attempting to stay true to what the Blackfoot wore. I thought it would be interesting to sketch an outsider who is accepted as part of the tribe. In this case, the simple headdress is very important in conveying the culture. Drawing a wing in her right hand gives her status within the community.

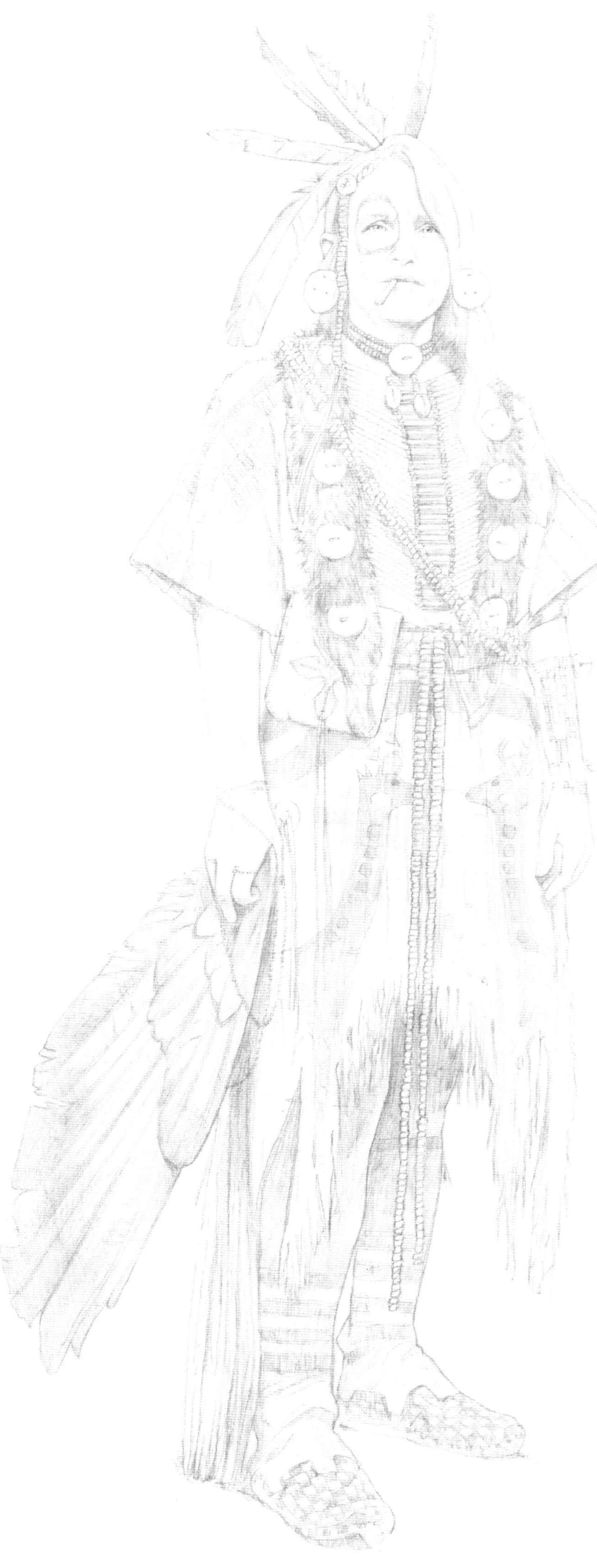

INSPIRATIONS & INFLUENCES

My inspiration mainly comes from other artists, and there are so many extraordinary artists out there! A number of contemporary practitioners that strike chords at the moment include Justin Mortimer and Nicolas Uribe. I adore the way they go about their business. Jason Shawn Alexander is another, from the graphic-novel medium, and Bryce Cameron Liston from more of a traditional figurative-art background.

There are a number of artists I looked up to in my youth who influenced me in many ways; Americans like Bernie Fuchs and David Grove, plus Holbein, Ingres, and Andrew Wyeth. Ray Harris Ching was another who played a big part in my early drawing practice, going some way to steering me towards becoming an artist myself.

White Squaw of the Blackfoot Indians, final detailed drawing

By adding tone and developing the drawing, I brought texture and a certain amount of 'lived in' feeling to the final image. I dropped any notion of background, as I felt it was too distracting when trying to tell the story of the costume.

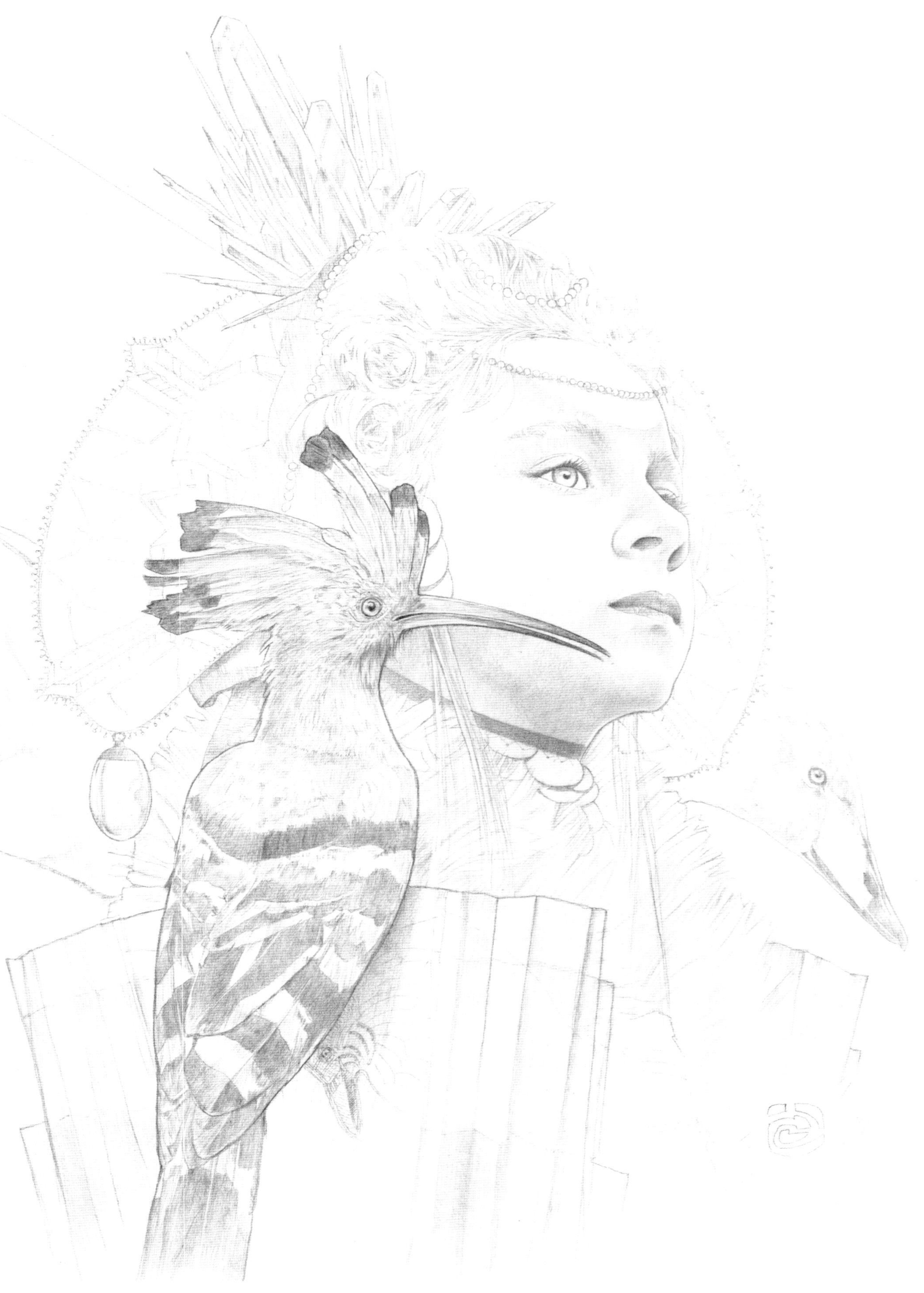

Princess Bewick of the Glaciervolk

The Glaciervolk is a story I've been developing for a number of years, as time allows. The idea behind it focuses on a number of civilisations who dwell on the glaciers and frozen tundra of the Artic. Four realms all vying for power to secure wealth and serve the crazed alternative human world. Princess Bewick is heir to and keeper of the natural world. She has the gift of beauty and kindness to all living things.

This sketch explores point of view. By selecting a lower eye level, looking up at the princess, I immediately elevate the status of the character, which is critical in selling her to the viewer. This sketch primarily functions as a starting point for the character and any number of sketches to follow. It is 'asking the question' of who and what she could be. This might be followed by further drawings exploring other profiles, adornments, or garment embellishments befitting her position.

Opposite page | *The legacy we leave for future generations*

After experiencing the effects of forest fires in Canada in 2017, I wanted to record the potential legacy this leaves on a rapidly heating world and future generations.

LEARN YOUR CRAFT WELL

My number-one piece of advice to artists just starting out would be to learn your craft well. Know your strengths and learn what it takes to make and visually sell an image. If you're impatient, find a style that works and excites you when you're young. Find a shorthand style that aids thinking. Explore genres and think outside the box, but always be informed by styles and ways of working that garner work. Stay true to yourself and what you believe in, while being brutally honest about your abilities, because you'll get found out very soon in this industry.

Know your strengths and learn what it takes to make and visually sell an image

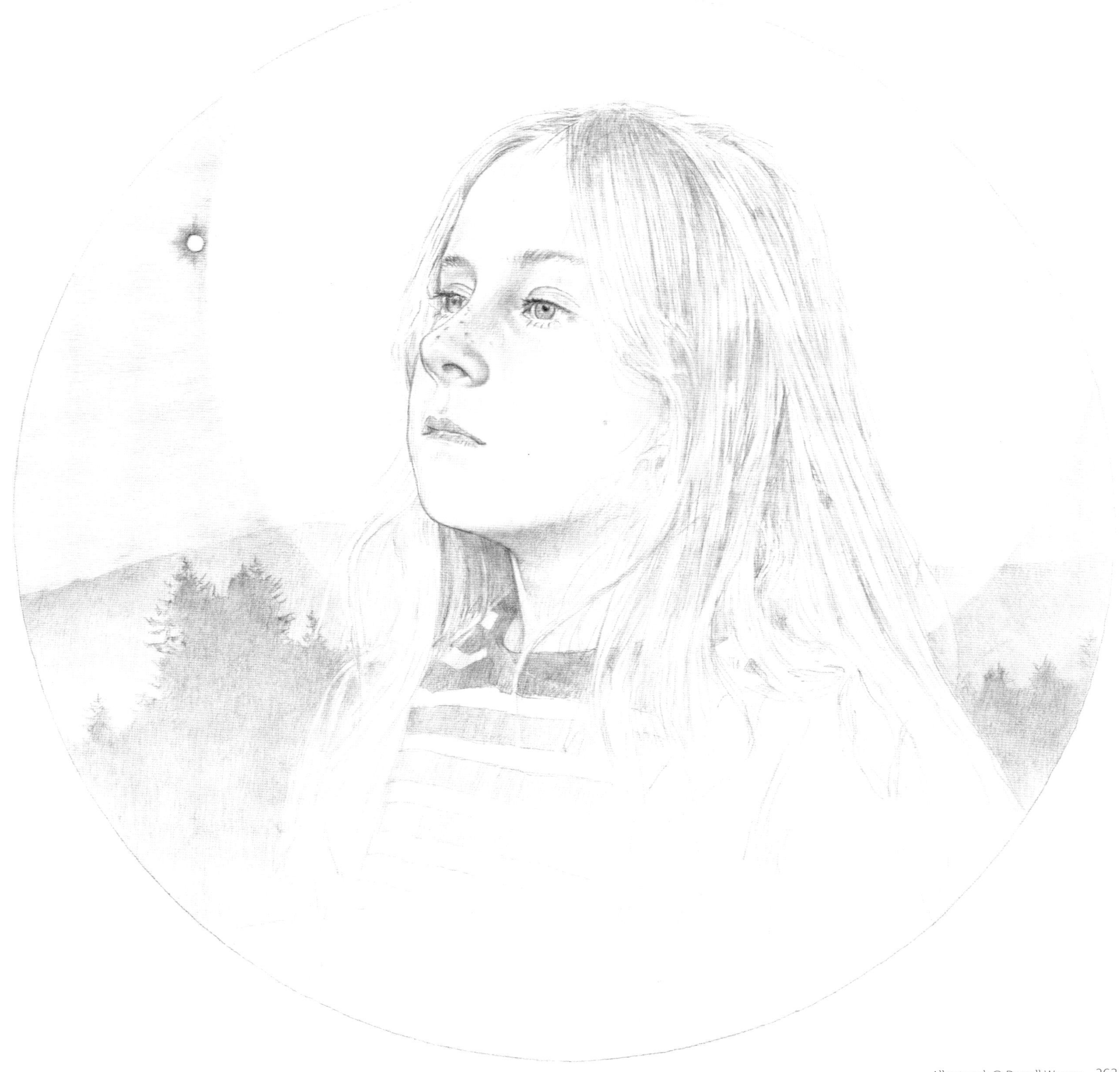

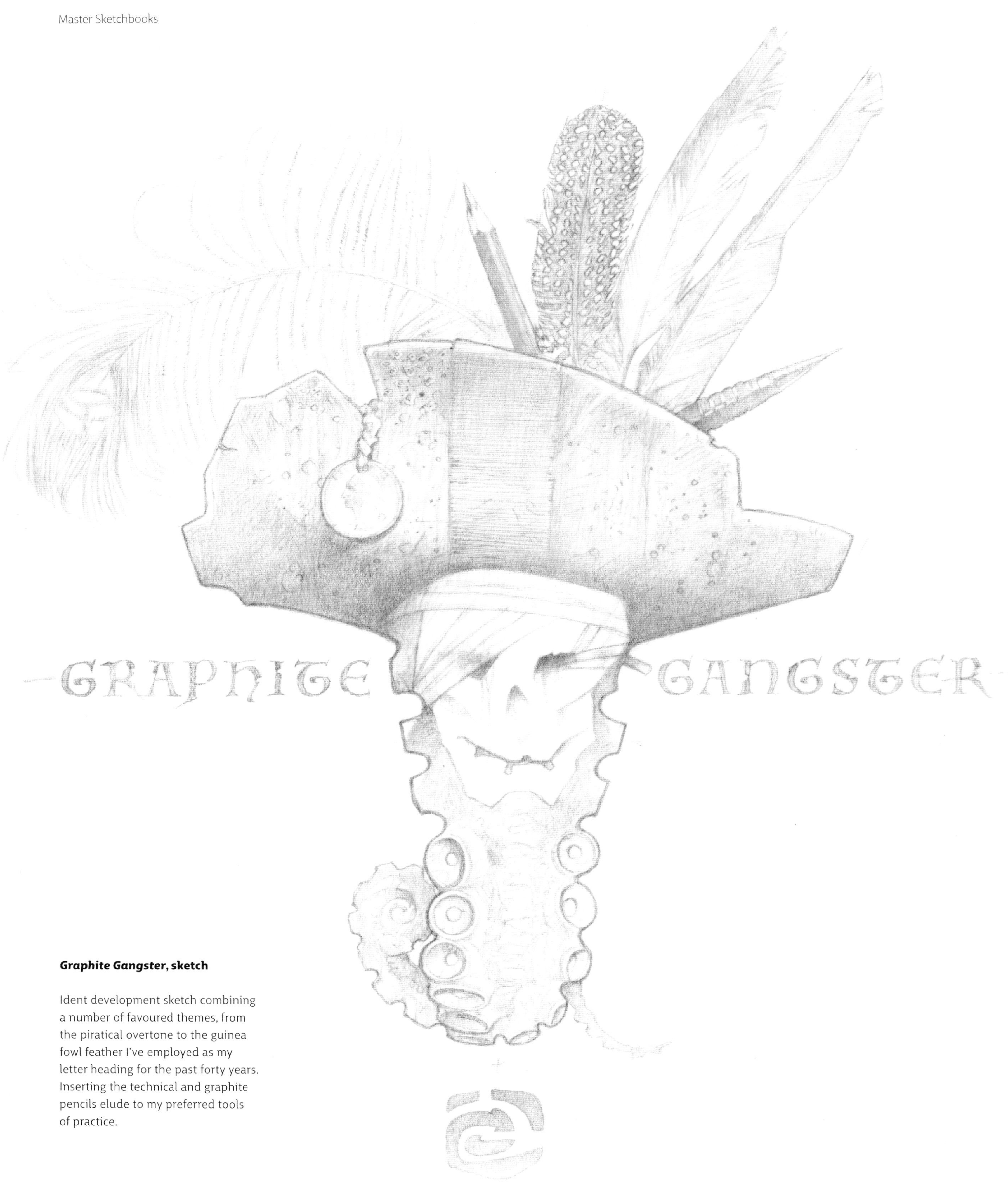

Graphite Gangster, sketch

Ident development sketch combining a number of favoured themes, from the piratical overtone to the guinea fowl feather I've employed as my letter heading for the past forty years. Inserting the technical and graphite pencils elude to my preferred tools of practice.

Medi-Weevil, sketch

Playing on the combination of the Medieval period
and the weevil insect by way of exploring the idea of
a northern European town in the Middle Ages being
inhabited by weevils in ornate period attire.

Contributors

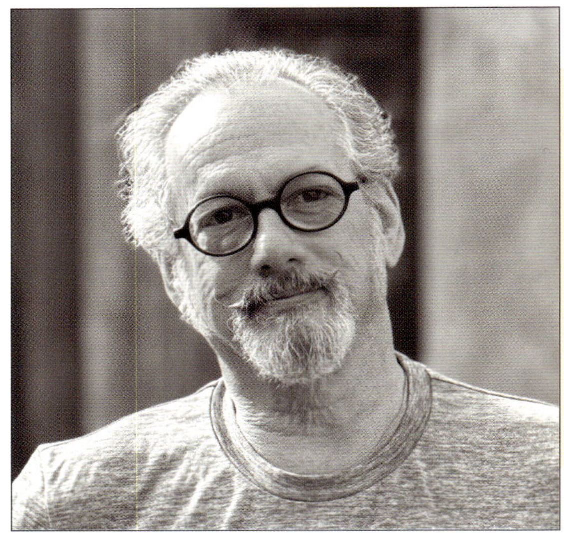

WAYNE BARLOWE - ARTIST & AUTHOR
waynebarlowe.com

Wayne Barlowe is an artist and author based in New Jersey, USA. He's spent nearly five decades creating art for his own written and illustrated books, as well as concept art for film, TV, and games. He is currently writing his third novel as well as illustrating a new *Hell* volume.

SANDRO CLEUZO - CHARACTER DESIGNER & ANIMATOR
instagram.com/sandrocleuzo

Born in Sao Paulo, Brazil, Sandro Cleuzo started working in animation at fifteen years old at a small animation studio that produced TV commercials. After four years learning the basics of animation, he moved to Dublin to work with Don Bluth on feature films. He then moved to Disney Feature, working as an animator and supervising animator on several films. He currently works for various studios as a freelance animator and designer.

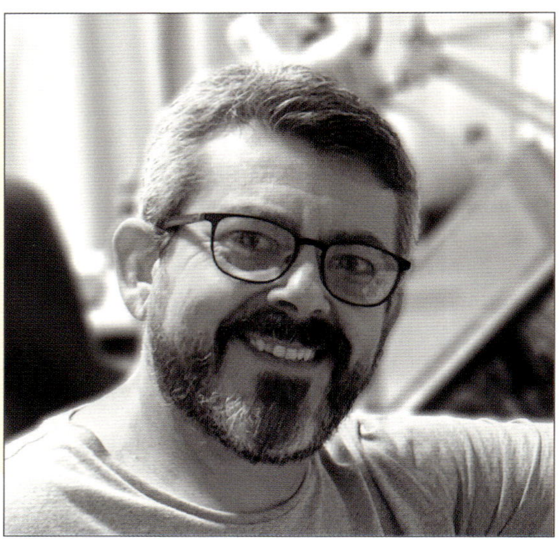

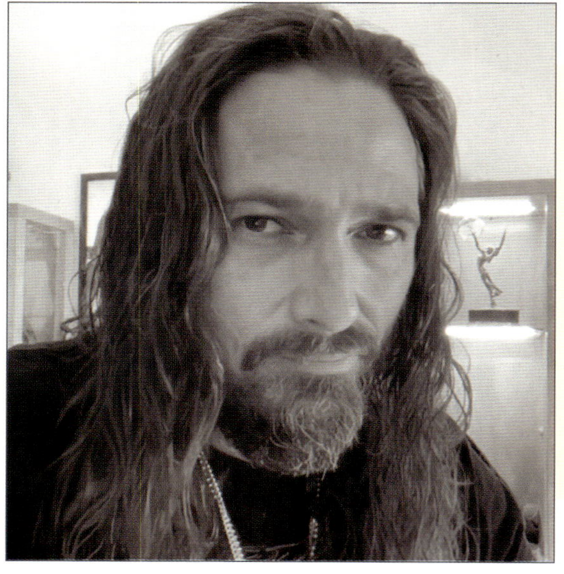

DAVID COLMAN - HEAD OF STORY
davidsdoodles.com

With an Emmy for design, David Colman is currently Head of Story at DreamWorks. He recently storyboarded *Tron: Ares* for Disney and *Mufasa: The Lion King* as Barry Jenkins' right-hand man. Along with extensive work on *Renfield* for Universal, he has worked with Robert Rodriguez and Ron Howard. David has a long list of projects with Sony, Paramount, Netflix, Legendary, Skydance, Apple, and many more. Widely known for his animal illustration outside of his studio work, he has self-published seven art books and owns a successful apparel line.

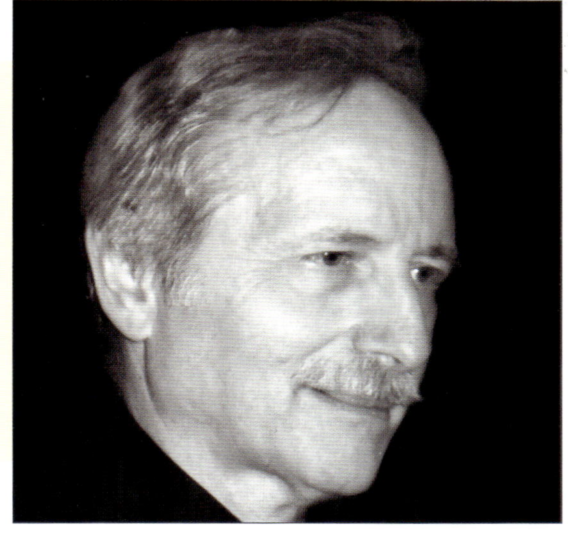

VINCENT DI FATE - ILLUSTRATOR

vincentdifate.com

Based in New York, Vincent Di Fate has worked for clients including IBM, *Reader's Digest*, The National Geographic Society, and NASA. He has received numerous awards for his art and is an inductee of the Science Fiction Hall of Fame (2011) and the Illustrators Hall of Fame (2019).

TONY M. DITERLIZZI - AUTHOR & ILLUSTRATOR

diterlizzi.com

A number-one *New York Times* bestselling author and illustrator, Tony M. DiTerlizzi has been creating children's books for twenty-five years. *The Spiderwick Chronicles* has sold millions of copies worldwide and was adapted into a feature film and television series. His bestselling trilogy, *WondLa*, is now streaming globally on Apple TV+.

Photograph © Jim Gipe

JAMES GURNEY - AUTHOR & ARTIST

jamesgurney.com

James Gurney is best known for his New-York-Times bestselling book series *Dinotopia*, detailing a fantastical world where humans and dinosaurs coexist. In the 1980s he painted science-fiction paperback covers and archaeological reconstructions. Gurney's original oil paintings have been shown in over thirty-five exhibitions in museums, including the Smithsonian, the Norman Rockwell Museum, and the Delaware Art Museum. He wrote *Color and Light* and *Imaginative Realism* based on his blog, Gurney Journey, and more than ninety articles for International Artist Magazine. His YouTube channel about painting on location has over 500k subscribers. His newest book is *The Artist's Guide to Sketching*, an expanded and remastered edition of his 1992 book co-authored with Thomas Kinkade.

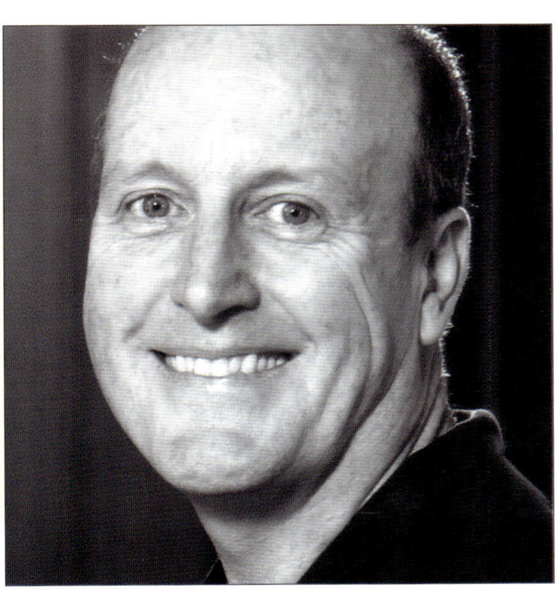

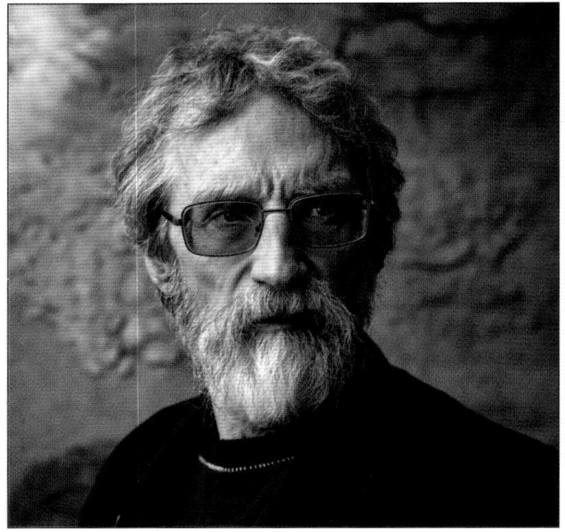

JOHN HOWE - BOOK ILLUSTRATOR & CONCEPT DESIGNER

john-howe.com

John Howe is a Canadian illustrator best known for illustrating the works of J. R. R. Tolkien. He worked alongside Alan Lee as chief conceptual designers on *The Lord of The Rings* and *The Hobbit* film series, and more recently as a concept artist on *The Lord of the Rings: The Rings of Power*. He has also illustrated card games, calendars, maps, and his own books.

Photograph © Lucas Vuitel

DAVE MCKEAN - ILLUSTRATOR & ARTIST

davemckean.com

Based in Kent, UK, Dave McKean has illustrated over ninety groundbreaking books and graphic novels, collaborating with Richard Dawkins, Ray Bradbury, David Almond, John Cale, and Heston Blumenthal. As well as his self-penned *Cages* and *Black Dog: The Dreams of Paul Nash*, he has directed three features – *MirrorMask*, *Luna*, and *The Gospel of Us* with Michael Sheen – and many short films.

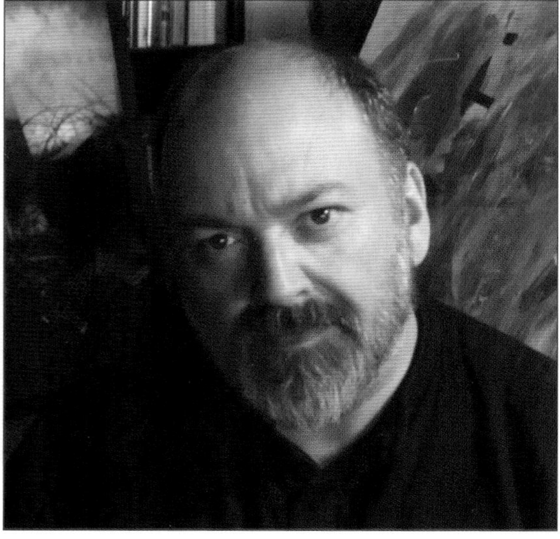

DARRELL WARNER - CHARACTER/ COSTUME ILLUSTRATOR

darrellwarner.co.uk

Darrell Warner is a British artist with over forty years of professional practice. He has worked in costume and character development, plus costume illustration, on over fifty major film titles, including the *Pirates of the Caribbean* franchise and *Wicked*. He is a semi-regular exhibitor at various Federation of British Artists society shows, won the Award for Excellence at the 2023 Royal Institute of Painters in Water Colours, and was a semi-finalist for Sky Arts Portrait Artist of the Year 2013.

TERRYL WHITLATCH - ANIMAL & CREATURE ARTIST

artstation.com/terrylwhitlatch

Terryl Whitlatch is internationally recognized as one of the top animal and creature artists working in entertainment today, as well as one of the pre-eminent animal anatomists working with the science community. Having made her debut as Principal Creature Designer for *Star Wars: Episode I – The Phantom Menace*, her clients include Lucasfilm, Industrial Light & Magic, Walt Disney Feature Animation, and countless others in the entertainment industry. Equally as versatile in the scientific world, her work has appeared in such publications as *Scientific American*, as well as in recent documentaries such as *Prehistoric Planet*. The author of several books on creature design, she is a highly sought-after educator and lecturer on animal anatomy, both real and imagined.

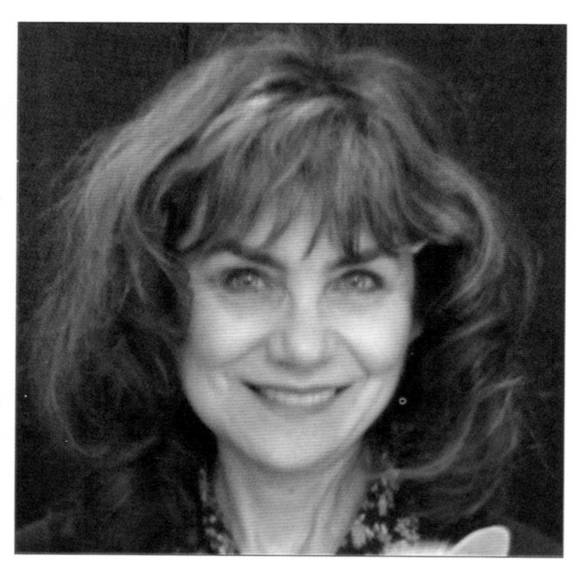

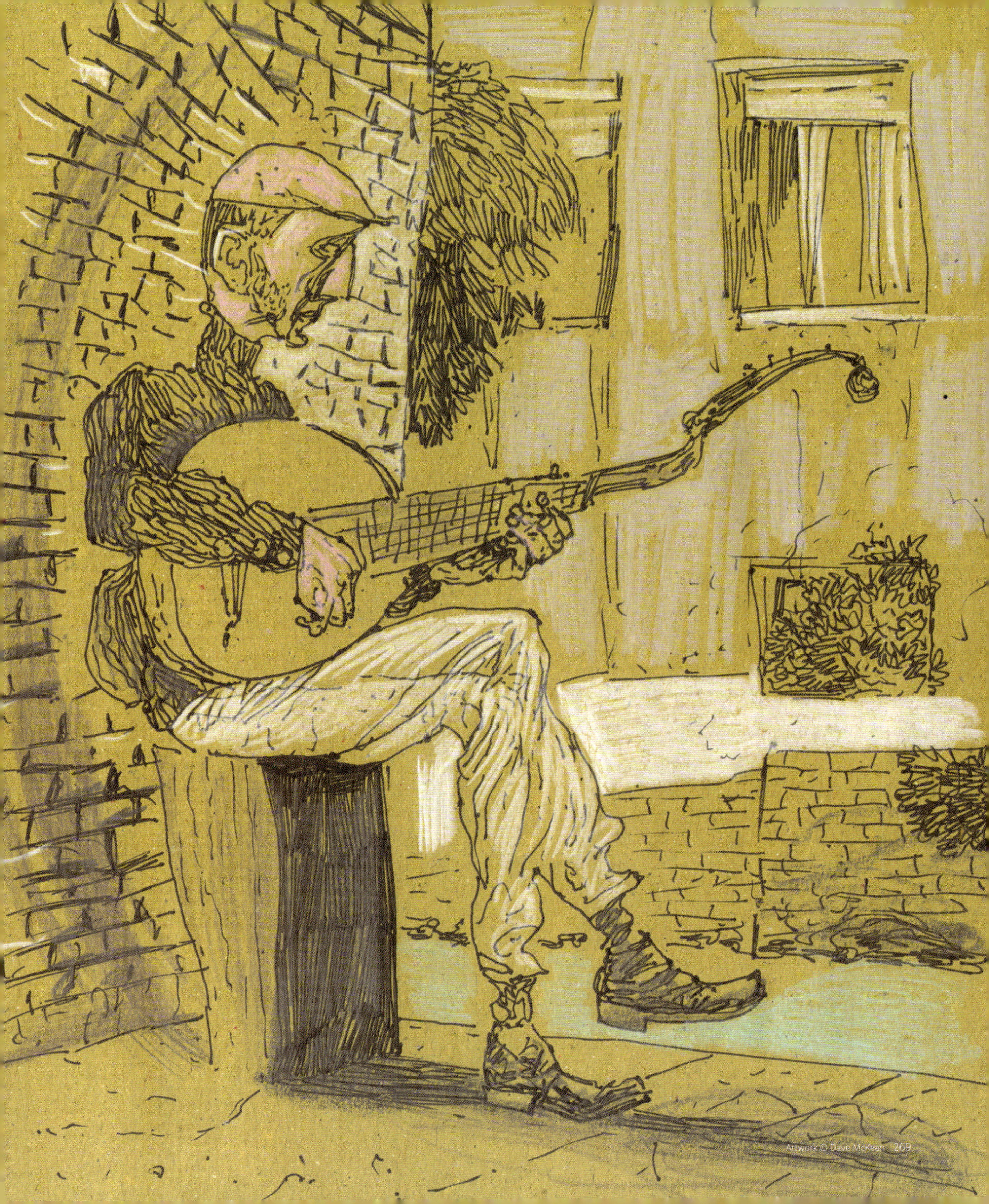

Artwork © Dave McKean 269

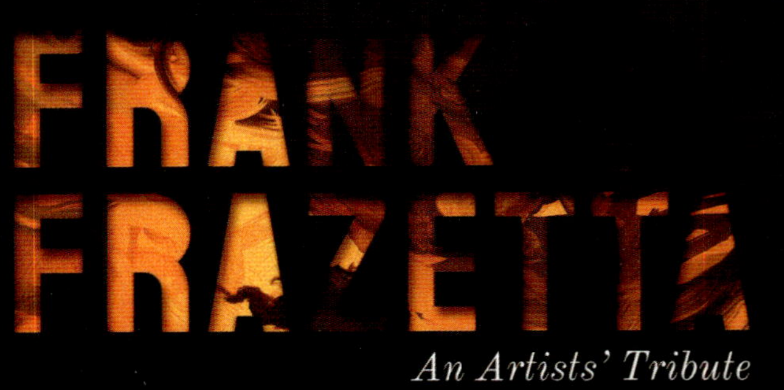

FRANK
FRAZETTA
An Artists' Tribute